Simple Steps to Organizing Everything

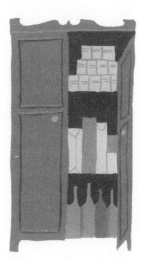

Simple Steps to Organizing Everything

BY DONNA SMALLIN

RODALE

Printed in the United States of America
Rodale Inc. makes every effort to use acid-free ∞, recycled paper ♲.

Illustrations by author
Cover design by Tara Long and Wendy Palitz
Interior design by Wendy Palitz

Rodale direct mail edition published under license from Storey Publishing, LLC.

Library of Congress Cataloging-in-Publication Data

Smallin, Donna, date
  Simple steps to organizing everything : 1,200 get-organized-fast secrets for curing everyday clutter challenges / Donna Smallin.
      p. cm.
  Includes index.
  ISBN-13 978–1–59486–389–9 hardcover
  ISBN-10 1–59486–389–X hardcover
  1. House cleaning.   2. Orderliness.   I. Title.
TX324.S537   2006
640—dc22
                                                                            2006001766

4 6 8 10 9 7 5 3 direct mail hardcover

We inspire and enable people to improve their lives and the world around them
For more of our products visit **rodalestore.com** or call 800-848-4735

For my mother-in-law, Audrey Smallin,
organizer extraordinaire
and
For every organizer who has gone before me—
and all those who will follow.

CONTENTS

INTRODUCTION

Life is short. What's that got to do with getting organized? Everything. I believe that the whole point of getting organized is to create more time, space, and energy in your life for the people and things that matter most to you.

You can spend precious minutes and hours every day looking for things you know are "around here somewhere," or you can find a place for everything so you always know exactly where to look. You can go through life in "catch-up" mode, with high levels of frustration and stress, or you can learn how to simplify daily living with the organizational systems and tools described in this book.

When I tell people that I have written several books about uncluttering and organizing one's home and life, they invariably ask whether I am super-organized. Well, I may be super-organized by some standards, but I like to think of myself as *simply* organized. By that I mean that I am as organized as I need to be. I could spend all day organizing, but instead I choose to spend only as much time as necessary to keep my life running smoothly.

Here's my secret: Don't make organizing difficult; keep it plain and simple. Find simple strategies, systems, and tools that work for you, and then use them regularly.

This may come as a surprise, but there is no one right way to get organized. That's why, in this book, I have presented many different solutions to the most common organizational challenges, so you can choose the one that appeals most to you; you might even try a variation of an idea. If a technique works for you, it's the perfect solution. If it doesn't work for you, try something different.

One of the aspects I find most rewarding about the process of organizing is that it helps you figure out what's most important to you. And knowing this can help to simplify your life. Organizing also brings with it a certain freedom. With less clutter to weigh you down, you have more time to pursue the things that bring you the greatest happiness and satisfaction. I wish you well!

Note: The Internet is a wonderful source of information on organizing. For this reason, I have referenced a number of Web sites throughout this book. Wherever possible, I have tried to include non-Web alternatives as well.

ACKNOWLEDGMENTS

In writing this book, I have had the honor and privilege of meeting dozens of organizing experts who readily contributed proven tips, strategies, and solutions. I am very grateful for their support, encouragement, and inspiration. I thank my research assistant, Danielle Francois, who helped me to get started on this huge organization project by setting up interviews, doing research, and handling lots of little details. I owe my husband, Terry, many hugs and kisses for helping me finish this book by running errands, doing grocery shopping, putting dinner on the table, and even decorating the house for the holidays (beautifully, I might add!). Lastly, I would be remiss if I did not acknowledge the patience and guidance of my editor, Dianne Cutillo, who really knows how to work with writers.

PART I

Getting Started

So, you want to get organized. Well, there's no better time than today to get started. After all, the sooner you start, the sooner you'll achieve your goal. But simply *wanting* to get organized won't make it happen. You have to make it happen by *choosing* to begin and then taking that all-important first step.

Getting started is often the most difficult part of getting organized. You may not know where or how to begin, but you can learn these things. More important is belief in yourself. Believe that with patience, perseverance, and a little know-how, you can accomplish anything. Choose to get organized and soon you'll enjoy the benefits of a simpler life. Organizing requires you to think about what's most important to you — what you really love and want — and to make decisions based on that knowledge. It can change your life for the better. So go ahead and take that first step.

CHAPTER 1

FIRST THINGS FIRST

Ask yourself why you want to get organized. What's in it for you? How did you come to your current disorganized state? Scrutinizing your relationship to clutter and disorganization is the first step toward getting organized. The more you understand about that relationship — and your role in it — the more successful you will be at bringing about lasting change. So don't skip this step!

The Rewards of Organization

The benefits of being organized go far beyond having an uncluttered home or being able to find things. Being organized can add hours to your day and days to your month because being organized saves time. The more organized you get, the more time you have to spend on the things in life that give you the greatest joy. And you'll reap physical, emotional, and financial rewards, too.

Disorganization creates unnecessary stress, and too much stress over a prolonged period can lead to serious health problems. And just think of the energy you waste each day searching for things. Getting organized can help increase your energy level and decrease your stress level.

If you have an abundance of clutter in your home, frequently miss appointments, or pay bills late, your self-esteem can really take a beating. Even low levels of disorganization can make you feel out of control and create feelings of dissatisfaction with yourself and your life. Good organizational systems, in contrast, instill confidence in yourself and your abilities.

Have you ever bought a replacement for something only to find the original item later? Do you often have to pay late fees on bills? Do you shop on credit and carry balances? Do you eat out frequently because you don't have the time to cook or don't have the makings of a meal in your cupboards or refrigerator? In the process of getting organized, you may discover that greater financial security and success is within your grasp. You might even be able to make money by selling belongings that are just taking up space in your home or office.

The Challenge

Perhaps you have tried to get organized in the past but only ended up with a bigger mess. Or maybe you succeeded, but your success was only temporary and now you're faced with the challenge of getting organized all over again.

Organizing *is* a challenge, not so much because of the time and commitment it takes, but because it requires us to change our behavior — and that's not easy. It takes time, patience, and awareness to change the way we do things. It also requires the proper motivation, planning, preparation, commitment, and action. Organization is not something that just happens; you have to make it happen. The way to do that is to **ACT**:

Assess your situation

Commit to a plan

Take action

Getting organized is really about taking control of your life, sorting through everything that demands your time and space, determining what's really important to you, and letting go of what's not. To get the wheels of this process in motion, start by assessing your situation.

What's Your Situation?

There are as many reasons why disorganization prevails as there are people. But if you really want to get organized, there's hope, even if you believe yourself to be the most disor-ganized person who ever lived. The following questions are designed to get you thinking about your unique situation, your relationship with clutter, and your specific challenges. (Taking the quiz on page 8 will provide you with further insights.)

- **Have you always been disorganized?** If so, think about this: Were you ever taught organization skills? Probably not. But you can learn organization skills at any age and, by applying these skills, you can turn chaos into order and regain control of your life.

- **Are you just temporarily disorganized?** Think back to a time when you were more organized. What has been the most dramatic change in your life since that time? Can you find a relationship between that change and your current disorganized state? What advice would you give to someone in your situation?

the cost of disorganization

Think about how much time you spend every day looking for your car keys, unpaid bills, checkbook, the belt that goes with your blue suit, or whatever. For the purposes of this exercise, let's say you spend fifteen minutes each day searching for things. How much do you earn at your job? If you earn $20 per hour, disorganization is costing you $5 per day. That works out to $35 per week, $140 per month, and $1,680 per year — a hefty price to pay.

- **Do you spend a great deal of time shopping?** It's America's number one pastime, and it helps explain the proliferation of clutter in our lives. We don't just buy an item to replace one that is broken or worn out. We buy because we can't pass up a sale or because we think we have to have the latest gadget or clothing style. It seems like the more we earn, the more we spend — and the more we own. We keep bringing stuff into our already cluttered homes and, in some cases, digging ourselves deeper in debt.

- **Are you secretly afraid of getting organized?** Because organization is a process of change, it is inherently an emotional process. We all have thoughts and feelings attached to the concept of organization, some of which can prevent us from reaching our goals. Many people, for example, fear that getting organized means having to get rid of things they are not ready to part with. Others envision "uncluttered" as "sterile" and fear that living and working in an uncluttered space will thwart their creativity. And some of us believe that we just can't do it because we've tried once, twice, or many times before and failed; we feel defeated before we even start. What are your thoughts and feelings about getting organized? What do you fear might happen in the process or as a result of getting more organized?

- **Are you a perfectionist?** You might think that a perfectionist would have a perfectly ordered home, but more often than not, the opposite is true. That's because perfectionists want to do everything just right, or not at all. So they keep putting off getting organized until they can do it perfectly. Judith Kolberg, director of the National Study Group on Chronic Disorganization, says, "Often, our best intentions are left in stacks." She calls this tendency *deferred decision-making*.

What's Your Plan?

If you want to be successful at getting organized, you've got to have a plan. A plan is the map that will get you where you want to go. A good plan includes what you want and why, when you want it by, and what you are willing to do to achieve it. To create your plan for success, write down your answers to the following questions:

- What made you choose to read this book?
- What do you hope to accomplish?
- How might getting organized improve your life?
- In what ways has being disorganized detracted from your life?
- What are you willing to do to get organized?
- Why is it important for you to do this now?

PUT IT IN WRITING

If you want to achieve something, whatever it is, write it down. Be as clear and specific as possible. You are more likely to realize your goals if you put them in writing. Maybe it makes them more concrete, I don't know. I only know that it works.

—Harriet Schechter, The Miracle Worker Organizing Service

Knowing why you want to get organized is vital to your success. This is your motivation to get started and to stick with it until you are satisfied with the result. Your plan should also include a deadline to keep you focused on your goal. It's difficult to predict how long it will take to undo weeks, months, even years of disorganization, however.

Rather than guessing or setting an unrealistic deadline, create a one-month plan. Choose five things you most want to accomplish during the month. List these items from highest to lowest priority. Be as specific as you can. At the end of the month, if you have not yet accomplished all five tasks, create a new one-month plan that outlines what you hope to achieve this month — and what you are willing to do to make it happen.

Taking Action

Once you have a plan, you're ready to implement it. Harness the power of your mind, and let it lead you toward your goals.

Remember, getting organized requires us to change our behavior, and that's not easy. Be patient with yourself. If you believe that you are an organized person, you'll have a much greater chance of becoming one. If you catch yourself saying or thinking negative things like "I can't do this" or "I'm so disorganized," counter with, "That's not true. I am a very capable person, and I can do whatever I set my mind to do."

It helps to envision order. If you can visualize your space as you would like to see it, you are more likely to achieve your goal. See yourself walking from one uncluttered room to the

---

sample plan

What I Want

- I want to organize my closets and drawers so I can get dressed more quickly in the morning.
- I want to learn how to keep track of important dates, appointments, and things to do so I don't forget them.
- I want to develop a system for paying my bills so that I don't owe late fees.
- I want to figure out how to make more time for myself so that I can exercise.
- I want to clean out my garage so that I can park my car in it.

When I Want It
By [insert date one month from today]

What I Am Willing to Do
Turn off the television from 7 to 8 P.M. every Tuesday and Thursday night and spend that hour working on organizing activities.

Do you need to get motivated? Consider enlisting the help of a friend. Tell this person what you want to accomplish by what date, and ask him or her to check in on your progress.

---

next. Picture a friend walking with you and complimenting you on your achievement. Feel the pride that comes from a job well done.

Affirmations are another way to take mental action toward your goal. An affirmation is a positive statement with personal meaning that you repeat often. Example: "I am organized out of respect for myself and others." Or "I am getting my life in order so I can more fully enjoy living."

Now, let's get started!

what's your organizing IQ?

Choose the number (1–4) that best describes your response to each of the following statements.

1 = Rarely or never
2 = Sometimes
3 = Quite often
4 = Almost always

☐ I get tired just thinking about what it will take for me to get organized.

☐ My co-workers or housemates think I am disorganized.

☐ Lack of time or space keeps me from getting more organized.

☐ I find myself wishing I could be more organized.

☐ I spend a significant amount of time looking for things every day.

☐ I am disorganized.

☐ I let mail pile up until I have time to deal with it.

☐ I save things that I think I might need someday.

☐ I feel guilty about throwing away things.

☐ I leave things out as a reminder to myself to do something.

☐ I have no time for myself.

☐ When it comes to clutter, I think, "Why bother? It will just get cluttered again."

☐ I can't bear the thought of parting with anything I own.

☐ I dread opening one or more closets in my home or office.

☐ When the profusion of clutter in my home gets to me, I go out.

☐ If someone stops by unexpectedly, I try to avoid letting them in.

☐ I miss scheduled appointments or forget important things to do.

☐ I have trouble keeping up with birthdays, holidays, and season changes.

☐ I feel like I accomplish very little in any given day.

☐ I equate busy-ness with success.

☐ I am pulled in three different directions at once.

☐ I use late notices as reminders to pay bills.

☐ I carry credit card debt from month to month.

☐ I live from paycheck to paycheck.

☐ I find it difficult to maintain a balance in my savings account.

_____ **TOTAL**

rating your score

81–100: You have so much to gain from organizing your home and life! Taking the time to get and stay organized will dramatically decrease your high level of stress and frustration, free up time and energy to pursue whatever brings you joy, and remove obstacles to achieving your definition of success. Make the commitment to get started today, and stick with it!

61–80: You are probably suffering because of the cumulative effects of disorganization. Clutter has been building for some time, and it seems like with each passing month and year, you get more and more disorganized. But there is no reason why you can't turn things around with the right combination of organizing systems and strategies. Just don't expect it to happen overnight!

41–60: You probably don't consider yourself a disorganized person, but for whatever reason, you may be feeling more disorganized than usual. Chances are, you are adjusting to a major change in your life — a new job, home, or relationship, or loss of one of these things. Taking the time to get organized will add the structure you need right now during this time of transition. If the disorganization in your home and life has always been at this level, learning some new organization skills will help.

25–40: Your organizational skills are very well honed, and you derive pleasure from being organized because you see the benefits. Because you stay on top of things, you accomplish most of what you set out to do each day. If you are looking for a new career in a helping profession, you might consider becoming a professional organizer.

CHAPTER 2

UNCLUTTERING YOUR HOME

You've got a plan. You're motivated and you're ready to get organized once and for all. Start by freeing yourself from clutter — all the excess stuff in your life that you could live without. Make it your goal to surround yourself with only things you love and use, and let go of everything else that's just taking up valuable space.

Where to Start

It really doesn't matter where you start. But starting in the room where you spend the most time is going to give you the greatest satisfaction, and motivate you to unclutter the rest of your home. An alternative place to start is in the room that contains the most frustrating amount of clutter or disarray. Once you decide on a room, make it your goal to start with the most visible clutter first, then work on uncluttering the stuff that's out of sight.

If just the *thought* of "weeding out" or "paring down" your belongings is scary or uncomfortable for you, relax. In theory, you could keep everything and still create a beautifully organized home. It will just take a little longer to find a place for everything so that you can find what you want when you want it.

However, if you're like most people, some (maybe even many) things in your home have outlived their usefulness or appeal. You could easily live without these things and never even miss them. Really! If you aren't using something or don't like it anymore, it's just taking up valuable space in your home. If you can bring yourself to let go of such things, you will create more space for what you really love and use.

When to Unclutter

Any time is a fine time to unclutter, but if you find it difficult to throw things out, you might want to plan your start date to coincide with trash day. That way, your throwaways won't be hanging around and tempting you to come and take them back. You might also plan your uncluttering around an upcoming church tag sale, neighborhood garage sale, or community trash day, but only if these events are taking place in the very near future. You want to get started now!

Uncluttering is best accomplished by focusing your time and attention on one clearly defined area. If you try to unclutter a whole room all at once, you'll probably make a bigger mess. The uncluttering process is also far less daunting and more manageable if you determine in advance how much "uncluttering time" you will spend in any given day.

Keep in mind that your home didn't get cluttered overnight, and it's probably going to take some time to get it organized. If you can spare a whole day here and there, great. But you don't have to put your life on hold to get organized. Just setting aside fifteen minutes to one hour each day can quickly add up to a job well done.

What's important is not how much time you spend on any given day, but that you get started. If you've allocated one hour for uncluttering, set a kitchen timer or alarm clock for one hour, or put on your favorite CD. When the timer sounds or the music stops, it's quitting time. There may be days when you want to continue on for another hour. But if you've had enough for one day, just walk away. The clutter has been there for awhile, right? It'll be there when you come back to it tomorrow.

How to Unclutter

Uncluttering is a great project for a rainy day. Wear comfortable clothes, put on your favorite music, and focus all of your attention on your

goal. Uncluttering takes time, but it's not complicated. It's a sorting process.

Charge in, but don't take on too much at once. Start with a defined space, such as a counter, table or desktop, or shelf. Empty that space of its contents. Then sort items into five categories. Use labeled boxes or bags to collect items that belong in categories two through five:

1. Things you love and/or use; you'll keep these
2. Things you could give to someone else
3. Things that belong in the trash
4. Things you could sell
5. Things that belong elsewhere

In the process of uncluttering room by room, you will come across things that belong in another room or somewhere else altogether, such as books and videos that need to be returned or something you borrowed from a friend.

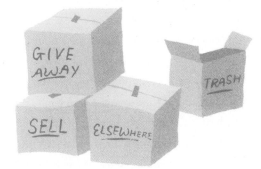

What You Need

- ❏ Four boxes or bags labeled "Give Away," "Throw Away," "Sell," and "Store Elsewhere"
- ❏ Small spiral notebook
- ❏ Pen or pencil
- ❏ Alarm clock or kitchen timer

An uncluttered house looks cleaner than a clean house that's cluttered.

—Judy Warmington,
Woman Time Management

Use the spiral notebook and pen or pencil to jot yourself a reminder to return these things, and make notes about other things you need to do that come to mind while you are uncluttering. Deposit these items in a box or bag labeled "Store Elsewhere." When you are finished organizing for the day, take these items where they belong. If items belong in the room you are organizing, but not where you found them (on the kitchen counter, for example), give them a temporary home somewhere in a space that you have not yet uncluttered.

Obviously, things you love are things you want to keep, even if you never use them. You'll also want to keep things you *do* use, even if it's only once a year. If you have more than one of something, however, ask yourself how many of these items you really need. If you're uncluttering a junk drawer, for example, and you find that you have an exorbitant number of pens or rubberbands, ask yourself how many is enough. Keep what you can use and give away the rest.

What about parts and pieces that you find? Or things that are missing parts and pieces? Set up a "lost and found" box somewhere, and put these items into it as you find them. You might also put in this box things that don't have a home yet and things you can't identify. When

you finish uncluttering your entire home, go through the box to see if you found any matches for these items or if you now have a home for them. Discard the junk.

If you're undecided about an item, take the "Keep or Toss" quiz. If you're still undecided, ask yourself, "What's the worst possible thing that could happen if I got rid of this?" Still undecided? Then keep it for now, along with the things you love and use. Or put that item in a box labeled "Undecided." When you finish uncluttering your home, seal the box, write the current month, day, and year on it, and store it away. If you haven't had a need to open that box one year from now, then you know that you don't *need* what's inside and you can let it go.

Don't worry about cleaning during the uncluttering process. That's something you can do later, when the room is organized to your satisfaction. Cleaning as you go might slow you down, and you don't want that. You want to work as quickly as you can so that you can see the end result that much sooner. Also, it's easier to clean an uncluttered room — one of the benefits of organizing that you're sure to appreciate.

MAKE A DATE

Consider making a daily or biweekly uncluttering appointment with yourself. Write it in your planner like you would any other appointment.

—Mitzi Weinman, TimeFinder

Letting Go

Uncluttering requires letting go and that can be difficult — even painful. Sandra Felton, founder of Messies Anonymous, says, "Be willing to take a risk that you may want later what you discarded. Also realize that it may cause temporary pain to throw something out. However, it also causes definite pain to keep it. Throwing it out is mild pain compared with the pain which comes from having to live helplessly with all the clutter that finds its way into the house."

Following are some tips to help you let go of material possessions you no longer love or use.

● **If you are afraid to let go of something, do it scared.** Once you get over the initial shock, you'll be amazed at how much lighter and freer you feel. You may find that letting go of material possessions helps you to let go of emotional clutter, because the physical act of letting go can trigger a release of frustration, anger, guilt, and other emotional baggage.

● **Imagine that you're moving.** Ask yourself: Is this item worth the effort and expense of packing it up, carrying it out to the moving van, and unpacking it at the new place? If not, give it a new home.

● **Get someone else to help you go through your things.** Have that person hold each object. Holding it yourself emphasizes your attachment to it. This is precisely why a good salesperson will encourage you to touch something or try it on.

keep or toss?

What if you're undecided about what to do with a particular item? It's probably something you could give away, throw away or sell, but for whatever reason, you're not quite ready to part with it. Ask yourself:

● Have I used this item in the past year? **Yes/No**
● Has anyone else in my home used it in the past year? **Yes/No**
● Do I have a definite use for this in the foreseeable future? **Yes/No**
● If it's broken, is it worth fixing? **Yes/No**
● Does this item serve a worthwhile purpose in my life? **Yes/No**
● Do I need to keep it for legal or tax purposes? **Yes/No**
● Is it more important to me to keep this item than to have the space it occupies? **Yes/No**
● Do I love it? **Yes/No**
● Does someone in my household love it? **Yes/No**
● Would it be difficult or expensive for me to get another one? **Yes/No**

Scoring: There are no right or wrong answers, but a "Yes" answer to any one of the above questions provides a sound reason to keep that item. A "No" answer, on the other hand, gives you good reason to toss it.

- **Think about your abundance.** If you have more than one of something, be honest with yourself. How many do you really need? Be grateful for the abundance in your life. Then make a decision from the heart to share your wealth with others who may be less fortunate.
- **Play Judith's game.** Judith Kolberg, Director of the National Study Group on Chronic Disorganization, developed an uncluttering game called Friends, Acquaintances, and Strangers which you can play with your belongings. As you look at each item, ask yourself if it is a friend, an acquaintance, or a stranger. An outfit you wear often is a friend. Something you bought but never wore is an acquaintance. Clothes that don't fit or that you haven't worn in a year or more are strangers. Find a new home for acquaintances that have overstayed their welcome. Kick out the strangers.
- **Give up the caretaker job.** The more stuff you have, the more stuff you have to take care of and the more space you need to store it. Make a conscious decision to let someone else take over the caretaking.
- **Come back to it.** If you've been doing pretty well with letting go but get stuck trying to decide between keeping a particular item or not, set it aside for a day. You may simply be too tired to decide. Or maybe there are other things going on in your life that are interfering with your decision-making ability.

The Great Giveaway

Uncluttering your home gives you the perfect excuse to get rid of all those things you really don't want or use anymore — everything from hair accessories to books to furniture. Just because you bought it or someone bought it for you doesn't mean you have to keep it forever. Wouldn't you prefer to surround yourself with things you love and use? Give yourself permission to give away the things that no longer suit your taste or lifestyle.

Think of someone you know who might enjoy having what you no longer want. Ask if that person would be willing to come and get whatever you are giving away. One thing you don't want is a box full of stuff that you have to deliver to every corner of the world, because you know what will happen: The box will just sit there and become a source of frustration.

It may be more convenient to donate your whole box of giveaways to one charitable organization and be done with it. Think first of the one place that accepts everything from toys to clothing to household furnishings. Or separate your giveaways into several bags for delivery to several donation stations. The chart below is a partial list of what you can take where.

You may be able to deduct your donation from your income taxes. Be sure to keep a list of the items you donated and the value of each item, and ask for a tax receipt from the charitable organization.

It Pays to Unclutter

For some people, selling unwanted belongings makes it easier to part with them. You won't get rich uncluttering your house, but you may end up with enough for a little splurge. The primary outlets for selling secondhand items are consignment shops, classified advertising, Internet auction sites and, of course, yard and garage sales.

Donation Stations

Item	Where to Donate
Clothing	Goodwill, religious organization, domestic violence shelter (women's and children's clothing), Dress for Success affiliate (women's suits and work apparel), thrift store, theater (for costumes)
Kitchen and housewares	Goodwill, religious organization, domestic violence shelter, thrift store
Toys	Police station (for holiday drives), religious organization, domestic violence shelter, thrift store, hospital
Books (except textbooks)	Library, thrift store, secondhand bookstore
Textbooks	Prisons
Fabric, sewing and craft materials	Senior citizen's center, grade school, theater (for costumes)

If you have clothes, furnishings, and other items in excellent or even like-new condition, consider selling them on consignment. Consignment shops will accept secondhand belongings and give you a percentage of the selling price, generally 40 to 50 percent. Items will remain for sale until the end of a specified contract period (usually 60 to 90 days), after which you can collect your earnings. Most shops offer to donate unsold items to charity. Take them up on it! There's no sense in bringing things back home. To find a shop near you, look in the Yellow Pages under "Consignment Shops" or "Secondhand Shops."

WHEN TO BRING CLOTHING TO A CONSIGNMENT SHOP

Clothing Season	Drop off In
Spring/summer	Mid-February
Fall	Mid-August
Winter	End of September/ early October

To maximize your earnings, check out a few stores before choosing one and compare their stock and policies. Also, take location into account. Don't choose a store that is off the beaten path unless you are sure that it does lots of business.

Consignment shops accept all kinds of things, including:

- Clothing and accessories
- Furniture
- Kitchenware
- Decorative household items
- Sporting equipment
- Toys
- Infant furniture and items
- Videos and books

Some stores specialize in specific items, such as used sporting equipment, books, or children's clothing. Clothes must be in excellent condition with no loose or missing buttons, no falling hems or tears in the material, and no stains. Newer clothes, designer labels, and classic styles sell best. Bring them to the store cleaned, pressed, and on hangers. Bear in mind that consignment shops want seasonal clothing that is coming into season.

If it's too late in the season to bring in your clothes, put them in storage and make a note to yourself to get them out before the beginning of the next season. (See page 157 to learn about an effective reminder system known as a tickler file.)

Perhaps best of all, selling on consignment lets you earn back at least some of your original purchase price, which may make it easier to let go of things that are just taking up space. And it's simple to do.

Selling Direct. You can sell larger items directly to buyers by placing a classified advertisement in one of your local newspapers or weekly shopping papers. Items to consider advertising include furniture sets, large appliances or power equipment, and computer equipment. Direct selling generally brings the best price, but you do have to pay a fee for the advertisement. Also you'll have to spend time on the telephone and in person with prospective buyers.

To sell valuable items, such as jewelry, antiques, coin collections, and musical instruments, look for stores that specialize in buying and selling these items. The Yellow Pages of the telephone book is a good place to start. You may wish to get more than one estimate to ensure that you're getting a fair price.

Selling On-line. You can sell just about anything on the Internet. The world's largest on-line marketplace is eBay. People use eBay to buy and sell all sorts of things, including:

- Antiques and art
- Books, movies, and music
- Business, office, and industrial items
- Clothing and accessories
- Collectibles
- Computers and peripherals
- Dolls and teddy bears
- Home and garden items

- Jewelry, gemstones, and watches
- Photo and electronic equipment
- Pottery and glass
- Sports equipment and memorabilia
- Tickets for events and travel
- Toys and hobbies

eBay assesses two selling fees: a nominal insertion fee to list each item (or quantity of same items) and a final value fee, which ranges from 1.25 to 5 percent of your final sale price. Additional fees apply for optional services, such as an on-line payment service that allows eBay to collect payment from buyers and deposit it directly into your bank account.

Selling at a Garage Sale. A time-proven way to get rid of unwanted stuff and make a few bucks in the process is to hold a garage or yard sale. Planning ahead will minimize time and effort while maximizing sales. The seven simple steps outlined here will help make any sale a success.

SALE-DAY MUSTS

• Try to be ready at least an hour earlier than your advertised start time, unless you indicated "no early birds" in your ad.

• Plan for a busy day. Dress comfortably (in particular, wear appropriate shoes) and eat a hearty breakfast. Make your lunch before the sale starts. Have a chair and beverage handy.

• For safety's sake, lock your house and do not allow strangers inside for any reason.

• Leash your dog or confine him to the house for the duration of the sale, especially if he is likely to bark, jump on people, or otherwise scare away potential buyers.

• When the sale is over, load unsold items in your car to donate to a pre-selected charity organization, such as The Salvation Army, or arrange ahead of time for a pick-up.

—Helen Volk, Beyond Clutter

1. Set a date. Check first to find out whether your municipality requires a permit to hold a garage sale or puts any restrictions on garage sales. Then pick a date for your garage sale, preferably a Saturday. One day should be sufficient, but if you have a lot of stuff to sell and time to spare, make it a two-day sale. Most buyers arrive in the morning; you may want to end your sale by 2 P.M. rather than waiting around for stragglers.

2. Write and place an advertisement for your sale. List your big-ticket items and some of the more desirable things. Unless you are willing to start selling at the crack of dawn, include the phrase "no early birds." List the hours of your sale. Run the ad three days before and on the day of the sale.

3. Designate a collection spot. Set up one area of your garage or home for collecting, sorting, and pricing items to be sold. Keep similar items together: for example, furniture, sporting equipment, books and videos, infant clothing and toys, kitchenware, and linens.

4. Put a price on everything. Use stickers or signs. It's easier on you when prospective customers don't have to ask, "How much is this?" If you are unfamiliar with garage sale pricing, go to some garage sales and look for items similar to those you will be selling. As you collect items for your garage sale, price them.

5. Make and post location signs. Check with your municipality or development association to make sure it's OK to hang signs advertising your sale and to find out whether there are restrictions concerning sign placement, when signs can be posted, and so forth. Post signs at strategic locations, including the nearest intersection with a main road, the end of your street, and your driveway. Write in large capital letters with black marker on a brightly colored card stock. Keep it simple:

GARAGE SALE
Sat., May 5, 8 A.M.–2 P.M.
125 Main Street

Draw an arrow pointing the way. Hang up the signs up to one week before your sale. Make a note of every location and be sure to take down every sign immediately after your sale.

6. Arrange your wares attractively. To display smaller items, use tables or lay a sheet of plywood over two sawhorses and drape with a tablecloth. Put all clothes on hangers, hang on a length of clothesline, and clip with clothespins. Or, if you have two stepladders, insert a long pole or broom between the two

PRICE TO SELL

Simplify pricing by group; for example, all ladies shirts $1 or all paperbacks 25 cents. Then you only have to create a few signs instead of many price stickers.

• Price cheap. Don't get hung up on value. Remember, your goal is to get rid of stuff.

• Use whole values such as $5, $1, 50 cents, and 25 cents to simplify addition and make it easy to make change.

—Treva Berends, The Organizing Specialists

for a clothes rod. Separate men's, women's, and children's clothing and accessories. Put out at least one long mirror so that shoppers can see if the style, color, and size is right. Run heavy-duty extension cords for testing electrical appliances. The more you can set up your sale along the lines of a retail store, the easier it is for customers to browse and find things. Remove from the garage sale vicinity any items that are not for sale, or attach a sign to them that reads "Not for Sale." Put a box of stuff out by the road with a "Free" sign to attract passersby.

7. Be prepared. Think about how you will handle money. Will you wear a fanny pack or apron, or use a cash box? Will you need a helper? Be sure that you have enough coins and bills to make change for two twenty-dollar

One Challenge . . .

I have certain items that I don't use or even like for that matter, but because these things were given to me as gifts, I feel compelled to hang on to them.

Three Solutions

1 FROM JULIE SIGNORE, *1, 2, 3 SORT IT*: If you feel that the person who gave you the gift will expect to see it in your home, ask your kids if one of them would like the item for when they leave for college or have a place of their own. The next time you see the person who gave you the gift you can say, "Gee, Susan, that gift was so special that Sally decided she wants to keep it in a safe place until she leaves for college." If you doubt you will ever be asked about the gift in the future and no one in the family wants the item, donate it to a charitable agency in your community. Remember, the worst part of receiving a gift or item that is not your style is not being questioned about its whereabouts in the future by the giver; it's holding on to something that is perfectly good and not using it, when there are others who need it!

2 FROM TREVA BERENDS, *THE ORGANIZING SPECIALISTS*: When you receive a gift you don't particularly like or need, make a choice to display or use it for a period of time. Then pass it along to someone who will appreciate it — maybe to someone who admires it in your home. If you choose to honor the giver, use or display gifts, but limit your own acquisition of similar items, for example, a picture frame. When giving gifts, keep in mind that consumable gifts are always a good choice, especially for people who have everything. Give a gift certificate to a spa, favorite restaurant, or store, or a basket of store-bought or homemade edibles.

3 FROM DOROTHY MADDEN, *ORGANIZE IT!*: If the giver is a person who plays a major role in your life, such as a mother-in-law, hold on to it for the sake of the relationship. People are more important than things. If, on the other hand, the giver is not someone who is likely to look for the gift in your home, give yourself permission to give it away. A gift is a gift. It's meant for you to do with it what you will.

bills — five fives, thirteen ones, and two dollars in loose change that fits your pricing system (for example, you may only need quarters). Have a calculator or paper and pencil handy for quick addition. You'll also want shopping bags and a few boxes, as well as newspaper for wrapping breakables. Set up as much as possible the night before your sale. Be sure you have enough light in your garage, or if you are having a yard sale, that you are prepared for rain. Consider selecting and listing a rain date in your advertisements, just in case. And to help move items in the last hour of your sale, consider reducing everything to half-price as the crowds begin to wane.

To encourage your children to unclutter their rooms, offer to let them keep whatever money they make from selling their stuff. If you don't have a lot of stuff or can't stand the thought of going it alone, invite friends and family members to join you in your garage sale effort, with the understanding that they do all their own pricing and set-up, they help you on the day of the sale, and they take all unsold items with them when they leave. You'll need a system to track who sells what to keep proceeds straight. If you're working with just one other person, you can simply direct buyers to the appropriate money-taker. Or you might use color-coded price stickers.

One way to draw a larger crowd to your garage sale is to make it a neighborhood or block sale. Let your neighbors know that you are planning a garage sale on such-and-such a date, and ask if they are interested in having a sale of their own on that day. A benefit of

recycling stuff

Rather than add to the landfill, recycle. For example, take plastic grocery bags back to the supermarket and return wire hangers to the dry cleaner. You can also recycle used inkjet printer and laser printer cartridges through the manufacturer or school fundraising programs.

Dare to be creative. Turn an old golf bag with wheels into a garden-tool caddy or umbrella stand. Or "plant" your old mailbox in your garden for storing hand tools.

Whatever you decide to do, do it within a specified time frame to keep this stuff from continuing to take up space in your home.

joining forces is that you can advertise the block sale together and split the cost of advertising. You may even be able to buy a larger ad, which is more likely to get noticed. Be sure to give your neighbors plenty of advance warning (at least one month) so they have time to go through their homes and set aside items they want to sell. A neighborhood or block sale also generates a strong sense of community, so get out there and have fun.

CHAPTER 3

ORGANIZING BASICS

Uncluttering is half the battle. Organizing is the other half. Without organizing, you'll find that you have to unclutter over and over again. Getting organized shouldn't be complicated; the more complicated your organizational system, the less likely it is that you'll be able to maintain it. So keep it simple. And remember that the only "right" way to get organized is the way that works best for you.

A Home for Everything

More often than not, things don't get put away because they don't have a home. How can you put everything in its place if you don't have a place for everything? The key to getting organized is to find the best possible home for all of your belongings, everything from measuring cups to memorabilia.

When choosing a home for an item, don't think, "Where shall I put this?" Instead, think, "Where am I most likely to look for this?" Ideally, the home you create will be close to where the item gets used and where others might be apt to look for it. As you look at where things are stored in a particular room, ask yourself the following questions to help you determine where each item belongs:

- How often do I use it?
- Where do I use it?
- How accessible is it?
  How accessible should it be?
- Does it belong in this room?

Things you use often should be visible or easily accessible. Store the things you use most often between neck and knee height and toward the front of a closet or cabinet. Store things you rarely use on higher or lower shelves or in your long-term storage area. You may find that the best place for some items, such as a broken lamp, is in the trash. Other items might belong in other rooms. Still other items, such as a suit you no longer wear, might belong better in someone else's home.

If you have a place for storing a particular item, but that place isn't being used, figure out why. Perhaps it is not conveniently located. A good example is the hamper. If your kids get undressed in the bedroom but the hamper is in the bathroom or the laundry room, it's no wonder their dirty clothes always wind up on the floor. Put a hamper in each bedroom.

Work with Clutter

Organizing your home and possessions to fit your lifestyle can go a long way toward minimizing clutter. Where do you tend to drop your keys when you come in the door? Where do you put things you need to take with you when you leave for work? Where do you pay bills?

Walk through your home and look at what's lying around. Consider how you use each room. Work *with* clutter by organizing these logical storage places. Ask these questions:

- What causes clutter in this room?
- What items end up here that should be somewhere else? Why?
- What things should be in this room that are not here now?
- What organizing products could I use here? (See page 26 for ideas.)

Is your dining room table or kitchen counter, for example, a dumping ground for anything and everything that comes in the door? Can you find or create a better place nearby to store these things, perhaps on a shelf or in a cabinet? You may not be able to eliminate clutter, but you *can* control it.

An effective way to minimize clutter is to set up work centers for specific activities, such as handling mail and bills, sewing, hobbies, and laundry. A workstation that includes all the tools you need close at hand saves you time. You also may find that it is most efficient to have certain things, such as scissors, in more than one location. You might want to keep a pair with your office supplies and another pair with your gift-wrapping supplies, for instance.

WHAT HAVE YOU GOT?

Look at an area of your home and ask yourself, "What have I got here?" First, eliminate the things that do not belong in that area. Put those items in the appropriate place, whether it be in the trash or another location. For the remaining items, ask yourself, "What have I got here?" Group the items into categories. For example, in the garage, categories might include automotive, lawn and garden, tools, and sports equipment. Plan your strategy on paper before beginning to physically sort the items. Once you've established the major categories, next determine the most convenient place to store each group of items. When you've decided on a location, take another look at the items in each category. Ask yourself again, "What have I got here?" and then decide what type of container, hook, or shelf will work best.

—*Judy Stern, Organize NOW*

Consider establishing clutter-free zones. Make the dining room a no-toy zone, or lay down ground rules for using the living room: for example, "If you carry it in, carry it out when you leave." You might also consider creating your own personal sanctuary — a space you can call your own, where you can read or write or think in privacy. If you live with others and cannot claim an entire room for yourself, claim a portion of a room and declare it off limits to everyone but yourself. As you begin to assert control over clutter, space by space, room by room, you will begin to regain control of your environment — and your life.

One Challenge . . .

I often leave notes and things out as a reminder to do something. If I put everything away, I'm afraid that I will forget something important that I was supposed to do or where I put something that I need.

Three Solutions

1 FROM DONNA D. MCMILLAN, MCMILLAN & COMPANY PROFESSIONAL ORGANIZING: Is that really the reason why you leave things out? Or do you leave things out because you don't know what else to do with them? Give everything a home or a place to live. Then, when you're finished with it, get in the habit of taking it back home. It could be cotton swabs that belong on the second shelf of the medicine cabinet to the right. When you give things a home, you can always find whatever you're looking for, even in the dark!

2 FROM JUDY STERN, ORGANIZE NOW: When you leave things out where you can see them, generally you don't see them again. They become part of the wallpaper. A more effective reminder system is to keep notepads available in locations where they'll come in handy for jotting down reminders. Once you've written something down on a list, you no longer need the item itself as a reminder, and you can feel comfortable putting it away.

3 FROM LORRAINE CHALICKI, YOUNEEDME.COM: Some visual cues are okay if you're disciplined. For example, near the door, you might allow only things that you will take with you on your next trip out the door. In your office, you might write "To Do Today" reminders on colorful sticky notes that you affix to a stand-up acrylic holder placed on your desk. As you address each item, pull the reminder off, throw it away, and congratulate yourself for getting it done.

Contain Yourself

Use containers to organize your belongings. Think of drawers, shelves, and clothes rods as containers, in addition to boxes, crates, baskets, and bags. Keep like items together in separate containers. This makes it easy to find what you're looking for, even if you never get around to organizing the contents of the container.

Group items together in whatever way makes sense to you. In your closet, clothes can be sorted and hung by shirts, pants, skirts, dresses, and suits, or by color. Small items, such as cookie cutters, can be put in resealable plastic bags to keep them separate from other small kitchen gadgets in a drawer. Familiarize yourself with organizing products designed to help you contain all kinds of things. You may be surprised at the variety of producers available.

To maximize existing storage space, think vertical. Think about what you might be able to hang on walls, from the ceiling, and behind closed doors. A shoe rack hung over the back of a door, for example, takes up less space than a standing shoe rack. Use same-size storage boxes that stack easily on shelves to make use of space at the top of closets. In cabinets, you might be able to mount an organizing product to the inside of a door to store spices or pot lids.

If you have a lot of wasted space at the top of your cabinets, try raising or lowering shelves to create more usable space. Or use freestanding shelving or hanging wire baskets under shelves to create additional storage. Consider replacing fixed shelves with adjustable shelving that rolls out, so that even items in the back are accessible. You can buy a do-it-yourself kit for this purpose at hardware and home stores.

Designate temporary storage areas for garage sale items, gifts purchased in advance of the occasion, clothing to go to the dry cleaner, library books, and rented videos to be returned. Store a marker and stickers with your garage sale items so that you can price them as you put them into storage.

Don't just toss things into storage. Take the time to put them where they belong, or create a home for them, so that you don't have to spend hours or days reorganizing your storage at a future date. But do keep an open, "catch-all" box in your storage area to gather all the things you find throughout the year that belong in one of the packed boxes. Rather than pull out all the boxes just to put away one item, you can put away everything in the "catch-all" box periodically.

Organizing Products

There are some terrific products available to
help organize your possessions. But remember:
For every one thing you buy, something must
go, and that goes for organizing products, too!
Be careful that you're not just organizing clutter; you want to pare down as well. Resist the
temptation to buy organizing products until
you know what you need to contain. And be
sure to measure your space so that you buy the
right-size product.

Organized and disorganized people alike
swear by clear plastic storage bins with lids.
Disorganized people throw stuff in them and
hide them just to get it out of sight — which is
a start. Organized people use them to store
everything from puzzle pieces to scuba diving
equipment, craft supplies, and holiday decorations. Why are these bins so popular?

- They're clear, so you can see at a glance
  what's inside.
- They come in lots of different sizes.
- They're stackable.
- They're airtight and watertight, so you can
  store things in the basement or garage with-
  out worrying about them getting wet.
- They keep out dust, dirt, and insects.
- They're fairly inexpensive and go on sale
  several times a year.
- They're readily available at mass merchan-
  dise stores.

Sometimes, the best organizing product is
something you have in your home that you
acquired but are not using. A magnetic knife
holder, for example, can be mounted inside a
cabinet door to hold nail clippers, tweezers,
and scissors. Hat boxes, decorative tins, and
woven baskets can contain clutter on shelves
while enhancing the decor of any room.

A filing cabinet or bookcase is probably a
worthwhile investment, but in general, you
don't have to spend a lot of money on organizing products. Check out your local dollar store
for inexpensive jewelry organizers and shoe
bags. Following are some ideas for recycling
everyday items into free organizers.

- In a bathroom cabinet or drawer, use empty
  baby-wipe containers to separate and store
  first-aid supplies, make-up, pain relievers,
  and vitamins.
- Stack plastic milk crates or wooden produce
  boxes against a wall or in a closet, open side
  out. Use them to store books or games.

- Use cardboard copier paper boxes or produce boxes with lids for long-term storage.
- To store odds and ends in the kitchen junk drawer, workshop, or office drawer, use recycled microwave food trays, check boxes, margarine tubs, or aerosol can tops.
- Use a liquor carton with cardboard partitions to store rolled-up artwork. Or use one in your coat closet to store dry umbrellas.
- Empty egg cartons can be useful for storing small items. Remove the lid and place it in a desk drawer to hold paper clips and other small items. Or keep the lid on and store small crafts supplies in it.
- Use shoeboxes to store photos or as dresser drawer organizers.
- Film canisters are very useful for storing small items, such as buttons, safety pins, screws, nails, even quarters and tokens. Use masking tape to label each container, or use a piece of clear tape to attach a sample item to the outside of the container.

Achieving Your Goals

If you find the challenge of getting organized too overwhelming, break it down. Take it one step at a time. Strive for excellence, not perfection. There's a concept called the *law of diminishing returns,* which states that perfectionism rarely pays out. Be the best imperfect person you can be, and get started on achieving your goal. Also, on completion of each step, reward yourself with something you enjoy that you don't often get to do, such as meeting a friend for lunch or getting a manicure or pedicure. That will help keep you motivated.

- **If you have the desire and determination, all you need is a plan.** Make a list of the rooms that you want to organize. Take a walk through each room and jot down the things that need to be uncluttered or organized. Be specific: for example, organize books or clean out refrigerator. Then prioritize your list. Write the number one next to the thing, area, or room that bugs you most. Focus on that challenge. When you're done, check it off your list, give yourself the reward you promised yourself, and decide what is your next priority. Focus only on that challenge.
- **Set a start date and an end date for your home organization project.** If you're not done by then, you can always adjust the end date, but it helps to have one. The end date might be a holiday or party, or a date that you set for a garage sale. Just be sure to allow yourself enough time. How much time is enough? That varies widely from person to person, and it depends on how large your home is and whether you have help. It wouldn't hurt to allow yourself three months or more to do the job right. If you finish earlier, you can enjoy the rewards of organization that much sooner.
- **Focus on the big picture.** For example, if you have papers strewn all over your home, gather them in one place and put them in a cardboard box or other container, maybe even an empty filing cabinet drawer. You can make individual files later. In the meantime, you've

reduced clutter, and you know where all your papers are. Use this same strategy to organize drawers, shelves, and any container. The important thing is to get started by sorting and containing things.

- **Commit to your goal.** Decide how much time you are willing to spend each day on organizing and then schedule it. Even if you commit only five to fifteen minutes a day, you will eventually reach your goals. It's better to get there slowly and surely than to try to do it all at once and get so overwhelmed that you come to a complete standstill.

Help Is on the Way

Don't be afraid to ask for help if you need it. For example, when you get ready to sort through your clothes, invite a friend to help you determine what does and does not look good on you. Minimize distractions during the time you've set aside for uncluttering. Let the answering machine take your calls, and let housemates know that you don't want to be disturbed.

What if you are so overwhelmed that you can't even get started, or you get overwhelmed in the middle of organizing your closet? Professional organizers can help you get and stay organized. These organizing experts can provide ideas, information, structure, solutions, and systems to help you regain control over your time and space. There are thousands of professional organizers in cities around the world. Professional organizers offer the following services:

- Behavior modification
- Closet design and organizing
- Computer consulting
- Errands and personal shopping
- Events and meeting planning
- Filing systems
- Financial/bookkeeping
- Office organizing
- Packing, moving, and relocating
- Paper management
- Project management
- Records management
- Residential organizing
- Seminars, workshops, and training
- Space planning
- Time management

Hourly rates range from $20 to $300, depending on the organizer's level of experience and areas of specialty. To find a professional organizer near you, look in the Yellow Pages under "Organizing Services," or request a free referral through the National Association of Professional Organizers. This group will provide a list of member organizers in your area. Members have pledged to follow a strict professional code of conduct, which includes complete confidentiality.

When choosing a professional organizer, ask about experience with situations similar to yours. Don't hesitate to ask for referrals. Be sure to choose someone you feel comfortable with, since you will be working together closely.

There are at least two support group programs for people who are chronically disorganized. One is Clutterless Recovery Groups, Inc., a nonprofit self-help organization run by clutterers for clutterers. In addition to providing on-line information and support, this group offers workshops and meetings in cities throughout the United States.

Another support group is offered through Messies Anonymous, an organization founded in 1981 to provide educational and motivational aid to chronically disorganized people. Messies Anonymous sponsors twelve-step support groups in which participants set goals, discuss problems, and celebrate victories.

The Internet is a wonderful resource for organizing. Use any search engine to conduct a search for "organizing," and you will find many excellent Web sites, including sites where you can post questions about organizing. (You'll find some of these sites listed in the Resources, which begin on page 322.)

Some people thrive on organizational challenges. If you're one of them, consider giving "the gift of organization" to less organized friends and family members. You might even consider becoming a professional organizer.

Typically, professional organizers are compassionate people who genuinely enjoy helping others discover the benefits of getting organized. Successful organizers are also the type who enjoy running their own businesses. For more information about how to become a professional organizer, contact the National Association of Professional Organizers (see page 322).

If you can't find something in thirty seconds, it's in the wrong place.

—Donna D. McMillan,
McMillan & Company Professional Organizing

CHAPTER 4

STAYING ORGANIZED

Staying organized is even more challenging than getting organized, because you have to train yourself to do things differently. It takes twenty-one consecutive days to establish a new habit, by making a conscious effort every day *not* to do the same old thing. Once you've uncluttered your home, staying organized involves picking up, putting away, and discarding excess stuff on a regular basis.

Simple Everyday Strategies

The best way to stay organized is to take care of today's things today. It's easier to keep up than it is to catch up. Procrastinating usually makes more work later, which can take more time. It can also create more stress and sometimes even more expense. Following are some simple everyday strategies for staying organized by taking care of the little things.

• **Don't put it down, put it away.** Before you put something down, ask yourself, "Is this where it belongs?" In the beginning, it will feel like work, but if you keep after yourself, it will soon become second nature to put things away. Take dressing and undressing, for example. Even when you're in a hurry, remind yourself

that it takes just a minute or two to put away clothes after undressing — far less time than it takes to pick up and put away several weeks' worth of clothing. And it's not just *that* time and work you save when you put away clothes immediately. How often have you had to launder or iron an article of clothing because it was left on the floor overnight or for a week?

• **Lay down the law with household members.** Whoever makes a mess is responsible for cleaning it up — now, not later. That means everyone cleans up their own bathroom mess, their own kitchen mess, and their own bedroom mess. Set minimum standards at first, especially for younger family members, then raise the bar. (For ideas on ways to motivate family participation, see page 35.)

• **Unclutter as you go.** Every morning or evening, walk through your home for five minutes with a basket or tote bag in hand, collecting stray items and returning them to their rightful homes. When you go to the basement, attic, garage, or upstairs or downstairs, take something with you to put away. When you file something in a folder, flip through the folder to see if you can toss anything. A few minutes here and there every day can add up to uncluttering in no time.

• **Leave your "campground" cleaner than you found it.** Make it your policy never to leave a room without improving its appearance. Toss the newspaper in the recycling bin. Straighten pictures and lampshades. Close cabinet doors and drawers. Put dishes in the dishwasher. Make your bed after your morning shower or breakfast — it not only makes the room look nicer, it feels nicer to get into a made bed. If you share a bed, make it a rule that the last one up makes the bed. If you get up earlier every day, you may never have to make the bed again!

For Simplicity's Sake

House Rules

- If you take it out, put it back.
- If you carry it in, carry it out.
- If you borrow it, return it.
- If you open it, close it.
- If you throw it down, pick it up.
- If you take if off, hang it up.
- If you break it, fix it.

Organizing is a process. It's not a one-day project.

—Donna D. McMillan,
McMillan & Company Professional Organizing

• **Make it easy to stay organized.** Designate a "drop off" box for library books and videos that need to be returned. Keep a "put away" basket in a central location, or one in every room, to collect things that belong elsewhere. Make putting away a daily family chore. (And if you get unexpected visitors, you can use these receptacles to pick up and stash clutter in a hurry.) If you find yourself picking up the same areas over and over again, see if you can come up with a simple, practical solution for preventing or reducing future messes. For example, if your kitchen counter is littered with empty beverage bottles and cans, move the recycling bin closer to that area.

• **Make standard "to do" or "to remember" lists.** Make lists for anything you do on a regular basis, such as closing up your summer home or packing to go to the beach. File all of these lists in the same folder in your filing cabinet. Or, if you prefer, keep individual lists with related items so that you'll be sure to find them when you start looking for your stuff. This technique works for the smaller things in life, too. For instance, in your gym bag, keep a list of what you need to take with you. That way, you won't waste energy thinking about what you need every time, and you'll never end up at the gym without your sneakers or a towel.

- **Set limits on recyclable items.** How many plastic shopping bags do you need to save? How many empty margarine tubs and yogurt containers are enough? Being frugal is fine, but if you have more than you need, you're wasting valuable space rather than money. Keep just a few and recycle the others. Do the same with cardboard boxes, rubber bands, twist ties, and similar items you've been collecting.

- **Buy less.** Do you really need more stuff? Think twice about buying things that require extra upkeep, such as knickknacks that have to be dusted regularly and clothing with special washing instructions. Think three times before buying souvenirs; take photographs or keep a journal instead.

- **Simplify your life with the 80/20 rule.** Most people use only about 20 percent of what they own. The other 80 percent is just taking up valuable space, getting in the way, and causing more work than is necessary. In other words, it's clutter. Keep your home clutter-free by making a conscious decision to surround yourself with only the things you love and use.

TAKE ACTION

If something needs to be done, do something about it in the first two minutes you think about it.

—*Judy Warmington, Woman Time Management*

Minimizing Paper Pile-up

If there's one thing that clutters up a home fast, it's paper in its many forms. The best strategy for avoiding paper pile-up has three parts.

1. Limit the amount of incoming paper.
2. Develop a system for storing paper items.
3. Recycle regularly. Keep trash cans handy wherever unwanted paper tends to accumulate.

Junk mail and catalogs are like door-to-door salespeople. Occasionally, you're interested in what they're selling, but more often, you're annoyed at the intrusion. The difference is that you can be as rude as you like to junk mail and catalogs. If you have piles of unopened mail offers, solicitations and catalogs, dump them. Don't even give it a second thought, because you know you'll get more.

Open and sort mail daily into five categories: not for me, action items, to read, to file, and trash. Immediately discard junk mail. (This is easiest to do if you sort your mail near a trash can or recycling bin.) Don't even open it; you know it's junk. Place items to be filed in a folder labeled "To File." Place items to read in a folder labeled just that, then take it to your reading place. If a piece of mail requires action, you don't have to respond immediately, but try to minimize the number of times you handle it. For example, put mail you need to take care of today in a folder labeled "To Do." Place mail for other household members into labeled stacking trays or a vertical file. This is also a good place to keep your filing, reading, and "To Do Today" folders.

When you receive bills, save only the bill and payment envelope. Recycle or throw away the outer envelope and advertising inserts. If you can't bring yourself to just toss them, scan quickly for information that may be interesting or relevant, then toss them. Be sure to read any important notices. Take bills to the place in your home where you write out the checks for them. Create a simple system for storing bills, such as a folder labeled "Bills to Be Paid" or a large, labeled envelope that you keep in a drawer. For tips on paying bills, see page 123.

File regularly to avoid build-up of paper clutter. Do it daily, weekly, monthly, or quarterly, depending on the volume of paper. If you don't file regularly, at least put all items to be filed in a "To File" folder or basket. As you file something, flip through the folder to see if something else can be thrown out. Once a

For Safety's Sake

Protect your credit. Open credit card and other financial offers to make sure that they do not contain live checks connected to one of your credit card accounts. If you aren't going to use these checks, destroy them immediately to prevent them from ending up in the wrong hands. It's also a good idea to destroy preapproved credit card offers in your name. Consider buying an inexpensive paper shredder to destroy these items, or burn the paper the next time you use your fireplace.

> *Every piece of paper has a decision attached to it.*
>
> —LaNita Filer, LFJ Organizing Concepts Plus

year, purge old folders and papers from your filing cabinet. Put only what you really need to keep in long-term storage.

Beware of the paper clutter you create. Think twice before duplicating documents on the copier or printing out e-mails. Use the copier only when absolutely necessary. Store e-mail messages in folders on your computer, or simply make a note of the information you need and delete them. Also, think twice before bringing home free brochures and pamphlets. Read them on the spot if you can and then put them back. Bring home just the information you need by jotting down a note in your daily planner or in a spiral-bound notebook that you carry with you. Finally, recycle or throw away cardboard boxes unless you have a definite or immediate use for them.

Periodic Purges

The easiest way to maintain a clutter-free home is this: For every one item you bring in the front door, send one packing out the back door. Apply the one-in/one-out rule to everything from household items to clothing to paper. Decide before you go shopping what you intend to let go of to make room for your purchase. When you receive a gift, do the same. Keep in mind that what goes out does not have to be equal in value or size to what comes in.

When your child receives a new toy, donate an old one to charity. A good time to ask kids for a donation is just before or just after Christmas, a birthday, or another occasion on which they typically receive gifts. Keep a cardboard box in each child's room for collecting outgrown toys and clothes. When the box is full, take it to your favorite charity, a consignment shop, or to your designated garage/yard sale collection area.

Set aside a specific time each day for picking up. For example, do it while your morning coffee or tea is brewing or just before you go to bed. If it takes longer than fifteen minutes, consider it an early warning that you may be falling back into old habits. When you catch yourself thinking "I'll do it later," stop and do it *now*. Take the extra thirty seconds or five steps it takes to put things where they belong.

Take an inventory of clothing and accessories at the end of each season. Seriously consider donating items that were not worn or used during the past season or that no longer fit. Or set them aside for a garage sale (but only if you are definitely going to have a garage sale!). Wash or dry clean all seasonal clothing before storing it; that way, they'll be ready if you wish to sell items on consignment. Place a reminder in your tickler file to take items to the consignment shop at the appropriate time of year. (See page 16 for more information on consignment shops.)

At least once a year, host a party. Getting ready for the party is fun and gives you extra

FOLLOW THE TWELVE-MONTH RULE

If you haven't touched something in the past twelve months, chances are that you're not going to use it in the next twelve. Clothes and sporting goods seem to be some of the worst offenders. It's natural for people to have a hard time letting go of the past. If an old outfit or a bowling ball really means that much to you, then put it away with your keepsakes. If you feel like you need to hang on to ancient financial paperwork, put it in a remote storage area of your home. Just don't take up valuable space in your active storage areas with items you don't use.

—Ramona Creel, OnlineOrganizing.com

incentive to do a thorough uncluttering. This is also a good time to rearrange your knick-knacks and framed photographs and get rid of any that are no longer meaningful.

In January each year, clean out your filing cabinet to make room for the new year's files. Save only what you need and discard the rest. Chapter 11, The Office, offers tips on filing and retaining records.

Kid Clutter Patrol

You have opportunities to teach your children organizational skills that will last a lifetime. Don't waste those moments by picking up after them. Help them find a place for everything, and train them to put everything in its place.

Establish a morning pick-up routine that might include making beds, hanging up towels in the bathroom, and putting away pajamas. The evening pick-up routine might include putting toys away and clothes in the hamper. Kids want some privacy. Let them know that if they keep their rooms picked up, you will not have to enter except for periodic, preannounced inspections.

Picking up is even more boring for children than it is for adults. Make it fun for children to help. Following are a few ways to make picking up after themselves more like a game than work.

- **Play clutter tag.** To make other family members more aware of their clutter trails, get a roll of peel-off stickers (the easily removable kind) and tag each item that's left out. Just making them aware may make them think twice about leaving things out. Children may enjoy helping you tag items, and the act of tagging will make them more likely to put away their own belongings.

- **Establish a "penalty box."** If Mom or Dad has to pick up something one of the kids left out, it will be forfeited until Saturday morning. To reclaim the item, its owner must pay a penalty of one extra chore. If anyone chooses not to do the chore, you know that the item isn't important to him or her. Give it away or throw it away without guilt.

- **Beat the clock!** This is a good way to make cleaning up a messy bedroom or playroom more fun. Assign a "put away" basket or pillowcase to each child. Set a timer for thirty seconds and see who can pick up the most stuff.

Repeat as necessary and keep score. Reward the winner with a couple of quarters, or allow him or her to stay up a little later that night.

- **"You be the boss."** Let your children take turns being boss for ten minutes. Their job is to supervise the other children as they pick up their belongings and straighten up their rooms. In learning to be a good supervisor, children also learn to pay more attention to details.

- **Blow the whistle on clutter.** Plan a fifteen-minute family pick-up time with a special reward at the end, such as a bowl of popcorn and a movie. Have everyone start in the same room. Blow a whistle as the signal for family members to start putting things away. When that room looks good, blow the whistle again and yell out a room name. "Players" run to the next room and start picking up in that room. Wrap up the game with praise for a job well done.

Sometimes you have to get tough. If family members leave their belongings where they don't belong, gather them up in a large garbage

One Challenge . . .

I've always been very neat and organized, but my husband is the exact opposite and it's driving me crazy. Can you give me some practical ways to cope with a messy partner?

Three Solutions

1 FROM LORRAINE CHALICKI, YOUNEEDME.COM PERSONAL SYSTEMS: Don't make the mistake of labeling your partner "wrong." For years, I would get on my husband's case about his messy desk, but after researching the differences between left and right brain thinkers, I realized that for him, a drawer is a black hole. He needs organizational systems that are very visual and hands-on. Once I understood this, we were able to organize his desktop with upright cascading files for storing folders out in the open, stacking wooden boxes for notebooks and CDs, and a big, white, erasable marker board for managing project deadlines. His desktop isn't "neat and tidy" by some standards, but it's organized for him and that's what matters.

2 FROM PAULA ROYALTY, WORKSMART PRODUCTIVITY CONSULTING: Set aside time to discuss the issue with your husband. Try to reach agreement on how you can live together more harmoniously. Ideally, you want the house to be clean, neat, and tidy, but in reality, what's your minimum standard? You might be happy, for example, if he would agree to leave nothing on the floor and put recyclables in a designated area.

3 FROM DONNA D. MCMILLAN, MCMILLAN & COMPANY PROFESSIONAL ORGANIZING: You shouldn't have to feel like you're nagging. Agree to bring in a professional organizer so that you don't have to be the "bad guy." I can't make anyone do what I suggest, but your spouse may be more likely to take advice from a professional who is not a family member or friend.

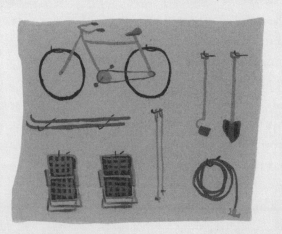

bag and take it out to the garage. When they ask if you've seen a particular item you picked up, tell them it's out in the garage. When they ask why, tell them you found it lying around and thought it was garbage. They should get the idea pretty fast.

Another "tough love" idea is to let your kids know that whatever you find lying on the floor at such-and-such a time will go into the garbage. Then carry through. Throw out or donate the first thing that gets left out. A variation that works well with younger children who can't yet tell time is to tell them that whatever the vacuum cleaner touches gets vacuumed up or goes in the garbage. Once they see that you mean business, they'll scramble to pick up their things when you get out the vacuum cleaner.

Establish playtime rules. Teach very young children to take out only a few toys at a time. If they've already got two or three toys out, they must put one away. Consider restricting toys to one room of the house.

Reminder Systems

Have you ever wondered how some people always manage to remember your birthday? It probably doesn't have anything to do with

memory at all. Much of being organized has to do with developing routines and reminder systems. You might, for example, get in the habit of doing laundry every Monday, cleaning out your refrigerator on trash night, or sweeping away cobwebs on the first of every month. After awhile, it just becomes habit. But many of us also need reminder systems for routine as well as nonroutine activities.

The tickler file described on page 157 is a simple reminder system that works great, as long as you use it. To remind yourself to check smoke detector batteries once a month, write a note to yourself and file it in next month's folder. When the first of the month rolls around, you'll find the note so you can act on the reminder and then refile the note in the following month's folder. To remember birthdays and anniversaries, type a list of special dates in calendar order and then file the list in your tickler file according to the first date on the list. It's best to file the reminder one week before the actual date to give yourself time to buy and mail the card. Refile the list according to the next date on your list.

If you like visual cues and you refer daily to a wall calendar, the best reminder system for you might be to note all important events and reminders on the appropriate dates throughout the year when you get your new calendar. If you learn of a new birthday or anniversary as the year progresses, write it on your calendar. At the end of the year, transcribe all of the birthdays and anniversaries onto your new calendar.

Another way to remember birthdays and anniversaries is by using a "Days to Remember" book. This is a perennial calendar of months and days that allows you to record birthdays, anniversaries, and other special days. You can also include the year of the birth or wedding for future reference. As new birthdays and weddings take place, write them in your book. You'll never have to transcribe these dates, but you will need to remember to check the book occasionally. This method works best if you get in the habit of buying cards in advance and filing them in your tickler file.

If you prefer a more high-tech approach to organizing, have your computer remind you of special days and things to do. Free Internet reminder services allow you to set up e-mail reminders for important dates and events. Several such services are listed in the Resources beginning on page 322.

If you have scheduling software installed on your computer, you can enter tasks, such as "Buy birthday card for Mom," and then specify the date and time you want to be reminded about that task. And, if you have a personal digital assistant (PDA), simply download your calendar from your computer, and you can be reminded of what you need to do even when you're away from home.

ORGANIZING GREETING CARDS

Buy greeting cards at random when you see ones you like. Store them in a file caddy or other sturdy container that accommodates 9×12-inch manila envelopes upended on their sides. Label envelopes by category:

- Adult Birthday/Children's Birthday/Belated Birthday
- Anniversary/Wedding
- Friendship/Thank You
- Get Well/Feel Better/Sympathy
- Congratulations/Baby/New Home
- Special Occasion/Holiday
- Blank

Using envelopes instead of file folders keeps the greeting cards in like-new condition. Labeling the envelopes along the top edge (upended side) makes it easy to flip through your collection to find the appropriate category. Having an assortment of greeting cards on hand saves you from having to run out and buy them when you may not have the time to do so.

—*Bette Martin, Necessary Indulgence Professional Organizing*

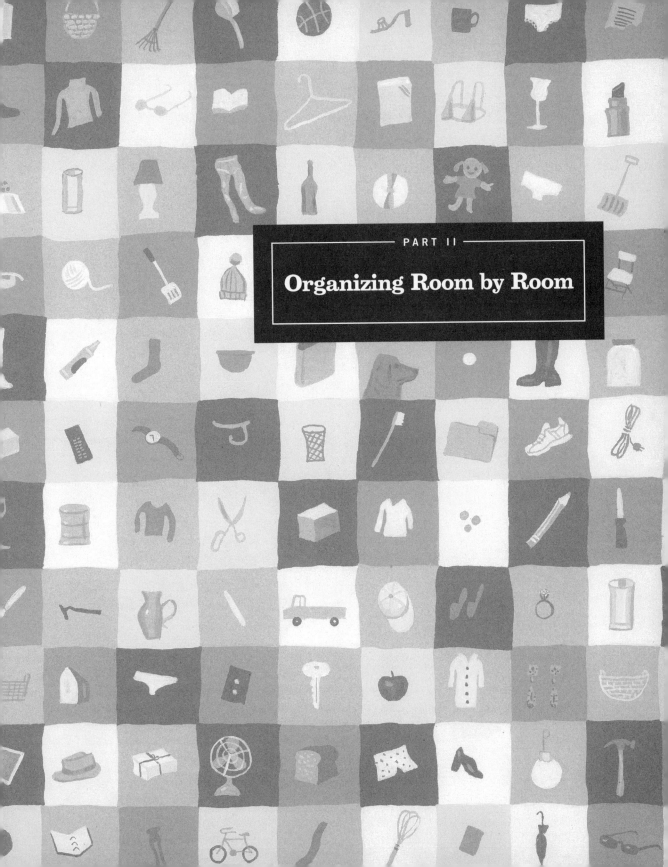

PART II

Organizing Room by Room

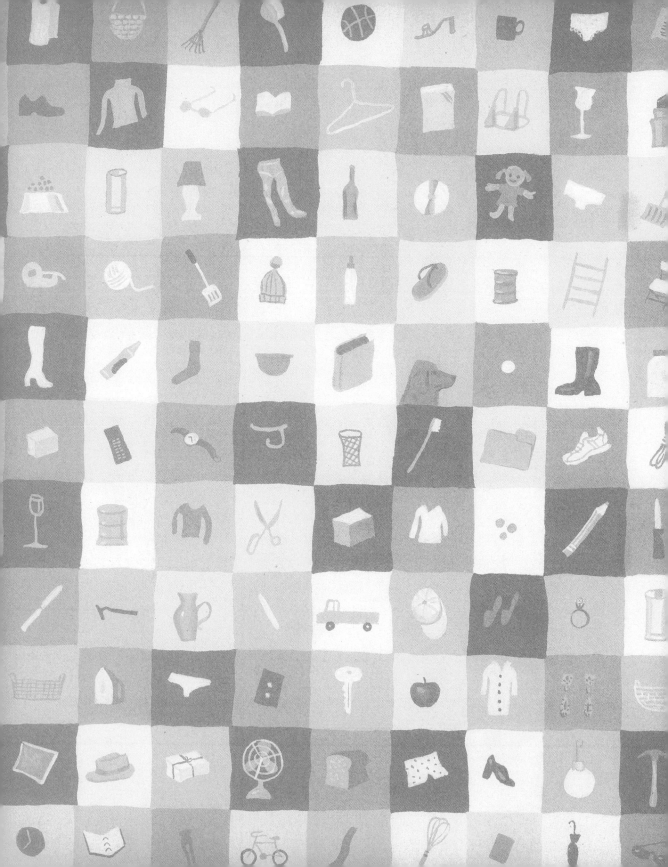

Any large organizing project is best accomplished by breaking it down into smaller, more manageable tasks. This is particularly true when organizing a home. The simplest way to divide this enormous project is to work one room at a time. Envision the rooms in your home as containers of related items. Organizing a single container is far easier than trying to organize many containers simultaneously. Simply choose the room that you want to organize first and begin. Within the room that you've chosen, organize one drawer, shelf, or defined space at a time.

The chapters in this section focus on a particular part of the home for quick and easy reference. Because there are so many different types and sizes of homes, some rooms, such as storage rooms, are grouped into chapters by utility.

CHAPTER 5

ENTRYWAYS

When you think of the entrances to your home, think of first impressions. An uncluttered entrance is open and inviting. Think of the feeling you get when you receive a warm handshake or greeting. Now picture a large, muscular man with arms crossed against his chest, blocking your doorway. That's the impression a cluttered entrance makes. What impression do your entryways make?

Uncluttering Entrances

The problem with clutter is that after awhile, you tend not to see it, unless you trip over it — and in that case, you see it after the fact. If you want to know what your entryways *really* look like, step outside for a moment and close the door behind you. Pretend you are a neighbor or friend who has never been to your house. Invite yourself in. Now, look around as if you are seeing your home for the first time. What's your first impression? On a scale of 1 to 10, with 10 being the most favorable, how would you rate your first impression of your home? How far off is your impression from the impression you would like to make?

Take a look at the things that are cluttering your entryways. Where do they belong? Is it easy or difficult to put these things where they belong? For example, if coats belong in the coat closet, but there are no hangers or the closet is already too crowded, putting away coats becomes impossible.

As you begin to unclutter your entryways one by one, use a box or bag labeled "Store Elsewhere" to collect items that belong elsewhere in your home. In another box, collect items that should go in your car so that you can take them where they belong. Such items include library books to return, clothes to drop off at the dry cleaner, and merchandise to be returned to the store. To avoid putting them in the trunk and then forgetting about them, post a sticky note on your dashboard as a reminder to deliver them or make a note in your calendar.

Homes for the Homeless

Now, look at what's left in your entryway. Put away things that have a home. Look at what's left. Is there anything you could throw away or give away? Do it. All that should be left now are those items that you need to create homes for, which might include the following:

- **Shoes.** Place a shoe rack, large wicker basket, or other receptacle near the front door to collect shoes. If you always take off your shoes at the door, you won't have to go searching for them later and your carpets and floors will stay cleaner.

- **Wet shoes and boots.** In winter or wet weather, set out enough rubber or plastic boot trays, bath mats, or towels, to accommodate wet shoes and boots for residents and visitors. If you use a shoe or boot rack for this purpose, be sure to cover the floor beneath it.

- **Mittens and gloves.** Use a hanging shoe bag with clear plastic pockets to keep pairs of mittens and gloves together. Hang it behind the closet door or from the rod. Reserve lower pockets for shorter household members. Or hang a nylon mesh bag from a hook or peg in the coat closet. At the end of the season, simply take the bag down, launder the contents, return them to the bag, and store with your out-of-season coats and clothing. To dry wet mittens and gloves, glue clothespins to a strip of  wood that you can nail into the wall above a heater. Varnish or paint the wood and clothespins to make them more attractive.

- **Hats and scarves.** Store brimmed hats flat on a shelf or in hatboxes. Hang caps and other hats on coat pegs, or store them with scarves in a hall storage bench or on a shelf in your coat closet. If you always wear the same scarf with the same coat, hang them together. Otherwise, fold and hang scarves on hangers in your coat closet. Keep these hangers together off to one side of the closet.

- **Umbrellas.** Store wet and dry umbrellas in an umbrella stand just inside the door or just outside the door (if that area is sheltered). Dry umbrellas can be hung on a standing coat rack, wall hook, or peg.

- **Backpacks and book bags.** Install a double coat hook that will accommodate one backpack and one jacket. Install one hook per child at the appropriate heights.

- **Other school paraphernalia.** Create a "launch pad" in a hall closet or along one wall of the hallway. Stack however many plastic crates you need — one for each child — for collecting lunchboxes, graded homework and tests, announcements, and paperwork to be signed.

Assign crates by color, or label with names. Encourage your children to put everything in their crate when they come home and to take everything out when they leave in the morning. That way, their stuff won't clutter up your hallway or kitchen, and they will know where to find it. You and your partner may want crates, too, for storing pocketbooks, briefcases, and anything else that will head out the door with you (for example, library books or dry cleaning). If you don't like the look of crates, try a bookcase with cubbyholes or a standard bookcase. Place same-size baskets or wire bins on the shelves for each family member.

• **Keys.** Hang your keys on a nail near the door, and get into the habit of putting them there as soon as you come in. If you don't like the look of a bare nail, buy a decorative key hanger. Or hang a door-

knob basket and drop your keys into it when you come home. If the basket is big enough, you'll also have a handy holding station for outgoing mail.

Everybody thinks that their mess is the worst mess I've ever seen. Relax, I say. You're working with a natural disaster here. Life is naturally messy.

— Sheila Delson, FREEDomain Concepts

CLEARING OBSTACLES

Feng shui (pronounced "fung shway") is the ancient practice of living in harmony with the environment. One of the basic principles of feng shui is to have a good flow of energy (*chi*) throughout your home. Clutter traps energy. If you have a messy office, for example, you have dead energy. Conversely, an uncluttered bedroom can help you to sleep well and enjoy harmonious dreams. The absence or presence of clutter in your entryway also has significance. The front door represents your journey through your life or career. Clutter in your entryway blocks the natural flow of your journey. This can prevent you from achieving success or even from recognizing your most harmonious path.

— Lorraine M. Duvall, feng shui consultant

Organizing Coats

Sort through coats and separate into two categories: in season and out of season. Then sort the out-of-season coats into two categories: coats you will most likely wear next season and coats you are not likely to wear because of fit, style, color, or age. Set aside the coats you won't wear again for someone who will. Give them to a family member or friend, donate to a charitable organization, or take them to a consignment shop before the start of the season. Now look at the out-of-season coats that you will wear again next season. If any coats need to be cleaned, bring them to your laundry room or put them in your car to take to the dry cleaner.

Next, sort through in-season coats. Are there any you didn't wear last season? Any you probably won't wear again ever? Put them with the coats you plan to give to someone else. Consider yourself fortunate that you are in a position to share. Hang all the coats you're keeping on sturdy hangers and arrange by type of coat (sporting, casual, and dress, or short and long) or by family member. Add a few extra sturdy hangers for hanging guests' coats. Replace wire hangers with sturdy coat hangers.

What else is in your coat closet? Hats, gloves, umbrellas, boots? Discard items that are worn or broken beyond repair. Put anything you don't use or wear in your "Give Away" box. Clean and put away all out-of-season items. If there's nowhere to put them except the coat closet, put them on the upper shelves, on the floor in back, or in a corner. Remove items that don't belong in the coat closet and put in your "Store Elsewhere" box.

If you don't have a shelf above the clothes rod or you have only one shelf, consider installing shelving that goes up to the ceiling to make use of all that wasted space. Upper shelves are great for storing out-of-season clothing and sporting gear, old photograph albums and memorabilia, or anything requiring long-term storage. Use clear plastic bins so you can see what's inside, or clearly label boxes. On the shelf just above the clothes rod, use wire bins to separate and contain accessories, such as gloves and mittens.

Most coat closets have only one long rod hung at about the shoulder height of an adult. If you want children to hang up their coats, make it possible for them by installing a rod at their shoulder height or Shaker-style pegs along the back wall, at one end of the closet, or in the hallway.

Neatness Counts

Many homes have a "formal" entrance and a "family" entrance. It's generally easier to keep the formal entrance clutter-free, simply because it isn't used as often as the family entrance. And it goes without saying that the more use a room or space gets, the more clutter it attracts; this is especially true of entrances.

The best way to combat this natural tendency to clutter is to find a place for everything that *belongs* in the entryway and to return those items to their homes when you are finished using them. But what about things that you leave in the entryway temporarily, such as books and videos to be returned? It's simple: Give them a home, too. Try a decorative basket by the door, or put these items in a tote bag that can be hung on a hook or peg inside the coat closet.

TIME-SAVER

60

Do you like to know how you look before you leave home? Avoid backtracking to another room by hanging a mirror in your entryway or behind the door of your coat closet.

CHAPTER 6

KITCHEN AND DINING AREA

In *Cooking as Therapy*, Louis Parrish wrote, "If you can organize your kitchen, you can organize your life." The kitchen is home to an incredible number of items, from gadgets, appliances, and tools to foodstuffs. It's also where we spend a great deal of time — not just preparing and eating food, but also managing the household and hanging out. It's no wonder this room attracts so much clutter.

Getting Started

Organizing the kitchen can easily be a full-day job. If you can't spare an entire day, break the task down into smaller jobs. Unclutter the counter today, tackle the refrigerator and freezer tomorrow, and unclutter everything else one day at a time until you are satisfied with the results.

The countertop is a good place to start. Just uncluttering your countertop can make your whole kitchen look neat and organized. Simply remove everything from the counter, and then put back only those things you use at least twice a week. Find a new home for everything else — possibly in another room or in the "Give Away" or "Sell" box. The next step is to organize for efficiency.

Where to Store What

Think about the types of activities that take place in your kitchen. They might include food preparation, cooking, washing dishes, eating, opening mail, and paying bills. Then think about where in the kitchen you do these things and what tools you need to do them. Now look at nearby storage areas in each of these activity areas. Tools should be stored as close as possible to where you use them. For example, keep the toaster near the breadbox, pots and pans near the stove, and the coffeemaker near the sink.

Before you start lamenting your lack of cabinet or counter space, look at your walls and ceiling as potential storage spaces. In a restaurant kitchen, the chef's main tools are hung up rather than stored away because it's more efficient. If you have a handsome set of pots and pans, consider hanging them on a wall or from a ceiling-mounted rack. Hang knives on a magnetic bar attached to the wall, and hang cooking utensils on a pegboard or rail system with hooks mounted near your stove.

When replacing small appliances, consider ones that mount under cabinets (coffeemaker, microwave, toaster, and can opener are good examples). Another way to gain counter space is to put your microwave on a rolling cart that has shelves and drawers, where you can store cookbooks and measuring cups and spoons.

Organizing Cabinets

Take everything out of your cabinets, one cabinet at a time. Throw away plastic containers without lids, and give away those in odd sizes

make your own

Hanging Rack

What You Need:
- Old ladder 3 to 4 feet in length
- Sturdy chain
- S-hooks
- Ceiling hooks

Cut an old ladder to the desired size. Refinish to match your kitchen decor. Use chains to suspend the ladder from hooks screwed into the ceiling joists. Hang pots and pans on S-hooks dangling from the ladder.

that you never use. If you have more than enough coffee mugs or glasses, get rid of some. Discard or hold aside for donation anything else in your cabinets that's just taking up space.

The most efficient place to store dishes, glassware, and silverware is close to your dishwasher or sink, so that it's fast and easy to put them away after being washed. You also might store them near the table, so a helper can get to the table without getting in the way of the cook in the food-preparation zone. A great way to optimize storage space for dishes is to install a wire shelf unit that attaches to the underside of your existing shelving. Also, consider using cup hooks underneath shelving for hanging coffee cups and mugs. Glassware should be stored upside down to keep the inside dust-free. Stemware can be hung by using an organizing product that clips to the underside of a shelf.

kitchen essentials

Following is a list of basic kitchen tools you'll need if you're setting up a new kitchen. If you already have more than the specified number of these items, ask yourself, "How many of these do I really need?" Only you know the answer. If you have an item that is not on this list, ask yourself, "Am I using this item?" If not, you could unclutter your kitchen by paring down your kitchen tools to those that you do use and need.

For food preparation
- Cutting board
- Bread knife with serrated edge
- 8- or 10-inch chef's knife, for chopping
- Paring knife
- Vegetable peeler
- Vegetable scrubbing brush
- Egg beater
- Grater
- Kitchen shears
- Can opener
- Set of nested mixing bowls
- Rubber spatula
- Dry and liquid measuring cups (2 sets)
- Measuring spoons (2 sets)

For cooking
- Small, medium, and large pots with lids
- Extra-large pot with lid
- Small, medium, and large skillets
- Whisk
- Tongs
- Metal spatula
- Wooden spoons (2 sizes)
- Slotted spoon

For baking
- Roaster pan with rack and cover
- Two oven-to-table casserole dishes (one 1-quart and one 2-quart)
- Oblong 13 x 9 baking pan
- Two baking sheets with edges
- 9-inch pie plate
- Muffin tin with 12 cups
- Two round layer-cake pans
- 9-inch by 5-inch loaf pan
- Large cooling rack or two small racks
- Rolling pin
- Flour sifter
- Pastry blender

For serving and cleanup
- Ladle
- Colander
- Carving knife and fork
- Potato masher
- Assorted plastic containers for leftovers

The Organized Pantry

Canned and packaged foods should be stored in a cool (below 70°F), dry area, away from light. Don't store these foods in cabinets near the oven or on shelves near the ceiling. In your food cabinets or pantry, designate specific shelves or sections of shelves for certain categories of foods; eventually, you won't even have to think about what goes where. Categories might include the following:

- Baking supplies
- Cereals and breakfast items
- Crackers and snack foods
- Canned meat and fish
- Canned soup and broth
- Canned vegetables
- Canned fruit
- Baby food
- Dry goods, such as pasta, rice, and beans
- Spices and seasoning packets
- Oils and vinegars

Start organizing by removing all foodstuffs from your cabinets. Throw away all outdated food items, and give away any others that you will never use. Line your shelves with easy-to-wipe shelf paper to keep them clean. Store opened bags of chips, cookies, rice, dry beans, and other dry goods in stackable plastic bins that let you see what's inside. One staple that should *not* be stored in your pantry is whole-wheat flour, which needs to be refrigerated to keep from going rancid. If you find spoiled or infested foods, throw out the food and clean the area with a weak solution of vinegar and water.

make your own

Pot Lid Holder

What You Need:
- Small towel rack
- Screws
- Screwdriver

Before mounting the rack, check that it will hold your lids and that it does not interfere with closing the door. Screw a small towel rack to the inside of your cabinet door. Slide the pot lid behind the rack until the handle rests on top.

To keep food items visible and accessible in your cabinets, use freestanding wire shelves, stepped organizers, or single- or double-decker turntables. Arrange cans, bottles, and boxes on shelves with the labels facing out. If you use a turntable, put tall items or extra supplies in the center of the turntable. On shelves, move older items to the front when adding newer purchases. Keep like items, such as baking supplies, easily accessible by storing them in a stack-and-slide basket.

Canned goods can pose problems in your cabinets. Because of the depth of the shelves, stacking the cans one in front of the other is just not practical. You will forget what you've got stored in the back because you can't see it. The staff at The Container Store recommend storing canned goods on a three-tiered shelf that resembles a staircase. This product is expandable to fit the width of your cabinet and provides you with a full view of your canned goods. A gravity-feed can rack is another popular choice. This rack serves as a dispenser for your canned food while allowing you to see your entire collection of cans.

Label shelves with what goes where so that other household members can put away groceries. Do this after your shelves are arranged to your satisfaction. Sometimes, in the process of organizing, you discover a better arrangement than the one you started with.

If your shelves are deep, store less frequently used items or extra staples behind those you use more frequently. Sliding drawer racks make good use of space in deep cabinets and make food items more accessible. You could also use the space in back to store infrequently used appliances. If you have a pantry

make your own

Under-Cabinet Storage

What You Need:
- Recycled food jars
- Two screws for each jar
- Power screwdriver

If you have sufficient clearance underneath your upper cabinets, you may be able to use that space for decorative and functional row storage using recycled food jars. Use two screws to fasten the lids securely to the underside of your cabinets. Fill the jars with rice, beans, peas, pasta, popcorn, tea bags, nuts, raisins, and spices. Then screw the jars to the lids.

with a door, use the inside of the door for additional storage by installing over-the-door wire rack shelving.

Go through your spices. Open each jar and sniff the contents. If you don't smell anything, you won't taste anything. Discard jars and tins of outdated spices. You can buy spice organizers that attach to the wall or inside the cabinet door, or you can use a double-decker turntable or expanding, stepped shelf organizer. A "pull-down" spice organizer is available that attaches to the underside of a shelf. Store spice jars and tins with the labels facing out. Group spices that are often used together, such as nutmeg, cinnamon, and cloves, or alphabetize your spice collection. Keep taller jars together

TIME-SAVER

If you have bottles that tend to drip, wipe them well and place a plastic lid from a coffee can underneath them to prevent dripping on clean shelves.

or behind smaller jars. "File" seasoning packets face forward in a narrow box that lets you flip through them easily.

Organizing Your Refrigerator

To organize your refrigerator, start by uncluttering it. The best time to do this is the night you put out your trash or just before going to the dump. Start with the top shelf and work your way down. Open and unwrap everything, and check expiration dates. Throw out anything that is clearly bad or questionable. Discard useless bits of food and consolidate small but edible amounts of food in small containers. Also consolidate any "twos" or "threes" of things in jars or bottles.

Take note of how many foods went bad because they were buried or forgotten. Organizing your refrigerator can help to reduce the amount of spoilage and save money. Planning your food purchases can also help. See "Smart Food Shopping" on page 211 for suggestions.

Another way to reduce spoilage is to hang a magnetic erasable dry-marker board on the front of your refrigerator that lists the leftovers, cold cuts, vegetables, and other perishables inside. This list also minimizes the amount of time the refrigerator door is open, which will save energy and help keep food fresher longer.

The outside of your refrigerator may also be in need of uncluttering. Remove items that are outdated or that don't serve a purpose for you any longer. If you like to display photographs, consider purchasing inexpensive, magnetic-backed plastic frames to keep photographs flat, clean, and neatly arranged. For a really uncluttered look, consider keeping the front of your refrigerator clear of all magnets and hanging items.

For Safety's Sake

Have you ever wondered how long food stays fresh in the refrigerator? Play it safe by disposing of foods according to this recommended schedule.

Food	Dispose of If Not Used Within
Fresh fish	1–2 days
Ground meat	1–2 days
Fresh chicken or turkey	1–2 days
Fresh pork, beef, veal, lamb	3–5 days
Hot dogs, bacon	7 days if opened
Smoked breakfast links, sausage patties	7 days
Lunch meats	3–5 days if opened
Raw eggs	4–5 weeks
Boiled eggs	7 days
Egg, chicken, tuna, ham, and macaroni salads	3–5 days
Soups and stews, cooked poultry, cooked meat and meat dishes	3–4 days
Ham, fully cooked	7 days
Store-cooked convenience foods	3–4 days
Commercial mayonnaise	2 months after opening

Source: U.S. Food and Drug Administration Center for Food Safety and Applied Nutrition (www.cfsan.fda.gov/~dms/fttstore.html)

Now that your refrigerator is uncluttered, organize it. The first thing to decide is what to store where. The meat/deli tray is the coldest spot in your refrigerator — do use it to store all deli meats and frozen meats that you want to thaw in the refrigerator.

The crisper drawer is designed to seal tightly to keep in humidity. Storing vegetables in the crisper will help them to retain moisture. Lettuce will stay fresher if you wash it, shake off the leaves, wrap them in a paper towel, and store them in a heavy-duty, resealable plastic bag; squeeze out air as you close the bag. Other vegetables best stored in plastic bags are broccoli, carrots, cauliflower, celery, green beans, and scallions.

Washing and storing these vegetables in a sealed plastic bag will not only help them last longer but also keep your crisper cleaner. As long as the food inside remains fresh until used, the plastic bags can be washed and reused.

To store peppers, eggplant, summer squash, beets, cabbage, and mushrooms, use a loose plastic covering and place them in the crisper.

Store fresh herbs unwashed and loosely wrapped in the crisper.

Some vegetables should *not* be stored in the refrigerator. Cold air destroys the flavor of cucumbers; instead, dip them in cold water and store in a cool, dry place. If you want to serve them cold, chill just before serving. Potatoes should not be stored in the refrigerator because the starch breaks down quickly. If you bake a potato that has been refrigerated, it will be mushy. Potatoes, winter squash, dry garlic, gingerroot, and mature onions are best stored in a cool, dry place.

Most fruits are best stored at room temperature until they ripen. This includes apples, melons, pears, plums, avocados, peaches, and pineapples. You can hasten ripening by putting fruit in a paper bag. Do not wash grapes and berries until you are ready to eat them; the dusty stuff on them is a preservative. Refrigerate grapes and berries in a plastic bag with perforated holes or covered loosely with plastic wrap. Never refrigerate tomatoes; store in a cool, dry place and eat when ripened. Bananas should be hung to encourage proper ripening. Ripened fruits (except bananas) and cut fruit should be refrigerated to extend their life. Citrus fruits are best stored at room temperature because they have a waxy coating that seals in moisture.

Load up the door of your refrigerator with bottled and jarred foods. Group like items together. You might, for example, use one door shelf for jams, jellies and syrups, and another shelf for condiments. Eggs should not be stored in the door. Every time the door is opened, the eggs are exposed to oxygen, which causes them to deteriorate faster. To keep eggs fresh longer, keep them in their cartons on a shelf, away from the door.

Many helpful refrigerator organization products are available. A turntable on one or more shelves helps prevent perishables from being forgotten and makes food items more accessible. You can also use a tray that pulls out.

Another way to make items more accessible is to store similar foods, such as cheeses, in a clear plastic bin (with or without lid) that you can pull out of the refrigerator. This is also a great way to contain jarred and bottled foods that don't fit on the door shelves.

For neat and uncluttered storage of leftovers, invest in a supply of stackable glass or plastic food storage containers. Square containers make more efficient use of space than round containers, and clear plastic allows you to take a quick visual inventory. It's also a good idea to label and date containers — simply write with a marker on a piece of masking tape. Always store leftovers in the same place in your refrigerator, and see what you have there every day to reduce the amount of food that goes to waste. Do not refrigerate opened cans of foods; transfer the leftover contents to a plastic or glass container.

If you have lots of hungry mouths in your house, consider keeping one large container labeled "Snacks" on a lower shelf. Use it to store hard-boiled eggs, string cheese, leftover chicken or pizza, and other perishable snacks.

You can also buy a container that neatly stores and dispenses up to twelve cans of soda

and a two-liter bottle holder that clips to the underside of a shelf.

Be sure not to overpack your refrigerator. Cool air must circulate to keep food from spoiling prematurely.

Organizing Your Freezer

Although frozen foods will keep indefinitely at 0°F, their quality will deteriorate over time. Take a look at everything in your freezer. Throw out meats that are covered with a thick layer of frost, anything you cannot identify, and anything that's been in there for longer than one year.

Many freezer units have little or no shelving, which makes it difficult to organize frozen foods. You can create your own shelving by using coated wire racks or stackable wire baskets. Store together similar items, such as vegetables, meats, poultry, fish and shellfish, breads, and desserts, to make retrieval and inventory easier.

When you buy meat, store the newest purchases behind or under previous purchases so that you use the food that's been there longest first. Label and date leftovers and repackaged meats. Store in the freezer door items that require frequent access, including frozen juice concentrates, frozen breakfast items, frozen confections, and coffee beans.

Organizing is a matter of making better use of the space you have.

—Melinda Louise, Organize It

Organizing Kitchen Drawers

In your kitchen, you probably have one or two drawers containing silverware and other cutlery and at least one junk drawer. You may be fortunate enough to have additional drawers for dish towels, potholders, and other items. Go through the drawers one at a time.

When organizing, start with your silverware drawer. Take out the cutlery tray (you do have one, right?) and everything else in there. Take everything out of the cutlery tray, then put back only the knives, forks and spoons. Put the cutlery tray back in the drawer. Look at how much room you have left in the drawer, and look at the remaining items to go back into it. Which of them are essential in your kitchen? Put those items in the front of the drawer for easy access. What's left? Is there anything that was just taking up space in the drawer? Give yourself permission to get rid of it. Put it in a box labeled "Donate."

There's nothing wrong with having a junk drawer. Where else can you store those odds and ends you need from time to time? But some of what ends up in the junk drawer really *is* junk, such as unfixable items, pens that don't work, expired coupons, and a piece to a game you sold at a garage sale five years ago. Take everything out of your junk drawer and sort it into two piles: what you definitely need and use, and what's just taking up space. If you can't decide which pile an item belongs in, be honest with yourself. Is it really worth keeping?

Before you put items back into your junk drawer, think about how you can organize the contents by keeping similar items together. An

old cutlery tray might work well for organizing melon ballers, olive forks, cheese knives, and serving spoons or for containing pens and pencils in your junk drawer. Adjustable drawer dividers are another option.

You may have organizing "products" right at your fingertips. Checkbook boxes are great for containing small items, such as matches or batteries. Use resealable plastic storage bags to store all kinds of small things that you need only occasionally, such as cookie cutters or birthday candles. Use rubber bands or twist ties to keep together sets of things like fondue forks, basting pins, chopsticks, and kebab skewers.

Throw out worn potholders and stained dishtowels or convert to dust rags, but *only* if you need more dust rags. Keep only as many of these items as you need. If you like to put out a clean towel each day and you do laundry once a week, seven to ten towels should be plenty.

Organizing Under the Kitchen Sink

Install sliding wire bins or a turntable under the kitchen sink to provide easier access to kitchen cleaning items, such as dishwashing detergent, scouring powder, steel wool pads, and sponges. If you keep your kitchen trashcan under the sink or close by, this is the perfect place to store trash bags.

If you have small children, be cautious about storing cleaning agents under the sink, even if you use child safety locks on the doors. Eventually, children learn how to get around these safety measures, and the results could be disastrous.

Organizing Wraps and Bags

There's probably a place in your kitchen — one section of your counter, perhaps — where you tend to use foil, plastic wrap, freezer bags, and other food wraps. Store these food wraps close to where you use them, ideally at or close to counter height. Wall-mount dispensers for various kitchen wraps are available; however, they don't hold all types of food wraps. The same goes for dispensers that mount inside cabinet doors. You'll still have to find a place for sandwich and freezer bags, for example.

A great product for organizing food wraps is a set of sliding wire baskets that you can place in a cabinet above or below your counter. Each basket generally holds up to four boxes of food wraps. Try to store food wraps and plastic containers for leftovers close together, since these products are often used for the same purpose.

A nifty place to store trash bags is at the bottom of the trash can or recycling bin. That way, you always have a new bag handy. And the unused bags don't take up room in your cabinets.

Get out of the habit of saving every plastic bag that you bring home from the grocery store. Think about how many you really need, and for what. See if you can survive with about ten. Store them where you are most likely to use them. Special dispensers that mount on the wall are available, or you can make your own storage container from an empty oatmeal or coffee can with lid, empty tissue box, or plastic milk or water jug. (See the simple instructions below.) Take any unneeded grocery bags back to the store for recycling.

make your own

Plastic Bag Dispenser

What You Need:
- One-gallon plastic milk jug, large oatmeal container, coffee can with lid, *or* empty tissue box
- Hook (optional)
- Scissors

Cut a 3-inch hole in the side of the container. Stuff plastic shopping bags into it one at a time; if you do this, you can almost always pull them out one at a time. Set the container on a shelf or hang it from a hook.

Organizing Cookbooks and Recipes

Ideally, your cookbooks should not take up space on your counter. If you don't have shelves in your kitchen, consider using the top of your refrigerator for storing cookbooks between two bookends or in your pantry.

While you're organizing your kitchen, go through your cookbooks. Are there any you never use or don't like? If you've been cooking for a long time, your style of cooking and level of expertise may have changed over the years. Get rid of any cookbooks that don't fit your new style of cooking or degree of know-how. You may be able to sell them at a secondhand bookstore and get store credit or cash in exchange.

If you have a lot of cookbooks, group them by category or alphabetize them by title or author. If you have just a few cookbooks, perhaps arrange them by height, from tallest to shortest.

Whereas organizing cookbooks is pretty simple, organizing loose recipes can be a challenge. The traditional method of organizing recipes is a recipe card box with alphabetical or cookbook-style dividers. This works well if you don't mind transcribing new recipes onto cards. The number of recipes you can save, however, is limited by the size of the box.

A less limiting and less labor-intensive method of storing loose recipes is to keep them in a three-ring binder with plastic photograph album sleeves. Simply insert recipes from various sources and in various formats. You may have to tape index cards in to keep them from slipping.

The three-ring binder allows you to create sections by adding divider tabs similar to those in store-bought cookbooks. You might even consider keeping all untested recipes together in one section. Start by creating one book of your favorite recipes. Eventually, you may wish to create several binders for different types of recipes, such as quick and easy dinners, holidays, or family recipes. If you use a computer to type and print out your recipes, you could easily create copies of your cookbooks to give as gifts for weddings, housewarmings, or other special occasions.

Another way to store recipes is on your computer. You can create an electronic folder for recipes and then create subfolders for different types of recipes, such as appetizers or desserts. You can easily print them on demand when someone asks you for a copy, and your paperless "cookbook" takes up no space in your kitchen!

Compact discs are another paperless source of searchable recipes. You can even subscribe to one of many general and special interest e-mail newsletters available for free from numerous Web sites such as FabulousFoods.com, Cooking.com, and 30DayGourmet.com.

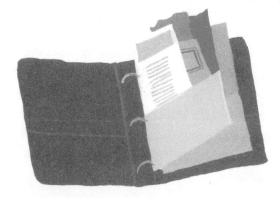

Don't forget to go through your self-assembled cookbooks, whether three-ring binders or computer file folders, from time to time and discard recipes that you didn't enjoy.

The Internet is a great source for recipes. You can cut and paste them into your word-processing program and store them in electronic folders. One of the most popular food-related Web sites is Allrecipes.com, a worldwide community cookbook that contains twenty-three chapters covering appetizers to vegetarian recipes. At this site, you can search for recipes by ingredient or category, create a personal recipe box, and make a shopping list for your weekly meal plan.

The Dining Room

A hutch in the dining room is the best place to store formal china, crystal and silverware, tablecloths and other linens, placemats, infrequently used serving dishes, and special occasion accoutrements for your table, such as candlesticks. If you don't have a hutch or china closet, store these items in an out-of-the-way spot in your kitchen.

Keep good china free of dust by using special covers or dishtowels. But if your dining room storage is limited and you never use certain items, remove these things from your house or put them in long-term storage to free up some space.

To prevent sterling silver items from tarnishing, use them often. Tarnish-retarding storage chests and wraps for silver flatware are available. Less frequently used pieces may be tightly covered with plastic wrap or placed in a resealable plastic bag to retard tarnishing. "Dip and shine" polishes are not recommended for finely engraved silver, as they tend to lighten the darker pattern areas that form part of the design. Polish silver periodically with good silver polish, and wash in hot soapy water before drying and putting away.

Discourage dumping of mail, books, and backpacks on the kitchen or dining room table by keeping it set with a tablecloth and place settings. This trick also reduces the amount of storage space you need for dishes and glassware. If you have children, have them reset the table each night.

For Simplicity's Sake

To organize and store holiday tablecloths, hang an over-the-door towel rod on the inside of your linen closet. Keep table linens from creasing by padding the rods with paper towel tubes; slice the tubes lengthwise and roll them over the rod.

CHAPTER 7

FAMILY ROOM

Whether you call it a family room or the living room, this is where you relax with your family and entertain guests. It may also double as a playroom or office. You might not mind the living room looking "lived-in," but it's frustrating to clear the coffee table for the umpteenth time in a week or to trip over things on the floor. The key to organizing the family room can be summed up in one word: contain.

General Room Organization

When decorating, keep it simple. The less you have out, the less you have to keep tidy. Unclutter your walls. Take down everything and put back only what you love in locations where you can enjoy looking at them. Do the same with knickknacks and collections on shelves.

Make clutter "invisible." No, this isn't a magic trick, but the right kind of storage does seem to make clutter disappear. Wire baskets tend to "disappear" into the background, and wicker baskets blend nicely with almost any decor. Store small, loose items, such as playing cards and pens, in a pretty bowl or woven basket set high enough on a shelf that you can't see the contents. Hide a corner office or play-room area behind decorative screens.

When buying furniture for your family room, look for pieces that are functional as well as comfortable and attractive. A chest-style coffee table, for example, doubles as a storage unit.

A Place for Everything

The biggest reasons why things don't get put away are that there's no place to put them or it's difficult to put them in their place. Look around your family room. Do the things on your coffee table belong there? Or did they get left there because they have no home?

Clear everything off your coffee table and put back only what belongs there. This may be coasters, or nothing at all. Find a convenient storage place for everything else, and get in the habit of returning these things to their homes. Keep remote controls in a basket on your coffee table, along with the television listings guide. Or attach them to their respective appliances with adhesive material (hook-and-loop fastener works well) and store the guide on top of the television set. Put a wastebasket in the family room to reduce littering. Create a home for pet toys and teach your pets where to find them. You might even want to teach them to put their toys away!

You might not need to find a place for *everything* in your family room. Stray items, such as coats, backpacks, toys, and school papers, may belong in another room. At the end of each day, or when visitors show up unexpectedly, pick up what needs to go somewhere else and put it in a "go to" box or basket near the door. Make it a weekly task to empty the "go to" box. You might also want to designate a holding place for rented movies and library books that need to be returned.

Think about all the activities that take place in your living area. Ideally, everything you need to perform these activities should be close at hand. For example, if you always clip coupons in the family room, store a pair of

TIME-SAVER 60

Storing books so that the spines are flush with the edge of the shelf prevents dust from collecting on the shelf edges, which means you'll need to dust less frequently.

scissors in the drawer of an end table or in a lidded box that fits under the sofa. You could also keep paper and pencil handy for jotting down notes or ideas.

The space under your sofa is great for hiding all kinds of things: games, puzzles, telephone books, photo albums, linens for the pull-out sofa mattress, or extra leaves for your dining room table. You might also use this space to store a collapsible tray for snacks or entertaining. If you store lots of small items under your sofa, place them on the lid of an old copy paper box for easy access.

Books, Books, Books

Are your bookshelves overflowing? You might think that the solution is to buy more bookcases or put up more shelves, and you might be right. But before you do that, go through your books shelf by shelf to see if you could free up space by giving some away or selling them.

Have you ever questioned why you hold on to every book that comes into your possession? Perhaps you love books and take pleasure in your growing library. But maybe you just got in the habit of shelving books, and now that you think about it, you'd be happy to sell some

books to the used bookstore in exchange for cash or credit. Remember, if you donate or sell a book and miss it later, it's generally pretty easy to get another copy, even if it means borrowing it from the library.

Organize your books into categories, such as fiction, nonfiction, reference, and children's. In libraries and bookstores, fiction is arranged alphabetically by author. You could also organize by genre, such as historical fiction, romance, or mystery. Nonfiction books are typically organ-

ized by subject: for example, gardening, parenting, or travel. If you have an extensive collection of nonfiction books, alphabetize by author within subject. Creating categories makes it easy to find books and even easier to return them to their proper spot. Keep children's books on the lower shelves or in bookcases in their rooms. If your bookshelves are overflowing but you have no room to add shelves, consider storing books horizontally rather than vertically. You may be able to fit more books on a shelf this way. The down side is that it's harder to find books and take them off the shelves.

Audio and Video Storage

Numerous products are available for organizing your videotapes, DVDs, CDs, and cassettes. It's worth doing a little research to find a system that's best suited to your space. Start by counting up your videotapes, DVDs, CDs, and cassettes so that you can select a system that will accommodate your existing collection and give you room to expand. Then look at your space and think about what storage system will work best.

You may find that it's simplest to store videotapes and CDs on shelves. Organize videotapes alphabetically by title or by genre, such as action, children's, comedy, drama, and suspense.

UNCLUTTER YOUR DECOR

Use the largest coffee table possible and eliminate end tables. Replace end-table lamps with swing-away wall lamps, which will eliminate clutter. They are available in all price ranges. For maximum versatility, choose lamps with a three-way switch. Simplify "the box" (the top, bottom, and sides of the room) by painting ceiling and walls the same color. Note that to achieve the illusion of the same color and to compensate for the effects of lighting, you'll need to paint the ceiling two shades lighter than the walls if the wall color is medium to dark. Group together collections of similar items, such as candlesticks and figurines, on shelves or on pretty trays. Paintings, framed photographs, and other wall hangings that are too small to stand alone look more stylish and impressive in groups.

—*Barbara Landsman, Dial-a-Decorator*

Organize CDs by such categories as jazz, classical, rock, and '70s, and then alphabetically by artist. Use separate shelves or sections of shelves for different genres or categories. Store videotapes and CDs like books — vertically, with the spines facing out — and use bookends to keep sections upright. Professional organizer Sheila Delson recommends storing VHS videotapes in 11 x 8 x 4½-inch photo boxes, which hold up to ten videos per box. Then simply assign each box a number, and make an index list of the contents by title. This makes access easier and saves time when looking for that one special title. You can also purchase shelving units that are specially designed for multimedia storage.

If you have space in a cabinet near your television or stereo, create a flip file for DVDs or compact discs by using narrow boxes or wire baskets. Stack-and-slide baskets are especially convenient. Store DVDs and CDs in their original cases. Organize alphabetically by title, or use separate boxes or baskets for different types of music or movies. If you like to take your music with you when you travel, you might prefer to remove CDs from their jewel cases and store them in a zippered carrying case with see-through pockets. Store audiocassettes in specially designed holders.

If your storage space is limited, consider CD and DVD organizers that mount to the wall, or mount shelves for this purpose. You can also buy over-the-door video racks that work well if you have a closet in your family room.

When buying a freestanding storage unit, match the color of the unit to the color of your

make your own

CD Storage

What You Need:
- Old dresser
- Plexiglas *or* fiberboard

Ever wonder what to do with that old dresser? Transform it into a unique CD library. Simply remove the drawers, then make shelves using Plexiglas or fiberboard. Store frequently used CDs in front and less frequently used CDs on the back of the shelves.

stereo components for a uniform, uncluttered look. Avoid CD towers with individual, preset slots; they can be difficult to reorganize when you buy new CDs. If your collection is alphabetized by artist, for example, you'll have to rearrange the entire collection to make space for a new CD in the appropriate slot.

Magazines, Newspapers, and Catalogs

Don't feel that you must catch up on back issues of magazines. Keep the latest issue only, and recycle or donate the rest. In fact, getting rid of back issues may make you feel good because you feel "all caught up" on your reading. Donate magazines to your local gym, a nearby hospital, doctor's office, nursing home, hospice, or wherever people are looking for something to help them pass the time. Before doing this, however, protect your privacy by clipping out the mailing label with your name and address.

Following are some tips for keeping magazines from piling up in the future.

• **Cancel subscriptions to publications you aren't reading.** If you haven't read the last three issues of a magazine, consider canceling your subscription. Maybe you're not as interested in the subject as you were when you subscribed, or maybe you don't have the time

to read it right now. Did you know that you can usually get a refund for the unused portion of magazine subscriptions? If you want to subscribe again in the future, you can respond to one of the offers you are sure to receive.

• **Save only the articles, not the whole magazine.** If you tend to do a lot of reading all at once, scan the table of contents and highlight the article you wish to read. Better yet, tear out those articles, put them in a "To Read" folder or a binder with magnetic photo album sleeves, and place the folder in a basket or rack near your favorite chair, at your bedside, or wherever you most often do your reading. If you tend to read in the bathroom, put a magazine rack in there. Or place reading material in a folder in your briefcase for something to do when you're waiting at the doctor's office, commuting via public transportation, or traveling. By saving only selected articles, you can reduce your reading pile by half or more.

• **Set aside a regular reading time.** If you're having trouble keeping up with your reading, but you don't want to cancel a subscription, set aside some time every day for

old news

Is your coffee table littered with old newspapers? Maybe you have a place to put them (a recycling bin in your garage, perhaps, or a basket near your woodstove), but it's not convenient to take them there every day. Create a temporary home for old newspapers where they can be stored after reading — a basket with a handle or a large tote bag might work well. When the basket or bag gets full, carry it where it needs to go.

reading. Do some recreational reading during your lunch break, try turning off the television at 9 P.M. or not turning it on until then, or read while riding your stationary bicycle.

- **Think twice before saving articles.** Can you look up the information elsewhere if you need it in the future? If you do save articles, file them where you are most likely to look for them. For more tips on creating filing systems, see page 97.

- **Toss the old with the new.** Get in the habit of tossing out the old issue when the new issue arrives. Better yet, recycle it as soon as you're done reading it.

- **Don't sign up for a subscription because of a sweepstakes.** Ordering does not increase your chances of winning. By law, all entries received must be included in the sweepstakes. You are not required to purchase anything.

Set up one rack, basket, or box for catalogs and one for magazines. If you prefer to keep magazines and catalogs together, keep all catalogs in front and all magazines in back so that you don't have to rummage through every-

RACK 'EM UP

The biggest mistake you can make in storing magazines and catalogs is to store them lying flat. Stand them up so you can flip through them easily and have them at your fingertips. Alphabetize them or group them into categories. This system allows you to find and replace a magazine or catalog with the latest edition in only a few seconds.

—*Nancy Black, Organization Plus*

thing to find what you're looking for. If you refer often to your catalogs and magazines, arrange them alphabetically or by subject, such as children's items, women's clothing, and sportswear.

When catalogs arrive, decide which ones you want to keep and immediately put them in the catalog box or basket. If you didn't request a catalog or have no interest in it, put it in the recycling box right away. If you have favorite catalogs, limit yourself to saving one issue at a time. When the new one arrives, throw out the old one, even if you haven't yet looked at it; it's outdated. If you are browsing through a catalog and see something you might like to buy in the near future, tear out the page, along with the order form and back cover (the order-takers always ask for the source code on the back of your catalog). Put only these pages in your tickler file (see page 157). Recycle the rest of the catalog.

If you need to save specific catalogs as resources for work, create folders for them in your filing cabinet. If necessary, categorize them to make it easier to find them in the future. Save only the most current version of the catalog. If you prefer to keep catalogs in plain sight or if they are too bulky to store in a file folder, store them in labeled acrylic magazine holders, which are inexpensive and available at office supply stores.

Organizing Photographs

There are only two ways to avoid photograph clutter: Don't take any photographs, or organize photographs immediately after developing. Not taking photographs probably isn't an option though you might impose a moratorium on picture-taking until you at least *start* organizing the photographs you have.

When you have film developed, order doubles only if you have a definite need for them. If the second set of prints is offered for free and you don't need them, decline the offer. You don't have to take them just because they're free. If you're offered a choice between a free second set of prints and free film, take the film. It may not be the brand you usually buy, but the quality may be identical. If you requested double prints, separate the first and second sets when you get them. Put the first set of prints into your photo album or photo boxes, and do whatever you planned to do with the second set — mail it to a friend right away, for example.

Save only good photographs. Throw away the ones that didn't come out right or are very similar to other, better photographs. Take bad photos back to the developer for credit. Some developers give credit for any photographs you don't like; look for a developer with this policy if you want to save some money.

If you have a computer, take photo processing to the next level: Have your developer deliver your photographs by e-mail or on a disk. Getting your photographs electronically eliminates having to file anything and allows you to share photos easily with friends and family via your Web site or e-mail.

When you need to replace your camera, consider getting a digital camera that allows you to upload and store images on your computer. To organize photographs on your hard drive, create a master file for digital images and subfolders for each set of photographs you take: for example, "Summer Vacation 2002" or "Tommy's Kindergarten Graduation." If you want prints, you can print them on your own color printer using special photograph paper, or send them to the Web site of a company that will "develop" them.

BEWARE OF BUGS

Insects, such as carpet beetles, sometimes attack color slides, negatives, and unprocessed film. Don't store slides, cameras, or film in drawers, closets, or cupboards where you keep clothing or fabric, or where lint has accumulated. These materials attract egg-laying adult insects.

—*Courtesy Eastman Kodak Company*

One Challenge . . .

I have years and years of loose photographs that I want to organize, but honestly, I get overwhelmed just thinking about where to start.

Three Solutions

1 FROM HELEN VOLK, BEYOND CLUTTER: Start by dividing photos into manageable segments. Think about your life and how you can divide it into three or four huge time periods or events, such as college days, wedding, or early married years. Sort photos, put them into separate boxes, and label them. If you do nothing else, at least you know what box to look in for a particular photo. The next step is to take one box and further sort the contents into smaller divisions until you get them down to shoe box size, so you can organize them. The nice thing about using shoe boxes as holding boxes is that you can just grab one and do your organizing anywhere.

2 FROM TREVA BERENDS, THE ORGANIZING SPECIALISTS: Start by organizing your most current photos and resolve to stay current from this point forward. Worry about the past later. When you have time, start with one particular event, time frame, or family member. Find all related photos and organize them. Choose the method of storage that works for you — photo boxes, albums, memory scrapbooks, or scanning into your computer.

3 FROM JUDY WARMINGTON, WOMAN TIME MANAGEMENT: Forget about trying to organize photographs chronologically. Organize instead by people or events, such as family vacations or holidays. Sort photographs by using labeled paper bags that have been cut down to about six inches high. Buy albums after sorting because you'll have a better idea of how many you need. Buy enough pages so that you can add to your albums if necessary. Make an appointment to start your photograph-organizing project. Decide how much time you can spend at any given session. When your time is up, put the project away and schedule another appointment.

The simplest way to organize and store recent photographs is chronologically, in a photo box with dividers to separate sections. You can also use shoeboxes and buy indexed dividers from an office supply store. It's best to store photographs on an open bookshelf, in a closet, or under your bed. Make sure the location is dark and does not get warmer than 75°F; otherwise the photos might be damaged.

Schedule some time each week to sort and organize photographs until you are caught up to date. Save only the best photographs; throw out the rest. Mail duplicates to a friend or family member, along with a quick greeting, or just throw them away. Do something fun with doubles of your favorite photos: Have them imprinted on a coffee mug, T-shirt, or computer mouse pad and give personalized gifts to your favorite people.

Whether you use albums or boxes to organize your photos, try to get them all in the same size for easy storage. Start a new album or box for each new child or grandchild. Consider putting formal portraits (baby, school, wedding, and family) in a family album.

When organizing older photographs, label each one with the name of the subject, date, location, and other details that you might not remember ten or twenty years from now. Use a soft-tipped, smudge-free marker to write on the back of the photo, or write on a piece of masking tape and affix to the back.

To preserve your most treasured memories, use archival photo boxes or archival pages. To keep negatives clean, use plastic sleeves or negative envelopes. Label them and store with your photographs. Or create an album for negative storage: Use three-hole punched negative sleeves, label with the month and year or event, and file them chronologically. Protect negatives from light, heat, and high humidity in storage.

Crafts Storage

Unless you have a room or area dedicated to sewing, quilting, or other crafts, you may gravitate to the family room to work on craft projects. If that's the case, the family room may be the ideal place to store your craft tools and supplies. Following are some tips for storing your craft supplies.

TUBS ARE TOPS

Stackable, clear plastic tubs with lids are great for storing crafts items. They come in so many different sizes, you're guaranteed to find a container that's just right for your particular supplies. Try to keep like supplies together — for example, all pom-poms in one tub and all glues in another — and use resealable plastic bags within tubs to separate different sizes or types of the same item, such as small googly eyes versus large ones or plastic beads versus wooden ones. Label your containers and stack them neatly on a shelf.

—Ramona Creel, OnlineOrganizing.com

- **Hang it.** If you have a closet in the family room, hang an over-the-door-style shoe bag with clear plastic pockets on the inside of the door. Use the pockets for storing scissors, paintbrushes, bottles or tubes of paint, spools of thread, and other tools and supplies.

- **Shelve it.** Store craft supplies with craft books on your bookshelves. Find a matching set of open tin boxes, hat boxes, or rectangular woven baskets with cloth liners. Use separate containers to hold different types of tools and supplies. Clear compartment boxes allow you to sort and organize small notions, such as buttons and beads, within each container, or you can use resealable plastic bags.

- **Stow it.** Can you make some storage room in a cabinet? Plastic multidrawer organizers are ideal for holding sewing and craft supplies. Many crafters use tackle boxes to store small, loose items such as beads. For larger items, clear plastic boxes that stack also work well, as do labeled shoeboxes. Old lunch boxes are stackable, sturdy enough to hold metal tools, and portable. Look for lunch boxes at garage sales and thrift stores.

- **Hide it.** You may be able to hide materials and supplies under the sofa in a flat, plastic storage box, or in a large storage trunk that doubles as your coffee table. Keep material on one side and supplies on the other.

- **Tote it.** If you can't create storage space for your crafts in your family room (or wherever you work on crafting projects), invest in a portable chest or rolling bin with drawers that you can keep elsewhere and bring out when you need it. A wheeled suitcase might also do

make your own

Crafts Center

Debbie Williams of Let's Get It Together says you can create a crafts center anywhere. Use a freestanding clothes closet to store craft or sewing supplies and works in progress. For a work surface, use a card table or metal banquet table that can be stored under the sofa or a bed when not in use. Disguise your workspace with a folding screen.

the trick. You could use plastic, lidded containers or even resealable plastic bags to keep like items together inside the suitcase. Large canvas tote bags are another option for separating, storing, and carrying things such as yarn and fabric scraps.

There are lots of ready-made solutions for organizing, storing, and carrying crafts tools and supplies. Look for these products at the back of crafts magazines, in mail-order catalogs dedicated to organization products, and through Internet retailers. You may even have the perfect organizing "product" right under your roof. Look around for unused boxes, bags, and other containers that may be perfectly suited to your needs.

CHAPTER 8

BEDROOM

If all you did in your bedroom was sleep, you could make your room look neat and organized just by making your bed. But you probably also use the bedroom to get dressed, watch television, read, play with your kids, or do craftwork. The solution is not to change the way you live but, rather, to implement organizing strategies that will create an uncluttered, restful environment that you enjoy.

Uncluttering Closets

Do you need more closet space for clothes? Create space by removing clothing items you don't wear because they don't fit, don't look good on you, need mending, or are out of season.

The best way to unclutter your closet is to pull *everything* out and put back only what you wear on a regular basis. Try on everything else. If the clothes make you look and feel good, keep them. If not, put them in a pile to give away, donate, or sell. Why keep clothes that don't make you feel good about yourself?

If you have clothes that no longer fit, you have two choices. You can donate or sell them, or store them elsewhere until they do fit — or until you're ready to let go of them. Maybe once another season or year has passed without

wearing these clothes, you'll come to accept the fact that they no longer serve a purpose in your life.

What's the worst possible thing that could happen if you got rid of clothes you aren't wearing? Let's say, for example, that you have a whole wardrobe full of size eight clothing, but you've been a size twelve for the past five years. If you gave away all of your size eight clothing and then did get back into the smaller size, the worst that could happen is that you would have to buy a new wardrobe. But wouldn't that be a great way to reward yourself for losing weight? You might have to buy new clothes anyway, if your clothes are no longer stylish or your tastes have changed. If it seems wasteful to get rid of perfectly good suits and whatever, think of it this way: They're going to waste hanging in your closet. Give away, donate, or sell clothes now, while they can be worn and appreciated by someone else.

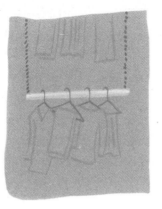

If you have clothes that need mending, look at each item and decide whether it's worth repairing. Do you still like it? Is it still in style? Put clothing you decide to repair in a bag or box to be delivered to your sewing place or to a tailor. Discard all other items, and make a note to yourself if you need to replace an item.

Simplify your wardrobe. How many outfits do you really need for dirty work like gardening or painting? Consider keeping only pieces that you can mix and match with other pieces. And pare down to only colors that really compliment your complexion. Most people look best in either brown and warm (yellow, red, orange, gold) tones or black and cool (pink, blue, green, silver) tones. If you don't know which category you fit into, notice what colors you are wearing when someone says, "You look very nice today." They may be reacting more strongly to the color than to the outfit itself.

Organizing Closets

Once you've uncluttered your closet and freed up some space, your next goal is to make everything visible and accessible. If a single clothes rod will suffice for hanging all of your clothes, great. But if your clothes are jammed together tightly, it's difficult to find things, let alone put them away.

A simple fix is to install a second rod a couple of feet below your existing rod to create hanging space for shorter items, such as shirts or blouses. You can buy a rod that mounts to the back wall, or you can hang a second rod from the first. To do this, you'll need a piece of PVC pipe, a sturdy chain, and two S-hooks. Cut the pipe to the desired length — perhaps half the length of the main rod. Thread the chain through the pipe, leaving enough length at either end for hanging. Attach the chain ends to the S-hooks and the S-hooks to the existing rod.

Installing a second rod maximizes existing space, which is the key to organizing your closet. Just be sure to allow room for longer hanging items, too.

THE HANGER TRICK

At the start of each season, when switching your clothes for the change in weather, hang all your clothes with the hanger head pointing out into the room instead of toward the wall. As you wear and return your clothes to the closet, put them back as you normally would, with the hanger pointing to the back closet wall. At the end of the season, see how many clothes still have their hanger heads facing out into the room. These are the clothes to consider discarding.

—Kim Cosentino, The De-Clutter Box, Inc.

Sort and hang similar clothing together. For example, hang all of your jackets together, and do the same for pants, skirts, dresses, and blouses. Or you might prefer to create separate sections for hanging casual, work, and dressy clothes. If you really want to get organized, use prelabeled rod dividers to keep groups separate. You might even arrange clothes within groups by color, from light to dark.

Don't overthink the grouping decision. Choose categories that make sense to you; you can always rearrange them later. Do hang the clothes you wear most often where they are easy to see and reach when you open the door. Also, hang things so that the fronts are facing you. It keeps your closet neater when everything is hanging in the same direction and makes it easier to identify items at a glance.

Use only plastic, wooden, or padded hangers. Wire hangers do not properly support clothes and often bend or sag, causing creases in your clothes and a messy-looking closet. Use plastic hangers to color-code clothing groups. For example, you can use three colors to divide clothes into casual, work, and dressy. To keep

jackets and shirts from twisting and sliding off hangers, always close the first few buttons.

Do you share a closet with one or more people? Since space is at a premium, weeding out what you don't wear is a critical first step. Then sort clothes into sections for each person. Store extra hangers between groupings. Or assign hangers of a different color to visually separate one person's section from another.

If your closet space is very limited, try using tiered hangers that allow you to hang multiple skirts and slacks together. Hanging swing-out trouser racks also save space.

Closet-organizing products provide affordable, do-it-yourself solutions that maximize existing space and make it easier to stay organized. You'll find closet organizer kits, individual organizing products, and custom-designed solutions in specialized mail-order catalogs, at most home centers, in the housewares section at large department stores, and at on-line organizing stores.

Some specialized organizing stores offer free closet and space planning service. Simply bring your closet measurements to the retail store, or request a consultation through an on-line store or by telephone. A closet organization expert will design a system of ventilated wire shelving and drawers to suit your space and needs. Another option is to hire a professional closet design company to come to your home. Look in the Yellow Pages under "Closets and Closet Accessories."

Clothes that you'll wear again before laundering, such as pajamas, don't have to be hung

TIME-SAVER

When you take an item out of your closet, remove it from its hanger and then place the empty hanger at one end of your clothes rod. Keeping empty hangers together makes it easy to find a hanger when you need one and keeps your closet looking neater.

up or put in a drawer after wearing; they need to be aired. But instead of leaving them on your bed or over a chair, find a place in your bedroom where you can screw in a couple of hooks or pegs — maybe on the back of your bedroom door or inside a closet door. A freestanding coat rack works well too.

Hang a nylon bag on a hook in your closet or behind a door to hold items that need to go to the dry cleaner. Hang another bag for pantyhose and other delicate items that require hand washing. This simple system will help to ensure that special-care items don't accidentally end up with the regular wash.

Accessories

Now it's time to do with your accessories what you did with your clothes: weed out the things that are only taking up closet space. If you can't bring yourself to let go of them, at least remove them from your closet. Box them up and store them with your out-of-season clothing.

If you have only one shelf or no shelves in your closet, you may be able to make use of the space above the clothes rod. Install one or more shelves for storing things like pocketbooks, hats, and bulky sweaters. Inexpensive, clip-on shelf dividers help to keep items separated. You might also use same-size clear plastic bins or wire baskets to contain like items. Plain cardboard boxes work fine too, as long as you label the boxes with what's inside.

An alternative to shelving is an organizing product with drawers, such as a sturdy cardboard dresser, roll-away wire bin organizer, or hanging garment bag with shelves. These work well if you lack dresser space but your closet is big enough to accommodate them.

How you store accessories depends on your storage space and personal preferences. Following are some suggestions.

Hats and Caps. Caps can be stacked or hung from hooks or pegs on the back of your closet door or along one wall. An accordion-style rack allows you to hang several caps neatly. Hang brimmed hats on a peg, or place them directly on a shelf. If you don't wear them often, protect hats from dust by storing them in a box. Or insert a hat in a brown paper grocery bag, staple it shut, use a marker to label the bag, and place the bag on an upper shelf.

make your own

Accessory Organizer

What You Need:
- Shower curtain rings
- Sturdy hangers

Slide a shower curtain ring over the hook of a sturdy hanger and let it rest around the top of the hanger. Clip other shower rings to it to create a chain of rings. Hang the hanger on the clothes rod. To hang belts and pocketbooks, simply unclip a shower ring, thread the buckle or strap through the ring, and reclip. Scarves and ties can just be threaded through the individual rings.

Pocketbooks. To keep them clean and dust-free, store pocketbooks and handbags in a plastic bin or labeled box on a shelf, or in a drawer. Store those you use often in open wire bins on a shelf for easy access, or hang them from pegs. You can keep pocketbooks without straps in a hanging canvas or nylon bag.

Belts, Ties, and Scarves. A hanging belt or tie organizer makes it easier to find what you want, when you want it. All you need is some space on a wall of your closet or behind a door. Count up your ties, belts, and scarves, and then choose an organizer with at least that many hooks. Or you can tap a row of nails or small hooks into the wall. If wall space is limited, consider using the back wall of your closet or the center support for your clothes rod. A hanging shoe bag with clear plastic pouches also works well for storing rolled belts, ties, and scarves. If you always wear certain accessories with a particular outfit, hang them together.

Shoes. Weed out shoes you aren't wearing, and then work on organizing. Put unwanted shoes into a box to be donated. If shoes are worn beyond repair, throw them away. Sort the shoes you do wear into categories such as work, dress, or casual, or group them by color. Count up your pairs of shoes and look for a shoe organizer that holds at least that many pairs. Multitiered, expandable shoe racks allow you to store many pairs in a small amount of space. Over-the-door shoe racks are also available.

If you want to keep shoes clean, especially seasonal or special-occasion shoes, save the original shoe box or store them in clear, plastic shoe boxes. If you use opaque boxes, take an instant photo and tape it to the front of the box to help you remember its contents. Store these boxes on shelves rather than floors, because keeping the floors clear makes it easier to vacuum.

Most shoe racks are not designed to hold men's shoes. Organizing experts at The Container Store recommend installing a series of short, closely spaced shelves from floor to ceiling to accommodate large shoes.

Organizing Drawers

The best way to organize drawers is to empty them completely, so you can see what you've got and then sort into categories. Use your bed as a sorting place. Categories might include the following:

- Undergarments
- Sleepwear
- T-shirts
- Active wear (gym clothes, bathing suits)
- Jeans and shorts
- Casual shirts
- Sweaters

Go through each category, one at a time. Sort each category into things you wear and things you don't wear, which might include socks with no matches, worn-out underwear, and jeans that are too tight. Take a look at quantities of each item. How many T-shirts do you really need? Try to reduce what you have to what you actually wear. Put things you don't wear in a box or bag labeled "Give Away" or "Throw Away."

Once you're done sorting, designate specific dresser drawers for specific items: socks and underwear, shirts, shorts, sweaters, and workout clothes, for example. You may have to combine similar categories, such as underwear and sleepwear or T-shirts and shorts. Now put everything back where it belongs.

Drawer organizers help keep things separate, especially the smaller items in your underwear drawer. If you have a lot of socks, you might separate them into dress, casual, and sport socks. Fold or roll socks; don't ball them up, because this causes them to lose their elasticity over time. If you really want to get organized, sort socks and undergarments by color within their sections.

To help keep shirts and sweaters neat and wrinkle-free in your drawers, fold everything the way retailers fold them. Lay the item face down with arms spread out. Criss-cross the arms behind the shirt or sweater, keeping the shoulders even with the sides. Fold in one whole side to the halfway point, then the other side. Fold up the bottom so that the hem touches the neckline and turn over.

If your drawer space is limited, store bulkier items, such as sweaters or jeans, on shelves in your closet. You might even decide to hang some things you used to store in your dresser such as jeans. Just because you've always stored something in a particular place doesn't mean that's the best place to store it forever and ever.

Organize the top of your dresser, too. Use a large canning jar or piggy bank to collect loose change. Corral everyday pocket items or jewelry in an attractive dish or tray. Give away perfumes and colognes you don't wear; throw away bottles that are virtually empty or make it a point to use them up.

Organizing Jewelry

Professional organizers agree that we wear about 20 percent of our clothing 80 percent of the time. The same applies to jewelry. You may even wear all of your *favorite* jewelry all of the time. The jewelry you don't wear doesn't take up much space, but it can be annoying to sort through it looking for the pieces you do wear. A jewelry box is useful for storing men's and women's jewelry, especially watches, bracelets, cuff links, tie clips, and rings. Other types of

For Simplicity's Sake

Provide every bedroom with a hamper of some sort for collecting dirty laundry. Put a mesh or nylon bag in the hamper to make it easy to carry dirty laundry to the laundry room or laundromat. The most efficient hamper is a basket that you can also use to carry clean laundry back to your room.

jewelry, such as necklaces and earrings, are better stored out of the box.

Hang necklaces to eliminate knotting and tangling and potential for breakage. You can buy a special jewelry organizer or use a tie rack. Cup hooks and nails also work fine. If you have just a few necklaces, you may be able to hang them over the top corners of a mirror. Another option is to hang only your fine-chain necklaces and keep pearl-type or costume jewelry in a glass bowl on your dresser top for easy access; this looks pretty, too. A baby-sized hanger with rubber bands stretched around it from top to bottom keeps necklaces from sliding into each other and getting tangled.

Earring trees reduce the amount of time you might spend looking for a set of earrings. If you store earrings in a jewelry box, clip hoop-type earrings together when you remove them to keep the set together. Another way to keep sets together is to store them in a clear plastic container with small compartments, such as a fishing tackle box. You can store bracelets, pins, and necklaces in the larger compartment below. It's not pretty, but it's functional. Earrings and fine-chain necklaces can also be stored in ice cube trays; place one set of earrings or chain in each "cube." The trays can be stacked in a dresser or vanity drawer.

Do you have every piece of jewelry you've ever purchased or received as a gift? If you love it all or wear it all, great. If not, lay out all of your jewelry on your bed. Throw away anything that is broken beyond repair or not worth fixing. Chances are, you have some things you know you won't ever wear again because they've gone out of style or your tastes have changed. Why hold onto it? Donate it to a local charity, sell it on consignment, or give it to your children or grandchildren for playing dress-up.

Off-Season Storage

Storing out-of-season clothing separately from in-season clothing allows you to find appropriate clothing without having to sort through the clothes you can't wear right now. But often, the big question is where to store seasonal clothes and linens. Some dwellings offer more options than others, especially those that have spare bedrooms with closets, and humidity-controlled basements. What's important is that you choose a place that is dry. Also, be sure that materials are completely dry before storing, to prevent mildew from forming.

Ideally, you'll have the space to move out-of-season clothing from your closet into another closet. If you can't do this, however, move out-of-season clothes off to one end of the closet and rotate them back in as the seasons change. A cedar storage trunk or closet is a great investment to keep moths and other insects from damaging garments or linens made of wool or wool blends. If you don't have one, put a cupful of cedar chips in a pair of old, clean panty hose and place in whatever storage containers you use. You can also use cedar blocks, mothballs, or moth crystals. Be sure that these repellents are fresh; otherwise, they won't work. Always clean clothes and linens before storing them for the season; the scent of your body is what attracts insects. Plan to thoroughly air clothes when you bring

"HOLY" CLOTHES!

With hundreds of dollars' worth of clothing and linens in your closets and drawers, it's wise to invest in pest protection products, such as cedar blocks and hangers, sachets, and sweater bags. Under the right (or wrong) conditions, virtually any fabric, cotton and synthetics included, can become dinner for a variety of pests. Without proper protection, clothing moths, carpet beetles, and even crickets can destroy an entire wardrobe in one season.

—*Staff, The Container Store*

them out of storage to get rid of the cedar/mothball odor.

If you have room in your bedroom, guest room, hallway, or finished basement, consider purchasing a freestanding closet for off-season storage of linens and clothes. Another option is to lay a broomstick or long pole over the backs of two same-size chairs for hanging shorter items, such as pants, jackets, and blankets. Cover with a sheet to keep the dust off.

Use a bed skirt to conceal convenient off-season storage under your bed. Store seasonal clothes or linens in suitcases, labeled storage bins, or drawers that fit under your bed; cedar drawers on wheels are even available. To create a little more storage under your bed, raise the height of your bed with risers. Be creative: Extra canned goods or paper goods can also be stored under a bed.

Items That Need Special Care. The following items require special care when they're stored for any length of time.

- **Blankets and comforters.** Make sure that blankets are clean and dry before storing. Down comforters should not be rolled too tightly or stored under heavy items, as this will compress the down. It's best to store these on a shelf, in a chest, or in a roomy bag. Tuck a few fabric softener sheets or cedar blocks between comforters and blankets to keep them smelling fresh.

- **Sweaters and casual clothing.** Wash or dry-clean sweaters and casual clothing. Sweaters should be stored flat. If you're storing them in the basement or attic, keep them in large plastic containers with tight-fitting lids to keep out mice and insects. If you're storing them elsewhere in the house, boxes or bags are acceptable. Label each box with its contents, and use separate boxes for each family member. You may find it easier to store children's clothing in boxes labeled by age or size and sex.

- **Suit jackets.** Hang suit jackets on sturdy hangers. Close all buttons. Stuff tissue paper into the sleeves of jackets to prevent creasing.

- **Leather, suede, and fine fabrics.** Do not store leather, suede, or silk in plastic. Plastic will cause leather and suede to dry out and other fine fabrics to develop yellow stains, rotting threads, or discoloration of buttons. If you want to keep clothing free of dust, hang items in canvas garment bags or cover each item with an old T-shirt, button-down shirt, or sheet of brown wrapping paper pulled down over the top of the hanger and folded in half over the shoulders.

- **Coats and accessories.** Hang clean, out-of-season coats on sturdy hangers. Hang out-of-season coats off to one side of your coat closet or in your off-season storage area. Mittens, gloves, and hats should also be cleaned at the end of the season. Store in a box on an upper shelf in your coat closet. Toss in a few cedar blocks for protection from moths, or pierce a small resealable plastic bag, fill it with mothballs, and put it in with clothes. If you store mittens, gloves, and hats in the basement or attic, keep them in a plastic storage bin with a tight-fitting lid. Label the bin.

- **Boots and shoes.** The end of the season is the ideal time to clean, polish, and waterproof boots and shoes. That way, they will be ready to wear at the start of the next season. Purchase an extra shoe rack for your off-season shoes. To prevent shoes and boots from getting dusty

ONE FOR THE ROAD

Keep an empty container under your bed for charity, filling it as clothing becomes outgrown or is no longer needed. When the box is full, take it to the charity of your choice. If you're really efficient, you'll itemize the contents of your box before dropping it off so that you will have a complete receipt for your tax records.

—*Debbie Williams, Let's Get It Together*

in storage, cover your shoe rack with an old sheet. Or wrap each pair of shoes and boots in a plastic grocery bag, tie the ends together, and toss them all into a large trash bag labeled "Sally's Summer Shoes" or "Jimmy's Boots." Off-season shoes and boots can also be stored in a large box or plastic storage bin with a lid. Because leather is particularly susceptible to mildew, avoid storing shoes and boots in your basement unless it is humidity-controlled.

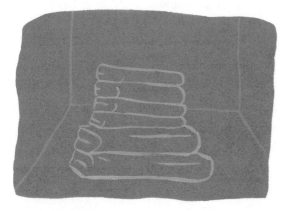

Linen Storage

Most people have more linens than they use or need. How many sets of sheets is enough for your household? It's nice to have extras, but why keep them if they're just taking up space? Sheets in good condition can be donated to several charities, including domestic violence shelters. Recycle old sheets into Halloween costumes for your kids, drop cloths for painting, or polishing rags. Or tear them into strips to be used in your garden to tie plants to stakes.

Organize your linen closet shelf by shelf. Arrange sheets by size: twin, full, queen, and king. Refold (if necessary) and stack same-size

Go to the library and look at decorating books. You'll find dozens of creative storage ideas. Then go home and analyze your particular needs in each room.

—Melinda Louise, Organize It

sheets. Labeling each section of each shelf will make it easy to find the sizes you need and also helps keep the closet organized.

Store sheets as sets by wrapping the fitted sheet and pillowcases in the flat sheet. Then, when you need a new set, you can just grab it with one hand. If you prefer to store sheets in stacks, store them folded side out. To fold fitted sheets, place a fist in one corner of the fitted sheet and then draw the opposite corner of the sheet over your fist. Now move your fist from the back to the front and lift the bottom elasticized corner up over your fist. Lay sheet down on a flat surface with the elasticized corners facing up. Fold edges in to form a square. Fold in half, and fold in half again.

It's nice to have a linen closet, but it's actually more efficient to store sheets in the rooms in which they are used. This way, when you're changing bed linens, you don't have to go somewhere else to get a clean set.

Store linens on a shelf in your bedroom closet, if you have the room. If not, a wooden chest or hall bench makes a convenient storage place for sheets, blankets, and comforters. It also makes a great place to sit when putting on your socks and shoes, which helps save your mattress from needless wear.

Another option is to buy underbed drawers that attach to your bed frame. You can use these drawers to store linens, pajamas and nightgowns, and out-of-season clothing. Plastic storage bins and drawers with or without rollers are also available. You can even store linens in a large, plastic zippered bag under your bed. These bags are often used as packaging for new quilts and comforters, and you might have some already. They're great for storing and keeping linens clean and dust-free. Be aware that you should *not* use a sealed plastic bag to store Vellux blankets because Vellux must breathe.

If you decide to buy a wooden chest or underbed drawers for storing linens, look for chests and drawers made out of cedar. They're a little more expensive but well worth the extra cost because cedar naturally repels moths and other insects. If you already have a noncedar storage box or drawer, slip in a couple of cedar blocks or fill a muslin pouch with cedar chips to protect against moth and insect damage.

Store extra bedspreads or blankets on upper shelves in your clothes closet, or hang them on hangers and keep them at the back of the closet. Another solution is to hang them from an over-the-door towel rod on the back of your bedroom door.

You say you have absolutely no place to store bed linens? Pare your collection down to two sets for each bed and store the extra set between the mattress and box spring or foundation. To do this, fold sheets in half horizontally and then several times lengthwise. Or keep only one set of sheets that you wash and put back on, eliminating the need for storage space altogether.

survey results

According to a recent customer survey conducted by The Container Store, people would be willing to give up bedroom and bathroom space (and even a spouse!) to have more room in their closets. The most common nonclothing items respondents reported storing in bedroom closets were handbags (70 percent), linens (30 percent), and gift wrap (21 percent). Receipts, tax information, board games, toys, household files, jewelry, and even silverware were also included in the mix.

CHAPTER 9

KIDS' ROOMS

You've probably resigned yourself to the fact that you will never be able to eliminate "kid clutter" completely. But you can control it, with a little creativity, patience, and a few proven techniques and systems. The key to minimizing the mess in kids' bedrooms and playrooms is to create a home for everything and to design storage spaces that make it easy for kids to put things away.

For Starters

It's important to get your kids involved in the process of uncluttering and organizing their rooms. You'll do them a big favor by helping them to learn organizational skills that will come in handy throughout their lives. Plus, allowing them to have input in the process of getting organized also helps to ensure that they will *stay* organized.

Be sure to unclutter your own bedroom first to set a good example. Then, when you are ready, you can say, "Okay, my room is organized. Now let's organize *your* room!" The more enthusiastic you are, the more likely your children will want to help. You might even promise a fun reward later. At the very least, be sure to praise children for their accomplishments.

There are three basic principles to keep in mind when organizing kids' rooms:

1. **Make it easy to put things away.** Provide plenty of containers for putting like items together, so kids can see at a glance what goes where.

2. **Organize from the bottom up.** Keep frequently used items accessible on lower shelves and in bottom drawers. Store less frequently used items higher up.

3. **Label everything.** Label shelves, drawers, and containers. For children who can't read, label with drawings, photographs, or pictures cut out of magazines or catalogs.

Do Some Weeding

Step one is to reduce the amount of clutter by weeding out clothing and toys that your children have outgrown. If you're planning to donate these items, explain to your children how they can help make a less fortunate child very happy by sharing the things they aren't using anyway. You might even give children a choice of charities to donate to so they feel more involved in the donation process. If you have a garage sale, let the kids keep the money they get for selling their toys and clothes.

A good time to weed out toys is just before a birthday or other gift-giving holiday. Explain the weeding-out process to your kids as making room for new things. With children who are reluctant to part with their toys, it helps to focus their attention on what they want to keep rather than what they are willing to get rid of. Ask them to choose their favorites and set these aside. Then ask, "What else do you like to play with?" Put what's left in a box or bag for donation or a garage sale.

Sort through clothing just before you go shopping for back-to-school clothes or at the start of a new season. Start by going through the current season's clothes and shoes. Pull out everything in the closet and then move on to drawers. Discard worn-out and stained items, as well as anything that's not worth mending. Have children try on clothes and shoes for the upcoming season to see what fits and to find out what clothing they do and don't like. If they don't like it, it probably won't get worn. Make a shopping list for each child by using separate pages in a small, spiral notebook that you can bring with you to the store. Be sure to include sizes.

Store items only if you are saving them for younger children, planning to have a garage sale, or planning to take them to a consignment shop before the start of the season next year. Box or bag up everything else, put it in your car, and make a note to take it to a local charity sometime during the next week.

For Simplicity's Sake

Store children's seasonal clothing and shoes in stackable storage containers or boxes labeled with season, sex, and size rather than by child's name: for example, "Summer — Girl's Size 10–12." That way, you'll know what's in the box without having to open it. Organize boxes by season or sex. Or put separate categories into plastic bags, seal them with twist ties, and toss into a 55-gallon trash can for storage in your basement, garage, or shed. Just be sure to label the lid!

Closets and Drawers

If you want kids to hang up their clothes, put hanging rods within their reach. To make an inexpensive child-height clothes rod, run a length of chain through a piece of sturdy plastic pipe that will accommodate hangers. Attach each end of the chain to a shower curtain ring and hang the rings over the original clothes rod. Or install a tension rod at the appropriate height and raise it as the child grows. Use the upper rod for hanging special occasion or out-of-season clothes or for a hanging shelf unit.

Divide your child's closet into sections for school, play, and dress clothes. For children who can't yet coordinate colors, hang matching outfits together. Use child-size hangers for younger children. Children's clothing fits better on these hangers, and they're easier for small hands to handle. Screw hooks or pegs on the back of the bedroom or closet door or along one wall for hanging everyday items, such as backpacks, sleepwear, or sports attire. Be sure to put these hooks at a height your child can reach easily.

Invest in a shoe rack with enough space to store all of your child's shoes. Show your children how to organize their shoes by keeping pairs together. If children are sharing closet space, assign one shoe rack to each child or assign separate shelves on a multi-shelf unit.

To organize collections of accessories, such as baseball caps or pocketbooks, look for an accordion-style coat or tie rack. Hang it on the back of a door or on a wall within easy reach. Organize barrettes by clipping each one to a length of hanging ribbon.

Designate specific dresser drawers for specific items, such as socks, underwear, shorts, T-shirts, pants, and shirts. Use drawer organizers to keep such items as socks and underwear separate from each other. You might also consider storing socks and underwear in a shoe bag with clear plastic pockets that you can hang in the closet.

make your own

Mini-Closet

What You Need:
- Old wood chest with hinged top
- Four screw-on furniture legs
- Tension rod
- Door pull
- Friction catch

Make a child-size closet. Screw legs into one end of an old wood chest with a hinged top; this will become the bottom of the closet. Stand the chest up, put a rod across the inside, and install a pull on the door. For safety reasons, install a friction catch to keep the door closed.

time to put them back. Examples of activity centers include:

- Reading center
- Play center
- Arts and crafts center
- Projects center
- Music center
- Computer center
- Homework center
- Entertainment center (television, stereo)
- Dressing center

Double or triple drawer space by installing slide-out drawers under your children's beds. Or put colorful, stackable crates or a ventilated wire bin system in the closet. These ideas are especially useful for younger children, who may have trouble opening heavy drawers or reaching the top drawer of a standard dresser. Cardboard and clear plastic drawer organizers are another alternative.

Tape pictures or photographs of what goes in each dresser drawer to the outside or bottom of drawers, so that even very young children can put clothes away. As they learn to read, you can replace the pictures with words.

Create Activity Centers

Take a cue from kindergarten teachers and organize your kids' room into sections designed for specific activities. Activity centers create natural homes for things and provide children with visual cues for where things can be found — and where they belong when it's

How you divide a bedroom or playroom will depend on your children's ages and interests, and the size of the room. In each activity center, store all items that are related to that activity. In the arts and crafts center, for example, you might set up a table and chairs and store supplies (paper, crayons and markers, stickers, tape, and scissors) in a cardboard drawer organizer under the table or in open bins on a nearby shelf.

Toys and Books

When organizing toys and books, think "open" and "visible." A proven technique for organizing toys is to use shelves wherever possible instead of a toy box. Things tend to get thrown into toy boxes and end up broken or buried. Storing on shelves make it easy for children to find the toys and books they want without having to pull out everything.

Organize toys on shelves by categories. Use colorful plastic dishpans on shelves to contain like items, such as building blocks, doll clothes, books, or small toys. Or use clear plastic, lidded bins that allow kids to see what's inside without opening them. Very young children may need assistance opening the lids; this may help parents teach the practice of getting out one toy at a time.

An alternative to using shelves for storage is to create cubbyholes for books, toys, and games with colorful, stacking crates. Interlocking crates are best, but you can secure non-interlocking crates to each other by using clear packing tape. Arrange the crates along one wall or in a closet.

If several children share a bedroom or play-room, consider keeping their toys and books separate. Use lower shelves and crates for younger children and higher shelves for older children. When children are very young, keep toys where they are convenient for you to access and put away. Store heirloom toys and toys that require adult supervision on "special" shelves that only you can reach so children have to ask for them. Or keep them tucked away in a "secret" place.

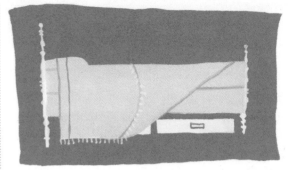

Designate and label specific spots for storing toys. Tape a little picture of the toy in its spot. This practice is also educational for toddlers, as it helps them with memory and matching skills.

Use the space under the bed for storing smaller items, like doll clothes or miniature cars. Look for plastic storage boxes with drawers. This is also a great place to store keepsakes. Provide each child with one lidded box for storing mementos. Make it large enough to hold all of their current keepsakes with room to add some more. When the box is full, help children go through the box to pare down the contents to the items that are most meaningful.

Stack game and puzzle boxes on shelves. If game boxes are falling apart, use empty egg cartons or recycled margarine tubs to store game pieces. Label the cartons or tubs with the name of the game and stack them on a shelf. Write the name of each game on the back of each game board along one side of the spine, and then fold and stack the game boards with the names facing out. Place instructions inside the folded board or inside a resealable plastic bag secured to the back of the game board with tape.

Reduce excessive toy clutter by putting some toys in storage for a few months. Bring them out on a rainy day or a day when your children could use a nice surprise. A good time to do this is right after a major gift-giving holiday when children are less likely to put up a fuss about your packing up a box of older toys.

The more you can keep things off the floor, the less cluttered a room looks and the easier it is to clean. Use hanging shoe bags on the back of a door to store beanbag toys, action figures, and other small toys. Hang it low enough so that kids can reach into all of the pockets. A great way to corral stuffed animals is to hang a nylon hammock in one corner of the room. Or hang a length of colored string or ribbon between two hooks at either end of a bare wall, and clothespins to clip beanbag toys and small stuffed animals to the string. You can use this same method to display artwork.

make your own

Comedy Central

What You Need:

- Magazine storage boxes *or* cereal boxes

You can buy magazine storage boxes to store collections of comic books, or you can make your own from empty cereal boxes. Use scissors to cut out a section of the right side panel of the box from the top down to about four inches from the bottom. Then cut diagonally from the top left corner of the front of the box down to that point. Cut out the back of the box to match the front. Store books with spines facing out. Store boxes side by side on a bookshelf. You can have kids make labels for the boxes, too.

Artwork and Loose Papers

Designate one space, such as the front of your refrigerator, as a "gallery" for displaying your children's drawings and paintings. Limit "shows" to one piece of artwork per child per week. Store post-show and unshown artwork in a sturdy portfolio that slips between the countertop and refrigerator. Or store artwork under your children's beds in boxes.

Ask your local pizza delivery store for a couple of clean pizza boxes. Give one to each child for storing their artwork. Have children write their names on their boxes and perhaps even decorate them. Make it their responsibility to file everything they bring home. At the end of the school year or when the box is full, have your child select his or her favorite, or select yours.

For long-term storage of favorite pieces, roll artwork in a paper towel or gift-wrapping tube. Write your child's name on the outside of the tube along with your child's age and the year. Or purchase an art portfolio or scrapbook for each child to save these treasures.

Consider recycling your children's artwork. Choose your favorites each year to create calendars that you can keep or give as a gift to grandparents and relatives. Create the calendar pages on your computer and then have the artwork and calendar pages laminated and spiral bound by an office supply store.

Loose school papers can quickly create a mess. It's important to contain them somehow, preferably in a place accessible to kids so that they can put them away after showing them to you. Following are three ideas for storing graded tests, school papers, photos, cards, certificates, artwork, and other loose papers. Whatever method you choose, be sure to put a large trashcan in each child's room to collect waste paper.

● **Purchase a large three-ring binder for each child.** Label the spine with your child's name. Have your child punch each paper and file it in chronological order throughout the school year, adding new papers to the top. Store nonpunchable items in the front or back pockets of the binder. Or purchase three-hole punched dividers with storage pockets for these items. Purchase additional binders, as needed, throughout the year.

● **Use a heavy-duty cardboard chest with drawers as a filing center.** Sort your child's papers into categories such as school papers (homework and tests); greeting cards and letters; and report cards, certificates, and awards. Then label and organize drawers by category. It's not quite as neat as filing, but it does make it easier to find things.

● **Invest in a small filing cabinet for storing all kinds of loose papers.** Show your child how to use hanging files and folders to organize by grade, classes, and projects — and how to purge files at the end of the school year. Buy colorful file folders and use color-coding for separate categories. If children share a room, assign one drawer to each child. If you are planning to buy a desk for doing homework, consider purchasing a desk with a drawer that will accommodate hanging files.

EVERYBODY'S A CRITIC

Keep children's art and school papers in an under-the-bed tub. Then, at the end of the year, you can sit down with your child and enjoy a little reminiscing as you go through the year's papers. Set a numeric limit (10 or 20 or whatever) or a spatial limit (whatever will fit in this manila envelope) and pick out your favorites together. It's a nice bonding activity, and it's easier to be discriminating about what you will keep when you view the entire collection all at once.

—*Ramona Creel, OnlineOrganizing.com*

CHAPTER 10

BATHROOM

Next to the kitchen, the bathroom gets more regular use than any other room in the house. With use comes more potential for clutter and disorganization. Happily, because the bathroom is generally the smallest room in the house, it's one of the simplest and easiest to organize. Start here if you want to see results fast.

Uncluttering

You may have more than one bathroom. If so, think about each bathroom as a large storage unit. Assign each unit to individual household members, groups (such as children), or guests. Then you can organize each bathroom in the manner best suited to its primary users. Having his and hers bathrooms is a good strategy to use if your partner's organizational style is vastly different from yours: for example, you like everything neat and tidy and your partner is oblivious to clutter. That way, your differences won't come between you every day.

Before you start organizing the bathroom, take a look around. What are your biggest challenges? A cluttered sink top? Messy drawers or shelves? Things on the floor that shouldn't be there? All of these challenges can be addressed with a thorough uncluttering, simple organizational techniques, and some inexpensive organizing products.

Your first step is to unclutter. How many toothbrushes do you have? How many do you need? Throw out worn toothbrushes. If you wish to save them for small cleaning jobs, keep only as many as you need — probably one — and put it with your cleaning supplies.

As you go through your medicine cabinet and drawers, you'll probably find duplicates of things like antibiotic ointment, adhesive bandages, makeup, and other partially used items. Consolidate whatever you can, but do *not* consolidate newer products with older products that may be approaching their expiration dates. Use the older product first, then the newer product. Some items, such as opened bottles of shampoo can be put to use in another bathroom. You can also use duplicates to create a first aid kit for your car or a toiletries bag for traveling.

To keep the sink top free of clutter, you'll need to create a home for everything. If you have enough drawers or shelves in your bathroom, assign one to each household member. Otherwise, organize drawers by categories, for example: makeup, hair care, and bath supplies. To keep drawers from becoming a jumbled mess, use ready-made drawer organizers to keep like items together, or make your own organizers from boxes, zippered or drawstring bags, baskets, or bins.

If your bathrooms could use more drawers and shelves, there are some simple solutions. If you're handy, you could install a few shelves along one wall. Another solution is ready-made storage units, including wall cabinets, freestanding shelf units and cabinets, and corner shelf units. Wire wheeled carts work well for storing extra towels, soaps, and other small items.

Eliminate clutter in the shower and tub with caddies designed to hold shampoo, soaps and bath gels, and razors. This will reduce clutter and make it easier to clean the shower and tub. If you have a lot of bottles, look for a tension-mounted shower caddy, which tends to offer

more shelf space than the kind that hang over the shower nozzle pipe. You might also consider installing wall dispensers for shampoo and liquid soap. Store bath toys in a nylon mesh bag that you can hang from the shower nozzle pipe, shower curtain rod, or a large hook attached to the shower wall by a suction cup.

The Medicine Cabinet

Empty your medicine cabinet and begin to sort through what you've got. Set aside expired prescription and nonprescription medicines, as well as antibiotics, regardless of expiration date. (Not completing a course of antibiotics places you at risk for developing resistant strains of bacteria, reducing the efficacy of the drug when it's needed most.) Also set aside any nonprescription medicines that are more than two years old or past their expiration date. Changes in chemical makeup over time causes them to lose their potency and, hence, their effectiveness. The same is true for sunscreens. Dispose of all old and outdated items properly (see the box at left).

Organize your medicine cabinet like you would any cabinet. Store the most frequently used items on the shelves that are easiest to reach, and store like items together. Group prescriptions and vitamins together by family member so that you don't have to search through all the bottles to find yours. Other

For Safety's Sake

Collect and return outdated and expired medicines to your pharmacist for disposal.

efficient groupings include cough and cold remedies, sunscreen and insect repellents, pain relievers, and first aid supplies.

Restock your medicine cabinet with labels facing outward. Use small plastic bins to contain small tubes and things you use together, such as antibiotic ointment and adhesive bandages. Consider labeling shelves so that you don't have to think about what goes where.

If your prescription plan requires you to bring refill labels to your pharmacist, keep them in the medicine cabinet along with your prescriptions. That way, when you need a refill, you know exactly where to find the label. When you get down to a one-week supply of a prescription, put the refill label in your wallet or purse and make a note to yourself to go to the pharmacy. Better yet, if your pharmacy offers an automated refill service, simply call, enter the refill number, and select the time and day you'd like to pick up the prescription; it will be ready when you are.

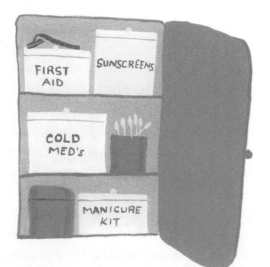

For Safety's Sake

Garbage disposal. Be careful when disposing of medicines, vitamins, cosmetics, and any potentially hazardous materials. Do not put them in the bathroom trashcan where children and pets may find them. Return outdated medications to your pharmacist; put everything else into a bag, tie up the bag, and put it into a lidded trash can out of reach of children.

Organizing Toiletries

The biggest challenge with toiletries, especially those you use daily, is being able to find what you need among the chaotic array of bottles, jars, and tubes. The best way to organize toiletries is to go through your shelves and drawers one by one, removing all containers of makeup, skin and hair care products, and other toiletries. Then sort by categories, which might include the following:

- Makeup
- Dental care
- Skin care
- Hair care
- Nail care
- Perfumes, powders, and deodorants

Examine each item carefully. Discard old, sticky nail polishes, makeup that is more than six months to one year old, and any empty bottles or jars. Discard or give away items that you no longer like or use. They're just taking up space that you can put to better use.

Where you store these things will depend on the set-up in your bathroom. How you store them may be as simple as grouping like items together on a shelf or in baskets or bins in a drawer. For a neat and uncluttered appearance, use same-size or same-style containers, especially if they will be placed on open shelves. When you store similar items together, it's not only easier to locate what you're looking for, but it also reduces the chance that you will buy duplicate items. If you like to keep extra supplies on hand, store them in back of the opened items. Keep in mind that most toiletries should be stored away from direct sunlight and heat, which can shorten their life.

How you store makeup will depend on how you use it. If you use the same few items daily, keep these items in a small basket, bin, or bag that is easily accessible. Store less frequently used items in a separate container. If you use a variety of makeup on a regular basis, contain it all in a makeup box designed like a fishing tackle box, with individual compartments for smaller items and a large storage compartment for larger items. Find one that will hold all of your makeup *and* fit neatly in its storage place. Take it out when you need it and put it back when you're done.

Hang It Up

If towels and clothing often get left on the floor, it's not necessarily because the previous occupants are too lazy to hang them up. It might be because there aren't enough places to hang wet towels or it's too difficult to do so. Both of these problems are easy to fix. From the few suggestions below, choose the ones that will work best in your situation:

- Add more towel rods behind the door or on the wall. If you have children, mount a few at child height.
- Hang an over-the-door towel rack.
- Bring in a freestanding coat rack to use as a towel rack
- Install hooks or towel rods near the sink for hanging washcloths and hand towels.
- Install pegs or hooks, at adult and child height, on the back of the door or along one wall for hanging pajamas and robes.
- Hang a mesh bag behind the door for collecting dirty towels.

All of these products are readily available through catalogers and retailers that specialize in home organization products and at discount stores. (See Resources, page 322.)

Towels and clothing aren't the only things you can hang in the bathroom. Take a tip from hair styling professionals and hang hairdryers and curling irons. Most of these appliances have hooks for hanging. All you need to do is tap a nail or screw a hook on the inside or outside wall of the vanity. Or hang a flat-backed basket with handle from a hook on the vanity, wall, or door and store all brushes, combs, styling products, and accessories along with electrical styling appliances.

Storing Bathroom Necessities

It may seem logical to store towels with sheets in a linen closet (if you have one), but because

the bathroom is where you use towels, it's the most efficient place to store extra sets. If you have few or no shelves, consider adding a free-standing, ready-made shelving unit over the toilet. If you need something to fit a narrow space, try a baker's rack. Here are a few more space-saving ideas for towel storage.

- Roll towels and washcloths and store them in a basket near the bathtub or shower.
- Use a wine rack for storing rolled hand towels and washcloths.
- Hang a three-tiered wire basket from the ceiling for storing extra washcloths, soaps, and bath products.

Whether you store towels on shelves in your bathroom or in a linen closet, consider folding towels as sets. Lay the hand towel and washcloth on top of the bath towel and fold all three together simultaneously. Then you can easily grab a full set when you need it. If you choose to fold and store towels individually, fold them all the same way to make them easy to stack and retrieve.

Sort through your towels and pull out any that are worn or frayed. Discard them or recycle them as rags, for pet baths, or for emergency use in your car. (If your vehicle gets stuck on ice, placing a towel in front or behind your wheels might provide enough traction to get you out.)

Consider storing bathroom cleaning supplies where you use them — in the bathroom. Keeping these items handy eliminates having to go get them from somewhere else when you need them. Use wire baskets that stack and slide for easy access. If your sink is the type with only a pedestal or legs underneath it, wrap it with a sink skirt under which you can hide cleaning supplies. If you have young children, be sure to use child-safety latches on cabinets and store cleaning supplies out of reach.

Store extra toilet paper and feminine products as close as possible to the toilets. Look for a decorative basket or canister with lid to keep these items accessible yet out of sight. Near the toilet is also a good place for a magazine rack if occupants enjoy reading in the bathroom. If extra toilet paper doesn't fit in storage near the toilet, hide it under the bed in the nearest bedroom.

In the guest bathroom, provide several sets of towels as well as basic toiletries such as soap, shampoo and conditioner, and hand or body lotion. It's also a good idea to provide at least one extra roll of toilet paper. Additional "nice-to-have" items in the guest bathroom include a hair dryer, an unused toothbrush (still in its original packaging), toothpaste, dental floss, and air freshener.

CHAPTER 11

THE OFFICE

Whether you are managing your home or pursuing a home-based career, you need a place to do your job. It might be a "corner office" in your dining room or a suite of rooms in your basement. The size of the office doesn't matter. What's important is that your office space is organized to accommodate your needs so that you can perform your work as efficiently and productively as possible.

Location, Location, Location

Where do you pay bills and file important papers? Do you keep bills to be paid in one place, pay them in another, and file receipts in yet another place? Having a designated office space makes it simpler and easier to handle incoming mail and paperwork, organize bill paying, and manage your household. You don't need a full-fledged office for home management, but you do need a work surface, something to sit on, somewhere to file important papers, and a place to store basic office supplies.

For many home managers, the kitchen is the ideal place to set up a household office. Your kitchen table or countertop may be the perfect work surface; all you need is a place to store files and supplies. Use the tips in chapter 3,

"Organizing Basics," and chapter 6, "Kitchen and Dining Area," to make some room in a cabinet below the counter near the work surface. On one shelf, place a crate or bin that accommodates hanging files. Use the space alongside your filing box to store envelopes and paper, a calculator, and stapler. Store loose items, such as pens and pencils, paper clips, and rubber bands in coffee cups and place them on a turntable for easy access. Or put all of your office supplies in a portable, lidded bin that you can pull out when you need it and put back when you're done. Use a napkin holder on the counter for outgoing mail.

Since you really don't need much space for a simple household office, you may find that you can set one up in the corner of the dining room, family room, or bedroom by using a secretary desk or other furniture that blends with your decor. Or you can hide your office area behind a couple of room dividers.

You may even be able to use a closet for your office. Build in a tabletop and shelves and add an electrical outlet or phone jack if needed. Or simply use the closet as a place to store a rollaway desk and file trolley that you pull out into a hallway or spare room when needed. You can also create a compact office center in an armoire. Open the doors, pull up a chair, and voilà! There's your office. Close the doors, and all you see is a beautiful piece of furniture.

Setting Up a Home Office

A work-at-home office requires more space than a household office because it needs to hold project and client files, reference books and materials, and office equipment. Location is also more critical. Ideally, your office is in a room with a door to afford privacy, and it's

located away from high-traffic areas, such as the kitchen. A separate entrance is good if you have business visitors.

Organizing for comfort can improve productivity — and your bottom line. Start with the basics: a good chair and proper lighting. A comfortable, supportive chair is a must. When shopping for a chair, try out different models to see how they feel. Look for a chair with lots of adjustability to create a perfect fit for your body. Pneumatic height adjustment lets you alter your seating position throughout the day with just a touch. A wheeled chair is great for rolling from one work area to another, but if you spend most of your day sitting in one place, consider getting a kneeling chair that helps to keep your spine in proper alignment.

Lighting is also critical for comfort. There are two types of lighting: ambient lighting for the room and spot lighting for office tasks. The best ambient lighting for computer work is indirect lighting suspended from the ceiling. Spot lighting is a must for focused paperwork. Desk or table lamps should be positioned to light work areas. A fluorescent lamp fixture mounted under a cabinet is another option for office task lighting. To reduce glare and reflections from nearby light sources and relieve eyestrain, mount a glare screen on your computer monitor. And keep it clean. Some kits with antistatic wipes and cleaner mount on the side of your monitor for easy access.

Efficiency begins at your desk. If you have only a standard desk, you're probably cramped for space. An L-shaped configuration is a more efficient set-up; a U-shaped configuration can accommodate an assistant or guest. A modular desk is a good choice because it allows you to reconfigure to adapt to future needs. When shopping for a desk, look for furniture that is easy to assemble. And make sure that your desk has at least one hole to collect computer and telephone wires and keep them out of the way. Make a sketch of your office layout before purchasing furniture, and take it with you when you go shopping. It's also a good idea to take measurements of the room, so you know the parameters of the space you're working with.

The right technology can also increase productivity. Invest in whatever office equipment you need to do your job well. Remember, it's tax deductible. If you can't buy it outright, consider leasing. Keep your future needs in mind when selecting equipment. And be sure to buy from a company that provides good technical support and quick turnaround on repairs. Avoid buying multifunction equipment, such as fax/copier/printers and telephone/answering machines. They save space, but if one function goes on the blink, you have to remove the whole unit for repair. If your budget is tight, look for rebate offers or check out reconditioned equipment. And if you're not sure if you really need a piece of equipment, wait sixty days and then reassess your needs.

Set up a phone number for your business that is separate from your home number. Consider getting at least one other line for your fax and Internet connection. Choose a telephone that has hold, redial, speakerphone, and caller identification features. It's also a

Put a period between the words home *and* office *to keep them separate.*

—Barbara Fields, PAPERCHASERS

good idea to get a phone that enables you to add a headset to keep your hands free for typing or writing.

Finally, stock up on office supplies so you won't have to waste time running out to buy an ink cartridge for your printer in the middle of an urgent project. But don't go overboard on supplies, especially if your storage space is limited. Many office supply companies will deliver just about anything within 24 hours with no shipping fees on orders more than a certain dollar amount. Set up an account with the company of your choice and keep a running list of supplies needed so that you can order them all at once.

Uncluttering Your Office

Your office probably contains more stuff than you need or use — everything from outdated computer equipment to invitations left over from an event that took place five years ago. Most of this stuff gets saved "just in case," but meanwhile, it's taking up valuable space. And the thing that generally takes up the most space is paper.

Start by moving all inactive files into storage. Your inactive files might include past client projects, the previous year's bookkeeping and tax records, research or coursework materials, and any files you do not need to access on a regular basis. Go through your filing cabinet drawers and piles of folders and pull out all of your inactive folders. Group them into categories, such as tax records or client projects, and put them in a lidded cardboard storage box that accommodates hanging folders. You can get these inexpensively at office supply stores and many discount department stores. Use a wide-tip marker to label the box. Store these boxes in a closet, attic, basement, garage, or off-site storage area. Or stack boxes on top of each other in one corner of your office and hide the whole lot behind a decorative screen.

Next, collect all of your office supplies in one place. Sort supplies into two categories: things you use and things you don't use. Give the things you don't use to charity. Then sort the ones you do use into categories by use, such as computer supplies, desk supplies, and paper supplies. Create a supply center, where you contain and store like items together by using labeled boxes or stacking trays on shelves.

For instant shelving in a closet, use a free-standing bookcase or shelving unit. If you don't have a closet, you can use an open bookcase (hidden behind a screen if you prefer) or a freestanding cabinet with doors. Or store supplies under your desk, out of kicking range.

You may be able to use the space behind your office door for storage. Hang a shoe bag with clear plastic pockets for containing smaller items, such as boxes of staples, paper clips, and diskettes. Or hang an over-the-door rack for storing videotapes, magazines, and file folders.

Sell or donate computer equipment you are no longer using. If you donate it to charity, you may be able to take a tax deduction. In the Resources (see page 322), you'll find contact information for several companies that accept computer donations. You also might be able to donate your computer to a local nonprofit organization or to a technical or vocational school where students are learning to repair computer equipment.

Now, about your desk drawer. Do you really need everything that's in there? Take everything out and put back only what you use on a regular basis. Store extra pens, pencils, and other supply items in your supply center. Make sure they work first! Discard any junk you find. Uncluttering your drawer will create more space, but if you make a home for everything in your drawer, you'll be able to find whatever you need without having to rummage through everything. A drawer-organizing tray may suffice to organize pens, pencils, scissors, stapler, staple puller, postage stamps, paper clips, and other items. If you happen to have an extra cutlery tray, that works well too.

Finally, unclutter your computer. Start by backing up your files. Then empty the trash can on your desktop. Run a disk clean-up program if you have one. Uninstall programs and components you aren't using. Run the disk defragmenter utility, which reorganizes your hard drive, making it quicker and easier for your computer to find files. To make it easier for *you* to find files, set up or reorganize your computer system by using the folder system to keep related files together. Create folders within folders; if you don't know how, consult the Help feature. Move files where they can be more readily found. Rename files or folders if necessary. Delete documents that you no longer need.

Organizing Your Workspace

Make a list of the things you use daily or weekly or collect them all in one place. Then sit in your office chair, pull yourself up to your desk or computer in your usual seated position, and extend your arms out from your sides. Now sweep your arms together in front. That semicircle you have just circumscribed is your primary workspace. This is where you want to keep the things you use at least several times each week.

Organize your primary workspace to accommodate the flow of work. For example, you might keep your incoming mail and "Bills to Be Paid" folder on one side of your primary workspace and your out box on the other. If you are right-handed, position your telephone to the left of your seated position. Lefties should position the telephone to the right. Keep your appointment book, notepaper, and writing implements within easy reach of your telephone.

Next, use your imagination to draw concentric circles around your primary workspace. The things you use occasionally should be closest to your primary workspace, and items you use less frequently should be farthest away. If you find yourself regularly getting up to retrieve certain files, use a vertical desktop file organizer to create an interim holding place for current project or client folders. Or get a rolling cart that you can keep close to your desk.

corraling your cords

Organize the cords that come out of your computer, telephone, fax, and answering machine. Get some plastic garbage bag fasteners, cable organizers, or hook-and-loop straps. Take a few minutes to straighten out all the cords. Fasten them together so that they form one big rope. If possible, drop the whole bundle through a hole at the back of your desk. You can do this with the wires of your television, VCR, and stereo equipment, too.

One Challenge . . .

I need help uncluttering my desk. I clean it off one day and within one week, it's a mess again. What can I do to keep my desktop organized?

Three Solutions

① FROM DEBBIE GILSTER, ORGANIZE & COMPUTERIZE: Put all loose papers, magazines, receipts, business cards, and other paper items in a box. Create "Action Files" using bins, hanging folders or stacking trays. Set up "In" and "Out" baskets. Label files "File," "Read," "Pay," "Do," and "Pending." Now sort your papers, one small pile at a time, until the box is empty. Just move each item into its new home based on what the next action is. Don't forget to use the trash can as much as you can.

② FROM JAN JASPER, JASPER PRODUCTIVITY SOLUTIONS: Set up a system for your working files by using a small, inexpensive file holder that you keep right on your desktop. Sort your current and pending papers into categories. Many people need folders for the following categories: papers to photocopy, papers pertaining to a meeting, an upcoming business trip, bills to pay (or expense receipts to turn in), things to read and decide about, several folders for current projects, and a "pending" folder for things on which you're waiting someone else to act. Label folders clearly so you'll know at a glance what's where. Once you get in the habit of using these folders in tandem with your reference files, you can keep your desk clear. The hard part is getting started. But once you start, you'll see immediate results, which will provide the motivation to maintain the system.

③ FROM RONNI EISENBERG WITH KATE KELLY, AUTHORS OF ORGANIZE YOUR OFFICE! (New York: Hyperion, 1999): Set aside a block of time to unclutter your desk. Have on hand a trash can, a pen, file folders, and labels. Clear the space you want to organize. Then make a big pile of all the paper. Evaluate each item, categorize it, and put it away in a desk drawer, file folder, or a desktop organizer. Throw out as much as possible. Even when you are feeling overwhelmed, just keep sorting and categorizing. If you devote the necessary time, your desk can be cleared. You might want to enlist the help of a partner — a spouse, secretary, or someone who can help you keep going.

Organizing your workspace can greatly enhance your productivity. Making simple adjustments to your workstation can do the same. Position your computer monitor a full arm's length away from your seated position. If you can read the screen, it's not too far away. As much as half of the viewing area should be below eye level. Tilt the top of the monitor slightly farther back than the bottom. If you have to reach for your computer mouse, move it closer. Keep the feet of your keyboard up.

Controlling Paper Chaos

Wasn't the introduction of the computer supposed to be the dawn of the paperless office? Instead, we have more paper than ever — and more misplaced files and lost paperwork as well.

Gather all loose papers in one place. Pick up the first piece of paper and make a decision: Do I need this? Keep it only if it serves a purpose. File it only if you will need to refer to it at a future date. If it is something that requires action, such as replying to a letter, or if you need the information to write a report, make a note on your "To Do" list. Then put the paper item in a folder labeled "To Do" or note on your "To Do" list where to find it. Tackle your filing one stack at a time or for ten to fifteen minutes each day until it's all done. If you're really uncertain about whether to save a paper, ask yourself what's the worst possible thing that could happen if you threw it away. Keep in mind that often, all you really need to keep is the information, not the paper. Make a note of favorite URLs or the name of a reference book, for example, and throw away the paper.

TIME-SAVER

File only what you really need to file. Research has proven that 80 percent of what is filed is never looked at again. So if you spend a total of one hour each month filing *everything,* you are wasting 48 minutes every month. If you know where to go to get that information should you need it in the future, don't file it.

Avoid piling paper. Use hanging files and vertical files that allow you to flip through papers more easily. Even your "To File" folder can reside in a hanging file until you get to your filing. The one exception to piling may be your in box and out box. It's easier to toss these items into baskets than it is to put them into file folders.

Use paper organizers to keep stationery and envelopes handy. Stacking paper trays do the trick. Use one tray for storing recycled paper. That way, you'll always know where to find a piece of paper to jot down a note, and you'll have less paper trash. If you're short on desk space, consider buying a paper organizer that resides under your printer or fax. You can also file stationery in hanging folders in a desk drawer.

Filing Systems

Files can be classified as active and inactive. Active files should be stored within arm's reach or very close to your primary workspace. Inactive files, also known as *archive files,* should be stored away from the main work area in a separate filing cabinet or labeled storage boxes.

The secret to a good filing system is to keep it simple. Whatever filing system you use should make it easy to find what you need, be easy to maintain, and make sense to everyone who needs to use it. One of the easiest systems is the A-B-C system. Label a set of hanging folders with tabs for each letter of the alphabet. Then use interior manila file folders with subject labels, such as "January Receipts," that you file under "R" for receipts. File the interior folders in alphabetical order within each lettered folder.

TO PRINT OR NOT TO PRINT

Has the computer brought more paper into your life because you print out your e-mails? Most e-mail messages (if they need to be saved) should be stored on your computer. Create folders in your e-mail program so you can file them by client, project, or subject. Better yet, use a contact management software that automatically links every e-mail to the record of the person who sends it to you. Not printing e-mails reduces filing time, speeds finding messages later, and reduces paper clutter. If you need to bring an e-mail to an off-site meeting, you can print it out, but that should be the exception, not the rule. Try it. It's amazing how much time and space you'll save!

—*Jan Jasper, Jasper Productivity Solutions*

Another system that is easy to set up is a simple numeric system with master index. Label a hanging folder with the number "1." Pick up the first piece of paper you want to file. Write "1" in the upper right hand corner and put in the hanging folder labeled "1" Then write "1" at the top of a sheet of paper that will become your master index. Write a three- to five-word description of the paper you just put in the folder; for example, Directions to Boston. Continue filing in this manner until you have about a dozen papers in the folder labeled "1." Create a folder labeled "2." Start filing papers in that folder. It doesn't matter that the papers are unrelated.

Type your index into a word-processing document on your computer and store it on your hard drive. When you need to find a particular document, use the search feature on your computer to locate the document and corresponding folder number by searching for a keyword, such as "directions."

Although alphabetical and numerical systems are the easiest to set up and work well for many people, subject files are generally the preferred method of filing. Set up hanging files for broad categories, such as "Accounting" or "Prospective Clients." Then set up interior file folders for papers to be filed within each category. For example, in the accounting category, you may have separate folders for accounts receivable, accounts payable, and monthly receipts. (*Hint:* Use box-bottom hanging folders to accommodate thick subject files.) File subjects alphabetically, or group related folders together in each drawer.

Remember that the reason you file something is so that you can find it again if you need it. When naming a new file, think of what heading you are likely to look under should you need a document in the future, not "Where should I put this?" Don't think too long about this. The first name that springs to mind is probably the best file name. Use a noun (person, place, or thing) as your file name.

Label all new folders immediately. Avoid labeling files and folders "Miscellaneous." Documents are either important enough to have their own label or not important enough to save.

Try using different-colored file folders to classify different categories of information. Color-coding makes it easier to identify which files are which without even reading the file name and makes finding the appropriate files a split-second task. It also looks nice, which makes filing a more pleasant task. If you color code files, keep your system simple. Limit the number of colors you use to four or five. For example, you could use green for accounting files (bills, receipts, and copies of invoices), blue for administrative files, and a few different colors for each client.

When filing by subject, try to sort everything into ten to fifteen categories or fewer. You can always add or eliminate categories later. Use broad headings for file folders that will allow room for several subcategories. For example, use "Advertising" as the name for one hanging file, and in that file, hang folders labeled "Yellow Pages," "Trade Journal," and "Newspaper."

Use separate drawers for separate broad categories. You may want to reserve one entire drawer for current client projects and another for business-related files, such as expense receipts, vendor account information, and membership files. Create "hot files" for those files you access frequently. Make space in a filing cabinet or desk drawer that is within arm's reach, or use a vertical desktop file or rolling cart file.

Once you have your filing system in place, align hanging file tabs in a zigzag pattern. Use the slot on the far left, then the middle slot, then the far right and repeat so you have just three columns of tabs showing and all tabs can be seen. (Use clear tabs for easy readability.) If you position tabs on the fronts of hanging folders, it makes folders easier to open; just grasp the tab and pull forward. Do not overstuff drawers; leave a couple of inches free so that it's easy to open folders without having to remove them.

Always put new documents in the front of the folder, so all your files are in reverse chronological order. Periodically, go through all of your folders. Throw away anything that's obsolete, and consolidate or add file folders as needed.

File papers in a loose-leaf binder only when you need to keep similar topics together for quick and easy reference or need to bring that information with you to a meeting. If you want to keep a binder in your filing cabinet along with related items, look for hanging binders in an office supply store. These are especially handy for storing newsletters, phone lists, manuals, or other reference materials.

TIME-SAVER

Set up the perfect filing system for you by using a ready-made filing system. FileSolutions is a manual system that offers customized versions for home, business, doctors, educators, and students. Kiplinger's Taming the Paper Tiger is Windows-based software that allows you to quickly find documents by using search keywords. (See Resources on page 322 for more information about both systems.)

For detailed information about organizing financial records, see page 125. Following are some general filing suggestions for personal records.

• Keep receipts and other tax documents in one place, so that they're handy when you're ready to do your taxes.

• Set up a file for automotive service and repairs. Keep it for as long as you own your vehicle.

• Set up a file for each child that includes Social Security numbers, medical forms, report cards, and any other records you wish to keep.

• File operating manuals and warranties in a hanging folder. If you wish, you can set up interior manila folders and file manuals and warranties by room. The important thing is to keep them all together in one place. Staple the receipt to the documentation. This will make it easier to follow up with the store or company if there is a warranty problem. Keep the warranties, manuals, and receipts for as long as you own the item. Or, if you prefer, file manuals, warranties, and receipts in an accordion-style folder that you can store on a shelf.

Table It. Debbie Gilster of Organize & Computerize recommends making a master index for your files. You can make this list by creating tables with word-processing software or spreadsheet software. Create a table with two columns. Think of a short name for each of your filing cabinet drawers. In the first column, list the name of the drawer. In the second column, list all of the file names in that particular drawer. (Judy Stern of Organize NOW recommends doing this with two people: one to read off the names of the files and one to type the names.)

Use the sort feature to alphabetize the list. You can do a sort within a sort to see only the files for a certain drawer, or you can do a single sort and see all of your files. When filing, refer to the master index to determine where a paper should be filed. Write the location and file name in the upper right hand corner of the paper and store it temporarily in your "To File" bin. With a master index, you can do your filing from anywhere. Just take the stack of papers and master index with you. You might even be able to delegate the physical filing of papers.

One Challenge . . .

What's the best way to organize reminders and little pieces of information I don't want to lose? I've got little scraps of paper and sticky notes everywhere, and still I can't find what I'm looking for when I need it.

Three Solutions

1 FROM MITZI WEINMAN, TIMEFINDER: I recommend creating a paper fact file by using a small, three-ring notebook with tabbed separators, A through Z. Put a few sheets of paper in each section. Write important bits of information directly into your notebook under the letter where you are most likely to look first for this information such as "D" for directions, "P" for passwords, or "B" for books you want to read. Once you've entered the information, you can discard the paper.

2 FROM PAT VOYAJOPOULOS, OASIS: Save bits as bytes! Create an electronic version of the paper fact file described by Mitzi Weinman using your spreadsheet program. Set up twenty-six worksheets, one for each letter of the alphabet, within one workbook. As you receive information, type it into your spreadsheet on the appropriate page.

3 FROM STAFF, THE CONTAINER STORE: The solution may be right at your fingertips. If you use a revolving card file for phone numbers and addresses, you can use it to record other information as well. Simply file it under the appropriate letter of the alphabet. Record deadlines and birthdays on your calendar. This will prevent little scraps of paper from piling up on your desk.

CHAPTER 12

STORAGE AND UTILITY AREAS

The basement, attic, and garage are often the most disorganized rooms in the house, because that's where we dump everything we don't want in the living area. The same goes for the back porch, sheds, off-site storage areas, and for utility rooms — workshops, laundry rooms, and cleaning closets. Organizing these rooms can save time, reduce frustration, and make household tasks easier.

Organize a Cleanup

Schedule some time to clean up and clean out storage areas. If you have adult children no longer living at home, let them know that you are planning to unclutter and organize your storage areas. Give them a deadline to come and get their stuff. Donate or throw away whatever is still there after the deadline.

You'll need all the help you can get in the cleanup, so get your family involved. Or invite a few friends or relatives to help you in return for helping them clean out their basements, attics, and garages. Once you get the job done, keep storage and utility rooms uncluttered by getting rid of things you are no longer using instead of storing them. Following are some suggestions for getting started.

• **Be prepared.** Before clean-up day, look at each area and make a list of what needs to be done and what you will need to do it. For example, you will need bags for hauling away trash and boxes for packing up donations, garage sale items, and things that belong somewhere else. Label these boxes clearly and set them up in the middle of the room, along with a supply of trash bags. You'll also need felt markers for labeling these boxes and storage boxes. You may need extra lighting so you can see what you're doing.

• **Plan to spend one entire day in each room.** If you're not done by the end of the day, you should have a pretty good idea of how much more time you need to finish. Schedule another clean-up day if necessary.

- **Wear comfortable clothing and shoes.** You'll be on your feet and moving around most of the day. Expect to get warm from your exertions (just think of all the extra calories you'll be burning!). And expect to get dirty.
- **Work in one room at a time.** In larger rooms, clear one section at a time. Assign sections to individual helpers or pairs of helpers.
- **Go through everything.** Open every box. Take everything off every shelf. Put back only what you want to keep. Consolidate boxes of similar items and label your boxes. You might even want to print out an inventory list and tape it to the outside of the box. Haul away what you decide to trash, donate, sell, repair, or move somewhere else.
- **Make clean-up more fun.** Let's face it. The last thing anyone *wants* to do is spend the day in a dark, musty basement, hot attic, or dirty garage. Make it more of a party. Play music, have refreshments on hand, and plan to take a lunch break. Also plan your reward — think of something fun that you and your helpers can do together when the work is done.

Basement, Attic, Garage, or Shed?

Should you store things in the basement, attic, garage, or shed? Base your decision on accessibility and climate. Easy accessibility makes a garage or shed ideal for storing frequently used sporting equipment, such as bicycles; lawn, garden, and snow removal equipment; trash cans and recycling bins; and automobile-related items. Basements also generally allow easy access to stored items. The attic is typi-

cally the least accessible storage place, especially if it's just a crawl space or if you have to climb a pull-down staircase to get up there. Limit attic storage to things you need to access only occasionally, such as holiday decorations, moving boxes, and tax records.

Don't put things in storage that should really be trashed, donated, or sold. Do store things you use only once a year or less in the back or bottom of your storage area. Store items you need to access more frequently in the front or on top. Label everything using wide felt tip markers. Store boxes and bins with labels facing out so you can find what you're looking for without having to move heavy boxes. Folks who are super-organized may even want to tape an itemized list of the contents to the front of the box.

Basement Storage. Basements tend to be very humid, which creates a breeding ground for mold and mildew that can damage clothing and furniture. Some basements may also flood, or you could end up with water in your basement because of a sump pump failure, leaking washing machine, or broken pipe.

GOT JUNK?

Look in the Yellow Pages under "Junk Haulers," or consider renting a Dumpster to haul away old furniture and appliances, construction debris, yard refuse, and other household junk for disposal or recycling.

a word about off-site storage

Off-site storage should be a last resort. If you are currently renting storage space, think carefully about the items you are storing. Is it really worth the money to store this stuff? Or could you get rid of some or most or even all of it? Periodically, sort through items in your off-site storage area and reevaluate what you really need to keep.

Designate one area for all stored items. Unless you have a heat- and humidity-controlled basement, don't store anything directly on the floor. Place boxes on shelves or pallets and furniture on pallets. If you buy or build shelves, make sure they're deep enough to store boxes safely and high enough to let you sweep or vacuum underneath. Hang clothes in a freestanding closet or canvas garment bag.

Store like things together in boxes or crates, and label everything. Open crates on shelves are great for things that require frequent access, such as camping or sporting equipment. If flooding is a possibility, store everything in watertight plastic tubs. Cardboard boxes are fine for dry, well-ventilated basements.

Attic Storage. Although the attic is often the driest storage area, its contents are subject to extreme heat, especially during summer. Heat can damage photographs, audio and video cassettes, albums, and some clothing. Your attic may also be a winter home for mice and a year-round home for insects that can do damage. Use plastic containers with tight-fitting lids to protect clothing, books, and paper products. Cover furniture with old sheets to keep the dust off; if water leaks are a concern, use waterproof tarps instead. Stack or flatten extra boxes and store them at the far end of your attic, along with other long-term storage items.

Garage and Shed Storage. Storage space is often limited in the garage or shed, but you can maximize it by using vertical storage systems. Use vinyl-coated hooks to hang bicycles, sleds, winter tires, folding lawn chairs, and ladders from the rafters. Look at what items you might be able to hang and then figure out how many hooks you'll need to buy.

Use wall-mounted long-handled-tool holders to hang brooms, rakes, shovels, and other long-handled tools, or simply use two well-spaced nails that support the head of these tools. Another variation is to cut the top and bottom off of any size can and nail the can to the wall with the open ends facing the floor and ceiling. Slide the long handle of a tool down through the can; one tool per can works best for easy access.

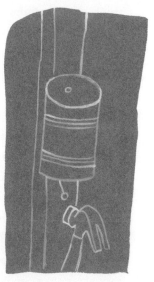

You can also create storage between exposed studs for long-handled tools. Purchase two 2 x 4 boards. Nail one board horizontally across the exposed studs approximately one foot off the ground and the second one approximately three feet off the ground. You can then slide long-handled tools in between the outside wall and the boards. Set up a metal or wood shelving unit along one wall for storing assorted loose items, such as automobile maintenance products, recycling bins, and in-line skates.

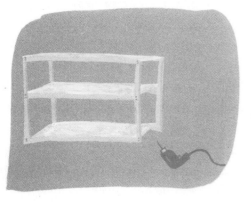

Workshop. Have you ever bought something from the hardware store only to discover days or weeks later that you already had it right there in your workshop? Is your workbench so cluttered that you have to push things aside to do anything? Once you get your workshop organized, your work area will be uncluttered and it will be easy to find the tools and supplies you need.

Before you start organizing, think about the way things are arranged in a hardware store. Broad categories of materials, such as plumbing and electrical supplies, are stored in separate sections. Hand tools are grouped by use. Screws, bolts, nails, and fasteners are organized in different compartments according to use and size.

Start organizing your workshop by sorting tools and supplies into major categories: electrical, plumbing, woodworking and building, household, and painting. Then sort within categories; for example, screwdrivers, wrenches, chisels. Use a box to collect tools and supplies you know you never use. Maybe you know someone who can use them, or perhaps you'll put them with other items you've been collecting for your next garage sale. Throw away all garbage, including broken tools and rusted hardware.

Next, designate storage areas for each of the major categories and find a place for everything. Try to keep categories as separate as possible.

THE ORGANIZED WORKSHOP

It's easier to get organized when you have items that will help you get organized.

❑ Sorting table (a sheet of plywood or an old door over two sawhorses works well)

❑ Large box for collecting giveaways

❑ Trash can or box for garbage

❑ Cardboard boxes or crates for containers

❑ Hardware organizer or assortment of lidded containers

❑ Label maker, or masking tape and wide-tip marker

You might assign separate shelves, separate cabinets or drawers, or even separate walls.

Accessibility is the key to an organized workshop. Keep the tools and supplies you use most often within easy reach. Store less frequently used items on upper shelves, under your workbench, or at the back of cabinets. If you can hang something, do it. Hanging is preferable to shelving because it keeps things more visible and accessible. Following are some storage ideas for your workshop.

- **Hang it up.** Use pegboard and pegs to hang power tools and large hand tools, such as saws and hammers. Use a marker to trace the silhouette of each tool onto the pegboard, for a visual reminder of where it goes. For tools with wooden handles, insert large eye screws at the end of each handle and hang them from hooks on the wall. If your ceilings are low, you might be able to attach wire shelving horizontally to the ceiling rafters and use S-hooks to

hang tools. You can also hang a length of heavy-duty chain from a stud in the ceiling and place S-hooks at intervals on it. Keep lumber in racks that hang from the ceiling. Color-code the lengths like they do at the lumberyard by painting the ends of the boards: red for 10 foot, green for 12 foot, and so on.

- **Divide and conquer.** Use cardboard boxes, empty joint compound buckets, and plastic crates or bins to store similar items, such as plumbing supplies, on shelves. Label containers and shelves. Use glass jars (such as those from peanut butter, spaghetti sauce, or baby food) to store hardware. Divide hardware by type (nuts, bolts, screws, nails, picture hangers, and fasteners) and size. Screw the lids to the underside of a shelf, then screw the filled jars into the lids. You can also use lidded coffee cans. Lay the cans horizontally with the lid facing out. Label the lid, or tape a sample of what's inside to the lid. Drive a long nail or furring strip into each end of the shelf to keep the cans from rolling off.

- **Contain yourself.** Use a hanging shoe bag with clear plastic pockets to store small hand

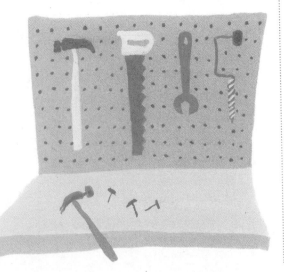

Many products have been designed to help you organize your essentials in the car. You can buy an inexpensive cell phone holder that attaches to the dashboard, so that you won't have to search for the phone when it rings. Portable carry cases provide easy access to the music of your choice and make it easier to exchange CDs and tapes with music from your main collection. A visor organizer is great for collecting gas, toll, and meal receipts or stashing a couple of business cards. You can also buy a pocketed bag that hangs over the back of a front seat to store children's essentials, such as toys or extra diapers. Or store these things in a tote bag on the floor behind the front seats.

If you don't have a door pocket, use the space under your seat to store such things as your CD carrying case, umbrella, flashlight, and maps. Buy a map case, or store maps in a zippered plastic bag. Use the compartment between seats or the glove compartment to store a small pad of paper and a couple of pens, napkins, a travel pack of tissues, wet wipes, or a small bottle of antibacterial soap that doesn't require water.

To keep your car litter-free, keep a small plastic bag in there for collecting trash. Hang it around the cigarette lighter, or secure it to a side window by using a suction cup hook. Organization, etc. (see Resources, page 322) sells a lidded leak-proof bag that hangs over the back of your seat. Get in the habit of picking up trash every time you get out of the car and emptying the trashbag every time you fill up your car with gasoline.

If you have room, leave your cooler in the car throughout the summer months. When you go grocery shopping, pick up some bagged ice and use the cooler to keep refrigerator and freezer items cold until you get home. To keep the cooler from sliding around in the trunk, set it on an old bathroom rug with the "grippy" back side faceup.

Since your car goes just about everywhere with you, it's a great place to keep things you might need while you are out and about. This includes the following items.

- A couple of rain ponchos
- Sunscreen and insect repellent
- Bungee cords or rope, for tying down large purchases
- Telephone book
- Change of clothes for each child
- Extra diapers, baby wipes
- Blanket
- Travel toys and books
- Small bag of toiletries including a toothbrush and toothpaste, dental floss, deodorant, nail clippers, nail file, and feminine products

Stash these just-in-case items in a crate, lidded storage box, duffel bag, or diaper bag in your cargo area. You might also want a separate container for automotive items, such as windshield washer fluid, oil, and a rag for checking oil.

If you use your car for business, consider getting a hanging file box for papers and files you need to have with you. You may also find it useful to keep some office supplies handy. A tackle box makes a nice portable storage box for postage stamps, paper clips, pens, pencils, markers, and notepaper.

Sports Equipment

Store only sports equipment that is being used regularly. Donate or sell outgrown bicycles and skis. Throw away broken equipment, or have it repaired. Get rid of exercise equipment that is not being used; sell it at a garage sale or through the classified section of your local newspaper.

If there's enough room in your garage, designate one wall as an indoor "parking" area for children's bicycles and riding toys. Ask children to "park" there whenever they're done riding. To encourage them, you could make parking signs with their names on them. For quick clean-up of smaller outdoor toys, designate a large, clean trashcan in the yard or garage.

Assign one area of your garage, basement, or shed for storing all sports equipment. Hang bicycles from the rafters or on the wall, or install a bike storage pole that extends from floor to ceiling and requires no mounting. Snowshoes, ice skates, and bicycle helmets can be hung on the wall. Store baseball bats, lacrosse and hockey sticks, fishing poles, skis and ski poles between exposed studs (see page 105). Or buy an organizing product specifically designed for sports equipment that has space for tall stuff and shelves and drawers for smaller stuff.

Keep balls in a large netted bag that hangs from the wall or ceiling of the garage, in a clean trashcan, or on a narrow shelf with a piece of wood or large nail at each end to keep them from rolling off. Another idea is to string a nylon hammock across one corner of the garage. You can use it to store balls, baseball gloves, bicycle helmets, and hockey pads.

Holiday Decorations

What do you do with a half-used roll of Valentine's Day tissue paper, the reusable Easter decorations, or a dozen cups and napkins with jack-o-lanterns on them that are left over from your Halloween party? Why, save them for next year, of course. But this year, store them so that you can find them again next year.

Gather all decorations and supplies for every holiday. Then place them into one box for each holiday. Get same-size boxes that you can store individually on shelves (the ideal situation) or stack in order of holidays and rotate as the holidays pass.

Label boxes in big bold letters on the side that faces out or decorate each box with wrapping paper, artwork, or colors from each holiday. This is a great project for young artists. If you decide to buy large plastic storage tubs, select tubs with different colored lids for easy identification. These tubs are a good choice if you plan to store holiday decorations in a damp garage or basement or in an attic that harbors mice.

Holiday ornaments require care when packing. Protect your ornaments from break-

HANG IT UP

Cover hanging decorations with clear plastic trash bags, tape the bags shut, and hang them from rafters in your basement, garage, or attic.

age by using ornament boxes, which are available wherever organizing products are sold. Or wrap ornaments in tissue or newspaper and store several in each partition of a cardboard liquor or wine box; your local liquor store will be happy to give these to you. Very small breakable ornaments can be stored in empty egg cartons secured with a rubber band around each end. To keep strands of holiday tree lights or garland from becoming a tangled mess, wrap them around empty wrapping paper tubes.

Keep year-round wrapping paper in an accessible yet out-of-the-way location, such as a shelf in your laundry room or cleaning closet or under your sofa or bed. If you have many rolls of gift wrap, a cardboard map/plans box from an office-supply store can help keep them organized. Keep the paper clean by putting several rolls in a clear plastic trash bag that's secured with a twist tie. Keep rolls of paper from unraveling by slitting an empty wrapping paper tube from end to end and sliding it over the new roll. With this system, you can also dispense paper neatly and easily through the slit. Or slip one leg cut from a pair of old pantyhose over one or more rolls and secure the open end with a twist tie. Consider limiting yourself to one or two kinds of gift wrap and one or two colors of ribbon and bows that will work for everything. A pretty pastel print will work for showers and weddings, and a brightly colored print makes a fine wrap for birthday presents for children, men, and women.

Managing Memorabilia

As you unclutter your storage areas, you will come across some (or many) things with sentimental value. What should you do with them? Do what feels right to you. You may look at some stuff and say, "What am I saving *this* for?" and not hesitate to throw it away. Or you may say, "I couldn't possibly part with this" — so don't. But do find a suitable home for the things you wish to keep.

Decide how much space you are willing to give to memorabilia; it might be a box or a shelf or an entire closet. When your stuff expands beyond that space, you'll know it's time to pare down. If space is at a premium right now, choose to keep the items that are most precious to you and offer the rest to your children or siblings. Or bring memorabilia out of hiding and out in the open, where you can see and enjoy it. Here are a few suggestions:

• Take photos of your children's artwork. Put the photos in your photo album and let go of the physical memento. (Remember, don't store photographs and scrapbooks in the attic or basement, where they are exposed to intense heat or high humidity. Store these in the main area of your home, away from light and heat.)

• Make a keepsake quilt from scraps of clothing, such as your father's flannel shirts, your favorite baby clothes, or your T-shirt collection. Or trace children's artwork onto cotton squares, sew them together, and use fabric paint to color them exactly like the originals.

• Drape one of your mother's pretty scarves over your dresser, use one to hang a decorative wreath, or artfully arrange a few over a curtain rod to create a unique valance.

• Laminate and use event tickets as bookmarks. Store them in a basket or box on a bookshelf.

• Create a mosaic plant pot or a picture frame from pieces of a broken vase or chipped dishes.

TRAVEL SOUVENIRS

If you're a born collector like I am, you enjoy keeping souvenirs from your trips. But then what do you do with them once you get them home? When it comes to inexpensive souvenirs such as lapel pins, coins, and matchbooks, I recommend collecting only one of each item from each place you visit. To keep souvenirs organized at home, invest in organizers designed for collectibles. Display pins in shadow boxes, using foam and black velvet to fill the frame. Arrange and display postcards in large picture frames or in scrapbooks or photo albums. Look for a nice display case for storing collections of items such as matchbooks, spoons, golf balls, and shot glasses.

— Stephany Smith Gonser, Put Simply Consulting

PART III

Organizing Finances

Whether you are living from paycheck to paycheck or off the interest from an inheritance, it pays to get your financial house in order. Whatever your financial situation, you can always improve it by learning to manage your money better, taking steps to reduce your debt (and spending), and developing strategies to increase your savings and investments.

Organizing your finances can have a profoundly positive effect on your life. In chapter 16, "Living on Less," you will find dozens of ideas for simplifying your life and gaining financial freedom by organizing your spending around needs rather than wants.

You would do well to consult with a certified financial planner who can evaluate your financial fitness, develop a plan for reaching your goals, and recommend specific steps for achieving those goals.

CHAPTER 13

MANAGING YOUR MONEY

Many think that managing money means making ends meet, but it's also about making the best use of your assets so that you can achieve your financial goals. Do you have a personal financial plan to achieve those goals? Are you and your assets protected? Do you have a budget and a system for paying bills? Are your financial records organized in one place?

Assessing Your Situation

Start taking control of your finances by looking at your current financial status and developing some goals. Put your goals in writing. Make them specific and quantitative: for example, "I want to become debt-free in two years" or "I want to retire by age sixty and have an income of $3,000 a month." Once you know where you are and where you are going, you can develop a personal financial plan.

Get a snapshot of your financial status by preparing a balance sheet or net worth statement. This is a simple financial planning tool that weighs everything you own (your assets) against everything you owe (your liabilities). Liabilities include mortgages, charge accounts, and loans. Assets include the following:

- Cash and cash equivalents (cash on hand, bank and credit union accounts)
- Liquid investments that can be easily converted to cash (CDs, cash value of insurance policies, bonds, trusts, stocks and mutual funds, securities and annuities, gold and silver, employee savings plans, and money owed to you)
- Nonliquid investments (individual retirement accounts and other retirement funds, investment real estate, business interests and partnerships)
- Personal possessions (house, cars, antiques, jewelry, other)

To prepare a balance sheet, make a list of all of your assets and liabilities. Calculate a total for each of the four categories of assets listed above. Then add up your liabilities. Subtract your liabilities from your assets, and you will have your net worth. If the figure is negative, then you owe more than you own. In that case, you'll want to concentrate your energies on developing and implementing a personal financial plan to reduce debt. You'll find lots of information about reducing debt in chapter 14, "Spending and Debt."

If your net worth is positive, take a closer look at your assets. Do you have enough cash or liquid assets for emergency reserves, or are most of your assets nonliquid? Conventional wisdom advises us to have on hand the equivalent of three to six months' take-home pay. This fund is meant to cover your expenses should you lose your job or be unable to work because of injury or illness. It's also nice to have emergency reserves in case you need to pay for an unexpected house repair, car repair, or medical bill. Stockpiling an emergency fund is a good savings goal to work toward once you have eliminated your debts.

Conversely, if most of your assets are in low-yield savings accounts and your goal is to retire rich or at least comfortably, you will want your financial plan to include more higher-yield investments. You'll find more information about savings and investments in chapter 15, "Savings and Investments."

Protecting Your Assets

Part of managing your money involves insuring your assets as well as your intentions regarding your assets. Without adequate insurance, you could lose everything you own. And,

Keep systems as simple as possible so that things fall into place with little or no effort.

— Pat S. Moore, The Queen of Clutter

if you don't update your will or the beneficiaries on your insurance plans, your assets could end up going to an ex-spouse.

Following are seven types of personal insurance. You may not need all of them, but you should consider each one and determine whether it should be part of your financial plan.

1. Health insurance. Without health insurance, a major illness or lengthy hospital stay could deplete your nest egg. Worse yet, you could end up owing tens of thousands of dollars in medical bills. However, many people overpay for health insurance. If you have an emergency reserve fund, you may be able to bring down your monthly premiums by choosing a policy with a higher deductible. Consider all of your options, but don't consider going without health insurance, even if it's just major medical insurance that covers only hospital expenses.

2. Life insurance. If your death would cause hardship for your spouse or children, you need life insurance. If not, you probably don't, unless you want just enough coverage to take care of your final expenses. The next decision is whether to buy a term-life policy or whole-life policy with a cash value. Most financial advisers agree that you may be better off getting term life insurance, which is available for a lower cost, and investing the difference for long-term growth. Do some research and consult with your insurer of choice to figure out what's right for you.

3. Disability insurance. If you're younger than age sixty, your chances of becoming disabled are much greater than your chances of dying. If you are the primary breadwinner, it's worth investigating disability insurance, which would pay a portion of your regular income.

ANNUAL CHECK-UP

As a financial planner, I like to look at the big picture. This is why I ask my clients a lot of questions, including:

- Who is named as the beneficiary on your life insurance policy?
- Who is the beneficiary of your retirement accounts?
- Do you have a will? When was the last time you reviewed it?

Sometimes we discover that the person named as the heir on a will or the beneficiary on a life insurance policy or retirement account is an ex-spouse or deceased relative. Things change. That's why I recommend periodically reviewing your will and updating it as necessary. Also periodically check to see that the beneficiary designations on your life insurance policy and retirement accounts are correct, especially if you are or have been divorced.

—*Bob Colley, Cornerstone Financial Advisors*

This type of insurance is pricey, but you may be able to reduce your premium by selecting to receive benefits after 180 days rather than 90 days. This is another reason to have an emergency reserve of cash.

4. Long-term care insurance. This type of insurance covers long-term hospital and nursing home stays. The earlier you start paying for this insurance, the less you have to pay each year. Alternatives to long-term care insurance include saving specifically for this possibility, tapping into your home equity, or relying on government assistance.

5. Homeowner's or renter's insurance. Homeowner's insurance covers your home (structure and contents) against virtually everything except war damages, earthquakes, floods, and nuclear power plant accidents. Renter's insurance covers contents only. Both types of insurance include coverage for belongings you might take away from your home and also protect against most non-business-related lawsuits, except those covered by your automobile insurance. Be sure that your insurance plan will replace property at its current value, not what you paid for it. Valuables such as jewelry and furs must be covered separately.

6. Automobile insurance. Some states do not require automobile coverage, but it's a good idea to have it anyway because it will cover you if you're responsible for an accident or if your car is damaged by an uninsured or underinsured driver. Get quotes from several companies. If you have an emergency reserve fund, you may be able to reduce your monthly premium by increasing your deductible.

7. Personal umbrella insurance. If you are sued as a result of an automobile accident or injury sustained on your property, your automobile or homeowner's/renter's insurance will cover up to $300,000 and $100,000, respectively. (Check your insurance policies to make sure that you are covered to these maximum amounts.) An umbrella personal insurance policy extends these limits to $1,000,000 or more, depending on the coverage you choose.

Establishing a Budget

The most critical component of managing money is budgeting. A budget allows you to track what comes in and what goes out. It's also a great tool for learning where you can cut expenses, thereby freeing up cash to reduce debt or invest for your future. In short, a budget can help you gain control of your finances — and your life.

There are two types of expenses: fixed and variable. Fixed expenses include mortgage and rent payments, property taxes, car and loan payments, insurance premiums, tuition, and day care. If you pay a set amount on a regular basis, it's a fixed expense. Everything else is a variable expense. This category includes utilities, groceries, clothing, eating out, haircuts, and entertainment.

thy will be done

Do you have a will? If not, your property will be distributed according to the laws of the state in which you live. Having a will is the only way to make certain that your assets and personal possessions are distributed in the way that you want, without unnecessary delays. It's also important to have a power of attorney that authorizes someone you trust to manage your financial and legal affairs if you are unable to do so. This document cannot be drawn up after the fact. (See chapter 27, "Organizing Your Estate," for more information.)

One way to get a handle on your actual expenses is to review your checkbook register. List all expenditures for the past six months in a budget sheet like the one shown in the chart on the next page, or use a spreadsheet program. Then break your list into fixed and variable expenses. Total up all expenditures in each category, such as groceries or parking, and divide by six to get the average monthly expense for each.

To create a budget that really works, you also need to figure out where your cash goes. Although it's a lot of work, the simplest and best way to track cash expenditures is to write down every penny you spend and for what. Don't change what you normally spend. Just write it down in a small spiral notebook that you carry everywhere. At the end of one month, total up what you spent in each category. Then add these expenses into your budget as variable expenses.

monthly budget

Expense Item	January	February	March	April	
Fixed Expenses:					
Rent or mortgage					
Car payments (list separately)					
Car insurance					
Other insurances					
Child care					
Prescription drugs					
Cable					
Internet access					
Savings and investments					
Variable Expenses:					
Credit card payments (list separately)					
Telephone					
Electric and heat					
Food (groceries, school lunches, snacks at work, eating out)					
Clothing					
Household furnishings					
Transportation (include gasoline, tolls, parking)					
Recreation and entertainment (include subscriptions, allowances)					
Personal grooming (include beauty, dry cleaning, laundry)					
Charitable contributions					
Memberships					
Other (pet care, gifts, cards)					
TOTAL					

	May	June	July	August	September	October	November	December

Once you know what you're spending each month, compare it to what you earn each month *after* tax. Earnings include take-home pay, commissions or bonuses, tips, alimony and child support, rental property income, dividends and interest, Social Security benefits, and retirement funds. Then evaluate your financial health.

- If your earnings exceed your expenses, you can use the surplus to reduce debts or contribute to savings or investments.
- If your expenses equal your earnings, you are probably living from paycheck to paycheck. Take a look at your variable expenses to see where you might be able to make some cutbacks without seriously affecting the quality of your life. Consider bringing your lunch to work at least a few days a week, carpooling, eating out less often, or buying clothing at discount stores. Use any "found" money to build savings for unplanned expenses and for retirement.
- If your expenses exceed your income, reduce expenses to avoid getting deeper in debt. If necessary, investigate extra sources of income. Eliminate or reduce all nonessential expenses until you can balance your expenses and earnings. Also take a good look at your fixed expenses. You may be able to find a comparable apartment for less money or trade in your car for a less expensive one.

Maintaining Your Budget

Once you have established a realistic budget, make a conscientious effort to stick to it for at least three months. At the end of each month,

A MUST FOR COMPUTER USERS

If you have a computer, you should be using a financial software package like Quicken or Microsoft Money. You won't believe how much quicker and easier it is to manage your money when you harness the power of your computer. You can use financial software to do everything from budgeting to paying bills to keeping track of tax-deductible expenses. The check-writing feature is a huge time-saver, especially for checks you write every month. You provide the information once, and next month, all you have to do is tell it to print.

—*Karen Simon, PC Tech Associates*

compare your budget figures to actual figures. It may be helpful to make a chart that allows you to do this easily. If you are way off course after the first month, don't give up. Look at what happened and see if you can make a couple of adjustments during the next month to bring those numbers closer together. After a few months, you should need to make only minor adjustments.

Saving up for a major purchase or annual expenses, such as vacations or holiday gifts, can be tricky. The key is to plan ahead and set aside some money every month. Divide the amount you will need by twelve and add that figure to your monthly budget. Then write a check each month to your general savings account, or open a special savings account specifically for annual expenses.

Paying the Bills

Processing bills is a routine task that you can simplify with a system that organizes the whole process, from where to store bills that need to be paid to what to do with bills and receipts after they've been paid. Your system should also take into account when, where, and how you process bills.

Is bill-paying a chore you dread? Consider trading off this responsibility with one of your partner's responsibilities. Or find a way to make it more pleasant. You could, for example, make it a point to play your favorite music or tie a reward to paying bills, such as writing a check to your savings account or treating a friend to lunch on what's left of your entertainment budget.

Designate one area in your home as a bill-paying place, and keep everything you need to pay the bills there. Store bill-paying supplies in nearby drawers or cabinets, or put them in a portable storage bin that you can stash somewhere when not in use.

Scheduling bill-paying days also helps to streamline the process. Get in the habit of paying bills on the first and fifteenth of the month or on every payday. That way, you're more likely to pay bills on time and will avoid having to pay late fees and interest charges. Paying bills on time also maintains (or re-establishes) a good credit record.

Store bills to be paid in one place close to where you open mail or where you sit down to pay bills. If you pay bills twice a month, you might try storing bills in a folder with two pockets, one for bills to be paid on the first of

the month and one for bills to be paid on the fifteenth. Keep a running list of each bill you need to pay, along with the amount due and the due date. As you pay each bill, cross it off the list. Add new bills to the bottom of the list. Write check numbers on paid bills and file the stubs in folders labeled by category, such as "Telephone" or "Car Insurance." (See page 125 for more information about organizing financial records.)

What You Need

Typical bill-paying supplies include:

❑ Calculator
❑ Postage stamps
❑ Envelopes
❑ Return address stamp or stickers
❑ Pen
❑ Calendar
❑ Stapler
❑ Paper clips
❑ Blank checkbooks and registers

To reduce the number of checks you write each month, consider paying bills electronically. You may be able to set up an automatic withdrawal from your checking account to pay your telephone or electric bill, insurance premiums, or credit card bill. Paying electronically saves you the time (and expense) of writing and sending checks. Of course, this has to be something you are comfortable with. And you still have to remember to write the amount paid in your checkbook register.

Many banks and independent companies, such as Paytrust, also allow you to receive, review, and pay all of your bills on-line. You decide who to pay, how much, when, and from which account. Paytrust even allows you to make a payment to someone who doesn't normally send you a bill, such as your babysitter or gardener. The best part is that you don't have to file anything — they store all of your bills on-line (securely, of course) for one full year and off-line for up to eight years. At the end of each year, you can purchase a CD-ROM with all of your bill images from the past year.

If you prefer to pay all bills by check, consider setting up two separate checking accounts. Use one account to pay fixed expenses (including payments to your savings and investment accounts) and the other account to pay variable expenses. Take enough out of each paycheck to cover all of your fixed expenses and put the rest in your variable expense account to pay for groceries, clothing, and entertainment. If you and your partner split the bill paying, you could set up a joint money market account into which you deposit all income and two separate checking accounts in your names for paying bills. Each month, you and your partner would then write a check to your respective accounts to pay whatever bills are your responsibility.

One simple bill-paying system that works well for families with limited income is the envelope or cash system. When you deposit your paycheck, leave enough money in your checking account to cover fixed expenses. Take the balance of your paycheck in cash for variable expenses. Based on your budget, divide that cash accordingly into separate envelopes for groceries, gas, entertainment, and other anticipated expenses, such as allowances for each family member. This system limits your spending to whatever cash you have on hand. If you run out of money for one expense category, you can borrow from another envelope, but in the end, there's only so much money you have to spend.

Whatever system you use, be sure to balance your checking account each month as soon as the statement arrives. One little mistake in addition or subtraction can end up costing you a fortune in overdraft and bounced check fees. And banks can make mistakes, too; you'll want to catch and address such errors promptly.

Organizing Financial Records

Most of us save more paperwork than is necessary, and we do it because we think we have to or because we've always saved everything. But really, how often do you refer back to your cable bill? If there's no need to save paid bills, filing them is a waste of time and energy, not to mention a waste of filing space.

Following is a guide to help you determine what papers you should save and which ones you can toss. This is only a guide. For complete and current guidelines for keeping tax-related papers, refer to Internal Revenue Service (IRS) publication 552, "Recordkeeping for Individuals," at www.irs.gov/.

● **Paycheck stubs**. Check each one for accuracy. Then toss them. Save only the most recent stub, which may be requested as proof of income or employment if you decide to apply for a loan.

● **Deposit slips, ATM withdrawal slips, and debit charge receipts.** Save them to verify amounts on your next bank statement, and then toss. Save debit charge receipts only if they represent a tax-deductible expense or will provide proof for a warranty claim.

● **Bank statements, canceled checks, and check registers.** Save bank statements for three full tax years. You may need them for a tax audit or to prove that you paid a bill if you don't have the receipt. You'll also need to produce bank statements if you apply for a mortgage loan to prove that the money you intend to use for the down payment is not borrowed money. After three years, you can shred or burn statements. Save canceled checks for one year, then destroy all but the ones that support tax-deductible expenses. Keep canceled checks in the envelope with the bank statement, label the outside of the envelope with the start and end dates of your statement period, and file in your current year's files. In an effort to reduce paper, see whether your financial institution will send your statements electronically and keep your canceled checks. Do save check registers, as these will help you to track down the canceled checks. Write start and end dates and starting and ending check numbers on the front of the register.

● **Non-tax-deductible credit card receipts.** If you use a credit or debit card to make purchases, save all receipts from these purchases to verify the amounts on your statement. You may want to save all merchandise receipts for thirty days as proof of purchase should you decide to return an item for a refund or exchange. If an item comes with a warranty, staple it to the warranty certificate or product guide. It's also a good idea to save receipts for expensive articles of clothing, so that you have documentation of their value if an item gets lost or ruined by the dry cleaner. You may want to save receipts for furniture and other large-ticket items (anything over $100, for example) in a safe deposit box or fireproof file cabinet, along with photos and a household inventory list to document replacement value. Toss receipts for items you no longer own.

● **Tax-deductible credit card receipts.** Verify amounts against your next statement, record in your bookkeeping system, and file with other tax records, which you should save for up to three full tax years. After three years, the government cannot ask for supporting documentation.

- **Credit card statements.** Check to be sure that your last payment was received and verify any new charges. When paying the bill, write the amount and date paid and check number on your statement. Save statements for credit cards that are used for tax-deductible expenses. Otherwise, you can toss last month's statement and keep only the most recent one.

- **Utility bills.** When the next bill arrives, check to make sure your account was credited for the correct amount, and toss the old bill.

- **Insurance policies and bills**. Save insurance policies for the period in which they are in effect. Save each monthly bill until the next one is received to check that your account was properly credited. Toss canceled insurance policies and related statements.

- **Tax returns.** The IRS has three years to audit your return, so keep tax returns for three consecutive full tax years. If you underreport your income by 25 percent or more, the IRS has six years to audit your return. And if you don't file returns at all or file a fraudulent claim, the IRS can audit at any time. All tax deductions must be backed up by receipts. Store tax returns and receipts in large manila envelopes. Label each envelope "Tax Return — 20XX." File it with previous years' returns in a cardboard storage box with lid and label the box. If you decide to destroy tax returns that are older than six tax years, it's best to shred or burn them. Before destroying, be sure that your income for that year is reflected on your most current Social Security benefits statement.

- **Investment records.** Save all investment records and bank statements related to investments. If investment summaries are cumulative, you need to save only the most current one. It is not necessary to keep the prospectus from year to year. Keep savings certificates, stocks, bonds, and other securities in a safe deposit box or fireproof file cabinet.

- **Property records.** Keep real estate records for the duration of ownership or longer if needed for tax purposes. Real estate records include real property deeds, title papers, abstracts, mortgage and other lien documents, burial lot deed, tax assessment notices, purchase contracts, records of capital improvements (including rental property), motor vehicle titles, and purchase receipts.

- **Other.** If you have had a history of bad credit, or if your bank or credit company has made mistakes on your billing, keep those bills and any correspondence you have sent or received, especially correspondence that confirms a satisfactory outcome.

In most households, one person is responsible for managing the files. Would your partner or children know where to look for important legal or financial information they may need in the event that you cannot tell them? It's a good idea to set up a folder in your filing system labeled "In Case of Emergency." Give the hanging folder a red or yellow plastic tab that makes it stand out in the drawer. In this folder, include bank account numbers and passwords; phone numbers for your attorney, accountant, financial planner, and investment broker; the location of important documents, such as insurance policies, will, and power of attorney, and the location of the key to your safe deposit box or combination to your lockbox. Let your partner, adult children, or a trusted friend know that you have created this folder and where to look for it if necessary. Update the file periodically.

Preparing for Tax Time

The simplest way to be ready for tax time is to prepare throughout the year. Keep good records and store all your tax-related documents and records in one place so that you can find them when it's time to prepare your returns. If you did not do this last year and the deadline for filing your tax return is fast approaching, refer to the Tax Preparation Checklist on page 129 for a list of the records, documents, and information required to prepare your return.

You don't have to have a fancy filing system. The important thing is to create *some* kind of system for recording income and expenses and storing corresponding paperwork throughout the year. Your record book could be as simple as a spiral notebook in which you note the date, item, and who it was paid to or received from. Your filing system might be as simple as a file folder, envelope, or even a shoe box labeled "Taxes 20XX." File all receipts immediately so you don't lose them. Separating receipts by month or by type of expense such as postage or utilities will make it easier to track down a particular receipt in the event you are audited. Also file all documents marked "Important Tax Information."

Avoid mixing business with pleasure. Deposit all business income into a business checking account and use this account to pay business bills. If you use a credit card for business expenses, use that card for business expenses only. Keep your bank and credit card statements with your tax records along with canceled checks. Refer to page 125 for details about how long to save financial records.

The Honorable Learned Hand, former U.S. Appeals Court justice, once said, "There are two systems of taxation in our country: one for the informed and one for the uninformed." Unless your tax income returns are extremely simple, it's almost always worth paying a professional tax preparer to do them for you. You may be very good at math and enjoy working with numbers, but do you know and understand all of the most recent changes in tax law that could affect your tax liability? The extra you may unknowingly pay in taxes can easily offset the cost of hiring a good tax preparer. And it's a tax-deductible expense!

Ask your friends, family members, and business colleagues to recommend a tax preparer or certified public accountant (CPA). The best way to determine how much it will cost to prepare your tax returns is to bring copies to your prospective preparer. Keep in mind that the cost of preparing your return is one thing.

If you bring your shoe box full of receipts expecting your tax preparer to sort through it all, you will have to pay extra for that service. On the other hand, you may be able to save money on the cost of tax preparation by using a computer program for record keeping if the preparer is able to use your data files.

Be sure to inform your tax preparer of any major life events that occurred throughout the year. Life events that might change your tax status include:

- Adopting a child
- Birth of a child
- Going back to school
- Sending a child off to college
- Getting married or divorced or becoming widowed
- Buying or selling real estate
- Moving
- Starting your first job
- Changing jobs or being laid off
- Retiring

When you think about preparing your taxes, think about what you can do now to reduce your tax liability next year. For example, if you are expecting a baby by the end of the year, you can expect an additional tax deduction. So, if you wanted to, you could decrease the amount of tax withheld from your check so that you don't end up overpaying. Or, if you receive a windfall, you may want to increase the amount of your withholding to offset the amount of additional tax owing at the end of the year.

tax preparation checklist

Whether you meet with a tax preparer or do your own taxes, the first step is to gather all tax-related documents and information for the entire year including the following.

❏ Social security numbers for you, your spouse, and your dependents

❏ Current residential address and other residential addresses during the tax year

Income Records and Documentation

❏ Employment (W-2 forms)

❏ Trust, partnership, or S Corporation income (Schedules K-1)

❏ Unemployment compensation (1099-G forms)

❏ Miscellaneous income (1099-MISC forms and/or bookkeeping records)

❏ Retirement plan distribution, pensions, and annuities (1099-R forms)

❏ Social security benefits (RRB-1099 forms)

❏ State and local income tax refunds (1099-G forms)

❏ Sale of your home or other real estate (1099-S forms)

❏ Interest income statements (1099-INT and 1099-OID forms)

❏ Dividend income statements (1099-DIV forms)

❏ Proceeds from broker transactions (1099-B forms)

❏ Records for any other income that may be taxable or reportable including alimony, jury duty pay, gambling or lottery winnings, prizes and awards, scholarships and fellowships

Tax-Deductible Expenses*

❏ Mortgage interest paid (1098 form)

❏ Other interest paid (second mortgage, student loan)

❏ Real estate taxes paid

❏ Moving expenses

❏ Auto loans and leases if vehicle used for business (need account numbers and car value) or mileage records

❏ Contributions to retirement plans, early withdrawal penalties on financial assets, and investment expenses

❏ Charity gifts and donations

❏ Unreimbursed expenses related to volunteer work such as mileage

❏ Unreimbursed expenses related to your job including travel expenses, uniforms, union dues, subscriptions, office supplies

❏ Job-hunting and job-related education expenses

❏ Child care expenses (need name, address, and tax ID or social security number for payee)

❏ Medical savings accounts

❏ Alimony paid (requires social security number for payee)

❏ Tax return preparation fees

❏ Self-employment business expenses, including health insurance premiums and estimated income tax paid (requires documentation)

Consult your tax preparer about allowable deductions in your situation.

One Challenge . . .

Every year, I find myself scrambling around trying to pull together all of the information I need to prepare my taxes. Last year, I was audited and it took me hours to find receipts for those tax-deductible expenses I had claimed in the previous year. Is there a simple way to keep track of my expenses that will also allow me to find whatever receipts I may need to produce in the future?

Three Solutions

1 FROM PAT S. MOORE, THE QUEEN OF CLUTTER: I like to keep things as simple as possible, especially when it comes to setting up something like a bill-paying center. I recommend having a separate spot for all unpaid bills — even a special napkin holder — to separate bills from other papers. I jot the due date on the envelope where the stamp goes and keep the bills in order of payment. When the bill is paid, the receipt (if you need to keep it for tax or legal purposes) goes into a file box, file drawer, or accordion file for the current year's records. At the end of the year, clean out the current year's records and archive anything tax-related to the tax file. Archive anything else you think you might need in a file out of your current box and shred everything else.

2 FROM JULIE SIGNORE, 1,2,3 SORT IT: I recommend what I call the *record book system,* which requires a sturdy, bound ledger. On the first twelve right-hand pages, enter the months of the year for the entire year. Leave the left-hand pages blank for recording all income. Under each month, enter the bills you pay regularly in that month. As you receive bills, fill in the amount due to the right of the entry and log the due date to the left. Store bills to be paid in your account book. Use the extreme left-hand column to record the date paid and use the extreme right-hand column to record the check number and amount paid. File all paid bills and receipts in manila envelopes (one for each month). If you need to find a receipt, the book will direct you to the envelope.

3 FROM JUDY WARMINGTON, WOMAN TIME MANAGEMENT: I usually recommend an eight-pocket portfolio folder for storing a year's worth of tax information. Label one pocket for each major expense category; for example, credit card statements, utilities, charitable donations, etc. Or buy a letter-size, accordion-style folder with compartments that are preprinted with the months of the year. File all paid bills, canceled checks, and receipts in the appropriate month. Either way, you'll have all of the documentation for your taxes in one place at the end of the year.

CHAPTER 14

SPENDING AND DEBT

The more we earn, the more we spend, and the more we dig ourselves deeper in debt. There's only one way out to get out of debt. Start spending less than you earn, and make debt reduction your number one financial priority. Set some goals, keep track of your progress, and before long your debt will be history.

Debt-Reducing Strategies

You don't necessarily need to make more money to reduce your debt. Rather, you probably need to change what you do with the money you have. It's easy to fritter away money unless you realize how a buck here and a buck there adds up. Here's a good example: If you spend one dollar on a can of soda or a snack from the vending machine each day, you're spending $5 a week, or $20 a month. If you brought your own soda and snacks from home, you could apply the difference toward getting rid of your debt that much quicker.

Let's say that you have a credit card balance of $1,000 at 18 percent interest and that $15 of your minimum monthly payment of $25 goes toward interest. If you continue to pay the minimum every month, it will take you 12.75

years to pay it off, and the total amount you will end up paying is $2,115.41.

The trick to reducing credit card debt is to pay back more than the minimum each month. If you make a fixed payment of $40 each month toward that same $1,000 debt, it will be paid in 2.67 years and the total amount paid will be $1,262.79. You might think that you can only afford to make the minimum payment, but as you can see from this example, paying the minimum ends up costing you more in the long run. Don't leave yourself short on cash for regularly occurring expenses, but do pay as much as you can each month on your debt. If it means going without a little luxury or two, that's probably appropriate.

If you can't pay more than minimum amounts due, just keep paying the *current* minimum amount due on each one of your card accounts. As your credit card balance goes down (because you're no longer charging things, right?), your minimum monthly payment will also go down, which actually lengthens the amount of time it will take to pay off your debt and puts more money in the bank's pocket. Look up the amounts you paid last month, and pay those same amounts every month.

Be sure to make credit card payments on time every month. If you make even one late payment or skip a payment one month, many credit card companies will increase your interest rate dramatically, making it take even longer to pay off your debt.

Work on paying off your debts one by one. List your debts in order of the lowest to highest amounts owed. Use whatever money you have freed up in your budgeting process to pay extra toward the first debt on your list. Pay the current minimum amount due on the other debts. Continue to do this each month until the first debt on your list is paid. Now, here's where you really start making progress. Combine the amount you've been paying on the first debt to the minimum monthly amount due on the next debt until it too is paid. Continue this process until all debt is paid. Then begin to apply your total debt reduction payment each month to savings and investments.

financial trouble?

In the last three to six months, have you:

- Paid only minimum payments on credit cards? **Yes/No**
- Had to borrow or take an advance to pay basic living expenses? **Yes/No**
- Consolidated debts by borrowing at a higher rate of interest? **Yes/No**
- Taken a cash advance on one credit card to pay another? **Yes/No**
- Missed one or more payments on charge accounts? **Yes/No**
- Paid your rent or mortgage late? **Yes/No**
- Received a collection notice or call? **Yes/No**
- Invested nothing in savings or retirement accounts? **Yes/No**
- Wondered how you would make it to the next paycheck? **Yes/No**
- Lost your spouse, been laid off, or unable to work due to illness? **Yes/No**

- Relied on credit cards to make ends meet? **Yes/No**
- Been afraid to open the mail or add up how much you owe? **Yes/No**

Scoring: Tally up the number of "yes" responses, then read below.

1–3 Take steps to protect your financial future by establishing a budget that includes debt reduction or regular contributions to savings.

4–7 Your "yes" responses are warning signs that you need to pay more attention to your finances. You may not feel like you're in trouble, but unless you learn to manage your money better, you are definitely headed for harder times.

8–14 You really didn't need to take this quiz because you know you're in trouble. Don't give up hope on your financial future. Seek the advice of a debt counseling service.

Keep in mind that banks want you to owe them because that's how they make money. From time to time, you may receive credit checks with an advertisement enticing you to use them to go on a well-deserved vacation, install a backyard pool, or get some other nice treat. Don't do it — it's a debt trap. Shred or rip up the checks (so that no one else can use them) and throw them away immediately.

Until you can pay off the entire balance every month, stop using your credit cards. Better yet, cut them up and throw them away. If you can't bring yourself to do that, put your credit cards in a small plastic tub filled with water and place the tub in the freezer. Freezing your credit cards will curb impulse credit card shopping by helping you make a conscious choice about what and when you will buy on credit. Once you get used to buying on cash (and you see your credit card balances going down), you may relish cutting up those credit cards.

Close unused credit accounts. It's a good idea to cancel credit cards that are paid in full for two reasons. First, it will keep you from getting sucked back into charging. Second, having too much open credit could result in a loan denial for a major purchase such as a home or car. When you cancel accounts you aren't using, the credit card companies will notify the credit reporting agencies that will update your credit file.

Trade credit cards for debit cards because a debit card combines the convenience of a credit card with the sensibility of paying cash. Debit cards are different from credit cards as they are tied to cash in a bank account. They are particularly useful for making airline, hotel, or car rental reservations over the telephone.

You can take steps to reduce your mortgage debt too. Pay extra monthly, annually, or whenever you can toward the principal in your mortgage. As little as $25 extra per month can add up to tens of thousands of dollars in savings in interest. It doesn't matter whether you pay this extra money monthly or in one lump sum at the end of the year. If you get a tax refund, consider applying it to your mortgage loan. When you are shopping for a mortgage or refinancing a home, consider a fifteen-year versus a thirty-year mortgage. The monthly payments will be slightly higher, but you'll own your house free and clear in half the time and save money in the long run.

Lowering Monthly Bills

One way to find more money for reducing debt or increasing your savings is to lower your monthly bills. Start first by looking at your largest expense — your home. We all need shelter, but your mortgage or rent payment may be eating up too much of your budget. One option for homeowners is to look into refinancing your mortgage. If interest rates have dropped since you financed your current loan, you may be able to reduce your mortgage payment. If you rent, look for a less expensive apartment or house.

Consider raising the deductibles on your insurance policies. Changing the deductible from $250 to $500 on your automobile could result in significant monthly savings. For self-employed individuals, choosing a higher deductible can make a huge difference in health insurance premiums. If you decide to raise your deductibles, be sure to have enough money in your emergency fund to pay the deductible without putting strain on your budget.

You may be able to reduce your telephone bill. Ask your telephone service provider whether you have the most economical plan for local calls based on your actual use. Ask your long-distance carrier for their best deal. Compare both plans with those of other providers and switch if it will result in savings. Make regional and long-distance calls during

off-peak hours. Look up telephone numbers in the phone book instead of calling information. If you are paying for optional services that you aren't using or really don't need, cancel them. Also shop around for the best cellular phone plan. There's no sense in paying for time and features that you are not using.

Take some simple steps to reduce heating and cooling costs. Consider installing energy-saving shades, especially if you live in a region with very hot summers or very cold winters. At the very least, lower your shades to keep the sun out on hot summer days and to keep heat in on cold winter nights. Turn lights off when not in use. A single light bulb left on twenty-four hours a day can cost you as much as $75 over the course of the year. In winter, turn your thermostat down at night and when you go to work. For every degree you lower your heat, you will save 2 percent on your total heating bill. You can safely lower your thermostat to 55°F if you will be away for an extended period of time. Ask your local electric utility company whether they offer a free home checkup and tips for reducing your energy use.

One way to save on your electric bill is to keep appliances operating at peak energy efficiency. Clean your dryer lint trap after every use, drain your hot water heater periodically, and vacuum refrigerator cooling coils twice a year. When purchasing new appliances, look for products that carry the Energy Star logo. (Energy Star is a program administered by the U.S. Environmental Protection Agency that offers energy-efficient solutions to consumers and businesses.)

Using Credit Cards Wisely

When you limit the number of credit cards you use, you reduce the number of bills you have to pay — and the time it takes to pay them each month.

If you are carrying debt on your credit cards, you can decrease the total amount you have to pay in interest by reducing the interest rate. To find the best rates available, go to Cardweb.com or Bankrate.com. If your credit history is good, you may be able to transfer balances from higher-rate cards to one lower-rate card. Be sure to read all the fine print that goes along with that great introductory offer. You may also be able to consolidate your credit card debt with a home equity loan. However, you could lose your house if you cannot pay back the loan.

At department stores, cashiers will often offer a discount on your purchases if you apply for the store's credit card on the spot. Your safest bet is to decline the offer. Take the offer only if you can *definitely* (not probably) pay off the entire balance when the bill arrives. Then cancel the account and cut up the card. Store credit cards generally have very high interest rates.

Consider choosing credit cards with a payback. Some cards offer frequent flyer miles or membership rewards. If you use it for everything (groceries, gas, restaurants, travel, and so on), you get back a little something. The Discover card offers 1 percent cash back on total annual purchases; you could invest this refund in savings or investments. You must pay off your balance every month, however,

For Safety's Sake

Guard against fraud. Sign new credit cards immediately and protect cards like you would cash. Destroy or file credit card receipts or any document that lists your account number. And never give out your credit card information over the telephone unless you are the one placing the call and you are confident that you are dealing with a reputable company.

otherwise the interest you pay will far outweigh the cash you get back. And be sure to choose a card that doesn't charge an annual fee, definitely an unnecessary expense.

Charge big-ticket items as soon as possible after your credit card's billing cycle closes. Look at a recent credit card statement to determine when that date is. By timing your purchases, you'll be able to use and enjoy them for one whole month before having to pay for them. But do this only if you are going to pay off your entire balance at the end of the month. Otherwise, you'll end up paying more in interest.

Kick the Shopping Habit

Most of us go shopping with nothing particular in mind. But we always come home with something. According to the American Consumer Credit Counseling Service, half of all purchases are made on impulse. Unfortunately, these are the things that end up cluttering our homes!

Before you make the decision to buy a particular item, ask yourself if it is something you *need* or something you *want*. If you think you need it, ask yourself: Do I already have one or more of these? Is it going to improve the quality of my life in any way? Do I really need it, or would I rather put the money I would have spent into my savings account? If it's a luxury item and you really "must" have it, save up for it.

Go shopping only when you need something. Go with a list and stick to it. To minimize impulse buying, leave your credit card at home. When you shop with cash, you tend to think twice about your purchases. If you really want to buy something, walk away from it. Go to a different store, get a drink, or use the restroom. Then decide whether it's worth the walk back. Better yet, go home and think about it for a few days.

Resist the urge to splurge. If you are trying to reduce your spending so that you can pay down debt or increase your savings, remind yourself that waiting has its reward. Work on changing your mindset from "I want it now" to "I can have this and more if I wait until I reach my goal."

PAY DAY

Request a change in your credit card billing date if you have a bill that comes due at an awkward time of the month for you. Banks are usually willing to accommodate you.

—Lynne Crew, Affairs in Order

Consider the real cost of your purchases. Every dollar you spend represents the time and energy you gave to earn it. Think in terms of how many hours you need to work to pay for each item you want to buy. For example, if you earn $15 an hour and an item costs $120, ask yourself whether you would be willing to work eight hours without compensation to have that item. Don't buy something just because it's cheap or on sale. Buy it because you need it or love it.

Buy clothes and accessories in coordinating shades. By doing so, you'll need fewer shoes and accessories to go with your outfits if you stick to the basics. Develop a wardrobe of classic styles — things you can wear year after year and always look fashionable. You can update your wardrobe each season with a few less expensive tops, shoes, and accessories. But remember the cardinal rule of maintaining a clutter-free home: For every item you add, one must go.

Need Help?

According to the American Consumer Credit Counseling agency, almost half the households in America report having difficulty paying their minimum monthly payments on credit cards. If you feel like you are in over your head, help is available. Several nonprofit credit counseling services will help consumers to work out their debt problems. These organizations can help you devise a debt repayment plan and learn practical budgeting skills so you stay out of debt. They typically negotiate with your creditors to do the following:

- Eliminate or reduce interest rates
- Eliminate late fees
- Lower monthly payments
- Consolidate multiple debts into one payment
- Improve your credit rating

In return, you will be asked not to use or apply for any credit for a specific length of time or until your current debts are repaid. To find a credit counseling service in your area, check the Yellow Pages under "Credit Counseling" or contact one of the companies listed in the Resources (see page 322).

Don't try to duck creditors. If you're getting calls at home or letters from creditors demanding payment, don't ignore them. You'll buy yourself more time (before they file a lien against you, garnish your wages, come to repossess, or sue for payment) if you show that you are willing to repay your debt. Contact your creditors. Settle on an amount that you can pay now or by a certain date, and then follow through on your promise.

Use bankruptcy as a last resort. Filing for bankruptcy may seem like an easy way out, but a bankruptcy remains on your credit report for ten years and will affect your ability to secure a loan for a car or home. It also may rear its ugly head in a routine employment check and cost you a job.

Achieving Your Goals

Owing money is like living your life in reverse. Every month, you are paying for things you did last month. Eliminating debt is the only way to

shift your life into forward gear and get ahead. You're the driver; you can do it by taking control of your spending and better managing your resources.

- **Come up with a realistic plan.** Figure out your total credit card debt. Then decide when you want to be debt-free. Divide the amount you owe by that many months. This will give you a rough idea of the total amount you need to pay creditors each month. If you can't afford that amount, adjust your goal.
- **Stick to your plan.** It's easy to slip back into old spending habits. But if you want to pay off your debt, you've got to stop using your credit cards. It's as simple as that. This may mean going without some things for the time being. Read chapter 16, "Living on Less," for suggestions on how to live on less.
- **Track your progress.** List your current debts on today's date in a calendar. Each month, write your new balances on the calendar. Or, use a personal finance package on your personal computer to track progress toward your goal.

CHAPTER 15

SAVINGS AND INVESTMENTS

Whatever your financial goals, budgeting is the first step, followed by reducing debts and expenses and learning to live with less. But thanks to the magic of compounding interest, saving and investing your money is the way to reach the ultimate goal of many Americans: financial freedom. All it takes is a little planning to get started and some discipline and patience to see it through.

Getting Started

If you're like many Americans, you're probably spending money as fast as you earn it. But if you overspend today, you will have nothing for tomorrow. The good news is that it's never too late to start saving. The sooner you start, the more you will have when you need it, whether you want to buy a home, finance your children's college education, or retire comfortably. So how do you get started?

● **Start by setting goals.** What do you want to save for? A new car? Vacation? New home? Remodeling the kitchen? College for your children? Retirement? Write down your goals, along with an estimate of the amount you need. Use a savings calculator, such as that

available at Bankrate.com (see Resources, page 322), to compute how much you have to save to reach your goal at various interest rates and how much you need to save every month. Or meet with a financial adviser.

● **Pay yourself first.** Take 5 to 10 percent (or whatever figure you came up with in the previous step) out of every paycheck and make a payment to your savings account or retirement plan. Then pay the rest of your bills. Learn to live on what's left rather than overspending and finding yourself unable to make regular contributions.

● **Break down your goals.** If your goal seems unobtainable, break it down into smaller goals. Let's say you want to save $10,000 for a down payment on a house over the next five years. To reach that goal, you need to save $2,000 each year. That works out to $5.48 a day. Now look at your daily expenses. Where might you be able to cut back by $5.48 each day? Start putting away that amount, in cash, every day, just as if you were spending it. Use a shoebox or coffee can. By the end of the week, you should have saved $38.36. Take it to the bank and deposit it in your savings account. If you do this every day for the next five years, you have saved $10,000. Actually, you'll have more than that because you will be earning interest along the way, which might just pay for closing costs or a mover. When you have enough in your savings account, open a money-market account or buy a certificate of deposit (CD) to maximize earnings with higher interest.

● **Contribute regularly to your savings.** Make it a habit to save something each month, even if it's only $10. Increase that amount as you pay off debts or get pay raises. Create a lifestyle around what you earn now, not what you hope to earn someday. When you do get a raise, continue to live on your current income and invest the extra income every month.

Strategies for Saving

Most financial planners will advise clients to save 5 to 10 percent of their pretax earnings. If that doesn't seem possible, pick an amount that you feel comfortable with and start saving that amount on a regular basis. Then gradually increase that amount. Remember that it's not how much you earn, but how much you save, that will determine your financial future.

Once you get started, you will probably find that saving money is not so hard after all. It might hurt a little in the beginning as you adjust to spending less. But the satisfaction and sense of achievement that come from having money in the bank will more than make up for any initial discomfort. Following are some painless ways to save.

● **Arrange for automatic contributions to your savings account.** Have your savings deducted automatically from your paycheck, or set up an automatic transfer from your checking account to an investment or savings account. It's easier to save when you do it automatically because you don't have to make a choice about what to do with your money each month. Think of that automatic payment as a down payment on your financial security.

● **Keep the change.** Get in the habit of putting all loose change into a jar or bowl every day. At the end of that week or month, deposit that money into your savings account.

FOLLOW THE RULES

Live within your means by using the 70-20-10 rule. Use 70 percent of your take-home pay for regular monthly bills plus other regular expenses, such as groceries, gas, and clothing. Set aside 20 percent for large-ticket items, such as a car or home. Save the remaining 10 percent for retirement.

You'll be surprised how quickly pennies, nickels, dimes, and quarters add up. You might even go so far as to never spend change from your purse or pocket. Break a dollar bill instead and save the change.

- **Invest all "found" savings.** Use coupons during grocery store shopping and deposit the amount of your savings into your savings account. Find a free parking area, take the bus or walk to work from there, and invest the savings. Make it a point to use your own bank's automatic teller machine to save processing fees. Any time you save money or make a decision *not* to spend money, make a conscious decision to invest it. Keep a running total in a small spiral notebook and write a check to yourself at the end of the week or month. Or keep the cash you didn't spend in a bank deposit envelope that you can hand to the teller next time you're at the bank.

- **Invest all extra income.** Whether you get a nice tax refund or win the lottery, plan to invest any extra cash that comes your way rather than spend it. This goes for those extra paychecks you get several times each year when there are five weeks in the month instead of four.

- **Consider adjusting the amount of tax being withheld from your paycheck for the purpose of investing the additional upfront earnings.** If you always end up getting a tax refund, that's nice, but it was your money to begin with. If you had invested it as you earned it throughout the year, you would have that amount plus interest. Divide the amount of your last tax refund by 12. That's about how much you could be investing each month without changing your lifestyle one bit. Use tax tables available through your employer or accountant to figure out how much tax to withhold so that you break even at the end of the year. If you are self-employed, work with an accountant to determine the amount of tax you should be paying quarterly to the state and federal governments.

- **Join a credit union through work or through a family member.** Credit unions generally offer higher interest on savings accounts than banks do. In addition, you can usually get lower interest rates on loans, which could give you some extra money for your savings and investments each month.

- **Involve the whole family in saving.** Ask your partner and children to think of ways they can save money each week. Keep a chart of the money saved so that you can monitor your progress. Set goals for your savings, such as paying off debts so that Dad doesn't have to work overtime or taking a family vacation.

- **Make and take food and beverages from home.** Eating breakfast or lunch out every day adds up fast, and so will your savings when you choose to eat breakfast at home and bring your lunch to work. Keep track of what you spend on coffee, breakfast, and lunch plus snacks and beverages from the vending machine every week. Add it up and multiply by four. That's how much cash you could be putting into your savings account every month, less whatever you spend at the supermarket buying these items. You could probably treat yourself to gourmet coffee beans and a coffee grinder and still save much more money than if you continued to buy coffee on your way to work.

● **Save on taxes.** When preparing your tax returns, be sure to take every deduction allowed by law. Because tax laws change frequently, hiring a professional tax preparer could result in big savings — and you can deduct the expense. If you are self-employed, save every little receipt as well as the big ones.

● **Shop smarter.** Before buying anything, ask yourself, "Do I really need this?" Always try to negotiate a better deal wherever you shop. (It can't hurt to try!) And never pay full price for anything. Shop around for car and home insurance before renewing if insurance rates are not dictated by state regulations. When you make hotel reservations, ask for their best rate. If you shop from catalogs and on-line stores that do not have a store in your state, you won't have to pay sales tax on your purchases. If you do your holiday shopping this way, minimize the cost of delivery by ordering multiple items from just one or two catalogs. Always save all shopping receipts for at least thirty days in case you need to return or exchange an item.

When shopping for a car, consider buying a good used car instead of a new car. Use the money you save by having a lower car payment to reduce your debt or increase your savings

and investments each month. Better yet, shop for a car at a government auction of automobiles repossessed by the Internal Revenue Service or confiscated from criminals.

● **Take advantage of membership discounts.** Organizations and associations frequently offer member discounts on various products and services, but most people don't use them because they forget that they are available. Write down on a slip of paper the discounts available to you and carry it in your wallet or purse as a reminder. Then get in the habit of shopping where you can get additional discounts.

● **Save as you spend.** You can save thousands of dollars toward college tuition through Upromise (see Resources, page 322), a free program designed to help families reach their college savings goals. Contributing companies, such as AT&T, General Motors, and McDonald's, give you back part of your spending as college savings. In addition, relatives and friends can contribute toward your child's education, or you can contribute toward theirs. Upromise also allows you to invest your savings in a tax-deferred college investing account managed by some of the world's leading financial services firms. Their Web site has a calculator for projecting your college savings based on current and anticipated spending with contributing companies.

Short-Term Savings. Once you start saving money, where should you put it? That depends on what your goals are, how fast you want to reach those goals, and how much risk you are willing to take. Generally speaking, the higher the yield, the higher the risk. Savings accounts and other cash accounts, such as CDs and money market funds, are recommended for building emergency reserves and saving for short-term needs.

Here's what *not* to do with your savings. Don't keep them under your mattress or in a non-interest-bearing account. Don't keep them in your checking account either, because it's too tempting to spend your savings when you have easy access to it. It's also difficult to keep track of how much is savings and how much is for expenses, which may lead to accidental spending.

If you are just getting started with a savings plan, you may want to put your money in a regular savings account. After three months, or when you are able to meet the minimum deposit requirement, you might consider putting some savings into a CD. A CD allows you to deposit a certain amount of money as an investment for a fixed length of time ranging from three months to five years. CDs are federally insured and pay higher rates of return, sometimes double the interest rate paid on savings accounts. They're a great way to save for large expenditures with a definite purchase date, such as a family vacation or holiday gifts.

The benefit of a CD is that it keeps your savings out of reach for a specified term. The down side is that you might have to pay a penalty if you need to withdraw the money before the end of your contract period. But some financial institutions allow customers to cash in CDs with no penalty, and variable-rate CDs allow you to make additional deposits during the specified term and sometimes a limited number of withdrawals. This might be a good way to save for a down payment on a house.

A money market account is another option for short-term savings. It's basically an interest-bearing checking account with limited check-writing privileges. A money market account also may require a minimum balance and you may be charged a monthly service fee if that balance is not maintained. The money market account is a good choice for your emergency fund because you can access your money at any time with no penalties, but the restrictions may keep you from raiding it.

Savings accounts, CDs, and money market accounts are all generally safe investments because they are insured up to a certain amount by the Federal Deposit Insurance Corporation. Another fairly safe savings product is a bond, through which you are lending

For Simplicity's Sake

Use the rule of 72 to figure out how many years it will take for your investment to double. Simply divide 72 by the rate of return on your investment. For example, if you currently have $10,000 invested in a fund that averages a 10 percent return, it will take 7.2 years to grow to $20,000. Keep in mind that the rule of 72 does not account for inflation.

your money to the government or a corporation. In return, you get paid a specified interest rate at intervals during the life of the bond or when it matures.

Long-Term Investments. It's easy to put off saving for the future when there are so many pressing needs and wants in the present. But the sooner you start putting money away, the more time your money has to make money for you through interest, dividends, and capital gains. If you have access to the Internet, use a search engine and enter the keywords "compounding interest" to find Web sites with calculators that demonstrate the power of compounding interest. Even if you are paying off high-interest credit cards and other debts, it makes sense to start saving for long-term goals now.

There are many different types of investment vehicles, some of which are designed for specific purposes, such as saving for college tuition or retirement. Do a little research to familiarize yourself with some of the options. Then seek the advice of a financial planning professional. When organizing your long-term investments, remember these three things:

1. **Hold a steady course.** Once you decide where to invest your money for long-term growth, be prepared to ride out the ups and downs of the market.
2. **Diversify your investments.** As your savings grow, don't keep them all in one place. Balance higher-risk investments, such as stocks, with safer investments, such as CDs and bonds.

3. **Invest comfortably.** Choose investments that suit your personality. If you are not a risk-taker, putting even a small chunk of your savings into a high-risk investment might keep you awake at night.

If your goal is saving for retirement, most financial planners will advise you to fund your 401(k) or 403(b) account to the maximum. Automatic deductions from your paycheck make saving for retirement painless. Many companies allow employees to invest up to 15 percent of their annual income (or up to $10,000). You don't have to pay tax on that money until you begin to withdraw it. Some companies even offer to match part of your contribution, which helps your balance grow quickly. And there's a plan for everyone. Self-employed individuals have similar plans through which they can save for retirement, including the Simplified Employee Pension, SIMPLE plan, and Keogh plan.

Make a contribution every year to an individual retirement account (IRA). Contributions to a regular IRA are tax deductible up to the maximum amount allowable. Your investment will then grow tax-deferred until you begin to withdraw it at retirement. Another option is the Roth IRA. Your contribution isn't tax-deductible, but your earnings grow tax-free until distributions are made. Check with your tax specialist for restrictions and eligibility requirements.

Invest regularly. Once you start contributing to an IRA, contribute every year whether you need the tax deduction or not. The amount you save on your taxes cannot begin to compare with the effect of compounding over time. One way to invest regularly is to set up an automatic withdrawal each month from your checking account to fund your investments. This is an easy way to get into the investment habit.

Saving for college tuition? You may be able to borrow against your retirement account or withdraw college expenses from your IRA with no penalty. You can also set up a 529 plan, which allows families to save for higher education without having to pay taxes on the earnings. And savings can be withdrawn tax-free when used at any accredited college, university, graduate school, trade school, or vocational school to pay for tuition, room, board, fees, books, and supplies. Another benefit is that you can change your designated future college student to another eligible college-bound family member. When saving for college, keep the money in your name, not your child's name, to increase your child's chances of receiving need-based financial aid.

Games People Play. The right attitude toward saving can go a long way toward helping you reach your goals. It's not about pinching pennies or denying yourself; it's about building wealth. And the more fun you have with it, the more likely it is that you will achieve your savings and investment goals.

- **Make it a contest.** Set an annual savings goal. Then come up with a reward that you will give yourself when you reach that goal.

- **Write checks to yourself.** You could simply transfer money each month from your checking account to your savings or investment account, but in the beginning at least, you may find it more rewarding and fun to write a check to yourself.

- **Make saving a social activity.** Join an investment club, a group of people who come together for fun and profit. Ask friends, family members, and business colleagues if they know of any local investment clubs.

- **Educate yourself.** The more you learn about investing, the quicker you will be able to achieve your financial goals because you will be motivated to do so. Read books, look for education information on-line, and attend lectures and workshops.

For Simplicity's Sake

Learn to be content with what you have. When you stop spending on useless or unneeded "stuff," you instantly have more money to invest. Remind yourself daily that the most important things in life are not things that can be purchased. Look for value in the things that no amount of money can buy. A smile on the face of your partner or child; a strong, healthy body; and the wonders of nature can be "bought" without spending a penny. Adding these "investments" to your portfolio will surely enrich your life.

CHAPTER 16

LIVING ON LESS

What are your beliefs about money? How much is enough? Many people are discovering that less is more. The less you spend, the less you may need to work, giving you more time for the things that really matter. You can reclaim control over your finances, and your life, by choosing to consume less. Though contrary to the trends of our consumer culture, it is the most direct path to a simpler life.

How Much Is Enough?

Learning to live with less requires knowing the difference between wants and needs. We *need* food, water, shelter, and clothing. We *want* things like gourmet meals, big houses, fancy cars, and stylish apparel. Do you really need twenty-three pairs of shoes? Or five sets of sheets for your bed? Or that gadget you just saw advertised on television? How many things do you own that are not being used?

Acquiring things has become such a habit that we often don't think about the cost of acquisition. Think about the cost of owning. On a practical level, your belongings cost you storage space as well as the time it takes to care for them. The more you own, the more you have to care for. If you're charging purchases and carry-ing balances on your credit cards, you're paying a lot more than the item is worth, even if you buy it on sale. Which is more painful: not having the latest widget, or looking at your credit card bill every month? You also pay the price of time spent shopping. You can always buy more things, but you can't buy more time.

Much of what we own was bought, consciously or subconsciously, to project an image of success. We tend to let our expenditures speak for our competence. Wouldn't you rather be recognized for who you are and what you have accomplished instead of what you own? No matter how much you acquire, you will never have it all. It's better to have a few possessions that you love and use than a thousand that weigh you down.

Simple Everyday Strategies

The key to living on less is being content with what you have. Look at the many things you own. Do you wear all of your jewelry and clothes? Do you use all the gadgets in your kitchen or workshop? Do you have everything you *need*? Be thankful for the abundance in your life and learn to appreciate the value of things that can't be purchased at any price — time to pursue whatever makes you happy, nature in its glory, a smile on the face of someone you love. Here are some strategies to help you.

- **Tune out commercial messages.** Advertising creates desire. Commercial messages are designed to make you and your kids feel compelled to buy this, that, and the other thing. Use television commercial breaks to get up and stretch, do quick household chores, or turn down the volume and talk to other members in your household. Consider watching less television in general.

- **Buy only to replace something that is used up, worn out, or broken beyond repair.** Also get in the habit of taking care of what you own. When you do buy items, shop around to compare prices, but don't go cheap, especially for things that will get daily use, such as mattresses or carpeting. High-quality, high-efficiency, durable goods will last longer and save you money in the long run. If your budget won't permit buying new items, look for high-quality items in good condition from second-hand stores, consignment shops, and thrift shops.

- **Borrow or rent things you use infrequently or will eventually replace anyway.** Borrow video and music tapes, and books from the library for free. Some libraries even lend framed paintings! Or rent movies instead of buying them. If you have one car that is not driven every day, compare the cost of owning it with the cost of renting a car or taking a cab on the occasions when you need a vehicle.

- **Learn to be a do-it-yourselfer.** If you can do some of your own repairs or make things you might normally buy, you can save a lot of money. See if you can find someone who is willing to teach you what you need to learn. Your local high school may offer continuing education classes. Or teach yourself by using books from the library. You can also save a bundle by making your own meals and gifts.

- **Maximize your spending power.** Train yourself to buy things like clothing, outerwear, and sporting goods out of season or during clearance sales, when you can get the most for your money. Shop for holiday cards and seasonal decorations right after the holidays and save 50 to 80 percent off the regular price. Consider buying holiday candy after the holiday at a fraction of the regular price and freezing it until the following year. There are also traditional annual sale dates for certain items, including new and used automobiles (December and January), tires (May), jewelry (January), lawnmowers and yard tools (August), mattresses (February), paint (April), and linens and towels (January and July).

- **Trade or barter services.** Think of goods and services you could provide in exchange for goods and services you need. You may be able to barter with produce from your garden, babysitting, baking, sewing, or professional expertise. If you and your partner would like to have the house to yourself for the night (a priceless treat!), make arrangements ahead of time to have your children spend the night with friends or family members with the understanding that you will take in their children another night.

- **Make the most of your children's clothing budget.** Purchase clothing in primary colors that can be mixed and matched and worn by either sex, now and as hand-me-downs.

Reducing Your Grocery Bill

One of the best ways to save money on groceries is to plan your weekly menu around specials at the supermarket. Get what you need for the week and then stock up on sale items to the extent that your budget and storage capacity allow. Some supermarkets offer "two for one" deals on perishable items. If you shop for yourself or a small family, you can still take advantage of these great deals: Split the goods — and the cost — with a family member or friend. Here are a few more simple ways to cut your grocery bill:

- **Eat vegetarian more often.** Replace one or more meat dishes each week with main dishes that feature less pricey protein sources such as eggs, beans, cheese, and tofu.
- **Avoid buying convenience items.** Single-serving packages, precooked or mari-

PRIORITIZING WANTS

Make a list of your wants and needs.
Try to be brutally honest about which category they fall into. Then, take a look at the items on your want list. Ask yourself how much each purchase will improve your quality of life. Rate each item with an "A" for a large improvement down to "C" for negligible improvement. If an item will actively detract from your quality of life in some way, don't rate it — just cross it off your list. Now take a look at your "A" list and think about how you can balance these high-priority wants with your budget. What are you willing to give up? Where can you compromise? Perhaps you can forgo a cup of coffee and a newspaper each morning to pay for a European vacation. Or buy your designer clothes at a consignment store so that you'll have enough left over for those skis. If you make these decisions based on how the purchase will improve your life — based on your own priorities, and not someone else's — you shouldn't go wrong.

—Ramona Creel, OnlineOrganizing.com

nated meats, bagged salads, cookie dough, and shredded cheese invariably cost more.

- **Substitute the real thing for paper goods.** Use dish rags instead of paper towels for more economical kitchen cleanup. Use newspaper to clean windows with less streaking.

Opt for cloth napkins instead of paper napkins. And if you're a new parent consider buying cloth diapers instead of store-bought diapers to save money and reduce waste.

- **Get a savings card.** If your supermarket offers an automatic savings card, get one and use it. If you don't have a savings card or forget to bring yours, ask if the cashier can swipe the manager's card so you can get the savings.

Clip Coupons. Coupons are a great way to save on groceries if you use them and you remember to bring them to the supermarket. If you clip coupons, organize them so you can find the ones you want when you need them. One method is to file them in a recipe or card file box or accordion-style canceled check file with alphabetical dividers. You could also file them by expiration date or by food category. Double your savings by shopping at supermarkets that offer double-coupon days.

TIME-SAVER

Don't bother clipping coupons for products you don't use regularly. Have your children go through your collection of coupons and throw out the expired ones. If you take the kids shopping with you, have them locate the coupon item for you. You might even offer them cash for the value of the coupons in return for helping to do the shopping, loading and unloading the car, and putting food away.

Some people believe that the best place to keep your coupon organizer is in the glove compartment of your car. That may work if you tend to make lots of trips to the supermarket or if you don't mind spending time at the store searching through coupons to see what you have. A more efficient way to shop with coupons is to make them a part of the planning process rather than the shopping process. Store your coupon organizer in the room where you clip coupons and write your grocery list. Pull the coupons you need for your shopping trip based on your list. While you compile your list, look for and discard expired coupons. Put your list and coupons together in an envelope that you bring to the store. You might also want to put a pen in the envelope so that you can cross items off your list as you pick them up. Also, bring a clothespin with you and, as you find the coupon items, clip those coupons to your shopping cart. Keep unused coupons in the envelope.

Coupons can save you money, but it takes time to clip, file, retrieve, and use them. Is it worth it? To answer that question, you have to weigh the cost of your time against the savings. You may even be able to save as much money, or more, simply by comparing unit prices or planning your meals around supermarket sales. Keep in mind that even with the savings, a coupon item may cost more than a comparable item with a different brand name or a store-brand item.

Buy in Bulk. Buying in bulk is another way to save, but only if you will use everything you buy and have a place to store it. If it goes bad before you use it, you've wasted your money. Also, it sometimes costs less to buy a smaller container on sale than it does to buy a larger container. Always check the unit price. If you prefer brand-name items, you can save by shopping at a warehouse store for food, pet food, paper goods, laundry detergent, and more. Keep in mind, though, that many supermarket brands are made by the name-brand manufacturers and are of similar quality. This is especially true with such items as bottled water, pastas and rices, and canned foods. Experiment to see where you can cut costs without sacrificing quality.

Cheap Eats

Eating meals out regularly can quickly get expensive. If, for example, you spend an average of $6 per day for lunch five days a week, that's $30 per week or $120 per month. You can make and take your lunch from home for a fraction of the cost. So why don't more people do this? Because making meals requires planning. You can't make a sandwich if you don't have sandwich fillings in the house. And if you don't stock your pantry with "quick and easy" meal fixings, you're more likely to take the family out for a fast-food meal or order a pizza. If you haven't already, you might want to read "More Organized Mornings," page 186, and "Meal Planning," page 210.

If all you really want from a restaurant is the food and not the ambiance that goes with it, place an order to bring home. When you eat out, you have to add an extra 15 to 20 percent to the bill for service, and you'll pay a hefty price for beverages. Ordering takeout allows you to save on the added costs of eating out while still enjoying your favorite restaurant food. Following are more simple strategies for eating out on the cheap.

- **Eat earlier in the day.** Go out for brunch or lunch instead of dinner, and get a comparable meal for up to half the price.
- **Eat earlier in the evening.** Take advantage of early-bird dinner specials, which are generally offered between 4 P.M. and 6 P.M. to get great meals for less.
- **Watch for special offers.** Restaurants will sometimes offer "buy one, get one free" dinner specials to bring in midweek traffic. Look for restaurant promotions in your local newspaper, or ask at your favorite restaurant if they offer any midweek specials.
- **Reserve eating out for special occasions.** Some restaurants offer a free meal on your birthday. Go there to celebrate family birthdays. Just be sure to bring some identification as proof.
- **Schedule and budget for going out to eat.** Avoid eating out on impulse. Schedule it as a treat.
- **Share appetizers, desserts, and entrees.** Restaurant serving sizes are often the equivalent of two or three standard servings. Sharing will save money, and calories!
- **Take home leftovers.** Bring leftovers to work for lunch the following day, or incorporate them into your next main meal. You might, for example, be able to slice and reheat steak

and serve with eggs for breakfast or add gravy and serve with a baked potato for dinner.

Affordable Entertainment

In many areas throughout the United States, you can buy an "entertainment book" that offers hundreds of money-saving coupons for restaurants, movie tickets, attractions, retail stores, and services, such as dry cleaning and oil changes. Usually sold as a fundraiser for schools, churches, and community groups, the book can quickly pay for itself just in discounts. All the other discounts are then a bonus.

Take advantage of off-peak freebies, discounts, and season passes. Some museums offer free admittance on certain days of the week or at certain times of the year. Some tourist attractions offer "locals" a discounted price. Plan to attend a movie matinee instead of a prime-time show, or buy movie tickets in bulk. Many movie theater chains offer tickets by mail that save you about 40 percent off the regular price. Go to plays on weeknights instead of weekends, or catch the preview performance. If you regularly frequent a local tourist attraction or other entertainment venue, it may be cheaper to buy a season pass.

See plays and concerts for free. Many theaters and concert halls recruit volunteer ushers, who get to enjoy the performance once everyone is seated and may even get to meet the performers.

Take a "learn to" class. Many local high schools offer inexpensive continuing education classes on topics ranging from starting your own business to writing poetry to learn-ing to swim. Arts and crafts stores sometimes offer free or low-cost classes for adults and children.

Join an outing or special-interest group. Nearly every community has groups that get together on a regular basis to go walking, hiking, or bicycling. You might also look for a writer's group or book club, or start your own with friends.

Visit your local library. Larger public libraries offer programs and services that are free and open to the public, such as the following:

- Free Internet access
- Community magazine swaps (bring one, take one)
- Writing workshops for children and adults
- How-to demonstrations and talks
- Mini-seminars on current topics
- Book and poetry readings
- Book discussions and discussion groups
- Current magazines and newspapers for browsing
- Special interest exhibits
- Free movie and audiocassette or CD loans

Check out what's happening at bookstores. Many bookstores, especially those with cafés, offer a regular schedule of free events and activities, including: book and poetry readings, writer's groups, book discussion groups (with discounts on books for members), live music (usually on Friday and Saturday nights), and special interest discussions.

If you enjoy entertaining but want to keep the cost of entertaining down, throw potluck dinner parties. Ask your friends to bring their favorite dish (and a canned good for a local relief kitchen if you wish). You can request specific courses or just see what kind of dinner develops.

Frugal Family Fun

You don't have to spend a lot of money for kids to have fun. Check your local newspaper for upcoming events and activities — free festivals, fairs, and other forms of entertainment — that offer frugal fun for the whole family. Here are some further suggestions.

- **Give yourself a visitor's tour of nearby towns.** This is a great way to spend an afternoon or day, alone or with friends or family. Go to the local chamber of commerce or visitor's center. Pick up some local interest brochures and maps, and ask about fun things to do that are inexpensive or free. Choose places and activities that are new to you. Repeat often.
- **Plan a picnic.** Pack a basket, knapsack, or cooler with the makings of brunch, lunch, or dinner, complete with the beverages of your choice. Be sure to include plates, cups, and utensils. You can use paper and plastic, or make it extra special with silverware, glasses, and dinnerware. Don't forget to bring along a blanket or cloth to spread on the ground. Choose a picnic spot in advance, or simply head out for a leisurely walk or drive and "discover" the perfect place to picnic along the way.
- **Plant a vegetable garden.** Kids love to watch things grow, especially if they have a hand in planting and caring for them. And

once those veggies are ready to pick, you save on produce.
- **Take a walk, and talk.** The exercise will do you good, but the most important benefit of going for a walk is that it allows you to give your partner, kids, or friends what they want most from you — your attention. Let them talk about whatever is on their minds.
- **Allow kids to become bored.** When kids get bored, their imaginations kick in and they come up with creative ways to entertain

themselves. It's a wonderful way to help children develop and enhance creativity, imagination, and resourcefulness.

- **Visit your library.** Many libraries offer free activities for children of all ages, including weekly storytelling hours, summer reading clubs, and writing workshops.

- **See what's happening at bookstores.** Like libraries, many bookstores offer free activities for children, including video release parties, storytelling times, and young readers' clubs.

- **Get tips and ideas on-line.** Whether you're looking for indoor or outdoor activities, arts and crafts ideas, or fun learning activities, you'll find hundreds of tips and ideas on-line. Enter the keywords "family activities, "family fun," or "family education" in any search engine to locate helpful Web sites.

- **Vacation at home.** It's simpler, less expensive, and can be far more relaxing than jetting (or driving) to and from a vacation destination. Create an itinerary just as you would for a regular vacation. Plan to see the sights that visitors come to see. Try out a new restaurant or two. Order takeout food, and have it delivered on some nights. Stock up on your favorite breakfast foods, snacks, and beverages. Unplug the telephone, television, and computer. Leave housework and yard work for when you "get back."

- **Take a camping trip.** Hotel stays and eating out make up the bulk of expenses on vacation. Camping and cookouts minimize those expenses, add fun and adventure to your trip, and create lasting memories. Choose your destination and look for a family campground. If you've never tried camping before, borrow a tent, sleeping bags, and other gear before you invest in your own equipment.

- **Bring your own snacks and drinks to amusement parks.** Why waste your hard-earned money on overpriced food and beverages when you can bring your own for a fraction of the cost? Load a child's wagon with a small cooler and tow it along with you. If there's enough room, young children can ride in the wagon when they get tired.

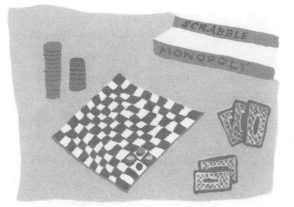

PART IV

Organizing Time

Do you wish that time would stop so that you could catch up? Instead, maybe you should slow down. When you're traveling at warp speed, as so many of us do (and on autopilot, no less), it's easy to get caught up in the "busy-ness" of living. And it's easy to forget that you are the master of your time. How much of what you do every day are you doing because you feel that you "have to" do it? Would anyone care if you didn't do something on your list? Are there things you could delegate? What do you wish you could do with your time? By making a conscious choice to organize your time around the people and things that are most meaningful to you, you can regain control of your life, at home and at work.

CHAPTER 17

MANAGING YOURSELF

We can't really manage time because we have no control over time. We do, however, have control over how we choose to spend our time — and how we choose *not* to spend it. Managing time is really about managing ourselves from day to day and moment to moment and making choices based on our values and goals.

Organizing Things to Do

We all have "things to do." Have you ever noticed that the mundane stuff always seems to get done? You don't have to put "empty the kitchen trash" on your list of things to do, because there will come a point when the trash can can hold no more. The urgent stuff also seems to get done, regardless of whether it's on your list. But what about all of those things that are important and not urgent? How many of the important things we accomplish in a lifetime, or even on any given day, depends to a large extent on how well we organize our priorities.

• **Watch your every move.** Over the next week, before you do anything, ask yourself why you are doing it. Is it important? Is it important enough to do right now? A ringing

telephone is a perfect example. Most people automatically answer the phone rather than *decide* to answer it. It's there for our convenience, but it's easy to become enslaved by it. Pay closer attention to what you are doing so that you can make more conscious choices about how you spend your time.

• **Create a list of goals you would like to accomplish over the next one to five years.** Each day, add something from your list of goals to your daily "To Do" list and make it the first thing you do. It could be as simple as making a phone call to get information or a stop at the library to do some research. Working toward your goals every day brings you one step closer to achieving them. Cross off your list any goals that were imposed on you by someone else.

- **Keep your daily "To Do" list manageable.** Some people like to write down every little thing because they enjoy crossing them off the list throughout the day. Others prefer to just write down the three most important things to do. Whichever person you are, include on your daily list only the tasks that you can reasonably expect to complete today. Next to each task, write how long you think it will take you to complete that task — then double that figure.

Many people (especially optimists) have trouble managing their time because they underestimate how long it takes to do certain things. If you are always late for work, try timing your drive tomorrow. You might find that it's a longer drive than you thought and that you haven't been allowing yourself enough time to get there. To start developing more realistic estimates, write down what you do each day and how long it takes, including breaks and interruptions. Do this for at least one week.

- **Prioritize your day.** Write the number one next to the task or activity that is the most critical or urgent. Which is the next most important task? Make that your number two priority. Continue prioritizing until you have a number next to each item on your list.

- **Keep track of action items with a tickler or reminder file.** Make one folder for each month of the year (January through December) and one file for each day of the month (1 through 31). Place these two groups of files together in hanging files folders in your desk drawer or rolling file cart. Use the monthly folders to file reminders to yourself and any paperwork you will need in the coming months, such as birthday cards to send, airline tickets, registration forms, and meeting agendas. If you will need something later this month, such as directions to a client meeting, file it in the appropriate day-of-the-month folder. Get into the habit of checking your tickler file every day to see what is in the current day's folder. Take care of everything in that day's folder and put it back in the file behind the other day folders. At the end of each month, take everything out of the next month's folder and file in the appropriate day-of-the-month folders. Once you start using a tickler file, you'll wonder how you ever managed without it.

TOOLS TO GOALS

Before you can decide how best to spend your time, you first have to decide what you want. Think about what's truly important in your life. These are your values. What do you want to see happen in your life? These are your goals. Once you acknowledge your values and goals, you can use time-management tools to help you achieve your goals and, ultimately, those things that are truly important.

— *Sheila Delson, FREEDomain Concepts*

Planning Your Day

Time spent planning and organizing your day is time well spent. Take whatever time you need to plan and organize your day by using whatever method works for you. It's helpful to have a planning tool that you can use to manage your time each day. There's nothing wrong with using the back of an envelope, as long as you don't misplace it. But most people find that they can make better use of their time if they have a calendar-type tool that lets them combine things to do.

The classic planning tool is what's known simply as a planner. Choose from daily, weekly, and monthly formats depending on how much room you need to record information. Most daily and weekly planners have a monthly planning guide that lets you see the month at a glance. If you spend a lot of time at your computer, you may choose to use a scheduling program to plan your day. If you decide to use a computerized planning tool, be sure to back up your data regularly.

Use your paper or electronic calendar to keep track of scheduled appointments as well as things on your "To Do" list. Block out time for daily routine tasks too. You might, for example, block out 8 to 9 A.M. every day to do long-range planning or 4:30 to 5:00 P.M. to do filing, return phone calls, or handle incoming mail. Schedule cyclical tasks, such as paying bills and doing laundry, for certain days of the week or month. Also schedule appointments with yourself to do things you enjoy, such as taking a walk or catching up on your reading.

Keep your schedule flexible. When looking at how much time you have in a day and what you want to do, create a buffer zone around each activity that allows more time than your estimate to accommodate unexpected delays. Give yourself a little breathing time between appointments. When you write appointments on your calendar, include a phone number to call in case you're running late or need to reschedule.

Whether it's first thing in the morning or late at night, you're generally most productive at a particular time of day. Use this time to accomplish the things that require the most energy or brainpower. Save your least productive time of day for doing routine tasks, such as filing.

At the end of the day, look back on your uncompleted tasks. Why were they left uncompleted? What held you up? How can you make sure they get done the next day? If you want to know where your time goes each day, use your planner to keep a record of what you actually did so that you can compare it to your plan.

Planning in Circles. According to Nancy Black of Organization Plus, people typically think in abstract rather than linear terms. So instead of keeping lists of things to do, she recommends a technique called *mind-mapping*. Orient a sheet of paper horizontally, and draw a small circle in the middle. Write today's date and the words "To Do" in the center of the circle. From that circle, draw lines (or rays) out toward the edges of the paper; draw one line for each task. Write one task on each line. Break down the task into steps, drawing additional lines for each step and noting what must be done.

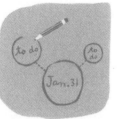

Planning this way allows you to see that many tasks involve multiple steps. It's a good reality check. When you're done, ask, "Can I really do all this in a day?" The next step is to prioritize. Choose the three most important tasks and get started. Mind-mapping is also an effective planning tool for kids.

Everyday Shortcuts

Have you ever thought to yourself, "There must be an easier way?" Often, we keep doing things the hard way because that's the way we've always done it. But if you took time to look at what you're doing, you could probably find ways to save time and energy every day, especially on routine tasks. Take cleaning the shower, for example. Why scrub soap scum when you can simply spray your shower after each use with a product that keeps soap scum from forming in the first place?

One way to simplify routine tasks and save time is to group similar tasks together and do them all at once, whether it's daily, weekly, monthly, or annually. For example, instead of filing each piece of paper as you are finished with it, put it in a "To File" folder and do all of your filing at one time. Check and respond to e-mail once or twice a day instead of many times throughout the day.

Group activities together as much as possible. If you're going to the bank, look at your master list of things to do and see if there's another errand you can do while you're in that area. Schedule routine office visits to the dentist and doctor on the same day. If you have children, plan to take them all for haircuts at the same time. Instead of shopping for cards one at a time, buy all the cards you'll need for several months or a whole year and file them in your tickler file. Saving just a few minutes here and there on routine tasks frees up time for more important things.

LISTEN UP!

Whether you use a calendar or a handheld organizer, begin to regard that planner as a highly paid assistant who is continually reminding you about your appointments and things to do. The more attention you pay to that assistant, the better service you will get from it.

—*Donna Cowan, Cowan & Company Professional Organizing*

Limit the number of choices you have to make on a daily basis. Plan weekly meals in advance and post the plan on the refrigerator so that you don't have to think about what's for dinner. Pare down your wardrobe to your favorite outfits to make it easier to decide what to wear each day. Limit how much you have to remember by writing everything down or using reminder systems such as those described in chapter 4, "Staying Organized."

Get into "wash and wear." First, go through your closets and drawers and then consider getting rid of clothing that requires special care, such as dry cleaning or ironing. When you buy new clothes, choose clothes that are machine washable and do not need to be ironed.

Get your hair styled in a way that is natural. If you have straight hair, get a good cut that accentuates the straightness. If you have curly hair, wear it curly. Try a new cut or styling product designed for your hair type. Going natural saves time and energy. If you've been thinking about getting a really short hair cut, do it. Most short cuts look great with little or no blow-drying or fuss.

Always fill your gas tank when it gets down to one-quarter full. The last thing you want to do when you're running late for work or an appointment is discover that your car is nearly out of gas.

You have to take time to make time.

—Judy Warmington, Woman Time Management

MAKE YOUR MOVE

When the lines at a cash register are equal, choose the line that's next to an unopened register. If it opens, you might be able to move from last to first in line.

—*Mitzi Weinman, TimeFinder*

Freeing Up Time

Research shows that Americans (with the exception of parents with young children) have about forty hours more of free time each week than previous generations. According to Geoff Godbey, a professor of leisure studies at Pennsylvania State University and co-author of *Time for Life*, about twenty-five hours of free time come during weekdays, usually in thirty- to forty-five-minute increments. But the typical American estimates his or her weekly amount of free time at nineteen hours. Perhaps that is because we watch an average of sixteen to twenty-one hours of television each week.

The number-one tip for freeing up time is, you guessed it, turn off the television. How often do you sit down to watch one show and end up watching several hours of television? Try turning the television on thirty minutes later than usual or turning it off thirty minutes earlier. Then take that time to do something you've been wanting to do. Alternatively, don't turn the television on unless there is a specific show you want to see, and turn it off when that show is over. Or tape your favorite shows and watch them when it is most convenient for you. This also allows you to fast-forward through all those commercials — a big time-saver.

Another way to save a substantial amount of time is to delegate. Spend your time doing things only you can do, and let go of the rest. If you can afford it, get a professional to clean your house or mow your lawn. Let a travel agent make travel arrangements. Teach your kids how to do laundry. Hire an assistant to handle routine office tasks, such as filing or scheduling appointments, or give more responsibility to your current assistant. It may help to remind yourself that you don't *lose* control when you delegate; you *gain* control of your time and life.

Fighting Procrastination

Do you tend to procrastinate? Do you know why? Most people think that we procrastinate because we're lazy, but that's not necessarily true. There are some valid reasons for procrastination, and some simple solutions to overcoming it.

One reason why we procrastinate, particularly when faced with a large project, is because we're so overwhelmed that we don't know where to start. The solution is to break the project into a list of smaller tasks or steps. The first step can be as simple as making a phone call or setting up a file. Once that's done, you can move on to the next step. If you find yourself procrastinating at any step along the way, breaking it down will help you get started again.

Loneliness is another reason why people procrastinate. The solution in this case is to solicit a little help from your friends. See if you can get a family member, friend, or colleague to tackle the project with you. Alternatively, you might want to announce your goals to select friends, family, or colleagues. Let them know what you are doing and when you hope to be done. Sometimes it helps just to know that there is someone rooting for you. You might also try imagining that a very important person in your life is right there with you. What would he or she say to inspire you?

Perfectionism also causes people to procrastinate. If you're a perfectionist, you want to do everything just right or not at all, so you keep putting off what needs to be done. If this sounds like you, try to let yourself be the best imperfect person you can be. Keep in mind that no one else expects as much from you as you do from yourself.

MASTER THE MINUTES

Use small blocks of time to accomplish tasks rather than waiting for large amounts of uninterrupted time to take care of things. Consider what can be accomplished in ten minutes. You can organize a drawer, clean out your wallet, write a note, or read a story to your child. In five minutes, you can make a few phone calls, sort your mail, or empty the dishwasher. In one minute, you can review your to-do list, make your bed, or stop and smell the roses.

—Linda Samuels, Oh, So Organized!

Set the stage for success. Don't put off an important project until the last minute. Schedule a regular time each day to work on it. Decide before you begin each day how long you will work before taking a break or moving to another project. Also do a quick attitude check before you get started. It's easier to work on a project if you *choose* to spend time doing it rather than feeling like you *have* to do it. Whether you're trying to unclutter a closet or write up a report at work, make a conscious choice to stay focused for a specified length of time. Limit distractions by turning off the telephone ringer or closing your door.

Slowing Down

Despite its seeming simplicity, it's not easy to "stop and smell the roses." We've trained ourselves to be constantly on the go, to always be doing something and thinking ahead. Try this exercise: Stand up and deliberately walk across the room in slow motion. Notice how making a conscious effort to slow down increases your awareness and expands time. That's what slowing down in life can do for you.

Try putting yourself in charge of the pace of your day. Think pace, not race. Have faith that everything that absolutely must get done will get done. You might think that moving faster or cramming one more thing into your already busy day is being productive, but it may be counterproductive if you make mistakes in your hurry. By living a frantic, rushed life, you may also be sabotaging your health and well-being.

Worry about right now. If you find yourself worrying about something that might happen tomorrow or some day, concentrate on today. Take it one day at a time. And if that's too much to think about, take it one hour at a time. Leave the past behind. Let the future be what it will be. Repeat to yourself as often as needed each day: Where am I? Here. What time is it? Now. Focus on the task at hand. Whether you are washing dishes, driving to the store, doing your job, or helping your children with their homework, try to focus all of your attention and energy on what you are doing.

Remind yourself every once in awhile that all you really *must* do today is breathe in and breathe out. The world won't end if you don't get everything on your list done today. Resist that urge to do just one more thing. Eliminate one activity that you do on a regular basis that provides you with little or no satisfaction and only adds to your sense of being overwhelmed.

Schedule a Vacation. Lorraine Chalicki of YouNeedMe.com Personal Systems offers the following advice for those who need a break from the "busyness" of their lives: You can begin to rediscover the art in your life and work by scheduling daily pauses or "mini-vacations" on your calendar. The word *vacation* comes from the Latin vacare, which means "to be empty." Pull out your calendar and for each day block out a fifteen-minute "vacation" designed to empty your mind. Slow your pace, shift your rhythm, turn your attention to your breathing, and give yourself time to just be. These silent breaks can promote solutions to problems and worries. With continued practice, you will discover that slowing down your pace and focusing on nothing but your breath will renew your energy. Do this daily and you might find that when your

annual two-week vacation rolls around, you won't waste the first two days relearning how to gear down from your usual hectic pace! (See chapter 21, "Organizing to Go," for more tips.)

Managing Stress. Change is the chief cause of stress. Even positive changes such as buying a new home or getting a promotion can cause stress. The key to managing stress is to regain control over those things that are within your power. Following are some ways to do just that.

- **Schedule quiet time.** Turn off the radio during your commute. Get up earlier than the rest of your family and enjoy some peace and solitude. Make time to read or write. You might even try meditating for ten minutes a day.
- **Minimize the effects of stress on your body by taking care of yourself.** Get more sleep. Find a form of physical activity that you enjoy, such as walking, and do it for at least twenty to thirty minutes every other day. And drink eight to ten glasses of water to your health each day.
- **Learn to replace your automatic stress response with a relaxation response.** Take a few deep breaths or count to ten and then respond. Leave the room, if you can, to put some distance between you and your stressor. Or look for something humorous in the situation.
- **Create a support network.** Research shows that people who have family and friends to help them through stressful times stay healthier and recover faster than those who do not have a social support system. So be open to making new friends. And keep in touch with the supportive people in your life.

CHAPTER 18

ORGANIZING YOUR WORK

Good organizational skills at work can pay off in enhanced productivity, better relationships with co-workers, and greater career satisfaction. The basic time-management tips and strategies presented in the previous chapter can be applied at work. This chapter focuses on some work-specific issues, such as planning your workday, managing projects, and handling routine tasks.

Planning Your Work

It has been said that if you fail to plan, you may as well plan to fail. This is particularly true at work. Planning is the blueprint or map that helps you to achieve your goals, individually and as a team. It allows you to organize your time effectively and provides a way to measure your progress.

- **Start with the big picture.** When planning your work, start with your ultimate goals and work backward to what needs to be done today. Take a look at your major projects or goals. Make a list of all the tasks required to complete each one, such as requesting bids, setting up a kick-off meeting, or writing a memo. Every project or goal consists of

smaller, more manageable jobs that you can schedule into your workday or delegate. Give each task a deadline, and then schedule it into your calendar. It's helpful to break down goals into monthly and weekly goals as well as daily goals.

- **Be more proactive by planning ahead.** You can't always manage your time optimally; emergencies do come up, and urgent matters need to be attended to. But in general, deadlines should not fall into either category. By thinking and planning in advance — that is, by being proactive — you'll spend less time in reactive mode.

- **Schedule only 50 percent of your day.** Allow time in between appointments and projects and at the beginning and end of your day.

That way, if a project takes longer than you expected or you have to break away to handle a more urgent task, there's still a chance you can finish what you planned to do. If you have time left over at the end of the day, use it to get a head start on tomorrow's tasks.

- **Delegate tasks that do not require your expertise or interfere with the important priorities you are trying to accomplish.** When delegating, be sure to clearly communicate what you need to have done. Keep your instructions simple and concise. Allow questions at this stage and throughout the project. Give the project a reasonable deadline. Make the delegatee want to help by making him or her feel like a partner in your project. And don't forget to say "thanks."

Managing Your Day

Schedule your work and stick to your schedule. Identify the things that waste your time and resolve to eliminate them. Don't allow procrastination to stand in the way of achieving your goals. Offer yourself a reward for finishing a particularly challenging or unpleasant task. See page 161 for helpful tips on overcoming procrastination.

- **Establish a daily routine.** Figure out what you want to do when, and then block out that time for that activity. If you spend a lot of time out of the office, you might want to schedule one day in the office each week when you can attend to administrative duties, including developing a plan for the following week. If you have a staff meeting every

Wednesday at 1 P.M., you might want to spend Tuesday afternoon preparing for that meeting. Schedule routine tasks for times when you are most likely to be interrupted. Arrive at work earlier or leave later to find quiet time for important work.

- **Focus on the task at hand.** Concentrate on the one thing you are doing and forget about everything else. If you're having trouble getting started on a task, cup your hands around your eyes for thirty seconds to direct your attention to the task in front of you. Decide before you start a task how long you will work on it. When the time is up, move on to the next task. Let your answering machine or voice mail take messages when you need uninterrupted time. Keep a notebook handy to jot down stray thoughts and ideas about other projects or things to do.

- **Beware of multitasking.** Sure, you can read e-mail while you're on hold waiting to place an order or talk to a client. But trying to carry on a conversation and edit a document at the same time could result in accidentally deleting that document. The more complex

> ### ORGANIZE YOUR DAY
>
> **Separate your work day into work time and recovery time.** Recovery time is time to put away papers, review the work of the day, and plan for tomorrow. It's every bit as important as your work time.
>
> —*Barbara Fields, PAPERCHASERS*

could you be better organized?

How organized are you at the office? Your responses will help you judge whether your organizational skills need improvement.

- Are you late for meetings and appointments more often than not? **Yes/No**

- Do you frequently need to ask for deadline extensions? **Yes/No**

- Do you routinely find the need to shift "things to do today" to tomorrow's list? **Yes/No**

- Do you feel totally overwhelmed when you think of everything you have to do at work? **Yes/No**

- Are you easily distracted from your work? **Yes/No**

- Do you have a hard time finishing what you start? **Yes/No**

- Do you frequently misplace or spend more than a few seconds looking for important papers? **Yes/No**

- Do you find it difficult to set realistic project deadlines? **Yes/No**

Scoring: One or two "yes" answers pinpoint potential problem areas for you. Three to five "yes" answers indicate room for improvement in your organizational skills. More than five "yes" answers indicates that you may not achieve your career goals unless you learn how to organize your time and work. If you had no "yes" answers, you are simply unstoppable!

the task, the more attention it requires. The cost of switching gears also grows as the complexity of the task grows. If it requires significant warm-up time to get going again, switching back and forth between complex tasks will actually slow you down.

Smart Systems

If you want to get organized, simplify your work with systems for managing projects, routine tasks, and communications. A good system is one that works for you. If you're happy with your current systems, don't change a thing. If, however, you have no systems or want to get better organized, following are some ideas for systems that you might consider implementing.

Managing Routine Tasks. Set aside specific times for routine administrative or management tasks, such as filing or writing daily reports. Perform such activities as returning telephone calls or checking e-mail at two specific times each day. Set up action folders on your desktop where you can temporarily store papers to file, read, copy, or send to other people or departments. Get in the habit of writing your daily "To Do" list at the end of each day. That way, when you come in to work, you know exactly what needs to be done and you can get to it. If you check your e-mail first thing in the morning, consider sending your "To Do" list in a message to yourself.

Work in Progress. Create and label a new folder for each new project. While you're working on the project, this folder will be your next Friday." If you delegate work to an assistant or co-worker, create a folder with that person's name on it. Use it to temporarily store paperwork that you intend to pass along or notes that you need to share about the project. Make a note in your calendar of when the project or task is due back to you.

Making and Returning Phone Calls. If you need to make a lot of phone calls in a day, minimize the time you spend on each call by having an agenda in front of you and sticking to that agenda. When you leave a voice mail message, keep it as brief as possible. Be sure to say your name clearly and leave a number

One Challenge . . .

I'm always busy at work, but I don't seem to be making any progress toward my goals.

Three Solutions

1 FROM MARIA GRACIA, GET ORGANIZED NOW!: What have you spent your time on lately? Are most of the things you're currently doing contributing to your life goals and dreams? If not, it's time to re-evaluate and re-establish your priorities. Make a list of the things you're spending your time on. Label each item A (highly contributes to my goals and dreams), B (somewhat contributes to my goals and dreams), or C (doesn't contribute to my goals and dreams at all). To achieve your goals and dreams, you must eliminate the Cs.

2 FROM ALLISON VAN NORMAN, ORGANIZING SOLUTIONS: Decide what your top three tasks are each day, and do them first. If you have a lot of trouble prioritizing, try this method. Number the tasks as they appear on your list. Compare task one to task two and decide which has a higher priority. Give that task one point. Then compare one to three, one to four, and so on. When you've finished, compare task two to task three, task four, and so on, until you've gone through your entire list. The tasks with the most points are your highest priorities. You might be surprised.

3 FROM CYNDI SEIDLER, HandyGirl PROFESSIONAL ORGANIZING: Make a catch-up list of tasks you have avoided or put on the back burner, and rank them from the most important to the least important. Resolve to do at least one task from this list each day.

working file. These files, also known as *hot files,* are the ones that you will refer to on a daily basis. If you have to get up to retrieve your working files every time you need them, they're too far away. Keep working files within arm's reach. Staple agendas and schedules to the inside front cover for easy reference. You might also want to develop a simple "Project Status" form that allows you to keep track of projects and tasks that you delegate to co-workers or to outside agencies. Keep the most recent papers on top so that your file is in chronological order. When the project is done, transfer your working folder to your filing cabinet.

Managing Notes. One way to organize myriad pieces of information is to keep a spiral-bound, pocket-sized notebook with you at all times. Start each day by putting the date at the top of a clean page. Throughout the day, jot down anything you need to remember: people's names, things to do, ideas, notes from telephone conversations or meetings. Clip a pen to the spiral binding so that you're never without one. If appropriate, later you can transfer this information to a more permanent location

OUT OF SIGHT, OUT OF MIND?

I find that the more things you leave out as reminders, the less you actually have a handle on what needs to be done. It's difficult to look at a pile of paper, for example, and know that the pile represents seventeen tasks and that this one is the highest priority and that one has a deadline of Friday. It is much easier to choose the next best thing to do when you're looking at a list. So transform stacks of papers into a combination of a "To Do" list and a filing system. If you're afraid you won't be able to find what you need later in your filing system, note on your list, near the "To Do" item, where the corresponding papers are.

—*Stephanie Denton, Denton & Company*

such as a project folder or telephone direc You can also use your computer to re notes in a contact management program.

Follow-up Systems. When you read and r memos, reports, and other documents, highlighter, marker, pen, or sticky flags to passages that you will need to refer back you won't have to waste time searching pertinent information. Respond to mer making a handwritten note on the o memo. Note important dates and deadl whatever calendar system you are using. be helpful to also include an advance re to yourself: for example, "estimated ta where you can be reached. Say the number slowly. If you don't require a return call, say so. If all you really want to do is leave a message and you want to avoid getting into a conversation, make the call at a time when you don't expect that person to be there. Use the telephone when you want to establish a personal connection, need an immediate response, or require two-way communication. Otherwise, send an e-mail, fax, or memo.

Working at Home

Working at home has distinct challenges. There's the challenge of working alone. And then there's the challenge of distractions ranging from the dog barking to kids screaming and the refrigerator "calling" your name. Good time management and organizational skills are even more important for those who work at home.

Working alone doesn't have to be lonely. Plan to get out every day, whether it's to run a few errands, go to the gym, or go for a walk. Stay in contact with business colleagues by phone and e-mail. Get involved with a professional association or community group. This is also a good way to network with potential clients and other entrepreneurs. Meet up with a friend for lunch occasionally, or take a client to lunch.

The biggest challenge most home-based entrepreneurs and employees face is keeping home and office separate, physically and mentally. Start by keeping personal and business papers separate. If you have to use the same filing cabinet, at least use separate drawers. Make a point to confine all office-related paper

> ### POWER ORGANIZING
>
> **Make your computer the central hub for all of your phone contacts, fax and letter correspondence, "To Do" lists, addresses, reminders, and calendar information. With personal information manager (PIM) software, such as Outlook, Act, Entourage, and Goldmine, you can do all that and even keep track of your e-mail. And the great thing is you only have to enter contacts once. The information in your contact database links to your PIM e-mail, calendar, and correspondence features. Have your PIM launch automatically by placing it in your start-up folder. If you're on the road a lot, download your information to your personal digital assistant (PDA) and take it with you. Using a PIM is a great way to stay organized and can help make possible the illusive paperless office.**
>
> —*Do'reen A. Hein, Artistic Designs*

and paraphernalia to your office. Make that space the most efficient, functional office you've ever had the pleasure to work in. Close the door to minimize distractions and let other family members know that you are not to be disturbed.

Set beginning and ending hours for work and be there — working — during those hours. At the end of the day, turn off your computer and close the door. Don't answer your business phone after hours. Don't respond to business e-mails. You don't have to provide service around the clock just because you work at home.

Hire help if you need it. Working at home requires you to wear many hats, from bookkeeper to chief garbage collector. Many tasks, such as bookkeeping, cleaning, filing, and other administrative work, are best hired out so that you can concentrate on doing what you do best. You can even hire a virtual assistant to do things like send out mailings and respond to voice and e-mail messages when you are on vacation. If finances are limited, look for a college student who wants a part-time job, or pay one of your children to help out with some of the simpler tasks.

Be sure that your home-based business projects a professional image. If clients come to your home office, keep it neat and organized. If you don't have a suitable space in your home, consider meeting clients off-site. If you spend a lot of time online reading e-mail or doing research, subscribe to a voice mail messaging service or get a second line so that your

clients don't get a busy signal. When you answer the phone, answer it with a professional greeting. State your company name and ask "How may I help you?" At the very least, state your name.

For tips on setting up a home office, see page 92.

Working on the Road

Business travel presents an additional set of challenges to organizing your work. The biggest challenges include staying in touch with the office and other business colleagues while on the road, making the best use of downtime when traveling, and organizing paperwork and getting work accomplished when you're on the go.

Staying Connected. There are so many high-tech options that make it easy to stay connected wherever you go. But do yourself a favor: Before going away, ask yourself how connected you need to be. Decide which method or methods of communication would be most efficient for each trip. For example, is it worth lugging your laptop just to check e-mail each day or will you be staying in a hotel that offers Internet access?

For many office workers, keeping up with the daily volume of communications is difficult enough, and being on the road makes it even more difficult. Fortunately, there are several simple ways to reduce the number of communications that require your immediate attention when you are out of the office.

- **Change the outgoing message on your voice mail or answering machine.** Let callers know that you are away and what date you will be back in the office. If possible, give callers an option for getting immediate assistance from another staff member in your absence.
- **Forward your calls to an assistant.** Or have your assistant check your voice mail periodically so that you don't have to. If there is a matter that requires your immediate attention, your assistant can call you. Your assistant can also respond to less urgent matters on your behalf. If you don't have an assistant, consider hiring a virtual office assistant. Refer to page 323 for a few options.
- **Set the "out-of-office" automatic reply to incoming e-mail messages.** If you have this option, you won't have to worry about check-

ing e-mail at all. Or, if you do check it, you can respond to just those messages that are most urgent and get back to everyone else when you return to the office.

- **Let current contacts know that you will be away.** In the days or weeks preceding your trip, make a point to let those people you are working with on a daily basis know that you will be out of the office, who will be covering for you, and how to reach you if necessary.

Managing Time Away. The secret to managing time and getting things done comes down to being realistic about what you can and cannot accomplish in any given situation. So plan your time and your work wisely. For example, if you need to work on your laptop while at a hotel, make sure that your room is equipped with a desk and dataport. Find out in advance what business services are available and at what cost. Also, be sure that your hotel is conveniently located so that you don't waste work time.

DO PASS GO

Here's a way to shave time off your daily commute and local business road trips: buy a pass that lets you go through toll booths without waiting in long lines. This type of pass, generally available for state highways, also saves you from fumbling for change and eliminates the need to save all those little receipts.

—*Diane Hatcher, Timesavers Services Professional Organizing*

- **Plan to use travel time as productive down-time.** Many business travelers say they do some of their best creative thinking in the air. Bring a notebook and pen to write down stray thoughts and ideas on current or upcoming projects. Or, if you are traveling by car, bring a handheld voice recorder to capture whatever jewels might spring to mind.

- **Prepare and organize in advance the work you plan to bring with you.** One type of work that lends itself well to travel is filling out forms and expense reports. Gather everything you will need for this project and put it into a folder or large envelope. If you decide to use travel time to catch up on your reading, organize the various types of reading (memos, reports, articles, newsletters, magazines) into these categories and keep them all together. If you decide that you will take advantage of uninterrupted travel time to make some headway on a particular project, you may want to download information onto a floppy disk or CD so you can access it on your laptop. If you need paper files, consider having them sent via overnight courier to your hotel so you don't have to carry them.

- **Make a list of the tools, supplies, and paperwork you need to bring with you.** Create this list on your computer so that you can add to or delete from it and print it for your next trip. Here's a list to get you started:

- Tickets and itinerary
- Laptop computer
- Maps and directions
- Cell phone
- Passport for international travel
- Notepads
- Reading materials
- Business cards
- Appointment calendar
- Address and phone directory
- Project folders
- Personal digital assistant (PDA)
- Prepaid or corporate calling card
- Pens, pencils, highlighters, markers
- Pocket calculator
- Special requirements

THREE E-MAIL TIPS

- **Use detailed subject headers when composing e-mails. This** saves time for the recipient, and it saves you time when you search for old e-mails. For example, "Question about Smith account" is a useful subject heading because when you see it two months later, you know exactly what the e-mail is about. "Question" is too general for a heading. No subject heading at all is even worse.

- **Delete unneeded e-mails. Some e-**mail messages can be deleted as soon as you've read them. Other messages you need to save for a short time but can safely delete later. Once a month, go back and delete any e-mails you no longer need, and archive those e-mails you must keep.

- **Use your in box as an extension of your "To Do" list. If you regularly** clean out your e-mail in box, all that remains there are things you have to act on. So your in box becomes a useful tool rather than a junk-filled, long-term storage area.

—*Jan Jasper, Jasper Productivity Solutions*

CHAPTER 19

BALANCING HOME AND WORK

Everything in moderation — that's the secret to happiness and good health, right? So why is it so difficult to maintain balance in our lives? Because it takes conscious effort and attention. How do you know when your life is in balance? When you function almost as well when things are going badly as when things are going well and your overall satisfaction with life remains the same.

What's Important to You?

Knowing what's important to you is the first step toward creating more balance in your life. Imagine that you had only one month to live. How would you spend your time differently? How would your priorities change? What would become more (or less) important to you? To assess your priorities, ask yourself the following questions.

- What makes me happy?
- What is the one thing I most want to accomplish?
- What do I value most?
- What do I want to be remembered for?

Then develop a strategy based on your answers.

- **Keep focused on your values.** Take five minutes at the end of each day to reflect on how you aligned your expenditures of time, energy, and money with your values throughout the day. You might want to keep a journal to chart your progress. As you plan your day, know what is most important to you today. The more time you spend thinking about your values, the more likely you are to express your values through your actions.

- **Don't be afraid to let the world see who you really are.** When you are being yourself, you give others permission to do the same. With no false fronts to keep up, life is much simpler and more satisfying.

- **Pare down your commitments.** Assess your involvement with various committees, boards, and clubs. Is the time you are spending on each of these commitments aligned with your values? Are you getting a sense of satisfaction or fulfillment from your involvement? When you volunteer your time, know why you are doing it. Do you enjoy it? Does it help you meet personal goals? If not, politely excuse yourself from commitments that are creating undue stress.

Finding Your Balance

It's not easy to juggle multiple priorities, especially when it means juggling the demands of family and career along with your own needs. But that's what we do day after day. On some days, we accomplish extraordinary things and even manage to keep everyone happy. But at what cost?

No matter how valiantly we try, we can't do it all, all of the time. And we can't do some things as often or as well as we would like to do them. So we wind up feeling like we've failed somehow. We're stressed out, tired, and maybe even a little angry. Because more often than not, we sacrifice our own plans and goals to meet the needs of others. Or we don't even make plans and goals for ourselves, because we figure, "Why bother?"

Every time you say yes to something, you are saying no to something you've already said yes to.

—Mitzi Weinman, TimeFinder

TEN-MINUTE GOALS

One of the oldest phrases in the book is, "I'll do that when I have the time." Problem is, that time never seems to come. If you really want to do something, the time can generally be found pretty easily. For example, if you just won an all-expenses paid trip to the land of your dreams, you'd probably find time to fit it into your busy schedule. It's time to begin fitting in those things you want to do, and ten-minute goals can help. Schedule ten minutes a day to catch up on your reading, begin learning a foreign language, or have fun with your children.

—*Maria Gracia, Get Organized Now!*

- **Bring balance to your life by focusing attention where attention is needed.** The next time you feel angry, frustrated, guilty, resentful, or stressed, note whether it is about home issues, career issues, or leisure or private time. Do you frequently feel this way about this area of your life? If so, resolve to bring your attention to this area and make an effort to make some changes that will bring your life into balance.

- **Imagine life as a game in which you are juggling five balls in the air.** Name those balls work, family, health, friends, and spirit. Work is a rubber ball; if you drop it, it will bounce back. But the other four balls — family, health, friends, and spirit — are made of glass. If you drop one of these, it will be nicked, damaged, or shattered.

● **Detach yourself slightly from your environment to become more objective about your role at home and at work.** As a more objective observer, you are more likely to find ways to improve your balance. Ask yourself this: Are you a hard worker or a workaholic? The difference between the two is state of mind. Working hard to achieve a goal is admirable. Workaholics work for the sake of working in the belief that work will somehow make them worthier. If others see you differently from the way you see yourself, imagine for a moment that their perspective is the true perspective. See if you can justify their position and then try to justify your own.

● **Structure your day for balance by scheduling specific times for work, home, and play.** When you are at work, engage fully in your job. When you are with your family, give them 100 percent of your attention and energy. And when you are playing, concentrate on your enjoyment. Live each moment to the fullest.

● **Spend less time talking about your need to relax and more time doing it.** Play hooky from work. If you've been swamped with deadlines, spend a whole day with no plans. Just do what you feel like doing, when you feel like doing it. If you have to make a lot of decisions at work, give yourself a time-out from making decisions. Let someone else decide where to go, what to do, and what to eat. If your job requires constant contact with people, escape into solitude. Go for a walk in the woods or paddle a canoe on a quiet lake.

● **It's okay to stop and rest.** If your life is a whirlwind of activity seven days a week, try balancing it with some true leisure time — a time to sit and rest — without feeling the need to be productive or busy doing something. It will refresh your spirit and make you more efficient when you return to your responsibilities. If an appointment or activity is canceled at the last minute, resist the urge to fill up that time slot with another appointment or activity. If you work particularly long and hard one day or if you feel exhausted, make a conscious effort to take it a little easier the next day. Sleep later if you can. Leave work half an hour early (or at least on time). Squeeze in a nap. Put your feet up and read a book. Or do nothing at all. A change from your regular routine can be just as relaxing as a rest, and maybe even more restful if you're the type that finds it hard to sit still. Try doing something you really love to do but haven't done in a long while.

Learn to Say No

Is it worse to say yes and feel angry, or to say no and feel guilty? The answer goes back to your values and beliefs. When you act from your values and beliefs, your decision feels right. Frustration is a signal that you are doing more than what feels comfortable.

Don't let guilt make you take on more than you can handle or take you away from what's really important to you. According to Miss Manners, the polite way to refuse is to offer an apology but no excuse. She suggests the follow- ing polite denials: "Oh, I'm terribly sorry, but I can't." "I'd love to, but I'm afraid it's impossible." "Unfortunately, I can't, but I hope you can find someone."

If you feel stressed most days, examine your schedule. Is there a commitment you can forgo? Or is there someone else who can do some of the things you are doing? Ask other members of your household which obligations they would be willing to pick up. You might find that your husband doesn't mind vacuuming or that your daughter actually enjoys ironing.

Minimize your shuttling responsibilities. A 1999 report by the Washington-based Surface Transportation Policy Project shows that American mothers with kids in school spend an average of 66 minutes each day driving. If it's safe, encourage children who are old enough to walk, cycle, or skate to school and to after-school activities, or use public trans- portation. If other mothers you know are in the same time bind, see if you can work out a weekly schedule of pick-ups and drop-offs that provide all of you with a little extra free time.

twenty ways to say no

Ramona Creel of OnlineOrganizing.com offers these suggestions for saying no.

- I can't right now, but I can do it later.
- I'm really not the most qualified person for the job.
- I just don't have any room in my calendar right now.
- I can't but let me give you the name of someone who can.
- I have another commitment.
- I'm in the middle of several projects and can't spare the time.
- I've had a few things come up and I need to deal with those first.
- I would rather decline than end up doing a mediocre job.
- I'm focusing more on my personal and family life right now.
- I'm focusing more on my career right now.
- I don't really enjoy that kind of work.
- I can't, but I'm happy to help out with another task.
- I've learned in the past that this isn't my strong suit.
- I'm sure you will do a wonderful job on your own.
- I don't have any experience with that, so I can't help you.
- I'm not comfortable with that.
- I hate to split my attention among too many projects.
- I'm committed to leaving some time for myself in my schedule.
- I'm not taking on any new projects.
- No.

Making Time for You

Yes, family is important. Yes, work is important. And yes, there's only so much time in a day. But if you don't take care of your own needs, who will? If you want to unclutter your life, begin by choosing to put yourself first. It's not being selfish; it's being self-caring. There's a big difference.

Caring for yourself — physically, emotionally, intellectually, socially, and spiritually — will make you happier, healthier, and better able to cope with the demands of daily living. In fact, by putting your own needs first and reserving even just a little more time and energy for yourself, you will have more to give to others.

You're in charge of your time, so go ahead and make some time for yourself. Schedule free time into every day. Block out some time in your calendar and write the word "FREE" in that time slot. Use this time for activities that you really enjoy, such as spending time with your children, visiting friends and family, or gardening. Then schedule everything else around those times. Why should it be the reverse? Allow some flexibility in your schedule, however. Don't try to plan every minute of your time. Leave some time to do whatever you feel like doing at the moment, which may be nothing at all.

Free up time by taking advantage of all that technology has to offer. Have your paycheck deposited directly into your checking account. Set up automatic payments for your bills. Shop on-line, especially if you don't like shopping. Use your computer to create a grocery list or to manage your finances. Let your answering machine take your calls during dinner or when you are trying to enjoy some quiet time. Just don't become a slave to technology. Remember, you are ultimately the master of your own time.

Try designating a night to do your own thing. If your children are old enough to fend for themselves, consider making one night a week a night when everyone is on their own. This can be your time to take a class, read, write, draw, or do whatever makes you happy.

UNCLUTTER YOUR MIND

It's hard to concentrate on work or home when your brain is overloaded with things you are trying to remember about one or the other. Here are two simple ways to clear mental clutter:

1. Keep a small notepad or voice recorder with you to capture thoughts, ideas, or anything you want to remember.

2. Call home or work to leave yourself a reminder on your own voice mail system or answering machine.

—*LaNita Filer, LFJ Organizing Concepts Plus*

Carve out a chunk of time that is your "do not disturb" time. Let everyone in your household know about this time and make it clear that you are to be interrupted only in case of emergency. Go through possible scenarios with them to make sure they understand what constitutes an emergency. If they see blood, smoke, or fire, that's an emergency. Everything else can wait. If one of your kids wants to go over to a friend's house and needs your permission, he'll have to wait a half hour until you are free. If your husband can't find his favorite golf shirt, he keeps looking himself, gets the kids to help him look, or wears another shirt. Hint: It's a lot easier on everyone if you spend your "do not disturb" time behind a closed door.

Make use of the free time you do have. If you have an hour for lunch, plan to spend thirty minutes eating and thirty minutes doing something that you want or need to do such as:

- Read a book.
- Take a nap.
- Take a walk.
- Pick up a few groceries.
- Make personal phone calls.
- Write a letter.
- Run a couple of quick errands.
- Listen to music on your headphones.
- Sit and think.

If you can't manage a whole hour or more of time to exercise or read or whatever, start with ten minutes. Ten minutes of time for yourself is better than zero minutes. If you can, keep your hobby stuff handy so that you can

One Challenge . . .

There are so many things I would love to do, but because I work fifty hours a week, I just never seem to have the time. How can I make more time for myself?

Three Solutions

1 FROM LORRAINE CHALICKI, YOUNEEDME.COM PERSONAL SYSTEMS: Include your personal passions in your workday. If you're a shutterbug, bring your camera to work and take photographs during your lunch hours. Or schedule a five-minute "fun break" or two throughout your workday to leaf through your favorite photo magazine or catalog. If you love music, bring your favorite CDs or tapes to work and take a lunchtime break with your headphones. As you begin to build these breaks into your workday, you'll quickly discover that they provide a major boost in energy and improve the quality of your work and mental processes.

2 FROM MARIA GRACIA, GET ORGANIZED NOW!: You really can't add anything to your schedule without subtracting something else from it. Think about what things you can choose to subtract so that you can add the things you really want to do. Do away with anything that is not helping you fulfill your goals and dreams.

3 FROM JAN JASPER, JASPER PRODUCTIVITY SOLUTIONS: Schedule appointments with yourself to make time for the things you keep "not getting around to." This works for everything from taking the next step on that back-burner project to making sure you get yourself to the gym twice a week.

make good use of spare moments throughout the day and of waiting and commuting time.

Time for Family and Friends

At the beginning of each month, put "fun stuff to do" on your calendar to balance the demands and responsibilities of home and career. If you wish you had more time for your family, think about how you can make more time for them. Where there's a will, there's a way. Perhaps you can try the following techniques to see what works best for you.

- Cut back on work hours.
- Change jobs.
- Trade full-time for part-time work.
- Cut commuting time by working closer to home.
- Work at home one or more days a week.

Unite the three Fs: family, friends, and fun. One way to make more time for friends without shortchanging your family is to invite friends to join in some family fun. Choose activities that everyone, even friends without children, can enjoy.

- Attend a sporting event.
- Go to a water park.
- Take a hike.
- Fly a kite.
- Rent boats or canoes on a nearby lake.
- Go camping for a weekend.
- Go skiing or cycling.
- Have a picnic at the beach.
- Make plans to go on vacation together.
- Celebrate the holidays together.

For more ideas on organizing togetherness for your family, see page 190.

Friends help us maintain the balance between work and play. It's so easy to get caught up in doing and achieving that we often neglect to make time to be with the people we care about most. Yet research shows that people who have family and friends to help them through stressful times stay healthier and recover faster than those who do not have a social support system.

Dedicate time to friendship time. Take a few minutes to send an e-mail message or a "just thinking of you" card. Make a quick phone call, or leave a "hello" message on a friend's answering machine. Make a standing date for coffee or lunch with your best friend once or twice a month.

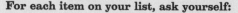

CUTTING BACK

Identify some specific areas where you might be able to cut back on your responsibilities. For each item on your list, ask yourself:

- How easy or hard will it be for me to let go?
- What consequence would ensue if nobody took up the slack when I let it go?
- Who is the logical choice to take up the slack in responsibility?

Now work your list. Start with the items that are the easiest for you to let go of, with the least dire consequences, and for which someone can pick up the slack. Select at least one per week to let go. Where appropriate, you'll want to inform those who will be affected that you're doing this. In some cases, that will mean training someone else in how or what is required for them to pick up the slack. And you'll need to accept their mistakes and the inevitable chaos that ensues. Ultimately, you'll reap the benefits of increased time, freedom, and a happier, more satisfying life.

—*Rose Hill, The Academy for Business Success*

PART V

Organizing Home Life

Most people will say that family and home life are their number one priority. The way to organize your home life — and maximize time with your family — is to implement schedules, simple routines, and systems that are easy to maintain. In chapter 20, "Organizing Your Family," you'll find suggestions for keeping track of who needs to be where when, as well as ideas for creating opportunities for family togetherness. Chapter 21, "Organizing to Go" offers tips for getting and staying organized before, during, and after your next vacation or business trip. Chapter 22, "Managing Your Household," outlines a plan for preparing meals and keeping your home presentable with minimal time and effort. And, in chapter 23, "Organizing for Safety," you'll learn ways to keep your family safer and more secure at home. All it takes to accomplish these things is a willingness to try something different.

CHAPTER 20

ORGANIZING YOUR FAMILY

Think of your family as a team, with you as the team's manager. Your job is to organize the team and minimize the chaos. As the manager, you need to know where all players are at all times. Players need to know the rules. You all need to work together as a team to achieve your goals, whether playing at home or away.

Managing Family Schedules

Trying to keep track of who needs to be where and when can be daunting. Try implementing a family planning system. It could be as simple as making notes on a calendar that hangs on the refrigerator. For families that are always on the go, consider a slightly more sophisticated interactive scheduling system that enables family members to make plans around each other's schedules.

A great tool for keeping track of family schedules is a large blank write-on/wipe-off wall planner with a spacious grid that provides plenty of room for writing in daily, weekly, or monthly events and activities. These boards sometimes include a separate planning area where you can note future events and activities. Assign a different color marker to each

family member for writing in appointments, meetings, practices, games, gym time, celebrations and outings, and such tasks as grocery shopping or taking garbage to the dump. Each family member should be responsible for entering his or her own schedule.

Another effective tool for family scheduling is a group practice appointment book. This is the kind of planner used in physician offices. Available for four- and eight-person groups, the group practice appointment book lets you block out the time in quarter-hour increments for each family member, so you can see everyone's schedule at a glance. Look for an undated planner that lets you make "appointments" from as early as 7 A.M. to as late as 9 P.M. Use a large, magnetic clip or two to attach the calendar to the refrigerator.

When coordinating your family's schedule, don't forget to block out time one day a week for family clutter control. During this time, everyone goes through the house picking up and putting away misplaced items that belong elsewhere. Setting up a specific time for uncluttering eliminates the need to nag, and without question the results are far more dramatic when every room gets uncluttered simultaneously. If once a week doesn't suit your family's style, try doing it for five minutes every night after dinner.

Rules and Routines

Kids need rules and routines. They may not always like the rules, but knowing what to expect — and what is expected from them — makes them feel more secure. The rewards and punishments that come with rules also teach kids that people are responsible for the consequences of their actions. But kids can't learn that lesson unless you apply rewards and punishments consistently, and that's the hard part. It may be easier to create and enforce several important rules rather than trying to enforce lots of little rules.

What is your family's daily routine? Routines help your family get organized and stay organized. They also help to reduce the stress and frustration that comes from having to nag kids about doing their homework and chores. If the idea of routines seems stifling, consider this: Having them may allow more time for fun because routines help kids, and you, manage time better. Following are some ideas for developing routines.

- **Morning routine.** In the morning, the goal is to get kids out the door on time with the least amount of whining and complaining. It might be easier to yell "Time to get up!," but why start your day yelling? Try waking your kids with a little tug on their big toes or a tickle. Or put on their favorite music, and turn the volume up. If your kids have trouble tearing themselves away from the television in the morning, try turning it off fifteen to thirty minutes before "go" time, or don't turn it on at all. Parents can get weather, news, and traffic reports from the radio and Internet. Post morning chores where kids can see them when they're getting dressed.

MAKE PLANNING FUN

Try using a paper calendar with large squares as your family planner. Any calendar will do, as long as the squares are big enough. Buy small stickers of different colors to signify different types of tasks or activities. For example, you might use green stickers to indicate any activity that requires money, blue stickers for school events, yellow stickers for family activities, and red stickers for doctor and dentist appointments. Let kids put their own stickers on the calendar. Next to each sticker, have them write their names and the time of the activity or event: for example, Jennifer, 1:30 P.M. Be sure to make a color key and keep a supply of stickers and a pen handy.

—Debbie Williams, Let's Get It Together

- **After-school routine.** Just like adults, kids need time to wind down after a busy day. Allow them time to have a snack, watch television, play computer games, or play outdoors with friends. Down time is important, but if homework or chores are not getting done, you may need to help kids manage their time better by setting up specific times for these activities. If you can, schedule a set "homework time" for all of your kids. This is also a good time for you to work on quiet activities, such as reading, writing, or paying bills. Get kids in the habit of putting all permission slips, forms, and notices in your "in box" when they come home. If there's something that has to go back to school, put it in your child's "in box" or directly into his or her school bag.

- **Bedtime routine.** It's important for kids (and you) to get enough sleep. Lack of sleep is one of the chief causes of daytime fatigue and is linked to poor performance in school. Get your children in the habit of going to bed each night at the same time. Reserve after dinner as time for quiet activities, such as reading, writing, working on homework or projects, and

watching television. Help young children wind down for the night with a bedtime story, singing, or some snuggle time. Establish a time for "lights out" and stick to it.

More Organized Mornings

Are weekday mornings hectic in your home? Take the madness out of mornings by getting as much as possible prepared the night before and by implementing workable routines for your family.

- **Select outfits the night before.** Have your children decide what they want to wear to school the next day, or take it one step further and get them to pick out school outfits for the whole week on Sunday. Hang the complete outfit on a single hanger in the closet or behind their bedroom door, or lay it out on a chair. Now do the same for yourself. Lay out everything you need, from underwear to shoes to jewelry, so you won't have to search for things in the morning or be forced to wear a wrinkled shirt or pantyhose with runs. Selecting outfits the night before also helps keep your bedroom neater, since you'll have plenty of time to put away any clothing you decided not to wear.

- **Prepack book bags and briefcases.** In the evening, get your children in the habit of putting their books, papers, and anything else they will need at school the next day into their book bags. Do the same with your gym bag and briefcase. If you are active on various committees or boards, consider keeping separate briefcases for each to ensure that you always have what you need for meetings. Place bags, briefcases, and anything else that should leave with you, such as library books and videos to be returned or clothing that needs to go to the dry cleaner, near the front door. If you check the weather forecast the night before, you can also select and place outerwear near the door.

- **Make breakfast before going to bed.** Put water in the coffeemaker and coffee in the filter, so all you have to do is turn it on in the morning. Have your children set the table the night before with breakfast cereals, bowls, glasses, and silverware. For a special treat on the first day back to school or for a birthday, you could make waffles the night before and reheat them in the toaster oven.

- **Make lunches ahead of time.** Consider making a week's worth of sandwiches at once. Your kids might enjoy being part of the production line. Freeze sandwiches in separate plastic bags, then place them all in a large airtight zipper bag labeled with the type of sandwich inside. Remove sandwiches from the freezer each morning, and they will defrost by lunchtime. Fillings that freeze well include peanut butter, deli meats, and tuna salad made with sour cream or salad dressing. Mayonnaise and jelly do not freeze well. Prepare and refrigerate separate sandwich bags of lettuce, sprouts, onion, or tomato to add to the sandwich once it's defrosted.

- **Develop wake-up routines.** Stagger wake-up times for better traffic control (and less fighting) in the bathroom. If this is a big issue at your house, use a kitchen timer to set limits on bathroom time and move such

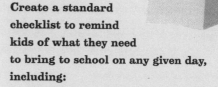

NO MORE HIDE-AND-SEEK

Create a standard checklist to remind kids of what they need to bring to school on any given day, including:

- Homework and project materials
- Permission slips or other school forms
- Band instrument
- Gym clothes
- Sports equipment
- After-school necessities
- Special items for events or activities
- Library books
- Lunch money

You can make a note of where the kids tend to leave things, if that helps: for example, "gym clothes — check the laundry basket." The goal is to make sure that everything they need for school is in one place when it comes time to leave. That way, your children can simply grab their bags on the way out the door instead of playing hide-and-seek with their school supplies. For kids who split their time between parents, you might want to create a standard list of things the child might need while at Mom or Dad's place, and use that list when packing for the visit. Consider keeping small, inexpensive items such as school supplies, toothbrush, socks, and underwear at both houses.

—Ramona Creel, OnlineOrganizing.com

activities as hair drying and getting dressed into the bedroom. It's also helpful if some family members shower or bathe the night before. Another way to stay on schedule in the morning is to set a kitchen timer or alarm to go off ten minutes before it's time to head out the door.

The Message Center

A message center is a must in a busy household. Designate one area for picking up messages and mail, preferably in a central location, such as the kitchen or wherever there is a telephone and some desk or counter space.

Hang an erasable board, bulletin board, or sticky board for posting messages, or keep a small notepad and pen near the telephone for writing down messages. Secure the writing implement to the phone with a string or cord so that it doesn't "walk" away with the last person who used it. Or keep a supply of pens and pencils within reach of the telephone.

For Simplicity's Sake

Use a message pad with carbonless duplicates for recording messages and conversations. You can tear off the note and feel comfortable that there is still a record somewhere. The message form also helps train children to take complete messages.

—*Debbie Gilster, Organize & Computerize*

If you use an answering machine to take messages, consider having family members use the "memo" feature to leave messages for each other when they go out. You can also use this feature to remind yourself to do something upon your return.

Make it clear to household members that the message taker must leave the message in the designated area. The message center is also the best place to store incoming mail. Use labeled stacking trays or a vertical file sorter to separate mail for each recipient. Be sure to have a large trash can or recycling bin nearby for collecting opened envelopes, junk mail, and other paper garbage.

Keep a list of emergency and frequently called phone numbers near the phone. If your message center is in your kitchen, you might tape the list to the back side of a cabinet door. The list should include telephone numbers for police, fire, and ambulance, and Poison Control Center (800-222-1222); it may also include numbers for family dentists and physicians, veterinarian, utility companies, plumber and electrician, day care and schools, and favorite restaurants and movie theaters.

Keep a current telephone book in your message center. It makes sense to store your own personal telephone directory here, too. When you receive cards and other personal correspondence, check the return address to see if you have the most current one in your directory. Consider using a revolving card file with individual A–Z tabs. If an address or phone number changes, fill out a new card and throw out the old one.

To ensure that you get all of your telephone messages, Stephanie Denton of Denton & Company recommends subscribing to a voice mail messaging service through your local telephone company. Set up separate mail boxes to route telephone messages directly to the appropriate party. This system also works well for keeping personal messages separate from work-related messages.

Household Chores

No one wants to do household chores, but they need to be done. The fastest way to get chores done is to divide the work between household members. This will probably require a family meeting to determine who will do what.

So how do you divide chores fairly? One way is to make a list of routine chores — those that need to be done on a daily or weekly basis. Once you've got your list, break it down into categories, such as preparing for meals; cleaning up after meals; doing laundry; vacuuming, dusting, and general cleaning; yard work, garbage and recycling; and pet feeding and dog walking. Then assign one or more categories of chores to

TIME-SAVER

In your revolving address directory, attach a tiny sticky tab to the cards you search for most frequently. These stickers are available wherever office supplies are sold.

each family member for one week. At the end of the week, rotate the schedule. A variation on this strategy is to ask family members to volunteer for the chores they don't mind doing on a regular basis and rotate the chores that no one likes to do. Obviously, there are some chores that only you or your partner can do, such as paying bills, grocery shopping, or cooking.

Create a "job jar" for jobs that fall outside the daily chores. Write jobs on slips of paper and assign a wage or points for each job. Put these slips of paper in a large jar or empty coffee can. One night a week, have each family member draw a chore from the job jar. Hang a write-on/wipe-off board on the refrigerator for kids to keep track of their weekly wages or points. If you like the idea of a point system, assign a reward for various point levels. For example, twenty-five points might earn the chance to stay up one half-hour later on a weekend night or to skip one weekly chore the following week. Let kids know that they may earn additional wages or points by doing additional chores.

Make an Agreement. Be sure to give a specific time frame for daily chores. For example, whoever has laundry duty needs to check the dryer

SLOW DOWN

- **Plan at least one day during the school week with no scheduled activities.**
- **Set a limit to the number of outside activities.**
- **Schedule weekly family meetings to review the coming week's events and commitments.**

—*Mitzi Weinman, TimeFinder*

each day after school and fold whatever clothes are in there. Make it clear that privileges depend on response to family requests. If assigned chores don't get done on time, no privileges are awarded. Privileges may include going to a friend's house after school or overnight, going to the movies or to the mall, or engaging in other extracurricular activities.

Offer children a per-job salary or weekly allowance as incentive. Inspect each chore as it's done and give praise to help reinforce good habits and build self-esteem. Even small children can help. While one family member is vacuuming, a younger one can follow along behind cleaning baseboards with socks on his hands. If you have two or more little ones, make it a contest to see whose sock puppet gets dirtiest.

Julie Signore of 1,2,3 SORT IT suggests creating a work agreement with your kids. Be very specific because kids will find any loopholes. Decide on the instances in which a concession may be made. Can chores be traded? Who is

responsible for seeing that they are completed? List the penalties of breaking the agreement. Whatever you do, create goals that are realistic. You are aiming to keep your home organized and enhance your kids' self-esteem, not set them up for failure. Create penalties that you will stick to. Do not create consequences that will be hard for you to follow through with. Kids test adults — it's the nature of being a child. Remember, the art of discipline is also an expression of love. You are not taking away from a child's childhood by teaching responsibility and self-discipline.

Organizing Togetherness

Togetherness is the key to building a strong family. Do you set aside time to be with your children, partner, sisters, brothers, parents, and extended family? In today's busy world, it's easy for families to drift apart. But you can cultivate togetherness by making an extra effort to "be there" for your children and for other family members — not just on birthdays and holidays, but every day. For many families, just sitting down to eat dinner or breakfast together would be a major step in the right direction.

One way to ensure that you get together on a regular basis is to hold regular family meetings. This is a time when you can share upcoming schedules and any past, present, or future concerns. Having an open forum helps kids to bring up subjects they might not otherwise have the courage to broach on their own. Call special family meetings as necessary to work on special projects, make an important announcement, or to discuss a controversial issue.

Carve out some "together time." Set aside one morning, afternoon, evening, or day every week to do something fun together. Take turns making suggestions about what to do next. You might go to a movie, sporting event, play, or concert. Visit one of the kids' aunts or uncles. Or stay home, make popcorn, play board games, and talk. Let the answering machine take messages or limit phone calls to a quick "I'll have to call you back" conversation.

Find ways in which you can get some exercise together, such as walking, hiking, cycling, or in-line skating. Recent studies show that nearly two-thirds of all school-age children can't measure up to the minimum standard of fitness. A recent Surgeon General's Report on Physical Activity and Health shows that about the same proportion of adults do not engage in the recommended amount of physical activity, and 25 percent are not active at all. Exercising together is a way to bring you closer as a family while helping to improve your health and fitness.

You can even make chore time into quality one-on-one time with your children. Try asking children to take turns helping you to prepare dinner. They might balk at first but will soon begin to look forward to their turn if, during your time together, you shower them with attention. Ask about school, extracurricular activities, friends, favorite subjects, and dreams.

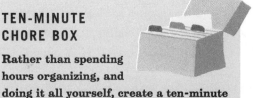

TEN-MINUTE CHORE BOX

Rather than spending hours organizing, and doing it all yourself, create a ten-minute chore box for yourself and one for each family member. Each person's box should contain chores or tasks that take a maximum of ten minutes to accomplish. Gear chores to abilities: For example, while older kids can help out with vacuuming, a three-year-old can pick up her toys. Write these chores or tasks on slips of paper. Each day, each person pulls one slip of paper from his or her box. When the chore is completed, that slip of paper is placed in a holding envelope until the chore box is empty. The boxes are then refilled, and the system starts over again.

This system also works well for getting tasks done at the office. Create a ten-minute chore box with individual slips of paper on which you write tasks that take ten minutes or less to do, including filing, purging files, reading articles or e-mails, doing on-line or telephone research, straightening up your desk, and dusting and watering plants.

—*Maria Gracia, Get Organized Now!*

Projects are another way to build unity within families. Work together to rake fall leaves, decorate the house for the holidays, or unclutter the basement to make room for a game room. Try setting some goals together as a family. You might work together to raise money for a charitable organization, volunteer your services in the community, train for and participate in a local race, or set up a family savings plan for a vacation.

One Challenge . . .

I am always having to rearrange my schedule to accommodate my family's schedule. Usually, it's because my kids leave it until the last minute to tell me that they have to be somewhere. How can we plan better together as a family?

Three Solutions

1 FROM RAMONA CREEL, ONLINEORGANIZING.COM: I suggest setting aside time once a week for a family planning session at which everyone can discuss their upcoming activities, appointments, events, and things to do. Record everything on your family calendar. Just taking time to discuss plans and making sure they gel with everyone else's plans is a huge step toward getting better organized.

2 FROM STEPHANIE DENTON, DENTON & COMPANY: Consider putting technology to work. Many families use handheld electronic organizers for keeping track of their schedules. Look for models with infrared ports that allow you to "beam" calendar entries to other family members. Being able to see everyone else's schedule at a glance helps to avoid scheduling conflicts and allows you do things like make your next doctor's appointment while at the doctor's office.

3 FROM GLORIA RITTER, PAPER MATTERS AND MORE, INC.: Keep your family calendar on the Internet so that everyone has access to it wherever they are. Yahoo! (see Resources, page 322) offers a free calendar tool that lets you share your schedules, find free times, and send appointment reminders. You can also use this tool for entering things to do along with deadlines.

CHAPTER 21

ORGANIZING TO GO

Planning a family vacation or a weekend getaway? Going abroad or out of town on business? You don't have to be a veteran traveler to organize a safe and memorable trip. But there *are* simple things everyone (even veteran travelers) can do to avoid unnecessary fuss, hassles, and expense. And, with a little know-how, anyone can learn how to pack like a professional and stay organized wherever you go.

Smart Vacation Planning

Rule number one: Plan ahead. If you're traveling for leisure, plan your trip at least one month in advance. For travel during peak periods (namely, winter holidays, spring break, and summer), you may need to book months in advance to ensure availability.

• **Be flexible.** The more flexible you can be in making your travel plans, the better deal you'll get. Virtually every vacation destination has its "off-peak" seasons when airfare, hotel rooms, and car rentals are offered at reduced rates. Consider planning your vacation around special offers from airlines that are trying to fill flights to various destinations. Go to the Web sites of the major airlines and sign up for e-mail

announcements of these reduced fares, including last-minute fares at a fraction of their regular price.

But what if the only time you can travel is when vacation demand and prices are at their peak? You may still be able to enjoy significant savings on airfare by being flexible about what days you can travel. Generally, lower airfares are offered midweek. Traveling midweek is also good because traffic is lighter. So even if your flight is delayed due to weather, you are more likely to experience only a short delay.

Adding a Saturday night stay almost always brings the cost of air travel down. Being flexible about the time of day you travel can also make a huge difference. For example, you may be able to get a cheaper flight by leaving your destination after noon on Monday or before 8 A.M. on Friday. Also, investigate the possibility of flying into and out of nearby airports that may offer lower fares. The savings can be well worth the extra drive at either end.

- **Consider electronic tickets.** Many leisure travelers prefer to have paper tickets, but electronic tickets actually provide more security and peace of mind. If you lose your paper ticket or it is stolen, you have to fill out a lost ticket claim with the airline and then purchase a new ticket. If the old ticket is not found within a certain time period, you will be reimbursed for one of the tickets. Though you will be able to get the new ticket at the original price you paid, you will need to pay a lost ticket fee, which can be quite steep. With an electronic ticket, there's nothing to lose. You simply present your photo identification (which you need anyway) to get your boarding pass.

- **Join a frequent-flyer program.** Frequent air travelers can earn free tickets and upgrades by becoming a member of one or more airline frequent flyer programs. Even if you are not a frequent air traveler on a particular airline, it doesn't hurt to "join the club" and collect frequent flyer miles. After all, there's no cost to join. With some frequent flyer programs, miles earned are valid indefinitely, so sooner or later, you might well have the requisite number of points for a free roundtrip ticket or upgrade. Overnights at selected hotels and car rentals also earn frequent flyer miles with most programs. Some programs even offer awards on qualifying foreign exchange transactions and on long-distance use with selected carriers.

- **Book to your advantage.** If you are traveling by air, book your flight first and then your hotel. You can often get a better rate on your hotel when you book it as a package with your flight. This is not true of car rentals. You can usually get a much better deal if you book your car rental separately. In both cases, don't assume that a 50 percent–off coupon you might have is always the best deal. Generally, the discount is off the regular rate, and you can get a better rate without it. If you are booking your hotel separately, be sure to compare apples to apples. For instance, one hotel might appear to be cheaper, but daily-parking costs may offset the savings. Conversely, a higher rate per night that includes breakfast might work out cheaper than staying in a hotel with a lower rate.

When booking your hotel, always ask if the rate quoted is the best rate available. Ask if any of your association memberships or credit cards entitle you to a discount; you can often save 5 to 10 percent off the best rate this way. You may be able to get a better rate on your hotel room by purchasing in advance and paying a deposit on all or part of your stay.

Also ask if the hotel has any special packages available, which may include breakfast, discount coupons to restaurants, room upgrades, or special amenities. Ask again when you arrive at the hotel if your rate is the best available, as rates do change.

• **Shop around for savings on land travel.** There are ways to save on land transportation costs as well. If you are traveling by train, Amtrak offers a discount to members of the Automobile Association of America (AAA). Riding the rails during off-peak hours — that is, before or after busy commuter hours — generally results in additional savings. Daily rates on car rentals can be pricey, but if you rent for five to seven days, you will get the weekly rate.

• **Be a savvy car renter.** Be aware that car rental companies usually quote a rate for a midsize car. If you don't need the extra room, ask for the rate on a compact-size car. A smaller car generally gets more miles to the gallon, which can add up to savings on gasoline as well, especially if you plan to do a lot of driving. Unless you expect to do very limited driving, look for a car rental that offers unlimited miles. Otherwise, the cost per mile above and beyond the free miles offered can add up quickly.

The car rental company agent will encourage you to sign up for optional insurance on the rental vehicle. Check with your automobile insurance agent beforehand to see if your policy covers a rental car; it usually does. Also, most credit card companies provide insurance coverage automatically when you use their card to charge the rental. To avoid unnecessary

hassles at the car rental company, make and bring with you a photocopy of your insurance policy or your credit card agreement. Most automobile insurance policies do not cover car rentals outside the United States. In that case, you would be wise to purchase automobile insurance in that country with coverage amounts similar to your policy at home.

Before driving away in your rental car, inspect it inside and out. If you notice any dents or scratches or damage to the interior that are not noted on the rental agreement, point them out to a company representative, who should then make those notations on the agreement.

For several years now, car rental agencies have offered a "prepay" option for gas, and many travelers find this convenient, especially when they're unfamiliar with the locations of area gas stations or will be racing to catch a flight for a plane when they return the car. The prepay option is more expensive, and if you prefer to fill the tank yourself, always remember to return the car with a full tank of gas. As you leave the car rental place, look for the nearest gas station and make a note of it on your map. You do have a map of the local area, right? If not, get one from your car rental agent.

too good to be true?

If a travel offer sounds too good to be true, it probably is, especially if the mail solicitation requires you to call a 900 number or the caller wants you to make an immediate decision without anything in writing. Those travel "awards" that require you to make a payment to collect your "prize" or to disclose confidential information such as your checking account or social security number are travel scams.

- **Organize your road trip.** If you will be traveling by car, plan your route in advance to minimize the possibility of getting lost. Free mapping services are available to AAA and other automobile club members. You can also get maps and written driving directions from several mapping services on the Internet. (See page 328 for several such services.) The other option is to buy a good road map and use a highlighting pen to mark your intended route. Separate and store change for toll roads in empty film canisters with a sample coin taped to the top of each lid for easy identification. If you have some spare room in your trunk, pack food and beverages from home in a cooler and plan to have picnics along the way. Look for good picnic spots on the map.
- **Put your affairs in order.** One last word about smart vacation planning: It's a good idea to have your affairs at home in order. Leave a copy of your current will, insurance documents,

and power of attorney with your family or a friend or let them know where they can find these documents. For more information about organizing your estate, refer to chapter 27.

Smart Money Moves

There are some smart things you can do to protect yourself financially from the time you make your travel arrangements until the time you return home. You may have heard of trip insurance. That's the first thing to consider. There are also simple things you can do to keep yourself from getting ripped off while away from home.

Trip and Travel Insurance. If you have to postpone or cancel a flight due to an illness or death in your family, regularly scheduled airlines will usually give a refund with a note from a doctor or a death certificate. But you may get no refund at all on a travel package unless you have trip insurance. Take the quiz on the next page to help you decide if you should get trip insurance.

Trip cancellation and trip interruption insurances provide financial protection for nonrefundable travel expenses. Cancellation insurance reimburses you if you are unable to depart for your trip due to an unforeseen accident or illness that affects you, a close family member, or a traveling companion. Trip interruption insurance reimburses you if an injury, illness, or other event prevents you from continuing your trip.

Trip cancellation and interruption insurances are usually bundled together at a cost of pennies on the dollar. If you are booking a travel package, your travel agent will almost always ask if you want to buy this insurance. Before signing, read the insurance policies carefully to find out if there are any exclusions such as preexisting medical conditions, mountain climbing, or terrorism in the country where you are headed. Look for a policy that will waive any of the exclusions you want to have covered. Also, make sure that trip cancellation insurance covers you while you are on the way from home to your departure point, as many policies do not.

Most other types of travel insurance are usually unnecessary because they duplicate coverage you already have. Unless you are traveling to a foreign country where your medical insurance is not valid, you probably don't need to buy a separate insurance policy that reimburses you for medical or hospitalization expenses incurred while traveling. If you have accidental and death and dismemberment insurance or life insurance, you're already covered for that wherever you go. Lost baggage is usually covered under your standard renter's or homeowner's insurance. Checked and carry-on luggage may also be covered by your credit card company policy if you used that card to make your travel purchase.

Credit Cards. Using a credit card to pay for your hotel or rental car, meals, and other incidentals is a good idea because you won't need to carry as much cash. Just be sure to check your available credit before you go. Bring an envelope to keep all credit card receipts together. When you return home, check the purchase amounts on your billing statement against your sales receipts to make sure they match. This is especially important if the charges are in a foreign currency. Without the receipts, it would be difficult to verify the correct amounts. If you find any discrepancies or transactions that are not yours, contact your credit card company immediately.

While you're out and about, protect your credit cards as if they were cash. Do not leave them unattended in your hotel room or car, on the beach, in a nightclub, or anywhere else.

should you buy trip insurance?

If you answer "Yes" to any of the questions below, it may be wise to purchase trip insurance.

- Are you buying a travel package, charter flight, tour, or cruise? **Yes / No**
- Are you booking a bargain vacation with a tour operator you've never used before? **Yes / No**
- Will you be traveling with a baby or young child? **Yes / No**
- Are you or any of your traveling companions in frail health? **Yes / No**
- Do you or any of your traveling companions have a chronic medical condition that could flare up before or during the trip? **Yes / No**
- Do you plan to participate in a risky sport or activity while on vacation? **Yes / No**
- Are you traveling to a country where you might need to evacuate due to political unrest or terrorism? **Yes / No**

Report a lost or stolen card immediately. Before leaving home, make a list of the credit cards you are taking on your trip, including the account number and expiration dates. Also include the phone number to call if your credit cards are stolen. If you are traveling abroad, you won't be able to call an 800 number so be sure to get another you can call. Keep one copy of your list in your checked luggage and one copy with you. Not all credit cards are accepted everywhere, so consider bringing a different brand of card with you as a backup. Leave unneeded credit cards at home.

"Safe" Money. Traveler's checks provide a safe, secure way to carry money, especially when traveling  abroad or when you prefer to spend cash instead of using credit cards. If you bring traveler's checks, make a list of your check numbers and make two copies. Keep one copy with your checked luggage, and leave one copy with someone at home. Also, in case of loss or theft keep your receipt for your traveler's checks separate from the checks. Cash checks as you need them, not all at once, and cross used check numbers off your list.

An even safer, more convenient alternative to traveler's checks is Visa TravelMoney. This is a prepaid travel card that gives you 24-hour access to your travel funds in the local currency at favorable exchange rates. You can access your Visa TravelMoney funds with a Personal Identification Number (PIN) at any Automatic Teller Machine (ATM) where Visa is honored. The value of prepaid funds with Visa TravelMoney is that the funds are stored on the Visa TravelMoney system, not on the card. So if you lose your card, you don't lose your money. Just be sure to memorize your PIN, or, if you do write it down, keep it separate from your Visa TravelMoney card. Another plus is that you can purchase additional cards for traveling companions or to keep in case your primary card is lost or stolen. Visa TravelMoney is available around the world through Travelex. See page 329 for contact information.

Of course, using your own bank ATM card is also an option as long as the ATM service you require is available where you are going. Most modern countries have ATMs that can be accessed by your local bankcard, and the exchange rates are comparable to the going rate of exchange. If you don't know for sure that ATMs are available where you are going, plan to use your ATM card as a backup rather than a primary source of funds. Again, memorize your PIN, or, if you write it down, keep it separate from your card. Using an ATM card allows you to withdraw cash as you need it rather than carrying around large amounts of cash. If you do have a sizeable sum of money with you, don't keep it all in one place.

Safeguarding Valuables. Keep in mind that in many vacation destinations would-be thieves are on the lookout for unsuspecting tourists. Leave expensive jewelry at home. If you carry a pocketbook, sling it over your head and across your body. Men should carry their wallets in a front pants pocket to deter pickpockets. If you do keep a wallet in a back pocket, wrapping rubber bands around it will make it more difficult for someone to slip it out unnoticed. In your wallet, fold larger bills inside smaller bills so as not to "flash" the larger bills when removing cash to make purchases. The safest ways to carry cash include money belts or pouches that are worn underneath clothing or hidden pockets sewn into clothing. It's also a good idea not to carry all cash and credit cards in the same place. If your hotel room has a safe, use it to store your passport, cash, credit cards, and other valuables when you go out. Never leave cash or valuables in your hotel room.

Phoning for Less. One final word about smart money moves: Be aware that making telephone calls from your hotel room can cost a small fortune, especially in countries outside the U.S. Using the card provided by your long-distance carrier can also be quite expensive with a cost per minute that may be up to five times more than you pay for calls dialed direct from your home. Plus, the company often tacks on a surcharge for calls made from a pay phone. Using your cellular telephone could also get expensive depending on where you are going and what type of plan you have. The least expensive way to make calls when you are away from home is to buy a prepaid phone card. If your hotel charges a connection fee to call 800 numbers, use the prepaid card at a pay phone. If you plan to use the card overseas, make sure before you buy that you can use it where you are going and get the access number.

Before You Go

When you're about to head off on vacation or a business trip, there always seems to be so little time, so much to do. Following is a checklist and timeline designed to speed you on your way by helping you organize things to do before you go. Jot down any other things you need to complete before going.

One week or more prior to departure:

- Start a "Don't Forget to Pack" list.
- Decide how you will get to the airport or train station; make any necessary arrangements.
- Arrange for a house sitter/pet sitter or make kennel reservations.
- Arrange to stop newspaper and mail delivery temporarily (unless you have arranged for a house sitter).
- Get traveler's checks if you plan to bring them.
- Make copies of your passport and visa(s), driver's license, credit cards, traveler's check receipt(s), and airline tickets; pack one copy with checked luggage and leave one copy with someone at home.

Up to one week prior to departure:

- Wash clothes.
- Make a list of clothes and accessories to bring.
- Gather books, magazines, and maps you plan to bring with you.
- Give a copy of your itinerary to someone at home; include names, addresses, and telephone numbers of hotels and persons you intend to visit.

24 to 48 hours prior to departure:

- Call the airline to reconfirm your flight and inquire about better seats (keep the phone number with your tickets).
- Pay all bills that will come due while away or make arrangements to have someone else pay them; leave a bank deposit slip if you are expecting a check that needs to be deposited in your absence.
- Recharge cell phone, cordless shaver, and other rechargeable items.
- Pack your suitcases; make a note of any last-minute items you still need to pack in each bag.

Day of (or night before) departure:

- Pack last-minute items.
- Turn off your pager.
- Back up your computer and shut it off.
- Synchronize your personal digital assistant (PDA) or pack your telephone and address book.
- Forward e-mail or put auto-response message on e-mail.
- Change voicemail or answering machine message (unless you will be checking in for messages frequently).
- Wash dishes.
- Water plants.
- Unplug television and other electrical appliances that consume electricity even when off and to safeguard them in the event of severe weather, power surges, or lightning strikes.
- Call the airline or go on-line to confirm flight status just before leaving home.

For Safety's Sake

Take a few moments to write down important medical information that could be used in the event that you require emergency care. Include blood type, drug allergies, heart problems, and other medical problems such as diabetes, and any prescriptions you are taking. Also list your physician's name and telephone number and your pharmacist's number. Write this information on the back of your business card or on a small piece of paper tucked into your wallet with your driver's license or into your passport.

If you are traveling with children, do the same for each one of them; also include their age and weight. Record information for each child on the back of a wallet-size school photograph and keep it with your emergency information. The photograph could also come in handy if your child gets lost.

The more you can simplify your travel preparations, the easier it will be to pack up and go anywhere at any time. If you usually hire a house sitter, pet sitter, or baby-sitter, create a form letter that includes detailed instructions as well as emergency contact numbers. Type the letter on your computer so you can update it when you need it again. Make a note to yourself on the form to attach your itinerary.

Organized Packing

The biggest mistake travelers make is packing too much. More stuff means heavier luggage, and that can be a real problem when you have to lug it on and off shuttles, through crowded terminals, and sometimes even up and down stairs. And if you can't handle it all yourself, you end up spending more for porters or for taxis at your destination rather than public transportation. Another advantage to packing light is that you have more room for whatever you might want to bring home from your travels.

The trick to packing light is to take half as much stuff and twice as much money. You might never need the extra cash, but you'll have it if you do discover that you need something you left at home. Another way to pare down what you bring is *not* to bring anything you think you *might* be able to use; you probably won't. Following are more ideas for helping you maximize suitcase space while lightening your load:

- **Shoes and socks.** Limit the number of shoes you bring to one pair for dress, one comfortable pair for walking, and one pair of sandals if appropriate. On travel days, wear the shoes that would otherwise take up the most room in your suitcase. Use the space inside shoes to stuff socks, underwear, and other small items.
- **Outerwear.** Instead of bringing one bulky coat, bring a cardigan-style sweater and light rain or wind jacket that you can wear together. Tie both around your waist rather than packing them. The sweater will come in handy if the temperature on the plane is cool. Even if you are going somewhere warm, you might need a

CREATE A PACKING LIST

Create and save standard packing lists for your carry-on bag and checked luggage. Sometimes the most obvious things are the ones you forget! A packing list also serves as a reminder for any items you need to obtain prior to your trip. Your packing list for your carry-on might include:

- Reservation confirmations, tickets, itineraries
- Passport or driver's license
- Wallet and purse
- Medical insurance cards
- Cash, credit cards, traveler's checks
- Prepaid phone card or calling card
- Keys (house and car)
- Eyeglasses and contacts plus lens cleaners
- Prescriptions and medications
- Camera and film
- Video camera and tapes
- Magazines and books
- Snacks and drinks
- Maps and directions
- Makeup and toiletries
- Jewelry
- Personal address book
- Change of clothes

Use your packing list as a checklist for your return trip so you don't accidentally leave something important behind. While away, if you think of something you wish you had brought, add it to your packing list for next time and keep the list in your suitcase. Once you get home, make a list of "things I didn't need" so that you won't take them next time.

sweater or jacket for cooler evenings or unseasonably cold days.

- **Clothing.** Bring clothes that are versatile, such as a T-shirt that can double as a nightshirt or beach cover-up, outfits that can be dressed up or down or layered, and separates that can be worn as part of more than one outfit. Weed out everything else. Avoid bringing any clothes you never wear at home; you probably won't wear them on vacation either, unless where you are going is the only place you would wear them. Keep in mind that while natural fabrics are cooler, synthetic fabrics tend to wrinkle less and often travel better.

- **Underwear.** Plan to wash lingerie and small articles of clothing in your hotel sink, especially if you will be away for more than a week. Bring a small amount of fine-fabric detergent with you in a small plastic container.

For Simplicity's Sake

Store all travel items such as a neck pillow, alarm clock, travel-size blow dryer, and jewelry pouch in your favorite overnight bag or suitcase. That way, you have everything you need right where you need it. If you travel often, prepack a toiletries bag with travel-size containers of the things you use every day including toothpaste, shampoo and conditioner, shaving cream, razor, skin care products, and cosmetics. Don't forget to include a toothbrush! Restock used-up items at the end of each trip.

- **Jewelry and accessories.** Leave all valuable jewelry at home, along with anything else you wouldn't want to lose. Limit accessories to one belt, one hat, and maybe two scarves or ties. If a scarf can double as a sash or shawl, that's even better.

- **Makeup and toiletries.** Do bring just the basics. Don't bring full-size bottles of anything (except maybe sunscreen lotion if you are going somewhere sunny). Look for sample-size toiletries at the drug store. Or transfer shampoo, conditioner, or shower gel into small, travel-size containers or even empty film canisters. Label everything. Instead of bringing perfume bottles, moisten cotton balls with perfume and store in a film canister. (Empty film canisters are also handy for carrying earrings and rings and for keeping foreign coins separated by country.)

- **Other.** If you are traveling with someone else, check with each other so that you don't bring duplicate items of things like travel alarm clocks and guidebooks. Instead of bringing an entire guidebook, use a razor blade to remove just the section you need. Find out if your hotel offers amenities such as a hair dryer and iron. If not, ask yourself if you really need them or if you can survive without them. Instead of bringing home souvenirs, bring a journal to keep a record of what you did each day, where you went, who you met, how much you spent, what the weather was like. Take photographs or buy postcards.

A Federal Aviation Administration (FAA) rule implemented in 2001 limits passengers to one piece of carry-on baggage per person plus one additional personal item such as a purse, briefcase, or diaper bag. All other luggage must be checked. The size of the carry-on allowed varies by airline, but most allow a piece with dimensions adding up to no more than 45 inches (length plus width plus height). Check with your air carrier to confirm carry-on size restrictions.

Be prepared to open all carry-on bags for airport security inspection. Avoid overpacking so that they can be opened and closed easily. Pack small items together in a clear pouch or resealable plastic bag. Do not pack wrapped gifts in your carry-on bag as you may have to unwrap them. Pack any objects that might be perceived as weapons, such as knives, cutting instruments of any kind, manicure scissors, knitting needles, ice picks, or straight razors in your checked luggage, not your carry-on bag. Make sure that each piece of checked luggage has a name tag on the outside and your name, address, and telephone number inside. It's also a good idea to add your dates of travel and contact information at your destination.

Do not pack cameras and electronic equipment such as portable CD players and laptop computers in your checked luggage, which could get lost or stolen. In your carry-on, pack a complete change of clothes in case your checked luggage gets lost or arrives later than you do. Also keep with you any other items you will need in the next twenty-four hours, including vitamins and prescriptions, eyeglasses, contact lens supplies, makeup and toiletries. Important papers are also best packed

PLAY FIVE QUESTIONS

If you tend to pack too much when you go away, ask yourself these questions:

1. **Where** are you going? If you're traveling for business, find out what type of attire will be required. Some destinations such as Europe require dressier clothing even during the day. But if you're going to a low-key resort area, casual clothes may be all you need to bring.

2. **When** (in what season) will you be there? Research weather conditions at your destination using a weather forecasting service on the Internet or on television. Then choose attire accordingly.

3. **What** will you do while there? Review travel brochures and have a plan for places to go and things to do before your trip so you know what you will need to bring; for example, hiking boots, sun hat, or snorkeling equipment.

4. **Why** suffer with excess luggage? Pack what you want to bring, and then pare it down to what you really need. KISS — Keep It Simple, Sweetheart — by making a packing list.

5. **How** can I avoid packing too much? Color coordinate your attire with "mix and match" clothing. Plan to hand wash some items, use hotel laundry services, or go to a local laundry center.

—*Donna D. McMillan, McMillan & Company Professional Organizing*

in your carry-on bag. Everything else you pack in your carry-on is pretty much a matter of personal preference.

Consider organizing the contents of your suitcase with packing cubes — soft fabric and mesh squares — that let you keep like items such as socks and underwear together in your suitcase. Just put clothing into various-size cubes and put the cubes into your suitcase. You might also be able to keep smaller items together by placing them in large plastic zippered bags. Keeping categories of clothing separate helps keep you organized while you are away, especially if you will be moving around.

Many seasoned travelers swear by the *rolling method* for saving space and reducing wrinkles. If you roll two or three of the same item, such as pants, you may be able to save quite a bit of space. And rolling several items together around a soft core item such as a travel pouch or zippered bag filled with socks may help to minimize wrinkles even better.

Store anything that might leak in a resealable plastic bag. Pack a tote bag or small backpack that you can use for shopping excursions or on day trips. When packing to come home, pack dirty clothes separately. Put all dirty laundry in one suitcase or use plastic bags to keep dirty clothes separate from clean clothes (if you have any clean clothes left!).

Traveling Abroad

Traveling to another country requires a little more planning and preparation than traveling within your country of residence. And there are some practical health and safety precautions that you should take as well.

- **Passports and visas.** The first thing you need to do is check your passport to make sure that it is valid. Some countries require that your passport be valid at least six months or longer beyond the dates of your trip. If your passport expires before the required validity, or you don't have a passport, you will have to apply for a new one. Allow two to three months before your departure to avoid having to pay expediting fees. Depending on where you are going and how long you are staying, you may also need to apply for a visa from the country you are going to and provide proof of required immunizations. (On page 328, you'll find contact information for visa services.)

When traveling abroad, do not carry your passport with your money or pack it in your checked luggage. Do fill in the emergency

LOOK MA, NO WRINKLES!

Wrinkles can't be avoided completely, but they can be minimized. Pack things tightly so they don't move around. Packing suits, dresses, shirts, and blouses individually in dry-cleaning bags helps. Placing a sheet of tissue paper between each layer of folded clothing is another way to minimize wrinkles. Consider packing a wrinkle-releasing spray product instead of a travel iron. Roll wrinkle-resistant clothes such as pajamas, T-shirts, and sweaters, and stuff them into small spaces, wherever they fit.

— Diane Hatcher, Timesavers Services Professional Organizing

contact information page in your passport using pencil (so that it can be updated for your next trip). Leave copies of your itinerary, passport data page, and visas with family or friends at home, so that they can contact you in the event of an emergency.

- **Required reading.** Before you go, it's always a good idea to familiarize yourself with the culture, people, history, and geography of your destination. Guidebooks are great, but you can also get lots of free information from the local library, your travel agent or from the Internet. Be sure to pack a foreign language phrase book or dictionary — and use it whenever attempting to converse with someone in a foreign country. If you make the effort, you are more likely to get whatever assistance you need.

- **Laws and customs.** Be sure to obey and respect local laws and customs. Remember that when you are in another country, you are subject to its laws. Be aware that in some countries, it is unlawful to enter or exit with that country's currency. Ask your travel agent about currency restrictions at your destination. It is also illegal in some countries to exceed your credit card limit. On a more pleasant note, in many countries, it is customary to present small gifts in return for a home-cooked meal or other hospitality. These gifts might include a handmade item, postcards from your hometown, souvenir pins, or chocolate.

- **Money and purchases.** You can usually exchange money at the airport or at your hotel, but local banks generally give the most favorable rate. Deal only with authorized agents when you exchange money or you may end up

REPLACING A LOST PASSPORT

If your passport is lost or stolen while you are traveling, it will be much easier to get a replacement if you plan ahead for this possibility. Photocopy the data page at the front of your passport and write down the addresses and telephone numbers of the U.S. embassies and consulates in the countries you plan to visit. (See page 327 for contact information.) Pack this information along with two recent passport-size photographs in a place separate from your passport. Write down your passport number and the date and place it was issued, and give this information to a friend or relative at home as backup.

in jail. Using your credit card or ATM card will also give you the current rate of exchange with no markup or fee. Keep receipts for any items you purchase abroad, as you will need to declare them upon your return to the United States. Be aware that you are not allowed to bring some items back into the United States and that the number of allowable duty-free items is limited.

- **Safety and security.** For up-to-date travel information, obtain the U.S. Department of State's Consular Information Sheet on the country or countries you plan to visit. In addition to other valuable information, these sheets include the location of the U.S. embassy or consulate, unusual immigration practices, health conditions, and general crime and safety or security information. Information about travel warnings in effect, terrorist threats, and other conditions that might pose a risk to American travelers is also available. (Contact information for the U.S. Department of State is listed on page 327.) Schedule direct flights wherever possible, and avoid stops in high-risk areas.

- **Health precautions.** Ask your doctor about any health precautions you should take prior to leaving the United States. Some countries may require proof of immunization against such illnesses as typhoid, polio, and hepatitis. Contaminated food and drink are the major sources of intestinal illness while

medical insurance

Should you buy it? If you answer "Yes" to any of the questions below, it may be wise to purchase extended medical and/or evacuation insurance.

- Are you traveling to a country with questionable medical facilities? **Yes / No**
- Are you in frail health or taking numerous required medications? **Yes / No**
- Do you have a chronic medical condition that could flare up during your trip? **Yes / No**
- Do you plan to participate in a risky sport or activity while abroad? **Yes / No**
- Are you traveling to a country where you may encounter a hazard to your health due to political unrest or terrorism? **Yes / No**
- Are you currently covered by the Social Security Medicare Program? **Yes / No**

traveling, especially when traveling to developing countries, where sanitation practices leave much to be desired. Drink only bottled, canned, or boiled beverages. Do not even use the tap water to brush your teeth. Avoid raw vegetables and fruit (unless you peel them yourself), unpasteurized milk and milk products, raw meat, and shellfish. Remember this rule of thumb: If you can't peel it or cook it, don't eat it. This includes ice cubes.

- **Medical insurance.** It's very important to review your health insurance policy to make sure that it will cover medical and hospital expenses while you are abroad. If it does, be sure to bring your insurance card with you and a claim form. If not, buy a short-term health insurance policy. You can and should also buy an insurance policy that will cover the cost of medical evacuation in the event of an accident, serious illness, or death, as this could cost thousands of dollars. Health and emergency medical assistance insurance usually includes other valuable benefits such as emergency consultation by telephone and interpretation services. Ask your travel agent where you can buy this type of insurance. If you have a preexisting medical condition or are over age sixty-two, read the policy carefully and make amendments as necessary to make sure that you are covered.

- **Other medical precautions.** Pack an extra pair of eyeglasses and prescriptions in your carry-on luggage. If you are traveling abroad with a preexisting medical condition, bring a letter from your physician describing your condition and any prescription medications, including the generic name of prescribed drugs. To avoid problems when passing through customs, keep prescription drugs and vitamins in their original, labeled containers. Pills in any other containers may be seized.

- **Emergencies.** If you encounter serious legal, medical, or financial difficulties or other problems abroad, contact the nearest U.S. embassy or consulate for assistance.

- **Reconfirming flights.** Don't forget to call the airline seventy-two hours prior to traveling to reconfirm your flight. Without this "reservation" call, you could find yourself stranded. When you call, provide the following information: your passport number, your date of birth, and your citizenship. This will speed the process of going through customs, as they will simply need to verify the information in the computer and not actually enter it.

Traveling with Kids

Planning ahead can make the difference between a fun family trip and a family disaster, especially if you're traveling by air. Prepare kids for the trip by showing them on a map where you are and where you are going. When possible, book nonstop flights so that you won't have the added hassle of changing planes. For long trips, consider booking a late evening flight; the kids might just sleep through it. Don't forget to bring your children's birth certificates; you may be asked for them by the airline, especially if you are traveling out of the country without the other parent.

If you're traveling with a child under two, a front pack or sling will make it easier to keep your baby on your lap. Consider buying a seat

for your infant on a long flight (usually available for half price). If you do this, you will need to bring a car seat. You'll probably need one anyway at your destination unless your car rental company has guaranteed to have one available for you. Even then, you may prefer the safety features of your own car seat.

Utilize gate-check service for your stroller so that you'll have it right away when you deplane. This is especially helpful if you have to make your way from one end of a terminal to the other to change planes. If you're planning to rent a stroller at your destination, a backpack carrier may be an option. You can check that at the gate as well.

Packing Tips. When packing for your children, plan on needing two outfits per child per day. You may be able to double up on some items such as sweatshirts or cardigans or dress clothes that may be worn for only short periods of time. All of this can go in checked luggage along with the bulk of the diapers, favorite videos, and whatever else you might want at your destination. Consider packing children's clothing in bundles that make up a complete outfit so you can just hand it to them when needed. Or pack outfits in individual resealable plastic bags labeled with each child's name.

Pack what you will need before, during, and immediately after the flight in carry-on bags. Every air traveler is allowed one piece of carry-on luggage plus a personal item such as a diaper bag or backpack — that goes for kids, too. Preschoolers and older children may enjoy having their own rolling carry-on bags to carry a sweatshirt, two extra changes of clothes, snacks, small games and books, a stuffed animal or two, or a favorite blanket. Just make sure it isn't too heavy for them to manage, or you'll end up carrying it.

Traveling can be especially hard on children. Pack some surprises to prevent them from getting bored or cranky. An inflatable beach ball or a game of cards might help time pass more quickly when waiting at the gate. To help prevent in-flight boredom, bring several small gifts for each kid that you can present at regular intervals or as needed. Older children will appreciate having a portable device for listening to music or books on tape. You can also show them how to plug into the onboard radio. Also, be sure to bring plenty of snacks (purchase individually wrapped packages or wrap them yourself) and beverages, preferably in resealable containers.

Other in-flight essentials include enough diapers for the flight plus two more just in case. You won't have a changing table on the airplane so consider using pull-up-type diapers if you can. Pack a quantity of diaper wipes in a large resealable plastic bag. Use a smaller bag to carry wipes for cleaning faces and hands. Bring plenty of baby food and formula if needed, as these items are hard to find at the airport. A pacifier, chewy fruit snack, or chewing gum may help keep your kid's ears comfortable during takeoff and landing.

Vacation. While on vacation, help children create their own special memories of the trip. One way to do this is to buy postcards of the places you visit. Have children write on the postcard what they want to remember about that place. When you return home, punch a hole in the corner of the cards and put them on a key ring. Or give each child a journal. Each day, write the date at the top of a new page and encourage children to draw or write about what they did that day. They can also paste postcards or brochures into their journals or ask people they meet for their autograph. Don't forget to bring along craft supplies, including scissors, tape, glue, markers, and crayons, for this project. Another great idea is to give kids disposable cameras of their own so they can take photographs from their own unique perspectives and create a special photo album when they get home.

Try not to overschedule your family. Resist the urge to see and do everything. Ask each family member what he or she most wants to do while on vacation. (You may need to give younger children some choices.) Make a list of these "must-see/must-do" activities and schedule them into your itinerary. Leave the rest of your vacation schedule free for making spontaneous plans or pursuing simple pleasures such as looking for seashells on the beach or bike riding.

Plan a vacation that offers something for everyone. If you're traveling with young children or teenagers, or as a single parent, consider travel destinations that cater to all ages and interests such as cruises, Club Med, and family resorts. Do you want an adventure? Consider going on a hiking or biking tour or exploring a foreign city. Wherever you go, find out what amenities are included, so there are no surprises when you get there.

For Safety's Sake

Check with your hotel to see if your room is or can be childproofed. If not, bring along a package of outlet covers. You might want doorknob covers, too. If you are traveling with young children, request a first-floor room rather than one with a balcony. Once you get there, take a good look around for possible hazards. Get down on the floor and look for any small items such as buttons, paper clips, coins, or pills that could end up in your crawling baby's mouth. Remove matches. Also remove plastic bags from trash cans. Bring a roll of masking tape to secure washcloths over sharp table corners and to tape down exposed electrical cords. Move hotel samples of soap, shampoo, and other toiletries out of reach of young children.

Packing a Diaper Bag

Keep the diaper bag packed and ready to go by creating a packing checklist. Creating a checklist makes it easy to delegate this project to a spouse or child.

Changing Needs
❑ Changing pad
❑ Disposable diapers (or cloth diapers, plastic pants, and extra diaper pins)
❑ Baby wipes or damp washcloth with a squirt of soap stored in a resealable plastic bag
❑ Diaper ointment
❑ Baby powder
❑ Waterless antibacterial hand cleaner
❑ At least one extra set of baby clothes
❑ Small plastic garbage bags (with twist ties) for disposing of dirty diapers or bringing home dirty clothes

Feeding Needs
❑ Formula, bottles with protective nipple covers, and bottle bags (or nursing pads if breastfeeding)
❑ Small bottle of water for making formula
❑ Burp cloth
❑ One or two bibs
❑ Baby food and utensils
❑ Bottle of juice with protective nipple cover
❑ Finger foods and beverages for older children

Rest and Play Needs
❑ Lightweight blanket or sweater
❑ Heavier blanket for cold weather
❑ Pacifier or teething ring
❑ One or two toys and/or books

Other Needs
❑ Small first-aid kit
❑ Any current baby medications (plus dispenser if needed)
❑ Hypoallergenic sunscreen

CHAPTER 22

MANAGING YOUR HOUSEHOLD

Most everyone admires an efficient, well-organized household. But for many people, it seems impossible to attain, let alone maintain. That's where systems come into play. With simple systems for meal planning, grocery shopping, house-keeping, and other routine household tasks, anyone can enjoy the benefits of an organized household with a minimal investment of time and energy. Yes, even you!

Meal Planning

Planning meals may be easier than you think. Just follow these four simple steps.

1. Make a list of your favorite meals and ask your partner or children to list their favorite meals. If you get stuck for ideas, skim through a cookbook or two.
2. Choose seven meals from your list and start a grocery list with the ingredients you need. Be sure to include vegetables, side dishes, and desserts.
3. Add your favorite breakfast, lunch, snack, and beverage items to your grocery list.
4. Post your meal plan on the refrigerator, along with any recipes you need or references to where you can find recipes.

If you have a computer with access to the Internet, you can do your meal planning and list making on-line at Myrecipe.com. Browse through the on-line cookbook. Then add the recipes you want to try this week to your personal recipe box. If requested, Myrecipe.com will create a detailed shopping list of ingredients based on the recipes you select. You can then delete items you have on hand and add other items you might need for the week such as beverages and ready-to-eat foods.

When you plan your weekly meals, consider doubling one recipe and freezing half for a night when you will be too busy to cook or just want a break. Be sure to label and date the freezer package and use within one month of freezing for best taste.

If your weekday schedule is hectic or inconsistent, stick with quick and easy meals and save gourmet recipes for your days off. If your budget permits, take advantage of prepackaged items, such as bagged lettuce mixes, cooked chicken, and frozen stir-fry meals. If you have a slow cooker, include at least one meal in your weekly plan that can be made in the slow cooker. You can assemble the ingredients in the cooker the night before and put it in the refrigerator. Then, in the morning, all you have to do is put the crock into the pot. It's great to come home in the evening and have dinner ready!

Save your list of favorite meals for planning the next week's meals. After several weeks of planning, you will have a variety of meals to choose from, so you won't have to spend so much time thinking about what to have for dinner. You may also save money on your groceries because you won't overbuy perishables. Meal planning also helps ensure that you and your family eat more healthy, nutritious foods rather than convenience foods.

Smart Food Shopping

To reduce the number of last-minute trips to the supermarket, post a running grocery list on your refrigerator or inside a cabinet door. As

you use up an item or notice that you are running low, add it to the list. Do this for refrigerator, freezer, and pantry items. Get other household members in the habit of adding items to the list as they use them up. If you buy paper goods and toiletries at the grocery store along with your groceries, add these items to your list, too.

At the supermarket, stock up on items you use often, such as canned tomatoes or tuna fish, when they are on sale. On the other hand, if you notice that your vegetable oil tends to go rancid or the honey crystallizes before you use it up, buy a smaller size next time.

Before each trip to the supermarket, clean out your refrigerator. Toss anything that is past its expiration date, along with anything that is questionable. If you need to replace an item, add it to your grocery list. Take note of items that will spoil within the next few days and plan to use them in your next few meals.

At the store, shop for nonperishable items first and fruits and vegetables, meat, dairy, and frozen food items last so that these perishable items stay cold. If you pack your own groceries at the checkout, pack refrigerated and frozen foods together to keep them cold. In hot climates or warmer seasons, keep a large cooler in your trunk for these items and purchase a bag of ice, especially if you have a long drive home.

Unpack purchases as soon as you get home, sorting foods into groups. Work first with items that can go directly into the freezer. Then sort the rest of your groceries into groups: dairy, meats and poultry to go into the refrigerator or to be rewrapped for freezing, fruits and vegetables that need refrigeration and those that don't, canned and packaged goods, and nonfood items. Sorting will make it easier and faster to put everything away.

TRIPLE RECIPES

In the course of your normal cooking, triple your recipes. If you're preparing lasagna, make three: one for eating tonight and two for the freezer. Tomorrow night, do the same thing with a different recipe. After one week of tripling your regular meals and freezing two, you'll have two weeks of meals with almost no extra effort. It's not much harder to prepare three lasagnas than it is to prepare one.

—*Deborah Taylor-Hough,* Frozen Assets Lite & Easy *(Fox Point, Wisc.: Champion Press, Ltd., 2001)*

If you buy dry, canned, and paper goods in bulk, look around your home for potential storage spaces. You might be able to install some shelving in a coat or linen closet, at the bottom of your basement stairs, or along one wall of your garage. An old kitchen cabinet would also make a great storage place in your basement or on your back porch. Cover it with a tablecloth and use as an end table. Another option is to store the overflow in boxes under your bed or a guest bed.

The Recycling Center

Most communities require recycling as a way to reduce the amount of waste that goes into our landfills. That means keeping recyclables separate from regular trash, which requires a system. How you set up your system depends on local recycling guidelines. If your recyclables get picked up at the curb, you probably don't need to do much sorting other than keeping paper separate from other recyclables.

If you take your recyclables to the recycling center yourself, you probably need to sort them into categories. You could collect all recyclables in one large bag or bin and sort them at the recycling center. Or you can do some or all of your sorting at home.

If you prefer to sort at home, write down the categories of recyclables that are accepted by your local recycling center; these may include glass (separated into green, brown, and clear), plastic, tin, plain paper, newspaper, catalogs, magazines, and cardboard. This is how many recycling containers you will need to sort your recyclables. And depending on the amount of recyclable glass you generate, you may need to sort further by color (green, brown, clear).

For recycling containers, use heavy-duty clear plastic bags or bins that you label accordingly. If you prefer bags, consider hanging the bags on hooks along one wall so that the bottoms of the bags touch the ground and one side is left open for easy collection. If your recyclables are clean, you can reuse these bags over and over. If you prefer bins, line them with bags that you can remove for carrying the contents to the recycling center. Since recyclables are similar to garbage, it's best to set up your recycling system in the garage or wherever you store your trash cans.

Because most recyclable material originates from the kitchen, it makes sense to set up a primary collection device there that you will empty daily or weekly, depending on volume. You can use a second garbage  can labeled "Recyclables Only" to collect all glass, plastic, and tin cans. If you generate a lot of recyclable paper (plain paper, newspaper, magazines, and catalogs), keep a collection device in the place where most of the recyclable material is generated.

Organized Housekeeping

When you save up all your housecleaning for one day, it seems like a lot of work because it *is* a lot of work. The trick is to do a little cleaning every day. The payoff is that you will never

TIME-SAVER

Line recycling bins with plastic bags to make it easy to haul away paper, cans, and bottles.

60

again feel overwhelmed by housecleaning — and you'll have a house that you'll enjoy coming home to.

- **Start with a thorough cleaning.** This might take all day or all weekend if you're really behind on housework. Or you can commit to cleaning one room each day until all rooms are brought up to par. Either way, make the commitment and stick to it. Put on some music or listen to a book on tape to keep you motivated. Better yet, enlist the help of family members, or work out an exchange with a friend.

- **Pick up clutter from floors, coffee tables, and other horizontal surfaces.** It's easier to do this if you have something to put things into such as a basket or a tote bag. Next, put all the tools and cleaning supplies you'll need in a bucket with a handle that you can carry from room to room. This will eliminate having to "go fetch," which adds unnecessary steps, time, and frustration to your cleaning session. Include a trash bag for emptying wastepaper baskets and for dumping other garbage. You'll also need a second bucket and a mop if you plan to wash floors. Choose cleaning products that are designed to handle more than one job, so you won't have so many to carry around. For example, use the same disinfectant product for cleaning toilets and bathroom floors. An old apron with pockets is also a great way to carry some cleaning supplies and is handy for picking up small items before they get sucked up in the vacuum cleaner.

- **Develop a routine.** Tackle the toughest rooms first, generally the bathroom and kitchen. Work in one room at a time, and work from top to bottom so that floors are the last thing you clean. Let cleaning products do their job while you do yours. Spray your shower and tub with a "scrub-free" cleaner, and pour a little cleaner in the toilet to let sit while you wipe countertops and clean the mirror. Or pretreat a rug stain while you dust the family room.

- **Do a little at a time, more often.** If you spend five minutes cleaning the bathroom three times a week, it takes only fifteen minutes total. But if you wait to do it once a week, it can take up to twice as long to cut through the build-up of clutter and dirt. Try cleaning the toilet, sink, and mirror while your children are taking a bath, and clean the shower stall while you're in it. Scrub the walls and floor, then scrub yourself.

- **If you're in cleaning mode, don't stop until you have finished what you set out to do.** If the telephone rings, don't answer it. You might not realize it, but when you really get into cleaning, you gain some momentum that works in your favor. Also save rearranging things and organizing for another time.

- **Enlist the help of family members, even if it means lowering your standards.** Two people can get the job done in half the time. Three people can accomplish even more in less time. The added bonus of getting family members involved in the cleanup effort is that they might be more inclined to keep things cleaner. See page 189 for ways to divide household chores.

Daily Speed Cleaning

There are lots of things you can do daily to make cleanup easier and reduce the total amount of time it takes to maintain a clean and uncluttered home.

cleaning supplies

To clean well, you must be prepared. Keep these basic supplies on hand at all times.

- Powdered abrasive cleaner
- Tile cleaner
- Glass cleaner
- Multipurpose disinfectant cleaner
- Wood floor and cabinet cleaner
- Furniture polish and rags
- Feather or lambswool duster
- Large scrubbing brush for floors
- Large sponge for shower, tub
- Smaller sponge for countertops
- Toilet brush
- Paper towels
- Trash bags
- Wet mop
- Broom
- Vacuum cleaner
- Mini-vacuum cleaner

• **In the kitchen.** When cooking or baking, fill a dishpan with hot, sudsy water and wash bowls and utensils as soon as used. Fill pots with water as soon as they are emptied and let them soak. If washing dishes by hand, do so immediately after each meal. Between meals, use a dishwashing wand to wash individual items. Wipe up spills and splatters on the surface of your stove at once before they dry. Wash burner trays with a sponge or cloth. Wipe up any spills in the refrigerator, in your oven, or on the floor as they occur. Get in the habit of sweeping the kitchen floor each night. Clean rings in jewelry cleaner while you wash dishes. Clean out your refrigerator while waiting for water to boil or empty the dishwasher while waiting for your coffee to brew.

• **In the bathroom.** Keep a roll of paper towels under the sink. Each time you use the sink, wet a paper towel and use it to wipe the sink and counter, or use a damp washcloth

TIME-SAVER

When making a bed, it's faster to spread the top sheet and blankets and then tuck in corners rather than walking around the bed three or four times to tuck in one layer at a time.

that is ready for the wash anyway. You can also buy antibacterial wipes to clean and disinfect countertops, the sink, and the toilet seat. After each shower, use a store-bought spray that promises to keep your shower clean. (It's best to start with a clean shower for this product to work effectively.) Hang towels after each use to keep them fresh longer between laundering.

• **In bedrooms.** Each morning, take a few minutes to make your bed, pick up and discard or recycle read newspapers and magazines, and return glassware, dishes, and foodstuffs to the kitchen. Before going to bed, hang up or put away clothes you will wear again and put everything else in the hamper or in a bag that you will take to the dry cleaner. When it's time to change sheets, take them off, wash them, and put them right back on the bed. It eliminates having to fold them, put them away, and get them out again later. For variety, switch to a different set when the seasons change.

• **Around the house.** Set aside some time each day for extra cleaning in one particular room. Then move on to another room the next day. Repeat until all of the rooms have been cleaned. Extra cleaning might include vacuuming, mopping, dusting, changing linens, cleaning the toilet bowl, or doing laundry. If you spend ten to thirty minutes a day on extra cleaning, you'll rarely have to spend any more time than that on housecleaning. And your house will always look presentable.

Doing Laundry

Laundry is a chore that seems endless, especially if you have a family. As soon as you finish folding all the clean clothes, it's time to wash another load of dirty clothes. But you can organize the whole process to save time and effort while ensuring that everyone has clean clothes to wear. For starters, don't wait until you run out of socks or underwear to do laundry. Do it every Monday night or Saturday morning or whenever — and let everyone know the schedule.

If you have to do laundry every day to keep up with demand, let everyone know that if they want something washed, it should be in the laundry room by a certain time and can be picked up after such-and-such a time.

● **Sorting dirty laundry.** Set up a color-coded system for sorting dirty laundry. Use three different-colored baskets: white for white clothes, pink for light colors, and dark blue for dark colors. Or invest in a triple clothes sorter with tubular steel frame and canvas bags that you can label "White," "Light," and "Dark." Make it the responsibility of each family member to bring dirty laundry to the laundry room and put it into the appropriate basket or bag. Consider marking each basket with the washing machine settings for that particular type of load.

● **Washing and drying.** Before putting dirty clothes into the washer, check pockets to make sure they are empty and zip zippers. Start a load of laundry in the morning and have the kids put it in the dryer when they get home from school. Or start the wash at night before going to bed and toss it in the dryer first thing in the morning. Never leave a dryer running when you leave the house, because lint buildup or a faulty dryer can be a fire hazard. Be sure to clean the dryer's lint filter after every load. To cut down on the number of towels you're washing, assign a set of towels to each household member and have them use it for one week, hanging it up after they're done in the bath.

● **Ironing.** Remove clothes from the dryer as soon as possible to avoid wrinkles. Do the ironing right away, or hang up unironed clothes in your closet. Then, when you need to iron something, iron as many items as you have time to iron. As an alternative to ironing, try spraying clothes with a wrinkle-releasing product. It's a little on the expensive side but works quite well and is worth the price if you don't like to iron.

• **Folding and sorting clean laundry.**
Color-code your children's clothing. Dot clothing tags and the toes of socks by using a different colored laundry marker for each child. Post a key to the coding system on your dryer so that whoever is doing the folding knows which clothes belong to whom. Folding is easiest if you have a flat surface at about waist height. Kids might find it easier (and more enjoyable) to carry laundry out to the family room and do their folding on the sofa in front of their favorite after-school television programs.

• **Distributing clean laundry.** Have baskets handy to carry clean and sorted laundry back to where it belongs. Consider assigning a laundry basket to each household member. Write their names on a piece of masking tape and affix to the baskets. Make it the responsibility of each household member to bring their clothes to their rooms and return the basket (empty or full of more dirty laundry to be done).

• **Doing laundry at a self-service laundry.** Make it easy on yourself to get the job done. Sort dirty laundry before leaving your home. If you have a lot of dirty laundry, consider putting it in large fabric bags that you can sling over your shoulder rather than in separate baskets that would require multiple trips from your home to the car and from the car to the laundry center. But do bring a basket or two along for collecting and carrying folded and sorted laundry. Premeasure powdered detergent for each load into resealable plastic bags. Leave economy-size bottles of liquid detergent, bleach, and fabric softener at home. Transfer the amount you need into small,

unbreakable bottles, properly labeled with their contents. As for how best to carry quarters, up to twenty fit in an empty film canister. Or you can ask for a roll of quarters at a bank. Most laundry centers have change machines, but if you bring your own you won't be frustrated by machines that are out of order or that don't accept worn or wrinkled bills.

For tips on how to set up your laundry room, see chapter 12, "Storage and Utility Areas."

Entertaining

The key to organizing a successful party is to plan ahead. That way, you can focus your attention on your guests, which will make the party more enjoyable for them and you. Follow these five steps for a seemingly effortless party.

1. Plan your menu in advance. Keep it simple. Choose dishes that you have prepared successfully in the past. The best choices are dishes that can be cooked ahead of time and either frozen or refrigerated, or dishes that can be put in the oven as guests arrive. If more than one dish must be cooked in an oven, be sure that they can be cooked at the same oven temperature. Also be sure that you will have enough room in your refrigerator for foods that need to be kept cold before the party. Plan to serve appetizers and desserts that require little or no last-minute preparation. Make a list of all the foods and beverages you plan to serve, along with notations of where to find the recipes.

2. Develop a timetable for preparation. Start with the day and time of your party and work backward to make a timetable. Your timetable should begin with a trip to the supermarket at least one day in advance, if not several days or one week beforehand, to make sure that everything you need is available. If there are any items you need to buy on the day of your party, such as fresh seafood, include that trip on your timetable. Estimate how much time you'll need to prepare each dish, and then add 20 percent to allow for distractions and unforeseen incidents. Start with the dish that requires the most preparation and finish with the one that requires the least preparation. The beauty of making a timetable is that you will know beforehand if your menu plan is overly ambitious, and you can adjust accordingly with no waste of time, effort, or money.

3. Make a shopping list. With recipes in hand, go through your pantry to make sure that you have everything you need, including the condiments you plan to serve with various foods. Don't assume that because you have a particular item, you're all set. Check to see that you have the quantity you need. Add beverages, paper goods, and nonfood items, such as toothpicks, to your list. Don't forget cream and sugar for coffee and garnishes for drinks and food.

4. Do as much as possible in advance. Plan which china, stemware, silver, and serving pieces you will use and make sure that everything is clean. Save the last hours before the party for simple preparations, such as setting the table or buffet and lighting candles. Plan to have everything ready at least one hour before your guests are scheduled to arrive. That way you'll have plenty of time to get yourself ready without having to race around.

5. Accept all offers of help. If your partner or children ask if they can help, put them to work on specific tasks, such as putting ice in buckets or taking coats. If you will be serving mixed drinks, you will need someone to do that so you are free to greet and mingle with guests. If guests ask if they can help, do not hesitate to delegate simple tasks that won't take more than a few minutes, such as putting music in the CD player, carrying something from the kitchen to the dining room, or refilling a bowl with chips or nuts.

CHAPTER 23

ORGANIZING FOR SAFETY

When it comes to your family's safety, prevention is the best protection. Keeping clutter off floors and stairs helps prevent falls, and safely storing hazardous materials can prevent fire or accidental ingestion. There are many simple things you can do to help prepare your family in the event of an emergency. When every second counts, being organized could prevent injuries and save lives.

Home Safe Home

While your home is generally a safe haven, some conditions and practices can be potentially hazardous, especially for younger family members. Play it safe. Take steps to protect your family by checking every room for safety hazards and making sure that everyone is aware of unsafe practices. Following are some home safety guidelines.

• **Kitchen.** Keep knives and sharp objects out of reach of children. Don't store things over the stove; you could be burned in the process of reaching for them while cooking. Never leave anything cooking unattended, whether it's on top of the stove, in the oven or toaster, or in the microwave. Keep cooking areas clear of combustibles, such as dishtowels or paper, and wear clothes with short, rolled-up, or tight-fitting sleeves when you cook. Turn pot handles inward on the stove, where you can't bump them and children can't grab them. Enforce a kid-free zone three feet around your kitchen stove. If grease catches fire in a pan, slide a lid over the pan to smother the flames and turn off the heat. Leave the lid on until the pan is cool. Make sure your hands are dry before using an electrical appliance to keep from getting a shock.

• **Bathroom.** Store medicines, vitamins, cosmetics, and any potentially hazardous materials out of reach of children or in cabinets with child-safety latches. Use caution when disposing of these products. Flush pills and medicines down the toilet; put all other items into a plastic bag secured with a twist tie and dispose of in a lidded trash can that children and pets cannot get into. Use nonslip mats in bathtubs and showers. Consider having grab bars installed in bathrooms for elderly family members. Make sure that your hands are dry and you are not standing on a wet floor before using an electrical appliance. Unplug hair dryers when not in use so they can't get turned on accidentally. Never leave a baby or young child alone in the bathtub. To avoid scalding, adjust the temperature of your hot water heater down to 120°F.

- **Family and living rooms.** Allow air space around the television and stereo to prevent overheating. Use a sturdy, metal fireplace screen. Have the chimney checked and cleaned annually or more frequently if you use your fireplace or woodstove often. Do not store newspapers near the fireplace or woodstove where they could be ignited by a stray spark.

- **Bedrooms and kids' rooms.** Buy fire escape ladders for bedrooms on upper floors, if needed. Make it impossible for younger children to get at toys with small parts. Store these items way up high on shelves that only you can reach. Explain the danger of choking to older children so that they do not leave games or projects with small parts unattended.

- **Baby's room.** Position the crib well away from potential hazards: heaters, lamps, electrical cords, wall decorations, windows, and furniture that could be used to climb out. Replace drapes and blinds that have cords that could accidentally strangle a baby. Buy window guards or locks that allow windows to be opened just a crack. Use the restraining strap on the changing table. Keep all toiletries out of baby's reach at all times. Keep the drop side of the crib up and locked. Once your baby can pull up to a standing position, remove the crib bumpers and keep the mattress in its lowest position. Before your baby is old enough to climb out of the crib unassisted, secure the room with a good-quality door gate. Cover electrical outlets with child-safety caps. Enclose heaters to prevent burns.

- **Office.** Do not plug multioutlet power strips into other multioutlet power strips. Distribute weight in filing cabinets; opening a full top drawer with empty or partly filled bottom drawers can cause the cabinet to tip over. For this same reason, close one drawer before pulling out another. Close all file cabinet drawers when not in use so you won't trip over them.

- **Basement, garage, and storage rooms.** Store gasoline and other flammables in tight metal containers away from heat sources. Do not store anything near your furnace or heater. Store lighter-weight items on upper shelves and heavier items closer to ground level to avoid potential breakage or injury when retrieving them. Have heating equipment checked and cleaned yearly.

- **Workshop.** Keep flammable objects away from spark-producing tools. If you have young children, keep the door to your workshop locked to prevent access to hazardous materials and sharp tools. Equip your workshop with safety equipment such as safety glasses, dust mask, and fire extinguisher.

FIRE SAFETY AND PREVENTION TIPS

For your own protection and for that of your family, read and follow these tips.

- Install at least one smoke detector on every level of your home, and outside each sleeping area.

- Unless you heat and cook solely with electric, install one carbon-monoxide detector on each floor of your home to provide early warning of faulty ventilation.

- Do not warm up vehicles in an attached garage without opening the garage door or use gas or diesel-powered machines indoors without proper ventilation.

- Purchase only smoke and carbon-monoxide detectors approved by Underwriters Laboratories or Factory Mutual.

- Test smoke and carbon-monoxide detectors every month.

- Replace smoke detector batteries once a year with fresh batteries or immediately if a detector "chirps." Never "borrow" a smoke detector battery from another appliance.

- Replace smoke detectors every seven to ten years and in any new residence.

- Equip each floor of your home with fire extinguishers, especially the kitchen and near fireplaces and woodstoves. Choose models rated "2-A:10-B:C" for use on any type of fire. Instruct household members in their proper use.

- Use only child-resistant lighters and store all matches and lighters up high, where small children can't see or reach them, preferably in a locked cabinet. Teach your children that matches and lighters are tools, not toys, and should be used only by adults. Instruct them to bring any matches or lighters they find to an adult.

- Never leave burning candles unattended.

- Never smoke in bed or when you are sleepy. Cigarettes are a leading cause of fire-related deaths in the United States. Use heavy, nontipping ashtrays. Discard butts and ashes in metal, sealed containers or in the toilet.

- If an electrical appliance smokes or has an unusual smell, unplug it immediately and have it serviced before using it again. If an appliance gets wet, get it serviced immediately.

- Do not use electrical appliances with cords that are cracked or frayed. Don't overload extension cords or run them under rugs. Turn off your television, stereo, and other electrical appliances when not in use.

- If a fuse blows, find the cause. Replace the fuse with one of the correct size.

- Keep portable heaters at least three feet from anything that can burn. Keep children and pets away from heaters, and never leave heaters on when you leave home or go to bed. Do not dry wet mittens or other clothing on space heaters.

Keeping Kids Safe

Many injuries that occur in the home are the result of falls. To protect young children (and older persons who may get up in the middle of the night and take a wrong turn), install safety gates at the top and bottom of stairs. Remove tripping hazards, such as papers, books, and shoes, from floors and stairs. Remove throw rugs that may slip, secure them with double-sided tape, or put rug pads underneath. Make sure that your home is well lit and that staircases have handrails.

Err on the side of overcautiousness when storing household chemicals. Store open containers of bleach, laundry detergent, and cleaning supplies on high shelves out of the reach of children to prevent accidental ingestion. Keep the phone number for the Poison Control Center (800-222-1222) handy and call it if you suspect that your child has been poisoned. Keep ipecac syrup and activated granular charcoal on hand to use if directed to do so by the

---

For Simplicity's Sake

For current information about known product hazards and recalls, visit the Web site of the United States Consumer Product Safety Commission at www.cpsc.gov. Check out the "New This Week" section on the home and the "Popular/New/Calendar" section. You can also subscribe to receive all recall notices by e-mail on the same day they are issued.

---

poison control specialists or your physician. If your child is not breathing, call 911 immediately instead of the Poison Control Center.

Small children have a natural tendency to put things into their mouths, which may cause them to start choking or stop breathing. Do not leave plastic bags, deflated balloons, cords, or small objects, such as buttons, coins, and beads, unattended. Also do not leave out candies or nuts. Supervise infants and children when they are eating so that you can respond immediately to choking.

Emergency Response Plans

All family members should know what to do in the event of a fire, earthquake, flood, or other disaster. It's important to develop a home emergency response plan for your family. Have a family meeting to discuss your plan and then practice it on a regular basis.

Fire. Does every family member know at least two ways out of your home in the event of a fire? Prepare for a fire emergency by developing an escape plan. Be sure that everyone knows at least two exits — doors and windows — from their bedrooms and from your home in general. If you live in an apartment building, plan to use fire exits, not elevators. Decide on a place outside, perhaps at the end of the driveway or at a neighbor's house where you can call 911, where everyone will meet. Practice your escape plan at least twice a year.

It's important to note that most deaths from home fires occur between the hours of 11 P.M. and 6 A.M. Have at least one fire drill between these hours. Practice yelling "Fire!" to alert family members in the event of a fire. You may want to keep a whistle in each bedroom. Be sure that all family members can operate the locks, windows, and doors. And get in the habit of sleeping with doors closed; this will keep searing heat and smoke out of bedrooms and allow additional time to escape. Teach children the five most important rules to remember in the event of a fire emergency (see box at right).

Power Outage. Your emergency response plan should also include what to do in case of a power outage. Check the fuse box, then call the electric utility company to report the outage. Keep flashlights in every bedroom and near every entrance. That way, if you come home to a power outage, you won't have to go bumping around in the dark to find a flashlight. Keep candles, matches, a flashlight, and extra batteries together in one place. Handy items to have include one or more oil lamps (filled and ready to light), fondue pot and fuel for heating up canned foods, nonelectric can opener, gas grill, battery-powered radio or television, kerosene space heater, and several large containers of water.

what to do in case of fire

1. Feel all doors before opening them. If a door is hot, don't open it. Find another way out.

2. Crawl under smoke. Because smoke rises, the air will be cleaner closer to the floor. Cover your mouth and nose with your pajama top to keep from getting smoke in your lungs.

3. Just get out. Don't waste time getting dressed. Don't search for your pets or anything else. We can buy new things, but we can't replace you!

4. Stop, drop, and roll if your clothes catch fire. Cover your face with your hands and roll over and over.

5. If you can't get out, don't hide. Stand by an open window, yell "Help," and wave a lit flashlight so that the firemen can see you. (Keep a flashlight in each bedroom.)

Evacuation. Some situations, such as an extended power outage, flood, or hurricane, may necessitate evacuation. Make a list of things you would need to take with you if you had to evacuate your home. Think first of those things family members need every day, such as medications, eyeglasses, or diapers. Plan to take a one- to three-day supply with you. You'll need money wherever you go, so be sure to put your checkbook on your list, along with some emergency cash or traveler's checks. Stash the cash and your list with your power outage emergency supplies.

Just in Case

It's always better to be prepared for the worst, just in case. A little organizing now could save you and your family a lot of unnecessary stress, legwork, and expense later.

Keep important legal documents, such as titles and deeds, in a fireproof box or bank safe deposit box. You might also consider making copies of your driver's license, passport, and Social Security card and storing these identification papers along with your legal documents. If you really want to play it safe, make copies of all legal documents and send them for safekeeping to a friend or relative who lives outside your geographic area. It's also a good idea to make a home inventory list and store that in your fireproof box or safe deposit box, along with appraisal documents and photographs or videotape of and receipts for big-ticket items.

The American Red Cross recommends that you keep a well-stocked first aid kit in your home and car and bring one with you when you go hiking, biking, camping, or boating. You can buy many types of ready-made first aid kits or make your own kit by filling a small duffel bag, tackle box, or plastic storage bin with the necessary supplies (see the checklist on page 225) and labeling it. In addition to the supplies recommended by the American Red Cross, it's also a good idea to include a working flashlight, first aid manual, emergency telephone numbers, and a list of allergies and medications for each family member. If you use anything from your kit, be sure to restock it. And be sure to keep your first aid kit out of reach of young children.

Although you probably don't like to think about it, you never know when you may be faced with a life-or-death situation. Would you know what to do if a family member started choking or stopped breathing? Consider getting certified in standard first aid and cardiopulmonary resuscitation. Make sure that your babysitter is certified as well. The American

For Safety's Sake

Evacuating your home. If you have to evacuate your home, post a note telling the date and time, where you are going, and with whom. Bring the following items with you:

- Money
- Food
- Water
- Plates, glasses, and flatware
- Battery-powered radio or television
- Flashlight
- First aid kit
- Medications and eyeglasses
- List of valuables
- Important documents
- Change of clothes and sturdy shoes
- Sleeping bag or blankets
- Keys
- Pet supplies

Source: *Natural Disasters* (Itasca, IL: National Safety Council, 2001). Permission to reprint granted by the National Safety Council, a membership organization dedicated to protecting life and promoting health.

Red Cross regularly offers programs teaching first aid and cardiopulmonary resuscitation to children and adults who want to learn valuable lifesaving skills.

Pet Safety and First Aid

Pets rely on us for protection. Remember that before you buy, use, or store household cleaners, pesticides, or other potentially hazardous substances. Read the labels. Even common household foods, plants, and other items can cause stomach upset and vomiting if a cat or dog eats them. Other substances, such as certain plants and antifreeze, can be deadly. If your pet is vomiting repeatedly, is having seizures, is losing consciousness, is unconscious, or is having difficulty breathing, contact your veterinarian immediately.

Never give human medicine to a dog or cat unless directed to do so by a veterinarian. Also do not give dog medicine to a cat; it could be fatal. Be careful when taking your medications that you don't accidentally drop a pill on the floor. And don't leave medications out on a counter or table, where your curious pet could find them. Store all medications, including ointments, out of reach of pets. Dispose of expired medicines by flushing them down the toilet or wrapping them in a plastic bag and carrying to an outside waste receptacle with a tightly fitting lid.

Pets get sick just like people. And sometimes, despite your best efforts, pets get injured. The American Red Cross recommends that you pay attention to what is normal for your pet so you can detect signs of something

wrong. If your pet is ill or has been injured, approach slowly and cautiously. Speak gently and quietly to calm your pet. Bear in mind that any sick or injured animal, even your own, can become aggressive when frightened or in pain. If your pet growls as you attempt to move him, protect your hands and arms with thick sleeves and gloves. You may be able to subdue a small animal by covering and wrapping him tightly in a towel or small blanket.

Pet Hazards. Following is a list of substances that are hazardous to the health of cats and dogs.

- Onions and onion powder
- Chocolate (all forms)
- Alcoholic beverages
- Yeast dough
- Coffee (grounds and beans) and caffeinated tea
- Salt
- Macadamia nuts
- Hops (used in home beer brewing)
- Tomato and potato leaves and stems (green parts)
- Rhubarb leaves
- Moldy foods
- Many plants, including azalea, oleander, cyclamen, daffodils, bird of paradise, castor bean, rhododendrons, sago palm, Easter lily (cats only), and Japanese Yew
- Flea control products and other insecticides
- Mouse and rat poisons
- Household chemicals, including mothballs, potpourri oils, fabric softener sheets, dishwashing detergent, and batteries
- Antifreeze and windshield washer fluid
- Medications

Source: American Society for the Prevention of Cruelty to Animals (ASPCA) (www.aspca.org)

Keep the following telephone numbers with other emergency numbers:

- Your veterinarian
- Nearest after-hours veterinary clinic
- ASPCA Animal Poison Control Center (1-888-426-4435)

If you have an after-hours emergency, call the clinic first to let them know you are coming. It's also a good idea to keep the address and directions, and maybe even a map, handy in case an emergency occurs in the care of a pet sitter or another family member. The Animal Poison Control Center provides a fee-based service, so you will need to have your credit card number ready.

Don't Panic. According to the ASPCA Animal Poison Control Center, if you suspect that your pet has been exposed to a poison, it is important not to panic. Although rapid response is important, panicking generally interferes with the process of helping your animal. Take thirty to sixty seconds to safely collect and have at hand the material involved. This may be of great benefit to the center professionals so that they can determine exactly what poison or poisons are involved. In the event that you need to take your animal to your local veterinarian, be sure to take with you the container for the product your pet ingested. Also bring any material your pet may have vomited or chewed, collected in a plastic bag.

PART VI

Organizing Transitions

Staying organized through change is one of life's most difficult challenges. But there are some simple steps you can take to make transitions easier, whether you are getting ready for the next season, moving into a new home, adopting a pet, preparing to welcome a child into your life or send one to college, or arranging for the transfer of assets to your heirs.

Your normal routines and schedules are bound to be upset by change. Organizing can help get you back on track. Prepare as much as possible in advance. And try to retain the organizing systems that have worked for you in the past. But recognize that a new situation may require that you modify some of your former habits and methods. Remember that there is never one right way to get and stay organized. This is especially true when you are preparing for and going through life transitions. Look for the simplest solutions.

CHAPTER 24

ORGANIZING FOR THE SEASONS

How can you be better prepared to greet the changing seasons? When is the best time to plant bulbs or reseed the lawn? How often should you clean gutters or drain the hot water heater? In this chapter, you'll learn what tasks and activities should be performed throughout the year to maintain your personal property, keep everything in good working order, and enjoy a clutter-free home.

Make Way for Spring

Once snow showers change to rain showers, it's time to put away snow removal equipment and supplies. If you have a powered snow thrower, follow the manufacturer's instructions for winterizing. Perform spring maintenance on your lawnmower or tractor as recommended by the manufacturer. Check fluid levels and inspect drive belts and blades. Get gasoline for your mower, propane for your gas grill, or lighter fuel and charcoal briquettes for your charcoal grill.

Around the time you stop heating your home, remove and store any removable storm windows and doors. If this is the first time you have removed them, be sure to indicate which windows go where. Write with a wide-tip permanent marker directly on the edges of the storm windows or on pieces of masking tape affixed to the edges. Label each window with its appropriate location, such as "Kitchen — Above Sink" or "Living Room — West Wall." Also, indicate the top of each storm window. Wash windows inside and out before putting up window screens.

Get out your garden hoses and check for leaks. Replace worn or frayed clothesline. If line is in good condition, clean with detergent, water, and an old washcloth or rag.

Springtime Home Maintenance

Doing simple home maintenance in spring can help to prevent small problems from becoming big problems. Take some time to walk through and around your house. Make notes of any repairs or problems that require your attention.

- Open windows or vents in the basement and attic to ventilate.
- Check for leaks or signs of water damage, especially in the basement, attic, garage and around your dishwasher and washing machine areas.
- Check washing machine hoses for cracks or bulges; replace if needed.
- Make a note of any stains or bulges on ceilings and walls that you want to have an inspector look at.
- Inspect caulking around tubs, showers, and sinks; recaulk if necessary.
- Check the roof for any needed repairs; secure loose shingles.
- Check to be sure that your television antenna is secure.
- Check for termite and other insect damage.
- Check siding for wood decay or popped nails; secure loose nails or replace.
- Check your foundation, masonry, or stucco for cracks; reseal as needed.
- Decide if and when you need to do any painting inside or out.
- Plan to reseal wood or slate floors or sand and varnish wood floors as necessary. Strip wax from linoleum floors and rewax.
- Have your central air conditioning system inspected.

Spring Cleaning

When you think of spring, what do you think of? Showers? Flowers? How about cleaning? The season of rebirth is the perfect time to clean and freshen up your home. Take advantage of the extra hours of daylight to tackle some of the big stuff. But don't expect to get everything done in one day. Look at what needs to be done and work it into your regular schedule. Make it a family affair: Get the kids to help, and enjoy the satisfaction that comes from working together as a team. When the work is done, plan to celebrate with popcorn and a movie or a trip to the park.

Get a start on your spring cleaning by washing windows inside and out so you can let the sunshine in. It's generally recommended to do this on a cool, cloudy day to prevent the glass cleaner from streaking. It's hard to see the streaks if it's sunny, and the cleaner sometimes dries too fast to wipe away when the windows are warm.

It's easier to keep track of your progress — and see the results of your labor — when you work in one room at a time. High-traffic areas, such as the kitchen and bathrooms, are a good place to start.

reminders for all seasons

Following are some of the routine and preventive maintenance tasks that should be performed every few months. The easiest way to remember these things is to get in the habit of doing them on the first day of every new season. Routine safety checks should be done twice a year. Do these when you turn the clocks ahead or back, or on April Fool's Day and Halloween.

When seasons change
- Clean and clear all household drains.
- Drain the hot water heater.
- Wash quilts and bedspreads, shower curtains, and throw rugs.
- Turn your mattresses.
- Add fresh mothballs or fresh cedar products in your storage area.

Twice yearly
- Replace the batteries in your smoke and carbon monoxide detectors.
- Clean smoke detectors. Remove and wipe cover with a damp cloth; vacuum interior.
- Inspect fire extinguisher; recharge if pressure is below operating range.
- Hold a family fire drill.
- Check refrigerator and freezer temperatures with an appliance thermometer. Refrigerated foods should be kept at 40°F, frozen foods at 0°F.
- Clean or change furnace or air conditioning filters.
- Clean ceiling fans and light fixtures; wipe bulbs and replace nonworking bulbs.
- Roll up large area rugs and vacuum underneath.

- Clean scuff marks, handprints, and other marks off walls and doors.
- Clean baseboards and polish woodwork.
- Wipe smudges and spills off cabinet doors.
- Vacuum your refrigerator coils to keep your refrigerator running at peak performance.
- Clean the top of the refrigerator and cabinets.

Nothing spruces up a home like the look and smell of clean carpets. In addition, some people like to redecorate for spring and summer by changing curtains and furniture slipcovers.

- Rent or hire a carpet cleaner, after the muddy season has passed.
- Clean curtains and rehang or put them away until fall.
- Replace flannel and dark-colored sheets with lighter-colored cotton sheets.
- Replace heavy bedspreads with lighter ones.
- Launder all winter quilts, bedspreads, and blankets and store. See page 77 for tips on off-season storage of linens.
- Clean and waterproof leather boots, outerwear, and accessories and store.

Unclutter your house, room by room (see chapters in Part II, "Organizing Room by Room"). Pack up unwanted items for a spring garage sale. Tag and price these items as you box them. See page 18 for tips on organizing a successful garage sale.

Super-clean the interior of your car. Vacuum and shampoo carpets, rugs, and seats. Wash windows. Clean and shine the dash. Wash doors, ceiling, and molding.

Early Spring Yard Work

If you live in a cold, snowy region, you probably can't wait to get your hands dirty out in your yard once spring arrives. On the first nice day, get to it! Start by picking up branches and other debris. As you're walking around, make a note of any repairs you might need to make to outbuildings and fences.

You might be able to promote early greening of your lawn. After the snow melts, rake debris from your lawn. If your lawn is still soggy, move quickly to avoid compacting the soil. When the soil is dry and firm enough, adjust your mower blade height to its lowest setting and mow, then rake and remove clippings.

Although fall is the best time to reseed your lawn, you can do it in spring, too. Rake the area with a heavy-duty garden rake to dig up the soil for planting, then seed and water. Fertilize your lawn after one or two spring cuttings. Then fertilize every eight to ten weeks thereafter (for example, May 15, July 30, and October 15). Apply fertilizer to a dry lawn and water. If you fertilized your lawn late in the fall, it is not necessary to fertilize in the spring.

Are you planning to plant late spring or early summer bulbs? Residents of southern

For Simplicity's Sake

Once your bulbs start coming up, set wooden stakes into the bare spots so you know where to plant new bulbs in the fall. Attach a piece of masking tape to the stake and write with a permanent marker what you wish to plant there.

states can do this as early as late February or early March. Northern dwellers should wait until late April or early May. Follow planting instructions on the packaging. Everyone else should be able to plant in late March or early April. Lettuce, peas, spinach, broccoli, and other hardy vegetables can be planted as early as you can work the soil. You can plant seeds for some flowers, such as annual phlox, California poppies, and sweet peas now, too. Also look for seedling violas and pansies. Spring is also a good time to plant trees and shrubs.

Summer's Almost Here

After the busyness of spring, reward yourself by getting ready for outdoor fun.

- Get your pool ready. Remove the cover, fill with water, and superchlorinate according to manufacturer instructions.
- Inspect bicycles; lubricate chains and adjust seat heights as necessary. Check that your children's bicycle helmets still fit. Also inspect outdoor play equipment for loose bolts or broken parts.

- Bring your outdoor furniture, grill, and play equipment out of storage; clean it off and set it up. If you see some rust, sand and repaint as needed. Get new cushions for your lawn furniture if necessary.
- Check your gas grill before using it. Use a pipe cleaner to remove possible blockage by insects or grease buildup in the tubes that lead to the burner. Check hoses for cracking, brittleness, holes, and leaks; replace as necessary.

Summer Garden Chores

For most people, working out in the yard is a pleasure rather than a chore. Regardless, certain things need to be done at certain times, and you can organize chores to keep your lawn and garden looking their best.

Let's start in the garden. When the danger of frost has passed and nighttime temperatures are holding steady at 55°F or higher, it's safe to plant annual flowers and vegetables. You can move houseplants outdoors then, too, and plant flower boxes. Dig up any spring bulbs you wish to transplant, but wait until after the foliage has died back. Save only the larger bulbs; the smaller ones will not bloom. Replant immediately and water. Or place in a mesh bag and store in your garage or other cool (50°F to 65°F), dry place until fall. Be sure to label the bag.

Once the soil has warmed up sufficiently, mulch vegetable and flower gardens to conserve water and prevent weeds from sprouting. Use grass clippings, straw, mulched leaves, or partially broken down compost.

If you wish to extend the growing season for your vegetables, plan to do this as soon as your first crop is gone. Remove all plant debris and weeds and fertilize soil. Plant cool-season vegetables, such as spinach, turnips, radishes, onions, or leaf lettuce from seeds. When seedlings emerge, apply a two- to three-inch layer of light mulch. Water thoroughly and regularly, preferably early in the day.

Delegate yard chores to family members. Rotate chores so that one person doesn't get stuck doing the same ones all summer. Regular chores may include cleaning the pool, watering the lawn, watering gardens, and mowing. If you remove no more than one third of the grass leaf at one time, it is not necessary to rake clippings.

PLANNING AHEAD

Order early spring flowering bulbs in August. If buying at a retail store, choose the biggest bulbs. Be sure to buy enough to plant in clusters. Store in original packaging in the "cool and dry" compartment of your refrigerator or another cool (40°F to 50°F), dry place.

Back to School

Don't wait until the last minute to get organized for the start of a new school year. As early as July, clothing stores start phasing out summer apparel and introducing fall items. Plan to shop on a rainy day or an exceptionally hot day, when it might feel good to spend time in an air-conditioned mall.

Before you go shopping, have your child try on last year's clothes to see what still fits. If you dislike shopping, try catalog or on-line shopping for everything from pencils to underwear to coats. There's a charge for delivery, but if you add up the time you spend getting to and from the store and waiting to check out, it may be worth the added cost. Try to do as much shopping as you can from one catalog to defray shipping costs and, if possible, choose catalogs that do not need to collect sales tax in your state.

Do whatever you can to make a smooth transition from vacation to school. If your child is new to a school, arrange to have your kids meet their teachers and some classmates before school starts. At the very least, spend time talking about school in a positive manner and give children an opportunity to express concerns. About one week before school starts, adjust bedtimes and wake-up times to coincide with school schedules. See page 186 for tips on managing morning madness.

A Season of Change

Take advantage of fall's bounty. Watch for end-of-season markdowns on summer items, such as suntan lotion, insect repellent, beach toys, lawn furniture, and summer clothing. Collect

leaves, pine cones, seeds, sticks, and other natural goodies for winter craft projects. Shop for fall mums and other hardy annual plants to replace fading summer blooms.

Of course, there's work to be done, too, inside and out. Do outdoor jobs on one of those beautiful fall days when the air is crisp and the sun is warm. Save your fall cleaning and redecorating for a rainy day. Indoor things to do include vacuuming refrigerator coils and heat vents before turning on your furnace. Following is a list of some of the major things to do outdoors each fall.

- Take down awnings and wash and store them.
- Clean window sills and screens.

- On the first cold day, check for drafts around windows; reglaze and seal drafty windows.
- Check your door sweeps; replace if you feel cold air coming in.
- Repair ripped or broken screens and replace or store.
- Wash and put away summer clothes and blankets. Bring out the winter clothes and blankets.
- Have your chimney and furnace inspected.
- Scrub mildew from decks, porches, and siding.
- Clean, drain, and cover your pool; winterize according to manufacturer instructions.
- Remove the oil and spark plugs from your lawnmower; perform routine maintenance as recommended by the manufacturer.
- After most of the leaves have fallen, clean accumulated leaves and other debris out of gutters and downspouts to prevent clogging or collapse.
- Clean and sand the wood handles on your garden tools. Apply a coat of wood preservative to keep wood from drying and splitting.
- Get your snow thrower ready for winter use. Follow manufacturer instructions. Get gas if you need it.

Fall Gardening

Fall and late fall are the ideal times to fertilize your lawn. Fertilizing now results in a healthier lawn in spring and summer. Rake leaves periodically as they begin to fall; it's easier to keep up than to

TIME-SAVER

If you don't need to remove screens for the winter, use a handheld vacuum cleaner to remove cobwebs, leaf pieces, and other debris rather than removing them and hosing them down.

catch up. Put some leaves in your perennial gardens and around bushes and shrubs to provide winter protection. Reseed bare spots in your lawn, if needed. Use a heavy-duty garden rake to dig up the soil for planting, then seed and water. Keep pets and children off that area of the lawn until the grass is hardy enough.

In your garden, protect tender plants from early frost. Cover plants with large cardboard boxes. Once the average daily temperature falls below 65°F, pick tomatoes and let them finish ripening indoors out of direct sunlight. Keep an eye on the weather forecast. Bring houseplants indoors before the nights start turning cold.

Plant early spring flowering bulbs in fall. Inspect stored bulbs and throw out any that are mushy or decayed. Residents of southern states can plant in late September or early October. Those who live in northern states must wait until late November or early December or just before the ground freezes. If you live somewhere in between southern and northern states, you can plant in late October or early November. Dig holes that are two to three times deeper than the height of bulb. If you're not sure which end is up, plant it sideways. Cover with soil, fertilize with bonemeal, and water. Your local nursery or Cooperative Extension service can provide more exact planting information based on your USDA Plant Hardiness Zone.

Last but not least, put your gardens to bed for the winter. Cover perennial beds with two inches of mulch made of leaves or other mulching material. Turn vegetables under along with some compost material.

Welcoming Winter

In the cold, dark winter months, plants bring special joy and hints of good things to come. Throughout the winter, check your houseplants frequently. You may need to water more often than usual because heating dries out the soil. Occasionally washing leaves with lukewarm water and a few drops of mild dishwashing liquid will help to enhance absorption of low light. Vacuum heat vents and dust radiators every time you vacuum your floors and carpets.

If you live in a cold place with temperatures below freezing, winter is a good time to defrost your freezer. You can put all your frozen items outside your door with no worries about spoilage.

Take advantage of after-holiday sales. After the first of the year, you'll find dramatic markdowns on boxed holiday cards, ornaments, wrapping paper, ribbon, and bows. Shop now and have more time to enjoy next holiday season. You'll also find good sales on toys, furniture, carpets, linens, winter clothing, and more.

Year-End Checklist

The first of the year is a great time to get your home and office paperwork in order. Following is a checklist of very important, but often overlooked, year-end "To Dos."

❏ Clean out financial files (including tax returns and supporting tax documentation that is no longer needed) to make room for the new year's paperwork; shred or transfer older documents to archive storage as appropriate.

❏ Remove other outdated documents from your active files; discard, or put into archive storage as appropriate.

❏ Gather all of your tax paperwork and finalize records for the year.

❏ Update your household inventories to include photos, receipts, and appraisals (if necessary) for any new purchases made in that year and upgrade the replacement value of your homeowner's or renter's insurance to match.

❏ Update your will and powers of attorney to take into account any changes in the tax and estate laws or a life change such as a move, marriage, divorce, birth of a child, or death of a beneficiary.

❏ Update your list of account numbers (bank, credit card, investment, insurance policies, for example) and important contacts such as your attorney, investment broker, doctors, accountant, insurance agent, and executor of will to include any changes since this time last year.

— Ramona Creel, OnlineOrganizing.com

Begin preparing your taxes in January and file as early as possible if you expect a refund. If you expect to owe, prepare your taxes early anyway, but hold off on mailing until April.

PLANNING AHEAD

- Order late spring/ summer flowering bulbs in January.
- Start planning in January if you wish to take the family on vacation during the summer holidays.

For gardeners, winter is the season to dream *and* the season for perusing seed catalogs. As spring nears, start seeds indoors under grow lights. While you're waiting for an opportunity to plant outdoors, try forcing a few bulbs indoors, which will add spirited splashes of color and even fragrance to your interior landscape. Another good indoor project for gardeners that really shows of houseplants is positioning shelving under windows to ensure that plants get appropriate levels of light. Consider removing drapes you never close and using the drapery rod for hanging plants.

Though you may have to wait for warmer weather to plant, there are several ways to tend your garden in winter. Cut and place branches from your holiday tree over bulb beds and perennial gardens for added winter protection. Take advantage of a warm, sunny day to repair broken arbors and trellises before spring growth makes this difficult. During the dormant months, you may also be able to move rocks, prepare raised beds, or dig a compost trench. You could even build a new bird feeder.

Winter is also a great time to unclutter and organize your home, especially for people who live "up north" and prefer staying indoors to going out in the snow and cold. Plan a "first day of spring" party and use it as motivation to get your house in order over the winter months. Work in one room at a time using tips from previous chapters. Or skip the party, and focus instead on an organizing project you've been meaning to get to for a while, such as organizing your photographs, recipes, or closets. When you're finished, reward yourself for a job well done.

new year's resolutions

Making New Year's resolutions is a tradition that dates back to ancient Babylonian times. New Year dissolutions have an equally long history! We begin with the best intentions, but keeping New Year's resolutions is challenging. Following are three tips to help you set goals that you can keep.

1. Make resolutions early. Choose resolutions that you've been thinking about. You're more likely to follow through on these resolutions than on those made last minute at the midnight hour.

2. Stick with one or two resolutions. Make a list of all the things you want to do. Then choose the one or two things you would most like to accomplish this year and focus on those goals.

3. Set obtainable goals. When making resolutions, think about what you will need to do on a daily, weekly, and monthly basis to achieve your goal. If it doesn't seem realistic, scale back your expectations.

CHAPTER 25

MOVING

Whether you're moving across town or across the country, there's no such thing as an easy move. But a little planning and organization can minimize chaos before, during, and after moving day. The more prepared you are, the less stress you'll feel and the sooner you'll be able to settle in and start enjoying your new home and community. Need help? Call in a professional organizer.

Planning a Move

Like any big project, an organized move begins with a plan. Start by creating a simple checklist to help prepare for your upcoming move. If you have access to the Internet, go to www.MoversGuide.com, where you can create a personalized moving checklist and timeline. At this site, you can also get maps and directions, purchase packing supplies, rent a moving truck, and make arrangements to connect utilities. You can also generate a personalized moving checklist at www.Homestore.com/moving. A Web site with a good standard checklist can be found at www.ClubMom.com. If you don't have access to the Internet, make your own simple checklist and timeline using the one on page 241 as a guide.

How Will You Move? The first decision to make is how to get your belongings from point A to point B. Should you hire a moving company or do it yourself? The answer depends on how much time and money you are willing to spend. Generally, the least expensive option is to rent a moving truck, pack up your stuff, and enlist the help of friends to load and unload everything. But cost shouldn't be the only consideration. Also consider your ability to lift and carry heavy furniture without damaging it, the walls, or your back. Keep in mind that your moving expenses may be tax-deductible, which makes hiring a professional mover more affordable. If you have more money than time, get an estimate for having the mover pack and unpack your belongings as well as move them.

If you are considering hiring a moving company, the United States Department of Transportation recommends the following:

- Get estimates from at least three companies. Ask about the conditions of each estimate (for instance, is it guaranteed not to exceed a certain amount?).
- Ask for each company's motor carrier number and call the Department of Transportation at 202-358-7000 to find out if they are properly registered and insured.
- Ask your moving company for a copy of *Your Mover's Rights and Responsibilities,* a publication of the Department of Transportation.

Don't base your selection on price only. If possible, get referrals from friends, family members, and business colleagues. Get a written estimate from each moving company you contact. If you are putting things into storage, you might want to get an estimate for having the movers do that for you. Don't forget to ask about payment policies. Will the mover bill for services? If not, will the mover accept a check on the day of the move, or do they require a money order?

Utilities. About three weeks before your move, arrange to disconnect utilities at your current residence and reconnect them at your new residence. You will need to cancel trash collection, lawn and yard care services, and delivery services. Use the spreadsheet software on your computer to create a chart like the one below. Print and keep this document with you on moving day so that you can follow up if needed.

Utilities and Services Record

New address: _____

New phone number: _____ New fax number: _____ New e-mail address: _____

Utility/Service	Date to Cancel	Date to Restart	Confirmation #	New Provider	Phone Number	Notes
Electric						
Gas						
Local phone						
Long-distance carrier*						
Cable** or satellite TV						
Internet						
Water and sewer						
Delivery services						
Garbage removal						
Lawn and yard care						
Other services						

*You will need to get your new phone number first.
**Make arrangements to have your cable box picked up to avoid charges.

Moving Checklist and Timeline

Following is a sample four-week schedule for moving. If you have more or less time, adjust the schedule accordingly. To allow yourself enough time for each step, get started as soon as you know you are moving.

When to Do It	What to Do
As soon as possible	• Select a mover or reserve a truck rental • Create a checklist and timeline
4 weeks before	• Submit official change of address form to post office • Notify banks, creditors, and other businesses of your new address • Arrange for transferring children to a new school • Get packing supplies • Begin packing belongings
2–3 weeks before	• Make arrangements to disconnect and reconnect utilities and cancel services
1–2 weeks before	• Drop off donations at a local charity or arrange for pickup • Begin your final house cleaning • Start saying goodbyes
1–2 days before	• Finish packing boxes • Back up computer files • Get traveler's checks if needed • Pack your moving day survival kit • Pack or give away refrigerator and freezer items • Clean refrigerator and defrost freezer
Moving day	• Direct movers • Vacuum and mop floors room by room
After your move	• Send moving announcements to friends, family, and clients

Plan to have utilities switched off at your old home the day *after* your move and switched on at your new residence the day *before* you move. Utilities are often switched off in the early morning hours; ask about this when you call and plan accordingly so that you are not without necessary services on the day of your move, such as electricity for vacuuming or telephone for emergencies. You may want to have a cellular phone on hand as a backup, especially if you are moving on a Friday or the day before a holiday. If you don't own one, you can rent one. That way, if your telephone service doesn't get connected, you can still make and receive calls. It's a good idea not to announce your new telephone number to the world until your service is hooked up. Sometimes, the number you get is not the number that was assigned when you placed your service order.

Easing the Transition. Are you moving with children? Contact the board of education in your new community to arrange for transferring or enrolling your children in schools there. Also make a point to talk to your children to learn how they feel about moving. This will give you an opportunity to address any concerns up front. Keep in mind that children will pick up on your emotions. If you're anxious and stressed out about moving, your anxiety may display itself in your children's behavior. In the weeks leading up to your move, find out as much as you can about your new community. You might try the following:

- Take a walk or drive around the new neighborhood.
- Make arrangements to visit the new school or day care facility.
- Stop by the local Chamber of Commerce to find out about things to do.
- Visit the local library or bookstores to find books on the area.
- Look on-line for information about your new community.
- Line up some extracurricular activities for your children at your destination.

Your Pets. Call your veterinarian to find out whether your pet will require any vaccinations before moving to your new location. Make arrangements to get copies of your pet's veterinary records, including a record of rabies vaccination if you do not have one. Call local officials in your new location to find out about pet licensing requirements, leash laws, and other ordinances. To find a veterinarian in your new neighborhood, ask your current veterinarian for a referral, check the Yellow Pages, or contact The American Animal Hospital Association at 800-883-6301 or at www.healthypet.com.

TIME-SAVER

Order new address labels or an address stamp with your new address as soon as you know it. If you receive your order early enough, you can use your labels or stamp to fill out change of address notifications, which will be faster than writing each one by hand.

Announcing Your Move

Make sure your mail moves with you by filing a change of address form with the U.S. Postal Service at least one month or more of your scheduled move date. You can pick up this form at any post office, or fill one out on-line at www.MoversGuide.com. First-class mail and packages will be forwarded to your new address for one year. Magazines and newspapers will be forwarded for sixty days. Catalogs and advertising mail will not be forwarded.

You can speed up the forwarding process by notifying personal and professional contacts of your new address. The Movers Guide packet available at post offices includes postcards you can use for this purpose. Or you can send a fax or e-mail form letter, or call everyone who sends you mail, including:

- Credit card companies
- Banks and savings and lending institutions
- Insurance agents
- Investment agents or institutions
- Physicians, dentists, and veterinarian (when you contact your family physician and dentist, arrange to have your medical records mailed to your new address or sent to your new physician and dentist)
- Attorney and accountant
- Schools and colleges
- Club memberships, including frequent flyer programs
- Magazines and newspapers
- Social Security Administration, if you are currently receiving benefits (800-772-1213 or www.ssa.gov)

MOVING ON

If you're moving to a new home, chances are you'll be buying new stuff to fit that home's decor. Remember that before packing. Give to charity any overabundance of linens, decorative items, duplicate kitchen gadgets, old cookware, and other items you don't use now or won't use later.

—Pat S. Moore, The Queen of Clutter

- Department of Motor Vehicles
- Board of Elections (for voter registration)
- Internal Revenue Service (800-TAX-FORM or www.irs.gov)
- Employer and previous employer (if you are expecting a wage statement for this tax year and if you have a pension plan with any previous employer)
- Clients (if self-employed)
- Friends and family

At www.Homestore.com/moving, you can create and send a free on-line postcard to family and friends by using one of the available photographs or one of your own. Or do an on-line search using the keywords "virtual postcards," and adapt a standard greeting card to suit your purposes.

The easiest way to notify anyone who sends you bills is to make a note of your new address on the next bill you receive. If you are paying the bill before your move, be sure to include an effective date for your new address. If you call magazines with your change of address, ask whether they handle address changes for any other magazines to which you subscribe.

Packing and Organizing

Moving is a good time to lighten your load, especially if you are moving to a smaller home or plan to change your decor. Resolve to take only what you can use at your new home and leave everything else behind. Less stuff means less time spent packing and unpacking and less expense for moving. And best of all, it also means more space at your new place!

As you are packing, ask yourself the following questions:

- Is this item worth the time it will take to pack and unpack it?
- Is it worth the expense of moving it?
- Will it fit in with the decor of my new home?
- Does it still fit my lifestyle?
- Am I the rightful owner of this item?

If you answer "no" to any of these questions, don't pack it and don't take it with you. For more help in determining whether you should take an item or leave it behind, take the "Keep or Toss" quiz on page 13.

As you start packing, keep a trash bag or box handy for those things that can be thrown away. Label one box "Give Away" and use it to collect items that you can donate to charity. When that box is full, start another one. Keep

all of your donation boxes together in one room, separate from moving boxes. If you want to have a garage sale, do it at your current location before you move. There's no sense in moving things you plan to get rid of.

Packing is a time-consuming job; get started sooner rather than later. If you're overwhelmed by the thought of packing up everything you own, take it one day at a time. Pack four boxes a day, and you'll have 112 boxes packed in four weeks. Enlist some help from family and friends, and it'll go even faster.

You're going to need lots of boxes, probably more than you think. You can purchase boxes from your mover or rental company, or if you are on a limited budget, ask at your local drug, liquor, or grocery store if they can set aside some boxes for you. Also look for lidded copy

Packing Supplies

❏ Packing boxes in assorted sizes
❏ Packing paper (plain newsprint is best)
❏ Bubble wrap for fragile items
❏ Wide-tip markers for labeling boxes
❏ Rolls of packing tape
❏ Packing tape dispensers

paper boxes that you can bring home from work. It's helpful to have an assortment of boxes for packing various items:

- Larger boxes for lighter but bulky items, such as pillows and lampshades
- Smaller boxes for heavier items, such as books and paper files
- Wine or liquor cartons for fragile items
- Dish-pack boxes for dishes
- Special boxes for artwork and mirrors
- Wardrobe boxes for clothes
- Banker storage boxes for hanging files and fragile items
- Lidded copy paper boxes for fragile items
- Large, clear plastic bags are convenient for transporting unbreakable, unwieldy items such as wicker baskets

You may be able to leave clothes in dresser drawers and files in file cabinet drawers. Just remove and carry each drawer into the moving

truck, then replace drawers once you load the dresser or file cabinet. If you hired a moving company, ask if they will do that for you. Also ask if you can borrow wardrobe boxes; if not, purchase them. On moving day, transfer hanging clothes from your closets to the wardrobe boxes. Once the boxes arrive at your destination, simply remove clothes from the boxes and hang them in your new closets. A wardrobe box is about two feet wide, so if you have a ten-foot closet rod, you will need approximately five boxes. You can use the bottom of each wardrobe box to transport shoes. Bag each pair individually so you don't have to match them up at the other end. Or pack sweaters and jeans in plastic bags and put them at the bottom of the wardrobe box.

Start in a room that does not get regular use, such as a guest room, attic, basement, or formal dining room. You may need to repack things like holiday decorations to reduce the possibility of damage during shipping. Also repack boxes that are ripped or missing flaps or lids. Stack boxes neatly along one wall so that you can still walk through the room.

Pack one room at a time, keeping similar items, such as pots and pans, together in boxes. In each room, pack things you don't use or won't be needing for the next few weeks first and leave more frequently used items to be packed last. In the family room, for example, you might start by taking down and packing wall hangings or books and pack audio and videotapes last. If you have tapes organized alphabetically or by category, use a rubber band to keep them together, especially if you have movers packing for you. Leave the kitchen for last. Plan to use plastic utensils and paper plates and cups for the last few meals before moving so you can pack all of your dishes. Or keep out just enough dishes for your family and include them with your moving day essentials.

Label each box with the room name on all four sides, at the top right of each panel. Use a wide-tip felt marker and print clearly, preferably in capital letters. Under the room name, add the word *Fragile* if contents are breakable, or "This Side Up" with an arrow if the box contains a lamp or other items that should not be tipped upside down. On one side of the box, list the general or specific contents of that box. Or label boxes with the room name and a number and then keep a master list of what is in each box.

Pack heavier items at the bottom of each box and lighter items at the top. Use blank newspaper sheets to wrap breakables. You can buy sheets from your moving company. If you're on a limited budget, ask your local newspaper publisher if you could have their "end rolls," which is the unusable paper at the end of each roll of newsprint. Do not use printed newspapers; the ink tends to rub off on things, which makes more work at the other end.

ABCs OF PACKING

Everything you pack does not have to be unpacked the first day in your new home. If it contains essential items, mark it A. If the contents are important, but not crucial, mark the box B. If the box contains out-of-season items, holiday items, and other things you won't need right away, mark the box C. Then unpack in A, B, C order.

—Maria Gracia, Get Organized Now!

When packing fragile items, crumple up newsprint to provide extra padding on the bottom of the box, between items, and on top of contents. To wrap and pad larger kitchen breakables, you can use dish towels. In the bathroom, use washcloths, hand and bath towels to wrap and pad breakable bathroom items. Use sofa and bed pillows or light blankets to pad boxes that contain larger fragile items, such as statues or jewelry boxes. Do not pack fragile items with heavy items.

Pack and fill each box tightly to prevent contents from shifting during transport. But don't overload boxes. Keep them to a manageable weight, especially if you are doing your own lifting and moving. If you have space at the top of a box, fill it tightly to the top with crumpled newspaper so that other boxes can be stacked on top without crushing it. Secure boxes by taping the flaps closed, and reinforce the bottom with a strip of packing tape that wraps around the edges of the box.

Some items require special care when packing to avoid mishaps and damage during shipping. There are also things you can do to help speed up the process of settling in. Following are some suggestions for both.

- Pack opened bottles, jars, tubes, and containers in resealable plastic bags in case they leak.
- Remove and wrap ceramic and glass lids separately from the main item.
- Pack small, fragile items in small boxes that can be packed together in a larger box.
- Wrap small items in colored tissue to help prevent them from getting lost in a carton.
- Wrap each piece of china and glassware individually.
- Pack albums and CDs vertically, not flat, with large hardcover books on either end and mark the box "Fragile."
- Pack same-size books together, either flat or upright.
- Use original packaging to pack computer and electronic equipment.
- Cover both sides of mattresses with fitted sheets to keep them clean (you can always wash the sheets).
- Use blankets to protect wood furniture from nicks and scratches.
- As you remove artwork and decorations from walls, tape hardware for hanging to the back of the item.
- Put hardware from disassembled items into a labeled bag; tape the bag to the item.
- Ask a nursery about the best way to transport your plants.
- Drain gas and oil from power equipment.

- Use clean and disinfected trash cans with lids to transport outdoor toys or gardening tools and supplies.

Keep in mind that moving companies cannot transport items that are flammable, corrosive, or explosive. This includes but is not limited to aerosol products, matches, paint thinner and paints, pesticides, cooking fuel, lamp oil, liquid bleach, ammonia, and other cleaning solvents. Dispose of these products before moving, or take them with you in your car. Moving companies

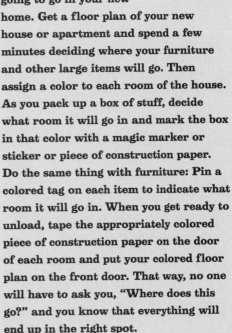

WHERE DOES THIS GO?

When packing up your stuff, think about where everything is going to go in your new home. Get a floor plan of your new house or apartment and spend a few minutes deciding where your furniture and other large items will go. Then assign a color to each room of the house. As you pack up a box of stuff, decide what room it will go in and mark the box in that color with a magic marker or sticker or piece of construction paper. Do the same thing with furniture: Pin a colored tag on each item to indicate what room it will go in. When you get ready to unload, tape the appropriately colored piece of construction paper on the door of each room and put your colored floor plan on the front door. That way, no one will have to ask you, "Where does this go?" and you know that everything will end up in the right spot.

—Ramona Creel, OnlineOrganizing.com

moving day essentials

Your moving day essentials might include the following:

- Maps and directions to your new home for you and mover (exchange cell-phone numbers, too, if available)

- Paperwork and payment for moving company
- Vital phone numbers
- Record of utility and service connections (page 240)
- Pen and notepad
- Medications for family and pets
- Aspirin or other pain reliever
- Basic tools and a flashlight
- Cleaning products and tools
- Trash bags
- Toilet paper

- Toothpaste, soap, shampoo, and shower curtain
- Snacks and drinks
- Disposable plates, cups and utensils
- Dish detergent, sponge, paper towels
- Telephone (not cordless)
- Knife for opening sealed boxes
- Alarm clock
- Night lights

also cannot transport food, plants, or living things that may die or spoil in transit. Decide beforehand where you will donate anything that you cannot take with you. You may be able to donate unopened foodstuffs to a food pantry; folks living in a nursing home might appreciate getting some houseplants. Items that are not recommended for shipping include items with sentimental or monetary value and furs.

Moving Day

The day before moving, have each family member pack an overnight bag that includes one complete change of clothes, night clothes, toothbrush, and other necessities for the next twenty-four hours. For children, necessities might also include diapers, a favorite stuffed animal, blanket, and toy or game. Pack these bags into your car, not the moving truck. That way, you won't have to go searching through boxes, and you'll have what you need if the moving truck gets delayed. If you are driving the moving truck yourself, load these bags into the truck last so that they are the first to be unloaded at your destination.

Pack a bag for your pets, too. Include enough food for the next twenty-four hours, food and water bowls, treats, toys, and leash. Be sure that your pets are wearing identification tags in case they get loose. It's a good idea to put your pets in kennels or carriers before the movers arrive. Or confine them to one room, close the door, and place a note on the door that says, "Do Not Enter — Pets Inside." As much as possible, try to maintain your pet's regular feeding and exercise schedule on moving day.

Other things to have in your possession on moving day include paperwork and payment for the mover, important documents or computer discs, medications, maps, jewelry, and other valuables. Pack these items in a briefcase or tote bag that you can keep at your side. If you have a fireproof lock box, put valuables inside and lock it in your trunk. Pack kitchen, bathroom, and bedroom necessities and other essentials in boxes labeled "Open First" and load

One Challenge . . .

I'm in the process of moving my eighty-year-old mother from the three-bedroom home where she's lived for thirty years into an efficiency apartment. How can I help her "downsize" without feeling like she has to give up everything?

Three Solutions

1 FROM HELEN VOLK, BEYOND CLUTTER: I find that it helps if you can get the elderly to concentrate on one thing, and that is, what they're going to take with them. With the smaller stuff, I suggest that they choose what *they* want first. Then make decisions about what to give to family members. Surrounding themselves with things they love will help them to feel more at home in their new surroundings.

2 FROM JAN LIMPACH, ORGANIZING PLUS: It's important that at least some items with sentimental value make the move to the new residence. I bring my clients catalogs so that they can choose bookcases and shelving to hold their most precious photos and mementos. For everything else, it's easier to let go if they know that someone will use and enjoy these things. Usually we start with "Who can this go to that I know?" Then we move on to "Who can this go to that I don't know?"

3 FROM PAT S. MOORE, THE QUEEN OF CLUTTER: It's helpful to measure the rooms in the new home and draw a simple floor plan. Many retirement homes provide such drawings. Many home improvement stores sell a simple kit with furniture templates that you can use to arrange the rooms on paper. This will help tremendously in deciding what goes with her and what just goes. Also, as you're trying to make the decision of what to keep, collect all of the same type of item together. When you see all forty lamps together, it's easier to choose the three you like or need.

these boxes on the truck last. Or, if you prefer to move them yourself, label them "This Stays Here" so that the movers do not take them.

Consider arranging for children to stay with a friend or relative on moving day. If the kids will be present, give them a job to do or direct them to a designated play area so that they do not interfere with the loading and unloading. Or you can put your children to work unpacking their own things. Older children may be able to help out and direct movers to the appropriate rooms or help you to make beds.

Unpacking and Settling In

Plan to set up one room completely as soon as possible so that you have a place to take refuge from all the boxes elsewhere in your house or apartment. If you can't set up a whole room on the first day, there are some things you can do to make the first night and day in your new home more comfortable and fun.

- Make up everyone's bed, or have the whole family camp out in the living room.
- Put beverages in the refrigerator and favorite snacks in a cupboard.
- Hook up your telephone and order takeout for dinner, or go out to eat.
- Hook up the television and VCR, find the nearest video rental store, and spend the evening watching a movie.
- Make sure there is toilet paper in every bathroom.
- Hang a shower curtain if needed and put out towels, soap, and shampoo.

> ### THE PAPERING TECHNIQUE
>
> **Show movers where furniture belongs in each room by writing the words "Bed Here" or "Desk Here" on a sheet of brightly colored 8x11-inch paper. Then place the paper where you want that particular piece of furniture to go.**
>
> —*Donna D. McMillan, McMillan & Company Professional Organizing*

Unpack one room at a time. Put furniture where you want it and then start unpacking boxes. Don't put things just anywhere; find a place for everything. If you can't find a place for something, put it in a box labeled "Store Elsewhere." Bring that box with you to the next room. If, after unpacking and organizing all rooms, you still have things in the "Store Elsewhere" box, you'll need to decide what to do with those things. In addition to the "Store Elsewhere" box, you'll need large trash bags for collecting all the newsprint, which you can burn in your fireplace or recycle. Remove tape from empty boxes and flatten. Save them only if you know you will be moving again within the year or if you have enough space to store them. Recycle boxes you do not need. Pack small and medium flattened boxes into a large box for easy removal.

Professional organizers Lynn and Kevin Hall of Clutter No More, Inc., suggest using a ticking kitchen timer to get things done. Set the timer when you feel overwhelmed looking at a stack of boxes to be emptied. The ticking timer keeps you going at a quick pace and helps you stay focused. Stop working on the project when the timer goes off. Reset the timer if you want to continue.

If you have pets, keep them confined for the first few days until they get adjusted to their new surroundings. If your pets go outside, keep them leashed to prevent them from running away in an attempt to get back to their old neighborhood.

It's natural to want to get settled in as soon as possible, but don't spend all your time unpacking. Take time to explore your new neighborhood and get familiar with your surroundings. Plan weekly outings with your family to explore cultural and recreational offerings.

Combining Households

One of the biggest moving challenges is trying to merge two fully furnished homes into one. Whatever you do, don't attempt to move everything from both homes and *then* decide what to do with it. It doesn't make sense to move things twice, and the sheer volume of stuff will put unnecessary strain on your relationship.

Make an agreement to make a fresh start. Bring to your new home only the things you really love or use on a regular basis, and give the rest away. Sometimes it's easier to let go of things if you can find new homes for them. Think of family members or friends who may have admired a particular item in the past or could use something you no longer need. Or donate items to a charity with the knowledge that someone will appreciate your gift.

You may be able to help each other decide what goes and what stays with this exercise: The next time your loved one is in your home, have him or her make a list of those things he or she really likes. You do the same at his or her place. Use your lists to start a master list of things that you will definitely want to move into your combined household.

Give yourselves plenty of time — anywhere from six weeks to six months — so you can do a really thorough job of uncluttering. How long you need depends on several factors, including the size of your existing and prospective homes, how long you've lived at your existing addresses, how much stuff you've collected over the years, and how much time you are willing to devote to uncluttering.

Spend some time uncluttering your home every day. You'll find plenty of helpful ideas in chapter 2, "Uncluttering Your Home." On weekends, help each other tackle bigger projects, such as uncluttering basements, attics, and closets, and sorting through memorabilia. Don't be surprised if you learn more about each other in the process! Be prepared to accept the fact that both of you are going to keep things the other one thinks are crazy to save.

Selling Your Home

As soon as you decide to move, you should put your home on the market. Four out of five home sellers use a realtor to list and sell their homes. To find a good realtor, ask people who have sold their homes recently if they would use their realtor again. The realtor you choose to list your home should work full time and have at least several years of experience in the business. It's a good idea to interview several realtors before signing with one. Ask where, when, and how often your property will be advertised. And don't get locked into a long-term listing contract without a reasonable cancellation clause so that you can change realtors if you are not satisfied with performance.

Selling your home directly to prospective buyers is the alternative to listing with an agent. The upside is that you might be able to sell your home without having to pay the agent's commission. The downside is that you may not be able to reach as many prospective buyers as you can when you list your home with a Multiple Listing Service (MLS), which is available through realtors. You'll also have to pay for your own brochures and advertising, field all telephone inquiries, be readily available to show your home to prospective buyers, and negotiate all offers on your own.

Regardless of how you decide to sell your home, you will need to locate the deed to your property, current tax bill, information pertaining to any liens, and Homeowners' Association documents if applicable. You'll also need to estimate the value of your property and set your price. A realtor can provide you with a comparative market analysis of recent home sale prices in your area. Or you can do a little research on your own by checking real estate listings for similar properties. Then consider how much you paid for your property, the condition of your property, how much you put into home improvements, and how much you want to make after all transaction fees are paid. Figure on 1 percent of the selling price for closing fees (attorney fees, title search, and recording fees) and another 1 percent if the seller pays the buyer's mortgage costs in your state. If you are using a realtor, you'll have the brokerage fee as well, which is typically 6 to 8 percent of the purchase price. But don't overprice your home in an effort to offset these fees, as overpriced homes are less likely to sell.

Real estate agents agree that a home shows best when it is clean, uncluttered, and nicely furnished. The next best way to show a house is completely empty. So if you need to move before you sell your home, plan to take everything with you and leave it spotless. If you can afford to make major repairs, you should, because some things, such as a leaky roof or rotting deck, could deter prospective buyers and make it harder to sell your home.

The Home Show

Don't underestimate the power of first impressions when it comes to showing your home. Here are some simple, inexpensive things you can do to increase the "curbside" appeal and marketability of your home.

Outdoors
❏ Take care of any minor repairs such as broken windows or gutters.

❏ Mow your lawn and weed your garden.

❏ Pick up any debris that may have fallen or blown into your yard.

❏ Put trash cans out of sight; keep the garage door closed.

❏ Plant a few annual flowers near the entrance or buy a few potted or hanging plants.

❏ Repaint the exterior of your home if needed.

❏ Wash windows.

Indoors
❏ Give your house a thorough cleaning, from top to bottom.

❏ Unclutter and organize every room including storage areas.

❏ Unclutter and organize closets and kitchen cabinets.

❏ Fix simple things like loose doorknobs, broken doorbells, and leaky faucets.

❏ Eliminate bad odors at the source.

❏ Make your home look, smell, and feel cozy for prospective buyers: put out vases of cut flowers, light scented candles or a fireplace, bake bread or cookies, or simmer something "homey" on the stovetop.

❏ Open blinds and curtains and turn on all lights to create a feeling of spaciousness and light.

❏ Turn off the television for "show time."

MAPPING YOUR MOVE

Get a detailed street map of your new neighborhood and study it before you move so you don't feel totally lost when you get there. Lessen relocation stress for your children by making a copy of the map for each child. Mark the location of your new home, their schools, community playgrounds, movie theaters, and other kid-oriented attractions. You can further relieve your children's stress by giving them photographs of your new home that they can show to friends.

CHAPTER 26

NEW BEGINNINGS

Life's big events come hand in hand with opportunities to test your organizational skills. Whatever your new adventure — adopting a pet, preparing to welcome a new baby into your home, or sending the kids off to college — you can be better prepared to handle the transition smoothly and efficiently with advance preparation. Grab a pen and start making a list!

Adopting a Pet

Now is not always the right time to get a pet. But when the time *is* right, the investment of time and energy pays off in years of companionship and love.

Are you ready for a pet? It's sad, but the main reason why so many dogs and cats end up in shelters is because their owners were unprepared for the realities of pet ownership. Cuddly kittens and puppies can be quite destructive and often require more work than expected. And, as they grow into full-sized pets, they demand loving care, training, and medical attention that can sometimes be costly.

Keep in mind, too, that having a pet means more housecleaning. Cats tend to track litter out of the litter box. Dogs come indoors with

muddy paws. Both shed. Expect to do more vacuuming, especially if you choose a long-haired pet.

Would this be your first pet? Talk to pet owners about the pros and cons of pet ownership. If you don't have the time or energy required to care for and train a puppy or kitten, you might consider adopting an older animal from a humane shelter. They're more difficult to place in homes than are younger animals, even though they often are already trained and make the best pets.

Do some research to find out what breeds are best suited to your personality and lifestyle. For example, Greyhounds are more suited than other dogs to being home alone all day because they sleep 90 percent of the day.

Others, especially large breeds, need a fair amount of exercise each day. Some breeds of cats, such as the American Bobtail, make great traveling companions. Others, such as the Maine Coon, tend to get along very well with the family dog. If you have children, talk to a veterinarian about what breeds of dogs and cats are best with children.

If you would like to buy a purebred animal, be sure to buy from a reputable breeder. It's a good idea to see the mother and father if possible so that you can observe their temperaments as well as physical traits. A good breeder is generally very particular about placing puppies and kittens with new owners and may even have you sign a contract stating that you will feed your pet a particular brand of food or that you will send photos of him on a regular basis.

Whichever type of pet you choose, you'll need to budget for medical care in addition to food and toys. Unless you plan to breed your pet, get your cat or dog neutered or spayed so that you don't end up with an unexpected litter. Also plan to take your pet to the veterinarian at least once a year for a checkup and vaccinations.

Bringing Your Pet Home. Cats and dogs, especially kittens and puppies, are naturally curious. Before you bring your pet home, take a walk around your home and look for accidents waiting to happen. Look high and low. Do you see any dangling electrical cords? Is there anything that could topple and fall if bumped? Keep in mind that cats like high places. You may want to move breakables into a safer stor-

age place, at least for a while. Cats and dogs sometimes learn to open cabinet doors, so be sure to store household cleaning products and other hazardous substances in upper cabinets or shelves. See page 225 for more information on pet safety.

Prepare as much as possible before bringing your new pet home. Where will he sleep? Who will be responsible for feeding or walking him?

What You Need

Pets need things, too. Here's a list of some essentials you'll want to have on hand.

- ❏ Water bowl
- ❏ Food dish
- ❏ Leash (for outdoor pets)
- ❏ Collar
- ❏ Identification tag
- ❏ Dry food
- ❏ Canned food (optional)
- ❏ Treats (especially good for puppy training)
- ❏ Litter, litter box, and plastic scooper (for cats)
- ❏ Scratching post (for cats)
- ❏ Safe chew toys (for dogs)
- ❏ Grooming brush
- ❏ Flea comb
- ❏ Nail clippers
- ❏ File folder for medical records
- ❏ Dog crate or cat carrier

What will you feed him? What will you do with him when you go to work each day? What will you do with him when you go on vacation or you are traveling? Will your new pet be allowed on the furniture? Have all the supplies you need before you bring your new pet home (see checklist on page 255). Make a list and bring it with you to your nearest pet supply store.

When you bring your new pet home, confine him to one room at first so that he can get familiar with his new surroundings. Then gradually, over the next few days, introduce him to the rest of the house. Right away, begin to establish sleeping, eating, and playing routines. Eventually, you'll want to expose your pet to other people and even other pets, but don't rush into it. Give your pet time to adjust to his new home. And play it safe. Confine your puppy or kitten to a room with a closed door when your attention is needed elsewhere or you need to go out. You may be able to use a baby gate to confine your puppy to one area of your home such as the kitchen.

Housebreaking Your Pet. Housebreaking a kitten is generally very easy. Just fill a box with litter and set your kitten in it after he drinks or eats. You might want to hold his front paws and make digging motions in the litter. If he doesn't use the litter box right then, don't worry. He'll be back. Place the litter box in a low-traffic, quiet area away from your kitten's food and water. If you adopt an older cat that is not using the litter box, call your veterinarian for advice.

Dogs present more of a housebreaking challenge. Paper training is best if you will be away all day. If you're home during the day or able to check in frequently, crate training is the preferred method for housebreaking.

Paper-Training 101. Paper training is a simple two-step method that helps puppies learn to use a specified area for elimination, then helps them make the transition to going outdoors.

1. Confine your puppy to a safe, enclosed area with a tile or linoleum floor. You may be able to use a baby gate as a doggy gate.
2. Cover the floor with newspaper. The puddles and piles may be random at first, but soon your puppy will choose one area far from his food and bed to make his "spot."
3. Layer several dirty papers on "the spot" to give it a strong scent so the puppy will be attracted there. Dogs prefer to eliminate where they have gone before.
4. Gradually shrink the paper-covered area until it is fairly small.
5. When you are home, help your puppy make the transition to eliminating outdoors by taking him out immediately after waking, playing, and eating; before going to bed; and any time your puppy heads for his indoor "spot" or the door.

Crate-Training 101. Dogs are clean animals and won't soil the place where they sleep. Crate training uses this natural instinct to help your puppy develop bladder and bowel control.

1. Introduce your puppy to his crate, which should be big enough for him to turn around and lie down comfortably. Or put a cardboard box at the back of an adult-size crate to make it puppy size.

2. Throw a treat or toy inside the crate and have your puppy go get it. Say a command like "In your crate!" or "Kennel!" Always praise him or give him a treat so that going into the crate is associated with pleasant experiences.

3. Crate your puppy at intervals throughout the day. Young puppies need lots of rest. Restrict your puppy to the safety of his crate whenever you cannot watch him closely, for naps, and at bedtime.

4. Take your puppy outdoors to eliminate. After waking, playing, or eating, ask your puppy, "Do you want to go out?" and then take him outdoors to the spot where you'd like him to go.

5. Praise your puppy for doing "it." Wait until your puppy starts eliminating and then say a command phrase, such as "Do it!" or "Go for it!" Lay on lots of praise.

6. Do not crate your puppy for any longer than 2 to 3 hours at a stretch. That's about as long as a 6- to 8-week old puppy can hold his bladder. For the first month or so, you'll need to get up a few times in the middle of the night to take your puppy out.

TIME-SAVER

60

To quickly clean pet hair from upholstery in your car and home, lightly wet your hand and run it across the fabric. Or don a latex glove and do the same thing — the hair will stick to the glove. A damp sponge or foam ball or masking tape also make quick picker-uppers.

Preparing for a Baby

A new baby brings so much joy — and so many organizational challenges. But getting ready is half the fun. Start your preparations early so you can savor the anticipation of your new arrival without feeling hurried or pressured.

Begin with the financial decisions surrounding your child's entrance into your world. The first thing your baby needs is adequate health insurance. Review your policy. Most health maintenance organizations cover maternity and well-baby care as well as hospitalization. More traditional plans do not always cover well-baby care visits. If you are pregnant now and don't have health insurance, you will need a plan that covers preexisting conditions. Your new baby (and other children) may be eligible for free or low-cost health insurance through the federal government's Insure Kids Now! Program, which is available in every state in the United States (see page 327).

Two other types of insurance to consider are disability and life insurance. Even if your employer provides disability insurance, you

baby basics

Following is a list of essentials for your baby's first month at home.

Coming home
- Newborn (rear-facing) car seat
- Outfit to wear home
- Six receiving blankets

Feeding and changing
- Baby bottles and formula (four to six 4-ounce bottles and six to eight 8-ounce bottles)
- Nursing supplies if you will be nursing (breast pump, two or more nursing bras, easy-access sleepwear)
- Six to eight bibs
- Up to a dozen burping cloths
- Five to eight diapers per day
- Diaper pail with locking lid (if using deodorizer cakes)
- Baby wipes
- Diaper rash ointment or petroleum jelly
- Three to four changing pad covers

Clothing
- Four to six nightgowns or sleeping sacks
- Four to eight one-piece coveralls with snaps
- Three to four short- or long-sleeved outfits (with feet for winter)
- Four to five undershirts
- One dress-up outfit
- One to two machine washable sweaters
- One to two hats
- Two pairs of booties
- Six pairs of stretchy socks
- Warm outerwear for cold weather

Bedding
- Crib bumper
- Three to four sets of crib sheets
- Two to three baby blankets
- Two to four waterproof mattress pads

Bathing
- Newborn tub
- Four to six washcloths
- Two to four hooded towels
- Baby shampoo and soap
- Baby lotion

Health care and grooming
- Cotton swabs and alcohol (for umbilical cord)
- Thermometer (rectal, tympanic, or axillary)
- Ear bulb or aspirator
- Saline nose drops
- Acetaminophen drops
- Baby nail clippers or scissors
- Brush and comb

Getting up and out
- Infant seat
- Cloth baby carrier
- Two or more pacifiers
- Diaper bag with portable changing mat
- Infant stroller or carriage

may wish to supplement it by buying additional coverage. Disability insurance pays benefits when you are unable to work. While life insurance is not necessary for single people or married couples without children, it's definitely something to consider when you have a young one counting on you for financial support. Both parents should be insured. See pages 117 and 118 for additional information about life and disability insurance.

With a child on the way, you need a simple will and trust that outlines how you wish to provide for your child in the event of your death. You'll need to name a guardian for your child and a trustee who will manage the inheritance. If you don't have a will, the state court will choose a guardian and trustee and split up your property in a way that might not be your first choice. Think about who you would want to watch over your child and your estate if you could not do so. Then make an appointment with an attorney to draw up a simple will and trust.

It may seem like a long way off, but your new arrival will be graduating from high school and heading off for college before you know it. The sooner you start saving, the more money you'll have to finance your child's education. See page 141 for tips on how to save painlessly. Then consult with your financial planner to determine the best plan for you.

Outfitting the Nursery

If you haven't started preparing your baby's room by your sixth or seventh month of pregnancy, now's the time. The first step is to furnish

and decorate the room where you will put your baby to sleep, change diapers, and store your baby's clothes and other necessities. Start by cleaning out the closet to make room for baby things. Consider adding shelving for easy access.

As you are decorating your child's room, keep in mind that nursery-themed wallpaper will become outdated as your little one grows. Look for wall decorations that can be peeled off later. Or paint the walls with washable latex paint and buy sheets, blankets, crib bumper, comforter, curtains, and other furnishings with your choice of decorative theme. When you want to update the look of the room, simply change the furnishings. Avoid throw rugs in the nursery that may cause you to slip or trip when carrying your baby.

Basic furniture for baby-to-be includes a crib, sturdy changing table, and dresser. The crib mattress should fit snugly in the crib with no more than two fingers' width between the crib and the mattress. Buy them together to make sure of a good fit. If you buy a used crib, check the labeling to make sure that it meets federal safety regulations and industry voluntary standards (those of the American Society for Testing and Materials). Consider getting a rocking chair or glider and ottoman if you don't have one. Babies love the comforting head-to-toe rocking motion. You might also consider getting a bassinet or cradle so you can keep your newborn in your bedroom. If your baby will be sleeping in the nursery, you might want to get a baby monitor.

You don't have to spend a fortune outfitting the nursery. Resist the urge to run out and buy stuff right away. Instead, set aside money each month while you are expecting. Look all you want, but do your buying in the last trimester.

Final Preparations. Tie up loose ends during your last trimester. Once your baby gets home, you'll want to be able to give him or her your full attention.

- Find a pediatrician.
- Set up interviews with child care professionals and choose one.
- Baby-proof your home.
- Learn baby cardiopulmonary resuscitation.

- Subscribe to a parenting magazine.
- Arrange for someone to care for pets and other children while you are in the hospital or picking up your adopted child.
- Create or shop for birth announcements and address the envelopes.
- Cook and freeze some meals.
- Do a thorough housecleaning before you bring your baby home.
- Set up the crib and changing table and organize baby things.
- Line up a friend or family member to help you during the first week or so.
- Make a list of people you want to notify right away by telephone. Prepare an e-mail message to send to a select group with or without scanned photos or photos uploaded to your computer from your digital camera. Or you can put photographs on your personal Web site, then send the address to friends and family.

As your due date approaches, memorize or keep your doctor's number with you at all times and don't hesitate to call if you have any questions or concerns. Pack an overnight bag with the things you want to bring to the hospital, including a comfortable, nonmaternity outfit to wear home. Make it a habit to keep enough gas in your gas tank to get you to the hospital; you won't want to stop on the way. Consider registering at the hospital in advance so that you don't have to fill out all the paperwork when you get there. It's also a good idea to map out and try more than one route to the hospital in case of road construction or closures.

Heading Off to College

Generally, colleges provide first-year students with a list of items to bring — and not to bring. Use these lists (or the one below) as a guideline for creating your own personalized list. Put a check in front of the items you already have. Estimate how much it will cost to buy what you don't have and establish a budget that will allow you to get everything you need before you leave for school.

If your list is long and you're short on cash, get "must-have" things first, such as bedding, books, and other school supplies. Then see whether you can borrow some of the "would-be-nice-to-have" things on your list. Or check out garage sales in your neighborhood.

One way to pare down your "to buy" list is to confer with your roommate about what he or she is bringing so that you can avoid cluttering your room with duplicate items, especially larger items, such as a television, stereo, and mini-fridge. For some things, such as area rugs, curtains, trashcans, and cleaning supplies, you can shop together and split the cost or divvy up what you need to buy.

Most likely, you won't be able to take all of your clothes with you. Choose to bring only the clothes you really love and wear on a regular basis and leave the rest at home. Also leave at home any seasonal clothing. You can always get these items when you come home on break. Bring a few week's worth of underwear

college basics

Following is a list of things you might need for your first year at college. If you are traveling by train or air or have a small car, consider buying some items when you get there.

- Two sets of sheets (most college dorm beds require extra-long twin sheets)
- Blankets, pillows, and bedspread
- Bedrest pillow (great for reading in bed)
- Two or three sets of towels
- Posters, wall hangings, area rug
- Television
- Stereo and music
- Mini-fridge
- Slippers, shower sandals
- Plastic shower caddy
- Personal hygiene items and cosmetics
- Multidrawer plastic storage unit for personal hygiene items and cosmetics
- Blow dryer
- Underbed storage containers
- Stackable crates or hanging bookshelves
- Large laundry bag and laundry supplies
- Backpack
- Portable umbrella
- School supplies (pencils, pens, highlighters, calculator, binders, notebooks, stapler, and paper clips)
- Clothing and accessories
- Major credit card with limit (for emergencies)
- Long-distance calling card
- First aid kit, sewing kit, small tool kit

and socks so you can spend more time studying and less time doing laundry. Good walking shoes are a must. Bring a bathing suit for the pool and some workout clothes, even if you think you won't do either. You might also want to bring one or two dressier outfits for special occasions. And don't forget your pajamas and robe.

You probably don't need as much stuff as you think. When deciding what to bring with you, look at what you use every day — things like your computer, television, stereo, sporting equipment, and telephone. If you forget something or realize that you need something, you can always go out and buy it or get it when you go home on break.

Organizing Your Dorm Room. Even if you don't bring a lot of stuff, it always seems like you brought too much. To avoid being overwhelmed by it all, make use of vertical storage space on walls and backs of doors. In closets, you may be able to install wire shelving to hold bulky sweaters or pegs to hold your laundry bag, pajamas and robe, book bag, or jacket. The more you can keep off the floor, the better. Stacking crates and hanging bookshelves also make good use of vertical space.

If available, use the space under your bed for storing extra sheets, shoes, and seldom-used items. A lidded plastic storage container does the trick. You might also be able to use a bookcase as a headboard, with storage for books and binders above and less frequently used items below your bed frame. A bed skirt will hide whatever you store underneath.

You'll also want to decorate your room. Bring things you can use to brighten up your room, express your personality, and help you feel more comfortable in your new surroundings. Hang your favorite posters, photographs, and artwork. Because space is limited, bring only the knick-knacks and mementos that are most meaningful to you. If an item is valuable, has deep sentimental value, or is desirable, such as an autographed baseball card or poster, it might be smart to leave it at home, to eliminate the possibility of its getting lost, stolen, or ruined.

great space-saving gadgets

Following are some organizational products that make efficient use of limited storage space in a dorm room.

- Under-the-bed storage containers
- Over-the-door towel rods
- Stacking, interlocking crates
- Rolling file cart or small filing cabinet
- Hanging book shelves
- Multitier shoe rack
- Stick-on plastic rods and hooks

CHAPTER 27

ORGANIZING YOUR ESTATE

No one likes to think about death and dying. But planning for the inevitable can alleviate a potentially huge emotional and financial burden on your family. Learn some simple things you can do to get your affairs in order today. In this chapter, you'll also learn what surviving family members need to do when a loved one dies — everything from obtaining the death certificate to settling the estate.

Estate Planning

Sooner or later, important decisions about your estate will need to be made. The best person to make these decisions is you. And the best time to make them is now.

An important part of estate organizing is estate planning. You may think that you don't need to do any estate planning because you haven't got "enough" in the way of assets. But estate planning isn't just for wealthy people. It's something that all of us should do for ourselves and our families.

Think of organizing your estate as a gift to your family — a gift that enables them to manage their grief without the added stress of trying to figure out what you would have wanted them to do. If you don't take the time to organize your estate, your heirs may lose part of it, whether it's to taxes, to probate fees, or simply because they are unaware of all of your assets.

Simply put, estate planning is doing *something* rather than *nothing* to prepare for the inevitability of death. Making a will, for example, ensures that what assets you do have are distributed as you wish — without controversy, wasted time, or unnecessary expense. It also establishes a plan for the physical and financial care of your dependents in the event of your death. And it can go a long way toward preventing the family upsets and bickering that often accompany the inheritance of property or its division when someone has not left a will specifying what should be done.

Another simple and smart thing you might want to do now is set up what's known as a *living revocable trust* for all of your titled property and assets. With a will alone, your estate must go through a court process before assets can be distributed. But by putting titled assets in the name of the trust ("The Jones Family Trust," for example) rather than leaving them in your name, you can pass these assets to your heirs quickly and easily — without federal estate tax, drawn-out estate proceedings, and unnecessary fees. A living revocable trust also protects your assets if you become incapacitated. For more information about the living revocable trust and other types of trusts, consult an attorney who specializes in setting up trusts.

Personal and Business Assets. The first step in organizing your estate is to identify and record all of your personal and business assets. This is important for three reasons:

1. In the event that you become incapacitated, the guardians of your estate will have to use your assets to take care of you.
2. All of your assets need to be found and accounted for before your estate can be settled.
3. Knowing what you have helps in planning to minimize or eliminate estate taxes.

Another good reason to do an inventory of your assets is that you may discover that your estate is worth more than you thought. Also, when you see an overview of your financial situation, you may decide to make some changes or decisions regarding your estate. For example, you may realize that you have more life insurance than you need or that you should get an appraisal on expensive jewelry, furs, or antiques. Your assets may include the following:

- Real property (home, rental, vacation, time-share, boats, etc.)
- Vehicles (automobile and recreational)
- Stocks, bonds, certificates
- Mutual funds, treasury bonds, notes, or bills
- IRAs and other retirement plans
- Annuities and royalties
- Life insurance benefits
- Money due you (bonus, alimony, child support, royalties, promissory notes)
- Prepaid assets (airline tickets not used, store credits, frequent flyer miles, etc.)
- Cash

Personal property is also an asset. But without a complete list of your personal property, it is difficult to put a dollar value on the possessions you've accumulated over time. Preparing a personal property inventory has the following benefits:

- It helps you to identify and record the location and value of your personal property.
- It helps you to decide what items you may want to bequeath to a particular heir.

- It can be used to ensure that you have the appropriate amount of homeowner's or renter's insurance.
- It serves as a valuable record of your possessions should you ever have a loss due to theft, fire, or other disaster.

Insurance companies and professional organizers recommend that you document the contents of every room. Working in one room at a time, record each item along with the year purchased, manufacturer's name and model (if applicable), and cost. If you have multiples of certain items, such as end tables, list the item once and write the quantity in front of it. If possible, create your inventory on a diskette so that you can update it as you acquire new items or dispose of items.

Back up your written inventory with a photographic inventory. Using a video camera or standard camera loaded with film that is recommended for taking indoor photographs, photograph the contents of each room,

including your attic, basement, garage, and porch or deck. Start by taking a photograph of each wall. Then take individual photographs of major pieces of furniture, appliances, electronic equipment, and other valuable or expensive items. Open cabinet and closet doors to photograph the contents. On the back of each print, write the date along with pertinent information such as general location shown or serial numbers. Store your personal property inventory, prints, negatives, and videotape along with receipts, appraisals, other important documents, and valuables. (See page 266 for safe, long-term storage options.)

Organizing Documents

One of the most helpful things you can do for surviving family members is to identify and organize your family's financial and legal documents and other important papers. Consider organizing documents into the following major categories of folders:

- Identification papers (birth certificate, citizenship papers, social security card, passport)
- Family papers (adoption, custody/guardianship, marriage, divorce)
- Military papers (DD214, discharge certificate)
- Estate documents and papers (will, trust, powers of attorney, letter of instruction, bank safe-deposit records)
- Deeds, titles, registrations (property, vehicles, cemetery plot)
- Personal property or home inventory (written and/or photographic with receipts and appraisals)

- Insurance papers (life, property and casualty, homeowner's, auto, health, disability, long-term care, plus supporting documentation for claims and awards)
- Statements for cash management accounts
- Statements for open bank accounts and related materials (canceled checks, checkbooks, passbooks, passwords)
- Debts (mortgage, outstanding loan records, credit card statements, promissory notes)
- Contracts and agreements (mortgage, lease agreements, IOUs, court orders)
- Investment certificates (CDs, stocks, bonds, and other investments)
- Retirement plan, survivor and annuity documents (IRA, military, other death benefits)
- Income tax returns, plus supporting documentation for last three or more years
- Business papers (incorporation, doing business as (d/b/a) certificates, computer backup disks, partner contracts or agreements)

Make a master list of all of your documents. Next to each item in your list, note where to find that particular document or related papers. Where appropriate, also note the name and telephone number for key contacts, such as your attorney, accountant, business partner, insurance agent, broker, and executor. If you have one or more bank safe-deposit boxes, record the number and location of the boxes. Also record the location of any assets, such as jewelry, that are hidden in your home or on loan to someone. If you keep this list on the hard drive of your computer, make a backup copy for your files.

Store originals of legal and financial documents in a bank safe-deposit box or a locking, Underwriters Laboratory (UL)–approved, fire-resistant file cabinet. Whichever storage method you choose, be sure to let someone else know where to find legal and financial documents and where you keep the key or combination. If you store documents in a bank safe-deposit box, be sure that the signature authorization card on file at the bank is up to date. Make copies for your home files of any original documents you choose to store in your safe-deposit box along with a list of any other contents.

IN CASE OF EMERGENCY

Take the time to record information that will be needed in the event of an emergency or your death, including but not limited to the following:

- Key contacts
- Location of important legal and financial records
- Location of safe-deposit box key
- Lock combinations and passwords
- Memorial wishes

Post your "key contacts" list near your telephone. Be sure that your contacts know where to find the information they will need to handle your legal and financial affairs. Do this now, while it is foremost in your mind, because later may be too late.

— *Donna D. McMillan, McMillan & Company Professional Organizing*

Be aware that a bank safe-deposit box registered in your name only will be sealed upon your death. If you store the original copy of your will here, your executor or trustee will, at minimum, need to present a copy of your death certificate plus a copy of your will in order to obtain access to your original will. In some states, opening the box may require a court order, which could take weeks.

Thy Will Be Done

A will is probably the most important legal document you will ever sign. And yet seventy percent of all Americans die without a will.

If you die without a will, someone will be appointed by the state to handle your affairs. That person could be someone in your family that you would never have chosen. If you have no children and no spouse, your assets may go to a remote family member instead of your closest friend. If you have children and you die without a will, a judge may decide who will raise your children. Dying without a will can also incur unnecessary taxes and expenses that may create a financial hardship for your heirs.

If you do nothing else in the way of estate planning, make a will. This will go a long way toward ensuring that your assets will go to the people and organizations you wish to receive them. It also lets you decide who should care for your minor children (if no other parent is living), who should manage any assets you leave to your minor children, and whom you want to carry out the terms of your will (your executor). In your will, you can also make provisions for your pets.

is a simple will enough?

If you answer "Yes" to the following questions, then a simple will is probably all you need.

1. Are you under age 50? **Yes / No**
2. Are you in good health? **Yes / No**
3. Is the total value of your estate less than one million dollars? **Yes / No**

Keep in mind that it is always a good idea to consult your attorney about current estate tax laws and how they apply to your particular situation. Generally, the older you are and the more assets you have, the more likely it is that you require *more* than a simple will.

Preparing a Will. A simple will can be prepared quickly and easily using inexpensive, standard legal forms or software (see page 331). Even if you hire an attorney to prepare a will for you, it's still relatively inexpensive.

Once you prepare your will, you may wish to discuss it with your family. Explain why you have decided to distribute your assets the way you did, especially if you are not dividing your assets equally among your heirs. Discussing the reasoning behind your decisions often makes it easier for everyone to understand and accept them.

Make a point to review your will periodically. If you get married or divorced, win the lottery, or want to change a beneficiary or any other terms, you will need to rewrite your will or update it with a codicil. If you move to another state, check to see if your current will is valid in that state.

Other Legal Wishes

It's important to make your wishes known — in life and in death. If you don't express your wishes, you put others in the uncomfortable and often stressful position of having to make decisions for you. This is particularly true of medical and financial decisions concerning the end of life. Taking time to make some critical decisions now can provide peace of mind for you and make things easier for your loved ones.

Just as preparing a will lets you make advance decisions about the handling of your estate, making a *living will* lets you decide in advance about critical end-of-life decisions that would otherwise need to be made by your family. If, for example, you suffered an illness or injury that caused your brain to stop functioning and your heart was beating only with the help of a life-support machine, would you want your body to be kept "alive" at all costs? Or would you want to spare your loved ones the overwhelming financial, emotional, and psychological costs of doing so? In a living will, you provide what's called an *advanced directive* to your physicians and family that guides them in deciding how aggressively to use medical treatments to delay death.

A *medical power of attorney*, or healthcare proxy, allows you to appoint someone you trust to act as your healthcare agent. With this legal document, the person you appoint is authorized to make medical decisions on your behalf if, at any time, you are unable to do so yourself. Ideally, this will be someone who is not afraid to ask questions of healthcare professionals to get information needed to make decisions. It should be someone who knows your wishes about medical treatment, is willing to take responsibility, and is assertive enough to ensure that your instructions are followed.

A living will and medical power of attorney are legal documents that you prepare in accordance with the laws of the state in which you reside. (You'll find sources for preparing your own documents in the appendix.) Sign and keep the originals of these documents and give copies to your physician, immediate family members, and your appointed healthcare agent.

There is another legal document you will want to prepare in the process of organizing your estate. Have you ever considered what would happen to your financial affairs if you were suddenly incapacitated? Who would pay your personal bills or keep your business in business? A *durable power of attorney* is a legal document that gives one or more people authority to manage your finances. In this document, you specify what this person is

One Challenge . . .

When it comes to sorting through property and possessions left behind, many family members end up with irreconcilable differences. What can be done to make the whole process as fair and equitable as possible?

Three Solutions

1 FROM JEANNE K. SMITH, EXIT, STAGE RIGHT: Together, go through all the items in each room, one by one. If only one person expresses interest in an item, move that item to that person's designated staging area or tag it. If two or more people express interest in an item, move it to a common room. If no one wants it, tag it for donation. Once you've been through every room, go back to the common area. Give the oldest family member first choice of items. Then allow younger siblings to make their first choice. Continue until all items are claimed.

2 FROM NORMAN ZALFA, ORGANIZE YOUR ESTATE, INC.: Minimize the potential for animosity by deciding beforehand who will get what. One way to do this is to invite family members to your home, give them each different-colored sticky notes to put on the things they would like to inherit. If an item is wanted by more than one family member, they can negotiate for it. Another option is to give photographs of selected belongings to your family members and have them identify those items they wish to inherit by indicating a "yes" or "no" and initialing the backs of the photographs.

3 FROM STEPHANY SMITH GONSER, PUT SIMPLY CONSULTING: You may want to call in a mediator to come up with a fair and partial distribution. It doesn't have to be a professional. It could be an impartial family member or friend of the deceased.

authorized to do on your behalf and for how long. You also specify how it should be determined that you are unable to manage your own affairs. This document should be prepared by an attorney.

If you wish to donate organs upon your death, tell your immediate family members because your body will need to be kept alive artificially for the surgical procedure. In many states, you can sign the back of your driver's license to indicate that you would like to be an organ donor. Or you can sign an organ donor card. Either way, it's important to get the signatures of the legally required number of witnesses. You may wish to bequeath or donate your entire body, in which case you should indicate that preference on your organ donor card or driver's license. Some medical schools and research institutions require that you make arrangements prior to your death and will not accept a body without that prior approval.

Last Wishes

It's not enough to verbalize your last wishes. What if your loved ones are not really listening to what you are saying to them because they don't want to talk about death? Or what if they forget what you said?

Make your last wishes known through a letter of instruction or "last wishes" form that provides instructions for what to do with your body after death, describes any arrangements you have made, and informs survivors of the location of important documents such as your will. This is not a legal document but rather a "love letter" to your family that can also include final words to loved ones and bequeathal of selected personal possessions.

Before you can write your letter of instruction, you will need to make some decisions. Remember that, as challenging as it may be to think about and make decisions about your death, it will be exponentially more difficult for others to make these decisions on your behalf.

Preplanning your death arrangements makes it so much easier for your family, especially if you die suddenly or unexpectedly. They won't have to try to figure out what you would have wanted; they'll know. And they won't overspend out of guilt or grief. Following are some questions to help you write your letter of instruction:

- **Do you want to be buried?** If so, what type of casket (wood or metal) do you prefer? What color do you want to be buried in? Would you like any personal possessions to be buried with you? Where would you like to be buried? What inscription do you want on your tombstone?
- **Do you prefer to be cremated?** Where and in what type of urn do you want your ashes kept? Or do you prefer them to be scattered? If so, where and by whom?

- **Do you want a wake so friends and family can pay their last respects?** If so, with open or closed casket?
- **Do you want a funeral service (with body) or memorial service (without body)?** Where would you like your service to be held? Do you want to have a particular type of flower or music at your service?
- **Is there anything else you would like survivors to do?** For instance, would you like them to send contributions to a particular charity or plant a tree in your memory?

You could meet with a local funeral director who can provide some of the choices available (as well as costs) to help you make decisions regarding your final arrangements. Find out what services are required in your state and which ones are optional. But don't feel obligated to prepay for any services. It may cost less to pay in advance for services or buy a cemetery plot for yourself and your spouse, but what if you move to another state or get divorced? It may make more sense for you to spell out your last wishes and let survivors make arrangements for you at the time of your death. Do make sure that you have a life insurance policy that will cover funeral costs so these do not create a hardship for your family.

If you have already made preplanning arrangements with a mortuary, crematory, or cemetery, include this information in your letter of instruction. List the company name, address, and telephone number to contact. Describe your arrangements. If you paid in advance or purchased insurance to cover the costs, list the contract or policy numbers.

With an average cost of $8,000 to $10,000, a funeral is one of the single largest expenses of a lifetime. Be aware that costs for goods and services vary widely. Call or visit at least three funeral homes and cemeteries to compare prices. One way to save on the cost of final arrangements is to join a memorial or funeral society. These are nonprofit, nonsectarian organizations that negotiate with local funeral homes to get special group prices on goods and services for their members. To become a member, you pay a lifetime fee of $20 to $45 and fill out a form to specify the goods and services you want. To find a memorial or funeral society, look in the yellow pages of

MISSING DOCUMENTS?

If you can't find important documents or papers, get new ones. It can take several months (or even longer) to obtain copies of some documents. (In the appendix, you will find contact information for government agencies through which you can obtain copies of vital records, military discharge papers, and tax returns.) This may not seem like much to you now, but a few months' delay in survivor benefits could spell hardship for others if you suddenly become totally incapacitated or die. This could even include loss of your home and/or business.

— *Norman Zalfa, Organize Your Estate, Inc.*

your telephone book under "Funeral Information and Advisory Services."

If you are a veteran, the U.S. Department of Veterans Affairs may pay a small allowance toward burial and funeral expenses. You may also be eligible for other benefits. Your survivors will need to present proof of your military service (DD214) for reimbursement, so be sure to let them know where to find that document. Determine the benefits available to you and note these benefits in your letter of instruction along with information on how to obtain the benefits.

Practical Matters for Those Left Behind

It's likely that you may be called upon someday to make final arrangements for someone who has died. If the deceased has left a letter of instruction or other form of last wishes, then you know exactly what kind of arrangements to make on his or her behalf. If not, you'll need to make these decisions on your own or with the help of a funeral director and family members. Notify relatives and friends as soon as possible so that they have the opportunity to grieve with you. Writing and placing an obituary in the newspaper is a good way to reach others who may have known the deceased. Another thing you should do is protect the residence of the deceased from unwanted visitors by making sure that all doors and windows are locked and perhaps placing a few lights on a timer to suggest that the house is still occupied.

The next step is to collect important papers. The first document you will need is the

death certificate, which you can obtain from the funeral director or county health department. If the deceased died overseas, request a multilingual death certificate so that you don't have the extra step of getting it translated. You will need to present one certified copy for each insurance benefits claim; to access each bank account; and to transfer ownership of vehicles, stock certificates, and other titled property. If you don't know how many copies you need, get at least a dozen.

The next most important document to locate is the original will. Other papers you will need in the first few weeks following a death include copies of all insurance policies; veteran's discharge papers; marriage certificate (for spouse); birth certificates (to claim survivor benefits for children); and social security cards or numbers for the deceased, spouse, and dependent children.

DON'T DOS

Even though some beneficiaries may be anxious to snag a piece of the estate, don't make financial decisions for at least a month. Don't take any interest or dividends from the estate if you don't have to and keep good records if you do. If you need the services of an attorney or other professional, do not agree to pay a percentage of the estate. Pay them by the hour for a specific project or job.

— *Norman Zalfa, Organize Your Estate, Inc.*

Once you have collected the necessary documents, apply for any and all benefits from life insurance policies, retirement plans, social security, and Veterans Administration. When you notify the deceased's employer, ask about life insurance benefits as well as monies due from salary, bonuses, commissions, accrued vacation or sick time, and other employee benefits such as pension or company stock options, and the continuation of health insurance for a spouse or dependents.

Don't hesitate to apply for benefits to any organization, including social or fraternal groups. The worst that can happen is that the claim is denied. Check with any professional organizations or associations to find out if the deceased was covered by a group life insurance policy. Check for the same with financial and credit institutions. Also find out if any loans, mortgages, or credit card accounts are covered by credit life insurance that would pay off the account balance.

Other less urgent but critical things to do in the days and weeks following a death include the following:

- Cancel medical, disability, and long-term-care insurance.
- Cancel credit cards and charge accounts in writing.
- Cancel magazine and newspaper subscriptions and any ongoing memberships (health club, book club); request reimbursement of the unused portion of prepaid fees.
- Cancel cable or satellite television and other nonessential utilities.

Immediate To Dos

Following is a checklist of the things that need to be done in the first few days and weeks following the death of a loved one:

- ❏ Protect the residence of the deceased so that it is not burglarized.
- ❏ Make funeral arrangements.
- ❏ Write an obituary and arrange for it to be published in the local newspaper.
- ❏ Contact all close friends and family of the deceased.
- ❏ Contact executor or attorney.
- ❏ Notify the deceased's employer.
- ❏ Get multiple certified copies of the death certificate.
- ❏ Locate the original will and give it to the executor or attorney.
- ❏ Locate or obtain a copy of all insurance policies.
- ❏ Notify insurance companies (in writing) of the death.
- ❏ Contact the Social Security Administration to apply for burial benefits (and spouse benefits if the deceased was already receiving benefits).
- ❏ Contact the Veterans Administration office to apply for benefits (if deceased was an honorably discharged veteran).

Consider waiting a month or so before canceling telephone and Internet provider services. In keeping these services "live," you may discover other friends and acquaintances of the deceased who would want to know the news.

Final Business

If you have been appointed as the executor of the will, your role is to find, secure, and manage assets until such time as they are transferred to the heirs. This includes such business details as identifying pension and insurance benefits, notifying banks, distributing personal effects, and paying debts and taxes for the deceased.

When a person dies without a written will, however, state law determines how the deceased's assets and property will be distributed. The court appoints a personal representative, usually a senior member of the family, to manage the deceased's final business.

If you have been appointed to settle the estate, establish a new bank account to be used to handle all financial matters involved in closing out the deceased's estate. Keep a detailed, dated diary of all activities done on behalf of the deceased. This will protect you in the event of future disputes or claims.

Locate and make a complete list of what the deceased owned, including real estate, stocks, bonds, bank accounts, deeds, and personal property. Keep all of this information together with associated documents and paperwork. In the process of looking for assets, search the house for hidden cash, jewelry, or other things of value. It is not uncommon for valuables to be hidden in the freezer, in medicine cabinets or pantries, in coat pockets, or sewn into drapes.

All assets have to be found before you can determine if the estate has to go to probate. Probate is the court-supervised process of paying the deceased's debts and distributing the estate to the rightful beneficiaries. Jointly owned property, property in trust, and assets with a designated beneficiary, such as life insurance policies and retirement plans, do not have to go through the probate process. Settling the estate also involves receiving claims against the estate (outstanding loans, for example), paying taxes and claims, and distributing assets.

Be aware that the probate process can take a full year or more. If probate is not necessary, the estate can be settled in a matter of weeks. (Avoiding probate is something that can be planned for in advance by putting assets into a trust or arranging for direct transfer to beneficiaries upon your death.) If you have any questions about the probate process or about settling the estate, you should consult an attorney. You may also wish to contact an accountant to help you file final income tax returns for the deceased.

One of the most time-consuming aspects of settling an estate is sorting through personal and household effects, deciding what to do with everything, removing items from a home, and preparing for sale of the home. (See chapter 25 for helpful advice on selling a home.)

Go through one room at a time, sorting items into four categories: give away, throw away, sell, and keep. Use labeled boxes or bags to help you sort and collect each category of items. Tape a note to larger items to indicate the appropriate action. If you're planning to have a yard or garage sale, it's easier to put a price tag on items as you are sorting through them. This keeps you from having to rehandle every item.

Take the time you need to sort through your feelings as well as through the material things. It's all part of the grieving process. Don't keep things out of guilt; keep only what you really want and let go of the rest. You may be able to disburse some belongings among friends and family members. If family members are scattered or there are bills owing, you may want to keep a few precious memory items for yourself and sell everything else.

Once you decide what you want to keep, you might want to contact an estate company to sell off the contents of the house in an estate sale. Or you can sell everything (including the junk) to an auction house or liquidator. This is often the quickest way to empty a house. Estate-sale professionals generally collect a percentage of the sale revenue so there is no out-of-pocket expense for you, the person selling the items. Be sure to get an appraisal on antiques, artwork, and collections from a third party before selling to an auction house or liquidator.

Another option is to hire a professional organizer who can assist with the details of a home closure, especially if you live far away or don't have the time. You can deduct the cost of these services from the estate, and you may be able to deduct this expense on the deceased's final federal income tax returns. A professional organizer can do the following:

- Help you decide what to keep, sell, give away, or throw away
- Suggest places to donate items
- Obtain appraisals for valuables
- Pack household effects
- Arrange for storage or shipping

Many professional organizers are beginning to specialize in estate organizing in response to growing need. Every one of them advises clients to do themselves, their family members, and their heirs one last big favor: Organize your estate now.

ONE LAST DONATION

If your loved one had a favorite charity, have an estate sale and plan to donate the proceeds to that organization. Keep in mind that it would have made that person happy to help a worthwhile cause — and everyone will benefit more in the end than if you packed everything into a storage unit to mildew and rot.

— *Ramona Creel, OnlineOrganizing.com*

One Challenge . . .

One of the most difficult challenges for those left behind is letting go of a loved one's personal possessions. We often feel guilty, even disloyal about selling or giving away someone else's things, especially when every item is a reminder of that person. But it is simply not practical or possible to keep everything. What are some ways we can feel better about letting go of these things while keeping the memories?

Three Solutions

1 FROM RAMONA CREEL, ONLINEORGANIZING.COM: Allow yourself to reminisce and grieve as you go through cleaning out the deceased's house. Don't be in such a rush to "be done with it" that you miss out on the opportunity to really say good-bye. Take photos of those treasured items you really want to remember. You might put together an album of your mother's favorite Sunday dresses or your grandfather's pipe collection or the furniture you grew up with. That way, you can look back fondly and reminisce, without needing an extra storage unit to keep it all.

2 FROM JEANNE K. SMITH, EXIT, STAGE RIGHT: If you decide to hold an estate sale, don't be there. It's too emotionally draining. Hire a professional and pay the fee. But do it after you've had a chance to relive memories by holding items, taking photographs, or simply sharing your remembrances with others.

3 FROM STEPHANY SMITH GONSER, PUT SIMPLY CONSULTING: Ask yourself this: If you could keep only one thing, what would it be? Focusing on what's really important helps to let go of the less important things. Keep only the best of the best. And keep only what you really like. If your space is limited, keep things that don't take up a lot of space. You may also need to put a limit on the number of items you will keep from collections of things like books, recipes, letters, or postcards.

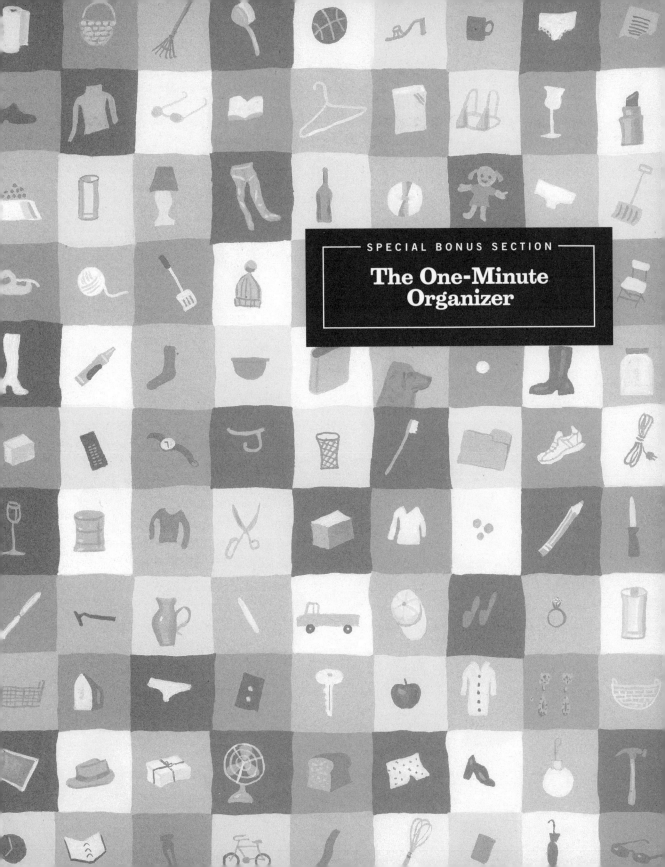

The One-Minute Organizer

In the first part of this book, you learned simple strategies, systems, and tools that, used on a regular basis, would help you get as organized as you need to be. Now, in this special section, you'll find 500 quick tips for getting your life in order—one minute at a time. In fact, you can read every tip in this section in a matter of seconds—and you can implement many in as little as one minute. (Look for the one-minute symbol.)

So got a minute? That's all you need to bring a little organization to your hectic life.

PART I

GETTING STARTED

Ninety percent of organizing is getting out of your own way. Think about the beliefs and behaviors that are contributing to the chaos in your life. Before you can change anything, you've got to recognize and accept responsibility for your role and be willing to change the thought patterns and habits that are keeping you from achieving your goal. If you start to think and act like an organized person, you will become one. Fortunately, the more you act the part, the more natural it becomes.

● Think about your motivation. What do you stand to gain from getting organized? What do you stand to lose if you don't?

● Create a one-month plan. Choose five things you most want to organize in the coming month. Number these items from highest to lowest priority. At the end of the month, if you have not yet accomplished all five tasks, create a new one-month plan that outlines what you hope to achieve this month — and what you are willing to do to make it happen.

● Take immediate action. Pick a single organizing tip from this book and **do it today.** Or take 5 minutes right now to organize your sock drawer.

● Make today the day you decide to get organized. Tell someone about it.

● Start each organizing session this way: Choose a space to organize. Then close your eyes and visualize what that space might look like without clutter and how that would make you feel.

*You don't have to stop everything to get organized. You just have to **START**. Make organizing a part of your daily life. Do it first. Do it fast.*

● Did you used to be organized? **Think back.** What happened between then and now? Did you move? Start a family or new job? Get married? Divorced? Lose a loved one? Good news: If you were organized at one point in your life, you can get organized again. Believe it!

- Start with the most visible clutter first. Seeing clear and obvious results will give you a boost of confidence.
- Talk with your family about why you want to get organized. Ask for their help. You may have to provide some incentive. *Ideas:* Establish a bonus allowance or system of rewards for adhering to new household rules; plan a family night out after a big decluttering project; or agree to put yard sale money toward a family vacation.
- Start with **today's mess.** Do whatever it takes to keep up with daily mail, dishes, and laundry. Then set aside time to catch up.
- **Commit** to spending a set amount of time every day on uncluttering and organizing activities. Schedule your organizing sessions for a time when you are mentally fresh. Make an appointment with yourself and write it in your daily planner. Then honor that appointment as you would any other appointment. If you absolutely cannot do this every day, try to schedule in two or three 30-minute sessions each week.
- Decide in advance what your reward will be for completing each organizing project or room. *Ideas:* Plan to buy yourself flowers, treat yourself to a pedicure or massage, or invite friends to enjoy coffee and dessert in your newly uncluttered family room.
- Tie your organizing goals into a larger **life goal.** Think about how getting organized will help you to save time or create space so that you can pursue your dreams or simply enjoy a more peaceful life.

Yes, organizing is work. But there's nothing all that difficult about it. The hardest part is getting ***STARTED.***

- Give yourself a **deadline.** Offer to host a family dinner over the holidays, plan a party at your house, or commit to participating in a neighborhood garage sale.
- Establish a daily organizing **reward.** You might, for example, allow yourself to surf the Internet, watch television, or chat on the telephone once your organizing time is up — not before.
- Ask a friend to check on your organizing progress one week from today.
- Without commitment, nothing gets done. Put your **goal in writing.** Post it on your bathroom mirror or put it in your make-up bag — someplace where it will be a daily reminder.
- Keep the **end in sight.** Think about how good you are going to feel about getting organized. Try to remember that feeling whenever you are tempted to dump a pile of mail on the kitchen counter or buy one more thing you really don't need.
- Look at what's working. If you have been successful in organizing one particular area, think about how you can apply that process elsewhere to create order.
- Familiarize yourself with all of the organizing products available. You're apt to find the perfect, ready-made solution for your biggest organizing challenge.
- Can't find time to organize? Make time by turning your television on 15 minutes later than usual or turning it off 15 minutes earlier.

- **Be realistic** about what you can and can't do. You can't unclutter your home overnight. You can unclutter a countertop or drawer in as little as 15 minutes.

- Get organized while you watch television. Pull out a **drawer** and dump the contents on the coffee table or floor. During commercials, sort the contents into four piles: throw away, put away (because it belongs in another drawer or somewhere else altogether), give away, and keep. Put back only what you love and/or use.

- Start right now. Spend the next 5 minutes picking up **five things** and putting them where they belong.

- Get your brain in gear. Complete the following thoughts:

I am disorganized because . . .
The top three things that keep me from getting organized are . . .
What really contributes to the clutter around here is . . .
Clutter makes me feel . . .
I could get more organized if . . .
I want to get organized because . . .
If I could get organized, I could . . .

> *Our experience is driven by our beliefs. If, for example, you believe that nothing you do makes a difference, that will be your EXPERIENCE. See if you can pinpoint one belief that may be limiting your ability to get organized.*

- Set a simple goal. *Example:* "Tonight I'm going to clean out my junk drawer, and then I'm going to stop."

- Tackle **one room** at a time. Organize that room one shelf, one drawer at a time.

- If you've never been organized it's very likely that you never learned *how* to get organized. You can learn by reading organizing books, attending workshops, and watching how organized people do things. Schedule time to learn organizational skills.

- **Plan** your approach. Random acts of organizing are all well and good, but if you really want to speed up the process, make a plan. Where will you start? How much time will you spend each day?

- Find an **organizing buddy** — someone who wants to get organized as much as you do. Decide to do it together. Make a standing weekly date to show off your accomplishments or discuss progress and share encouragement over the phone.

- Ask a friend or family member to help you organize your closet or garage in return for babysitting or help with his or her yard work. Or offer to help with an organizing project.

- Organize a progressive **cleaning party.** Invite a few local friends or family members to spend a Saturday at your house, decluttering your basement or garage. Make it fun with food and music. Continue the party next Saturday at the next house.

- Consider hiring professional help. Find a local professional organizer through the National Association of Professional Organizers (www.napo.net). A few hours with a professional organizer might be just the jump-start you need.

• Keep a **daily journal** of your organizing activities. Take a few minutes each day to jot down how long you spent organizing, what area or things you organized, how you felt afterward, and your goal for tomorrow.

• Make organizing time more fun. Turn on the radio or play your favorite CD.

• Schedule a personal **victory celebration** for three months from today. Write it in your calendar.

• Keep track of your progress. Use a colored marker to mark an **X** in your **calendar** for each day that you spend at least 5 minutes on uncluttering and organizing activities.

Use the two-pass approach to organizing your entire house. Start by gathering and getting things to the rooms where they belong. In the second pass, you can begin to organize the contents of each room.

What are you doing that contributes to the clutter and chaos in your life? Pick your single worst disorganizing HABIT and work on changing that behavior over the next month.

• Tackle large projects one step at a time. Start by making a list of all of the steps. Then rearrange the steps in order of importance. Working backward from your project deadline, create due dates for each step and incorporate them into your daily calendar. If you don't have a project deadline, create one.

• Set a **ticking timer** for the length of your organizing session to help keep you focused on what you are doing.

• Give organizing your full attention. Let your answering machine or voicemail take calls during your organizing sessions.

• Did you ever try to get organized but gave up, thinking you were a failure? *You* didn't fail. Your plan failed. Maybe you tried to do too much too fast. Think about what happened and what you learned. **Do it differently** next time, and you will get a different result.

• Make a list of organizing projects, such as filing, photographs, recipes, kitchen, garage. Select one. Break down that project into mini projects. In the kitchen, for example, mini projects might include countertop, under the sink, cutlery drawers, pantry, refrigerator/freezer, recipes, and coupons.

• For 5 to 15 minutes each day, work on one **mini project** at a time until the entire organizing project is done. Then check it off your list and move on to the next one.

• Resist the urge to get creative with your organizing systems. It just makes the job harder. Channel your creativity into other areas.

• Five ways to motivate a family member to get more organized:

• Gently communicate what is bothering you and why.

• Change the way you are asking (negotiating vs. demanding).

• Offer your support in helping to make the change.

• Be willing to make compromises.

• Be willing to accept that it might not be done exactly as you would do it.

❶ To make getting organized a priority, tie it to a **financial reward.** What will you do with the money you make selling things you no longer want or need? Use the financial reward as your incentive: The more you get rid of, the more cash you'll have.

• Organize your **purse.** Empty it completely. Throw out the trash. Remove items you don't need to carry with you. Make it easier to find things by minimizing the number of units in your purse. Use zippered plastic bags to contain like items, such as lipsticks and other cosmetics.

CLEARING CLUTTER

Unclutter first; then organize. It's so much quicker and easier to get organized when you have less stuff. If you aren't using something and don't have an immediate need for it, it's just taking up valuable space — and making it difficult to find the things you do use and need. Schedule 15 minutes a day to unclutter your space. Even 5 minutes of concentrated effort is better than 0 minutes. Once you get started, you may decide to keep going for the full 15 minutes or longer.

Start with the **easy stuff** — things that don't require any decision making on your part. Grab a trash bag and start tossing in things that are clearly garbage: food wrappers, expired coupons and flyers, stretched-out socks, stained clothing, rusted kitchen utensils, broken items that have since been replaced. Keep going until that trash bag is full.

• When uncluttering a shelf, drawer, cupboard, or closet, take everything out. Then put back only those things you love and use.

If you are saving something because you *might* need it someday, ask yourself, *"Could I get another one pretty easily and inexpensively if I needed it someday?"* If the answer is yes, **let it go.**

Can't decide what to keep and what to toss? Ask yourself, *"What's the worst thing that could possibly happen if I decided to let this go?"* If you can live with the consequences, you can live without the thing.

Pick a room — any room. Now pick **one drawer** or shelf in that room, and start there. Remove everything from a single drawer or shelf and sort stuff into five piles:

1. Throw away
2. Put away
3. Give away
4. Sell
5. Keep

Throw the garbage away. Put away the stuff that belongs elsewhere. Bag or box your donations and anything you plan to sell. Put back only the keepers — those things that you are currently using or absolutely love and can't live without.

- Do you find it difficult to make decisions? Create an **umbrella rule** about when to get rid of things. At what point are you most likely to be willing to part with something you no longer need or use? Six months? One year? Two years? Creating a personal decision-making rule now will eliminate the need to make lots of individual decisions later.
- **Be honest** about what you really need to keep.

To keep or toss? Ask yourself:

Have I used this item in the past year?
Will I need it on a definite date in the future?
Do I need to keep it for legal or tax purposes?
Would it be difficult to get another if I needed it again someday?

If you answer no to every question, toss it.

◉ Still undecided? Ask: *What useful purpose does this thing serve in my life?* If it isn't something you use, is it something that makes you feel good? If not, it's just taking up space. Let it go.

◉ The final step of each clutter-clearing session is the most important: **Schedule your next session.**

- Move out of your living space anything you aren't using but can't bring yourself to let go of. **Box it up.** Write on the box what's inside, and date it. If you haven't needed anything in that box six months or a year from now, donate the whole box.

◉ If you have trouble letting go, think instead in terms of what you want to keep. Make a decision to surround yourself only with **things you love** and use, and remove the rest.

◉ Recognize that you are not the same person you were 10 years ago. Your **interests, tastes, and styles** have changed. Aim to surround yourself with things that are a part of who you are today. Get rid of anything that is no longer useful or meaningful.

◉ Pretend that you are moving. Ask yourself: *Is this item worth the effort of packing up, carrying out to the moving van, and unpacking at the new place?* If not, give it a new home.

◉ Holding an object increases your attachment to it. Have someone else hold items as you make decisions about what to keep and toss.

◉ A heavy layer of dust on an item is a telltale sign that it's something you don't use. **Give it a new home.**

*Too much **STUFF?** Getting a bigger house or apartment is not the solution.*

◉ Establish limits on things like plastic **shopping bags** (20 is probably plenty), margarine tubs and yogurt containers (how many do you really need?), rags (only what will fit in a tote bag or bucket), and recycled computer paper (only what fits in a paper tray). Decide in advance what is a reasonable amount to have at any one time. Recycle the excess.

◉ Things have a useful life, and then they become useless. Sure, you can use an old T-shirt as a rag, but do you really need another rag? Give yourself permission to get rid of it.

- Decide to play by the rule: If it's ugly or unfixable, it's out of here.

◉ We often hold on to things we no longer use because we paid "good money" for them. But what is the value of a designer suit that just hangs in your closet, getting older and dustier every year? Zero. **Donate** that suit, and it could be worth $30,000 a year to the woman who wears it to an interview and gets the job.

◉ Try to make decisions quickly. If it takes you longer than 60 seconds to decide whether to keep an item, you probably don't really need it.

• Once you've made the decision to let go of things, get them out of your home as quickly as possible.

1. Schedule a pickup for your donations, or drive them to the nearest drop-off box.
2. Toss trash the night before your garbage collection day, or take it straight to the dump.
3. Hire a junk removal service.

*Aim to surround yourself with **BEAUTIFUL** and useful things. Give yourself permission to let go of the rest. It's just taking up space and weighing you down.*

• If clutter is interfering with your relationships or job, look into joining a **support group.** Check out Clutterless Recovery Groups (www.clutterless.org), Clutterers Anonymous (www.cluttersanonymous.net), or Messies Anonymous (www.messies.com).

◉ If it's not your clutter, you are not responsible for it. Give the responsibility — and the stuff — to the rightful owner.

Do not save things to sell at a garage or yard sale unless you have set a definite date for that sale. Donate those items instead.

◉ Recognize that your time is valuable. It takes a lot of time and energy to plan and hold a successful **garage sale.** You may be better off taking the tax deduction if you itemize on your tax return. If you make a donation valued at $400, you will save a percentage in taxes equal to your highest ending tax bracket. Do the math.

• Create a list of your tax-deductible donations, and assign values to each. Check out the valuation guide at www.salvationarmyusa.org.

• Look for a **local charity** that accepts donations of everything from books to clothing to household furnishings. *Better:* Find one that will send a truck to pick up your donations.

◉ Schedule a pickup with a local charity to come and get your donations one week from today, or make a note in your calendar to drive your donations to their destination.

◉ When making decisions about **sentimental items,** decide to keep only those things that hold happy memories.

*Some **PROGRESS** is better than no progress.*

• **Don't waste time** trying to sell junk. Trash stuff that's become outdated or obsolete, such as college textbooks, old computer equipment, and anything that's unfixable. No one wants it — not even as a donation.

◉ Weigh the pain of letting go of stuff you aren't using against the pain of living with it all. Sure, there's a slight chance that you might miss something after it's gone. But 99 percent of the time, you'll never think of it again. **Have faith** that you will make the right decision!

- Don't think of uncluttering as getting rid of stuff. Think of it as giving to someone who needs it more than you, or as **recycling.**
- If something holds a great deal of sentimental value and you absolutely cannot part with it, don't!
  - Take photos of your child with favorite artwork or school projects. Put the photos in your photo album and let go of the physical items.
  - Take a photograph of sentimental items before parting with them.

*If you have clutter, you are richer than you think. Look at uncluttering as an opportunity to **SHARE** your abundance — the stuff you don't need — with people who could really use it.*

- Accept that you can't control life by holding on to things. The secret is to let go.
- Decide to have a "giving away" party for **inherited** estate items. Invite family and friends to tag items they would like to take. Donate any untagged items after the party.
- What's the point of keeping **memorabilia** in storage? No one can enjoy it there. Look for ways to display, and even use, cherished items.
  - Instead of saving everything that once belonged to a loved one, find a way to **honor the memories** attached to various things. *Idea:* Videotape a family gathering where family members are invited to share their

remembrances about particular items. Then donate or give the items away. Or sell valuables and make a donation in the deceased's name.

- Create a **keepsake box** for saving love letters, cards, artwork, and other memorabilia. If you have little storage space, limit boxes to one per household member.
- If you are afraid to let go of something, do it scared. The act of letting go of material possessions can also help you let go of guilt, grudges, and other **emotional garbage.**
- Turn clutter into cash by:

  - Having a garage or yard sale.
  - Advertising big-ticket items.
  - Selling items on consignment.
  - Selling to a secondhand store.
  - Selling online.

- Unclutter your **work space.** Create a main storage area for office supplies — in a drawer, cabinet, or closet. Put like items together. Doing so will make it easy to see what you have and what you need.
- Clear your **desktop,** and put back only what you use daily. Store everything else in drawers, on shelves, or in your supply closet.
- Set up **clutter collectors** where clutter naturally tends to collect: a bowl on the counter for keys and loose change, a set of tiered baskets for collecting mail and school paperwork, a coat tree or wall hooks in the entryway for hanging outerwear and backpacks.
- Unclutter your walls. Take down everything, and put back only what you love. Group framed photographs together in one

space, for a more dramatic, less cluttered look. If you have too many **wall hangings** to display at one time, put some into storage and rotate them when the seasons change.

• Get rid of bath and shower items you haven't used in more than a month. Move extras into a guest bathroom, or pour them into travel-size containers. Donate the rest.

• Clear **bathroom** countertops. Put back the soap and anything else that absolutely must remain out. Store everything else in cabinets and drawers. Use handled baskets or bags for easy storage and removal of daily toiletries.

• Clean out your **medicine cabinet.** Throw away leftover doses of medicines, expired prescriptions, and over-the-counter products.

• Toss makeup products you never wear.

• Check expiration dates and toss:

• Perfume more than three years old.
• Makeup more than one year old.
• Sunscreen more than two years old.
• Anything past its expiration date.

• Use caution when disposing of unused medicines, vitamins, cosmetics, and any potentially hazardous materials. Flush pills and liquids down the toilet; put all other items into a lidded coffee can or plastic bag secured with a twist tie, and dispose of them in a lidded trash can that children and pets cannot get into.

• Clear out enough space on shelves and in cabinets and closets to make it easy to see what you've got and to **allow room** for future storage.

• Clear **kitchen** countertops, and put back only what you use at least twice a week. Store everything else in cabinets and drawers.

❶ Designate certain shelves or areas of your refrigerator for storing **leftovers.** It will increase the likelihood that the leftovers won't be forgotten.

❶ Label and date all leftover containers. Keep labels and markers handy.

❶ Add a carousel tray to one or more shelves in your **refrigerator** to enable easy access to items in the back. Or corral like items, such as snacks or condiment jars, in a large plastic container that you can pull forward as needed.

• Schedule some time to play "dress-up" in your **closet.** Try on everything. If it fits and you love it, hang it back up.

• Separate castoffs into categories: donations, repairs and alterations, consignment/yard sale.

❶ Move special-occasion **clothes** and **accessories** to one end of your closet to make it easier to get to everyday clothes.

❶ Starting at one end of your closet, work your way across and remove any items you haven't worn in the last year. If you haven't worn them in the past year, you are not likely to wear them in the coming year. Donate them now rather than later, and enjoy the **extra space** in your closet.

• Keep in your everyday closet and drawers only those clothes that fit you. Remove anything you don't wear because it doesn't look or feel good on you.

❶ If you can't bring yourself to let go of clothes you are not wearing, decide to put them with your out-of-season clothes. You may be ready to donate them six months or a year from now when you see them again.

◉ Toss promotional items and other freebies you are not using.

- As you unclutter closets and drawers, make **three piles:** A, B, and C. The A pile is for clothes you wear and like and definitely want to keep. The B pile is a "maybe" pile. The C pile is for things you haven't worn in ages. Put the A pile away. Then go though the B pile again. Donate clothes in the C pile.

PAPER STUFF

Paper is a daily part of modern life. But left unchecked, it can quickly grow into a bigger part than we would like! The secret to minimizing pileup is to establish a plan for dealing with each category of paper — everything from newspapers, catalogs, and magazines to mail, notes, lists, and receipts. It means making decisions. What do you really need to save? How and where should it be filed? Start by organizing your most important day-to-day papers first. Then tackle the less urgent papers.

• Start by making a **first pass.** Gather in one place all the piles of papers that are strewn throughout your home or office. Do a quick sort of papers. Put into boxes everything except your most important papers — generally project-related, financial, or papers with a deadline. In the second pass, you can begin to begin to make decisions about each piece of paper. Meanwhile, you know where all your unfiled papers are.

• Turn piles into files. First step: Take a sample pile and make a list of the types of papers you find. This will help you figure out what type of files you may need to create.

• Sort day-to-day papers into **action files:** bills to pay, receipts to enter, papers to photocopy, data for reports, items to file or discuss with your boss or spouse, or papers to forward to another department or family member. Create labeled folders for these action files, and store them upright in a stepped desktop organizer.

• Establish a home for unpaid bills. *Ideas:* Create an action file for your desktop or a folder for a filing cabinet drawer. Or file all bills and receipts in an expandable file with pockets for each month so you can pay bills and do your filing anywhere.

• Make it easier to **pay bills.** Keep handy a supply of envelopes, return-address labels, stamps, pens, a calculator, and a stapler.

• A **simple system** for bi-monthly bill payment: File bills that need to be paid in the second half of the month in a folder labeled "Due 16–31," and file those that need to be paid between the 1st and 15th in a file labeled "Due 1–15." Put both files in a hanging folder labeled "Bills Due." Or file the two categories in a two-pocket folder. Make a note in your calendar to pay bills on the dates you choose as your bill-paying dates.

• Sort before filing. Use hanging files in an empty cardboard file storage box or a rolling file cart to sort papers into **filing categories** such as insurance, taxes, and receipts. Attach a sticky note to the top of each hanging folder to identify the category — these are your sorting folders. Once you've sorted all your papers, transfer the papers from each category into an existing folder in your filing cabinet or, if necessary, add a file tab to your sorting folder and file the folder and all. The beauty of this sorting system is that you can do your sorting in front of the television or wherever it is comfortable.

❂ Remember that the reason you file something is so that you can retrieve it. When naming a new file, think of what heading you are likely to look under should you need that document. Don't think too long about this; the first name that springs to mind is probably the best file name.

❂ Do not store **your will** in a safe-deposit box rented in your name only. The box will be sealed on your death, which could delay the transfer of your assets. Make a photocopy for your home files, and have your attorney keep the original.

❂ Avoid labeling files and folders as **"Miscellaneous."** If the information isn't important enough to have its own label, it either belongs in another folder or it's not important enough to save.

• Align hanging-file tabs in the same position on every hanging folder. It makes it easier to see the labels when they're all in a line. Plus you can add and subtract folders from the drawer without messing up a zigzag pattern.

• Refer to the following standard home filing categories as a guide to setting up your own:

- Insurance: auto, home, life, disability, medical
- Financial: bank accounts, credit accounts, mortgage statements, investments
- Property: receipts for home improvements, furnishings and valuables, product manuals and receipts, automotive purchases and repair receipts
- Taxes: current-year receipts and other tax documentation
- Medical records
- Veterinary records

❂ If the stack of paper in a file folder is more than one inch thick, separate the stack into two folders.

❂ Choose staples over paper clips for keeping papers together in a file. Paper clips tend to fall off or get attached to unrelated papers.

❂ Insert hanging-file tabs on the front of the folder so that they're visible even when the folder is full. When you want to look in the folder, just pull the tab forward to open the file in the drawer.

Color-code hanging file tabs to distinguish between different types of files such as financial or insurance records. Also use **color coding** to separate business and personal files or to differentiate project or client folders.

Information gets **OUTDATED** *quickly. If you know where to find the most current information, there's no need to file the paper.*

• Don't waste time filing papers you don't need to save. For example, there is no legal or tax reason to save your cable bill and other utility bills after paying them unless needed to **document** business expenses. You may wish to keep just the most current paid bill as documentation that your last payment was received or for easy reference to customer service numbers. Shred the rest.

◉ If you like to compare utility usage from month to month, simply note amounts on a single sheet of paper or spreadsheet.

◉ It's a smart practice to save product purchase **receipts** for 30 to 90 days in case you decide to return an item. Create a folder labeled "Current Receipts." File the newest receipts up front. Periodically shred older receipts.

• To document value for property insurance claims, create an itemized list of high-value items such as jewelry, furniture, and artwork. Store receipts in a **safe-deposit box.**

◉ Keep credit card receipts until you receive your credit card statement and verify each purchase. Then shred them unless (a) you need the receipts to document business expenses or (b) you want to document your purchase for warranty or other purposes.

• Create hanging file folders for all **owner's manuals,** or store them in one or more three-ring binders with three-hole punched clear plastic pockets. Organize them alphabetically by category — for example, television or refrigerator — or by the room in which the product resides.

◉ Staple product receipts to owner's manuals. Shred receipts for items you no longer own.

If you had 20 minutes to evacuate your home and could take only what you could fit in your car, what would you take? Most things can be easily replaced. Once you realize this, it's easier to **LIGHTEN** *your load.*

• Once reviewed and paid, **credit card** statements don't need to be saved except to document business expenses for tax purposes. If you feel more comfortable saving them, limit yourself to 12 consecutive monthly statements.

◉ Keep only the current billing statement for property and automotive **insurance policies.** Discard the previous year's statement and documentation when you receive the new policy information.

• When your annual **investment** statement arrives, shred the quarterly statements. Keep only the most current year's prospectus and addenda.

• Unclog filing cabinets by tossing papers and files you no longer need. Start in one drawer, and work from front to back. Flag wherever you stop for when you return.

• Try a numerical system for "idea" files. Label a hanging folder "ideas." Label a manilla folder "1". Write "1" in the upper right-hand corner of the first 10–12 "idea" papers and put them in the manilla folder. On your computer, create a master index with two to five keywords to describe each paper. Create and number as many folders as you need to file all your papers. To retrieve a particular document, use the keyword search feature in your word processing program.

Shred all **financial documents** and any paper with personally identifiable information, including prescription labels, to minimize the possibility of identity theft or fraud.

• For complete and current guidelines for keeping tax-related paperwork, refer to IRS Publication 552, "Recordkeeping for Individuals" at www.irs.gov/pub/ or ask your tax adviser.

*Don't worry about coming up with the **perfect** organizing system for bills or filing. Done is perfect.*

• Set up a tax file. File all tax documentation immediately. Create labeled file folders for the following:

- Income — Pay stubs, W-2s, 1099s, interest and dividend statements
- Donations — Receipts for charitable donations (cash and noncash)
- Medical — Receipts for medical expenses
- Real estate — Mortgage interest statements, real estate tax statements
- Child care — Receipts for child care payments

• Also file any correspondence you receive from the Internal Revenue Service or state revenue department.

• Studies show that 80 percent of what gets filed never gets looked at again. Before filing a piece of paper, question whether you really need to. *Do you need it for legal or tax reasons?* Save it. Is there a copy filed somewhere else? Toss it.

• Store inactive files away from active files. You might think you need to buy more filing cabinets when all you really need to do is free up space by **archiving** inactive files. Tax files and completed project folders are good examples.

• Remove archived files — hanging folder and all — to an upper shelf of a closet or in your attic, dry basement, or garage. It's helpful to **store** these files in same-size boxes that can be neatly stacked. Look for sturdy white cardboard file boxes with lids that you can buy in any office-supply store. These boxes are designed with a rim around the inside for storing hanging folders. Label the front of each box — for example, "TAX RETURNS 1990–1999."

• Rent a safe-deposit box to store important financial and legal documents and any other items that would be difficult or impossible to replace, including:

- Marriage, birth, death certificates
- Settlement and divorce papers

- Adoption, custody, citizenship, military papers
- Trust papers, living will, powers of attorney
- Property deeds, motor vehicle titles
- Stock and bond certificates
- U.S. Savings Bonds
- All contracts
- Home inventory list, photos, receipts for valuables

❂ Rather than save entire magazines for future reference **tear out** and file only the articles.

❂ Put magazines and other reading material where you are most likely to read it — in your briefcase for the commute home, for example, or on your nightstand.

    • **Binders** are a simple, convenient way to store reference material. To decide between binder and file storage, ask yourself:

Would it be helpful if this information were portable?

Do I need to cross-reference information?

Do I have convenient shelf space for binder storage?

    • If the answer to all three questions is no, a filing drawer may be a better solution.

    • Use binders to file newspaper and magazine **clippings.** Create one binder for each main category, such as "Home Decorating Ideas" or "Vacation Ideas." Insert articles in top-loading clear plastic sheet protectors. Use tabbed index sheets to create sections — for example, "Bathroom," "Bedroom," "Kitchen."

❂ If you're a little behind on your reading material, schedule reading time into every day so you can catch up.

❂ If you're way behind on your reading, scan the table of contents of each magazine. **Highlight** only the most interesting articles, and read just those before recycling the magazine.

❂ Get caught up on your reading in less than 60 seconds. Toss everything in your **"to read" pile,** and vow to keep up from this point forward.

*Next time you hear yourself complaining about not having **TIME** to get organized, stop. All we have is time. How we choose to use it is up to us.*

    • Consider canceling subscriptions to **magazines** you haven't read in the past three months. You will likely receive a refund for the unused portion of your subscription. You may also have the option to temporarily suspend your subscription. Or you can donate the remainder of your subscription to a friend or family member by requesting to change the mailing name and address.

❂ **Put a limit** on the number of magazines you subscribe to, which might be half the number you receive now. If you miss any of them, you can always buy an issue or resubscribe at a later date.

❂ Don't keep every issue of every magazine. **Decide** now how many of each you would like to keep or have room to store. Recycle the rest.

    • If you have piles of **unopened mail** offers, recycle or trash them. Remember, more of the same are already on the way.

◑ Save only the newest versions of **catalogs.** Toss those you rarely or never order from.

- Let go of beliefs such as:

  • It's just going to get messed up again.
  • I don't know where to start.
  • I don't have time.
  • I don't know how.
  • I've tried to get organized before and failed.

- Reduce the amount of **unsolicited mail** you receive. Send a postcard or letter to the Direct Marketing Association, Mail Preference Service, P.O. Box 643, Carmel, NY 10512. Ask to have your name and address removed from all of their mailing lists. Allow several months for the deluge to subside.

◑ Here's a nifty trick for storing professional or office supply catalogs in a filing cabinet: Open the catalog to roughly the center and then hang it over the top edges of a hanging file.

◑ Designate a basket or paper tray where children can put all **school papers** that require your attention: permission slips, graded homework and tests, and notices.

- Set up a system for returning paperwork to children. *Ideas:* Create a folder for each child to check each morning or hand out paperwork at the breakfast table.
- Use large magnetic refrigerator clips to organize upcoming **event flyers** in date order, collect take-out menus, or post schedules for team practices and games.
- Cardboard dressers are a simple, inexpensive solution for storing school papers, art-

work, and mementos. Give each child a dresser or assign drawers to children in a shared room.

- School-age children will benefit from having their own filing cabinet or drawer. **Teach children** how to set up hanging file folders for each subject and how to file and purge papers at the end of the year to make room for next year's papers.

*Recognize that it's natural to feel some fear about getting organized even when the change is desired. Getting organized one minute at a time **ALLOWS** you to make a gradual adjustment from familiar territory into new territory.*

- Organize **recipes** in a three-ring binder. Use tabbed index sheets to create sections for "Appetizers," "Desserts," and "Untried Recipes." Sort recipes by category. Then insert same-category recipes back-to-back in top-loading clear plastic sheet protectors. Affix odd-size clippings, notes, or recipes to a sheet of $8\frac{1}{2}$-x-11-inch paper for easier insertion.
- Determine whether the savings you get from **coupons** are worth the time it takes to clip, file, and retrieve them. If you decide to continue using coupons, toss all expired coupons. If you haven't used grocery coupons in the past three months, toss them all.
- Store coupons in a mini expandable file with dividers for food categories or your store's aisle numbers.

SPACES & THINGS

Find a home for every homeless thing. Look at the stuff that never gets put away. Chances are it has nowhere to go. Organizing is about finding a place for everything so you can always put everything in its place — and put your hands on it when you need it. A good place for a particular item is one that is convenient to where the item is used. Once you decide on a home for something, you never have to think again about what to do with it. Just put it in its place.

• Organize one room at a time.

❶ Question the placement of everything. Ask: *Why is this here? Is there a better place for it?*

• To decide what goes where in any space, use the "HOT/WARM/ COLD" rule. If it's used frequently (HOT), keep it handy. If it's used occasionally (WARM), you can get up and walk to it. If it's rarely used (COLD), you can climb for it.

• Arrange the contents of cabinets and closets so that **frequently used items** are the most accessible. Store less frequently used items on very high or low shelves in a closet or at the back of a cabinet.

• Store items used most frequently at about waist height. If you have to choose between higher and lower, choose higher.

• Move anything you are not using out of your everyday living/working space.

• Set up **workstations** for activities such as handling mail and bills, sewing, hobbies, and laundry. Organize your workstation with all the supplies you need.

❷ Put scissors, tape, pens, paper, and other tools in places where you commonly use them.

• Pay attention to the areas that frustrate you. Could better organization diffuse your frustration? Make a note to organize that area in your next organizing session. Or take a 15-minute time-out and get a start right now.

• Walk through your home. Look for ways to use doors, walls, and even ceilings as **vertical storage** space: back-of-door organizers, shelving, hooks, racks, and grid systems.

- Look for and use **hidden storage** spaces:

  - Store wrapping paper and supplies in an under-the-bed box. Or stand paper rolls in the corner of a closet; hang ribbon and bows in a plastic bag clipped to a hanger with a clothespin.
  - Keep remote controls and small "cluttery" items in a decorative basket or tin on a shelf where you will see only the container.
  - When buying furniture, choose items that double as storage spaces: trunk-style coffee tables, beds with drawers, and covered benches.

*People have power over things — not the other way around. Vow to use that power to **REGAIN CONTROL** of your space and time.*

- Label everything: folders, home videos, boxes, bins, binders, shelves. Use a marker or a label maker to create neatly lettered, easy-to-read labels.
- When looking for more storage space, don't forget to look up. Sometimes the best solution is to hang items.
  - Collect all clothing with missing buttons, fallen hems, or rips and put it in a bag for **mending.** Schedule mending time, or take those items to a seamstress or tailor.
  - Need to frame a picture, repair shoes, or get a new battery for your watch? Put these items in the trunk of your car, and schedule a time to take them where they need to go.

- Designate a place near the door you use most often, where you can put **videos** or library books that need to be returned, outgoing mail, and items to go to the dry cleaner.
- Keep a small spiral notebook handy during organizing sessions. **Jot down** any organizing projects that should be dealt with in a separate session. Making a note will help to keep you from getting sidetracked.
- Place a basket or a shoe rack near the front door to collect shoes.
- Use a decorative **screen** to hide a shoe bin in the entryway, to partition off a workstation, or to keep archived storage boxes out of sight.
  - No office? File household papers in a rolling file drawer. Store it in a closet, and take it out as needed.
  - No coat closet? Install **pegs** along one wall, or get a coatrack for collecting backpacks, jackets, and hats that would otherwise end up where they don't belong. Be sure to hang hooks for children at an appropriate height.
  - Use adjustable dividers, drawer organizers, small boxes or trays, or even zippered plastic storage bags to organize similar things.
  - Arrange **books** the way they are organized in bookstores and libraries. Separate fiction from nonfiction. *One step further:* Organize fiction alphabetically by author. Organize nonfiction by type — biographies, history, and travel, for example—and then alphabetically by author.
  - Group collectibles together in one display for a less cluttered look.

- On the back of any door hang a **shoe bag** with clear plastic pockets to create instant, convenient storage for magazines, cleaning supplies, small toys, pantry items, craft items, or hand tools.
- Store out-of-season blankets, comforters, coats, sweaters, and other **seasonal** clothing in vacuum-compressed bags to save space.
- Use empty **suitcases** to store out-of-season clothing or bedding in a closet or under a bed. Use locking suitcases to store things you don't want the children to find.
- Store an extra set of sheets between the mattress and box spring at the foot of the bed.
- Clear **plastic storage bins** with lids are the organizer's favorite product. Figure out how many you need. Buy same-size boxes for neat and easy stacking.
- Copy-paper boxes are the next best thing to plastic storage bins. They're lidded, sturdy, stackable, and free. Bring some home from work and use them to store holiday decorations, memorabilia, hand-me-down toys, or out-of-season shoes and accessories. Or use them to store and carry donation items.
- Clearly label the front of each storage box.

*There's a difference between being organized and being **NEAT** and tidy. Stashing stuff in drawers and putting folders and papers in tidy stacks isn't necessarily organized. Always choose "organized" over "neat."*

- Store boxes and bins with labels facing out so you can find what you're looking for without having to move heavy boxes.
- Consider numbering each box and keeping on your computer a **master index** that includes the box number, list of contents, and location of the box. If you need to retrieve an item, use the "find" feature in your word processing program and a keyword to locate items or tape to the box an itemized list of the contents; you'll be able to find a particular item without having to open boxes.
- Designate a storage zone in your basement or garage where you can keep all storage items.
- Use open **plastic crates** on shelves for categorizing and storing items that require easy access, such as camping, biking, or skiing equipment or lawn games.
- Keep an open catchall box in your storage area to collect items that need to be added to packed boxes. Put **catchall items** where they belong the next time you pull out the boxes.
- In your garage, basement, or shed, create storage between exposed studs. Nail two-by-fours at one-foot intervals to create vertical bins for long-handled lawn and garden tools and sports equipment.
- Recycle lidded glass jars and coffee cans into containers for sorting, separating, and storing **hardware** in the workshop.
- Decide to use off-site storage as a last resort. If you are currently renting storage space, schedule a visit to your storage unit. Evaluate: *Is it really worth the money to store this stuff, or could you get rid of some or most or even all of it?*

*If you begin to doubt your **ABILITY** to organize, remember this: You can do anything you set your mind to do.*

- Arrange your **office** so that you can reach your telephone, keyboard, printer, and wastebasket without getting up.
- Be sure to distribute weight in vertical filing cabinets; opening a full top drawer with empty or partly filled bottom drawers can cause the cabinet to tip over.
- Organize your **desk drawers** so that each contains like items — for example, office supplies in one drawer, stationery and notepads in another.
- Solve the problem of what to do with bathrobes and wet towels with an over-the-door peg rack.
- If bathroom storage space is minimal, give each family member a portable **shower caddy** for transporting toiletries from bedroom to bathroom and back.
- To make more room for everyday bathroom items, consider storing first aid supplies and common, over-the-counter remedies in the guest room bathroom or in a kitchen cabinet.
- Store **kitchen items** where you use them: pots and pans near the stove, food-storage wraps and containers near the refrigerator, dishes and silverware near the dishwasher or table.
- Store items in a way that makes sense to you. You might, for example, store coffee filters, the sugar bowl, and coffee spoons with your coffee cups or store measuring cups and spoons in a large mixing bowl.

- Pull out large and seldom-used kitchen items — the turkey roasting pan, clam steamer, and punch bowl — and store in a more out-of-the-way area, such as a hall closet shelf, the garage, or the basement.
- Don't store frequently used items in cabinets above the **stove;** if you reach for them while cooking you could burn yourself.
- Organize a messy cabinet or pantry by making use of empty vertical space. Use double-decker turntables, sliding baskets, hanging shelves, stackable containers, and other inexpensive organizing products, including cup hooks.
- In the **kitchen pantry,** organize shelves and areas by type of food such as pastas, cereals, and soups. Categorizing makes it quicker and easier to find a particular item. Labeling shelves enables anyone to help put away groceries.

The average woman has 40 pairs of **shoes.** The average man has 10. Count yours.

If you have an above-average number of shoes, pull out those you no longer wear, and donate them. Somebody somewhere could really use them.

Separate shoes into regular wear and occasional wear. Keep those you wear regularly visible and accessible on a **shoe rack** or in clear plastic shoe boxes, stacked on shelves. Store special-occasion shoes on upper shelves, in a corner, or against a back wall.

If you store shoes in their original boxes, take an instant photograph of each pair of shoes and glue it to the front of the box to identify what's inside.

Trying to organize your entire home IN A DAY is like trying to eat an entire piece of cake in one bite. You'd choke. Work on organizing projects in small chunks.

• Try storing panty hose and socks in a hanging shoe bag with clear plastic pouches. Organize by color and type, such as knee-highs, dress sheers, and sports socks. The best part about this organizing trick is that you don't even have to fold them when you put them away. Just stuff them in the pockets.

• Hang like items together in your closet. Sort clothing in categories such as special occasion, business, and casual. Further sort into subcategories, such as pants, skirts, and long- and short-sleeved shirts. Or organize by color.

• Double **closet space** for shorter items by attaching a hanging clothes rod to your existing rod.

❶ Set a goal to keep things off the floor of your closet. It's less cluttered and makes it easier to vacuum.

• If your dresser drawers are overstuffed and you have room in your closet, consider getting a hanging **garment bag** with shelves. It will give you easy access to bulky sweaters, T-shirts, and jeans.

• Organize your dresser one drawer at a time. Organize your closet in sections. Otherwise you may create a bigger mess than you started with.

• Screw hooks in your bedroom closets to **hang robes,** pajamas, and other clothing that will be reworn. Add one hook where you can hang the entire outfit you plan to wear the next day.

❶ Hang a nylon or mesh bag on a hook in your closet to collect items that need to go to the dry cleaner.

• Organize **jewelry** in ice cube trays. Store one set of earrings or one fine chain necklace in each cube. Stack in a drawer.

❶ Place a pretty dish on dresser tops and nightstands to collect jewelry, loose change, and pocket paraphernalia.

• String a nylon hammock across a **child's room** to store stuffed animals or in a corner of the garage to create a home for balls, gloves, helmets, knee pads, and other sports gear.

• Organize and store toys in colorful plastic dishpans on shelves. **Toy boxes** tend to create clutter, because kids have to take out everything to find the one thing they want.

• In a young child's closet, install a tension rod at a reachable height and raise it as the child grows.

❶ Make it easy and fun for kids to put things away, and they will be more likely to maintain a clutter-free room. *Example:* Place a basket or crate on the closet floor to throw shoes into.

• Stack plastic crates in a child's closet for storing folded sweaters, T-shirts, and jeans.

• Colorful interlocking plastic crates make great **cubbyholes** for storing books, toys, and games.

• Organize toys in see-through plastic bins by themes. *Examples:* building blocks, cars, animals.

- **Bed elevators** are a great way to create instant under-the-bed storage space for toys or seasonal bedding and clothes. Some lift the bed high enough to create a little play area or room for a desk.

- On a **tight budget?** Try these no-cost ideas:

  - Ask for a clean large pizza box to use as a child's artwork portfolio that can be stored under a bed.

  - Give kids shoeboxes for storing their tiniest collectibles.

- Schedule a regular time each week to sort and organize photographs until you are up-to-date. Wait to buy photo albums or photo boxes until you know how many you need.

- Divide **photographs** into five to seven broad categories, such as "Friends," "Family," "Grandchildren," "Places We've Lived," and "Places We've Visited." Or categorize by events (graduations), time frames (college days), or family members. Sort photographs by category into labeled shoe boxes or photo boxes.

- Sort one category of photographs into subcategories. For example, if the category is vacations, sort photographs into separate vacations you've taken.

- Use labeled paper grocery bags cut down to about six inches high as temporary holders for organizing subcategories of photographs. Or use an **accordion file** with labeled folders.

- Select your preferred photo-storage medium and stick with it: photo albums or archival photo boxes with dividers.

- Throw away photographs that didn't come out right or are very similar to other, better photographs.

- Throw out duplicate photographs, or put them in an envelope marked **"Duplicates"** and store at the back of the album or box that holds the originals.

PART II

EVERYDAY STRATEGIES

It's a lot easier to keep up than to catch up. So start by organizing the everyday stuff. Set up systems to help you stay on top of appointments, pay bills, and manage information. Don't worry about setting up the perfect system. You can always perfect it later. Do be on the lookout for ways to simplify everyday tasks. Take note of the tasks you tend to avoid doing. Organizing these areas will make it simpler to complete these tasks and also bring you the greatest reward.

- If you're feeling a little stressed, it may be that things are getting out of control. **Regain control** by taking time out to organize something. You'll feel better immediately.

- Before you set something down, ask yourself, *"Is this where it belongs?"* If not, take an extra minute or two to put it in its place.

- Create a home for new acquisitions right away.

- Get into "wash and wear." Look for and buy clothes that are machine washable and don't need to be ironed.

- Use the time it takes to brew a pot of coffee to organize a cutlery drawer, remove out-of-date food from the refrigerator, or write a grocery list.

- Limit the number of **daily decisions** you have to make. *Examples*: Plan weekly meals in advance and post the plan on the refrigerator. Pare down your wardrobe to your favorite outfits to make it easier to decide what to wear.

- Jot all notes, reminders, and phone numbers in a small spiral notebook. It eliminates all the little bits of paper and sticky notes that are apt to get lost. And if you need to retrieve a piece of information, you know where it is.

- Get your **hair** styled in a way that is natural so you don't have to spend so much time fussing with it.

- Unclutter your **mind.** Get in the habit of writing things down rather than trying to remember them.

• Want to **keep track** of things like books to read, movies to see, restaurants to try, places to go? Simple ways:

- Use a notebook with divided sections to make and keep separate lists.
- Create a "Wanna" folder with lists for the things you "wanna" do.
- Use your contact management software or PDA to create electronic notes for each category.

• Establish **routines** to help you get things done in a timely manner. *Examples*: Back up your computer every Friday, change bedsheets on Saturday, enter receipts in your bookkeeping system on Monday, clean out the refrigerator before going grocery shopping.

• Make your bed every morning. It instantly neatens up your bedroom. Time how long it takes. Challenge yourself to do it under 60 seconds.

• File **contact information** for services under the business category, such as landscaping or accounting. This way you can still find the service contact even if you can't remember the name of the person or company.

• Use your Rolodex file to store odd bits of information that you may need to access while on the telephone or filling out forms: frequent-flyer numbers, driver's license and social security numbers, health insurance numbers, credit card numbers, lock combinations, passwords, and PINs.

• Rather than save an entire brochure or flyer for one piece of information, such as a tele-phone number, save just the information and discard the paper.

• If you look up a telephone number in the phone directory, **highlight** the entry. If you look up the same number again, add it to your personal phone directory.

• Create a list of **frequently called numbers,** such as your pet sitter, babysitter, veterinarian, and dentist. Post it near the telephone.

• If you don't have time to put photographs in albums right away, schedule 15 minutes to do it by the end of the week.

- If you really dislike putting photos in albums, consider taking all of your photographs with a **digital camera.** Download and store photos electronically. Just be sure to back up your computer regularly.
- Consider keeping all formal portraits (baby, school, wedding, family) in a formal **family album.** Use extra prints to create gift albums.
- Scrap any photos that didn't come out right. Or put them with your photo developing receipt and bring them back next time you develop film. Some developers will give you a refund on those.
- When a child is born, start a videotape to **record birthdays** and special events for that child.

• Have you ever forgotten your gym shoes or towel when packing your workout bag? Write a checklist and store it in a pocket of your bag. You can also create standard **packing check-lists** for volunteer meetings, children's overnights, or family camping trips.

Keep your **suitcase** packed with items you need to bring along on every trip: travel-size toiletries, folding umbrella, travel hair dryer, wrinkle releaser, and other necessities.

*Think about how you can make each **LIVING** space more pleasant. You'll be less likely to mess it up.*

• At the beginning of each season, hang clothes so that the open end of the hanger faces toward you. As you rehang items throughout the season, turn the hanger right way around. At the **end of the season,** you'll be able to see what you wore and what you didn't wear.

• If getting dressed in the morning creates a mess, figure out in the evening what you're going to wear the **next day.** It will give you time to hang up and put away whatever you decided not to wear. You'll also have more time to iron an outfit or do some laundry, if necessary.

❶ Stock extras of items that you use on a regular basis, such as ink cartridges and paper towels. Determine your needs for the next 3, 6, or 12 months, and buy in bulk.

• Create a **grocery shopping** form that includes all items currently in your pantry and any others you buy regularly. List like items together: fresh fruits and vegetables, dairy, frozen items, soups, and so on. Create bold headings for these categories and leave a couple of blank lines at the end of each category for write ins.

❶ Don't buy something because it's on sale. Buy because you need it.

• Post your shopping form. Circle or high-light each item you need to buy on your next trip to the store.

❶ To minimize impulse buying, leave your credit card at home. When you shop with cash only, you tend to think twice about your purchases.

❶ Consider the **real cost** of your purchases. Think in terms of how many hours you need to work to pay for each item you want to buy. Then ask yourself if it is worth the price of your time and energy.

❶ Before purchasing something, think about where you will put it when you get it home. If you have nowhere to put it, don't buy it.

• Buy clothes in coordinating shades. You'll need **fewer shoes** and accessories to go with your outfits — and you'll have more space in your closet.

• Develop a wardrobe of classic styles and outfits that you can mix and match.

❶ When you buy clothing for children, keep the **child-size hanger.** It's easier for adults and children to hang small clothes on small hangers, which makes it more likely that they will get hung up.

*Remember that nothing **WORTH** doing is easy.*

❶ Make a decision to purchase new items only to **replace items** that are worn-out. It will minimize clutter and save money.

❶ Go shopping only when you need something in particular. Make a list and stick to it.

❶ Keep a **running list** of items you need to buy. When you run out of an item or notice that you are running low, write it on your list. Do this with groceries, office supplies, pharmacy items. Keep your list handy so you can add to it easily.

❶ Aim to keep your clothes closet about half-empty. It's easier to take out and put away things when clothes are not crammed together.

• Tape to the outside of drawers pictures or photographs of what goes in them so even very young **children** can keep their clothes organized.

• Hang or fold matching outfits together for children who have not yet learned to coordinate colors. It will speed the process of getting dressed.

• Got filing? Set your **kitchen timer** or electronic calendar for 15 minutes and start filing. When the timer goes off, stop what you are doing until next time.

• Turn downtime into organizing or **catch-up time.** In 5 to 10 minutes, you can:

  • Balance your checkbook.
  • Clean out your wallet.
  • Stay on top of reading.
  • Write a quick note.
  • Sew a button back on.

❶ Keep reading material and portable organizing projects with your briefcase or purse so that you can just grab and go.

❶ Never leave a room without improving its appearance. Pick something up. Put it away.

❶ **Question everything** you file. *Do you really need to save the cable television statement after paying the bill? Why save paper that you will never look at again?* Shred it.

❶ Designate one basket or tray as your in-box. Do not return papers to your in-box once you remove them. Move them along to the appropriate folder or to the recycling bin or wastebasket.

FINISH what you're doing before starting something new.

• Use available technology to speed routine tasks:

  • Sign up for automatic bill payments.
  • Set up an autofill program to automatically fill forms online.
  • Program frequently called numbers into your telephone, cell phone, and fax machine.
  • Buy postage stamps on-line.

• Take the time to learn how to put **technology** to work for you. You don't have to become a computer wiz. Just choose the features that could simplify your life and learn them one at a time.

❶ Triage your mail as soon as it arrives. Toss the junk. File important things, like bills, immediately. Sort the rest into categories such as "To Read" or "To Call" or "For Bob."

❶ To prevent **paper pileup,** decide what to do with each piece of paper as it comes in: delegate, forward, file, toss, read, or respond. Set up action folders for the most common next steps.

❶ Get in the habit of developing photographs immediately upon finishing a roll. Make a note to drop them off.

- Put developed photographs in albums right away.
- Create a calendar file with 12 folders for the months of the year and 31 folders for the days of the month. Use it to store papers that you will need on a **future date,** such as birthday cards purchased in advance, directions to a party, or airline tickets. Store items in the appropriate day or month folder. Add "Check calendar file" to your daily to-do list to get into the habit of looking in it every day.
- Buy an assortment of **greeting cards** to have on hand for unexpected events: get well, sympathy, congratulations, new baby, thank you, birthday, anniversary, blank. Store them in a hanging file folder, binder, or special card box.
- Schedule **filing time** at least once a week or when your "To File" folder gets full.

If you find yourself backsliding into old behaviors, be glad! If you recognize a behavior, you can change it. Recommit to your GOAL and go back to trying on the new behavior.

- When bills arrive, quickly scan the inserts for any helpful or important information. Then save only the bill and the return envelope. This eliminates about half the volume of paper.
- Pay bills as they come, and you won't have to set aside a chunk of time to do them all at once. Or set up **automatic bill payments.** You'll have less incoming mail to open, sort, and file. And you'll spend less time writing checks and stamping and addressing the envelopes.
- Reduce the volume of mail and number of checks you have to write each month. **Consolidate** bills wherever possible — long-distance, local, and cell service; home and auto insurance; and credit cards. You might even save some money.
- If you don't need to save utility bill statements for tax purposes, keep just the current month's statements for easy reference to customer service contacts.
- Consider having credit card and bank statements delivered via **e-mail** to reduce the amount of mail you get. If you do this, set up electronic folders to store statements. And be sure to back up files regularly.
- Have your bank store your canceled checks. If you need to retrieve one, you can request it. When you file a paper, take a **quick look** through the folder to see if there's anything in there you can toss.

Monitor your self-talk. If you think to yourself, "I'm such a slob," immediately negate that thought with "I'm getting MORE organized every day."

- Always put new documents in the front of a file folder so that your papers are filed in reverse chronological order.
- Avoid placing folders and papers directly on your **desk** unless you are physically working with them.
- Create new project folders immediately, to give all related paperwork a home.

• Put papers back in a file folder as soon as you are done with them.

• Use business card holders in your **purse** for storing frequent-flyer cards, frequent-buyer cards, or membership cards. Or type and print the numbers on a sheet of paper and have it reduced to fit in your wallet.

• Organize ATM, debit card, credit card, and other receipts in your purse or car with a mini expandable file or coupon organizer. Schedule time to go through them daily, weekly, or monthly.

• Keep anything you might need on the road in your **car trunk,** and you won't have to worry about storing it anywhere else.

Examples: maps, beach blanket, folding chair(s), first-aid kit, rain slicker.

Always fill your **gas tank** when it gets down to one-quarter or one-half full.

Balance your checking account on-line every few days. Then you can shred ATM and debit charge receipts that have been posted, instead of hanging on to them for the entire month.

Slow down. Practice the concept of "pace, not race." Walk and talk more **SLOWLY.** *Give yourself more time to get where you're going and to complete your work*

CLUTTER CONTROL

Daily organizing is the best line of defense against clutter. Don't just put things down; put them away. And clean up as you go. Also keep in mind that clutter doesn't let itself in the door. The more trouble you have parting with things, the more careful you need to be about acquiring things. Keep in mind that unplanned purchases often end up as clutter. Make the decision not to bring something into your house, and you won't have to make a decision later about what to do with it.

• Do a quick **5-minute pickup** every night before going to bed. Assign family members to each room. Hand little ones a pillowcase so they can help with nightly clutter rounds.

• When you have 10 minutes free, pick up and put away 10 things that belong somewhere else.

• If you see something in a catalog that you might want to buy, tear out the page and the order form and throw out the rest. Staple the page(s) together with the order form and put them in a file labeled **"To Buy."** This makes it easier to find what you were interested in without having to save the whole catalog.

🅾 Never place a larger item, like a folder, on top of a smaller thing, like a receipt; you'll spend less time looking for things.

🅾 Live by the **one in/one out rule.** For every item you bring in the front door, send one item out the back door. Apply this rule to everything from clothing to paper to household items and gifts. Decide before you purchase an item what you intend to let go of to make room for your purchase.

🅾 Plan to **periodically purge** your belongings. Once a year is good. Twice a year is better. Or set up a schedule of regular mini household purges. Scheduling suggestions:

January: Files
May: Storage areas
June: Winter clothing
July: Children's clothing
October: Summer clothing
November/December: Toys and household furnishings

- Declare one day in the spring and fall as **"donation days."** Make a note now in your daily planner or calendar.

  - On self-proclaimed donation days, rummage through your home looking for things that are just taking up space in your closet, things you can donate. Box or bag them up and take them to a local charity.

- Decide to make an annual purge part of your **spring cleaning** ritual. Cleaning your house will be easier with less stuff in it.

  - Do an inventory of your children's clothing *before* going **back-to-school shopping.** If they haven't worn something in the past 12 months, either it doesn't fit or they don't like it. Add it to the donations or hand-me-down pile and make a list of any items that need to be replaced.

- Designate a family donation box for collecting items throughout the year. When the box is full, take it to a local charity.

  - Just before Christmas or birthdays, **ask your kids** for donations of toys, books, and clothes they no longer use or want. Help kids get into the spirit by letting them know that last year's gifts would make great gifts this year for kids who might not get any otherwise.

- When you redecorate your bathroom or buy new sheets for your bed, don't allow the old stuff to take up valuable space in your closets for the next five years. **Donate it now,** and let someone else share in the joy of redecorating.

- Establish a house rule that all **newspapers** go into the recycling bin at the end of each day, whether they've been read or not. By tomorrow, it will be old news.

- Hang clothes up or put them away immediately when you take them off.

*No matter how much you acquire, it's virtually impossible to have it all. There's always something newer and better being introduced. Try to be **HAPPY** with what you already have.*

- **Play clutter tag.** Give a roll of stickers to the kids for tagging any item that's not where it belongs. Making family members aware of their clutter trails may make them think twice about leaving things around.

- Make it clear that leaving personal belongings unattended may result in their being held for ransom. If a family member wants his or her stuff back, he or she will have to do an **extra chore.** If anyone chooses not to do the chore, you know that the item isn't important enough. Give the item away without guilt.

- If **family members** leave their things where they don't belong, gather them up and take them out to the garage. When they ask if you've seen a particular item tell them it's in the garage. When they ask why, tell them you found it lying around and thought it was garbage. They should get the idea pretty fast.

- When it seems like you need more storage space, it's probably time to eliminate some stuff. Schedule a **decluttering session.**

- Put a wastebasket in every room.

- Keep a litter bag in your car.

- If you're having a yard sale, plan to drop off whatever is left at a local charity, or schedule a pickup in advance.

- **Pack up toys** your children have outgrown. Write today's date on the box. If your kids are looking for something you packed up, you can pull it back out. But if the kids haven't missed anything in that box in six months, donate the items.

- Planning a **yard sale?** Give children an incentive to sell toys and games they no longer play with and books they don't read anymore. Let them keep whatever money they get for their stuff.

- If something breaks and you replace it, get rid of the broken item. It is officially garbage.

- Maximize your earnings by **selling used items** while they still have value. Make a decision to sell clothing while it is still in fashion. Sell books, toys, and games while they're still in demand. Sell sporting gear before it becomes outdated. Sell your cell phone, computer, or other high-tech equipment before it becomes obsolete.

- Remember that all donations made on or before December 31 are tax deductible in the current tax year.

- To reduce virtual clutter:

  - Delete all e-mail that requires no further action on your part.
  - If you want to save an e-mail, create a folder for it on your hard drive.
  - Avoid printing e-mails unless you absolutely need to have a hard copy.
  - Periodically schedule some time to delete files.

- When creating electronic folders, set them up the same way you would set up physical folders. Use subfolders within folders to organize files the same way you organize manila folders inside hanging folders.

Let go of the belief that once a thing enters into your POSSESSION, you are its keeper forevermore.

- Lots of well-intentioned gifts end up as clutter. Strategies:

  - Don't ever gush over a gift you don't like. Just say thanks.
  - If a gift giver asks what you want, speak up.
  - Spread the word that you don't need any more of whatever it is that you keep getting.
  - Drop hints about what you would love to get.
  - See if you can exchange a gift you don't like or can't use.
  - Keep gifts for a set time; then donate them.
  - Pass the gift along to someone who will appreciate it.

- If a gift giver learns that you no longer have the **gift item** given to you, you can simply respond, "I did appreciate your gift, but I ended up giving it to someone who really wanted/needed it."

- Talk with your family about gift-giving strategies at **holidays.** Consider having each family member draw one name to buy for. It's more likely that everyone will receive something they really want or need.

◉ Consider limiting yourself to one or two kinds of wrapping paper and one color of ribbon and bows that will work for every occasion.

◉ If necessary, restrict kids' toys to one or two rooms, to keep the rest of the house from getting cluttered.

◉ Consider creating one or more **clutter-free zones** in your home. Pick a room and declare it off-limits to clutter. Establish rules for that room:

- If you bring it in with you, take it out with you.
- If you take it out while you're in here, put it away before leaving.

◉ Think twice before buying souvenirs on vacation. Take photographs or keep a journal instead.

◉ Keep a handled **basket** in the family room for quick pickup and containment of clutter.

*Having less means being able to **ENJOY** what you have more.*

• **Set your table** for a formal dinner, to discourage household members from using it as a dumping ground for backpacks, mail, books, and everything else that comes in the door.

◉ When you finish reading a book, pass it along. Or periodically purge your **book collection,** keeping only the ones that you might want to reread or save for reference.

◉ Help kids see the relationship between clutter and time. On an evening when the house is in order, let kids know that because there's no clutter to pick up, you have time to make popcorn or cookies or whatever they're always asking for.

◉ If you "shop until you drop," clutter is the price you pay. Next time you are shopping, make a decision to postpone all impulse purchases by 24 hours. Most of the time, you'll decide it's not worth the effort to go back for it.

*If you want your children to grow up understanding that the **BEST** things in life aren't things, decide to stop giving them so many things.*

HOME MANAGEMENT

There is no one right way to organize anything. So don't be afraid to experiment. If your organizing system works, then it's perfect. If your system is not working, it's time to try something different. Know that the best home organizing systems are those devised by the end users. Try to get the whole family involved. Just be aware that not everyone in your household sees the benefits of getting organized. To get your family on board, you may have to get creative with incentives.

❂ Establish the household rule: Whoever makes a mess is responsible for cleaning it up — now, not later.

• Make regular organizing a **family project.** Tackle one room at a time together, and use the time to catch up on what's going on at school or in your child's head.

• Set up an **in-box** for each family member. Have kids put permission slips, forms, and notices in your in-box when they come home. Train them to look in their in-boxes by putting dollar bills and love notes in them.

• Help children learn organization skills that will last a lifetime:

• Get them in the habit of doing homework at a set time each day.

• Help them organize their schoolwork and homework assignments with folders and binders.

• Purchase a small day planner for each child for writing down assignments and due dates.

• Encourage kids to select their outfits for the next day and pack their backpacks before going to bed.

❂ If kids are hard to wake up or have to get up very early, put them to bed in their school clothes.

• Consolidate efforts to save time and energy:

• Shop for groceries once rather than three or four times a week.

- Iron a bunch of things at one time, rather than just one.
- Double a dinner recipe and freeze half for another night.
- Buy all the birthday and other special-occasion cards you need one month in advance.

• Establish a **household budget** based on actual expenses. Using your checkbook register, make a list of all expenditures by category for the past six months. Total each category and divide by six to get the average monthly expense for each.

• If you spend 5 minutes cleaning the bathroom three times a week, it takes only 15 minutes total. But if you wait to do it once a week, it can take a half hour to cut through the buildup of clutter and dirt.

• Designate one area in your home as a **bill-paying place,** and keep there everything you need to pay the bills, including: unpaid bills, calculator, pens, pencils, stapler, stamps, envelopes, and blank checks. Store bill-paying supplies in nearby drawers or cabinets, or put them in a portable storage bin that you can stash somewhere when not in use.

• Type standard lists of instructions and directions for your **babysitter** or pet sitter so you can just print them as needed.

Recognize that when you make changes, it takes time for others to adjust to those CHANGES. If you've always been the messy one, it's possible that family members have been using your messi-

ness as an excuse to be messy themselves.

◑ Designate one drawer or basket as a temporary holding place for **stray items:** buttons, eyeglasses, single socks, and anything that appears to be homeless. If a family member is looking for something, you can say, ìDid you check the basket?î Periodically, have family members claim whatever is theirs and put it away.

◑ Sometimes the best strategy for dealing with a teen's messy room is to close the door.

• Develop a schedule for **laundry:** Designate certain days for certain types of laundry, or if you do laundry daily, let everyone know that anything that needs to be washed should be in the laundry room by a certain time and can be picked up after such-and-such time.

• Laundry is quicker and easier to do when clothes are already separated into wash type. Train family members to sort their laundry into whites, lights, and darks. Use three separate baskets or a triple-compartment laundry sorter in the **laundry room.** Use a permanent marker to label each basket or compartment: whites, lights, and darks.

◑ **Teach your family** to turn shirts, pants, and socks right side out so you don't have to do it for everyone. Establish a reward for doing it.

• Put a dirty clothes collectorî in each bedroom. Ideally, this is a lightweight basket or bag that can be easily carried to the laundry room.

• If more than one family member is responsible for doing laundry (or you wish other family members *would* do laundry), try this: Write or type the washing and drying instructions for each type of wash on a slip of paper and pin or tape it to the outside of each basket or compartment.

◦ If **missing socks** are a problem, have everyone pin pairs of socks together. Wash and dry them with pins still in them. Have a place in every bedroom, preferably near the dirty-clothes hamper or basket, for keeping a supply of safety pins handy.

• Color-code your children's clothing. Dot clothing tags and the toes of socks, using a different-colored laundry marker for each child. Then anyone can do the job of sorting and folding without having to know whose clothes are whose.

• Fold or hang each item as you remove it from the **dryer.** Use the dryer top for folding and sorting; place folded clothes in the basket at your feet. Use the basket to carry clean laundry.

◦ Don't do laundry that isn't prepared as requested.

◦ **Premeasure** laundry detergent into zippered plastic food bags to take to the Laundromat. Use a film canister to take along 20 quarters.

• Spend some time organizing your laundry room and cleaning closet. It makes chores more pleasant when you can easily reach the supplies you need without getting hit on the head with dust mops and brooms.

• Simplify meal planning and shopping. Keep track of your **dinner menus** for a month. Write each complete menu on the front of an index card, and list the ingredients on the back. At the end of the month, you will have 28 dinner ideas to choose from each week. Simply add the ingredients you need to your weekly shopping list.

◦ With older children and teenagers, make it clear that privileges depend on response to family requests. If assigned chores don't get done on time, no privileges are awarded.

• Experiment with precooked, ready-to-cook, and **ready-to-eat items** from the supermarket. They cost a little more, but sometimes it's worth it. *Ideas:* marinated meats for the barbecue, bagged salads, roasted chicken, and frozen stir-fry meals.

◦ If your children go grocery shopping with you, have them locate the coupon items for you. You might even offer them cash for the value of the coupons in return for helping to do the shopping, loading, and unloading the car and putting food away.

• Look for Web sites that offer recipes searchable by ingredient. It's a big help when you have an abundance of a perishable item.

◦ Use a dishpan to collect all the dirty dishes from the table.

◦ Sort knives, spoons, and forks as you put them into the **dishwasher** to make it easier to put them away when they're clean.

• Trade the chore you most hate doing with another household member's most hated chore.

◦ If there's a chore you put off doing because you hate it, time it. It may not take as long as you think, and once you realize that, it will be easier to make yourself do it.

*Organizing is not a one-time-and-you're-done kind of job. It's an **ONGOING** process.*

- Do quick little cleanups often:

  - Use a no-wipe daily shower cleaning spray to prevent soap scum buildup.
  - Wipe sink, faucets, and countertop after the final use every morning. Use a washcloth or hand towel that's headed for the laundry.
  - Keep frequently used cleaning supplies in your bathroom and kitchen so that you can clean at your convenience.

❶ Stagger wake-up times for better traffic control (and less fighting) in the bathroom on school days.

  - Tackling all the **housework** yourself is not doing your children any favors. Get your children to help with laundry, dishes, cleaning, and other chores. Offer a per-job salary or weekly allowance. Reward points as incentive. Give praise for a job well-done to help build self-esteem.

❶ If you haven't already, make it a point to try revolutionary new **cleaning products** like cleaner-on-board wet mops, pre-moistened wipes, and ready-to-use toilet brush cleaners.

  - Make a list of chores that need to be done on a regular basis. Have family members initial the chores they don't mind doing. You do the same. Each of you can then take responsibility for those chores and rotate the ones everyone dislikes.
  - Try the **job jar** method of assigning chores: Write regular chores on individual slips of paper and put them into a jar. Each week, have family members take turns pulling out the slips of paper.
  - Create a separate job jar or envelope for jobs that fall outside the weekly routine.

❶ Keep a **log book** near the phone for recording phone messages and other notes for family members. It's a handy reference if you ever need to find a phone number that's not in your personal directory.

❶ If you think of something at work that you need to do at home, leave yourself a **voice mail** message.

SCHEDULES & TO-DO'S

Organize your schedule around your priorities. The more control you exert over your schedule, the more control you will have over the direction of your life. Accept the fact that you are not likely to accomplish everything on your to-do list. It's okay. Sometimes you just need to "be" rather than be doing. The most important things will always get done. Do make a point to focus on the task at hand. Recent scientific studies prove that multitasking is not as efficient as you might think.

Keep the same calendar for business and personal use. Use different-colored pencils or highlighters to distinguish between work and personal commitments.

- Find a calendar or **day planner** that really suits you. You'll be more inclined to use it every day.

Keep your schedule flexible. Create a buffer zone around each activity to accommodate for the fact that things take longer than you think and to allow for unexpected delays.

- Map out your day in 15- or 30-minute increments. You can often accomplish more by using small blocks of time to focus on a particular project.

- Build a little **relaxation** time into your schedule. Your body, mind, and spirit need it.

Block out one hour of time each day to work on long-range planning or goals.

Block out one morning or afternoon each week for administrative tasks: filing, paying bills, ordering supplies.

Schedule your most difficult tasks — those that require creative thinking and decision making — for the time of day when you have the most energy.

- Schedule **routine tasks,** such as housecleaning and grocery shopping, into regular time slots on your calendar. It will help to keep your household running smoothly and ensure that you don't overbook yourself.

- Do at least one thing each day that will bring you closer to a **long-term goal.** *Ideas:* Make a phone call, set up a folder, attend a meeting, set up a bank account, brainstorm an idea, ask an expert for advice.

- Free up time by consolidating like tasks:

  - Check e-mail messages and return telephone calls once or twice a day, instead of all day long.
  - Pick up and drop off dry cleaning at the same time.
  - Make a list of what you need from the supermarket, and shop weekly instead of daily.

○ Schedule a regular time for running routine **errands,** and run them all at once.

- Group errands together geographically to save time. Make a list and number stops in order.
- Don't forget to schedule routine maintenance on your **car** and home to avoid costly and untimely repairs.

○ When you write appointments in your planner, also write in a **phone number** to call in case you're running late, want to confirm, or need to reschedule.

○ Set your electronic calendar alarm, your watch, or an alarm clock to remind you when it is time to leave for an appointment or make an important call.

- Keep track of **family schedules** with a physician's group practice appointment book (available at office-supply stores). Multiple columns allow you to see where each family member needs to be at any given time.

○ Schedule a family meeting once a week to review upcoming agendas.

- Keep the family calendar in a central location so every family member can enter appointments and events.

If you keep doing things the same way, you're going to keep getting the same **RESULTS.** *Accept the fact that you're going to have to change your ways.*

- Create a **master list** of things to do. From this list, create your daily to-do lists.
- Put the **80/20 principle** to work. Only 20 percent of the things on your to-do list are priority items. If you have 20 things on your master to-do list, identify which four (20 percent) are the most important, and focus all of your energy on getting those things done.
- Evaluate every item on your master to-do list. Move any tasks that would be nice to do, but aren't necessary, to a separate "would be nice to do" list.

○ Decide which **one thing** on your daily to-do list is the most important. Do that first.

- End your work day by writing a to-do list for the next day.
- The secret to getting through your daily to-do list is to put fewer things on it. Just list the three most important things to do that day. If you have time left over at the end of the day, you can always add another task from your master list.

○ Add "Unclutter my desk" to your daily to-do list until it becomes a habit.

○ Every Monday morning or Friday night, pick a project or area to organize in the **coming week.**

❶ Schedule 15 minutes each day to work on **weekly** organizing projects. If you finish before the week is up, use the rest of the scheduled organizing time to spend with your kids, work on your novel, or do some long-range planning.

❶ If you have trouble getting started each day, add to your daily to-do list a simple task, such as "Make coffee" or "Check calendar." As soon as you do it, cross it off your list and move on to the first real task of the day. A sense of accomplishment helps to get your day going in the right direction.

• Make a decision about what to do next with each piece of paper you pick up. If it's not practical to take immediate action, file the paper in an action folder. For example, if you need to reply to correspondence but must first make a phone call to obtain information, file the paper in an action folder labeled "To Call."

• Go through your in-box daily.

• Keep in your **e-mail in-box** only those messages that you have yet to respond to. Delete or move other messages to subfolders within your in-box.

❶ Minimize distractions while you work. Let voice mail take messages. Close your e-mail program or lower the volume of your speakers so you can't hear incoming mail notification.

*It doesn't matter where or how you start. All that matters is that you **BEGIN** somewhere, anywhere. **START** right now.*

• At the beginning of each week, create time in your schedule for each one of your **priorities.** Then schedule everything else around those things.

• If having more free time is a priority, schedule your free time first. Then schedule focused work time. Use the time in between for completing routine tasks.

❶ Before you take on another responsibility, ask yourself if it fits with your priorities.

❶ Go on a **commitments diet.** If you are involved in activities that are not aligned with your values or priorities, consider resigning from those activities. It's okay. People will understand. Keep in mind that in stepping aside, you are giving someone else an opportunity to step forward.

• Choose two or three things that you consider to be the most important to you, such as career, family, fitness, or whatever you are passionate about. Design your to-do list around these priorities.

❶ If you have trouble **saying no,** say "Can I get back to you?" You may find it easier to bow out when you don't have the pressure of giving an immediate reply.

• Apply the on/off rule to commitments. Before you agree to be on a committee or board, get off a committee or board.

• **Delegate** anything that doesn't require your knowledge and skills. Delegate to household members or hire an outside service.

• Remember that in the big picture of life, your to-do list is not nearly as important as your to-be list. Schedule time to be with the people you love, in the places you love, doing the things you love to do.

❂ If it will take less than a minute to file a paper, write a check, or whatever, do it now.

❂ Beware of the practice of leaving papers out as reminders of things to do. *Better:* Make a note of what you need to do and file the paper in a to-do folder or in a hanging file with related papers.

• Simple ways to remember important things to do while you are out:

  • Put objects that need to leave the room or house with you near the door or on the driver's seat of your car.
  • Post a sticky note on the doorjamb.
  • Post a sticky note on the dashboard of your car as a reminder.

• Stay on track. As you begin to do something, ask yourself why you are doing it. Is it important enough that you need to do it right now? Or can it wait until later?

• Make dreaded tasks more enjoyable. **Listen to music** while performing the task, or give yourself a little reward after.

• Make a note in your calendar or day planner to start gathering all your **tax documentation** on or around January 15.

❂ Schedule an appointment with your tax preparer in late January/ early February.

• Deliver all tax documentation to your tax preparer no later than February 15, or use that as your start date if you are preparing your own taxes.

• At the end of the year, transfer special dates to remember to your new calendar.

❂ Make a note in your calendar to do a back-to-school clothing inventory in July and a toy purge in December. (See related tips on page 285.)

• Note birthdays, anniversaries, and special dates in your electronic calendar, in your day planner, or on a wall calendar. Also, pencil in reminders for routine automobile maintenance (inspections, oil changes, tire rotation) and for routine home maintenance (change air conditioning and heating filters and check smoke detectors).

❂ **Plan ahead** as much as possible to save time, money, frustration, hassles, and disappointments later. *Example:* If you know you have a week off in July, start making vacation plans in January or February.

Don't **OVERWHELM** *yourself by thinking about all the work you have to do. Just do what you can do today.*

❂ Never forget a special occasion again. Sign up for a free or fee-based e-mail reminder on the Internet.

• Schedule time in late December/ early January to go through all the files in your filing cabinet. Toss or shred any papers you no longer need to save. Consolidate or add file folders as necessary. Use a binder clip to mark the file where you left off, if you need to finish the project another day.

Appendixes

RESOURCES

Professional Organizer Services

National Association of Professional Organizers (NAPO)

4700 W. Lake Ave.
Glenview, IL 60025
847-375-4746
www.napo.net
Information about professional organizers and referral to professional organizers in your area. Order forms for "Golden Tips for Getting Organized" booklet from Golden Circle Members also available.

OnlineOrganizing.com

P.O. Box 1942
Clinton, MD 20735
301-659-2203
www.onlineorganizing.com
Free home and office organizing tips; products to help you regain control over your time, space, and paper; and free referral to a professional organizer near you.

Professional Organizers Web Ring (POWR)

P.O. Box 298
Mt. Ephraim, NJ 08059
www.organizerswebring.com
Post an organizing question or join the discussion forum for advice from professional organizers.

Search by state to find a professional organizer near you.

Day Planners

Day-Timer

1 Willow Lane
East Texas, PA 18046
800-457-5702
www.daytimer.com
On-line store plus information resource for time-management articles, productivity tips, and other time-related information.

Franklin Covey

800-819-1812
www.franklincovey.com
Productivity solutions — from paper and electronic organizing products to leadership training— for home, family, and business.

GO MOM! Planner

26037 Talamore Drive
South Riding, VA 20152
703-327-7722
www.gomominc.com
The ultimate daily planner system for busy moms who want to manage time more effectively, plan ahead, and keep track of their family's busy schedules. System includes an

undated weekly scheduler and 18-month flip calendar, plus pages for planning menus, grocery and bulk shopping lists, and for writing to call, to do, and to buy lists and other important notes and reminders.

Planner Pads

P.O. Box 27187
Omaha, NE 68127
800-315-7526
www.plannerpads.com
A unique, two-page-per-week format lets you organize all your business and personal activities in one place. Each page works like a funnel to find priorities, organize workflow, and plan your day. It also funnels events from idea stage to point of action, which helps to establish a productive workflow.

Yahoo!

www.yahoo.com
Offers a free calendar tool that lets you share your schedules with other people, find free times, and send appointment reminders.

Virtual Office Assistants

Pat Voyajopoulos, Oasis

51 Valley Road
Dedham, MA 02026
781-329-2236
pat@oasisadmin.com
Oasis provides administrative support to small and home-based business owners. With an MBA (concentration in Marketing and Computer Systems) and more than twenty years of professional experience, Pat Voyajopoulos can help you complete tasks that you don't have the time or desire to do.

Type4U Business Support Services

1580 Misty Valley Dr.
Lawrenceville, GA 30045
770-682-8636
www.type4u.com

A fully staffed and equipped office for your administrative support on an as-needed basis. Hire the services of an on-staff secretary, administrative assistant, or bookkeeper without the cost of a full-time employee. Staff includes experts on office support services, transcription, contact management, and desktop publishing.

Filing Systems

FileSolutions Filing Systems

800-336-2046
www.filesolutions.com
Custom-designed filing systems for home, business, doctors, educators, and students. Each complete system includes a set of preprinted and blank adhesive labels, guidebook for selecting file names, and alphabetical FileIndex to help you find documents. Available at The Container Store, Stacks and Stacks stores, Organized Living stores, and Storables stores; through distributors and professional organizers; and direct from the makers.

Kiplinger's Taming the Paper Tiger

The Monticello Corporation
4060 Peachtree Road, Suite D-339
Atlanta, GA 30319-3020
800-430-0794
freetrial@thepapertiger.com
www.thepapertiger.com
A revolutionary software product that combines an easy-to-use computer indexing system with proven paper-management methods. The complete kit includes Windows-based software, multimedia tutorial, preprinted labels, and a user's guide. "Find any document in your office within five seconds or your money back."

"Office-on-the-Go" System

301-659-2203
www.onlineorganizing.com
Designed to fit in the trunk of your car, this traveling office puts the tools you need at your fingertips. Comes with color-coded and prelabeled files, organized into either standard business or

personal categories. Includes storage for business cards, letterhead, and forms; ten hanging folders and eighteen interior folders; and side pockets for pens, stapler, and other supplies. The bottom is edged with hook-and-loop fastener to keep it from flipping over in your trunk.

Tax Tabs
P.O. Box 54513
Atlanta, GA 30308
www.onlineorganizing.com
Provides a mechanism for storing receipts gathered throughout the year, making them easy to retrieve in order to prepare your personal or business income tax returns quickly and conveniently. Includes preprinted filing labels, instructions for integrating Tax Tabs into your current system, and more. Available in home and sole proprietor versions.

On-line Office Supplies

Office Depot
800-Go-Depot
(800-463-3768)
www.OfficeDepot.com
On-line business solutions center and products.

Office Max
800-283-7674
www.OfficeMax.com
One-stop shopping for home and office organization products and business services.

Staples
800-378-2753
www.Staples.com
Home organization products, office supplies, electronic organizers, and business services, with weekly specials and a business-reward program.

Electronic Reminder Systems

www.NeverForget.com
Download a free trial of NeverForget Personal Reminder Software to set up and send e-mail reminders on a one-time, weekly, monthly, or annual basis.

www.RememberIt.com
Allows you to set up e-mail reminders for important dates and events.

Clutter Support Groups and Services

Clutterless Recovery Groups, Inc.
1714 54th St., Apt. B
Galveston, TX 77551-4717
409-744-1289
www.clutterless.org
A nonprofit self-help organization for clutterers by clutterers, Clutterless Recovery Groups sponsors workshops in cities across the United States. At the Web site, you'll find helpful information about hoarding.

Messies Anonymous
5025 S.W. 114th Avenue
Miami, FL 33165
800-MESS-AWAY (637-7292)
www.messies.com
Contact Messies Anonymous for support group information or a free introductory newsletter. (Send a self-addressed, stamped envelope to receive the newsletter.)

National Study Group on Chronic Disorganization
P.O. Box 1990
Elk Grove, CA 95759
916-962-6227
www.nsgcd.org
Call or go to Web site to get a referral to a professional organizer in your area or to order a reading list of books for chronically disorganized people.

Organizing Products

Contact the following companies to request a catalog, shop on-line, or for more information about retail stores and distributors in your area.

California Closets

888-336-9709
www.calclosets.com
California Closets specializes in restructuring traditional pole-and-shelf closets into more efficient, less cluttered storage areas. Call or visit the Web site for the location of stores worldwide.

The Container Store

888-CONTAIN (266-8246)
www.thecontainerstore.com
A store devoted to helping streamline and simplify lives by offering an exceptional mix of storage and organization products.

Hold Everything

800-922-4117
www.holdeverything.com
Well-designed, attractive storage solutions for the home, from closet and shelving systems to furnishings for the home office.

Ikea

www.ikea.com (www.ikea.ca in Canada)
Through retail stores around the world, Ikea offers functional, beautifully designed storage solutions for every room in the house — at affordable prices. Visit the Web site to find the store nearest you or to browse the on-line catalog.

Kitchen Accessories Unlimited

1136–1146 Stratford Ave.
Stratford, CT 06615
800-667-8721
www.kitchensource.com
Designer kitchen accessories and storage solutions, including simple, do-it-yourself cabinets and pantries.

Organization, etc.

800-600-9817
www.org-etc.com
Quality home organizing products and ideas for simplifying daily routines, making better use of space, and increasing productivity.

Stacks & Stacks

1045 Hensley St.
Richmond, CA 94801
800-761-5222
www.stacksandstacks.com
Thousands of storage and organization products to organize your home and office and simplify your life, including hard-to-find but useful items.

Lillian Vernon

800-901-9291
www.lillianvernon.com
Call to request a catalog, browse catalogs on-line, or search the Web site for a specific organizing product or category.

Recipes and Meal Planning Tools

www.Allrecipes.com

3317 Third Ave. S.
Suite D
Seattle, WA 98109
206-292-3990
A twenty-three-chapter on-line cookbook. You can search for recipes by ingredient or category, create a personal recipe box, and make a shopping list for your weekly meal plan.

www.Cooking.com

2850 Ocean Park Blvd.
Suite 310
Santa Monica, CA 90405
Recipes, menus, cooking tips and techniques, and entertaining ideas from award-winning chefs online and through free e-mail newsletter.

www.FabulousFoods.com

Dedicated to teaching and inspiring people "to cook, entertain, to interact, and most importantly to create lasting memories between themselves and the important people in their lives.

www.30DayGourmet.com

P.O. Box 272
Brownsburg, IN 46112
Make-ahead-and-freeze menus and recipes to save you time and money. Free e-mail newsletter.

Financial Planner Referrals

Certified Financial Planner Board of Standards

888-237-6275
www.cfp-board.org
A professional regulatory organization that fosters professional standards in personal financial planning so that the public values, has access to, and benefits from competent financial planning.

Financial Products and Services

Bankrate.com

11760 US HWY 1
Suite 500
N. Palm Beach, FL 33408
561-630-2400
www.bankrate.com
Bankrate.com provides objective financial data and research and editorial information to help consumers make informed decisions about loans and credit cards, savings, and investments.

Upromise

www.upromise.com
A free program designed to help families reach their college savings goals. Contributing companies, such as AT&T, General Motors, and McDonald's, give you back part of your spending

as college savings. They also allow you to invest your savings in a tax-deferred college investing account managed by some of the world's leading financial services firms.

Credit Counseling Services

American Consumer Credit Counseling, Inc.

130 Rumford Avenue, Suite 202
Newton, MA 02466-1316
800-769-3571
www.consumercredit.com
A nationally recognized consumer credit 501(3c) nonprofit organization helping people regain financial control through debt consolidation and credit counseling.

AmeriDebt

12800 Middlebrook Road, Suite 300
Germantown, MD 20874
800-408-0044
www.ameridebt.com
A nonprofit organization dedicated to assisting consumers who are having difficulties with their personal finances.

National Foundation for Credit Counseling

801 Roeder Road, Suite 900
Silver Spring, MD 20910
800-388-2227
www.nfcc.org
A national nonprofit network of more than 1,300 locations designed to provide assistance to people dealing with stressful financial situations.

Money-Saving Tips

The Dollar Stretcher

P.O. Box 14160
Bradenton, FL 34280
941-761-7805
www.stretcher.com
Search for and read articles and tips on such topics as home organization, space management,

and time management. Or send $2 (U.S.) to the address above for a sample issue.

Yearning for Balance Action Kit

The Center for a New American Dream
6930 Carroll Avenue, Suite 900
Takoma Park, MD 20912
301-891-ENUF (3683)
www.newdream.org
Tips and resources for people who subscribe to the belief that "more" is not necessarily better.

Government Services

Insure Kids Now!

877-543-7669
www.insurekidsnow.gov
A program of the U.S. Health Resources and Services Administration, Insure Kids Now! provides free or low-cost health insurance program for infants, children, and teens. Eligibility rules vary from state to state, but in most states, uninsured children 18 years of age or younger whose families earn up to $34,100 a year (for a family of four) are eligible.

Internal Revenue Service

800-TAX-FORM (829-3676)
www.irs.gov
Request IRS Form 4506 if you cannot locate a copy of the most recent income tax return for yourself or on behalf of a deceased individual. Use the forms and publication finder on the Web site to search for "Recordkeeping for Individuals," which contains complete and current guidelines for keeping tax-related papers.

National Center for Health Statistics

Division of Data Services
6525 Belcrest Road
Hyattsville, MD 20782-2003
301-458-4636
www.cdc.gov/nchs

Provides information on how to obtain vital records (birth, death, marriage, divorce certificates) in every state.

National Personnel Records

9700 Page Avenue
St. Louis, MO 63132-5100
Write in care of the branch of the military in which you served for a copy of your discharge papers.

Social Security Administration

800-772-1213
www.ssa.gov
Information about social security benefits and payments, including on-line forms for address changes and how to apply for benefits, including survivor and death benefits.

U.S. State Department (Consular Services)

Office of Overseas Citizens Services
Bureau of Consular Affairs,
Room 4811
U.S. Department of State
2201 C Street NW
Washington, DC 20520-4818
888-407-4747
(317-472-2328 from outside U.S.)
www.travel.state.gov
Go to the Web site or call the hotline for up-to-date Consular Information Sheets, Travel Warnings, and Public Announcements for any country. Or send a self-addressed, stamped envelope and request for information about a particular country or countries. Information is also available at any of the thirteen regional passport agencies, field offices of the Department of Commerce, and U.S. embassies and consulates abroad.

U.S. Department of State (Passport Services)

Office of Overseas Citizens Services
Bureau of Consular Affairs Passport Services,
Room 6811
U.S. Department of State
Washington, DC 20520-4818
900-225-5674
www.travel.state.gov
Go to the Web site for information about passport services and to download a passport application. Information is also available 24 hours a day via an automated 900 number for a cost of thirty-five cents per minute. Information is also available at any of the thirteen regional passport agencies, field offices of the Department of Commerce, and U.S. embassies and consulates abroad.

U.S. Department of State (Visa Services)

Office of Overseas Citizens Services
Bureau of Consular Affairs Visa Services
U.S. Department of State
Washington, DC 20522-1225
202-663-1225
usvisa@state.gov
www.travel.state.gov
Call, send e-mail, write, or go to the Web site to obtain visa requirements and contact information for countries worldwide.

U.S. Department of Veteran Affairs

National Cemetery Administration
800-827-1000
www.cem.va.gov
Information about eligibility and application for burial and memorial benefits for veterans.

Family Resources

Disney On-line Family Fun

www.familyfun.com
Ideas for indoor or outdoor activities, arts and crafts ideas, and fun learning activities, as well as money-saving tips.

Learning Network

www.familyeducation.com
Features learning activities by age group. Select an age group and then click on an activity topic. You also can sign up for a free e-mail newsletter.

ParentSoup

www.parentsoup.com
An iVillage Web site with ideas for parties and crafts as well as a variety of parenting information.

Travel Services and Products (also see Government Services)

AAA Map 'n' Go

DeLorme
2 DeLorme Drive
Yarmouth, ME 04096-6965
207-846-7000
www.delorme.com
Mapping and trip planning software for your computer that includes the latest AAA information and ratings on lodgings, restaurants, campgrounds, museums, parks, fairs, and family events.

Magellan's

110 W. Sola St.
Santa Barbara, CA 93101
800-962-4943
www.magellans.com
An award-winning mail-order catalog featuring a wide selection of state-of-the-art, high-quality travel organizing products from adaptor plugs to wrinkle-free clothing.

Rand McNally

www.randmcnally.com
Detailed electronic road maps include turn-by-turn directions, road construction updates, and estimated travel times from the makers of "indispensable guides to where things are and how to get there."

Travelex Worldwide Money

877-394-2247

customerservice@travelex.com

www.travelex.com

Order foreign currency online, track currency rates, and be notified when you want to buy. The Web site also features a currency converter to see how much your dollars will buy. Travelex is also a global source for Visa TravelMoney.

The Weather Channel

www.weather.com

Detailed weather reports and forecasts for anywhere in the world including airport weather forecasts, travel advisories, and flight on-time status.

Home Safety

National Lead Information Center

800-LEAD-FYI (532-3394)

For answers to questions about lead poisoning, free publications, and referral to a listing of lead-service professionals in your area.

United States Consumer Product Safety Commission

800-638-2772

www.cpsc.gov

Provides current information about product hazards and recalls. You can also subscribe to receive all recall notices by e-mail on the same day they are issued.

Trash and Recycling Information

Computers & Education Computer Recycling Center

3249 Santa Rosa Avenue

Santa Rosa, CA 95407

707-570-1600

www.crc.org

The mission of the Computer Recycling Center is "to promote the highest and best reuse of computer and electronic equipment, and recycle unusable items to keep them out of landfills." This nonprofit organization provides refurbished computers to public schools and community nonprofits. Check the Web site for recycling center locations, then drop off your old equipment and receive a charitable receipt.

Computers for Schools Program

3350 N. Kedzie Avenue

Chicago, IL 60618

800-939-6000

www.pcsforschools.org

This nonprofit organization welcomes contributions of color monitors, computers with high-speed microprocessors, and quality peripherals. Equipment is refurbished at various sites (correctional facilities, vocational centers, community colleges, etc.) and then placed in schools according to local program parameters and/or the preference of the donor. A donation receipt is provided.

Dress for Success

www.dressforsuccess.org

A nonprofit organization that helps low-income women make tailored transitions into the workforce, Dress for Success affiliates accept donations of interview suits. Check the Web site to find a donation location near you.

Earth 911

7301 E. Helm

Bldg. D

Scottsdale, AZ 85260

480-889-2650

800-CLEANUP (800-253-2687)

www.earth911.org

Information about environmentally friendly recycling and disposal.

Got Junk

300-1523 W. 3rd Ave.

Vancouver, BC, Canada

V6J 1J8

800-GOT-JUNK (468-5865)

www.1800gotjunk.com

Fee-based service that hauls away old furniture and appliances, construction debris, yard refuse, and other household junk for disposal or recycling.

Moving Resources

American School Directory
www.asd.com
Facts about local schools, including district phone numbers and statistics on class sizes.

Current Address Labels
www.currentlabels.com
On-line resource for address labels and stamps, stationery, and pet tags.

ForSaleByOwner.com, Corp.
60 E. 42nd St.
Suite 3007
New York, NY 10165
888-367-7253
www.forsalebyowner.com
The official Web site for buying and selling real estate without brokers or commissions.

Homestore.com
www.homestore.com/moving
Research cities, find local services, get tips for packing and unpacking, make arrangements to hook up utilities, and more.

United States Postal Service
www.moversguide.com
Lets you create a personalized moving checklist and timeline, get maps and directions, purchase packing supplies, rent a moving truck, and make arrangements to connect utilities.

Pet Care and Safety

The American Animal Hospital Association
800-883-6301
www.healthypet.com
To find a veterinarian in a new neighborhood.

ASPCA Animal Poison Control Center
424 E. 92nd Street
New York, NY 10128
888-4ANI-HELP (426-4435)
www.aspca.org
The only animal poison control center in the United States. Staffed by veterinarians and veterinary toxicologists 24 hours a day, 7 days a week. The center receives no state, federal, or hospital funding; therefore, they charge a $45 case fee to maintain their expert veterinary staff around the clock. The center's hotline veterinarians can quickly answer questions about toxic substances found in our everyday surroundings that can be dangerous to animals. The Center will do as many follow-up calls as necessary in critical cases and, at the owner's request, will contact his or her veterinarian. The Center also provides specific treatment protocols by fax. They accept VISA, Master Card, Discover, and American Express.

American Kennel Club
260 Madison Avenue
4th Floor
New York, NY 10016
www.akc.org
Information about selecting and buying a puppy, health care, nutrition, AKC events and registration.

The Cat Fanciers' Association, Inc.
P.O. Box 1005
Manasquan, NJ 08736-0805
732-528-9797
www.cfainc.org
Information on cat shows, cat breeds, and cat care from the world's largest registry of pedigreed cats.

Pet First Aid: Cats and Dogs
(St. Louis: StayWell, 1997) by Bobbie Mammato, DMV, MPH
Information to help you learn more about caring for your pet in an emergency. This book can be purchased through your local branch of the Red Cross or a bookstore.

Estate Organizing Products

Estate Organization Portfolio

Exit, Stage Right
P.O. Box 60794
Palo Alto, CA 94306
650-493-3948
www.exitstageright.com
A 70-page guide that includes all the information you and your family will need to handle the practical and administrative issues surrounding loss — be it from disaster, incapacity, or death. Deluxe binder includes data sheet pages to record personal choices and information as well as legal and financial data.

Personal Assets Inventory Workbook

McMillan & Company Professional Organizing
12021 Wilshire Blvd., Suite 670
West Los Angeles, CA 90025
310-391-7392
www.organizer4me.com
A safe-deposit–size workbook for recording locations of important documents and records, a room-by-room inventory of household possessions, and key people to contact in an emergency.

Estate Planning Documents

Nolo

950 Parker St.
Berkeley, CA 94710
800-728-3555
www.nolopress.com
Software and forms you can use to prepare your own will; manuals included.

LegalZoom

7083 Hollywood Blvd.
Suite 180
Los Angeles, CA 90028
www.legalzoom.com
LegalZoom uses Internet technology to help you prepare wills, living wills, powers of attorney, and other legal documents on-line. Once you complete a simple questionnaire, your documents will be prepared within 48 hours for significantly less than you would pay an attorney to prepare similar documents.

Legaldocs

www.legaldocs.com
At this site, you can prepare customized legal documents on-line, including a free living will that is written in accordance with the laws of the state where you reside. All documents can be previewed free of charge. Fees vary according to type and complexity of document.

PLAN4ever

310-734-5590
www.plan4ever.com
At this site, you'll find an easy-to-use Last Wishes form that will help walk you through the many end-of-life issues you may want to consider. After completing the form, you can print it out to file with your personal records and to distribute as necessary. Free.

Aging with Dignity

888-5-WISHES
www.agingwithdignity.org
This nonprofit organization offers Five Wishes, a legal document that helps you plan for such end-of-life issues as whom you want to make health-care decisions for you if you can't make them, the kind of medical treatment you want or don't want, and what you want your loved ones to know.

CONTRIBUTING EXPERTS

Following is a list of experts whose organizing tips, strategies, and solutions appear in this book. *Note:* Some contact information has been omitted at the request of the organizers.

Professional Organizers

Sally Allen • A Place for Everything, LLC(SM)
23735 Bluestem Drive
Golden, CO 80401
303-526-5357
sa@sallyallenorganizer.com
www.sallyallenorganizer.com

Treva Berends • The Organizing Specialists
3430 Shady Place N.E.
Grand Rapids, MI 49525
616-669-4855
104240.464@compuserve.com
www.theorganizingspecialists.com

Nancy Black • Organization Plus
14 Palmer Road
Beverly, MA 01915-2710
978-922-6136
nancy@organizationplus.com
www.organizationplus.com

Lorraine Chalicki • YouNeedMe.com Personal Systems
Box 31503
Seattle, WA 98103-1503
206-286-9052
lorraine@youneedme.com
www.youneedme.com

Kim Cosentino • The De-Clutter Box, Inc.
228 Robinson Lane
Westmont, IL 60559
630-968-7557
DeClutter2@aol.com
www.declutterbox.com

Donna Cowan • Cowan & Company Professional Organizing
P.O. Box 500728
San Diego, CA 92150-0728
858-451-2344
donna_cowan@compuserve.com

Ramona Creel • OnlineOrganizing.com
ramona@onlineorganizing.com
www.onlineorganizing.com

Lynne Crew • Affairs in Order
Sarasota, FL
941-907-6064
aioorganize@aol.com

Sheila Delson • FREEDomain Concepts
5 Oak Bend Road
Poughkeepsie, NY 12603
845-463-4140
freedomain@aol.com

Stephanie Denton • Denton & Company
1220 Paxton Avenue
Cincinnati, OH 45208
513-871-8800
dentonandcompany@compuserve.com

Ronni Eisenberg • Ronni Eisenberg & Assoc.
7 Turtleback Lane
Westport, CT 06880
203-227-1222
ronni@reisenberg.com
www.reisenberg.com

Paulette Ensign • Tips Products International
13146 Vellam Ct., #133
San Diego, CA 92130
858-481-0890
paulette@tipsbooklets.com
www.tipsbooklets.com

Barbara Fields • PAPERCHASERS
180 West End Avenue
New York, NY 10023
212-721-4991
organize@paperchasers.com
www.paperchasers.com

LaNita Filer • LFJ Organizing Concepts Plus
6140 S. Hwy. 6 , #176
Missouri City, TX 77459
281-431-2527
lanita@lanitafiler.com
www.lanitafiler.com

**Stephany Smith Gonser •
Put Simply Consulting**
209-814-2665
stephany@putsimply.com
www.putsimply.com

Maria Gracia • Get Organized Now!
611 Arlington Way
Watertown, WI 53094
920-206-1172
getorgnow@charter.net
www.getorganizednow.com

Lynn & Kevin Hall • Clutter No More, Inc.
11808 Rancho Bernardo Road, Suite 123#27
San Diego, CA 92128
800-953-3295
clutternomore@compuserve.com
www.clutternomore.com

**Diane Hatcher • Timesavers Services
Professional Organizing**
5249 SW 117 Terrace
Cooper City, FL 33330
954-252-7511
diane@timesaversusa.com
www.timesaversusa.com

**Barbara Hemphill • Hemphill Productivity
Institute**
1464 Garner Station Boulevard, #330
Raleigh, NC 27603-3634
800-427-0237
barbara@productiveenvironment.com
www.productiveenvironment.com

Barbara Landsman • Dial-a-Decorator
54 Riverside Drive, Suite 11-AA
New York, NY 10024
800-486-REDO (7336)
dialadec@aol.com

Jan Limpach • Organizing Plus
6909 Pratt Street
Omaha, NE 68104-2528
402-571-4397
Jan@OrganizingPlus.com
www.organizingplus.com

Melinda Louise • Organize It
Phoenix, AZ
602-997-0559
organizzitusa@aol.com

Dorothy Madden • ORGANIZE IT!
10 Park Place
Rochester, NY 14625-2165
585-381-5511
dmadden@organizeit.biz

Bette Martin • Necessary Indulgence Professional Organizing
11684 Ventura Boulevard #656
Studio City, CA 91604
818-753-2927
www.necessaryorganizing.com
bette@necessary.com

Donna D. McMillan • McMillan & Company Professional Organizing
12021 Wilshire Boulevard, #670
West Los Angeles, CA 90025
310-391-7392
donna@organizer4me.com
www.organizer4me.com

Pat S. Moore • The Queen of Clutter
10321 Doyle Boulevard
McKenney, VA 23872
804-478-5537
patsmoore@verizon.net
www.queenofclutter.com

Gloria Ritter • Paper Matters and more, inc.
202-441-0079
gloriaritter@cs.com

Linda Samuels • Oh, So Organized!
202 Cleveland Drive
Croton on Hudson, NY 10520
914-271-5673
linda@ohsoorganized.com
www.ohsoorganized.com

Harriet Schechter • The Miracle Worker Organizing Service
P.O. Box 90922
Santa Barbara, CA 93190
858-581-1241
HS@organizedwoman.com
www.miracleorganizing.com

Cyndi Seidler • HandyGirl Professional Organizing
10800 Otsego St.
North Hollywood, CA 91601-3929
818-508-1555
info@organized-living.com
www.organized-living.com

Julie Signore • The PHOENIX Organizational Consulting Services/1,2,3 SORT IT
P.O. Box 1112
Kula, Maui HI 96790
808-878-2617
sortit@maui.net
www.123sortit.com

Jeanne K. Smith • Exit, Stage Right
P.O. Box 60794
Palo Alto, CA 94306
650-493-3948
jeanne@exitstageright.com
www.exitstageright.com

Judy Stern • Organize NOW
244 Schenck Avenue
Great Neck, NY 11021
516-829-0862
judynstern@cs.com

Jackie Tiani • Organizing Systems, Inc.
P.O. Box 5085
Glendale Heights, IL 60139-5085
630-681-9080
jtiani@compuserve.com
www.organizingsystems.com

Helen Volk • Beyond Clutter
100 White Pine Dr. #413
Albany, NY 12203
518-640-9663
helen@beyondclutter.com
www.beyondclutter.com

Debbie Williams • Let's Get It Together
P.O. Box 590860
Houston, TX 77259
281-286-9512
debbie@organizedtimes.com
www.organizedtimes.com

Norman Zalfa • Organize Your Estate, Inc.
4645 4th Road North
Arlington, VA 22203-2348
703-522-5813
nzalfa@msn.com
www.organizeyourestate.com

Business and Personal Coaches

Rose Hill, Certified Business and Professional Coach
President, The Academy for Business Success
9114 SW Becker Dr.
Portland, OR 97223
503-245-4188
rose@coachrose.com
www.coachrose.com

Kathy Paauw, Productivity Consultant and Life Coach
Paauwerfully Organized
Redmond, WA 98052-5922
425-881-6627
kathy@orgcoach.net
www.orgcoach.net

Computer Organization Experts

Debbie Gilster • Center for Growth and Productivity
Aliso Viejo, CA 92653
949-389-0440
info@c4gp.com

Do'reen A. Hein • Artistic Designs
2124 Broadway, Suite 167
New York, NY 10023
212-592-3745 or 203-855-9363
103275.734@compuserve.com

Karen Simon • PC Tech Associates
2118 Wilshire Boulevard, #257
Santa Monica, CA 90403
310-390-3370
karen@yourpctech.com
www.yourpctech.com

Time Management Experts

Jan Jasper, Productivity Trainer and Speaker
Author, *Take Back Your Time: How to Regain Control of Work, Information, and Technology*
(New York: St. Martin's Press, 1999)
New York, NY
212-465-7472
jan@janjasper.com
www.janjasper.com

Judy Warmington • Woman Time Management
1159 E. Beltine NE
Grand Rapids, MI 49525
616-669-4855
j.warmington@comcast.net
www.womantimemanagement.com

Mitzi Weinman • TimeFinder
55 Nichols Road
Needham, MA 02492
781-444-3220
800-410-3220
mitzi@timefinder.net
www.timefinder.net

Feng Shui Consultant

Lorraine M. Duvall, Ph.D.
Styles Brook Road
Keene, NY 12942
518-576-9109
lduvall@kvvi.net

Financial Advisor

Bob Colley, CFP, CEBS
Cornerstone Financial Advisors
P.O. Box 788
Clifton Park, NY 12065
518-877-8800
bobcolley@cornerstone-fa.com

Home Organization Experts

Deborah Taylor-Hough, Author
Frozen Assets Lite & Easy: How to Cook for a Day and Eat for a Month (Fox Point, Wisc.:
Champion Press, 2001)
Champion Press, Ltd.
4308 Blueberry Rd.
Fredonia, WI 53021-9465
414-540-9873
info@championpress.com
www.championpress.com

Molly Gold, Founder • GO MOM !NC.
5405 Merion Station Drive
Apex, NC 27539
919-387-3848
mgold@gomominc.com
www.gomominc.com

Productivity Consultants

Paula Royalty • WorkSmart Productivity Consulting
13735 15th Ave. N.E. #A-8
Seattle, WA 98128-3121
425-562-3147
smartpro@worksmartpro.com
www.worksmartpro.com

Virtual Office Assistant

Pat Voyajopoulos • Oasis
781-329-2236
51 Valley Road
Dedham, MA 02026
pat@oasisadmin.com

Index

INDEX

<u>Underscored</u> page references indicate sidebars and tables. **Boldface** references indicate illustrations.

Credit counseling services, 136–37
Credit problems, saving records on, 127
Credit unions, 140
Crib, selecting, 259–60
Curtains, freshening, 231

D

Day planning, 158–59, 317
"Days to Remember" book, as reminder system,
    37–38
Death
   handling practical matters after, 272–76
   preparing for (*see* Estate planning)
Death certificate, 272
Debit cards, 133
Debt-reducing strategies, 131–33, 137
Desk
   organizing, 96, 288, 307, 318
   selecting, 92–93
Diaper bag, packing, 209
Dining room, organizing, 57
Disability insurance, 118
   for new parents, 257, 259
Discounts, membership, 141
Dishes
   dirty, collecting, 315
   storing, 47
Disorganization
   analyzing relationship to, 4
   assessment of, 5–6
   cost of, 5
   effects of, 4–6
Documents. *See also* Banking documents;
    Financial documents; Legal
    documents
   collecting, after death of loved one, 272
   filing, 307
   missing, obtaining copies of, 271
   organizing, for estate planning,
    265–66
   safekeeping of, 224, 266–67, 294–95
Dogs. *See* Pets

Donations
   of computer equipment, 94
   from estate sales, 275
   of garage sale leftovers, 18
   of items found when moving, 243, 244,
    248
   organ, 270
   tax-deductible, 311
   toy, 34
   from uncluttering process, 15, 15, 285, 287, 289,
    290, 300, 310
Dorm room
   necessities for, 261–62, 261
   organizing, 262, 262
Drawers
   organizers for, 26, 27, 54
   organizing, 282, 285
    in bathroom, 87
    for clothing, 73, 81–82, 301
    in desk, 94–95, 300
    in kitchen, 54
Dresser
   for CD storage, 61
   organizing, 74, 301
Dryer safety, 216
Dumpsters, 103
Duplicate items, assessing need for, 12
Durable power of attorney, 269–70
DVDs, storing and organizing, 61

E

Earrings, storing, 74
Eating out, saving money when, 149–50
eBay, for selling unwanted items, 17
Egg cartons, for storage, 27
Eggs, storing, 52–53
80/20 rule, 32, 318
Elderly persons
   home safety for, 222
   preparing, for moves, 249
Electric bills, reducing, 134
Electronic folders, creating, 311

Electronic tickets, for air travel, 194
E-mails
    avoiding printing of, 33, <u>98</u>, 311
    deleting, 311, 319
    as special-occasion reminders, 38,
        320
    at work, 171, <u>172</u>
Emergencies
    handling, 224–25
    locating financial or legal information in,
        127
    pet, 225–26
Emergency contacts
    for estate planning, <u>266</u>
    for message center, 188
    for pet care, 226
    for school, <u>235</u>
Emergency fund, 117
Emergency kit, for car, <u>109</u>
Emergency response plans, 222–23
Energy use, reducing, 134
Entertaining, preparation for, 217–18
Entertainment, affordable, 150–51
Entryways
    organizing coat closet in, 44–45
    storage in, 43–44
    uncluttering, 42, 45
Errands, 158, 318
Estate planning
    importance of, 263–64
    for new parents, 259
    steps in
        designating items for heirs, <u>268</u>, <u>269</u>
        expressing other legal wishes, 268–70
        funeral planning, 270–72
        identifying assets, 264–65
        organizing documents, 265–67
        preparing will, <u>119</u>, 196, 263, 267–68,
            <u>267</u>
        recording emergency contacts, <u>266</u>
    before vacation, 196
Estate sales, 275, <u>276</u>
Estate settling, after death of loved one,
    272–76
Evacuation, emergency response plan for, 223,
    <u>224</u>

F

Fall
    gardening in, 236–37
    outdoor chores for, 235–36
    school preparation in, 235, <u>235</u>
Falls, preventing, 222
Family activities, affordable, 151–52,
    <u>151</u>
Family room
    audio and video storage in, 60–61
    book storage in, 59–60
    crafts storage in, 66–67
    decorating, <u>60</u>
    general organization of, 58
    photo organization in, 64–66
    preventing paper pileup in, 62–64
    safety in, 220
    storage places in, 58–59
Family schedules, managing, 184–85, <u>185</u>, <u>190</u>,
    <u>192</u>, 318
Family togetherness, organizing, 179–80, 191–92,
    319
Fear of organization, 6
Feng shui, <u>44</u>
Files, office, storing, 93–94, 97–98, 294
Filing cabinet, cleaning out, 34, 293, 320
Filing system
    for home office, 97–101, <u>97</u>, <u>99</u>, <u>100</u>
    for papers, 33, 85, 292, 293, 294, 296, 306,
        307–8, 319, 320
    scheduling time for, 307
Film canisters, for storage, 27
Financial documents
    organizing, 125–27
        for estate planning, 265–66
    shredding, 294
    storing, <u>126</u>, 266–67
Financial goals, 116, 117
Financial planner, 115, 117, <u>118</u>, 138, 143,
    259
Financial software, <u>122</u>
Financial status, assessing, 116–17
Financial trouble
    getting help for, 136–37
    signs of, <u>132</u>

Health insurance, 117
    for new baby, 257
    for travel, 197, 206, <u>206</u>
Holiday decorations, storing, 111, <u>111</u>
Holidays, gift-giving on, 311
Home equity loans, 135
Home maintenance tasks
    springtime, 230–31
    year-round, <u>232</u>
Home office. *See* Office, home
Homeowner's insurance, 118, 197
Home selling, 252–53, <u>253</u>
Hotel stays
    booking, 194–95
    childproofing for, <u>209</u>
Housebreaking, for pets, 256–57
Housecleaning. *See also* Cleaning
    daily speed cleaning, 215–16
    general guidelines for, 213–14
    supplies for, <u>214</u>
Household chemicals
    pet poisoning from, 225
    safe disposal of, 289
    safe storage of, 222
Household chores. *See* Chores
Household management tasks
    entertaining, 217–18
    food shopping, 211–12
    housekeeping, 213–16
    laundry, 216–17
    meal planning, 210–11
    one-minute organizers for, 313–16
    recycling, 212–13
Houseplants, care of, 234, 236, 237, 238
House rules for clean-up, 30, <u>31</u>, 313

I

In-box, 306, 313, 319
Index
    for filing system, 98, 100–101, 294
    of stored items, 299

Individual retirement account (IRA),
    143–44
Information, miscellaneous, storing, 304
Inheritances, designating items for, <u>268</u>, <u>269</u>
Insects
    attacking photographic materials, <u>64</u>
    protecting clothing from, 75, <u>75</u>
    protecting linens from, 78
Insurance
    car, 118
    for car rentals, 195
    disability, 118, 257, 259
    health (*see* Health insurance)
    homeowner's or renter's, 118
    life (*see* Life insurance)
    long-term care, 118
    organizing, before vacation, 196
    personal umbrella, 119
    raising deductibles on, 134
    trip and travel, 196–97, <u>197</u>
Insurance policies and bills, saving, 126, 293
Insure Kids Now! program, 257
Internet
    organizing Web sites on, 29
    recipes from, 56, 57, 315
    reminder services on, 38
    for selling unwanted items, 17
Inventory, personal property, 264–65, <u>265</u>,
    293
Investment records, saving, 127, 293
Investments. *See also* Savings plan
    calculating doubling of, <u>142</u>
    from extra cash, 140
    long-term, 143–44
    short-term, 141–43
Ironing, 216

J

Jackets
    storing, 76
    for trips, 201–2

Jewelry
    organizing, 74–75, 301
    packing, for trips, 202
Journal, of organizing activities, 283
Junk, preventing accumulation of, 37
Junk drawer, organizing, 54
Junk haulers, 103
Junk mail
    discarding, 32, 295
    stopping, 296

K

"Keep or Toss" quiz, for uncluttering process, 12, 13
Keys, hanger for, 44
Kitchen
    daily cleaning of, 215
    organization in
        cabinets, 47
        countertops, 46, 47, 289
        drawers, 54
        freezer, 53
        pantry, 49–51
        refrigerator, 51–53
        under sink, 54–55
        starting, 46
        storage options for, 46–47, 300
        wraps and bags, 55
    safety in, 219
Kitchen sink, organizing under, 54–55
Kitchen tools, recommended, 48
Kitchen wraps, organizing, 55
Knives, storing, 47

L

Labeling, of storage areas and items, 50, 108, 298, 299
Label maker, 26
Ladder, as hanging rack, 47

Laundry
    hamper for, 74, 82
    procedure for, 216–17, 314–15
    storing, before washing, 70–71, 74, 82, 314
Laundry room, organizing, 107, 314, 315
Lawn care, 233, 236
Lawnmower, care of, 230
Lead paint, 260
Leather fabrics, storing, 76
Leftovers, storing, 53, 289
Legal documents
    organizing, for estate planning, 265–66
    storing, 126, 224, 266–67
Letting go of items
    difficulty with, 34
    for uncluttering, 13–14, 285, 286, 288
Life insurance, 117–18
    beneficiary of, 118
    for new parents, 257, 259
    trip coverage from, 197
Lighting, office, 92
Linens, storing, 77–78, 299
Liquor cartons, for storage, 27
Lists, "To Do." See "To Do" lists
Living revocable trust, 264
Living room, safety in, 220
Living will, 268
Long-term care insurance, 118
Luggage
    insurance coverage for, 197
    packing, 201–4, 201
Lunches, advance preparation of, 187

M

Magazines
    preventing pileup of, 62–63, 295
    storing, 63, 63, 295
Mail
    changing address for, 243–44
    junk
        discarding, 32, 295, 306
        stopping, 296

message center for, 188

sorting, 32–33, 306

Makeup

packing, for trips, 202

storing, 89

Manuals, filing, 100, 293

Meal planning

everyday, 160, 210–11, 315

for parties, 218

Meats, storing, 52, 53

Medical information

for trips, 200

updating, for school, 235

Medical insurance. *See* Health insurance

Medical power of attorney, 268

Medical precautions, during travel abroad, 206, 207

Medicine cabinet, organizing, 87–88, 289

Medicines

organizing, 87–88

as poisonous to pets, 225

safe disposal of, 87, 88, 289

Membership discounts, 141

Memorabilia

managing, 112, 112, 287

photographing, 288

safeguarding, 274

storing, 83

Message center, organizing, 188–89, 188, 189

Messies Anonymous, 29, 287

Messy family members, coping with, 36, 314

Microwave, location for, 47

Mind, uncluttering, 178, 303

Mind-mapping, as planning tool, 159

Mirror, entryway, 45

Mittens, storing, 43, 76

Money

alternatives to, for travel, 198

exchanging, on trips abroad, 205

safeguarding, on trips, 198–99

Money management guidelines

assessing financial status, 116–17

assets protection, 117–18

bill paying, 123–24

budgeting, 119–22

organizing financial records, 125–27

reducing debt and spending, 131–37

tax preparation, 127–30

Money market accounts, 142

Money-saving strategies

analyzing wants vs. needs for, 145, 147

for college, 141, 144, 259

for eating out, 149–50

for electric bills, 134

for entertainment, 150–51

everyday, 146–47

for family activities, 151–52, 151

for food, 140–41, 147–49

organization, 4–5

Morning routines, establishing, 185, 186–87

Mortgage

reducing debt from, 133

refinancing, 133–34

Motivation, for organization, 280, 283

Moving

announcing change of address when, 242, 243–44

checklist and timeline for, 239, 241

combining households when, 251–52

downsizing for, 249

hiring moving company for, 239–40

packing for, 244–48

planning utilities and services for, 240, 240, 242

preparing children for, 242, 250, 253

selling home before, 252–53, 253

storing paperwork for, 245

unpacking and settling in after, 250–51, 250, 251

Moving day, preparing for, 248–50, 248

Multitasking, 165–66

N

Necklaces, storing, 74

Negatives, photo, care of, 66

Newspapers, recycling system for, 62, 310

New Year's resolutions, 238

Nursery, outfitting, 259–60

O

Office, home
file storage for, 93–94
filing systems for, 97–101, _97_, _99_, _100_
locating, 91–92
managing, 169–70
organizing desktop in, _96_
organizing equipment cords in, _95_
organizing workspace in, 95, 97, 288, 300
safety in, 220
setting up, 92–93, _94_
uncluttering, 93–95
Office chores, system for, _191_
Office equipment, selecting, 93
Office supplies, 93, 94
Off-site storage, _104_, 299
One-minute organizers
for clutter control, 309–12
everyday, 303–8
for getting started, 280–84
for home management, 313–16
for papers, 291–96
for schedules and to-do's, 317–20
for storage spaces, 297–302
for uncluttering, 285–90
On-line selling, of unwanted items, 17
Organ donation, 270
Organization
achieving goals for, 27–28
basics for
finding storage places, 22–23, _23_, 297–99
minimizing clutter, 22–23
using containers, 25
using organizing products, 26–27
benefits of, 3, 4–5
getting help with, 28–29
keys to
assessing your situation, 5–6
establishing a plan, 6–7, _7_
taking action, 7
maintaining
by avoiding paper pile-up, 32–33
everyday strategies for, 30–32, 303–8, 309–12
with periodic purges, 33–34, 309
starting, with one-minute organizers, 280–84

Organization IQ, quiz for assessing, _8–9_
Organizing buddy, 282
Organizing products, 25, 26–27, 281, 299
for pantry, 49–50
for refrigerator, 53
Organizing projects
"grab and go," 306
making note of, 298
mini, 283
planning, 318–19
winter, 238
Outdoor furniture, care of, 234
Outdoor table necessities, storing, _54_
Overcommitment, avoiding, 176, _176_, _177_, 319

P

Packing guidelines
for diaper bag, _209_
for moving, 244–48
for trips, 201–4, 207–8, 304–5
Paint, lead in, _260_
Pantry, organizing, 49–51, 300
Panty hose, storing, _71_, 301
Paper(s)
filing system for, _14_, 33, 85, 97, 292, 293, 294, 296, 298, 306, 307–8, 319, 320
school, storing, 43, 85, _85_, 296
wrapping
limiting, 312
storing, 111–12, 298
Paper pile-up, minimizing, 32–33, 306
one-minute organizers for, 291–96
Paper scraps
alternatives to, 303
organizing, _101_
Paperwork
for moving, _245_
year-end checklist for, _237_
Parties
planning, 217–18
progressive cleaning, 282
uncluttering for, 34, 238

S

U

Umbrella personal insurance policy, 119
Umbrellas, storing, 27, 43
Uncluttering. *See also* Clutter
  best time for, 10–11
  giveaways from, 14–15, _15_
  letting go in, 13–14, 285, 286, 288
  making appointment for, _12_
  methods of, 11–12
  one-minute organizers for, 285–90
  for party preparation, 34
  recycling items from, _21_
  scheduling family time for, 185, 310
  selling unwanted items from, 15, 288
    on consignment, 16–17, _16_
    at garage or yard sales, 18–19, _18_, _19_,
      21
  for spring cleaning, 232
  storing loose papers from, 14
  supplies needed for, _11_
  time needed for, 11, 285
  when combining households, 252
  where to start, 10, _17_
  in winter, 238
Underwear, packing, for trips, 202
Unused items, difficulty letting go of, _34_
Unwanted items, selling, 15–19, 21, 288
Upromise, for college savings, 141
U.S. Department of State, travel information from,
    205–6
Used items, selling, 311
Utility bills
  recording amounts of, 293
  saving, 126, 307

V

Vacations. *See also* Travel
  with children, 208–9
  mini-, 163
  planning, _238_, 320

Values, analyzing, _157_, 173
Vegetables
  in garden, 233, 234, 237
  storing, 52
Vertical storage space, 25, 297
Veterans, benefits for, 272
Veterinarian, finding, 242
Videotapes
  of special events, 304
  storing and organizing, 60–61
Visas, 204–5
Visa TravelMoney, 198
Visualization, for achieving goals, 7
Voice mail
  reminders on, 316
  using, at work, 319

W

Wake-up routines, 185, 187–88, 316
Walls, uncluttering, 288–89
Warranties, filing, 100
Will
  executing, 272, 273–74
  importance of, _119_, 263, 267
  living, 268
  for new parents, 259
  preparing, 267–68, _267_
    before trip, 196
  reviewing, _118_
  storing, 292
Windows
  cleaning, 231, 232
  storm, removing and storing,
    230
Winter, chores for, 237–38
Work(ing)
  balancing, with home, 173–80
  e-mail for, 171, _172_
  at home, 169–70
  learning technology for, _170_
  managing day for, 165–66, _165_

Work(ing) *(cont.)*
  minimizing distractions at, 319
  organizational systems for, 166–69
  personal information manager (PIM) software
    for, 169
  planning, 164–65
  rating organization at, 166
  reaching goals at, 168
  reducing commute time to, 171
  on the road, 170–72
Work centers, for minimizing clutter, 23,
    297
Workshop
  organizing, 105–7, 105
  safety in, 220
  storage in, 299

Wrapping paper
  limiting, 312
  storing, 111–12, 298
Wrinkles, clothing, minimizing, 204, 204, 216

Y

Yard sales, organizing, 18–19, 18, 19, 21, 311
Yard work
  early-spring, 233
  fall, 236–37
  summer, 234
  winter, 238

THE UPSIDE-DOWN CHURCH

THE
UPSIDE
DOWN
CHURCH

GREG LAURIE

WITH
DAVID KOPP

Tyndale House Publishers, Inc.
WHEATON, ILLINOIS

Visit Tyndale's exciting Web site at www.tyndale.com

Edited by Vinita Hampton Wright

Book jacket design by David Riley+Associates, Corona Del Mar, CA

Library of Congress Cataloging-in-Publication Data

Laurie, Greg.
  The upside-down church / Greg Laurie.
    p.   cm.
  ISBN 0-8423-7812-X (hc : alk. paper)
  ISBN 0-8423-7847-2 (sc : alk. paper)
  1. Church growth. I. Title.
BV652.25.L38 1999
254'.5—dc21   98-51016

Printed in the United States of America

05	04	03	02	01	00	99
7	6	5	4	3	2	1

CONTENTS

ONE

THE UPSIDE-DOWN CHURCH
God's Original Plan Was
the Right One

I SUPPOSE I should be the last person writing a book on what a church ought to be. I have been a Christian only since 1970. I was not raised in the church. In fact, I had no background whatsoever in an understanding of the evangelical culture. I was your garden variety unbeliever. It's not that I was *somewhat* ignorant of spiritual things—I was *completely* ignorant of them. But Jesus Christ came into my life in 1970 and dramatically turned it around. I began preaching about a year and a half after my conversion, and I was pastoring at the ripe old age of nineteen. It seems crazy, doesn't it? But it happened.

We recently celebrated twenty-five years of ministry. As I look back on my life, I don't know what I would have done much differently. It was never our goal, per se, but we have become one of the largest churches in the country, with some fifteen thousand attending on an average Sunday. We see an average of three to four thousand people come to Christ every year in our church services alone. Thousands of others come to faith through our various outreach ministries, including the Harvest Crusades. One-fourth of the people in our congregation are actively involved in some type of ministry today. More than 60 percent of them came to faith at our services.

I know what you're thinking: This guy's bragging, and he's going to try to get me to buy into some program or seminar that will tell me how to do it for a small fee. And if I act now, he'll throw in some Ginsu knives! I guess I am bragging a little bit. But if I am, I am bragging on God, because I am about as ordinary a guy as you are going to meet. And that is why I have written this book. To give hope and some words of encouragement on how God can do extraordinary things through very ordinary people—people like me and maybe you. In this book I will share with you our theology, philosophy of ministry, and some practical advice as well.

I have been asked many times what verse best sums up my life and ministry. There are many things that I would love to quote that would position me as someone with great vision or faith. But if I were totally honest, it would be 1 Corinthians 1:26-29 (NIV): "Brothers, think of what you were when you were called. Not many of you were wise by human standards; not many were influential; not many were of noble birth. But God chose the foolish things of the world to shame the wise; God chose the weak things of the world to shame the strong. He chose the lowly things of this world and the despised things—and the things that are not—to nullify the things that are, so that no one may boast before him."

It is hard to explain all that the Lord has faithfully done in our ministry over the last twenty-five years. I'm reminded of a statement Warren Wiersbe made: "If you can explain what is going on then God didn't do it." I think there's truth to that. God has blessed our ministry. Yet we didn't use many of the techniques being touted today—surveys, studies, or attempts to have a more "friendly" approach to unbelievers. If you came to a service at Harvest Christian Fellowship, it would probably seem very contemporary to you. We have a relatively simple building, with no religious symbols to speak of. The music is clearly contemporary, and the dress style is casual. But underneath all of that are timeless biblical principles. This ministry could be compared to a

Windows 98 operating system. On the surface it is brightly colored, with simple icons to click. But underneath it is a DOS infrastructure. A healthy and thriving church must have a strong infrastructure. If you don't have a good foundation, trouble is coming, regardless of your growth, be it numerical or financial.

I would like to tell you our story. It may surprise or even shock you at times. I think you will laugh a bit. It has been and continues to be an adventure.

Humble Beginnings

After I became a Christian, I was afraid that God might "call" me to preach. I feared that it would happen at a really awkward time, such as when I was standing in line at the supermarket. I thought that maybe the Lord would force me to turn to the people behind me and say something really clever like, "I see that some of you are purchasing bread today. You know, Jesus said, 'I am the bread of life. He who comes to Me shall never hunger, and he who believes in Me shall never thirst'" (John 6:35, NKJV). Then I could say something like, "How many of you would like to come to Jesus right now?" The thought of the whole thing terrified me.

The day I first preached publicly did come. But it was not in the supermarket. In fact, it happened as the result of a misunderstanding. The church I attended was holding a mass baptism down at a beach in Newport Beach, California. I thought it was later that day, but it had already taken place, and I had missed it. When I rolled out of bed that

WE DIDN'T UTILIZE MANY OF THE NEW TECHNIQUES BEING TOUTED TODAY—NO SURVEYS, STUDIES, OR ATTEMPTS TO HAVE A MORE "FRIENDLY" APPROACH TO UNBELIEVERS.

3

morning, it was a day like any other day—no visions, no audible voices from heaven, no signs or wonders. But that day was about to alter the course of my life. I arrived at the beach, and instead of finding a few thousand people, as would be gathered for a baptism, I found only a handful. I was disappointed to have missed the baptism but glad to find some fellow believers to sing and fellowship with. As I joined their group I quickly noticed that no one was really leading. One person would sing a song, and others would join. Then another would sing a song, and we would sing again. I had read a passage of Scripture that morning that was sort of burning inside, and I sensed God nudging me to share it with this little group.

"Excuse me, but I read a Scripture this morning that I would like to share!" I blurted out nervously. Everyone seemed agreeable to the idea, so I stammered away, and when I was done, I was so relieved. I was saying to the Lord, quietly in my heart, *Lord, thank you for that wonderful opportunity! I can't wait to tell some of my Christian friends how you used me.*

I thought I was done that day, but the Lord was just getting started. While I was speaking, a couple of girls had joined our little group. When I finished, one of them said to me, "Excuse me, Pastor, but we missed the baptism, and we were wondering if you could still baptize us?"

"Pastor"?—what, is this girl nuts? I thought. "I'm sorry, I am not a pastor, and I don't even know how to baptize someone!" I protested.

"But we want to be baptized. Can't you help us?"

And then the Lord gave me a great sense of peace and impressed it upon my heart to go ahead and do it. "Uh, OK, I guess I could do that. Umm, let's go on down to Pirate's Cove."

Pirate's Cove is a charming little natural amphitheater, a spot etched in rock overlooking a small beach. Many times during the year, Calvary Chapel would have hundreds sit up on the rocks and watch as Pastor Chuck Smith and others baptized people. I had been baptized there myself, so it held fond memories for me. Except this time I was leading a little group that had now grown to about thirty down to Pirate's Cove, and I had no idea what I was going to do once I got there. As we went to the water's edge, I racked my brain, trying to remember something I had never really paid much attention to. The actual technique of baptizing a person! I remembered watching Pastor Chuck Smith holding a person's nose as he supported his back and gently lowered them backwards into the water. So I did the same and awkwardly baptized the first girl. She was still breathing afterwards, and I was greatly relieved. Then I baptized the second and was starting to feel like an old pro! As I came out of the water once again, I quietly rejoiced in this wonderful opportunity God had opened up for me.

While I was preparing to leave, I noticed that a crowd had gathered up on the rocks, taking all of this in. Then the thing I feared most came upon me. God clearly spoke to my heart and said one thing: "Preach!" Instead of being terrified, I had a great sense of calm and to the best of my ability proclaimed the gospel in my first little crusade. I even invited people to come down to where we were and receive Christ. A few did, and I had the privilege of baptizing them that day, too. Now I was ruined. I had the bug. Deep down, I knew that I was called to do this.

Early Days at Calvary

In those early growth days I couldn't get enough Bible study. I had no hostilities or hang-ups about the church because I knew nothing of it. In fact, I was like a sponge, drinking it all in and loving it. I wanted to serve the Lord somehow, and the only real skill I had to speak of was in graphic arts. In fact, my goal in life up to that point had been to become a professional cartoonist. Most of the Christian literature back in those days was pretty outdated. It was way out of step with the culture and, frankly, embarrassing to hand out.

So one day I decided to take one of Chuck Smith's sermons on John 4 and illustrate it in an easy-to-read comic-book format. I called it "Living Water." I wrote and drew it in about two hours and was so excited, I went over to his house and knocked on front door. When he came to the door, I held out my primitive little drawing and told him a bit about it. He really seemed to like the piece and suggested I redraw it in a tractlike format and then it could be printed up and distributed to the church. We printed about 10,000, and they were gone in a week. We printed 100,000, and they were soon gone. When all was said and done, upwards of 2 million of those little tracts had made their way out. Now I was really ruined. I knew that I was called to serve the Lord.

I began to support myself doing graphic arts on the side, but my real hope was to preach and teach others about Jesus Christ. I hung around Calvary Chapel, just hoping for opportunities to come my way. I set up my drawing board in one of the extra Sunday school rooms and would just wait for anything to do. When the pastors went out for lunch, I would firmly plant myself in the church office, hoping the secretary might shoot a counseling call or two my way. When a speaking opportunity arose in some faraway city no one wanted to go to, the other pastors would say, "Let Greg go. This would be a great opportunity for him!" I didn't mind a bit. I was eager to be used.

One day the ultimate leftover was dropped in my lap.

Leftovers from Heaven

An Episcopal church in a city called Riverside wanted to see if what God was doing in the Jesus movement down in Orange County could happen in their city as well. Some of the leaders of that church approached Chuck Smith and asked if he would send up some of the associate pastors to teach a Bible study aimed at young people. They rotated, each doing it for a few weeks and then handing it off to another. One particular week no one really wanted to go. They were talking about it among themselves as I quietly listened. One of the pastors said, "Hey, why not have Greg go up there?" They all agreed and said I could take the next Sunday night. I studied hard that week and desperately wanted to do well.

When I showed up at the church, I quickly realized no one had told them I was coming. They were expecting a pastor they already knew. The elder in charge reluctantly agreed to have me preach and said that he would be watching and listening very closely that night. Not exactly a vote of confidence! But I made my way through it and was told I could come back again the next week. So each week I spoke, and attendance actually began to grow. People started to receive Christ, and I was beside myself with joy! In fact, it grew into a group of about three hundred, and some of the people were starting to call me Pastor Greg. Here was the "pastor" thing again. It was almost laughable. I was twenty years old! I had been a Christian for only three years. I hardly felt qualified to be a pastor. Besides, I really felt called to evangelism, not pastoring. But this crazy Bible study just kept growing.

This little Bible study that I had the privilege of leading had now, for all practical purposes, become a church. We had outgrown the facilities at the Episcopal church where we began, so we looked for our own building. I was told of a Baptist church in the middle of town that had had a split and was available for lease or rent. We had no money in the bank and were really a bunch of kids just trying to do what we thought God wanted us to do. I called Chuck Smith and asked him if he would come and check this thing out with me. As we walked around the building, taking it all in, Chuck spoke with the Realtor who had listed it. I saw Chuck take out his checkbook, write out a check, and hand it to the Realtor. They shook hands, and Chuck came over to me and said, "Well, congratulations, Greg. You just got yourself a church!" He had to get back to Costa Mesa, so he climbed into his car and drove out of the parking lot, and I just stood there stunned.

What was I going to do? Who was going to help me? Was I really called to do this? As it turned out, Pastor Chuck had provided the down payment, but the rest was up to us. The next Sunday we made the announcement at the Episcopal church that we were moving to this new building. I was terrified that no one would follow us. But the next week they showed up in force. We were now five hundred strong!

I felt called primarily as an evangelist. Prior to taking on this Bible study, in addition to doing graphics I had become something of an itinerant preacher. I traveled with a number of the early contemporary Christian music groups, and I sort of emceed the evening and then got up and preached the gospel and gave an invitation for people to come to Christ. As itinerant, or traveling, preachers often do, I had developed five or six messages that I gave over and over, and they were well honed.

Yet now, here I was, called upon to teach every single week in the same place in this new and growing church that I had somehow become the pastor of. We had not only our Sunday night services but Wednesday services as well. I had to learn how to really study. I decided to teach through the books of the Bible as I had seen modeled at Calvary Chapel. I decided to start with Ephesians. The commentary *In the Heavenlies*, by Harry Ironside, was recommended to me, and I used that as my guide. For all practical purposes I stole Ironside's outlines, illustrations, and antidotes lock, stock, and barrel, but I was beginning to develop my own style. The numbers were not huge for our midweek studies, but I gave my all, sometimes learning things for the first time as I prepared during the day and delivered it to the people who came out that night.

Sunday nights were another issue altogether. I gave all my traveling messages and some new ones I developed and invited people to come to Christ as I had done on the road. But the response was dismal. I soon realized that these people needed to be fed the Word of God, and healthy sheep would reproduce themselves. So on Sunday nights, instead of topical evangelistic messages, I taught through books like the Gospel of John, Revelation, Genesis, Daniel, etc. Then I still gave an invitation for people to come to Christ. Now they were responding. And we began to grow even more.

You have probably noticed that I did not mention Sunday morning yet. This is because, as strange as it may sound, we did not yet have a Sunday-morning service. We were still largely a group of young people meeting together, and we decided we ought to do some kind of outreach for the older folks. What a reverse of what we normally hear! Instead of older people trying to reach the young, here were young people trying to reach the old. I hardly felt qualified, being only twenty-one at the time. So I asked a friend of mine who was in his fifties to teach on Sunday mornings; I could do the Sunday evenings and Wednesdays.

CHUCH CAME OVER TO ME AND SAID, "WELL, CONGRATULATIONS, GREG. YOU JUST GOT YOURSELF A CHURCH!"

The Sunday-morning services averaged about sixty people in attendance. This was odd, considering that we were running about a thousand in our evening service at that point. This man, Keith, had a wonderful heart and gave it his all, but to be honest, I think God wanted me to be preaching that service, too. I sort of used Keith as a security blanket because I was so apprehensive about speaking to a more adult audience. One week Keith had a heart attack. He was not able to do the Sunday-morning services, so I was on. (Keith recovered and was called to mission work in China—God has plans for everybody!) I continued teaching Sunday mornings, and the Lord blessed our efforts. Today our Sunday morning services are our best attended.

Evangelistic Doors Open: The Harvest Crusades

We have always given people an opportunity to come to Christ in our services. In fact, most of our associate pastors either came to faith at our church or began attending as very young believers. We have seen thousands and thousands walk the aisles over the years to make a commitment or recommitment to follow Jesus Christ. You might say our philosophy of ministry, in a nutshell, would be to know Christ and make him known.

Our Sunday evening service was always a bit more evangelistic than the others, and it was still my desire to see large-scale outreaches in our community. We booked a relatively large auditorium in a neighboring city and held our first crusade-type meetings, which we called Harvest celebrations back then. The Lord blessed, and we saw many respond. But as hard as I tried, I could not get those events to the next level, where other churches would come on board and help. I just stopped worrying about it and got on with doing the job of a pastor that God had set before me.

I read a story about young Charles Spurgeon, who had some visions of grandeur for himself and his ministry that was opening up in London. The Lord reminded him of a passage in Jeremiah: "Do you seek great things for yourself? Do not seek them" (Jer. 45:5, NKJV). It's hard not to be accused of egotism when you suggest that a huge meeting be held and you are to be the one doing the preaching. I just stopped worrying about trying to make it happen and concluded that maybe this was not God's will for my life. I was reminded of Paul's words when he said, "I have learned in whatever state I am, to be content" (Phil. 4:11, NKJV). There is a real temptation for those of us who are called to serve the Lord to see the grass as greener elsewhere—to think that bigger is always better. That we should be moving up some sort of ladder of spiritual success. But I have found, in retrospect, that we should be thankful for any opportunity God has opened up for us, no matter how large or small it may be. As Warren

Wiersbe has said, "You can never be too small for God to use, only too big."

What God requires of us is faithfulness. And if we are "faithful in the little things," He will give us more to do in His perfect timing. Scripture reminds us to not despise "the day of small things" (Zech. 4:10, NKJV). You are learning important lessons—lessons you will treasure for years to come—through what God is doing in your life right now. A minister of a smaller church once met the great C. H. Spurgeon, who was at the zenith of his ministry, and complained about the small size of his congregation. The minister voiced his envy of the thousands who came to hear Spurgeon each week. Spurgeon asked him, "How many people attend your church?" The minister replied, "About one hundred." Spurgeon replied, "I think that is enough to give an account of on the Day of Judgment." Ouch! What has God set before you right now? A home Bible study? A Sunday-school class?

As Warren Wiersbe has said, "You can never be too small for God to use, only too big."

A small congregation? An individual you are discipling? That's enough to give an account of on the Day of Judgment!

It was when I honestly found this contentment in what God had put on my plate that some very unexpected opportunities opened up for us to touch not only our community but also our state and our nation. They were to be called Harvest Crusades.

Like so many other things in my life, the opportunity to do crusades came when I least expected it. Chuck Smith asked if I would speak at a Monday night Bible study at Calvary Chapel, a study he had led for many years. I had attended it myself. It was a great honor to be asked to do this, and though our church was going strong and there were many things pulling on me, I sensed the Lord's leading to go for it. I applied the same format we have used for years at Harvest on Sunday nights: a time of contemporary praise and worship; often a guest musical artist (not usually announced ahead of time); and then a forty-five- to sixty-minute Bible study with evangelism woven through it.

Before we knew it, we were averaging twenty-five hundred people each Monday night, with anywhere from forty to eighty people coming to Christ each week. We were thrilled with the response. This would be great on a Sunday or Wednesday night midweek study, but Monday night? After this had gone on for about a year, I was at a meeting with some other pastors down in Costa Mesa, and Chuck Smith took me aside for a moment and dropped something on me that would change the course of my life and ministry. In his matter-of-fact way he said, "Greg, I've been noticing the Lord's blessing on the Monday-night studies this last year and thought we should take it to a larger venue, say, the Pacific Amphitheater, and do a Billy Graham–style crusade."

I was dumbfounded. "Isn't the Pacific Amphitheater a pretty big place, Chuck?" I asked.

"Yes, Greg, it is," Chuck said, with a twinkle in his eye. Then he added, "But we serve a big God!"

We had no idea how many people to expect for that first crusade. I wanted to take what God had been blessing in our Sunday-/Monday-night studies and combine it with some tried-and-true principles of large-scale evangelism. I had long studied the ministries of evangelists like D. L. Moody and Billy Graham. I wanted this crusade to build on the principles of what God had blessed over the years, combined with contemporary style and music. So we went about designing a new approach to the crusade format. My associate, John Collins, helped to brilliantly execute this first event and continues as our crusade director to this very day. The Lord has been faithful these last ten years, and we have seen over 2 million people in combined attendance, and over 150,000 people have walked the aisles to make commitments and recommitments to follow Jesus Christ.

After the crusade ministry began taking off, I was often asked when I was going to leave the pastorate and go into full-time evangelism. It seemed like the next logical step to everyone, even, at times, to myself. Yet, strangely, the very thing I had dreamed of for so many years held no appeal to me whatsoever. I loved (and still love) going out and sharing the gospel in venues large and small. At the same time, given a choice, I prefer to speak to our own congregation. I enjoy the interaction, the rapport, the contact of speaking to a group of people you can actually make eye contact with. In a stadium, all you see are little dots, and your voice bounces back to you as you speak. I'm not complaining. It is thrilling to see hundreds of people come forward to put their faith in Christ. But there is a price to pay for it, and that's another story I would like to tell at another time.

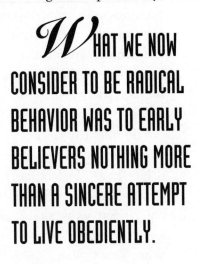

WHAT WE NOW CONSIDER TO BE RADICAL BEHAVIOR WAS TO EARLY BELIEVERS NOTHING MORE THAN A SINCERE ATTEMPT TO LIVE OBEDIENTLY.

The First Disciples: Radical or Right?

Let me ask you a question. Do you really want to change the world? You might be thinking, *Of course I do, Greg, but I'm a pretty ordinary person. Most days I can hardly manage to change my printer cartridge, much less the world.*

I understand that response. But consider this: Two centuries ago a group of believers, led by twelve men armed with little more than the message of the gospel, turned the world completely upside down. This was a relatively small group of believers who began meeting in an obscure upstairs room. They lacked almost every advantage we enjoy today. They didn't have mass media, computer and satellite technology, or stadium rallies. They didn't have the ability to publish their materials or the financial resources to build beautiful cathedrals.

And yet the church these Christians founded together in that small room upstairs not only survived but flourished. While being attacked spiritually and physically, this small group of men and women spread the message of salvation abroad and performed countless miracles in Christ's name. From every possible perspective—spiritual, historical, political—they left the world a different place from the way they had found it.

You might say, "These guys weren't like you and me. They were a bunch of radicals, right?"

Not at all. In fact, here's a truly radical thought: The early church leaders were simply living their Christian lives according to what Jesus taught. *What we consider to be radical behavior was nothing more than a sincere attempt to live obediently.* What many of us consider normal Christian living today— compared to what the first church experienced—is not normal at all. It's woefully inadequate and, as a result, pitifully ineffective.

When unbelievers said of the early Christians that they "turned the world upside down" (Acts 17:6, NKJV), it was clearly not meant as a compliment. In fact, it was an accusation and a criticism. Everywhere the disciples preached the gospel of Christ, they upset the norm. They changed the way people saw religion, God, politics, church, and personal relationships.

Jesus said in John 18:36: "My kingdom is not of this world. If it were, my servants would fight to prevent my arrest by the Jews. But now my kingdom is from another place" (NIV). He was saying, in essence, "My people aren't going to act the way you expect because I operate from completely different principles and goals."

Then, as now, it was really the sinful people whose ideas were all turned around, backwards, and upside down. So when the early Christians were said to be turning the world upside down, they were actually putting *right* what had been wrong since the fall of humanity in the Garden of Eden.

This is why the greatest compliment the church today could receive would be to have people complain that we Christians are turning the world on its ear. And if we aren't being accused of this, it's most likely because we're operating according to the principles of this world instead of according to God's upside-down kingdom principles.

Of course, most Christians and churches readily agree, on an intellectual level, with the principles Jesus taught. But how we respond in everyday life is usually another matter. How many of us truly love Him more than anything or anyone else, or really take up our cross daily and follow Him?

Yet anything short of this kind of "radical" discipleship—which is really what ordinary Christian living should be—is settling for less than what God desires.

CAPPUCCINO OR CHURCH?

Question: If Christians are the body of Christ, then why does church need to be in a building called "church"? Why can't I just have fellowship with a friend over lattes?

Answer: Many people question the validity of the church as an institution. But the church is the only organization that Jesus himself established.

Church is an *of course* to Jesus. It was also an *of course* to the early apostles. They encouraged one another, wrote to one another, exhorted one another. Paul agonized, in fact, about his desire to go and be with Christ versus his desire to be on earth with the church, his first family.

Of the church, Jesus said, "The gates of hell shall not prevail against it" (Matt. 16:18, KJV).

Unfortunately many of us hardly care about the church at large. We feel entitled to a good church, but most of us aren't doing anything more than spectating. We want the pastor's sermons to be good, but we also want them short because we have other things we want to do on Sunday besides warm the pews.

Instead of asking, "Why do I have to go to church?" we should be asking, "What can I do to minister to and build up Christ's own precious body, of which I am a part?"

I heard the story of a husband and wife who got up one Sunday morning as usual to get ready for church. It was just about time to walk out the door, and the wife noticed that her husband wasn't even dressed yet. She asked, "Why aren't you getting ready for church?"

"'Cause I don't want to go!"

"Do you have any reasons?"

"Yes, I have three good reasons. First, the congregation is cold. Second, no one likes me. And third, I just don't want to go."

The wife replied, wisely, "Well, honey, I have three reasons you *should* go. First, the congregation is warm. Second, there are a few people there who like you. And third, you're the pastor! So get dressed!"

What Kind of Person Can This Book Help?

Maybe you're a young Christian who's excited about living out your faith with your new family of faith—but you don't know where to start. What should you expect? How can you plug in?

Maybe you're a longtime Christian who feels ineffective or hampered at every turn. Too often your church body behaves just like the world you're trying to influence. Some days you feel as if you all got a new paint job but underneath you're still the same old Plymouth. How can you be like one of those first-century "upside-down" believers?

Or maybe you're among the many Christians in the so-called boomer and buster generations who have grown a bit cynical. You're not so much disappointed with God as you are disappointed with church. I mean, why put up with confusing liturgies and trite sermons? Why be associated—even remotely—with some of those TV preachers who wave Bibles but look and act like idiots? Along with plenty of friends, you're thinking, *Why should I even attend?*

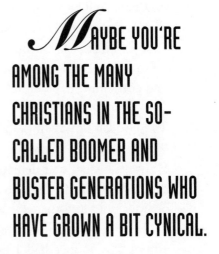

Perhaps you are a pastor who is trying to understand why nothing seems to be happening in your church. People aren't turning their lives over to Jesus Christ and being transformed; attendance is down; morale is low. Is this all your call to ministry is supposed to amount to? Should you bring in a marketing firm? Should you stop saying *Jesus* so much?

If you find yourself in any of these profiles, this book is for you. My prayer is that it can be part of God's plan to nudge you, along with other believers in your life, toward the kind of church experience that Jesus had in mind.

In some ways you might say that this book is a "church growth" book. However, my goal is not to show you how to be part of a church that is growing numerically or is catering to a certain segment of society. My goal is to show you how to be part of an "upside-down" church that is growing in power and impact because it has healthy foundations and operates according to God's kingdom principles.

The principles I want to share with you may not be what

you'd expect. I won't be proposing that you learn to do church exactly the way we do it at Harvest Christian Fellowship, although I often use our church as an example. I won't be telling you how to double the size of your congregation necessarily, although I believe a healthy church will naturally grow.

What I will be saying is that we don't need more programs or slick techniques. These principles aren't "Greg's Gimmicks for Success" or the latest buzz at some cutting-edge seminary. Instead, my intention is that everything you read will be timely and contemporary but at the same time completely biblical.

The Foolish Power of God

When I came to faith, God didn't exactly catch a big fish for Himself. I wasn't a celebrity. I wasn't a former this or a former that. I was a mixed-up seventeen-year-old. But God took this ordinary kid and turned his life around.

Let me tell you a little story that took place when I was in high school. No sooner had I become a Christian than I decided I didn't want to hang out with what we used to call the "Jesus freaks." In my newly converted state, they seemed just a little too intense for me, talking nonstop about God and quoting Scripture all the time. I thought, *I don't know if I want to go that far. I think I'm going to go solo. Me and God. We will work it out.*

One day, shortly after this, I was walking across the campus, and some guy approached me and said, "Brother Greg, I have something for you. I got you a Bible, bro!"

It was one of the Christian guys I didn't really want to hang out with. He held up this large, cowhide-covered Bible with two Popsicle sticks glued in the shape of a cross on the front. "I want you to have this, brother," He said, obviously very pleased with himself.

I said, "Oh, gee, thanks. What am I supposed to do with this?"

"Start reading it, brother. It's the Word of God!"

My eyes darted around, hoping no one would see me talking

with this guy. It's not that I did not have respect for the Bible; I just didn't want to carry one around on my high school campus. And certainly not one with Popsicle sticks glued together in the shape of a cross!

The fact is, I was embarrassed. As soon as this guy walked away, I shoved the Bible into my coat pocket so hard I ripped the seams. I was on my way over to a friend's house, and I certainly didn't want to be caught with this thing.

When I got to the door of my friend's house, I noticed a planter out front with some bushes in it. I looked to the left. I looked to the right. I pulled the Bible out and hid it in the bushes.

When my friend opened the door, I walked in, trying to look cool. Several of my friends were there. "Hey, guys," I said. "How's it going?"

"Hey, Greg, where have you been lately?"

"Nowhere." My heart was beating fast. I didn't want to tell them that I'd decided to be a Christian.

Then one of the guys said, "Do you want to go get stoned?"

"No. No. Not at all."

"What's wrong with you?"

"Nothing is wrong. I'm totally fine." They were all looking at me as if I'd lost my mind when suddenly the front door flew open and there stood this guy's mother. She asked, "Who does this belong to?" and held up the big cowhide Bible with the Popsicle-stick cross on the front. Every eye in the room looked at the Bible, and then every eye in the room looked at me.

"It's mine," I said sheepishly.

My so-called friends had a great laugh at my expense. One of them said, "Oh, praise the Lord, brother Greg! Are you going to be a nice Christian boy now and read the Bible, pray, and go to church?"

"No, I'm going to hit you in the mouth right now if you don't shut up!" (I hadn't yet read the part in the Bible about loving people.)

This was especially hard for me to take because I was always the mocker in school. I was the guy with the fast quip and smart-alecky response to the teacher. I had raised mockery to an art form. And now I, the mocker extraordinaire, was the one being mocked.

But I realized that if I was going to be a real follower of Jesus Christ, I had to make a break with these old buddies.

I would realize later that this Bible I was so ashamed of was the very Word of God that would change my life and the lives of others I would have the privilege of sharing its message with.

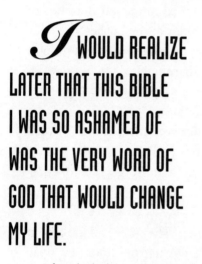
I WOULD REALIZE LATER THAT THIS BIBLE I WAS SO ASHAMED OF WAS THE VERY WORD OF GOD THAT WOULD CHANGE MY LIFE.

And you know what? Nothing's been the same since. Now that Bible I was ashamed to hold up is the book I speak from. It is my only authority, and it contains the only message I proclaim. As Paul said, "I am not ashamed of the gospel of Christ, for it is the power of God to salvation for everyone who believes" (Rom. 1:16, NKJV).

I firmly believe that God can turn any life upside down, just as He did mine. And through the "foolishness" of those who are willing to follow him, God can remake your church experience. He can turn the course of a generation and a world—one silly Popsicle-stick cross at a time.

"You Have a Little Strength"

We've been talking about the first church, which is described in the book of Acts. But when we look at a description of the church of the last days, which I believe we are a part of, the message of Jesus to the church in Philadelphia is relevant to us.

To the angel of the church in Philadelphia write,
"These things says He who is holy, He who is true,
'He who has the key of David, He who opens and no
one shuts, and shuts and no one opens': I know your
works. See, I have set before you an open door, and
no one can shut it; for you have a little strength, have
kept My word, and have not denied My name." Rev.
3:7-8, NKJV

There are a number of ways we can interpret what Jesus means by "I have set before you an open door." But one way is that He is speaking of a door of unprecedented opportunity. Paul used this same picture in 2 Corinthians 2:12, where He says, "I came to Troas to preach Christ's gospel, and a door was opened to me by the Lord" (NKJV).

In essence, Jesus is saying to His followers, "Hey, look. I have opened a door for you. What will you do with it?"

Today we have a unique opportunity to get the gospel out. Countries that were previously closed are now open. And we have technology to project the gospel message to more people than ever before.

> ARE YOU SENSING GOD'S CALL TO WALK FORWARD INTO A BOLD NEW WAY OF LIVING OUT YOUR FAITH?

But just as important are the doors that are open in your own life. Are you seeing the openings among family members or people you work with? Are you sensing God's call to walk forward into a bold new way of living out your faith?

The next thing Jesus says to the church is, "You have a little strength." This is very much like the picture of a sick person coming back to life. You know what it is like to lie around when you have a fever. If you jump to your feet too quickly, your head throbs, and you wobble a little bit. But you know you're getting better because you feel your strength coming back.

Jesus uses this image to describe the church of the last days. We're not a superchurch. We're not a perfect church. But we are a church that is coming back to life. And you are a key part of that church.

Will you accept God's challenge to penetrate this culture and not be ashamed of this life-changing message God has given us? It is the only hope for America.

PASTOR TO PASTOR
From the Inside Out

A lot of good books about how to do church take an approach that works from the outside in.

Let's face it. A lot of pastors don't have money to finance a demographic survey. Maybe you've tried every possible technique to get your church to feel that it's going somewhere, but your congregation is still letting out one long yawn.

In this book I'm more interested in the heart of the church, the passion of its people, the inner fire that changes things *in spite of size, programs, or numbers.* Too many of us are caught up in the outside stuff—focusing on numbers, building programs, and the latest ways to attract new members. And in the process, we've lost sight of our first love. We've lost our light, our burning fire, to see people turn to Christ.

What I'm proposing is something simple. It's too basic to be impressive. It should be easy—even obvious—but it's not. And so I hope to help you dig beneath the layers of "church" to get to the heart of what makes any church a force to be reckoned with—regardless of size.

I firmly believe that a vital small-town church that is ignited for God is far more capable of setting the world on fire than a huge church that has turned into a social club.

For the Believer in Jesus Who Wants an Upside-Down Life
Listen. The observers are many. The critics are many. The fair-weather followers are many. The compromisers are many. But the laborers are few. Will you become a laborer? No one can honestly pray for this work to be done who is not willing to help do it.

WE'RE NOT A PERFECT CHURCH. BUT WE ARE A CHURCH THAT IS COMING BACK TO LIFE.

Perhaps you feel that your spiritual resume is weak. Maybe, like Peter, you smell of fish. Or maybe your church's resumé falls short of the mark, and you wonder if it can rise to God's challenge. Maybe you've tried so many times before that you're reluctant to pin your hopes again on what God can do. But God has purposefully put in your heart those hopes for how His people can have an impact on the world.

Will you ask the Holy Spirit to stir your heart to answer the desire of Jesus? Will you pray, "Lord, use me"?

The story is told of an old preacher who was aboard that fateful trip on the *Titanic*. After he was thrown into the freezing Atlantic, he swam from lifeboat to lifeboat, raft to raft, piece of ship to piece of ship, crying out to people, "Trust Christ. Take Him as Savior. Receive Him into your heart. Call upon the name of the Lord, and you will be saved."

Today people are drowning all around those of us who are safe in Christ. We need to follow the example of this old preacher and get out the message: Trust Christ!

Remember, God makes us able to do whatever He's called us to do. And we have *a little strength*—exactly enough to turn our country, our town, our church, our neighborhood, our family, and ourself upside down for Christ.

TWO

A FEW GOOD CHRISTIANS
How Twelve Men Turned
the World on Its Ear

LET'S TAKE a closer look now at those first-century believers and see if we can get a handle on what they believed and did.

They lived upside-down lives, walking in obedience to God and applying the truths of His kingdom. Here's another way to look at it: God has told us, "My thoughts are not your thoughts, nor are your ways My ways" (Isa. 55:8, NKJV). In fact, most of the time God's purposes are exactly the opposite of our human impulses.

This means that in order to truly follow Him we must think and behave in ways that feel unnatural, or upside down, to us. This is what the early church did. How did they do it? In Acts 2:42-47, we find a snapshot of how the early church was working.

> *They continued steadfastly in the apostles' doctrine and fellowship, in the breaking of bread, and in prayers. Then fear came upon every soul, and many wonders and signs were done through the apostles. Now all who believed were together, and had all things in common, and sold their possessions and goods, and divided them among all, as anyone had need. So continuing daily with one accord in the temple, and breaking bread from house to house, they ate their food with gladness and simplicity of heart, praising God*

and having favor with all the people. And the Lord added to the church daily those who were being saved. NKJV

When we read this passage or think of the disciples, as well as the early apostles like Paul, we tend to see them as superhuman. We imagine saintly figures in stained glass, people who were somehow different from the rank and file of humanity.

If YOU WERE GOING TO SELECT A DOZEN GUYS TO CHANGE THE WORLD, WOULD YOU HAVE PICKED THE GROUP JESUS PICKED?

But any honest examination of the Scriptures reveals just the opposite. They were ordinary people who were subject to the same weaknesses and shortcomings we all experience. Jesus appeared to go out of His way to find a group of followers who had little claim to greatness apart from their willingness to believe and obey Him.

If you were going to select a dozen guys to change the world, would you have picked the group Jesus picked? Imagine if Jesus submitted the resumes of His team to a modern management group. The results might read something like this:

> *Thank you for submitting the resumes of the twelve men you're considering for management positions in your new organization. All of them have taken our battery of tests, the results of which we've run through sophisticated computer analyses. We've also arranged personal interviews for each candidate with our psychologist and vocational-aptitude consultant.*
>
> *It is our staff's unanimous opinion that most of the nominees are lacking in qualifications for the type of enterprise you are undertaking. We recommend that you continue your search for persons of experience and managerial ability and proven capability.*

We find that Simon Peter is emotionally unstable and given to fits of temper. He seems far too impulsive to be put in a position of oversight. Andrew has absolutely no qualities of leadership. The brothers James and John place personal interest above company loyalty. And they seem to be impatient with others. Due to this impatience and ambition, they could one day become disgruntled employees.

Thomas demonstrates a questioning attitude that could tend to undermine morale. We feel it is our duty to tell you that Matthew has been blacklisted by the Greater Jerusalem Better Business Bureau.

In closing, one of the candidates shows great potential. He is a man of ability, resourcefulness, and ambition. We recommend Judas Iscariot as your comptroller and right-hand man. All the other profiles are self-explanatory.

Sincerely yours,
Jordan Management Consultants, Jerusalem

These were the men God put His hand upon and used to turn the world upside down! And just imagine how Saul of Tarsus, who later became Paul the apostle, would have fared as a candidate for Jesus' team.

Once again we see how God's ways are upside down to us.

As we look at the people God used in Scripture and in contemporary history, we see that God has always gone out of His way to find individuals who didn't look as

GOD HAS ALWAYS GONE OUT OF HIS WAY TO FIND INDIVIDUALS WHO DIDN'T LOOK AS THOUGH THEY WOULD AMOUNT TO MUCH.

though they would amount to much. This is great news because it gives you and me assurance that God can use us just as surely and as powerfully as He used those men and women.

27

In fact, the Bible tells us, "The eyes of the Lord run to and fro throughout the whole earth, to show Himself strong on behalf of those whose heart is loyal to Him" (2 Chron. 16:9, NKJV). It doesn't say He is looking for a strong man or a strong woman but rather someone whom *He* could be strong *on behalf of.*

So how do we become the kind of person—or the kind of church—God is searching for?

When we look to the disciples, we can see three things that made them people God could use to build His upside-down church.

- They walked according to the Spirit, not the flesh (human inclinations).
- They kept in mind the purposes of God, not the priorities of people.
- They acted according to God's methods, not their own.

According to the Spirit

I believe one key reason the church is not affecting the world today as it ought is that it is not relying on the Holy Spirit. Far too often we are relying on programs or on surveys and entertainment. We are relying on other means instead of depending on the Holy Spirit to do His work. As a result, we fail. We can't turn this world upside down on our own power.

People who have put their faith in Christ have had the Holy Spirit come to live within them. He dwells inside them. But Jesus promises a dimension of power even beyond this. In Acts 1:8, He said, "But you shall receive power when the Holy Spirit has come upon you; and you shall be witnesses to Me in Jerusalem, and in all Judea and Samaria, and to the end of the earth." (NKJV)

Jesus was saying here that we need this power to gain supernatural courage and boldness to be witnesses. When we are filled with the Spirit, He gives us a supernatural power to know and do His will, to share the gospel, to resist temptation, and to live a life that is pleasing to God.

The word *filled*, specifically in Ephesians 5, where it says, "Be filled with the Spirit," has many shades of meaning. One translation of the word is the idea of the wind's filling the sail of a ship as it carries the ship out to sea. So to be filled with the Spirit is to allow God to fill your sails and guide your course through life, with His commands being sources not of drudgery but of delight.

But in the original language the idea of being filled with the Spirit also implies something being permeated. The picture here is that God wants His Holy Spirit to permeate the lives of His children in what they say, think, and do. It is not some emotional experience or a brief time during which I am filled with the Spirit.

WE ARE RELYING ON PROGRAMS OR ON SURVEYS AND ENTERTAINMENT INSTEAD OF DEPENDING UPON THE HOLY SPIRIT TO DO HIS WORK.

To be filled with the Spirit means that God's Spirit is infiltrating every aspect of your life. He is permeating your prayer life and your worship life. He is permeating your business, too, and the way you treat others. He is permeating all that you say and do. To be filled with the Spirit means that I am carried along by, and under the control of, Jesus Christ. It means I fill myself with the Word of God so that His thoughts become my thoughts, His standards my standards, His will my will. When we are filled with the Spirit, we are walking thought by thought, decision by decision, act by act, under the Spirit's control.

This implies an ongoing process. We are being filled again and again.

Let's suppose someone you know just bought a new car, and after a week it stopped running. The person says, "This piece of junk! I can't believe it—it just stopped running."

"Really?" you say. "When was the last time you put gas in it?"

"When I bought it."

"Have you gone to the gas station since then?"

"No."

The problem is not the car. The car simply needs its gas tank refilled. And the tank will need to be refilled as long as the owner wishes to drive around in it.

THE SPIRIT DOESN'T GIVE US POWER JUST SO THAT WE CAN FEEL GOOD ABOUT OURSELVES OR HAVE A WONDERFUL TIME AT CHURCH.

A lot of churches and individuals are wondering what is wrong with their lives. They put the key in the ignition, but it won't start. Maybe it's just time for a refill. You need to be filled with the Spirit. Don't misunderstand; God doesn't supply His power merely so that we can have an emotional experience. He doesn't give us His power just so we can feel good about ourselves or have a wonderful time at church. The Holy Spirit's power is the practical means for us to have an impact on the world. Every person should pray that God will fill him or her with His Spirit today.

And every pastor should pray, "Lord, there is no way we can make a difference in our culture through our own strength. We can't do it through programs or gimmicks. We can't do it through any of our own devices. We need a power beyond ourselves."

CHRISTIANS ANONYMOUS

Question: Greg, I'm a little turned off to the whole church scene—at least as we see it here in the States. Look at TV Christianity. Look at mainline denominations "blessing" same-sex marriages. Why shouldn't Christians distance themselves from the church?

Answer: True Christians should distance themselves from

any "church" that violates biblical standards. At the same time, we don't want to throw out the baby with the bathwater.

You want to find a church that has a balanced approach, which must include clear and strong biblical teaching, heartfelt and God-honoring worship, warm and loving fellowship, and vital, engaging evangelism.

The only "organization" Jesus ever started was the church. The day we received Him as Lord and Savior we became members of the body of Christ, or the church as a whole. We need the interaction, accountability, and outlet for our gifts and talents that only the local church can provide.

According to God's Purposes

The second principle we see at work in the disciples is that they walked according to God's purposes. But it didn't start out that way—at least not for all of them.

Remember Peter's mistake? When Jesus explained that He must go on to Jerusalem to suffer and die, Peter took Jesus aside and began to rebuke him. "Never, Lord!" he said. "This shall never happen to you!"

In many ways this was a natural response. When someone we love predicts that something terrible must happen, we want to say, "Oh no! Things are going to be fine." This was a genuine, well-intentioned response. But, unknown to Peter, there was another spirit behind it.

But Jesus turned and said to Peter, "Get behind me, Satan! You are a stumbling block to me; you do not have in mind the things of God, but the things of men" (Matt. 16:23, NIV).

This is one of the harshest rebukes recorded in Scripture, and it demonstrates an important point. If we miss this, we can be a stumbling block instead of a stepping-stone to furthering Christ's kingdom. *If we want to become part of an upside-down church, we have to keep in mind not our own priorities but God's.*

We can know Jesus well. We can even be walking with Him, loving Him, wanting to do what is right. But if we're just going along on our impulses, we're most likely going to do and say the opposite of what God has in mind.

THROUGHOUT THE BIBLE, GOD REMINDS US TO CHANGE OUR THINKING, TO SEE WITH SPIRITUAL EYES, TO REMEMBER THAT HIS THOUGHTS ARE NOT OURS.

God's ways—His goals and purposes—are so radically different from ours. That is why we have to be ready to live and to think in ways that may feel upside down to us.

Throughout the Bible, God reminds us to change our thinking (among other things), to see with spiritual eyes, to remember that His thoughts are not ours. The Bible is, among other things, a collection of stories about people who discovered this. Consider Saul of Tarsus, Mary, Gideon, and Abraham. At some point they were surprised by what God had in mind. Imagine what some of their incredulous questions might have been:

- Gideon: "You want me to lead an army of three hundred against an army numbering well into the thousands?"
- Mary: "You want the Messiah to be born in a stable?"
- Abraham: "You want me to sacrifice my son Isaac?"
- Saul: "You want your worst enemy to preach to the Gentiles?"

What's on *your* mind? Insert your name below in place of the word *God* in the following list. If you're a pastor, repeat the process with the name of your church. Are the statements still true?

- God is more interested in God's eternal goals than in our temporary plans.
- God is more interested in what's in a person's heart than in what's in our religious practice.
- God is more interested in making us more like Jesus than in our temporary happiness or comfort.
- God always prioritizes the spiritual ahead of the physical.
- God is often more interested in revealing God through people's weaknesses than through their strengths.

According to God's Methods

We've seen that the disciples operated according to the Holy Spirit and according to God's purposes. But the third important thing we notice about the early Christians is their methods. They not only had in mind the things of God (Peter had learned his lesson!), but they went about accomplishing God's work in God's ways.

The first Christians didn't out-argue pagans—they outlived them. It is worth noting that Christianity made no attempts to conquer paganism and dead Judaism by reacting blow by blow. Instead, the Christians of the first century outthought, outprayed and outlived the unbelievers. Their weapons were positive, not negative.

As far as we know, they did not hold protests or conduct boycotts. They did not put on campaigns to try to unseat the emperor. Instead, they prayed and preached and proclaimed the message of Christ, put to death on the cross, risen from the dead, and ready to change lives. And they backed up their message with actions: giving, loving.

> *THE FIRST CHRISTIANS OUTTHOUGHT, OUTPRAYED, AND OUTLIVED THE UNBELIEVERS. THEIR WEAPONS WERE POSITIVE, NOT NEGATIVE.*

Today the church as a whole (I speak of the evangelical church in this context) has never been better organized politically across the country. We get the word out quickly through our grapevine when legislation comes up that is not good for the nation morally and spiritually. We speak up and make a difference. That is good.

But has our passion for what is temporarily good displaced our passion for going about God's business God's way? When did our *work* for Jesus begin to overtake our *worship* of Him? Are we more inclined to protest than we are to pray? Are we more interested in who is in the White House than in who is in God's house? Are we more interested in boycotts than we are in the salvation of family and friends?

Social and political action have their place; they are not wrong in themselves. But it's tempting to battle with only those weapons. Our primary weapons are spiritual, and our job is to be ambassadors to the world—ambassadors who understand our Leader's policies and employ only His upside-down tactics (taken from Matthew 5):

- Give to those who take.
- Love those who persecute us.
- Bless those who curse us.
- Humble ourselves.
- Lay down our life.

We are in a war. But it takes only a glance through this list to see how radically different God's weapons are from the weapons typically used in moral, political, and social battles.

The early Christians recognized this. They knew that the nature of their struggle was essentially spiritual, for "we do not wrestle against flesh and blood, but against principalities, against powers, against the rulers of the darkness of this age, against spiritual hosts of wickedness in the heavenly places" (Eph. 6:12, NKJV). And because of the spiritual nature of this struggle, they understood the spiritual nature of their weapons, as seen in 2 Corinthians 10:4: "The weapons we fight with are not the weapons of the world. On the contrary, they have divine power to demolish strongholds" (NIV).

As a result, the early Christians prevailed. Where is Rome today? There is still a place called Rome, but it is no longer a world power. Now it happens to be a very polluted tourist attraction. We go to Rome today to see the ruins of an ancient civilization and eat some really good food.

*W*HEN DID OUR WORK FOR JESUS BEGIN TO OVERTAKE OUR WORSHIP OF HIM?

Where is Caesar today? Most of us know very little about Caesar—there's a salad named after him. Do we remember the names of the great emperors of Rome? For the most part, no.

One of them, Diocletian, relentlessly persecuted the church, causing it to go underground. He thought he had been successful in obliterating Christians. He actually had a commemorative coin struck, with these words engraved on it: "The Christian religion is destroyed, and the worship of the Roman gods is restored."

Where is Diocletian today? Gone. Where are Christians today? Everywhere.

Over the centuries there have been many attempts to destroy the Christian faith. But they have always failed for one simple reason: Christians make up the body of Christ, which is the church. And Christ said that the gates of hell would not prevail against it. Jesus Christ will prevail in the end and establish His kingdom. But He'll do it His way through His people, His church.

You and the Church
One of the most important key to becoming part of God's upside-down church is caring about His church, both universally and locally.

The early apostles cared desperately about one another and

about all the Christian churches that were forming. They encouraged one another, wrote to one another, exhorted one another.

We have all heard this one: "Well, you know, I would go to church, but there are so many hypocrites there. I just can't stomach a hypocrite." I must say, what exactly are you looking for? A place filled with perfect people? Are you really shocked when you find that the church is filled with people just like you? People who are flawed, who make mistakes? Yes, even people who are sinners?

A lot of people are pretending to be something they aren't. The story is told of a man who was desperate to make some money. So he went down to the city zoo, hoping to get a job feeding the animals. The manager at the zoo had no openings, but seeing how big this guy was, he offered him another position.

"Our gorilla died the other day, and that was one of our most popular exhibits! If we got you a special gorilla suit, would you put it on and imitate him for a few days? We'll pay you well for it."

The guy was so desperate that he agreed. He actually did quite well at it for the next few days, dressed up in his gorilla suit, beating his chest, shaking the bars of his cage. Huge crowds were soon gathering, and the money was good.

But one day, while he was swinging on his trapeze, he lost his grip and landed right in the middle of the lion's den! The huge beast gave a ferocious roar. The man in the gorilla suit realized he couldn't cry for help without revealing that he was a fake. He slowly walked backwards away from the lion, hoping to climb back into his cage. The lion, however, with a very hungry look on his face, followed him.

Finally in desperation the gorilla cried, "Help!"

Immediately the lion whispered loudly, "Shut up, stupid, or you'll get us both fired!"

I have often said that if you are looking for the perfect church, don't join it because you'll spoil it. There is no church that does not have some flaws. The church is not supposed to be a museum for saints but a hospital for sinners. It's supposed to be a place where we can come and learn, grow, and help one another. And it's a place where we can go to be transformed.

Listen to what the Bible says in Hebrews 10:23-25:

> *Let us hold fast the confession of our hope without wavering, for He who promised is faithful. And let us consider one another in order to stir up love and good works, not forsaking the assembling of ourselves together, as is the manner of some, but exhorting one another, and so much the more as you see the Day approaching.* NKJV

The Bible is clearly saying that we should make time to be with other believers.

We are living in critical times. The Bible warns us that one of the signs of the last days will be an apostasy—a falling away from the faith: "Now the Holy Spirit tells us clearly that in the last times some will turn away from what we believe; they will follow lying spirits and teachings that come from demons" (1 Tim. 4:1, NLT).

If you are looking for the perfect church, don't join it because you'll spoil it.

We need to be together. We need to stand together. And when we face hardship, challenge, or temptation, we can come and be with God's people and say, "Pray for me this week. Help me." Or, we might be helpful to someone else.

Your Potential

Will you let Him fill you with His Holy Spirit? Will you value His purposes over people's priorities? Will you work according to His methods, not worldly ones?

If so, when God looks at you, He sees potential. You may see only a blank canvas, but He sees a finished painting. You see a Simon. He sees a Peter. You see a Gideon. He sees a mighty man of valor. God can do a lot with a little.

It's interesting to stop and look at how these men's lives ended. These were heroes of the faith. These were the few people who were faithful. And yet church tradition tells us that Matthew was slain with a sword. Luke was hung on an olive tree. James was beheaded. Philip was hanged. Andrew was bound to a cross from where he preached until he died. Thomas was thrust through with a spear. Simon Peter, the man who denied his Lord three times, was crucified upside down because he said, "I'm not worthy to die in the same way that my Lord died." That's not the same Peter I read about in the initial stages; that's a changed man.

John was the only apostle who was not martyred. Church tradition tells us that he was banished to the island of Patmos, where he was put into a pot of boiling oil—but John wouldn't cook. There on the island of Patmos he was given the message of the book of Revelation.

These were great men on whom God put His hand. Their greatness was not because of who they were; it was because of Christ, who lived in them and worked through them. God can make you into a great man or a great woman. Are you willing?

In the next chapter we'll look more closely at growing a healthy church, not just a large one. Believers who are world changers know that numbers are the result, not the goal, of the gospel. After all, in the days of the early church the Roman coliseums had the really big crowds. But across the empire, in marketplaces and jails and catacombs and rooms up back-alley stairs, something incredible was taking shape. Lives were changing. A new movement was being born.

The world was about to be tipped on its head.

And we can do the same today.

THREE

CONSUMERS OR COMMUNERS?
Church Growth Rules That Could Be Making Yours Sick

THE CHURCH I pastor today actually began as a small Bible study over twenty-five years ago. Back then I had long hair parted down the middle, a full beard, and—well, you get the picture. Let's just say it was another place and time.

You see, I never expected to pastor a large church (I didn't even expect to pastor). We simply concentrated on learning and doing what Scripture teaches—and over time the Lord brought growth. We did not seek to be a big church; we sought to be a strong church. No one here at Harvest Fellowship gave size too much thought until a market research firm called one day and said, "Congratulations! You are one of the ten largest churches in America."

As a result of pastoring a large congregation, I'm frequently asked about our success. What kind of church growth formula do we follow? Can what we do at Harvest be applied to any church, anywhere, with similar results? In other words, "What's your secret fertilizer, and could we please have some?"

I understand these questions, and I know that the motivations behind them are often sincere. Very few pastors are interested in church growth solely to finance fat salaries or to feel more popular than they were in high school. But something would be terribly wrong if motivated Christians—pastors and laypeople alike—weren't interested in seeing their churches flourish and grow.

Over the years, some people have objected to our announcing how many people have become Christians in a particular service or rally at Harvest. They say, "You're not supposed to care about numbers." But why shouldn't we care about numbers?

Every number represents a soul. And I'm supposed to care about souls. So are you. The Bible tells us that the angels in heaven rejoice over every soul that is saved. We read in Acts that the early church kept count, too: "Then those who gladly received his word were baptized; and that day about three thousand souls were added to them" (Acts 2:41, NKJV).

It's quite possible to have a human body that's growing large—but not necessarily healthy.

We should do our best to get more people into church so more can hear the gospel, grow in Christ, and go out to multiply God's work in the world. This is our goal at Harvest Fellowship, and I believe it is the goal of almost every pastor I speak with.

So we agree that growth is good. Yet growth alone does not necessarily indicate that a church is healthy. When we see a church with high attendance, we can sometimes assume that the people there are doing some things right. But numbers don't tell the whole story.

Think of it this way. Paul told the Corinthians that the church is like a body with many different parts (1 Cor. 12:14-18). But as you know, it's quite possible to have a human body that's growing large—but not necessarily healthy. In fact, it's also possible for people to appear healthy even while their cholesterol count is off the charts or their liver is slowly disintegrating.

The simple truth is that size or growth rate alone does not indicate health. But health, on the other hand, almost always leads naturally to growth. This is particularly true when it comes to the church. That is why in this book we're focusing on health as a means to growth, not the other way around.

More and more pastors today are looking for ways to boost numbers. The past two decades have witnessed a dramatic increase in the number of "megachurches"—congregations of one thousand or more—around the country. Professionals have labeled the trend the "church growth movement."

But we have to ask what these trends mean for the church as a whole. Are we witnessing a second era of Christians who are really shaking up their world? Or are believers just shuffling their club memberships around to get the latest, most attractive deal?

I want us to look at how this new emphasis on growth is affecting today's church.

GROWTH OR HOAX?

Question: Isn't it a good sign that there are a lot of huge churches cropping up? Why doesn't this mean there are more Christians than ever?

Answer: In a recent article entitled "The Myth of Church Growth," published in *Current Thoughts and Trends,* David Dunlap cites some troubling statistics. For example, at the very time megachurches have sprouted across the landscape, the proportion of Americans who claim to be "born again" has remained a constant 32 percent.

According to Dunlap, growth isn't coming from conversions but from transfers; they account for up to 80 percent of all growth taking place today. He goes on to quote C. Peter Wagner, one of the leading spokesmen for the movement, who admits, "I don't think there is anything intrinsically wrong with the church growth principles we've developed . . . yet somehow they don't seem to work."

I would suggest that one reason they don't work is that they tend to approach church as if it were a business. But a business-driven response may only make things worse. In the long run, if we train people to be consumers instead of communers, we'll end up with customers instead of disciples. It might fill up an auditorium, but it'll never turn the world upside down for Christ.

The New Consumer Church

In my conversations with many pastors from around the country, I've noticed that a new word has entered church lingo: consumer.

IF WE TRAIN PEOPLE TO BE CONSUMERS INSTEAD OF COMMUNERS, WE'LL END UP WITH CUSTOMERS INSTEAD OF DISCIPLES.

Experts are telling us that people no longer attend a fellowship of believers to commune with God. They come to consume. And in order to thrive, churches are going to have to adapt to the needs of the "spiritual consumer."

When you label someone a consumer, you're zeroing in on one thing: consumption. That means it's all about appetite—what goes down the hatch. And churches that adopt a consumer-oriented approach in order to bring in the crowd often look to marketing experts to help them find out what consumers are hungry for.

In the past a group of leaders and believers might pray and ask God to show them where to plant a new church. Today they're likely to add a few steps. They'll say, "Let's do a market survey, find out where the growth is, figure out the demographics. Let's ask our target population what they want in a church. Then let's deliver it."

To better understand this shift in thinking, imagine the church as a business. You, as a church leader, are the owner/operator. You are trying to meet the needs of church "consumers," and you must compete with other nearby providers for the same customer.

Suddenly your concerns would change, although the change may be unnoticeable at first. You'd spend a lot more time asking questions such as:

THERE'S ALWAYS A NEW CHURCH DOWN THE STREET THAT HAS SOME NIFTY NEW PROGRAM OR WIDE-SCREEN TV THAT WE DON'T.

- What can I do to make my product more appealing and unique?
- How can I improve customer service?
- How can I adjust what we offer to meet and beat the competition?

This shift toward consumerism is being driven, directly or indirectly, not by pastors but by demands and expectations of church "customers."

"People expect a full-service church," one young pastor told me. "And there's always a new church down the street that has some nifty new program or wide-screen TV that we don't."

Listen to this: In a recent survey of a thousand church attendees, respondents were asked, "Why does the church exist?" Among laypersons polled, 89 percent said the church's purpose was "to take care of my family's and my spiritual needs." Only 11 percent said the purpose of the church is "to win the world for Jesus Christ."

The pastors from those same churches gave nearly the opposite answer. Only 10 percent said the church exists to meet the needs of members. The vast majority chose as the purpose of the church "to win the world for Christ."

Clearly the drive for a new way to do church is partly the result of a conflict of expectations between pastors and laypeople. The pastor is asking, "What will it take to get you plugged in to this church?" And people in the pew are answering, "Meet the needs of my family and make church a place we want to come to."

PASTOR TO PASTOR
Risky Rules for Growing

Could any of these church growth rules be making yours sick?

> Risky Rule #1: If it brings people in, it pleases God.
> Risky Rule #2: The less confrontational or overt the gospel message, the better.
> Risky Rule #3: Feed a church what it seems to be hungry for.
> Risky Rule #4: Target your church to a particular demographic group.

New Ways of Doing God's Business

Now would be a good time to pose the question What's so wrong with thinking of people as consumers and churches as marketers?

From a pastor's perspective I see many good reasons to consider church from a consumer's viewpoint. Frankly, I think it's better to be sensitive to what people want and need rather than ignore those needs for the sake of religious agendas, which has caused so many traditional churches to become irrelevant in today's culture.

Some good things are happening as a result of the church growth movement. Motivated believers are trying harder than ever to be relevant to people's real needs. Christians are finding new ways to reach out into their communities. And people who would never have showed up before are walking through church doors.

But I see dangers as well. If we let ourselves get trapped into relying solely on slick marketing ploys when it comes to doing God's business in this world, we've shifted the focus from the message of the gospel to the way we package it.

The last thing I want to do is discourage any person or ministry or cause some unnecessary division. Christians are reaching for new ways of doing things because they see real needs in the world around us—and they care! I thank God for the diversity of church expressions in the body of Christ. And we should be careful about putting our own limits on the ways God can work or the approaches God can bless if He chooses.

> *WE* SHOULD BE CAREFUL ABOUT PUTTING OUR OWN LIMITS ON THE WAYS GOD CAN WORK OR THE APPROACHES GOD CAN BLESS IF HE CHOOSES.

But at the same time, we need to be aware of choices—even well-intentioned, highly attractive ones—that take our focus, time, and energy away from God's original plan for the church that we see reflected in the book of Acts.

MOVEMENTS VS. MARKETING

Question: Wasn't the Jesus movement of the late sixties and early seventies market driven in many ways? For instance, you did church on the beach and used guitars for worship. What's the difference between that and surfer churches or yuppie churches today?

Answer: I can't speak for the entire Jesus movement around the country at that time, only for what I was a part of at Calvary Chapel in Costa Mesa, California. The pastor of Calvary, Chuck Smith, allowed the young people to express themselves in the way and with the music that was a part of their culture. It was not at all contrived or even thought out. It was sponta- neous. Looking back now, I believe it was a spiritual revival. There was a sense of expectancy in the air, a sense that God was truly at work.

Chuck had no master plan to speak of, just a desire to teach these young people the Word of God and help them mature spiritually. In fact, Chuck had built what for him was the ideal church sanctuary. It seated about three hundred in an intimate Spanish-style chapel. When the young kids starting showing up, they had to literally blow out walls to accommodate them. No surveys were taken, no market data analyzed.

God's Original Church Growth Plan

Recently I was at a gathering with some other pastors. Many of them were expressing frustration with the lack of numerical growth in their churches and were trying to figure out how to make their churches larger. One of them said, "My feeling is, whatever works, and if it pleases God, that is what I want to do."

I said, "You know, I don't want to be nitpicky, but I really have to correct that statement. It's not whatever works. It is whatever is pleasing to God. Period."

If it's pleasing to God, it will work.

God can meet the needs of our generation with or without a lot of spiffy marketing techniques to help Him out. At best they're optional. But what the church can never do without is God's own blueprints.

If there was ever a church growth plan that worked, it was the one used by the first-century church. Talk about numbers. Talk about effectiveness. This church exploded. Why? Because the believers knew why they were there and what they were supposed to do.

Eventually this little church scattered, divisions came, and persecution forced perseverance and, ultimately, growth. They certainly weren't perfect Christians or problem-free churches. However, when

I BELIEVE THAT WHEN GOD SET UP THE FIRST CHURCH, HE DID IT RIGHT.

we talk about the upside-down church described in Acts, we're seeing the Original Plan in action. The apostles' letters to the churches complete the picture.

In the rest of this book I want to focus on that picture. What are the principles for "doing church" God's way? What should a world-changing body of believers really look and feel like? And what can we expect to see happen in our own congregations if we get it right?

In chapter 2, we quoted Acts 2:42-47, which describes the first church. In this passage we find four foundational qualities:

1. They were a worshiping church.
2. They were an evangelizing church.
3. They were a learning church.
4. They were a loving church.

Think of the word W-E-L-L: Worshiping, Evangelizing, Learning, and Loving. At a glance, these four foundations don't appear to be remarkable or, for that matter, upside down. They may not have the marquee appeal of a star-studded Sunday program.

But I believe that when God set up the first church, He did it right. Churches that try to consistently prioritize these areas the same way the first church did will discover two things: just how contrary to conventional wisdom they can run and how powerfully they work as a plan for church growth God's way.

Original Church Growth Rule #1:
Become a worshiping church.

"They continued steadfastly . . . in the breaking of bread, and in prayers. . . . And many wonders and signs were done through the apostles. . . . They ate their food with gladness and simplicity of heart, praising God."

*A*LTHOUGH PRAYER AND WORSHIP SOUND LIKE AUTOMATIC RESPONSES TO GOD'S MIRACLES, THEY OFTEN AREN'T.

The early church was built on prayer and worship. We might read this and think, *That's a no-brainer,* or *I'd worship and pray a lot too if I saw signs and wonders happening all around us.*

When we read the book of Acts—the record of the early church's history—we might conclude that the believers had miracles happen every single day! But we need to remember that Acts is an overview of about twenty-five years of church history. There were likely many days when miracles did not happen. But the believers continued on "steadfastly" because they did not follow signs and wonders. Rather, signs and wonders followed the believers.

Although prayer and worship sound like automatic responses to God's miracles, they often aren't. Actually, we see throughout the Gospels that a more common response is "Wow! Do that again, and I just might believe. In fact, if you keep providing this way, I might keep following you." But Jesus consistently refused to deliver to these consumers. King Herod wanted to see Jesus, so Jesus was brought before him. But the Bible says that what Herod really wanted was to see Jesus perform a miracle. Not only did Jesus not perform a miracle for Herod, He never even spoke to him (Luke 23:8-9). Herod was not interested in Christ himself or in His message; he just wanted to be dazzled.

When it comes to worship and prayer, one contemporary church growth rule seems to be: "Make your church a happening place. Lots of miracles. Lots of emotions. And people will come." I saw a notice permanently painted on a church sign the other day: "Miracle service every Wednesday night, 7 to 9." That amazed me. I just hope God knows when His window of opportunity is.

An expressive, worshipful church results from sincere praise and sincere communion with the Savior. It's not something you schedule in order to draw a crowd.

To become a worshiping people means that we've been turned upside down. Our natural inclination is to worship—with our time, energy, and affection—other gods. But the Bible teaches that we are put on this earth primarily to know and walk with the God who made us and to bring glory to His name.

Original Church Growth Rule #2:
Become an evangelistic church.
"The Lord added to the church daily those who were being saved."

As we read the accounts of the first church, it becomes clear that literally everything they did culminated in evangelism. Proclaiming Christ was never seen as optional. It was never a job handed out to a special committee.

Evangelism happened regularly as the early believers lived their lives upside down in every way. As they did so, they aroused not only curiosity but also admiration and earned an audience with unbelievers.

HEALTHY, WELL-FED, WORSHIPING BELIEVERS WILL REPRODUCE THEMSELVES.

Today, many in the church actually debate Jesus' command to go into all the world and make disciples for Him. Some churches go so far as to say, "We're not called to evangelism. We are called to body ministry." Or,

"We're called to get into the Word together. There are other churches called to outreach."

Healthy, well-fed, worshiping believers will reproduce themselves. When I am glorifying God, when I am built up as a believer, I want to then go and share my faith.

One positive aspect of the recent growth movement is the emphasis on getting unbelievers to join us at church. More churches are trying to make their service sensitive to the needs of unbelievers. Cut out the Christian jargon. Don't actually preach from a Bible, just refer to it. Make visitors feel welcome—no pressure, no appeals.

This is a great goal, and it has brought thousands of people into the church who would never have attended otherwise. The result has been a growing awareness of our need to abandon Christian jargon and communicate the gospel clearly. In some cases it's pulled us out of our cliques and clubs and forced us to relate to unbelievers.

CREATIVE APPROACHES SHOULD WORK TO STRENGTHEN THE GOSPEL'S IMPACT, NOT OBSCURE IT.

However, I believe there is a potential downside. Sometimes a church tries so hard not to be offensive or confrontational that the gospel message is not preached in its entirety. I'm totally in favor of meeting people with Christ's message in creative ways. But this should work to strengthen the gospel's impact, not obscure it. If people walk away having a good feeling but no idea who Jesus is, we've really missed the boat.

This does not mean that drama is wrong or that using videos, music, or any other means to communicate the gospel is wrong. We do some of those things at Harvest. But it does mean that we must be sure that gimmicks don't take the place of the gospel, and that we are actually proclaiming the whole gospel—including judgment, sin, and salvation.

Paul put it this way, "How, then, can they call on the one they have not believed in? And how can they believe in the one of whom they have not heard? And how can they hear without someone preaching to them?" (Rom. 10:14, NIV).

We must realize that God's primary method of converting people is through biblical preaching. Scripture reminds us, "For since in the wisdom of God the world through its wisdom did not know him, God was pleased through the foolishness of [the message] preached to save those who believe" (1 Cor. 1:21, NKJV).

Notice that the verse does not say people would be saved by foolish preaching, though there is plenty of that. Nor does it say that people would be saved by the foolishness of Christian music, as wonderful as that can be, or by the foolishness of drama and skits. But rather, through the foolishness of *the message preached*.

I do believe that we make a grave mistake when we discourage people from bringing their Bibles to church. George Barna's book *The Second Coming of the Church* mentions that in the seventies, seeker churches wanted to make visitors feel welcome. So they did not make it necessary for people to locate Bibles or find passages in them. Churches didn't want visitors to feel that they were surrounded by what could be perceived as a bunch of "Bible thumpers." Barna says, "Two decades later, it is clear that this experiment has had a more sinister consequence. People don't even know where their Bibles are anymore!" In many churches, the core membership—not just the visitors for whom the tactic was originally embraced, has lost its familiarity with the Bible. He concluded, "Sadly, the shift away from promoting the personal responsibility to bring a Bible along has sent a signal to many people that the Bible is not important."

Original Church Growth Rule #3: Become a learning church.
"They continued steadfastly in the apostles' doctrine and fellowship."

This most basic essential of any healthy church is a commitment to preaching and learning God's Word. At the time of the first church, this meant listening to the apostles' teachings and reading the Scripture they had at this point.

But also notice the words "they continued steadfastly." Keep in mind that this means not only that the apostles taught faithfully and continually but that the congregation was faithful to "continue in"—learn and keep growing in—what was taught. They were attentive.

This may not appear to be upside-down behavior. But if you continue to follow the story of the first church, you see how the more common approach was to neglect sound teaching or to change the gospel's message. Paul wrote to the churches in Galatia:

> *I am astonished that you are so quickly deserting the one who called you by the grace of Christ and are turning to a different gospel—which is really no gospel at all. Evidently some people are throwing you into confusion and are trying to pervert the gospel of Christ.* Gal. 1:6-7, NIV

I do believe that in some churches the Bible is simply not being preached and taught with a view to giving the congregation a deepening understanding of Scripture.

It's true that many people today want church "lite" and hassle free. No heavy meals or five-course messages. They want to just drive in, place their order, and drive out.

But the danger here is that people develop an appetite for what they are fed. A church with a steady diet of feel-good sermonettes in place of good theology or solid teaching from Scripture will eventually raise up a congregation that is weak.

The writer of Hebrews expressed it this way:

We have much to say about this, but it is hard to explain because you are slow to learn. In fact, though by this time you ought to be teachers, you need someone to teach you the elementary truths of God's word all over again. You need milk, not solid food! Anyone who lives on milk, being still an infant, is not acquainted with the teaching about righteousness. But solid food is for the mature, who by constant use have trained themselves to distinguish good from evil. Heb. 5:11-14, NIV

Original Church Growth Rule #4: Become a loving church.
"Now all who believed were together, and had all things in common . . . continuing daily with one accord . . . and having favor with all the people."

Having all things in common. This is definitely upside down, and it's hard for many of us to even picture it. Of course, others of us think it sounds great: "Hey, the Carlson's would have to share their boat with us. . . ."

But this description wasn't intended to describe some socialist plot. It illustrates just how literally we're called to love one another. The reason the early church could share their possessions was that they were actually living out the second great command to love their neighbor as themselves. We see that their unity and love were so powerful that "all the people" thought well of them.

Who wouldn't want to join in on such a love fest where everyone was cared about and accepted? As a result, their numbers exploded and thousands came to Christ.

I think most people would agree that today the church at large doesn't live out this kind of unity or love. Many local congregations struggle to keep their own church from splitting in two. And meanwhile various church denominations squabble and spit at each other across the aisles while the world looks on. We seem to have forgotten that our commitment to love and unity in the church is one of the most powerful ways we witness to the world. And this is tragic.

*T*ODAY IT SEEMS THAT WE'RE WILLING TO LOVE AND ACCEPT EACH OTHER ONLY IF WE BELONG TO THE SAME CLUBS OUTSIDE OF CHURCH.

Today it seems that we're willing to love and accept each other only if we belong to the same clubs outside of church. One of the latest trends in church growth is the attempt to try to "niche" churches in a particular segment of society. You might call them designer churches. "Let's have boomers," or "Let's get the Generation Xers."

There's nothing wrong with trying to make a connection with a specific segment of society. Or choosing common interests as springboards to evangelization. We naturally invite to church our friends and others who share our interests.

But the problem with designing a church to cater specifically only to a certain group of people is that we miss out on the great beauties of diversity.

Jesus said, "Go into all the world, and preach the gospel." He did not say, "Go only to the people you can personally relate to" or "Pick a particular demographic group, and then go love them." Paul wrote to the Colossians, "So, naturally, we proclaim Christ! We warn everyone we meet, and we teach everyone we can, all that we know about him" (Col. 1:28, Phillips).

I think it's wonderful when someone walks into the church and sees different ages, different cultures, different tastes, different races—with one thing in common: Jesus Christ. That is a truly loving church. And that church will grow.

Beyond Formulas

The acronym I've used here—W-E-L-L—is simply a way to remember these four key principles. But the foundations of the first church are not just another formula. They are God's original design for a healthy, growing church. Throughout the rest of this book we will be focusing on how to live upside-down lives and create upside-down churches, based on these four key areas.

Yet while every church and every Christian's life should be built on these four foundations, each one should go about this differently. Your goal should not be to have a church that looks just like mine or anyone else's. Your goal should be to become part of a healthy, balanced, diverse church that is bringing souls into God's kingdom.

I believe that the church in our generation has a unique opportunity to make a difference in the world. God has opened the doors wide to us at this time in history, and we can use this opportunity to get the gospel out and to turn the world upside down.

We shouldn't think, however, that this is the first time the church has been tempted to treat itself like a gathering of consumers instead of communers. Remember Jesus' outrage at the marketplace? "Then he entered the temple area and began driving out those who were selling. 'It is written,' he said to them, '"My house will be a house of prayer"; but you have made it "a den of robbers"' " (Luke 19:45-46, NIV).

Every one of us has a vital part to play in helping our house of prayer grow healthy. But as we do, let's remember that God's church is not a business. It may grow larger when it's treated like one. But what will be the long-term prognosis? God's church is based on principles that go against the world's grain. So healthy growth cannot come from applying worldly methods.

FOUR

"GO THEREFORE . . ."
God's Upside-Down Plan to Save the World

FEW THINGS in the Bible are more upside down than God's plan to save the world. Think about this for a moment. The all-powerful God of the universe chose limited, fallible human beings as His main vehicle to spread the most important message the world has ever known.

He could have chosen angels to do the job. He could have parted the clouds and spoken audibly and said something like, "Hello, humanity. I'm God and you're not!"

In the past He spoke through a burning bush, appeared in visions, and carved His laws on stone tablets. But in our day He has clearly chosen ordinary men and women to carry His message of salvation to the world.

The Great Commission
If you've been a Christian for long, you've probably heard of the great commission. Some of you can't hear the words without worrying that God will send you to Siberia as a missionary. Or maybe you're not familiar with the term at all, and you're thinking, *The great commission . . . is that some kind of spiritual kickback we get every time we lead someone to Christ?*

Well, yes and no. I know of nothing in life so rewarding as

57

leading people to Christ. But technically the great commission refers to Jesus' command in Matthew 28:18-20:

> *Jesus came and spoke to them, saying, "All authority has been given to Me in heaven and on earth. Go therefore and make disciples of all the nations, baptizing them in the name of the Father and of the Son and of the Holy Spirit, teaching them to observe all things that I have commanded you; and lo, I am with you always, even to the end of the age."* NKJV

It's important to note that although Jesus was speaking to His disciples here, this commission is intended for the entire church—not just pastors, evangelists, and missionaries. And the great commission is not something Jesus said only once. It's emphasized many times throughout the New Testament.

Remember the parable of the virgins, or bridesmaids, found in Matthew 25? In this story about a first-century wedding, when a shout indicated that the bridegroom had arrived to escort the bride to the wedding, five bridesmaids had enough oil in their lamps and were ready to go. But five were foolish and said, "We don't have enough oil in our lamps. Can you give us some of yours?" The wise ones essentially answered, "Sorry, go get it for yourself." The door was shut, and they never got in.

THE GREAT COMMISSION IS INTENDED FOR THE ENTIRE CHURCH—NOT JUST PASTORS, EVANGELISTS, AND MISSIONARIES.

Clearly this parable is a warning from Jesus to the "pseudobeliever" (who is really not a believer at all) who sits in the pew every Sunday but has no real relationship with God. The oil Jesus mentioned in this story could be taken to symbolize the Holy Spirit in the believer's life. These five virgins without oil are a picture of those who may outwardly appear to be Christian but really aren't. Most messages I have heard on this text tend to emphasize that aspect of the parable, and I have given more than one message myself doing that very thing.

But something else strikes me about this story, something that speaks to true Christians also. Notice that those who had oil had no plan to give some to those who didn't: "Then the five foolish ones asked the others, 'Please give us some of your oil because our lamps are going out.' But the others replied, 'We don't have enough for all of us. Go to a shop and buy some for yourselves'" (Matt. 25:8-9, NLT). Our attitude as Christians can easily slip into "I got mine. You go get yours. I'm going to heaven—too bad you're not."

WE AS CHRISTIANS CAN BE ASLEEP WHEN WE OUGHT TO BE PREPARING OURSELVES AND OTHERS TO MEET THE BRIDEGROOM.

Notice, too, that when the cry went out to announce the bridegroom's arrival, both the wise and the foolish were sleeping. I think that is an important point. It clearly shows that we as Christians can be asleep when we ought to be preparing ourselves and others to meet the Bridegroom.

Jesus also told a story about a shepherd who had one hundred sheep. One went astray. The shepherd didn't say, "Win a few, lose a few." He left the ninety-nine. He went after that one sheep. Why? Because God doesn't value just multitudes; He values individuals. He values humans. He values the human soul.

We saw in chapter 3 that evangelism was one of the four foundations of the first church. But as we read about the early church in Acts, we notice that whether we're talking about learning, loving, or worshiping, all these things are ultimately part of making the church more equipped for evangelism. We might call "the equipping of the saints" our marching orders.

So how is the church responding?

The Great Concession

Some time ago *Christianity Today* magazine conducted a survey among its readers and found that most of them, 89 percent, agreed that faith in Jesus Christ was the only way to salvation. And 87 percent of the readers agreed that every Christian is responsible for evangelism. But only 68 percent of the respondents agreed or strongly agreed that the most important task for Christians is to lead non-Christians to faith in Christ. And only 52 percent said, "I have been more active in telling others about Christ in the past year than ever before."

I think these findings are fairly representative of the rank-and-file Christians in today's church. Most of us know that Christ is the only way to God. And we realize that evangelism is part of our calling, yet we respond to the great commission with something like, "Oh yeah, we're supposed to go tell every nation. . . . I'm pretty sure part of my offering goes to one of those missions groups."

SO HOW DID THE GREAT COMMISSION BECOME THE GREAT CONCESSION?

So how did the great commission become the great concession?

The readers responding to the *Christianity Today* survey named a number of problems, including: (1) A feeling that I am not able to do evangelism as well as the professional; (2) I'm too timid; (3) I fear how people will respond. These feelings are very real, and in the next chapter we address some of them. But I believe the biggest reason we in the church are not carrying out the great commission is that we don't care enough. We're simply not that concerned about the souls of others.

General William Booth, the founder of the Salvation Army, once said that if he could have his wish, part of the final training for preachers and evangelists would be to have them hung over the open fires of hell for twenty-four hours "so those that were sharing this gospel message would recognize the urgency of it," he explained.

The early church understood this urgency. Paul put it this way to the church at Corinth:

We are therefore Christ's ambassadors, as though God were making his appeal through us. We implore you on Christ's behalf: Be reconciled to God. God made him who had no sin to be sin for us, so that in him we might become the righteousness of God. 2 Cor. 5:20-21, NIV

Notice that God is making His "appeal" through us. And Christ is "imploring" unbelievers through us. The God of the universe is pleading with fallen humanity through us. If this doesn't inspire us, I don't know what will.

The first church was persecuted for preaching, and yet listen to this:

They called the apostles in and had them flogged. Then they ordered them not to speak in the name of Jesus, and let them go. The apostles left the Sanhedrin, rejoicing because they had been counted worthy of suffering disgrace for the Name. Day after day, in the temple courts and from house to house, they never stopped teaching and proclaiming the good news that Jesus is the Christ. Acts 5:40-42, NIV

Did you catch that? This is definitely upside-down behavior: rejoicing because they suffered. Here in the U.S. there's not much sales appeal for that kind of attitude. We have the opportunity to proclaim Christ without serious persecution for the most part. Yet the church is often casual about it.

In sharp contrast, these early Christians continued to do the very thing that had caused them to suffer. If I saw men behaving like this, it would get my attention. I'd want to know exactly what cause or person they believed in so passionately.

Meet a man named Andrew Meekin.

You may remember reading about the jet that was hijacked, then crashed with 163 passengers and 12 crew members on board. As it turned out, these hijackers bungled their plans, and there was not enough fuel to get to their destination. So the pilot announced to the passengers that he was going to have to do an emergency landing on water.

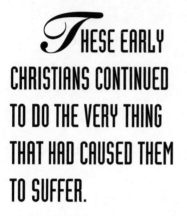

THESE EARLY CHRISTIANS CONTINUED TO DO THE VERY THING THAT HAD CAUSED THEM TO SUFFER.

Enter Andrew Meekin, a man on his way to a Bible conference. Andrew was a member of the evangelical church in Ethiopia, in Addis Ababa, the capital. Even though he was a soft-spoken man and not a preacher per se, when he heard that the plane was going to make an emergency landing, he stood up. In the final anxious minutes between that announcement and the crash, Andrew Meekin quickly shared the gospel message with the passengers and invited people to respond. A flight attendant who survived said that twenty people received Christ.

Andrew Meekin seized his opportunity. And I know what you're thinking: *OK, next time I'm on a plane that's going down I'll do that. I think under those circumstances, I'd feel urgent, too.* We probably would. But the Christian who is living according to Christ's upside-down principles believes and acts as if the plane could always go down. He is prepared and poised to seize the moment.

Be honest with yourself. Measure your response by your behavior and your choices, not by your feelings or intentions: Do you really care about the plight of the unbeliever? Every unbelieving person you meet today is in danger of dying without Christ at any moment.

I know these words are hard. So let me encourage you that if you're becoming painfully aware that you don't care enough about lost souls, that in itself is a good indication that you do care. I know that many believers fall into bed at night discouraged. Many of us are embarrassed that we've never led others to Christ. And we're not sure why, but it seems that our Christian walk lacks results.

May I suggest to you that the answer is simple. It's as simple as asking God to wake you up. As being

*W*INNERS OF SOULS MUST FIRST BE WEEPERS OF SOULS.

willing to take steps of faith and try to initiate conversations about Christ. It's as simple as asking God to give you a sincere burden for the lost. It's as simple as looking around every day to see what part you can play in God's amazing plan of redemption.

PASTOR TO PASTOR
"Weepers of Souls"

Some time ago I was asked to speak to a group of pastors on the subject of church growth and evangelism. I told these pastors that the reason many of their churches were not growing was that many of them really didn't care about evangelizing lost people.

Later, one pastor wrote me a letter saying, "My first reaction to your message was, 'How dare you say to me, a pastor, a man of God, that I don't care about lost people?' But then I began to think about it. I began to pray about it. And I realized you were right. I cared about my flock and our own ministry but not the lost.

"So I asked God to give me a burden, and He changed my heart. Now we are inviting unbelievers to Christ in our services, and every week people put their faith in Jesus."

We can talk endlessly about the need for evangelism. And we can create programs designed to mobilize our church with resources and tools. But it is of no consequence if the body of Christ doesn't care. We've got to start on the inside and work out.

It was C. H. Spurgeon who said, "Winners of souls must first be weepers of souls." And I would add that pastors must be weepers of souls if we want our congregations to become winners of souls.

Ask yourself with me, "When was the last time I wept because people need Christ?"

A Part to Play: Our Role in the Great Commission
The great commission is a joint effort.

When you think of your own conversion, you will remember that, yes, there was a moment when it all came into focus and you made that commitment to Christ. But probably a series of things brought you to that decision. It might have been the foundation your parents laid or a talk you had with a friend. It might have been something you were exposed to on TV or radio.

We all have a part to play. Some of us break down an intellectual barrier. Some of us come along and penetrate a heart's stubborn defenses with our own story about what Christ has done for us. Others of us sense when someone is ready, and we're led to actually pray with a person to receive Christ.

The apostle Paul put it this way in 1 Corinthians 3:6-8:

> *I planted the seed, Apollos [another preacher] watered it, but God made it grow. So neither he who plants nor he who waters is anything, but only God, who makes things grow. The man who plants and the man who waters have one purpose, and each will be rewarded according to his own labor.* NIV

Meet another guy, Edward Kimball. He sold shoes. But that's not how he changed the world.

Edward Kimball was an ordinary Christian who taught Sunday school in his church and made a living down at the shoe store. But his real passion was sharing the gospel. One day Edward determined that he was going to look for an opportunity to explain the gospel to a salesman named Dwight, who had just joined the staff.

Edward was really nervous. He hemmed and hawed and paced back and forth. Dwight was in the back room putting shoes away. Finally Edward mustered up his courage and launched into the story of Jesus' birth and death and resurrection. That day young Dwight gave his life to Christ.

Maybe you've already guessed. Dwight's last name was Moody. You may know him as D. L. Moody. So Edward Kimball, a shoe salesman, led to Christ one who would be one of the greatest evangelists in church history. This is the great commission in action. It's not just about what pastors and evangelists do from the pulpit. It's about what you do and say while you're selling shoes or programming computers or shuttling neighbor kids to soccer practice.

If the story stopped here, that would be amazing. But it continues. One day Dwight L. Moody was preaching, and a pastor named Frederick Meyer was listening. He was deeply stirred by Moody's message and went on to establish a nationwide preaching ministry. Later, while he was preaching, a young man in the audience named Wilbur Chapman accepted Christ.

Eventually Chapman felt called to evangelism. As he was proclaiming the gospel in various places, he decided he needed some help. He knew a young former baseball player named Billy Sunday, who was looking for a job, and Chapman hired him. Billy asked if he could preach every now and then. Billy Sunday ultimately emerged as the greatest preacher of the early 1900s.

One day Billy Sunday preached in Charlotte, North Carolina, where a great movement of God was taking place. Many people believed. They were so stirred up in their new faith that they invited a relatively unknown preacher, Mordecai Ham, to set up his gospel tent in Charlotte and keep preaching. On one of the final nights a tall, lanky farm boy walked down the aisle. His name was Billy Frank, but more of us know him today as Billy Graham. And he has personally delivered the gospel message to more people than any other man in human history.

IT'S WORTH NOTING THAT NO PERSON IN THE NEW TESTAMENT CAME TO FAITH APART FROM THE AGENCY OF A HUMAN BEING.

Think about that. Edward Kimball reached D. L. Moody, who reached F. B. Meyer, who reached Wilbur Chapman, who touched Billy Sunday, who touched those who brought Mordecai Ham to town to preach the gospel to Billy Graham.

We don't always celebrate the Andrew Meekins and Edward Kimballs of the world. We remember the D. L. Moodys and the Billy Sundays and the Billy Grahams. But God has placed His faithful ones everywhere. And we all have a crucial part to play.

It's worth noting that no person in the New Testament came to faith apart from the agency of a human being. Why didn't the angel of the Lord just go straight to the Ethiopian and skip Philip? And what about Cornelius? He was commanded by an angel to send for Simon Peter, who "will tell you what you must do" (Acts 10:6, NKJV). Why didn't the angel just tell him?

Because God has chosen to work through people. Even in the unique case of Saul of Tarsus, a person prepared the way. Before Stephen was stoned, as Saul stood by, approving, Stephen fearlessly proclaimed the gospel message. And then after Saul encountered the Lord on the road to Damascus, God sent a man named Ananias to lay hands on him and pray for him.

Does this mean that God can't save the world without people? Is God actually dependent on us? No. God can get the job done without you or me. But in His wisdom God has chosen people to communicate His message. And although God could get the job done without us, we could never get the job done without Him.

A Mission Possible: God's Role in the Great Commission

God's role in the great commission is greater than you may realize, because even though God gave this assignment to humans, He didn't leave it at that. When He commissioned us, He also committed Himself to helping us.

You'll notice that the word *commission* doesn't appear in Matthew 28. My thesaurus lists the synonyms *entrust, authorize, empower*. And each one of these is reflected in the words of Jesus and helps us understand God's part in the great commission.

GOD ENTRUSTS US. Have you ever had to entrust someone with an important message? You hope they get it right. You pray it gets delivered. Above all, you want the messenger to value the message as much you do. Just before Jesus announced the great commission, "the eleven disciples went to Galilee, to the mountain where Jesus had told them to go. When they saw him, they worshiped him; but some doubted. Then Jesus came to them and said . . ." (Matt. 28:16-18, NIV).

In His next words to the disciples, Jesus entrusted them with the most important message in the world. He gave them the great commission— *even while some were still doubting!*

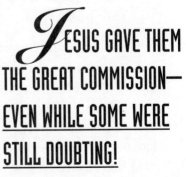

JESUS GAVE THEM THE GREAT COMMISSION— EVEN WHILE SOME WERE STILL DOUBTING!

Jesus didn't give the command only to those who firmly believed or had a special gift for talking to people. He gave it to all of them. He chose to trust this group with His appeal. Even if we have fears or doubts, we are still called. God has chosen to trust us with this precious mission.

HE AUTHORIZES US. Notice these words in the great commission: "All authority . . . has been given to me." Jesus was saying two things here. The first was: "I have total authority and control here. I am in charge of everyone and everything. You can't appeal to a higher power. And so you can rest assured that this assignment comes from the top."

Those of you with a military background understand this concept well. Your superior officer has the authority to tell you what to do. And when he speaks, you jump. Others of us can remember a baby-sitter who used this line on us. She said, "I'm in charge now. Remember that your parents have given me all authority. You have to do what I say." And we knew she was right.

Listen to Paul describing to the Colossians our authority through Jesus:

> For by him all things were created: things in heaven and on earth, visible and invisible, whether thrones or powers or rulers or authorities; all things were created by him and for him. He is before all things, and in him all things hold together. And he is the head of the body, the church; he is the beginning and the firstborn from among the dead, so that in everything he might have the supremacy. Col. 1:16-18, NIV

The second aspect of what Jesus is saying is this: When someone with ultimate authority has sent us to do something, we suddenly have authority ourselves. We read in Matthew 10:1 that before Jesus sent them out, "he called his twelve disciples to him and gave them authority to drive out evil spirits and to heal every disease and sickness" (NIV).

Think about a time when you had to accomplish a particular task at work. You went to a coworker and said, "I need thus and so."

And he or she said, "Hmmm, I'll think about it."

But then you piped up and said, "The boss sent me. And he needs this by 2:00 P.M."

"Oh. OK. I'll have it ready, no problem."

The great commission is not just something God told us to go out and do apart from him. He backs us up. He is our authority, and He lends us His authority as we go out into the world to do His will.

HE EMPOWERS US. Let's go back for a moment to the military analogy. You've been entrusted with an important message. And now you've been given authority to deliver it. But what if you have no means? "That's great, Sarge, but

JESUS WON'T EVER ABANDON US IN THE MIDDLE OF A MISSION.

don't I get any backup? How am I supposed to accomplish this?"

We all know what it's like to be asked to do a task that seems impossible, either because we don't know how to do the job or we don't have the resources we need. We may feel this way about evangelizing. *How can I ever get brave enough? What do I say?*

But the great news is that when God commissions us, He also empowers us to be His witnesses.

After the great commission in Matthew, we read in the book of Acts how Jesus appeared to the disciples yet again and said,

> *Do not leave Jerusalem, but wait for the gift my Father promised, which you have heard me speak about. For John baptized with water, but in a few days you will be baptized with the Holy Spirit. . . . You will receive power when the Holy Spirit comes on you; and you will be my witnesses in Jerusalem, and in all Judea and Samaria, and to the ends of the earth. Acts 1:4-8, NIV*

Basically God is saying here, "Wait! Don't think you can just go out and do this on your own. You need special power; you need my very Spirit within you."

A. W. Tozer said that if the Holy Spirit were taken away from the New Testament church, 90 percent of what they did would come to a halt, but if the Holy Spirit were taken away from the church of today, 10 percent of what we do would come to a halt.

Jesus promises to personally empower us. And He won't ever abandon us in the middle of a mission.

A FIRE IN THE PULPIT

Question: How can I be sure my congregation is really getting the message of the great commission? What can a pastor really do to set his congregation on fire?

Answer: It's been said, "The best way to get a fire in the pews is to first start one in the pulpit."

If you are a pastor or a Bible study leader, your heart and attitude will show themselves in what you say and how you say it. It was Moody who reminded us that we should never preach about hell without a tear in our eye or about heaven without a smile on our face.

Your people need to see that the plight of lost men and women is important to *you*. Reinforce the need to share the gospel often by teaching what Scripture says about responsibility. Perhaps the most important thing you can do is to be sure that you are consistently obeying the commission yourself by offering—from the pulpit—invitations for people to follow Christ.

When the people you speak to hear this kind of emphasis, it will remind them of the importance of seeking to lead others to Christ.

FIVE

DO YOU KNOW JESUS?
Practical Principles
for Witnessing

THE FIRST time I led someone to Jesus Christ, I did not expect the gospel to work. Not through my mouth anyway. My only plan was to fail.

I was two weeks old in my commitment to Christ. I didn't know much about Christian living or the Bible, but I'd heard that I should go out and share the Good News with others. So one day I went down to the beach—the same one where I used to make a point of avoiding any Bible-toting Christians who might try to witness to me.

Now here I was, a bona fide member of the Soul Patrol, out prowling for unbelievers to convert. But I wasn't exactly full of confidence. My main goal was to find someone who wouldn't argue or get angry at me. I thought if an unbeliever just ignored me or walked away, that would be fine.

Eventually I spotted a lady who looked about the age of my mom. I imagined that she might be sympathetic to me. When I walked up to her, my voice was shaking. I said, "Excuse me, but can I talk to you or something?"

She said, "Sure. What about?"

"Uh, about, like, God and stuff." (Remember, I was a teenager.) She said, "Go ahead. Sit down. Talk to me."

So I pulled out a copy of an evangelistic tract I had stuffed in my pocket for a moment like this. Since I couldn't remember exactly what it said in there, I read through the entire booklet verbatim. The whole time I read, I was shaking like a leaf and thinking, *This isn't going to work. Why am I doing this? This is not going to reach her.*

But the woman didn't leave.

When I got to a part that said, "Is there any good reason why you should not accept Jesus Christ right now?" I realized that I should direct this question to the woman. I hesitated. Feeling awkward, I looked up and asked her, "Is there?"

She said, "No."

"OK," I said, slightly confused. "Then that would mean you would like to accept Jesus Christ right now?"

She said, "Yes, I would."

I was so shocked that for a moment I didn't know what to do. I had planned only for failure. Frantically I searched the tract for some kind of prayer to lead her in. Finding one, I said in the most reverent tone I could summon, "Let's bow our heads for a word of prayer." But even as she prayed after me, I was still thinking, *This is not going to work!*

After we were done, the woman looked up and said, "Something just happened to me." And at that moment, something happened to me, too. I got a taste of what it was like to be used by God.

I had completely underestimated the power of the gospel. But I determined that from that point on, no matter what else I did in life, I wanted to share my faith with others.

It's Time to Hit the Beach

By now you understand that the great commission applies to everyone in the body of Christ. And I hope you've asked God to give you and your church a burning desire to see people come into God's kingdom. Now it's time to actually hit the beach. Or the streets. Or wherever it is you or your congregation meets unbelievers.

In this chapter we'll look at the practical aspects of how to actually approach unbelievers and be effective witnesses for Christ.

Remember the *Christianity To-day* survey I mentioned in chapter 4? The reasons most Christians listed for not witnessing were: (1) A feeling that I am not able to do evangelism as well as the profes-sional; (2) I'm too timid; (3) I fear how people will respond.

One thing Christians and non-Christians have in common is that they're both uptight about evangelism. Christians are uptight about witnessing to unbelievers, and unbelievers are uptight about being witnessed to by Christians. I can relate to both sides. Before I met the Lord, I was definitely the person on the beach you'd least want to pick on. I became pretty skilled at hanging out that Do Not Disturb sign to any would-be evangelists.

When you think about it, witnessing is sort of an upside-down thing to do. It goes against our natural avoidance of rejection or telling people something they may not want to hear. The idea doesn't exactly appeal to the church's new consumer mentality. Add to this the deep terror many of us feel about the idea of speaking in public, and you have a lot of reasons to stay home and keep your faith to yourself.

I have seen surveys taken where people are asked to identify their greatest fears. The predictable responses are these: fear of flying, spiders, being audited by the IRS, etc. But what always amazes me is that the number one fear is not death (that's number two) but rather having to speak publicly.

You may have heard the story from the days of the Roman

Empire about a Christian who was thrown to a hungry lion in the Colosseum. As the bloodthirsty spectators cheered, the lion pounced on the Christian. But the Christian quickly whispered something in the lion's ear, and the beast backed away in terror. After this happened several times, the emperor sent a centurion to find out what magic spell could make a ferocious lion cower in fear. A few minutes later the guard returned and said, "The Christian told the lion, 'After dinner you'll be required to say a few words.'"

Yes, witnessing can seem scary. But the lessons I learned that day at the beach still hold true. For those willing to risk a little personal rejection, the rewards go way beyond any awkward moments they might experience. And any Christian—no matter how young in the faith or terror-stricken or awkward or doubting—can learn how to effectively lead an unbeliever to Christ.

> **YOU CAN BE SHAKING LIKE A LEAF AND STILL SHAKE THE WORLD.**

I know firsthand that it doesn't take a lot of training for someone to be able to proclaim the gospel. The story proves this point. And have you noticed that often the most effective evangelists in a church are usually the youngest Christians? They have no idea that they might not be up to the task. Their passion and sincerity more than make up for any lack of knowledge or training.

However, I don't believe that hoping all the baby Christians will witness is a good plan for turning the world on its ear. Let's face it. As the church has responded to the great commission with a great concession, few are taking the time to say, "You need to do this—and here's how." I'm always amazed at the number of pastors and church workers who admit they haven't trained their people to witness with any kind of confidence.

What I'm about to show you won't necessarily make evangelism easy for you or your congregation. Some people will always feel uncomfortable proclaiming the gospel. But you know what? It doesn't have to be comfortable. In fact, I know this from experience: *You can be shaking like a leaf and still shake the world.*

PASTOR TO PASTOR
A Message Worth Repeating

You might be surprised to learn that many pastors feel as awkward preaching the gospel from the pulpit as their laypeople do sharing it on the job. In fact, some consider it unseemly to preach the gospel from the pulpit.

It's much more comfortable to preach about some other aspect of Christian living, such as fellowship or kindness. Everybody pretty much agrees with these things. But the true gospel message is inherently confrontational. In fact, some pastors have had complaints from their congregation when they have tried to accurately present the gospel from the pulpit. One pastor said, "Every time I preach about repentance and give an invitation, I can see my congregation squirm." Other pastors find that the gospel message doesn't measure up to their loftier themes and sounds slightly ridiculous.

I don't always succeed, but I try, in most messages I give, to present a simple gospel message and include at the end an invitation for people to come to Jesus. I believe that if there's a single thing I do as a pastor that has contributed to my church's growth and health, this is probably it.

For not only is it an opportunity to "throw out the net" and give people a chance to receive Christ, but it also models for the congregation how the gospel should be presented: simply and sincerely.

Salvation in the Desert

We find the story of Philip in Acts 8.

> *Now an angel of the Lord spoke to Philip, saying, "Arise and go toward the south along the road which goes down from Jerusalem to Gaza." This is desert. So he arose and went. And behold, a man of Ethiopia, a eunuch of great authority under Candace the queen of the Ethiopians, who had charge of all her treasury, and had come to Jerusalem to worship, was returning. And sitting in his chariot, he was reading Isaiah the prophet. Then the Spirit said to Philip, "Go near and overtake this chariot."*
>
> *So Philip ran to him, and heard him reading the prophet Isaiah, and said, "Do you understand what you are reading?"*
>
> *And he said, "How can I, unless someone guides me?" And he asked Philip to come up and sit with him. The place in the Scripture which he read was this: "He was led as a sheep to the slaughter; and as a lamb before its shearer is silent, so He opened not His mouth. In His humiliation His justice was taken away, and who will declare His generation? For His life is taken from the earth."*
>
> *So the eunuch answered Philip and said, "I ask you, of whom does the prophet say this, of himself or of some other man?" Then Philip opened his mouth, and beginning at this Scripture, preached Jesus to him. Now as they went down the road, they came to some water. And the eunuch said, "See, here is water. What hinders me from being baptized?"*
>
> *Then Philip said, "If you believe with all your heart, you may."*
>
> *And he answered and said, "I believe that Jesus Christ is the Son of God."*
>
> *So he commanded the chariot to stand still. And both*

Philip and the eunuch went down into the water, and he baptized him. Now when they came up out of the water, the Spirit of the Lord caught Philip away, so that the eunuch saw him no more; and he went on his way rejoicing. Acts 8:26-39, NKJV

Who was this Ethiopian man? First of all, we know he was a man of great importance and position. At this time in history, Ethiopia was a large and powerful kingdom located south of Egypt, and the treasurer would be similar to our secretary of finance. He would have been a cabinet member, and he would have traveled with a large entourage, including guards.

Picture a stretch chariot with tinted windows. Guys running alongside wearing sunglasses and little radio wires in their ears. He would have been hard to miss.

The Ethiopian diplomat had everything this world can offer. Yet he was on a search for God. We know this because he went to Jerusalem to worship. But instead of finding the vibrant faith of the glory days of Solomon and King David, he found a cold, dead religion that was laden with rules and regulations. Maybe he even tried, as a non-Jew, to keep some of these laws. But there was something missing in his life.

The other man in the story, Philip, did not have earthly power, wealth, or fame. We read early in this chapter that Christians had suddenly turned into public enemy number one. They were being hunted down and killed throughout Judea and Samaria. And yet Philip had the spiritual hope that the Ethiopian was searching for.

All of us are surrounded every day by people just like this Ethiopian man. They're in our churches, our families, our neighborhoods, and our workplaces. They have tried to be religious. Maybe they've prayed, read the Bible, been baptized, gone to church. But something is still missing in their lives, and we have the answer.

MASS VS. ONE-ON-ONE EVANGELISM

Question: Which is better? One-on-one evangelism or stadium evangelism? Why isn't it better to bring a friend to a crusade and let the pros handle things?

Answer: In Acts chapter 8, God gives us a great picture of the upside-down church in action, and we see both kinds of evangelism demonstrated. We see mass, or "crusade," evangelism, which happens in crowds and in group settings. We also see personal evangelism, which happens one-on-one. Both are valid tools.

In the early part of this chapter we read, "Philip went down to the city of Samaria and preached Christ to them. And the multitudes with one accord heeded the things spoken by Philip, hearing and seeing the miracles which he did" (vv. 5-6).

Of THE PEOPLE WHO COME FORWARD AT OUR CRUSADES, AN AVERAGE OF 85 PERCENT ARE BROUGHT BY A FRIEND.

Philip didn't have a stadium, but he might as well have. And this is just one of many examples in Scripture that clearly validate a large-scale approach to evangelization. In part, what kept the crowd attentive to Philip's message were the signs and wonders from God. A similar dynamic is often evident today in our stadium rallies as unbelievers see God in action among thousands of people. Many of these people would never come to church, but what's happening at the stadium captures their attention and makes them more attentive to the gospel message.

As we'll see, most of the principles that apply to personal evangelism also apply to mass evangelism.

The two types often work best in combination. Of the people who come forward at our crusades, an average of 85 percent are brought by a friend.

Keep in mind that both kinds of evangelism—group and individual—are valid and necessary if we're going to change the world.

Our Invisible Needs

Often people don't appear to need a thing, so we pass them by without sharing the gospel. But I'm here to remind you that these are facades. I used to be one of those people. You used to be one of those people, too. And we responded to the gospel.

So before we talk in practical terms about how we witness, let's look at four needs all humans have.

1. PEOPLE ARE SPIRITUALLY EMPTY. Every person has an essential emptiness within that only Christ can fill. In a recent interview Barbara Walters asked highly accomplished actor Richard Dreyfuss a revealing question: "If you could have one wish, what would you wish for?"

Without hesitating, he said, "Every time I have a birthday, every time I blow out candles, every time I see a shooting star, I wish for the same thing—I wish for inner security." Now here is a talented, successful man who still feels something's missing inside.

2. PEOPLE ARE LONELY. We tend to imagine the lonely as shut-ins or widows or people who recently moved to town. We think that the wealthy or famous or important could never be lonely. But everyone who doesn't know Christ is lonely for His companionship. People can only come so close to each other. The great physicist Albert Einstein once wrote to a friend, "It is strange to be known so universally and yet be so lonely." Only Christ can actually come and dwell within us and make His home in us.

3. PEOPLE ARE GUILTY. The Bible tells us that "all have sinned and fall short of the glory of God" (Rom. 3:23, NIV).

Because every person is capable of sin and does sin, every person experiences guilt. Now, not everyone has a strong sense of shame. We can sear our conscience by repeatedly sinning without experiencing repentance. We can also mask our shame with alcohol or suppress feelings of guilt until we convince ourselves that we're essentially good. But deep down every person knows that he or she is out of sync with the Creator.

Everyone is empty. Everyone is lonely. Everyone has a sense of guilt. Everyone is afraid to die.

4. PEOPLE ARE AFRAID TO DIE. Actor Dennis Hopper was asked about his greatest fear. He gave a one-word answer: "Death." Then he was asked, "What is your greatest regret?" He answered, "Mortality. That you don't live forever."

I know that many unbelievers will strut around and say, "Not me. I'm not afraid to die." But without a sure knowledge of belonging to God, all of us are afraid of death. The only way to truly have peace about our death is to know that heaven awaits us.

We need to allow the Holy Spirit of God to burn these truths into our heart and memory. Everyone is empty. Everyone is lonely. Everyone has a sense of guilt. Everyone is afraid to die. That way, when we look at people, we'll see past the superficial layers to the genuine human needs that make the message of the gospel our only hope.

The Philip Principles

Philip was a little-known disciple, but he became a great evangelist. How did he do it? What were his techniques, and what can we learn from his experiences?

We can learn quite a lot from this ordinary Christian. There are seven vital principles that give us practical guidelines for witnessing. Not only do these principles apply as we evangelize one-on-one, but they also show the way for churches and speakers as they try to reach others for Christ.

1. Go where people are.
Remember that Philip had gone to Samaria and preached the gospel. We could read that and not think much of it. But it brings out an important point. The Samaritans and the Jews hated each other. Remember how the woman at the well said to Jesus, "You are a Jew and I am a Samaritan woman. How can you ask me for a drink?"(John 4:9, NIV).

When Philip went to Samaria, he gave up his natural prejudice to bring the gospel to a group of people he would not even have communicated with under normal circumstances.

This reminds us that we should seek to communicate with people who *don't* look just like us. God wants us to take His gospel to *all* people. They may be younger or older or of a different race. There is no room for bigotry, prejudice, or bias in the life of a child of God.

If you want to witness to unbelievers, you need to go to where they live. Maybe it's the beach. Maybe it's the mall. This holds true for mass evangelism or deciding where to start churches. God doesn't tell us to go where people are most likely to come to church and support it financially. God sent Philip to people who needed salvation. It wasn't a great plan for church growth, but it was exactly God's plan for evangelization and soul saving. God did not say that the whole world should go to church but that the church should go to the whole world.

2. Obey the Spirit's leading.
Notice these verses from Philip's story: "Now an angel of the Lord spoke to Philip, saying, 'Arise and go toward the south along the road which goes down from Jerusalem to Gaza.' . . .

Then the Spirit said to Philip, 'Go near and overtake this chariot'" (Acts 8:26, 29, NKJV).

You may be thinking, *God never speaks to me.* But consider that the Spirit speaks to you all the time—and maybe you're not listening very well. Some of us tune out things we don't want to hear. We say, "Speak, Lord, your servant is listening." But when He does speak, what we hear doesn't suit us.

SOMETIMES WE DON'T REALIZE THAT WE'VE HEARD GOD UNTIL LATER.

What does God's voice sound like? Thunder? Charlton Heston or George Burns? When God generally speaks to us, it's through our spirit, not through our ears. We have an idea or thought that seems to be from Him. Or we feel what a non-Christian would call a "gut instinct." It may be through a circumstance or even through our own inclinations.

Sometimes we don't realize that we've heard God until later. Did God tell me to talk to the lady at the beach? I believe He did.

But don't miss this: *We don't need to wait to be sure we've heard from God before we evangelize.* He has already spoken to us through His Word. In no uncertain terms He has commanded us to go and preach the gospel. If we see a person bleeding by the side of the road, we don't wait to hear from God about whether or not we should help. We should be taking advantage of every possible opportunity to share our faith. Remember, we scatter our seed wherever we go in the hope that some of it will land on good ground and bring a harvest.

So let's say you've heard the Spirit's leading. Now be sure to obey—no matter how ridiculous the idea may seem. Look at my paraphrase of Philip's story:

> *When Philip hit the streets of Samaria, revival was beginning to break out. Demons were coming out of people. People were being cured of horrible diseases and putting*

their faith in Christ. Then an angel showed up and said,
"Go down toward the desert. That area known as Gaza.
It is about eighty miles from here." Acts 8:5-7, 26

To go eighty miles today, you would hop in your car and be
there in just over an hour. But for Philip it meant a very long, hot
walk. How easily Philip could have said, "Excuse me, Lord, but
with all due respect, the apostles and the other believers in Jerusalem are at least thirty miles closer. Couldn't you call one of
them? Great things are happening right here."

But Philip responded and seized the moment. And it's a good
thing, because God had uniquely equipped him to deal with this
man from Ethiopia. And God has uniquely equipped each of us
as well if we'll obey His leading.

3. *Approach with tact.*

So you've decided to approach some middle-aged lady on the
beach with God's good news. Where should you start? Probably
not with, "Hey, sinner!"

Philip used tact. I love the way he
approached this Ethiopian in the
chariot. He didn't walk up to him
and say, "Excuse me, are you
saved?" or "Did you know you are
going to hell?"

Instead, he sought to establish a
dialogue. "Excuse me, do you understand what you are reading?"

I wonder if that Ethiopian

TACT HAS BEEN
DEFINED AS THE INTUITIVE
KNOWLEDGE OF SAYING
THE RIGHT THING AT THE
RIGHT TIME.

thought, *And you are? . . . Do you normally hang out by yourself*
in the middle of the desert?

Tact has been defined as the intuitive knowledge of saying the
right thing at the right time. And I hate to say it, but this skill is
sorely lacking in many Christians. When the Bible says preach, it

doesn't necessarily mean you have to yell or be rude. Some perfectly friendly people turn into "droids" or tape recordings when they start to talk about Jesus.

But we can preach the gospel conversationally. We're not speaking from the steps of the Lincoln Memorial. We can stumble a bit, ask questions, look the person in the eye. We can remind ourselves that we're talking to someone who is just like us.

IN CONVERSATION, UNEXPECTED DOORS OF OPPORTUNITY CAN OPEN AS WE LEARN MORE ABOUT A PERSON.

Which brings up a possible language barrier: I call it "Christianese." Say you approach an unbeliever and begin, "Hey, you reprobate! Has anyone ever told you that you are lost, perishing, damned, and headed for perdition? What you need to do is be regenerated. Converted through repentance. And then you need to get on the straight and narrow!"

Now what exactly does that mean? For an unbeliever it means don't maintain eye contact and leave as soon as possible. If we use biblical terms—and some of them, like *salvation, redemption,* and *justification* are indispensable—we need to define our terms as we go. Effective evangelists always explain key concepts in familiar terms.

4. Establish common ground.
Philip took time to assess the Ethiopian's situation and relate to him as a person, not just as a potential convert. Here was this guy, reading from Isaiah 53. So Philip offered his help, conversed with him, and got to know him a little bit.

Sometimes it's only as we talk to people about life in general that we perceive the best way to bring the gospel to them. In conversation, unexpected doors of opportunity can open as we learn more about a person. And if we first affirm the other's feelings—"I understand. . . . I used to think that. . . ."—then the person is more open to our explanation of what we know to be true.

This also means that we adapt to people. It doesn't mean we change or adapt the gospel; we simply acknowledge that although everyone is essentially the same—empty, lonely, guilty, and afraid to die—we are at different stages in life and are facing our own unique joys and challenges. If we're going to share the gospel message with someone, we need to be willing to put ourself in that person's shoes for a moment and to express ourself so that we can be understood.

Paul put it this way in 1 Corinthians 9:19-23:

> *This means I am not bound to obey people just because they pay me, yet I have become a servant of everyone so that I can bring them to Christ. When I am with the Jews, I become one of them so that I can bring them to Christ. When I am with those who follow the Jewish laws, I do the same, even though I am not subject to the law, so that I can bring them to Christ. When I am with the Gentiles who do not have the Jewish law, I fit in with them as much as I can. In this way, I gain their confidence and bring them to Christ. But I do not discard the law of God; I obey the law of Christ. When I am with those who are oppressed, I share their oppression so that I might bring them to Christ. Yes, I try to find common ground with everyone so that I might bring them to Christ. I do all this to spread the Good News, and in doing so I enjoy its blessings.* NLT

Jesus, the master communicator, never dealt with any two people in exactly the same way. The woman at the well had spent a lifetime trying to fill a void with men. Jesus spoke of her deep spiritual thirst. To an expert in theology, Jesus spoke in almost childlike terms as He told Nicodemus in John 3 that he must be born again.

*A*SK YOURSELF, WHAT GOSPEL STORY OR IMAGE WOULD THIS PERSON CONNECT WITH?

Keep this point in mind whenever you are talking to someone about the gospel. Establish relationship, and then, based on what you learn, ask yourself, *What gospel story or image would this person connect with?*

That leads us to our next point: We need to know the Bible.

5. Use God's Word.

"Then Philip opened his mouth, and beginning at this Scripture, preached Jesus to him."

This, of course, is an essential for any person who wants to lead others to Jesus Christ. We are told in 2 Timothy 2:15 (paraphrased), "Study or exert yourself to be approved by God, a workman that does not need to be ashamed, rightly dividing the Word of truth."

Why is it important to share Scripture? Because the Word of God will not return void. I have found that when I am sharing the gospel, whether through preaching or one-on-one, the most powerful tool I have is the Word of God. Greg's word returns void. God's Word does not.

God says in Isaiah 55:10-11:

> *As the rain comes down, and the snow from heaven,
> and do not return there, but water the earth, and make
> it bring forth and bud, that it may give seed to the sower
> and bread to the eater, so shall My word be that goes
> forth from My mouth; it shall not return to Me void, but
> it shall accomplish what I please, and it shall prosper in
> the thing for which I sent it.* NKJV

Billy Graham once said, "Time and time again in my ministry I have quoted a Bible verse in a sermon, sometimes without planning to do so in advance, only to have someone tell me afterwards it was that verse that the Holy Spirit used to bring conviction and faith to him."

What if Philip had not been a student of the Bible when he was asked, "Of whom is the prophet speaking? Of himself or another?" If Philip hadn't been a student of Scripture, he would have said, "I don't know. A good question. Can I get back to you?" But fortunately Philip was well versed in what the Bible taught.

This doesn't mean you shouldn't witness because you don't have a lot of Scripture memorized or that the person who knows the most Scripture is the most effective witness. I'm saying that this is a powerful tool, an important tool, and you should always be trying to grow in your knowledge of the Word. We need to study and prepare ourselves as effectively as possible.

First Peter 3:15 says, "In your hearts set apart Christ as Lord. Always be prepared to give an answer to everyone who asks you to give the reason for the hope that you have. But do this with gentleness and respect" (NIV).

THE BIBLE IS THE WORD OF GOD WHETHER PEOPLE ACCEPT IT OR NOT.

Notice that it's not just the Word quoted but an appropriate passage that relates to the person or situation you are addressing. Scripture reminds us, "A word fitly spoken is like apples of gold in settings of silver" (Prov. 25:11, NKJV).

And if you don't have the answer? That's OK. Simply let that propel you back into the pages of Scripture to find it.

Some people might say to you, "I don't believe the Bible is the Word of God. That is *your* truth. Don't push your truth on me." They can say whatever they want. The Bible is the Word of God whether they accept it or not. And it is going to touch their life.

They may get angry. They might be resistant. But Scripture has a way of penetrating. Use it, know it, learn it, and memorize it.

6. Tell your story.

When you present the gospel, one of the most effective tools is the story of how you yourself came to Christ. It's a great way to share the gospel with people without making them feel preached at. And it is also a great way to offer proof that an intimate relationship with God is possible.

The book of Acts is full of examples where those preaching used their personal testimony. So often Paul would tell his own story, explaining how he used to persecute Christians and how he met the Lord on the way to Damascus. Keep in mind that Paul had a great intellect. He not only had a tremendous grasp of Scripture, but he was schooled in Roman culture and debate. Yet in so many cases when appearing before the elite of Rome, he would begin with that simple story of how he personally came to Christ.

Let me throw in a caution here, however. A good testimony is one that does not glorify the past. It glorifies what God is doing in your life in the present. I have heard people get up and talk about their life before the Lord and all the horrible things they used to do. And as they were describing it, it almost seemed that they had more fun before they became a Christian.

You also want to avoid focusing on what you have given up. "I had the success and the fame and fortune. But I gave it all up for Jesus!" When you say something like that, you are putting the emphasis on the wrong thing. You ought to be emphasizing what

> A GOOD TESTIMONY IS ONE THAT DOES NOT GLORIFY THE PAST BUT GLORIFIES WHAT GOD IS DOING IN YOUR LIFE IN THE PRESENT.

Christ gave up for you. Prior to knowing Christ, you were an empty, guilty person headed for certain judgment. All you gave up was an eternity separated from God. That was no sacrifice.

7. *Pursue a decision.*
Philip read the account of the death of Jesus to the Ethiopian. He pointed out that it was Jesus whom Isaiah was speaking of. Jesus was the Son of God, who went to the cross. Jesus was the one who shed His blood for us and died and rose from the dead. Jesus is the one we need.

The man said, "I want it." He invited the Lord into his life. And we're told that he "went away rejoicing."

It's tempting to just chitchat and call it good. "Wow. We had a great conversation about all kinds of spiritual issues." That's OK. But Jesus cut to the chase: "But who do you say that I am?" (Matt. 16:15, NKJV). There may be situations in which we are employing a long-term strategy, say, with a family member or coworker. But whenever possible after we share the gospel, we should ask the person to respond. The worst thing that could happen is that we get killed for asking. Since that is highly unlikely, consider two other alternatives.

The person might simply say no. That is a disappointment, but that may change tomorrow, so there's still hope.

But what about this alternative: A person might say yes and commit his or her life to Christ. If so, you will have had the privilege of personally leading someone from darkness to light.

Look Up
You might say, "God never gives me these opportunities."

But I suggest to you that He does. They are there. As Jesus pointed out, "The harvest is plentiful, lift up your eyes." The harvest is there, but the laborers are few. The observers are many. The critics are many. The complainers and "pew potatoes" are many. But the laborers are few.

Start where you are. Reach your world. Reach the people who are around you. You can reach them more effectively than many others can.

"But I'm not a professional!"

I'm so glad of that.

May God deliver us from many of these so-called professionals, who often do more harm than good. We need to do what we can to reach with the gospel the people God has already put under our influence. If you're not a professional, that's probably more an asset than it is a liability. You're just a regular person, nonintimidating, who speaks their language.

It's easy to spend a lot of time preparing to witness, working up our courage, thinking through our approach—only to discover that we're still pretty vague about the message we're delivering. We're still a bit mystified about what happened in that brief space in Scripture between when Philip met the Ethiopian and the Ethiopian believed, because it doesn't always go that smoothly.

We need to know exactly what the gospel message is and how best to explain it.

SIX

THE GOSPEL ACCORDING TO GOD
There's Good News—and
Some Bad News

I HEARD a story once about a group of servicemen who had a new chaplain appointed to them. These guys weren't believers, and they wondered what kind of religion this fellow really had. They approached the new chaplain and said, "Tell us, do you believe in a real hell?"

"A literal hell?" the chaplain asked.

"Yes, that's the one," one of them answered.

The chaplain, who was rather liberal in his theology, said, "No, rest assured, boys, I don't believe in a literal hell."

He thought this would make them happy. But their response surprised him. They said, "Well then, you are wasting your time and our time, because if there is no hell, we don't need you. But if there is a hell, you're leading us astray. Either way we're better off without you."

Sometimes I wonder if we Christians honestly believe what we claim to believe. Do we *really* believe the wages of sin is death? Do we *really* believe in heaven and hell? If that's the case—if we believe there really is hell—why are we not doing more to reach people with the gospel of Jesus Christ?

In the previous two chapters we looked at two reasons we don't evangelize. We're uncaring, and we're uncomfortable.

91

Now we're going to look at a third possible problem: We're unconvinced. Do we really know the gospel message? And do we really believe it?

Many years ago in England a criminal named Charles Peace was arrested. He was a burglar and a forger, and he was guilty of double murder. He was condemned to death. As he was on his way to the gallows to be executed, the chaplain who walked by his side went mechanically through his speech about the power of Jesus Christ to save from sin. Suddenly this criminal stopped, spun around, and looked at the minister and said, "Do you believe that? Do you really believe that? If I believed that, I would willingly crawl across England on broken glass to tell men it was true."

Today's church finds itself unable to turn the world upside down because in many ways it has compromised the very message that would accomplish this.

I believe the church today finds itself unable to turn the world upside down because in many ways it has compromised the very message that would accomplish this. Instead of proclaiming the gospel according to God, we are so often tempted to preach the gospel according to what we or our hearers might like. We can't evangelize if we're unconvinced—or if we don't really believe the whole gospel.

I read in a recent survey that 75 percent of the American public do not know what John 3:16 says. And 60-some percent don't know what the word *gospel* actually means.

Certainly *gospel* is tossed around loosely today. We describe a certain kind of music as gospel music. Or if we are stating something that we want people to know is true, we might say, "That's the gospel truth, I'm telling you!"

Or we will hear someone preaching and that person will say, "I am an evangelist. I am preaching the gospel." But then as we listen carefully, we realize that we are not hearing the gospel of Jesus Christ.

We need to know what the gospel is. What elements does the true gospel contain? This is important for two reasons. First, we want to make sure we've heard the true message and have responded to it, lest we build our faith on a false foundation. And second, Jesus has commanded every one of us to go into the world and preach this message—so we'd better know exactly what it is.

The Heart of His Message

The heart of the great commission is God's amazing upside-down message of salvation. A good summation is given to us by Paul in 1 Corinthians 15:2-4: "By this gospel you are saved. . . . Christ died for our sins according to the Scriptures . . . he was buried . . . he was raised on the third day according to the Scriptures" (NIV).

This is the gospel in a nutshell: Christ died for our sins, was buried, and was raised on the third day. But what exactly does this mean to the new believer? And why does it mean so much?

It's easy for us who have been Christians a long time to forget the basic principles of this incredible life-changing event we call salvation. We may think we know this message well, but as we seek to articulate its principles to an unbeliever, we often find ourselves stumbling.

WE MAY THINK WE KNOW THIS MESSAGE WELL, BUT AS WE SEEK TO ARTICULATE ITS PRINCIPLES TO AN UNBELIEVER, WE OFTEN FIND OURSELVES STUMBLING.

As we take a closer look at the meaning of salvation, we see that through salvation, we are acquitted of sin, allotted Christ's righteousness, and adopted into God's family. Those sound like a lot of lofty words, and for that reason alone we need to look at what they mean so that we can explain salvation clearly and simply to unbelievers.

1. We are acquitted of sin.
The apostle Paul put it this way in his letter to the Romans:

> *Therefore, having been justified by faith, we have peace with God through our Lord Jesus Christ, through whom also we have access by faith into this grace in which we stand, and rejoice in hope of the glory of God.*
> Rom. 5:1-2, NKJV

There's a phrase here I don't want you to miss: "justified by faith."

Justification sounds like a complicated word, but the idea is simple. It describes a legal act of God whereby you are declared guiltless before Him and are acquitted of every sin. Not because you are worthy or innocent—but because Christ stepped up and took your place.

It's as if Christ announced, "Hey, I did it. I'm guilty. Kill me instead." And because you agreed to let Him take your place, you were acquitted. Paul put it this way: "Christ redeemed us from the curse of the law by becoming a curse for us" (Gal. 3:13, NIV).

And to the Romans he wrote, "[We] are justified freely by his grace through the redemption that came by Christ Jesus. God presented him as a sacrifice of atonement, through faith in his blood" (Rom. 3:24-25, NIV).

Now if justification simply stated that my past was forgiven, that would be more than enough. But as they say in those commercials, "Wait, there's more!"

2. We are allotted Christ's righteousness.

Justification not only speaks of the sin God has taken away but of what He has allotted to us in its place. The word *justified* can be translated "put to one's account." When God justifies people, He places to their credit all the righteousness of Jesus Christ. And in doing so, He balances the moral and spiritual budget for us.

Philippians 3:9 says, "Not having my own righteousness, which is from the law, but that which is through faith in Christ, the righteousness which is from God by faith" (NKJV). This is not something that happens over a period of time, if you earn it. It is something that is instantaneously allotted to every person who has put his or her faith in Christ. No matter what they have done. It is not gradual; it is immediate.

Here's one way to think about it. Imagine that you were in debt for $10 million. You had charged yourself into oblivion, and there was no conceivable way you could pay back those debts. You had exactly $1.34 in your checking account.

Now imagine that a stranger came to you and said, "I love you so much that I am going to pay off your debts." And he paid off your debt of $10 million.

"Thank you so much!" you'd exclaim. "I can't believe I'm debt free!"

Then the stranger says, "I think you ought to go down and check your account balance."

So you go down to your local ATM machine and put in your card and code. The machine prints the little report. You have a balance of $20 million! Not only did he forgive you a debt of $10 million and pay it for you—he put into your account $20 million. Think about that. What God did for you is infinitely greater than that. God not only acquitted you of your sins, but He also allotted to your account the righteousness of Jesus Christ.

But wait. There's still more!

3. We are adopted into God's family.

Not only has God forgiven you, not only has God justified you, not only has God given you free access into His presence, but God has also adopted you into His family. The Bible tells us in Galatians 4:4-5: "When the fullness of the time had come, God sent forth His son, born of a woman, born under the law, to redeem those who were under the law, that we might receive the adoption as sons" (NKJV).

I can stand in awe of a God who has the power to forgive me and the desire to put His righteousness into my account. But by adopting me God is saying, "Don't just stand there in awe of me. Come close to me."

Justification speaks of an incredible thing done on my behalf. But adoption speaks of relationship. God says, "I want you as my son. I want you as my daughter."

Years ago, when I was in Israel, I saw a little Israeli boy chasing after his father, crying out, "Abba, Abba, Abba." I knew what that meant. It would be the same as if we saw a child chasing after his or her father saying, "Daddy, Daddy, Daddy." *Abba* is a Hebrew word that speaks of affection and intimacy between a parent and a child.

Galatians 4:6 continues: "Because you are sons, God has sent forth the Spirit of His Son into your hearts, crying out, 'Abba, Father!'" And then in Romans 8:15: "You did not receive the spirit of bondage again to fear, but you received the Spirit of adoption by whom we cry out, 'Abba, Father.'" Remember, this was a revolutionary thought to the people at that time. One didn't think of approaching the almighty, all-powerful, holy God and saying, "Abba." But Jesus was saying, "Yes, I have justified you. Yes, I have forgiven you. And what's more, I want you to come close.

This is the message we need to make known to a lost and dying culture. Remember, the gospel is the same for every person. We may relate it to different people in different ways. But the basics, the essentials, never change."

The gospel is capable of reaching every person. It cuts through cultural barriers, racial barriers, economic barriers, and age barriers. Everybody can grasp it because God honors and blesses it and somehow drives it into the heart of the listener.

Whether we're evangelizing one-on-one or in a church setting, we don't need to candy coat the gospel. We don't need to gloss over it. We don't need to soften it or harden it. We don't need to take away from it or add to it. We need to proclaim it in its simplicity and power and stand back and watch what God can do.

THE GOSPEL CUTS THROUGH CULTURAL, RACIAL, ECONOMIC, AND AGE BARRIERS.

Paul said, "I am not ashamed of the gospel of Christ, for it is the power of God to salvation for everyone who believes" (Rom. 1:16, NKJV).

Remember, Paul was a great orator. He was a student and a communicator. Paul could have called upon his ability to convince. He could have called upon his powers of oratory to bring his listeners around. But instead Paul concentrated on that simple-yet-profound gospel message because he recognized that it, not he, is the power of God that brings people into God's kingdom.

When we give invitations for people to come to Christ here in our church and at our crusades, we believe it is a work of God. My goal is not to get as many people on the field as possible. My goal is to proclaim the gospel as accurately as I can and leave the work of conversion up to the Holy Spirit.

EVANGELISM OR ENTERTAINMENT?

Question: How does Harvest Christian Fellowship decide what kinds of entertainment, drama, music, and recreation are an appropriate part of spreading the gospel, and what kinds aren't? Any criteria?

Answer: I look for a clear and uncompromised message. Otherwise, why would the church want to sponsor it? I also look for high quality.

If we are going to have a musical artist, I want to have personally seen the artist in action or have an endorsement from someone I can trust. Merely listening to the CD or reading the press packet is not really very helpful in making the evaluation.

I want musicians, actors, and worship leaders who are talented and relevant, but what is most important is that they use their gifts to minister to people rather than to put on a show. We like to embrace many musical styles at Harvest. Our criteria are authenticity, compassion, and a heart for God's kingdom and people.

PASTOR TO PASTOR
"Come On Down!"

Some time ago I saw a preacher on TV giving an invitation for people to come to Christ. The choir was singing "Just As I Am." (This was not Billy Graham, by the way). The pastor said, "If you want to come to Christ, get up and come forward now."

The camera went in for a long shot, and you could see the whole congregation. A couple of people trickled down front. Obviously the pastor was not happy with the number of people who were responding. So he said, "If you would like to make a recommitment to follow Jesus Christ, then you get up and come down." A couple of other people got up. But it was still pretty empty up there. And then the pastor actually said, "If you would like to know more about joining the church, come down now."

When he got to "If you want to join the choir, come down," I thought to myself, *Why doesn't he just say, "If you want to examine the veneer of the wood on my pulpit, come on down. Just don't leave me up here alone!"*

Sometimes we pastors get to thinking that our objective is to make people respond to God. But that's not your job or my job. Our job is to make the message clear and leave the results up to God. If people believe, that is the work of the Holy Spirit.

The Gospel Unplugged

We've looked at how to overcome some of our practical inhibitions about witnessing to other people. In fact, we followed Philip through a lot of key steps, right up to the point of baptizing the Ethiopian.

Sometimes we pastors get to thinking that our job is to make people respond to God.

But now I want to talk to you about the presentation of the gospel. It doesn't always go as smoothly as it did for me that day at the beach or as it did for Philip and the Ethiopian. As we all know, it's one thing to understand the gospel message and quite another to present it, especially when our audience is skeptical or argumentative. We tend to get sidetracked, and sometimes we lose the basic message.

Think about music. There are a million ways to dress it up—add electric guitars, keyboards, strings. Have you ever known a song really well and then one day you heard a version of it that was "unplugged"? Probably the beauty and simplicity of it was stunning. Suddenly you heard the simple melody and message of that song.

It's the same with the gospel. Presentation matters. We have a lot of high-tech approaches, especially in churches that are aiming at consumers instead of communers. The same tactics that work for other kinds of messages—such as business ads or political campaigns—backfire when it comes to the gospel.

From the world's viewpoint, God's kingdom operates upside down. So why would we imagine we should sell it as if it were any popular club or zippy new philosophy? Why do we think it's necessary to disguise its key points? I think we often underestimate the raw, even explosive, power that is inherent in the "unplugged" gospel message.

THE SAME TACTICS THAT WORK FOR OTHER KINDS OF MESSAGES—SUCH AS BUSINESS ADS OR POLITICAL CAMPAIGNS—BACKFIRE WHEN IT COMES TO THE GOSPEL.

The gospel according to God is simple. It is uncompromising, powerful, and complete. If you want to present Christ's message so that people become Christians in your church, or outside your church, keep the following principles in mind.

1. The gospel doesn't need our help.

I am amazed time and time again when people say, "Greg, what are you going to preach on this year at the crusade?"

"Same thing I preached last year. I am going to preach the gospel."

"What is your text?"

"The text may be different. The illustrations may be different. But it is going to be the same message."

"Yeah, but what about the Generation Xers? How are you going to communicate with them?"

Well, God doesn't change the basic truths according to who's attending the crusade. And God's Holy Spirit can convince anyone—Gen Xers included—that they need to be saved from their sins. If we tell the truth, God will use it.

2. The most effective message is a simple one.
Someone once asked the great British preacher C. H. Spurgeon if he could put in a few words what his Christian faith was all about. Spurgeon said, "I will put it into four words for you. Christ died for me."

It's as simple as that. Christ died for me. That is the essence of the gospel message. I love the way the apostle Paul said that God "loved me and gave himself for me" (Gal. 2:20, NIV).

Some time ago I had the privilege of watching Billy Graham receive the Congressional Medal of Honor in our nation's Capitol building for his faithfulness in preaching the gospel. The ceremony took place in the rotunda, a very imposing and intimidating room with a giant ceiling and incredible paintings and statues of presidents and other figures of American history.

Many members of Congress, as well as the vice president, were present. On a raised platform in the back of the rotunda, cameras from around the world filmed the event. Now if ever there would have been a temptation to soften the gospel a bit, to simply say a few nice things, that would have been it.

But one of the things I love about Billy Graham is that he is so tenacious. And he knows what he is supposed to do. He got up there and opened with a few pleasantries. And then he began to preach the gospel. He said, "I want to tell you that many years ago I was a young boy, and I went to a meeting. A man was telling us that we were sinners and we needed Christ. And he said,  'All have sinned and fallen short of the glory of God.' And right then, I realized I needed Christ to come into my life."

After presenting the gospel in simple, beautiful terms, he brought it all home. "As I look around at these statues of all of

THESE GREAT LEADERS . . . HAVE ONE THING IN COMMON. THEY ARE ALL DEAD. AND YOU ARE ALL GOING TO DIE.

these great leaders, I realize that they have one thing in common. They are all dead. And you are all going to die. Are you ready to die? Are you ready to meet God?"

I loved that. Remember, fellow communicators, that you and I can actually hinder the message of the gospel by complicating it. The same thing goes for you, layperson, when you're talking one-on-one with an unbeliever in some coffee shop. And so we need to be careful to present the simple, powerful, yet profound truth. Christ died for our sins. He was buried. He was raised again on the third day. Are you ready to die?

3. The good news of the gospel includes some bad news.
The word *gospel* actually means "good news." But before I can appreciate the good news of forgiveness, I need to know the bad news about judgment. If we don't deliver the whole truth of the gospel, we are not proclaiming the gospel.

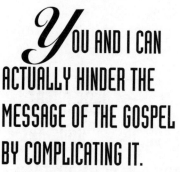

YOU AND I CAN ACTUALLY HINDER THE MESSAGE OF THE GOSPEL BY COMPLICATING IT.

This is where I take issue with people who offer Jesus as though He were some kind of a wonderful additive to life. "Accept Jesus Christ, and your teeth will be whiter, and your clothes will be cleaner, and your life will be better. Everything will be great."

But Christianity is not just about being happier. It's not about being a little bit more fulfilled. *It's about not going to hell,* and if you reject God's offer of salvation—you will face certain judgment.

The other day I was with my wife in a department store. She was looking at dresses, and I was wandering around. A salesgirl came up to me and said, "Are you Greg Laurie?"

"Yes, I am."

She said, "I can't believe you're here. My girlfriend and I were just talking about you. Actually, we were just talking with a friend who works in another department. He is living an immoral lifestyle. He was saying it's OK to be a Christian and live that way. If you could just talk to him, we think he would really listen to you."

I said, "OK. But tell him what he is getting himself into. Tell him that I'm a pastor and that I am going to tell him what the Bible says. I don't want him to think that he's being trapped."

So she and her friend went and got this guy and introduced us. "By the way, he's a homosexual," they announced.

This guy was obviously not happy about talking to me, and for a few moments we both just stood there,

> ## WE MISTAKENLY OFFER GOD'S FORGIVENESS WITHOUT ANY MENTION OF REPENTANCE.

feeling somewhat awkward. "I don't really think it's appropriate to talk about this here," he finally said. "But let me just say this really quick. I believe in Jesus Christ. But my God is a god of love, and I don't believe He'd send someone to hell for doing what I am doing. I believe that if two consenting adults agree to do something, it can't be wrong. How can you say that's sin?"

My response to him was, "Because God says it's sin."

I know that sounds simplistic, but that really is the bottom line. "You say that you believe in a God of love," I said. "I believe in a God of love, too. But when you say 'my God,' you are implying that you can remake Him in your image. You can't throw out the things about God that bother you and keep the ones you like. Who determines what is right and what is wrong? Do we reach it by consensus? No. We need a higher authority. And it's the Bible."

We talked for quite a while about what the Bible says. Finally he said, "I don't believe that God would say I can't do this one thing. I am going to keep doing it. I don't care what happens."

I knew I had to tell this guy the truth, so I said, "Well, I have to put it to you bluntly. If you continue living that way, you will face judgment for it." I spoke to him of God's plan and purpose. He didn't make a decision for Christ, but he said he was going to come to church.

So often we're tempted to offer a watered-down gospel with no teeth in it. We offer God's forgiveness without any mention of repentance. I've heard people use phrases like "All you have to do is ask Him in. That's it. It's wonderful."

Wait a second. What about repentance? What about obedience?

WE HAVE TO TAKE TIME TO LOOK AT THE BAD NEWS—SIN AND JUDGMENT—BEFORE THE GOOD NEWS HAS MEANING.

We have to take time to look at the bad news—sin and sure judgment—before the Good News has meaning. We have to acknowledge the exceeding sinfulness of humanity. We are hopelessly separated from a holy God whom we have all offended. There is nothing good in ourselves, and we desperately need His help.

And then comes the good news. In spite of our condition, regardless of all of the wrong things we've done, God did the ultimate for us. Romans 5:6 says:

> When we were still without strength, in due time Christ died for the ungodly. For scarcely for a righteous man will one die; yet perhaps for a good man someone would even dare to die. But God demonstrates His own love toward us, in that while we were still sinners, Christ died for us. NKJV

4. A compromising gospel is no gospel.
In 1 Timothy 4:16 Paul says, "Watch your life and doctrine closely. Persevere in them, because if you do, you will save both yourself and your hearers" (NIV). We must know what we believe.

We must know what the Bible teaches, especially on the topic of the gospel. Why? Because there is a counterfeit gospel out there.

Make no mistake about it. The devil is a master manipulator and imitator. One of the greatest tactics that he has used with tremendous effect over the centuries is to imitate "good news"— to offer a counterfeit version of it that is close enough to be believable to some but far enough from truth to be damaging to the person who believes it.

Paul wrote in Galatians 1:6-8:

> *I am astonished that you are so quickly deserting the one who called you by the grace of Christ and are turning to a different gospel—which is really no gospel at all. Evidently some people are throwing you into confusion and are trying to pervert the gospel of Christ. But even if we or an angel from heaven should preach a gospel other than the one we preached to you, let him be eternally condemned!* NIV

One consistent criticism of Christianity is, "How can you say as a Christian that Christ is the only way to God? Are you saying that people who have other religious beliefs are not believing the true thing? Are you saying that your way is the only way? How narrow of you. How bigoted of you."

It can be tempting to soft-pedal this issue and say something along the lines of "We all worship the same God. And you can choose your path. I have chosen mine. Mine is Christ. But if you want to worship some other way, that is fine."

It's not fine. And you can't say it if you are a true Christian. We must believe that Jesus is the only way to God, because none of the other gurus and prophets and religious leaders that have come

NONE OF THE OTHER GURUS AND PROPHETS AND RELIGIOUS LEADERS THAT HAVE COME DOWN THE ROAD WERE GOD.

down the road *were* God. Therefore, none of them could put us in touch with God. Even if they had been crucified as Jesus was, it would not have mattered. Jesus, who was God, was the only one who could bridge the gap and shed His blood in our place.

Jesus himself is the one who said this. He said in John 14:6, "I am the way and the truth and the life. No one comes to the Father except through me" (NIV). The apostle Peter echoed these words when he said in Acts 4:12, "Salvation is found in no one else, for there is no other name under heaven given to men by which we must be saved" (NIV). Paul says the same thing in 1 Timothy 2:5: "There is one God and one mediator between God and men, the man Christ Jesus" (NIV).

Therefore, to properly represent Jesus' message I can say nothing less.

Some of you may be thinking, *But if I say that to people, they will be offended.*

Maybe they will be. Then again, maybe they will believe. Who am I to edit the gospel? Who am I to say, "Lord, we need to update this whole thing for this new century. The words you spoke were insensitive and politically incorrect. We don't talk about hell anymore. We don't talk about sin anymore. This stuff is out, Lord."

We need to give His message and not change it—not even a little bit. Because there's nothing more exciting than the message of the gospel. And when we embrace it in its simplest, truest form and determine to preach it in a radical, upside-down way, we are in for the greatest thrill of our life.

PASTOR TO PASTOR

The Gift of Evangelism

Now and then I have a pastor say to me, "I'm just not very gifted at evangelism." If this is your case, I suggest that you find someone in your body who does have the calling and gifts of an evangelist and give him a platform for ministry.

All of us are not "gifted in evangelism," but *all of us* are called to evangelize and to support evangelism in its various forms. Paul wrote to Timothy, an overseer of a church, and told him to "do the work of an evangelist" (2 Tim. 4:5, NIV).

We often think that the work of the evangelist is done only outside the church. But that is not true. In Ephesians 4:11-12 we read, "And He Himself gave some to be apostles, some prophets, some evangelists, and some pastors and teachers, for the equipping of the saints" (NKJV). A person gifted for evangelism will not only bring the gospel message to the lost but will often have a special exhortive ability (to motivate, stimulate, excite to action) for the church. This is a simplification, but in one sense a pastor tells you how to do it while an evangelist makes you want to do it!

SEVEN

WALK THIS WAY
The Meaning of Upside-Down Discipleship

DON'T YOU love it when you're reading along in the Old Testament and suddenly God slows everything down to tell an important story? Time and again we pause in the history of God's people to zoom in on an unlikely hero, a conflict that threatens, and a detailed account of how things were finally resolved God's way.

The account in Judges of Gideon's battling the Midianites is one of these amazing stories. At the time, the Israelites were being plagued by their enemies, the Midianites, and an alliance of other hostile nations. God's answer was to choose a regular guy named Gideon to lead an army against them. The story begins in Judges 6.

Just how ordinary was Gideon? Well, the angel sent as a messenger from God caught Gideon in the act of being a coward. Gideon was so afraid of being seen by the enemy that he was secretly threshing his wheat inside a winepress—not on the community threshing floor—so no one would see him. But the angel greeted him with a memorable one-liner: "The Lord is with you, mighty warrior!"

We can almost hear Gideon laugh (or maybe it's the angel).

Gideon answers the angel as many of us would. "Hey, if God

is with me, then why are all these bad things happening? We're all at the end of our rope here. And in case you didn't notice, my family happens to be the weakest one around, and what's more, I'm the least among them! You must be looking for someone else!" (see Judg. 6:13-15).

Isn't it interesting how we always feel certain that God has the wrong man or woman whenever He's recruiting us? But the whole time, God is thinking, *You're just what I had in mind.*

In Judges 6:14 the angel of the Lord turned to Gideon and said something very important. "Go in the strength you have and save Israel out of Midian's hand. Am I not sending you?" (NIV).

Remember that line: "Go in the strength you have. Am I not sending you?"

So Gideon raised up an army of men to war against their enemies. But even with a thirty-two-thousand-man force the Israelite army was still far outnumbered by the Midianite alliance. Naturally Gideon wondered how and where on earth he'd find more men.

But here's what God said to Gideon. "You have too many men for me to deliver Midian into their hands" (Judg. 7:2, NIV).

Obviously Gideon was coming face-to-face with a God whose ways are upside down in relation to ours. And as Gideon tried not to choke on his breakfast, God set about reducing the size of Israel's army. First, He told Gideon to ask those soldiers to leave who were afraid. So Gideon did. Twenty-two thousand said, "Sure thing. I wasn't in the mood to die, anyway." And they left.

Gideon must have thought: *God sure underestimated how many were afraid!*

Not at all. In fact, God said to Gideon, "Still too many men are left." Then He told Gideon to take the remaining ten thousand men down to the river to drink. God instructed Gideon to let the very thirsty men drink their fill. He was to then watch for the ones who brought the water to their mouth cupped in their hand. Presumably they would be the watchful, alert, prepared ones, aware of a potential enemy ambush.

Gideon now had a mighty army of a few hundred men. Only those who were bravest and who were wholeheartedly committed to the battle were left. Finally God was ready to go to work. In a daring night raid, God gave Gideon's army a stunning victory over the Midianites. You can read more about how God went about doing this in Judges 7.

Through stories like Gideon's, God makes it abundantly and repeatedly clear that He can do more with a few committed folks than He can with thousands who are following Him only halfheartedly. Today God is still looking around to see who He really has. He is seeking those men and women who will follow Him with total abandon—against all odds, without questioning His directions or His methods.

GOD CAN DO MORE WITH A FEW COMMITTED FOLKS THAN HE CAN WITH THOUSANDS WHO ARE FOLLOWING HIM ONLY HALFHEARTEDLY.

God is looking for true disciples who are willing to think and act according to God's upside-down terms. God is looking for churches and pastors who are ready—no matter how small their congregations or poor their people or old their buildings—to turn their cities upside down for Christ.

"Am I not sending you?" He asks. "So go in the strength you have."

Hard Words

In many ways the first church found itself in a position similar to Gideon's. They were completely outnumbered, and their task appeared ridiculous, even impossible. To spread the gospel to every nation? To make the whole world believe in this Jesus who came and died and was resurrected? To get the world to follow a man they couldn't see?

In the last few chapters we saw how the early believers succeeded in their mission. But why were they able to do this? Not because they were mighty or numerous, or because they were brilliant strategic thinkers and marketers. But because they were true disciples who were taking directions from God.

Let's look first at the statements of Jesus concerning what is required in order for us to become His disciples. But let me make this doubly clear: These statements are *not* Jesus' requirements for salvation. When we first come to Jesus Christ to receive the

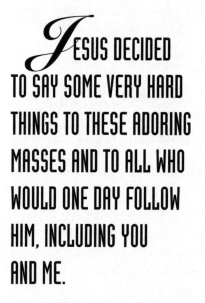

Jesus decided to say some very hard things to these adoring masses and to all who would one day follow Him, including you and me.

salvation He has offered us, we are at the beginning of a lifelong process. We are new to faith; maybe it's the first time in our life we've accepted anybody's authority. But as we grow in our faith and truly follow Christ, we're able to understand the realities of spiritual battle and of how radical our lifestyle is in an unbelieving world. Becoming a Christian requires a change of heart and a choice; continuing on in discipleship, becoming part of God's spiritual army on earth, has its own requirements.

First, let me set the scene. A great crowd had begun to follow Jesus at this point in His ministry. He'd become very popular with the common people because they resonated deeply with His message. They appreciated Jesus for deflating the religious establishment, for revealing the Pharisees to be the hypocrites they were, and for preaching about a kingdom that was available to everyone.

So here were all these people listening raptly to Jesus. These were Jesus' fans, and they loved Him. When things are going this well, most of us would be inclined to give the crowd what they want. Make them glad to be here. Make them want to stay—and, more important, get them on our computerized mailing list!

But Jesus did something very upside down. Just when you would think Jesus would be wanting to gather an army of followers, He made a Gideon move. He decided to say some very hard things to these adoring masses and to all who would one day follow Him, including you and me. Three times in the verses that we're about to read He says, "cannot be my disciple." He is saying, "You must do these things or you can't be my disciple."

Now great multitudes went with Him. And He turned and said to them, "If anyone comes to Me and does not hate his father and mother, wife and children, brothers and sisters, yes, and his own life also, he cannot be My disciple. And whoever does not bear his cross and come after Me cannot be My disciple. For which of you, intending to build a tower, does not sit down first and count the cost, whether he has enough to finish it—lest, after he has laid the foundation, and is not able to finish, all who see it begin to mock him, saying, 'This man began to build and was not able to finish.' Or what king, going to make war against another king, does not sit down first and consider whether he is able with ten thousand to meet him who comes against him with twenty thousand? Or else, while the other is still a great way off, he sends a delegation and asks conditions of peace. So likewise, whoever of you does not forsake all that he has cannot be My disciple. Salt is good; but if the salt has lost its flavor, how shall it be seasoned? It is neither fit for the land nor for the dunghill, but men throw it out. He who has ears to hear, let him hear!" Luke 14:25-35, NKJV

113

These were some of the most solemn and searching words that ever fell from Jesus' lips. And of all His upside-down statements, these were perhaps, and often still are, among the most misunderstood.

In fact, the multitudes shrank because of these radical and provocative statements. They were disappointed, as God knew they would be. Some wanted to be dazzled by miracles. Others wanted to be fed because they had heard about His wonderful miracle of feeding the five thousand. Some were hoping that He would overthrow the empire of Rome and establish His kingdom on earth.

They couldn't receive this message because they were thinking in ordinary terms instead of in kingdom terms.

Just as with Gideon, God was willing to thin the ranks because He really wanted only those who were truly committed to Him. He's simply not interested in huge crowds or personal popularity. Here He comes along and says, "Don't misunderstand what it means to follow me. This is what I'm really after. Are you willing? If not, go on home."

The Requirements of Discipleship
So often, people tend to misinterpret the meanings behind the four qualifications Jesus gave us for discipleship. Either we make them too literal: "I'm supposed to hate my mother, and I can't own so much as a pillow" or we make them laughable: "Having a crabby boss must be your cross to bear in life."

As we study the principles of discipleship from the passage we just read in Luke, it's important that we interpret them not just according to Jesus' words. We need to interpret them also in light of other Scripture and in light of Jesus' own example. Remember, this is not radical or abnormal behavior we're talking about—only what should be considered *normal Christian living*.

With this perspective in mind, let's look at the four important requirements of discipleship that Jesus Himself laid out for us twenty centuries ago.

Requirement #1: Love God more than anyone else.
Verse 26: "If anyone comes to Me and does not hate his father and mother, wife and children, brothers and sisters, yes, and His own life also, he cannot be My disciple."

Jesus is obviously not requesting that we hate our families. We know that He loved His mother and that while He was on the cross, He instructed the disciple John to take care of her. What's more, the Bible tells us over and over again that we are to love all others, including our enemies.

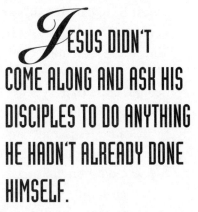

JESUS DIDN'T COME ALONG AND ASK HIS DISCIPLES TO DO ANYTHING HE HADN'T ALREADY DONE HIMSELF.

So what did Jesus mean? Well, let's look at what He did. Matthew records an incident that sheds some light on this statement.

> *While Jesus was still talking to the crowd, his mother and brothers stood outside, wanting to speak to him. Someone told him, "Your mother and brothers are standing outside, wanting to speak to you."*
>
> *He replied to him, "Who is my mother, and who are my brothers?" Pointing to his disciples, he said, "Here are my mother and my brothers. For whoever does the will of my Father in heaven is my brother and sister and mother."* Matt. 12:46-50, NIV

As Jesus was prone to do, He saw a teaching moment and took advantage of it. His family's arrival and their request to see Him was going to interrupt His work for God. Notice the phrase "While Jesus was still talking to the crowd." Jesus made a point of saying, "God's will is more important than My family. And My spiritual family, which includes those who do My Father's will, is now My first priority, even above My earthly family."

So why did Jesus use the word *hate?* The word used here is meant to indicate the opposite of love. This method of sharp contrast was a common oriental practice. Jesus was saying essentially, "If you want to be my disciple, your love for others must be like hatred in comparison with your love for God." We could retranslate this: "If you are going to be His disciple, you must love God more than anyone or anything else. Your love for Him must be so passionate, so profound, that no other love even comes close to it."

So why is this a requirement for discipleship?

Because Jesus understood that close relationships and our desire to please our families could also hinder our commitment to serve God. I often hear about new Christians who go home and tell their family that now they're going to follow Christ. Sometimes parents, friends, or others in the family oppose this. And then the temptation is strong for the new believer to say to God, "I don't want conflict here. So I'll wait until my husband or my mother changes her mind, and then I'll follow You."

If you are going to be a follower of Jesus, you are not going to get along with everyone. It's not that you shouldn't be a loving, considerate, and caring person. You should be more so. But if you are a true follower of Jesus, some people will be offended by this. They may think that now you feel you're superior to them. Or they may miss the way you used to party with them. Or they may suddenly feel less comfortable swearing up a storm when you're within hearing.

For whatever reason, we have to expect some conflict. And here's the bottom line: Either you are going to have harmony with God and friction with some people, or you are going to have harmony with people and friction with God. If there is no conflict with any person in any area of your life because of your faith, I would suggest that you consider this principle very carefully.

Remember that Jesus said,

> *Don't imagine that I came to bring peace to the earth! No, I came to bring a sword. I have come to set a man against his father, and a daughter against her mother, and a daughter-in-law against her mother-in-law. Your enemies will be right in your own household!* Matt. 10:34-36, NLT

Jesus knows that faith is something that can divide families. And this is how serious Jesus is about discipleship. He is saying that it may mean a conflict with loved ones. It may even lead to severing of a romantic relationship because that person doesn't want to follow the Lord with you. But this is necessary. In fact, sometimes it's that very conflict that finally brings about an unbeliever's awareness of his need for God.

CLOSE RELATIONSHIPS AND OUR DESIRE TO PLEASE OUR FAMILIES COULD ALSO HINDER OUR COMMITMENT TO SERVE GOD.

Are you willing to risk conflict with someone you love in order to help God save her soul? Are you willing to follow Jesus into battle no matter who decides to stay at home?

Requirement #2: Bear your cross. Verse 27: "And whoever does not bear his cross and come after Me cannot be My disciple."

That is a radical statement. Once again Jesus was asking His followers to do something He Himself would have to do and was planning to do literally. "Carrying his own cross, he went out to the place of the Skull (which in Aramaic is called Golgotha)" (John 19:17, NIV).

Keep in mind that this statement doesn't have nearly the same impact in our culture that it would have had upon the original hearers. Sometimes when these people went down to Jerusalem to buy food for dinner or to visit a friend, they would hear the clanking of armor and spot a contingent of Roman soldiers leading a man bearing his own cross. Immediately they knew that this man was going to his death. It was a shameful thing to be crucified in Christ's time. It was a long and torturous death reserved for the most hardened of criminals.

"*B*EAR YOUR CROSS" MEANS THE SAME THING TO EVERY MAN AND EVERY WOMAN: "BE WILLING TO DIE."

This is what the hearers of the time would have pictured, and to many the image would have been offensive. None of them would have imagined, as many people today are prone to do, that to bear their cross might mean something as silly as dealing with a mother-in-law who won't mind her own business.

Jesus wasn't referring to some unique trial we each have in our life. "Bear your cross" means the same thing to every man and every woman: "Be willing to die." It would have clearly indicated a spiritual call to suffering and death.

The dramatic point Jesus was trying to make here is an important principle of discipleship. He had just told us that we must love Him more than our family and friends. And then He said that we must love Him even more than we love ourselves. In fact, we must be willing to die, to surrender our very life to follow Him.

Certainly He doesn't mean we should offer ourself to be crucified. But what He does mean is that we need to be ready to put to death anything in our selfish nature that keeps us from Christ. Paul put it this way:

> *Therefore, brothers, we have an obligation—but it is not*
> *to the sinful nature, to live according to it. For if you live*
> *according to the sinful nature, you will die; but if by the*

Spirit you put to death the misdeeds of the body, you will live, because those who are led by the Spirit of God are sons of God." Rom. 8:12-14, NIV

God isn't asking us to put to death anything good. We are putting to death *that which leads us to death: sin.* And ultimately, this putting to death of our sinful impulses leads to life. Notice that Paul says if you do this, "you will live." And in his letter to the Galatians, he wrote, "I have been crucified with Christ and I no longer live, but Christ lives in me" (Gal. 2:20, NIV).

Jesus is trying to get us to understand a key dynamic principle. When we give up our tight grasp on our own life, we discover life as it was meant to be lived. When you really die to yourself, you find yourself. When you lay aside your personal goals, desires, and ambitions, that is when God will reveal the goals, desires, and ambitions that He has for you. Christian author A. W. Tozer once said, "In every Christian's heart there is a cross and a throne. And the Christian is on the throne until he puts himself on the cross. If he refuses the cross, he remains on the throne."

Too often, we want to be saved, but we insist that Christ do all the dying. No cross for us. No dethronement. We remain king within the little kingdom of our soul, and we wear our tinsel crown with all the pride of Caesar. It's hard to lay our life down. It feels upside down *not* to put ourselves first. It goes against our natural impulse to pursue our selfish desires and lusts.

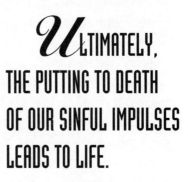

Ultimately, the putting to death of our sinful impulses leads to life.

But whom do you want on the throne of your heart?

Requirement #3: Forsake all you have.
Verse 33: "Whoever of you does not forsake all that he has cannot be My disciple."

Once again Jesus drives a hard bargain. What does He mean, forsake all I own? Do I have to have the world's largest garage sale and sell everything I possess, including my kids' bikes and that brand-new home computer I got last Christmas? I'm willing to endure some conflict with family. I'm willing to die to selfish desires. But now You want my boat, Lord?

Once again, we can't take Jesus' words to their literal extreme. And yet to ignore *any* literal sense of interpretation would also be a mistake. We need to look at things from God's upside-down perspective, which always puts the spiritual before the physical. And we need to look to Jesus' life for help. In Matthew 8:19-20 we read, "Then a teacher of the law came to him and said, 'Teacher, I will follow you wherever you go.' Jesus replied, 'Foxes have holes and birds of the air have nests, but the Son of Man has no place to lay his head'" (NIV).

This is how literally Jesus lived out this principle. He had no home. We don't read about His possessing anything at all except perhaps His tunic and cloak. And yet Jesus visits Mary and Martha in *their* home, and various times the Bible instructs us to show hospitality to strangers. If Joseph of Arimathea had sold all he had, he couldn't have bought Jesus' burial tomb.

Jesus wants us to dig deep and grasp the principle behind His words. Let's understand what the phrase *forsake all you have* means. It could be literally translated "surrender your claim to, say good-bye to." How often we say things like, "We painted our house the other day." "We drove our car." We refer to these things as *ours*. "That's my husband. That's my career." But in reality, if I am a disciple, I realize that all of this is under the ownership of Jesus.

I heard the story of a woman who had been working very hard one long day and decided to reward herself with a little treat down at the local mall. She found a Mrs. Fields cookies store and ordered a whole bag of fresh hot cookies just for herself. Then she went next door to Starbucks and got herself a grande latte, half-calf, with light foam and a touch of vanilla (whatever happened to a regular cup of coffee?). She then pulled out a *USA Today* from her purse, found a nice quiet table, and sat down to enjoy her cookies and latte.

A couple of minutes later a man sat down across from her. As she was reading her paper and munching on her first cookie she heard a rustling in her cookie bag on the table. Folding down the top of her paper, she thought she saw this man's hand pull out of her bag. He popped a cookie in his mouth. She thought to herself, *Surely that isn't possible; he wouldn't just take one of my cookies.* She heard the cookie bag rustle again, and this time she caught him in the very act of swiping one of her cookies. He didn't seem concerned at all. He just reached in and took another and another.

She would eat a cookie and he would eat one, all the time with a broad smile on his face. This lady was furious, but she was afraid to confront someone who would so blatantly steal her food. Finally there was only one cookie left in the bag. They reached for it at the same time and came out of the bag, each hanging on to a half of that final cookie. Smiling again, the man broke off half and gave it to her. He then ate the other half.

The woman was so angry that she bolted up from that table and walked away in a great huff. As she walked back to her office, she opened her purse to put the newspaper in it. There was her bag of cookies! The man hadn't been eating her cookies; she'd been eating his! And he was nice enough to even share the last one with her.

We boast of our future, our possessions, our plans, our cookies. In the process of doing this we forget the passage of Scripture that says, "Do you not know that your body is the temple of the Holy Spirit who is in you, whom you have from God, and you are not your own? For you were bought at a price; therefore glorify God in your body and in your spirit, which are God's" (1 Cor. 6:19-20, NKJV).

Jesus is asking, "Are you willing to give up *anything* to follow Me? Not only must you love Me more than your family, but you must love Me more than your home, your bed, your comfort. I don't guarantee these things as part of the 'follow Me' package." This enables us to demonstrate God's love to others in a tangible way. It also reminds us that everything we have is a gift from Him.

As we've seen, the first church lived out this principle in a radical way: "All the believers were one in heart and mind. No one claimed that any of his possessions was his own, but they shared everything they had" (Acts 4:32, NIV).

Are you ready?

Requirement #4: Count the cost.

Verse 28: "For which of you, intending to build a tower, does not sit down first and count the cost, whether he has enough to finish it—lest, after he has laid the foundation, and is not able to finish, all who see it begin to mock him, saying, 'This man began to build and was not able to finish.' Or what king, going to make war against another king, does not sit down first and consider whether he is able with ten thousand to meet him who comes against him with twenty thousand?"

I wanted to address this statement of Jesus last because in many ways it is a summary of the others. He's told us the price: potential conflict with loved ones; a decision to die daily to selfish sins; and a willingness to forsake, or let go of, our claim to all our material possessions. Now He's asking us to count up these costs and decide whether or not we're willing to pay the price.

You'll notice something important here. Christ is not asking us to pay the price for salvation. That's a free gift if we repent and put our faith in Him. However, to become a true disciple, a follower who doesn't turn back but goes forward and helps to gain ground for God, we must sit down and carefully weigh our motives and our commitment.

Have you ever made an impulse purchase and bought some-thing you didn't need? Cars are the worst. You are planning to buy a car within a certain price range. It's all you can afford. The salesman says, "Have you looked at this hot new model that came out? This baby is fast."

"No. I'm a practical person," you say. "And I could not afford that."

To BECOME A TRUE DISCIPLE, WE MUST SIT DOWN AND CAREFULLY WEIGH OUR MOTIVES AND OUR COMMITMENT.

"Want to take it for a spin?" he asks.

"What's the point?" you ask.

He smiles big at this. "What if I were to tell you that you could drive this off the lot for the same price you would have paid for this other car you were looking at?"

"I would say I'm interested." So you take it out for a test drive. It feels good. You like it. And there's that intoxicating smell of fresh new leather.

Back at the car lot you ask, "If you could get this to me for the same price . . ."

He says, "Let me talk to my manager. Just wait here."

He disappears for thirty minutes. You might imagine they're really talking about this. But you know what? He's probably just having a cup of coffee with his buddies. He is not going to take that offer to the manager. Never intended to. He's waiting for you to get even more hooked and to invest even more time.

He comes back and says, "I'm so sorry. The manager said we can't do it. But we can give it to you for this price."

It's not much less than the sticker price. But before you can think about it, before you've really counted the cost, you sign a paper that you'll probably regret for five years.

Jesus is saying, "Don't follow Me impulsively. Think about this. Count the cost. Mean it."

Why does God require this? Because He's not like some pushy used-car salesman. He won't sign you up if you don't really qualify or if you don't understand all the issues. He's looking for spiritual soldiers who are wholeheartedly committed to their mission.

Gideon didn't have to worry that one of his soldiers would turn back halfway through the attack. In the same way, God is looking for disciples who have decided to risk everything in order to follow Him into enemy territory.

Jesus set the ultimate example of counting the cost when He went to the cross. In the Gospel of John, Jesus declares, "The reason my Father loves me is that I lay down my life—only to take it up again. No one takes it from me, but I lay it down of my own accord" (John 10:17-18, NIV).

Jesus had counted the cost and made His decision. This does not mean that when the moment came to follow through, He wasn't wishing it cost less. It doesn't mean it was easy. And neither do we have to follow Christ like a bunch of robots. Sometimes it hurts to pay the price. That's a legitimate response. But it's a lot easier to pay a price that you've already decided you can afford.

Salty Salt

"Salt is good; but if the salt has lost its flavor, how shall it be seasoned? It is neither fit for the land nor for the dunghill, but men throw it out. He who has ears to hear, let him hear!" (vv. 34-35).

After stating the requirements for discipleship, Jesus made this final statement by way of explanation and warning. In Bible times, salt wasn't just another spice or something used to make popcorn taste good. It was often used to preserve food. And because they had no refrigeration, they wrapped meat in salt so that it would not putrefy and rot. Our modern equivalent would be beef jerky.

So when Jesus said, "You are the salt of the earth" in Matthew

5:13 and again in this passage, He was saying something about how we influence the world and preserve what is good. If we lose the main qualities that make us His disciples and therefore distinct and visible in the world—if we stop making a difference—we stop representing God. We're no longer salty.

Another use for salt was to stimulate thirst. If you are being a salty Christian, so to speak, your lifestyle will stimulate in others a thirst for God. They will watch you. They might laugh at you. But they will watch you and wonder, *What is it with this person? What makes her tick?*

If you are looking for a life of ease with no conflict or sacrifice, then the life of a disciple is not for you. But let me also add that if you don't want to be a disciple, then you don't want to be a true follower of Jesus Christ. A true follower naturally becomes a disciple, and the normal disciple's life looks abnormal to an unbelieving world.

> *IF YOU ARE BEING A SALTY CHRISTIAN, SO TO SPEAK, YOUR LIFESTYLE WILL STIMULATE IN OTHERS A THIRST FOR GOD.*

When we see all of this in Scripture, it's easy to say, "I believe these things." But what about when we are tested? What about when we really need to walk by faith and not by sight or feeling? What about when we need to trust God in an area where we are facing need or sickness or some other calamity?

Remember in Acts 4, when Peter and John were called before the elders and the teachers of the law and questioned? If you take only one idea away from this chapter, this would be a good one and should be the goal of every true disciple:

> *When they saw the courage of Peter and John and realized that they were unschooled, ordinary men, they were astonished and they took note that these men had been with Jesus.* Acts 4:13, NIV

Does your behavior astonish people? Is it obvious to those who speak with you that you've spent time with Jesus? Can they taste the salt?

The true tests of discipleship don't come in glorious moments. The war is ordinary, long, and sometimes quite ugly. Will you say, "Lord, I want to be like one of Gideon's three hundred. I would like to be a man or a woman who will stand in the gap for You and be Your real disciple and live an effective Christian life"?

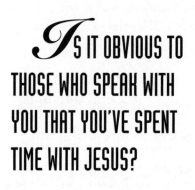

Is it obvious to those who speak with you that you've spent time with Jesus?

A little salt makes a big difference. And godly living in an ungodly situation can make a huge difference. God can do a lot with a little. It starts with you. Soon one disciple becomes two, and two become four, and four become eight, and eight become sixteen.

Evangelist John Wesley said many years ago, "Give me a hundred men who love God with all of their hearts and fear nothing but sin, and I will move the world."

I think that is still true. If we can find a few men and women who love God with all of their hearts and fear nothing but sin, we can build an army of disciples capable of turning the world upside down. We may lose a battle here and there, but we are not going to lose this war.

Remember God's exhortation: "Am I not sending you? So go in the strength you have."

THE IMPORTANCE OF "LITTLE" JOBS

Question: How does Harvest involve "the little people," not just to get the work done but as lay ministers? How do you make them feel that they're turning the world upside down by ushering?

Answer: Warren Wiersbe said, "You can never be too small for God to use, only too big."

We have ministry opportunities for everyone at Harvest, no matter what their gifts and calling are. Yet even if a person has a gift of communicating, we would not immediately place such a person in leadership.

We believe faithfulness is of the greatest importance.

We will intentionally give relatively menial tasks to people who want to serve so that we can test that faithfulness, much as Stephen and Philip waited on tables.

If they are faithful, in time they can advance to greater opportunities. If a person objects to this, it shows me that he or she does not have a true "servant's heart," which I believe is essential for effective leadership.

Even if people do not feel called to teach or preach, there are many opportunities for them to serve in ministries ranging from new-convert counseling to helping people find a parking space.

EIGHT

A READY ANSWER
Learning to Love
God's Word

HAVE YOU ever had one of those golden opportunities to share the gospel, and you really weren't prepared?

When I was young, I had a friend whose name was also Gregg. We attended elementary school together, and as we got older, we hung out, experimented with drugs, and got into trouble together.

After I became a Christian, I promised Gregg that I would not turn into a religious fanatic. "Listen," I said, "I know these Jesus freaks are weird. But don't worry. Your good buddy Greg Laurie will never become one of those weirdo Christians walking around carrying a Bible, talking to total strangers about God, wearing a cross around his neck, and saying stuff like 'Praise the Lord.' I am going to be cool about this."

Gregg seemed reassured. But, of course, I hadn't taken into account the power of the Holy Spirit in a person's life and the dramatic changes He can bring about.

One day a couple weeks later, I was walking around in Newport Beach. I wanted to get out and do something with my faith, so I had gone down there to share the gospel with whomever God might send across my path. Who do I run into but Gregg!

I hadn't seen my friend since our last conversation. And here I was with a big Bible in my hand and a cross around my neck. We started talking. And before I could catch myself, I said, "Praise the Lord."

Gregg looked at me, and I looked at him. We both started laughing. I had become one of those crazy Christians.

I said, "I know this looks weird, but I have been on both sides of the fence now. I know the way that you think, because that is how I thought for my whole life up to this point. But now I have seen what God can do. And, Gregg, I've got to tell you, Jesus Christ is real."

As I started witnessing to Gregg, he appeared to be listening and seemed open. I was getting excited, feeling sure that I was making progress. Then suddenly another guy came up and joined us. He'd seen me walk up to Gregg and had been listening to our conversation. He happened to own a "head shop" nearby, which is what we used to call stores that sold drug paraphernalia. "I have a few questions for you," he said.

"Sure," I answered. *Not a problem,* I thought. *I have been a Christian for a couple weeks now. Fire away.*

He proceeded to direct four or five pretty tough questions my way. Today I can't even remember what they were. All I remember is that I was dumbfounded. I didn't have a clue as to how to answer. Meanwhile, my good friend Gregg kept turning to me and saying, "Yeah, Greg, what about that? He's right, why does God do that? Why doesn't God do this?"

I was ashamed and embarrassed. But worst of all I felt that I had let the Lord down. I made a commitment that day to study the Bible, to know what it had to say so I would not be caught in that position again. I am not suggesting that now I have the answer to every question or that I can resolve any difficulty. But I realized then and there that I wanted to equip myself with God's Word so I could become an increasingly better witness for Christ.

A Matter of Life and Death

In the previous chapter we saw that a "learning church" is filled with true disciples—those who are trying to become like Christ based on what He said and what He did. Now I want to talk with you about imitating Christ by becoming a student of Scripture. The word *disciple* can actually be translated "learner."

Keep in mind, however, that the kind of learner that makes a true disciple is not just a student who listens passively. A disciple is someone who is completely intent on watching and listening to his teacher and who is drinking in every word with an intense desire to apply what he's learning. The early church studied the Scriptures wholeheartedly. Remember what we read in Acts 2:42: "And they continued steadfastly in the apostles' doctrine and fellowship, in the breaking of bread, and in prayers" (NKJV). Paul told Timothy, "Devote yourself to the public reading of Scripture, to preaching and to teaching" (1 Tim. 4:13, NIV).

Now at first glance, studying the Bible steadfastly or preaching the Bible in church or some other public venue doesn't sound too upside down. But you know what? That's not always happening in churches and among Christians. And it's definitely not what's happening in the world in general.

The Bible has been used to decorate coffee tables, to wave in the air while preaching, to put your hand on while taking an oath, to look spiritual on a nightstand, or to record the family tree. It has been read as great literature or a history text. The Bible is used for all these things every day.

But to use the Bible as a basis for your life choices, to desire to read it as you desire food to sustain you physically, to have an appetite for it so strong that when you don't read it, you feel empty, to believe that every word of it applies to you somehow, to try to obey it every day, to learn and to teach it all you can . . . that's definitely upside-down behavior, even in our "Christian" subculture.

I would be so bold as to say that if you know someone who

reads the Bible this way, that person's life does not look ordinary. You can tell at a glance that something is radically different about that person.

As a pastor I've been given clear direction from God as to what I should be doing. Paul said to Timothy, "Preach the word! Be ready in season and out of season. Convince, rebuke, exhort, with all longsuffering and teaching" (2 Tim. 4:2, NKJV). In the original language there is an urgency here, just as there is an urgency in the passages about evangelizing. Paul is essentially saying, "Preach the Word with alertness, with carefulness, with insistence. With passion."

PREACH THE WORD WITH ALERTNESS, WITH CAREFULNESS, WITH INSISTENCE, WITH PASSION.

But this command is not just for me as a pastor. It is for all of us as we take God's Word to the world. We should all be urgent about the Bible. We should treat this message as a matter of life and death.

I travel by plane quite a bit, and I have heard a few hundred times the speech the flight attendants give about safety and seat belts and oxygen masks. (Isn't it disconcerting how they quip so breezily, "In the event of a water landing . . ." as if this would constitute only a slight shift in plans?) I usually just flip through magazines while they make these announcements. I note where the emergency exits are, and then I go on with what I'm doing.

But what if the plane were actually going down? What if I knew that I had twenty minutes before impact, and the flight attendants gave that announcement one more time? I would not merely listen carefully; I would be frantically studying every word of that safety card for myself.

Remember the story in chapter 4 about Andrew Meekin? Christians who are really living an upside-down life for Christ approach evangelism as if the plane were going down every day.

And you know what? They also study the Bible *as if their life depended on knowing what it contains.* Because in many ways it does.

Unfortunately many churches and individuals just aren't studying, preaching, and learning the Bible this way. It amazes me how many preachers have lost sight of this urgency. Just turn on the TV on Sunday mornings. Go channel surfing and listen carefully. It's rare to hear someone actually speak from the Bible. And in many churches it's rare to hear the pastor say, "Please turn in your Bible to . . ." I have to confess that the sweetest sound to my ears is when I say this phrase and then hear the responsive rustle of Bible pages all through the sanctuary.

It's hard to understand this lack of passion for the Bible. What's gone wrong? Why are so many of us failing to turn those pages, preach from those pages, and feed our soul from them?

The rest of the passage Paul wrote to Timothy provides some clues. It continues,

> *For the time will come when they will not endure sound doctrine, but according to their own desires, because they have itching ears, they will heap up for themselves teachers; and they will turn their ears away from the truth, and be turned aside to fables.* 2 Tim. 4:3-4, NKJV

I want you to notice the bold parts of the above verses, because I believe that this time has come. And I believe these verses point to the three biggest reasons we have turned away from our love for the Word. We have spoiled appetites; we think we need more than the Bible; and we have ears that want to be tickled instead of taught.

1. We have spoiled appetites.

I was talking with a man back in North Carolina some time ago who is an expert in so-called church growth. He told me about another pastor who had started a church for Gen Xers.

I said, "Tell me; I'm really interested. What distinguishes a church that is targeted toward Xers or baby busters?"

He said, "For starters, they have televisions lining the walls on both sides of the sanctuary all the way from the front to the back."

"What's the purpose of that?"

"Well, the pastor speaks for about ten minutes, and then they break and have a video. Then he speaks a little more. Then another video. They do this because they know that people's attention span is too short to listen to the pastor for too long."

I think this is dangerous. Remember the phrase from Timothy? "They will not endure sound doctrine." Apparently these folks will not endure any kind teaching for more than ten minutes at a time.

What's happening here? Has our attention span shrunk since the first century? I don't think so. I think we've lost our ability to endure Bible teaching because we've have had our appetite spoiled by sweet stuff and fluff in place of the meat of the Word. The simple fact that we would have to *endure* teaching versus *desire* teaching is a bad sign. We *endure* liver and onions (at least I do).

People will develop an appetite for what you feed them. *Yet the fact that people develop an appetite for what they're served over time doesn't mean that they're consuming what their spirit is truly hungry for.*

I believe people are deeply hungry for the Bible. I think they want to hear what the Bible has to say. When they come to church, they don't expect the pastor to be a pop psychologist or a comedian or a political activist. They actually expect a preacher to preach from the Bible. Whether they are Gen Xers or boomers, everyone wants to know what the meaning of life is. Everybody wants to know God. And the answers are found in the Scriptures. We are going to have to learn how to sit down, slow down, and learn to enjoy the feast that's in the Bible.

2. We think we need more than the Word.

One undisputed leader of the church growth movement has said something I think is surprising. "If somebody has been sexually molested, if someone has grown up in the home of an alcoholic father, if someone has been beaten as a child, there are some deep psychological wounds that have to be carefully treated by trained Christian counselors before these wounded people can thoroughly appropriate the promises and precepts of Scripture." He closes: "Traditional preaching alone is not enough to restore many people to wholeness."

I understand that this pastor is being sensitive to the deep wounds of people. However, I disagree with the idea that the Word preached is inadequate to restore people to wholeness. I guess part of the problem has to do with how we interpret "wholeness" and whether or not that is our goal.

WHEN SEEKERS COME TO CHURCH, THEY DON'T EXPECT THE PASTOR TO BE A POP PSYCHOLOGIST OR A COMEDIAN OR A POLITICAL ACTIVIST.

Notice the phrase from 2 Timothy: "according to their own desires." Somewhere along the way we got the idea that the goal of a Christian is personal well-being. We desire healthy egos and high self-esteem and peace with our past, etc. We no longer believe in the power of salvation to make us new. Consider what Christ says: "My grace is sufficient for you, for my power is made perfect in weakness" (2 Cor. 12:9, NIV).

This subtle idea that the Bible is not sufficient has crept into our churches, and as a result we're neglecting the study of the Bible. Instead, many churches lean more and more heavily on books, philosophies, and small groups that focus on making us well and happy rather than on how we can live abundantly by denying ourselves for Christ.

Do you want healing? Everything you need is in the Bible. Psalm 107:20-21 says, "He sent His word and healed them, and delivered them from their destructions. Oh, that men would give thanks to the Lord for His goodness, and for His wonderful works to the children of men!" (NKJV).

The gospel preached is sufficient for you. Listen to Paul:

> *When I came to you, brothers, I did not come with eloquence or superior wisdom as I proclaimed to you the testimony about God. For I resolved to know nothing while I was with you except Jesus Christ and him crucified. I came to you in weakness and fear, and with much trembling. My message and my preaching were not with wise and persuasive words, but with a demonstration of the Spirit's power, so that your faith might not rest on men's wisdom, but on God's power.* 1 Cor. 2:1-5, NIV

*O*PERATING ACCORDING TO HIS UPSIDE-DOWN PRINCIPLES WILL WORK FOR YOU NO MATTER WHAT YOUR PAST OR HOW DEEP YOUR PAIN.

If you need counseling, get it. Just make sure it is biblically sound. If you need medical attention, by all means, seek it! However, don't forget for a moment that the ultimate healer is God. And His ways are not always like ours. He works through our weaknesses. He shines through our cracked parts. In fact, He prefers to work through people who let Him use their brokenness rather than focusing all their attention on becoming "whole."

His Word is where the real answers to life are found. And operating according to His upside-down principles will work for you no matter what your past or how deep your pain.

3. We have itching ears.

When Paul mentions to Timothy that people will have "itching ears," he is using a phrase that means "an itch for novelty." Another translation is "looking for spicy bits of information."

This is a perfect description of our culture. We are seeing an explosion of bizarre and aberrant philosophies and teachings today under the banner of "spirituality."

Why are people always surprised to discover that there are spiritual forces at work in the world? This stuff has much of society absolutely fascinated. Just go down to your local bookstore at the mall, and you will see what I'm talking about: dozens of weird, bizarre books dealing with all sorts of spiritual, novel topics—none of them coming from a Christian worldview. All of them offer to titillate the curious who have itching ears.

WHY IS IT WE THINK EVERYTHING THAT IS OLD IS OUT OF DATE AND EVERYTHING THAT IS NEW HAS THE ANSWERS?

But here is the problem. This desire to be tickled by spiritual mumbo jumbo is happening in the church as well. We are itching for new experiences. And we are even willing to disguise our penchant by cloaking it in a spiritual quest of some kind. Some will say, "It's a new move of the Spirit. We want a new thing from the Lord. Have you heard about . . . ?"

This reminds me of the mentality of the people on Mars Hill in Athens when Paul went to preach to them. These people believed in and would embrace just about anything remotely spiritual. And in Acts 17:21 we read, "All the Athenians and the foreigners who lived there spent their time doing nothing but talking about and listening to the latest ideas" (NIV).

We want something new. We don't want the old Bible stuff. Why is it we think everything that is old is antiquated and out of date and everything that is new has the answers?

I like what God says in Jeremiah: "Thus says the Lord: 'Stand in the ways and see, and ask for the old paths, where the good way is, and walk in it; then you will find rest for your souls' " (Jer. 6:16, NKJV). The old paths are the words of God, and we need to return to them, learn them, and preach them. If it is "new," it isn't true. If it is true, it isn't new.

This is not to say that God can't take His Word and make it fresh and new to our life. But when Paul said, "Preach the word," he didn't intend for me to preach politics, psychology, or social issues. He didn't tell me to preach morality in and of itself. He meant for me to preach God's Word, no matter what the topic—as clearly, honestly, and thoroughly as possible. I'm called to teach, not to tickle itching ears. And you in the pew are called to hunger for teaching.

Good Reasons to Read

So often we think of reading or preaching the Word as a Christian duty we perform so we can check it off our list of things good Christians do. But we truly need to study the Bible for more reasons than we realize.

Reading the Bible is kind of like exercising. The doctor says we need to exercise, so we reluctantly make our way down to the gym. But six weeks into it, we're not thinking anymore about what the doctor said. We want to go because we've discovered how many aspects of our life are improved by exercising.

The greatest reason to learn and to preach the Bible is so that we are all better equipped to turn the world upside down even when challenged by difficult questions from guys like the one I encountered while witnessing to my friend Gregg. But a great ability to evangelize is just one reason to read.

Here are five other important reasons why you will want to continue to study the Bible once you get started. And why you who are pastors need to keep preaching the Word to your people.

1. The Bible helps you learn theology (right ideas about God).
I make it a point to teach Bible-based theology on many Sunday mornings at my church. I want us all to have the right ideas about God and to have a grid that we can examine things by so we know what we believe and as a result know what we don't believe.

I've heard people say proudly, "I don't have any theology. I just love Jesus!" But if you have no theology, how can you share the gospel clearly? We all have a theology. We all make assumptions, either based on the Word or not, about how God works in the world. As C. S. Lewis once put it, "If you do not listen to theology, that will not mean that you have no ideas about God. It will mean that you will have a lot of wrong ones."

When we become not just lovers of the Word but students of the Word, we base our theology on the truth, and we obey God. Paul said to Timothy, "Do your best to present yourself to God as one approved, a workman who does not need to be ashamed and who correctly handles the word of truth" (2 Tim. 2:15, NIV). A wonderful place to start would be with *The New Believer's Bible*. It contains hundreds of notes on subjects ranging from the deity of Christ to how to pray effectively.

Remember when Jesus was tempted by Satan in the desert? Satan used Scripture outside its proper context, and Jesus answered him by using Scripture correctly. If you have no understanding of theology, then when Satan tries to confuse you by using the Word of God wrongly, you won't be equipped for combat. Study the Word, learn how it all works together, and you will be ready to say to Satan, "Scripture also says . . . "

> *IF YOU DO NOT LISTEN TO THEOLOGY, THAT WILL NOT MEAN THAT YOU HAVE NO IDEAS ABOUT GOD. IT WILL MEAN THAT YOU WILL HAVE A LOT OF WRONG ONES.*

2. The Bible prepares you to recognize false teaching.

You can try to be an expert on every weird, crazy concept that comes down the pike. But the best thing is to know the Bible so well that when you hear something, you can say, "No. That's not right because the Bible says this. That couldn't be true because the Bible says this. That's exactly right because Scripture says this."

The story is told of an inspector who worked for England's Scotland Yard in the counterfeit department. It was his job to distinguish false currency from the genuine. So someone asked, "Well, you must spend a lot of time handling counterfeit money." He said, "No, actually I don't. I spend so much time handling the real thing that I can immediately detect the counterfeit." That's the best way.

In the book of Acts we read of those who lived in Berea and had the privilege of hearing the great apostle Paul preach. Now, I have to be honest with you, if I heard Paul preach, I probably wouldn't check him out according to Scripture. This is *Paul* after all. This is the man who wrote a good portion of the New Testament. I would just kick back and take it all in.

But the Bible tells us, "Now the Bereans were of more noble character than the Thessalonians, for they received the message with great eagerness and examined the Scriptures every day to see if what Paul said was true" (Acts 17:11, NIV). This should be the model for all believers.

Now, of course, when we read his writings in the Bible, we don't have to question whether or not these writings are right. Those are inspired by God. But these people scrutinized the Scriptures to see if what was being taught to them checked out. And if these people checked out the words of Paul the apostle, how much more should we check out our preachers and so-called apostles and prophets today?

John wrote, "Dear friends, do not believe everyone who claims to speak by the Spirit. You must test them to see if the spirit they have comes from God. For there are many false prophets in the world" (1 John 4:1, NLT).

I encourage anyone to do that with me. Never accept what I say because I say it. Who am I? A fallible person. Make sure that what I say agrees with what the Scripture teaches. If you have a good working knowledge of the Bible, you will be able to detect false teaching quickly.

3. The Bible is spiritual food for your soul.

When you get up in the morning, what is the first thing you think about? The Bible? If you do, I tip my hat to you. But when I get up in the morning, the first thing I think about isn't the Bible or church or ministry or even my wife. I usually think about food. That's just human nature. *I must eat soon.*

IF YOU HAVE A GOOD WORKING KNOWLEDGE OF THE BIBLE, YOU WILL BE ABLE TO DETECT FALSE TEACHING QUICKLY.

Now let's try to broaden that idea to include spiritual food. If I am going to neglect a meal because my schedule is so hectic, wouldn't it be great if I neglected a physical meal and made time for the Word of God instead of neglecting the Word of God to eat that physical meal? I love what Job said: "I have treasured the words of His mouth more than my necessary food" (Job 23:12, NKJV).

Experts tell us that we are what we eat. That's also the case spiritually. If the right spiritual ingredients, which can be found only in the Bible, are missing, then we are spiritually deficient and malnourished. As a result, we are spiritually weak and vulnerable.

If we feed on God's Word, we will develop an appetite for it. And every day we will say with the psalmist, "As the deer pants for streams of water, so my soul pants for you, O God. My soul thirsts for God, for the living God. When can I go and meet with God?" (Ps. 42:1-2, NIV).

This is how Jesus felt about God's Word, and this is the attitude we should imitate if we want to be disciples: "Man does not live on bread alone, but on every word that comes from the mouth of God" (Matt. 4:4, NIV).

4. The Bible enables you to know God's will.

So many of us spend hours praying, "God, show me your will."

But the greatest key to knowing God's will in almost any situation is knowing what the Word says. We need to base our decisions on biblical principles as well as on the common sense God gives us—what God speaks to us personally, as well as what He speaks to us through those we respect.

I would like to say that every day God speaks to me audibly. After I wake up and think of food, God whispers, "Good morning, Greg; how are you?"

"I'm good, Lord. How are things up there?"

"Really great. Greg, here is the plan for today. And here is My will for you. I want you to leave the house at 7:46. When you get to the office, I want you to call this person."

But He doesn't. So how do I know God's will? I read the Word, and I operate by faith on biblical principles. When I come to a difficult situation or choice, I ask myself, *What biblical principles can guide me here?*

What does the Bible say? Then that is what I will do.

A lot of us are looking for this mystical, supernatural thing to happen, a loud voice from heaven declaring, "This is My will. . . ." But reading the Bible is what helps us to have the mind of Christ. It is how we can get our brain into a mode where everything goes through the grid of scriptural thinking. That is primarily how we are going to know the mind of Christ—and the will of God.

5. The Bible is one way God speaks to you personally.
After Jesus was crucified, two discouraged followers were traveling on the Emmaus road. They were devastated. They had thought Jesus was going to establish a physical kingdom and overthrow the tyranny of Rome, but instead He'd gotten Himself killed.

Now, He had told them repeatedly, "I am going to die. I am going to rise again on the third day." But they didn't understand this.

As they were walking along and talking, a stranger joined them, and they welcomed Him to walk along with them. They started to converse. He asked, "What are you talking about?"

They said, "Haven't you heard about all of the things concerning Jesus of Nazareth?"

"What things?"

And they began to tell Him all of the things that had happened. "And besides all of this, it's the third day since He was crucified."

He said, "You fools and slow of heart to believe" (see Luke 24:25). And the Bible says that beginning with Moses and the prophets, He opened to them all the things in the Scriptures concerning Himself. As He spoke, they listened.

When He acted as though He was going to go farther than they, the two people insisted, "Oh no. Stay with us." They sat down, and when the stranger broke the bread, their eyes were opened spiritually, and they realized it was the Lord. Immediately He disappeared from their midst.

I love this next statement. They said, "Did not our heart burn within us while He talked with us on the road, and while He opened the Scriptures to us?" (Luke 24:32, NKJV).

We all need a good case of spiritual heartburn. We will have that when Jesus Christ speaks to us personally through His Word.

Martin Luther said, "The Bible is alive. It speaks to me. It has feet. It runs after me. It has hands. It lays hold of me." Isn't that what we want? For God to speak with us and run after us and lay hold of us? He does that through the Word.

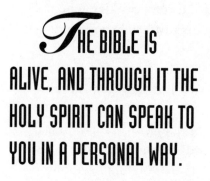

THE BIBLE IS ALIVE, AND THROUGH IT THE HOLY SPIRIT CAN SPEAK TO YOU IN A PERSONAL WAY.

The Bible is not just words on a page. Its words are alive, and through it the Holy Spirit can speak to you in a personal way. You're reading along, and suddenly you feel Christ highlighting a key point or speaking to your sorrow through a psalm. The Bible is a key part of our personal conversation with God. Get into the Word of God. And let the Word of God get into you.

PASTOR TO PASTOR
Five Ways to See If God's Word Is in Your Word

MEASURE CONTENT. Ask yourself: Are my stories and observations helping to illuminate the Bible passage, or is the Bible there simply to help justify the importance of my stories? Is the Bible my swimming pool, where I spend the most time, or is it simply my diving board?

2. MEASURE COVERAGE. Ask yourself: If my church were a lawn and my Bible teaching fertilizer, would my lawn be turning evenly green or a weird pattern of stripes and burn holes? We should be striving to preach the whole Word as thoroughly as possible over the course of time. Paul said he had not failed "to declare the whole counsel of God." Could you make that same claim?

3. MEASURE CONSUMPTION. Ask yourself: What kind of food is my church consuming? Are the people growing

mature on the meat of the Word, or are most of them still eating out of the blender? If you looked at a sampling of your sermons, would you find enough to feed a hungry church family? Are you explaining complex ideas and cutting them into smaller pieces for new believers? For the "grown-ups," have you offered further reading ideas, posed challenging questions, and gone beyond the basics of salvation?

4. MEASURE CREATIVITY.   Ask yourself: Am I doing justice to the Bible's amazing stories and surprising insights and principles? Or am I putting people to sleep with the truth—just giving them what they expect? Jesus communicated Bible truth through stories that were full of color, smells, and life. The Bible isn't boring, but as one old-time seminary professor used to say, one proof of the inspiration of Scripture is that it has withstood so much poor preaching.

5. MEASURE YOUR CONCERN.   Ask yourself: Do I preach the Word as if I'm on that airplane that's going down? Martin Lloyd-Jones described this urgency as "logic on fire." Some have the fire with no logic, or content. Others have the content but no passion. We need to combine the two.

SIGNS OF LOVE

Question: What are key indicators in a church that a love of God's Word is alive and well?

Answer: For starters, when you see people coming to church with their Bibles, that's an indication that things are on the right track. There have been times when I have spoken at other churches, and I will often begin my message with the words "Let's turn in our Bibles to . . ." It's always a cause for concern when people get that blank look on their faces because they don't have Bibles with them.

Second, you will sense an anticipation and eagerness to get into Scripture. I believe there is a need for genuine Spirit-directed preaching today, but I also believe there is a need for genuine Spirit-directed listening. Listening not only with our head but with our heart, having an openness to receive God's Word. First Peter 2:2 says, "You must crave pure spiritual milk so that you can grow into the fullness of your salvation. Cry out for this nourishment as a baby cries for milk" (NLT). We must come not only to hear the Word, but we should come also with a desire to apply it.

Third, if there is a love of God's Word in a church, I also think you will see this reflected in people's desire to attend other Bible studies during the week in addition to Sunday-morning services.

NINE

PASSING IT ON
Making Disciples
of Others

I BECAME a Christian in high school. But even as I prayed to receive Jesus Christ into my life, I was unceremoniously interrupted by the ringing of the bell to go to fifth period. No one told
me that I needed to read the Bible. No one told me that I should
pray or go to church. No one gave me any materials to read,
much less a Bible.

For a few days I was in sort of a spiritual no-man's-land. Suddenly I didn't feel as comfortable hanging out with my old
friends. Yet I didn't feel that I fit in with the Christians either.

I felt isolated until God directed a young man named Mark to
come and take me under his wing. Mark had noticed me at the
Bible study on the day I turned my life over to Christ. He approached me and said simply, "I would like to encourage you
and take you to church with me."

I was more than open. Mark took me to Calvary Chapel, and
he began to help me grow spiritually. He taught me how to read
the Bible, and we prayed together. Mark wasn't a great Bible
scholar or especially gifted to teach. But he was the first actual
Christian I came to know personally who could model for
me what it was to be a disciple of Jesus and to be a discipler of
others.

Beyond New Birth

Several chapters back we examined the great commission. We saw that it is God's assignment for all of us and that we need to care about evangelizing people who haven't yet found God. Now there's a key point that we should revisit. Somewhere along the line we in the church have separated evangelism from discipleship. But the two are inseparably linked.

Though one applies to Christians and one to non-Christians, evangelizing and discipling are, and should be, part of the same process. Jesus said, "Go therefore and *make disciples* of all the nations, baptizing them in the name of the Father and of the Son and of the Holy Spirit, teaching them to observe all things that I have commanded you" (Matt. 28:19-20, NKJV; italics added).

What exactly does it mean to make disciples? Part of verse 20 defines it for us: teaching people to observe all things that He has commanded. Simply put, it means to show others how to obey what Jesus has taught us. To disciple people is to live out our faith, to teach it by word, and to model it by example. We seek to lead people to Christ and then, to the best of our ability, help them get up on their feet and become spiritually mature.

*W*OULD WE EVER CONSIDER ABANDONING A NEWBORN BABY IN THE HOPES THAT HE WILL FIND WHAT IT NEEDS IN ORDER TO GROW?

In Colossians 1:28 Paul puts it this way: "So, naturally, we proclaim Christ! We warn everyone we meet, and we teach everyone we can, all that we know about him, so that we may bring every man up to his full maturity in Christ" (Phillips).

In a previous chapter we talked about what it means to become a true upside-down disciple of Christ. But a key part of being disciples ourselves is to be involved in making yet other disciples. And if Jesus is our ultimate example of a disciple, we should be trying to imitate His careful nurturing of His own followers.

We can also see discipleship as a key part of God's reproductive plan for His kingdom. Of course, we don't actually create Christian "babies"; God does that. But you might say that we assist at the birth. Would we ever consider abandoning a newborn baby in the hopes that he will find what it needs in order to grow? You wouldn't do that any more than a doctor would deliver a baby and then immediately give the little tyke a box of Pampers, put him out on the sidewalk, and say, "OK, son, God bless you. It has been good to be with you for this short time. Now go make something of yourself!" We need to take great care to nurture, protect, and guide those we lead to Christ.

Saul's Story

Did you ever notice in Scripture that even the apostles needed discipling? And often more than one person participated. Just as it may take more than one person to bring someone to the point of following Christ, we all have a part to play in discipling others so that they can in turn go out and shake the world for Christ.

God gives some great examples through the story of Saul. After Saul's conversion, many believers were uncertain about whether or not his Christianity was real. This is understandable. Saul was a dangerous man and had been a relentless persecutor of the church. Some people worried that Saul was pulling some kind of trick. What if he only claimed to be a Christian so that he could infiltrate the ranks of believers, get all their names, and have them arrested?

Having Saul become a Christian would be like hearing today that Saddam Hussein or Howard Stern or Marilyn Manson had turned his life over to Christ. The world, and even many in the church, might doubt that for a while.

In Saul's case, God sent a man named Ananias to help out. He said, "I want you to go and visit Saul. He is your brother, and he is in prayer."

Ananias must have been shocked to hear this. *Are we talking about the same Saul here?* He replied to God, "I have heard many reports about this man and all the harm he has done to your saints in Jerusalem. And he has come here with authority from the chief priests to arrest all who call on your name" (Acts 9:13-14, NIV).

Isn't it humorous how we think we're giving God a news flash? But the Lord replied to Ananias, "Go! This man is my chosen instrument to carry my name before the Gentiles and their kings and before the people of Israel. I will show him how much he must suffer for my name" (Acts 9:15-16, NIV).

Once again God's plans run counter to what we would do. God chose an enemy at present to become His "chosen instrument."

*B*ECAUSE ANANIAS WAS OBEDIENT, HIS INVESTMENT IN THE APOSTLE PAUL WOULD BE MULTIPLIED A MILLION TIMES OVER FOR CENTURIES TO COME.

Fortunately Ananias was obedient, even if he didn't fully understand God's purposes. He went and found Saul, called him brother, baptized him, and took the time to pray with and encourage him (see Acts 9:10-19).

Are you willing to disciple any person God sends your way— or sends you to help? Even the most unlikely of candidates or those you don't appear to have much in common with? Ananias's role in Saul's life can't be overestimated. You never know who you are discipling or what God has planned for that person. Because Ananias was obedient, his investment in the apostle Paul would be multiplied a million times over for centuries to come.

Excuses, Excuses

The most common excuse we give for not being actively involved in discipling others is that we don't feel qualified. We don't know enough about the Bible, and we're sure there's someone else out there more spiritually mature who has a gift for this kind of thing.

Besides, if we happen to be parents, we're discipling our own kids at home, aren't we? And those people who need discipling can always go to a Bible study or something, can't they?

But if we are brutally honest, often the reason we don't disciple others is that we're not living the Christian life we know we ought to be. We don't want to disciple others because we're going through the motions ourselves. Why set ourselves up to fail or to expose our inconsistencies to others? I mean, we don't want to cause a brother or sister to stumble. Maybe later, when we're not struggling so much ourselves . . . down the road. . . . But wait a second. Let's look at what Saul did after Ananais went to him.

> *Saul spent several days with the disciples in Damascus. At once he began to preach in the synagogues that Jesus is the Son of God. All those who heard him were astonished and asked, "Isn't he the man who raised havoc in Jerusalem among those who call on this name? And hasn't he come here to take them as prisoners to the chief priests?" Yet Saul grew more and more powerful and baffled the Jews living in Damascus by proving that Jesus is the Christ.* Acts 9:19-22, NIV

Notice that Saul didn't say, "Wow! I've been such a terrible example. I'm such a bad person; I can't possibly go out there yet and proclaim Jesus or teach others that He is the Christ!"

Instead, he immediately began to pass on to others the Good News he had received. And what happened? People were shocked; some probably snickered in disbelief. But this, too, was part of God's plan. If a very good and righteous person had begun to proclaim Christ, no one would have thought much about it. *But Saul's testimony was amazing proof of God's power to dramatically change any person's life, no matter what he or she has done.*

Disciple Making Is the Natural Outlet for a Disciple

What I really want you to see is what happened to Paul himself as a result of his efforts. We're told that he "grew more and more powerful." Paul thrived spiritually because he was doing what he was supposed to do—even though he was technically the least qualified to do it.

Maybe you're at a place in your Christian walk where you simply feel that you're in a spiritual desert. You read the Bible, and you think, *It's just not speaking to me the way it used to.* You come to church and think, *This is all good stuff, but I feel as if I've heard a lot of these things before.* You're trying your best to love God and live the Christian life, but the fire that once burned in your soul feels as if it's smoldered down to a smoking log.

Guess what? You probably don't need to attend more Bible studies. You may not even need to read more Christian books or go to more church services. The real problem may be that you don't have an outlet for what you are taking in. And if you do not have an outlet for spiritual truths in your life, you are going to lose heat and energy. You can keep blowing on those coals all you want. But what you really need is to share what you know with others; then your fire will grow.

The truths that God gives us are designed to be passed on. And when we give away what God has given to us, it actually *replenishes* our spiritual supply!

Have you ever discipled anyone? Have you ever taken a new believer under your wing and helped her along? Then you know, or at least you remember, that when you give your life away to disciple others, you get back so much more. It sounds cliché, but it's true. The new believers need our wisdom, knowledge, and experience. But we need them, too! We need their zeal, spark, and childlike simplicity of faith.

When you have a child, you begin to see things through a child's eyes again. As you watch a toddler discover ice cream for the first time, you're reminded about how wonderful and cold and creamy and amazing it is. That's why it's so fun to watch a child see the ocean for the first time. Or walk on sand or pick up snow. If you can see something through the eyes of a child, it can be like being a child all over again. And if you can see things through the eyes of a new believer, it can reignite you spiritually.

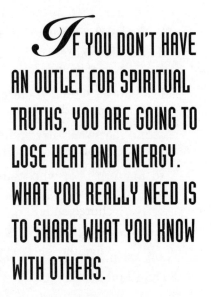

If YOU DON'T HAVE AN OUTLET FOR SPIRITUAL TRUTHS, YOU ARE GOING TO LOSE HEAT AND ENERGY. WHAT YOU REALLY NEED IS TO SHARE WHAT YOU KNOW WITH OTHERS.

That's why, for our sake as well as theirs, we need to be involved in making new disciples. It's all a basic part of God's process of spreading His gospel. And all of us can do this. It doesn't have to entail knowing the Bible front to back. It may be as simple as inviting a new believer out to coffee after a Bible study. You may be discipling people right now and not even know it.

Real Needs of New Believers

OK, so you're ready to start discipling others or to learn more about the process. Where do you start? What do young believers *really* need?

They need love and support to feel comfortable in church.
A lot of people who are raised in the church one day make their commitment to Christ and continue to attend that same church. They already know their way around.

But many, many people are new Christians like I was. They don't have a clue as to what's going on in church—why church is necessary or how to get the most out of it. For all they know, the number flashing on the monitor during the service is somebody's guess for how many days till Christ comes back instead of a signal to parents that their child needs them in the nursery.

We have a ministry for new believers called the Discipleship Team. The people in this group take up where the new-convert counselors leave off. Their objective is to help new believers adjust and get settled in our church. There is a lot of lingo and terminology they may be hearing for the first time, and we have found that what they really need is a friend.

I am so thankful that at Harvest Christian Fellowship we have so many people who come to us from an unchurched background. But I'm also aware of what this means to them. They are really in need of someone who will become a friend to them and say, "How are you doing? Have you met anybody? Do you have any friends? Have you been to church here before? Did your child find his class OK?"

On a deeper level, think of some of these young kids who come from broken homes. Maybe one or both parents are not involved in their lives. They decide to follow Jesus. Here you are, a Christian couple. How wonderful it would be if you could take that young one in and become almost like spiritual foster parents. Show them what it is to love one another. Show them what it is to have a stable home. You can influence a child for the rest of his life.

They need help and encouragement to
understand the Bible correctly.

One couple mentioned in Acts, Aquila and Priscilla, illustrate how we should help new converts. We read in Acts 18 how a man by the name of Apollos was filled with enthusiasm for the Lord. However, he had a few doctrinal problems. So Aquila and

Priscilla took him into their home. The Bible says they explained the way of God to him more accurately. As a result, Apollos became even more effective in what God had called him to do.

Remember the parable of the sower? The first thing that Satan will try to do when someone receives the Word is to come and pluck it away. How crucial it is for us to care for the spiritual ground of those souls who receive Christ! I can't overstate how important it is for you to be willing to disciple one of these believers, helping to snatch back, to hold firm, what Satan would distort or try to uproot.

BE WILLING TO DISCIPLE A NEW BELIEVER, HELPING TO SNATCH BACK, TO HOLD FIRM, WHAT SATAN WOULD DISTORT OR TRY TO UPROOT.

One of the simplest ways to provide this opportunity is through home Bible studies. At Harvest we have many such opportunities through the week. Here, older Christians can mingle with new Christians, and the wonderful process of discipleship can take place. Of course, these studies only function because of those who are willing to take the time to disciple others. I'm aware that a Bible study can turn into a gab session or a debate-a-thon. How important it is for us to take seriously the teaching of simple, basic truths in the Word.

One ministry that has been very effective at our church is something that we call the men's and women's Bible study fellowship. These groups simply meet and go through a book of the Bible together. Often there's a beneficial dynamic to having men meet together and women meet together. There will be a time of teaching, and then they will break into smaller groups and discuss what they have heard. A facilitator helps to keep the discussion on track.

This is a simple but great way to provide discipleship for new believers as well as to provide an opportunity for church members to grow in their teaching and discipling skills.

They need to see a Christian life in action.
New believers can get only so much information from a pulpit. What they need is to see God's principles at work in real life on a day-to-day basis. How does a Christian behave at work? How does a Christian behave when he drives? How does a Christian man treat his wife and children? Or how about single Christians? How do single Christians relate to members of the opposite sex? How does a Christian spend his or her free time? That is why Paul reminds Timothy: "Now you have observed my teaching, my conduct, my aim in life and my faith" (2 Tim. 3:10, paraphrased).

They need your help to mature in their own gifts and ministries.
John said his greatest joy was in seeing his children walk in the truth (3 John 1:4). As an evangelist I love to see people make that initial commitment to follow Christ. Yet as a pastor I find great joy in seeing people continuing in the faith and even leading others to faith.

> *NEW BELIEVERS CAN GET ONLY SO MUCH INFORMATION FROM A PULPIT. WHAT THEY NEED IS TO SEE GOD'S PRINCIPLES AT WORK IN REAL LIFE ON A DAY-TO-DAY BASIS.*

Almost all of our associate pastors at Harvest either came to Christ in one of our services or began attending as very young believers. And I could cite many examples of people who have come to faith at our church and have not only continued in the faith but have gone on to start their own ministries. We conducted a survey recently and found that one-fourth of the people at Harvest are actively involved in service in some capacity.

I have found that people who are the most enthusiastic about sharing their faith and ministering to others are often those who are youngest in the faith. Our new converts often want to immediately get involved in service. This isn't always a good idea. We require that new believers attend our church and be discipled for at least a year before they can serve. This is a way to protect them and to help them get a good spiritual foundation. Paul warned about putting new converts in such positions, where they would be targeted by the devil (1 Tim. 3:6).

Once new believers have met that requirement, we also ask them to go through some training, depending on what positions they are filling.

Six Keys to Discipling Others

Discipling others is mostly an informal matter, and it should happen naturally in the course of our life if we're walking tightly with the Lord. However, sometimes we want to be more focused in our approach. We want to "take someone on," the way Mark did with me or the way Aquila and Priscilla took on Apollos. Here are some things to keep in mind that will help in such situations:

1. EVALUATE THE PERSON'S NEED. Is this a new Christian, a person who's been a Christian a long time but who has slipped back into a sinful lifestyle, or just a struggling young person who wants someone to look up to?

2. EVALUATE THE FIT. Sometimes we're not the right person to disciple someone, and God has other options. It's almost always better, for example, to let women disciple women and men disciple men.

3. EVALUATE YOUR GIFTS. Some of us are especially good at helping others apply Scripture to real-life situations. Some of us are good encouragers. Others are gifted to help people in concrete, practical ways. We all have something to offer. Some are

gifted communicators; others are not. Discover your gifts, and give whatever you have to offer.

4. EVALUATE CHURCH RESOURCES. What Bible studies or other opportunities can you help a new believer take advantage of? Can you accompany him? Or could you call someone who's already going and try to make a connection?

5. EVALUATE YOUR COMMIT MENT/ TIME FRAME. In the case of formal discipleship, sometimes it's helpful to set up a time line. "Let's get together every Tuesday for three months" can help a new believer feel more willing to sign on.

6. EVALUATE PROGRESS. How is the new believer doing? Are there signs of growth? Does this appear to be a good match? What's the next step? Are you learning from this experience as well?

> *SOME OF US DISCIPLE THROUGH HOSPITALITY; OTHERS ENJOY TALKING OVER THEOLOGICAL ISSUES. DISCOVER YOUR GIFTS, AND GIVE WHATEVER YOU HAVE TO OFFER.*

Jesus said in Matthew 13:12, "Whoever has, to him more will be given, and he will have abundance; but whoever does not have, even what he has will be taken away from him" (NKJV). Do you see the importance of giving out what God has given to you? Proverbs 11:25 says, "The generous soul will be made rich, and he who waters will also be watered himself" (NKJV).

As I am ministering to others, God is ministering to me. As I am giving out, I'm also taking in from God's resources. The more I give, the more God gives. You cannot out-give God. Did you know that? You have your little spoon dishing out. He has a steam shovel coming at you. God says, "I will give you more."

It's the way that God designs His wonderful truth. It is designed to be passed on. Discipleship is not a suggestion; it is a command. It is essential.

Let me close by saying this: For the sake of those who don't yet know Christ, don't forsake God's command to go and make disciples. For the sake of the young believer, don't let apathy rob you of helping him or her on the journey. For the sake of maintaining an exciting, fruit-bearing walk with God, don't ignore these commands of Jesus. There's a world full of people ripe to hear the Good News. But there are so few workers for the harvest. We need disciple makers.

As I am ministering to others, God is ministering to me. The more I give, the more God gives.

May God help us be just that. Remember: It takes one to make one.

WHO'S ACCOUNTABLE HERE?

Question: Greg, how seriously do you think a church should take discipleship when it comes to accountability, people dealing with their sins, etc? Don't a lot of people go to a big church just so they don't have to be a true disciple because no one is watching?

Answer: That can happen. Some people do attend large churches for that very reason. They can retain a certain anonymity.

I think people who are visiting for the first time resent it when someone is overbearing with them, trying to get their address or invite them to do something. People will take that next step when they are ready. We know that we have unbelievers visit our church, and we want them first and foremost to make a commitment to Christ.

However, if we found out that a person who had allegedly made a commitment to Christ was living an ungodly lifestyle (sleeping with the boyfriend or girlfriend, for instance), they would be confronted and told to stop. If they persisted, we would ask them not to attend until there had been what we call "fruits in keeping with repentance."

For people to interact and develop spiritually in a large church, they need to get involved in one of our smaller group studies (men's or women's Bible fellowship, a midweek study, home Bible study, etc.). Every person in ministry is under some person who is accountable to a ministry leader, who is accountable to one of the people on our pastoral team.

PASTOR TO PASTOR
Balance of Power

As a pastor, you are ultimately a full-time discipler. That is not only your ministry but also your occupation. Sometimes it can be frustrating, in the same way a teacher wants to wring her hands when her students don't seem to want to learn. She's giving them key insights, and they're looking out the window. You're called to disciple, but the decision to follow is out of your hands. Remember these key points, and teach them to your church:

- *Growth takes time.* You are called to instruct "with all patience."
- *This is not a performance.* Authenticity and effort need to rate as high in importance as the appearance and polish.

- *Those who lead are vulnerable to temptation.* You yourself need prayer and guidance from others.
- *Some truths are caught more than taught.* Jesus taught His disciples a lot just by being with them. He was often with the multitudes, but He made time for the twelve disciples He had chosen to be with Him. People absorb a lot by being close to the little tasks you carry out daily, the comments you make that are unprepared, and the attitude you have when you aren't in front of a crowd.
- *You can't control another's journey.* Ultimately you have to let people choose—and choose to let them learn from consequences.

TEN

UPSIDE-DOWN LOVE

The Way to Show the World

IT'S IMPOSSIBLE to study how to become an upside-down church and not talk about Jesus' second greatest command: Love your neighbor as yourself (see Matthew 19:19).

How important is it? God says it's so important that getting everything else right won't matter if we don't get this right. We can evangelize right. We can get discipleship right, teaching and learning until the sun goes down. But a church, or a person, who doesn't get love right is not getting much else right (see 1 Cor. 13).

The Bible teaches that one of the characteristic signs of the last days is that there will be more self-love than ever. Second Timothy 3:1-2 says, "Mark this: There will be terrible times in the last days. People will be lovers of themselves" (NIV).

If that doesn't describe American culture, what does? Then it goes on: "lovers of money, boastful, proud, abusive, disobedient to their parents, ungrateful, unholy, without love, unforgiving, slanderous, without self-control, brutal, not lovers of the good, treacherous, rash, conceited, lovers of pleasure rather than lovers of God." All these characteristics are but outgrowths of loving ourselves rather than loving God.

Of course, putting others first goes directly against our inclination to care about ourselves above all. But if we really want to reveal Christ to our world, our most powerful tool is love—and not just the kind of love the world is accustomed to but the kind of upside-down, outrageously forgiving, and generous love that Jesus lived out and spoke to us about.

This kind of love has as its primary concern not its own welfare but the welfare of others. This kind of love will turn the world on its ear.

But before we talk more about becoming this kind of a loving church, we need to clear up some misconceptions. First of all, what does God really mean when He says, "Love your neighbor as yourself"?

Self-Love vs. Selfless Love

This command, to love our neighbor as we love ourselves, has often been mishandled in our "me first" age. Both Christians and unbelievers have interpreted this verse to support the theory that we need to learn to love ourselves more. The logic goes like this: Before you can effectively love others, you have to first learn to love yourself. So what we really need is more self-love or "self-esteem."

But is that really what that verse is saying? That certainly would not fit the context of Scripture. Jesus is not saying we should learn to love ourselves and then, as a result, go and love our neighbor. If that's what He meant, that's exactly what He would have said. He is assuming—rightly of course!—that your first concern when you wake up in the morning is for yourself.

You may be thinking, *No, Greg, you are wrong. I hate myself.*

I understand that reaction, but why do you hate yourself so much? *Because I'm ugly. Because I'm stupid. Because I'm a loser. I just hate myself.* That may be true. But the whole point is that you want to be different because you care so much about yourself. Even in your self-loathing, you are focused on yourself. As we all are.

When you walk past a mirror or one of those storefront windows, do you ever shoot a glance at yourself? *Am I looking OK? Those pants are a little high. What's going on? I'm getting heavier.*

And how about when someone gives you a picture of you and a bunch of people—whom do you look for first? You look for yourself. You love yourself. I love myself. We need to begin there. Then we will understand what Jesus meant when He said, "Love your neighbor as yourself."

What would happen if we truly began to take Jesus at His word and lived this way? What would this do to our churches? Can you imagine what kind of world we would live in if people operated by this principle? What would it be like if we really were as concerned about others' happiness, problems, and disappointments as we are about our own?

JESUS WAS ASSUMING—RIGHTLY OF COURSE!—THAT YOUR FIRST CONCERN WHEN YOU WAKE UP IN THE MORNING IS FOR YOURSELF.

No wonder the upside-down principles of love are also our greatest witness to the world; they back up everything else we are trying to do and say to unbelievers.

Remember how in Acts all the believers were as one? The response was a daily adding to their numbers. People came to Jesus because they saw how Christians loved each other.

Too often we see the opposite. I fear that we Christians are more often known for what we are against, not what we are for.

As it is, too many of us treat the world as the "enemy," and we respond to conflict or difficult people the same way the world would. Love leads people to God. Why? Because, as John says, "God is love" (see 1 John 4:8, 16). And if God is love, there can be no greater demonstration to the world of His existence than when we truly love them as God does.

PASTOR TO PASTOR
Do You Know What Your Congregation Is Reading?

B*usiness Week* magazine made this astute observation in an article on Christian retailing: "The books selling in Christian bookstores today are the touchy feely ones that focus on self-esteem, self-fulfillment, self-analysis. While devotionals, and missionary biographies gather dust on the shelves, so do books encouraging self-sacrifice."

It's embarrassing that even we believers can be obsessed with self. One popular Christian author made this statement in his book: "Christianity is an adventure of self-discovery that helps believers to become aware of their innate goodness." Innate goodness? Not according to Romans 1 and 2.

Another book said, "The Bible makes people feel good about themselves. Many try to use it to make people hate themselves, but the Bible promotes psychological and emotional health." Is that so?

What about the statement Jesus makes to the church of Laodicea (Rev. 3:17): "You are wretched, miserable, poor, blind, and naked" (NKJV). Or James 4:8-9, which says, "Cleanse your hands, you sinners; and purify your hearts, you double-minded. Lament and mourn and weep! Let your laughter be turned to mourning and your joy to gloom" (NKJV). The Bible will lead us to spiritual health, but it will

> THE BIBLE WILL LEAD US TO SPIRITUAL HEALTH, BUT THROUGH THE TRUTH ABOUT OUR SINFULNESS AND THE HOPE OF FORGIVENESS AND RESTORATION.

do so through the truth about our sinfulness and the hope of forgiveness and restoration. It's not just a feel-good-about-yourself book. Most of the time, Jesus (and all the prophets, Old Testament and New) are trying to get people to wake up to what *isn't* good—so that healing can begin.

I'm not against self-esteem, and I'm certainly not against emotional healing. But we need to be careful not to misuse Scripture to support these quests as ends in themselves. And we also need to make sure we're going to God, to His Word, for help.

HATE VS. HUMILITY

Question: Greg, are you saying that the Bible teaches us to hate ourselves? And how come humility gets no respect these days?

Answer: Let's understand. The Bible does *not* teach self-hate. The Bible does not teach that I am to be some miserable, always-down-on-myself person. The Bible is saying that you should see yourself as you are. You love yourself. But God is asking that instead of being so concerned about yourself, you give that same energy to others. That's part of what it means to deny yourself.

The Bible's main purpose is not to promote psychological encouragement or emotional health (although these are natural results of a thriving relationship with God). The Bible is given to reveal who God is. It is here to tell us how to come in contact with Him and how to be like Him. That is going to require that we see ourselves as we really are: Sinners separated from a God whom we have offended by our willful disobedience and the breaking of His commandments.

God's Upside-Down Love

It has been said that "Christians are living epistles; written by God and read by men." You are the only Bible some people are ever going to read. Upon hearing that you are a Christian, they will carefully watch your every move. They will want to see if your faith is real.

We may protest and say, "Well, no one is perfect, and people shouldn't expect too much of me!" That may be true, but like it or not, people are basing their opinion about God on you. We as a church are here to represent Jesus Christ to this world.

Most of us don't have a problem loving those who love us or giving to those who can give something back. We easily love our Christian friend who likes the same books and music we do. But Jesus said, "If you love those who love you, what reward will you get? Are not even the tax collectors doing that? And if you greet only your brothers, what are you doing more than others? Do not even pagans do that? Be perfect, therefore, as your heavenly Father is perfect" (Matt. 5:46-48, NIV).

Jesus is saying, in essence, "If you love those who love you and hang out with your friends and treat them well . . . so what? What does that prove? Even non-Christians love people who love them. I'm asking you to be different."

Just as Jesus has given us radical principles of discipleship, He repeatedly asks us to go one step farther. Consider these upside-down commands about relationships found in the Sermon on the Mount (Matt. 5–7).

- *Love your enemies and pray for those who persecute you.* Our tendency is to hate our "enemy"—that guy at the office who keeps trying to take credit for everything and make us look incompetent.
- *If someone strikes your right cheek, turn to him the other also.* Our tendency is to slap back—cut off the guy on the freeway who cut us off.

- *If someone forces you to go one mile, go with him two miles.* Our tendency is to make sure no one takes advantage of us.
- *Freely forgive those who don't deserve it—over and over again.* Our tendency is to wait for—or demand— an apology before we even consider forgiveness.
- *Judge yourself first—and more harshly than others.* Our tendency is to be hypercritical of others and to be slow to see our own errors.

We live in a culture that tells us to forget about others. Think only of yourself. Other people are out for themselves, and if you lower your guard, they will rip you off. They will take advantage of you. Your main job in life is to look out for number one.

We think, *What about me? What about my needs?* What if we adjusted our thinking to *Forget about me. What about that person over there?*

GOD'S LOVE IS NOT ABSTRACT OR PASSIVE. IT ENGAGES, WORKS, AND MOVES.

And if someone hurts you, we think it's OK if you hurt them back, get your pound of flesh. We exalt vengeance as a virtue, and we scoff at the person who forgives or turns the other cheek. If someone offends you, sue them. That's the operative phrase of the day.

Jesus is saying here that we have to do a flip-flop. We can't let this world squeeze us into its mold.

None of this comes naturally. But that's just the point, and that's the reason this love is powerful. Love isn't a feeling; love is fully love only when it acts. God's love is not abstract or passive. It is active. It engages, works, and moves. And that's good news, because it means that we can learn to love. We can grow in love. We can learn to love God's way.

169

God's Love Lessons

When one wants to get a clear picture of how this love Jesus commands us to have is supposed to look, 1 Corinthians 13 is a great place to start. It is perhaps the most definitive chapter on love in the Bible, and it goes straight to the heart of our struggles to love in the most daily and intimate settings.

But this section about love is useful to us because it does not focus so much on what love is. Rather, it focuses on what love does and does not do. The purpose of Paul's little prism here in 1 Corinthians 13 is not to give a technical analysis of love but to break it into understandable pieces so that we can more easily apply it in practical ways. If you really want to feel uncomfortable, go to 1 Corinthians 13, take out the word *love,* and put your name in its place. That can be discouraging. But there's another name you can insert in there that fits very well: Jesus. And as we read these verses, you will see that this passage is a true portrait of who Jesus is.

> *Love suffers long and is kind; love does not envy; love does not parade itself, is not puffed up; does not behave rudely, does not seek its own, is not provoked, thinks no evil; does not rejoice in iniquity, but rejoices in the truth; bears all things, believes all things, hopes all things, endures all things.* 1 Cor. 13:4-7, NKJV

The first thing we are told is that love is patient. Another way to translate that phrase is to say that love is long tempered. The word used here is common in the New Testament and is used almost exclusively with reference to being patient with people rather than being patient with circumstances or events. Love is willing to be inconvenienced or taken advantage of by a person over and over again.

Stephen's last words as he had his young life taken from him are a good example of patient love. As he was being stoned to death, he said, "Lord, do not hold this sin against them" (Acts

7:60, NIV). This is the same kind of love Jesus spoke of that turns the other cheek. This kind of love has as its primary concern not its own welfare but the welfare of others.

God's love is patient. It is long tempered.

Perhaps there is a person you work with or maybe a member of your family. This person may not be a Christian and seems to always be giving you a hard time. He makes jokes at your expense, quickly reminds you when you are not practicing what you preach, bombards you with difficult questions, and so on. You have thought about letting him really have it; you know, just giving him a piece of your mind. God knows he deserves it.

But instead, you just keep loving him. You try your best to answer his questions. You thank him when he points out that you are not living as you ought. Don't you realize how powerful that attitude and behavior are when coupled with the message you proclaim? It's a practically irresistible combination!

Remember Stephen. I believe it was his love that penetrated the hardened shell around the heart of Saul of Tarsus. Saul was holding the robes of the people who were stoning Stephen. He must have heard Stephen praying that God would forgive all of them.

The next attribute mentioned is kindness. To be kind means to be useful, serving, gracious. It is active goodwill. It does not merely desire the welfare of others; Philippians 2:3-4 says, "Let nothing be done through selfish ambition or conceit, but in lowliness of mind let each esteem others better than himself. Let each of you look out not only for his own interests, but also for the interests of others" (NKJV).

Love is active. If you wait for this emotion to come, you may never experience kindness. You may say to yourself, "I just don't feel kind; therefore it would be hypocritical of me to help that person. I don't feel the emotion, so it wouldn't be sincere if I were to reach out to her."

Just be kind, even if you don't feel kind. That's what God's love is.

Paul goes on to give us eight descriptions of what love is *not,* beginning with envious and jealous.

There are two kinds of jealousy. One says, "I want what someone else has." If they have a better car, house, job, even wife or husband, we secretly, and maybe not so secretly, wish we had the same. Isn't it amazing how you can be completely content with what you have until you see someone who has more of something or simply something different?

When I was a little boy, I had gotten a great haul one Christmas—lots of toys. I was so happy—until I went over to my friend's house. He had gotten a toy I'd never seen before. It was a little plastic scuba diver. You put batteries in him, and his little flippers kicked in the water. I thought that was the coolest toy ever made, and suddenly all of my toys were meaningless. I figured that my mom didn't really care about me. I actually went home and said, "Why didn't you get me this toy?"

Why did I feel that way? I was jealous. I wanted what he had.

Just accept the fact that there are always going to be people better off than you are. No matter how high you climb your ladder, how handsome or beautiful you are, or how successful in your field, someone is going to walk right over you. They are going to go past you. *How come they can do that?* Jealousy possesses us.

The second kind of jealousy is more subtle. I don't want what someone has. I wish *that person* didn't have what he or she has. I am so jealous of what they have that I would rather it be taken away from them. That's more than selfishness. It's actually desiring evil for someone else.

A familiar story in the Old Testament illustrates this kind of jealousy well. There were two mothers who both had babies, and they were all asleep in the same room. One night one of the mothers rolled over on her newborn and suffocated it, and it died. So she took the live baby from the other sleeping mother and put it in her bed and replaced it with her own dead baby.

When they woke up the next morning, the other mother saw immediately that this dead baby was not hers. "This is your baby. Why did you do this?" she asks the other woman.

"That's your baby. I can't help it if it died," she answers.

"You took my baby."

"No. It's my baby."

So they went to see King Solomon, who was renowned for his God-given wisdom. Both mothers were claiming to be the baby's mother. Solomon asked for wisdom from the Lord. Then he said, "I have the answer. Let's cut the baby in half. You can have one half. You can have the other."

The real mother said, "No. Just give the baby to her. She can have it."

The other woman said, "I like the idea. Cut the baby in half."

Then Solomon said, "I know who the real mother is. Give it to this woman, the one who wanted the child to live."

Jealousy in its extreme is willing to see all kinds of people suffer. James 3:14-16 says, "If you are bitterly jealous and there is selfish ambition in your hearts, don't brag about being wise. That is the worst kind of lie. . . . For wherever there is jealousy and selfish ambition, there you will find disorder and every kind of evil" (NLT).

TRUE LOVE HAS GOOD MANNERS. THAT'S SOMETHING THAT IS LARGELY LOST TODAY. WE SAY, "IF MY BEHAVIOR OFFENDS SOMEONE ELSE, THAT'S THEIR PROBLEM."

God's love is not jealous. And as we read on, it "does not parade itself."

Some people want everybody else to know how much they paid for a certain item or how high their IQ is or even how spiritual they think they are. They may brag about how much time they spend in prayer or how many people they have personally led to the Lord. They may go on and on about their church—its programs and big budget. God's kind of love does not brag.

Bragging is the other side of jealousy. Jealousy is wanting what someone else has. Bragging is trying to make others jealous of what we have.

In verse 5 of 1 Corinthians we're told that love does not behave rudely. True love has good manners. That's something that is largely lost today. We say, "If my behavior offends someone else, that's their problem. They have to get over it." But you are part of the body of Christ, and you should consider what other people are experiencing.

In this day of "road rage" and downright rudeness practically everywhere, a bit of kindness and some good manners can go a long way.

Verse 5 tells us that God's love is not provoked. It is not aroused to anger. It thinks no evil, which means it doesn't keep a record of the wrongs that are done to it. Unlike a common human response:

Someone wrongs you, and you say, "I can't believe you did that again."

"Again? When did I do it?"

"Fourteen years ago. Actually, fourteen years, three months, two weeks, ten hours, twenty-eight minutes, and four seconds."

"Are you crazy?"

"I keep records. Because I don't get mad; I get even."

That's not God's love.

Someone took advantage of you. Forget about it. They do it again. Forget about it. Don't worry about it. Just let it go. It doesn't matter. That's how God's love is.

Listen to this: Love "believes all things." Another way to translate this statement in verse 7 is to say that love believes all *good* things or love believes the best. It means that as a member of the body of Christ, a Christian who is loving, you are not always suspicious of others. You are not a cynic. If a fellow member of the church is accused of something wrong, you will consider him or her innocent until proven guilty. Not only that, you will stick up for that person.

But how often someone will come and say, "Did you hear about so-and-so?"

"No. What?"

"He has been accused of this and that."

"I always knew it." How often we will believe a rumor.

Rather, you should say, "Stop right there. Have you gone to so-and-so and talked about it?"

"No. I can't go to him. He would deny it."

"Maybe he didn't do it. Let's go to him right now. Because I don't believe he would do such a thing."

You should stick up for that person. But, no, in these days so often we will believe the worst. And then we will even add to it.

But then how sad it is and how embarrassing it is when we find out this was a complete fabrication and we actually fanned the flame of the gossip/slander fire by believing it and even spreading it to others. How hard it is when something unkind or untrue is said about us and we find that people believe it without even asking us. That's not the way we should be. God's love believes the best of every person.

Finally, verse 7 says that love *endures* all things. It refuses to give up. It refuses to surrender, to stop believing or hoping. Love will simply not stop loving.

You may be thinking, *Now, Greg, please. How could we ever live up to these standards? It's impossible.*

Yes, it is. By human effort it's impossible. But this is what we should be aiming toward. The Bible says God's love is shed abroad in our heart by the Holy Spirit. We need to cooperate with that by saying, "Lord, I am not this way. I am not always thinking the best of every person. I am not always mannerly, kind, or long tempered. Lord, I acknowledge my weakness, and I want to change."

The Bible tells us that the fruit of the Spirit is love. And this fruit will come as a result of abiding in Christ, of seeking to be more like Him each and every day.

PASTOR TO PASTOR
Five Ways to Love the World

James tells us that people will know we have faith by our works (see James 2:14-24). Faith justifies us before God. Works justify us before people. This world is desperate to see tangible demonstrations of the church loving, not condemning.

Here are some practical ideas (ones that we have practiced at our church).

1. Run a home for unwed mothers.
People know that we Christians are against abortion. Instead of waving placards down at the local abortion clinic, how about establishing a home for unwed mothers? We should provide a place where these mothers-to-be can be encouraged and given the means to carry their pregnancies to term, whether that means helping them make motherhood work for themselves or finding adoptive parents for the baby.

In addition to a home, our church also has a hotline for pregnant women; it's called Heartline. They call, maybe thinking we will refer them to the local abortion clinic. Instead, we encourage them to carry their pregnancy to term.

2. Minister to people in convalescent homes.
So many of our elderly people have been forgotten and, in some cases, completely abandoned by their family and friends. A little love on the part of a Christian there can go a long way.

We send people from our church over at Christmastime to sing Christmas carols for them. But all through the year, teams of people from our congregation go and read to them, sing to them, just be there. Many have come to know Christ as a result.

3. *Feed hungry people.*
We go out on Saturdays into the local parks and set up a little kitchen and feed people.

We have our worship group get up and sing some songs; then someone shares a gospel message; then we feed them a great meal.

During Christmas we also distribute special baskets filled with food for a Christmas dinner (with all the trimmings!), along with gospel tracts.

4. *Distribute clothing.*
Our church has a ministry called The Lord's Closet.

We ask people from our congregation to give us their unwanted clothing. We store it and give it to people who are in need. We also take clothing to the parks when we're feeding people and distribute it there.

5. *Visit prisoners.*
Visiting prisoners who, like the elderly, have been forgotten by family and friends, can really make a difference in their life.

We have teams that go into our prisons and juvenile halls and share the gospel with the inmates, and the result has been many of them coming to know Jesus Christ.

One in Spirit
Until now we've been talking about how to express love in relationships and to the world in general. But what about love in the church—locally and at large? The world needs to know God's

love. We must remember that the world is watching. And ultimately it is our love for each other in the church that is one of our greatest illustrations of who Christ is.

We, the church, are God's representatives on earth. And if we present to the world a church that is full of dissension, how can we effectively present Christ? He said that a building divided against itself cannot stand. And yet the church today is so often a setting for squabbles and dissension. We behave just like the world, only we do it in a beautiful building and attach spiritual terms to our ugly behavior.

Remember the love and unity of the early church described in Acts 2? That is our example. The original language used to describe this kind of love, here and other places in the Word, is the Greek word *koinonia*. We have many translations of this word into the English language, the most common being the word *fellowship*. But it can also be translated into the words *communion, distribution, contribution, partnership, partakership*. It describes a kind of love that is based on joint effort and purpose.

You know, some Christians actually have a hard time with Christians. It's easier to love people in the world because they don't know any better. They're supposed to be sinners. But those in the family of Christ . . . sometimes it's hardest to love those nearest to us in the pew. We expect more of them and from them (and they of us). And too often the result is bitterness and dissension.

The upside-down church is a church that is committed to loving at all costs. It is ready to make peace, to promote harmony, to lay aside pride and differences. A lot of churches are looking around for the right growth plan or the right inner framework. And that's great. God's church needs administration and organization. But what if we really worked on love?

When the world peeks in the windows of your church, what does it see? Does it see a bunch of people who really love each other? Does it see unity? fellowship? Or does the world look in your church and see just another organization or institution where people compete and strive and argue? Do they see us competing to serve or struggling for positions of power? Jesus said "By this all will know that you are My disciples, if you have love for one another" (John 13:35, NKJV).

It was this very thing that originally got my attention as an unbeliever. It was 1970. The sixties
were over, but the ideas of love and
brotherhood were still being
talked about. There was still the
belief that we, the younger generation, would not go the way of the
Establishment. We would cast
aside labels and prejudice and
really love each other as brothers
and sisters in the human family.

THE UPSIDE-DOWN CHURCH IS READY TO MAKE PEACE, TO PROMOTE HARMONY, TO LAY ASIDE PRIDE AND DIFFERENCES.

A sweet sentiment—it just didn't work. I quickly realized that we were chasing after a mirage. I still loved the idea; I just felt it was basically unattainable. Then I began to notice this group of very committed Christians on my high school campus. We very unaffectionately referred to them as the "Jesus freaks."

They seemed to really be experiencing what others only talked about. They called each other brother and sister but somehow seemed to mean it. After a class was over, I would see them hugging each other and saying strange things like, "I'll be praying for you!"

Having always been quite skeptical, I had a hard time believ-
ing this was not all some kind of act. So I started watching the Christians very carefully. They were starting to bug me a little bit, because if they were right, then that meant I was wrong. If God could actually be known and they had a relationship with

Him, that meant that I did not. So I watched them day in and day out, just waiting for one of them to slip up or break ranks and announce, "This has all been a big act."

But that never happened—for one simple reason. It was real. They actually did love one another. It was that fact that initially got me looking into the claims of Christ.

How would you, and how would your church, hold up under such scrutiny?

ELEVEN

KNOCK, KNOCK, WHO'S PRAYING?
The Power of
Upside-Down Prayer

SOMETIMES the Bible reminds me of the number one rule of fiction writing. It goes something like this: Get your character into a terribly hopeless, perilous position, a real dilemma with no way out. And then, just when things can't get any worse for your hero—make them much, much worse.

Of course, in the Bible this is usually where God steps in. And unlike a fiction story, God's stories are intended to do more than keep us on the edge of our seat. He wants us to understand how His kingdom principles work. And so He doesn't just say, "Pray." He *shows* through the lives of others what happens when people pray—and when they don't.

In Acts 12, starting in verse 1, we read a great story about how God redeemed a desperate situation through the power of prayer.

First, let's meet the bad guy—Herod. This name, *Herod,* appears quite often in the New Testament because there were actually a number of Herods, all related. The first Herod we read about was Herod the Great. He was king during the time of the birth of Christ. He had a son named Herod Antipas, who was eventually responsible for the beheading of John the Baptist. This Herod also had a son named Herod (Did anyone suggest

"Frank" or "Sam"?). This is Herod Agrippa, and he's the Herod we read about in Acts.

> *Now about that time Herod the king stretched out his hand to harass some from the church. Then he killed James the brother of John with the sword. And because he saw that it pleased the Jews, he proceeded further to seize Peter also.* Acts 12:1-3, NKJV

Immediately we learn that Herod Agrippa was a typical politician in the most negative sense. He wasn't interested in serving the people he represented but in being popular and powerful among them. Whatever made them happy, he'd do. Today he'd be one of those scandal-plagued politicians who shapes his policies around opinion polls and knows how to make use of a pandering media.

We read on:

> *Now it was during the Days of Unleavened Bread. So when he had arrested him, he put him in prison, and delivered him to four squads of soldiers to keep him, intending to bring him before the people after Passover.* Acts 12:3-4, NKJV

Herod had a reason for stationing so many soldiers around Peter in jail. He didn't want another resurrection episode—or another escape attempt. In the forefront of his mind was the tomb fiasco—the men guarding Jesus' tomb had fallen asleep. He was probably thinking also about the last time Peter was in prison. Just when Herod was sure Peter was under lock and key, he'd escaped.

Picture it. Someone said, "Hey, Peter is out there in the streets preaching."

"No," replied Herod with confidence, "Peter's in prison. Put him there myself."

"Oh, really? So then why is he out there preaching Christ?"

"What?!"

Peter must have seemed to Herod like James Bond does to his enemies in the movies. So it's not surprising that this time Herod took every precaution against Peter's escape—short of sitting on top of Peter himself.

Now let's consider Peter's position for a moment. He's the good guy in this story, and he's not just in prison; he's behind two locked gates, chained to two guards, and guarded by fourteen more. His fellow apostle James has been killed, and the situation for the church, as well as for Peter, has gone from grim to seemingly hopeless.

So what does the church do? We read on: "Peter was therefore kept in prison, but constant prayer was offered to God for him by the church" (Acts 12:5, NKJV).

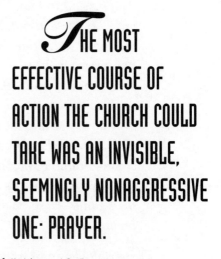

THE MOST EFFECTIVE COURSE OF ACTION THE CHURCH COULD TAKE WAS AN INVISIBLE, SEEMINGLY NONAGGRESSIVE ONE: PRAYER.

Notice that we don't read "The church boycotted all products made by Rome" or "The church had a sit-in in Herod's court." They didn't write to their local representative down there at the Roman Senate to do something about this immediately.

Some of the political options I mentioned do have their place. But the church at large must remember that these actions aren't the solution. They're human methods, and they are attempts to change people. *The most effective course of action the church could take was an invisible, seemingly nonaggressive one: prayer.*

We pick up the story again in verse 6.

> *And when Herod was about to bring him out, that night Peter was sleeping, bound with two chains between two soldiers; and the guards before the door were keeping the*

prison. Now behold, an angel of the Lord stood by him, and a light shone in the prison; and he struck Peter on the side and raised him up, saying, "Arise quickly!" And his chains fell off his hands. Then the angel said to him, "Gird yourself and tie on your sandals"; and so he did. And he said to him, "Put on your garment and follow me." So he went out and followed him, and did not know that what was done by the angel was real, but thought he was seeing a vision. When they were past the first and the second guard posts, they came to the iron gate that leads to the city, which opened to them of its own accord; and they went out and went down one street, and immediately the angel departed from him. And when Peter had come to himself, he said, "Now I know for certain that the Lord has sent His angel, and has delivered me from the hand of Herod and from all the expectation of the Jewish people." Acts 12:6-11, NKJV

There is power in prayer, and Peter knew it. The early church knew it. Though all of the doors were closed, one remained open: the door of prayer. This was and is the church's secret weapon and its source of power.

A Question of Faith

If this story stopped there, it would make the point that prayer works. However, if you read on, you'll notice that the disciples didn't do *everything* right. They prayed, yes. They prayed continually—earnestly, in unity. But they also doubted.

So, when he had considered this, he came to the house of Mary, the mother of John whose surname was Mark, where many were gathered together praying. And as Peter knocked at the door of the gate, a girl named Rhoda came to answer. When she recognized Peter's voice, because of her gladness she did not open the gate, but ran in and announced that Peter stood before the gate. But they said to her, "You are beside yourself!" Yet she kept insisting that it was so. So they said, "It is his angel." Now Peter continued knocking; and when they opened the door and saw him, they were astonished. Acts 12:12-16, NKJV

Picture this scene. Peter runs over to the house. He knocks on the door. Inside, the gathered church is praying. "Oh, Lord," they may have pleaded, "this is the last night before our beloved Peter is to be executed, as James was. Dear God, please deliver our—"

A knock sounds, but they keep praying, "Deliver our brother, and somehow get him out safely—"

There's the knock on the door again. Finally Rhoda gets up to answer it. She reappears moments later and interrupts. "Excuse me—"

"Lord, this is Peter, the Peter that you love. We pray—"

"Excuse me."

"What is it?"

"Peter is at the door."

"Are you crazy?"

Notice now the plural pronouns. "They" opened the door and "they" were astonished. It seems that for safety's sake the believers decided to open the door cautiously and face together what was on the other side. They are peering out . . .

And there's Peter, smiling. "Hi, everybody. God answered your prayers. Here I am."

I am so glad this is in the Bible. Not just because it's comical but because it reminds all of us that the apostles and leaders of the early church were people just like us.

But let's not miss the spiritual point. Not only does God answer prayer, but His power is not dependent on our praying perfectly. This passage, among others, debunks the popular teaching among some that says our faith makes all the difference in prayer and that faith is some kind of active force that we have to harness and use. We are told that we have to say the right thing. We have to give a "positive confession." We have to speak the miracle into existence. According to this theology, almost everything about prayer revolves around the quality of our faith.

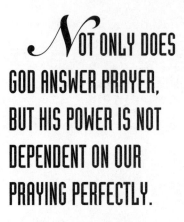

Not only does God answer prayer, but His power is not dependent on our praying perfectly.

It certainly was a good thing for Peter that this isn't true! Faith has a crucial place in prayer, but we should never say or think, "I want to pray for this, but I don't think I have enough faith." Instead, we should pray anyway, saying, "Lord, I believe; help my unbelief."

We must remember that there are certain things only God can do. We must do what only *we* can do. Only I can repent of my sin. Only I can believe the promises of God. Only I can discipline myself.

But only God can convert people. Only God can create a soul. Only God can forgive sin and take our guilt away. I have got to do my part, and God will do His part. My part is to pray in obedience and with as much faith as I can muster. God's part is to answer prayer.

An Upside-Down Approach to Prayer

How easy it is for us to approach prayer—our communication with God—from a human perspective. We begin to think of prayer as if it were a Coke machine. Insert the requests, and wait for the answers to come out. Or we may begin to think of prayer as a way to get God to conform to our wishes rather than help us conform to His.

Prayer in itself is a completely spiritual act. And effective prayer operates on God's upside-down kingdom principles. God describes these principles for us clearly in His word. Again and again He tells how we should pray, what we should pray for, and when we should pray.

1. Pray as the first resort—not the last.
When the believers learned that Peter was in prison, they said, "All right, we need a big gun here. We have trouble. What are we going to do? Let's pray."

Unfortunately, this is usually not our first inclination. We pray after we've exhausted all our own means of rescue. We pray when it becomes clear that we are completely helpless. For example, let's say you don't have enough money to pay your bills. If you're like most of us, first you might borrow the money from a credit card. If it's maxed out, you might call a friend to borrow some money. If that fails, you might go so far as to call a relative. And then finally, perhaps after trying strangers from the phone book, you reluctantly pray. At this point, what have you got to lose?

But what you should be asking yourself is, *What have I lost by not praying?*

The Bible says, "You do not have, because you do not ask God"

I HAVE PRAYED FOR SOME REALLY STUPID THINGS. AND I AM SO GLAD THE LORD OVERRULED AND SAID, "OH, GREG, FORGET IT. I'M NOT GOING TO DO THAT TO YOU."

(James 4:2, NIV). It is my firm conviction that many Christians don't have God's provision, healing, and blessing in their lives simply because they have not asked for it.

I don't believe that God heals everyone or will give you everything you might ask for. But many of us are missing out on many of the things God has for us simply because we don't ask. Prayer should not be a last resort. It should be the first thing we do.

2. Pray for what God wants—not what you want.

Our natural impulse is to pray for what we want, but upside-down prayer is in line with what *God* wants. Prayer that is powerful is offered according to God's will. First John 5:14-15 says, "This is the confidence that we have in Him, that if we ask anything according to His will, He hears us. And . . . we have the petitions that we have asked of Him" (NKJV).

This is reassuring because it means that nothing lies outside of the reach of prayer except what lies outside of the will of God. And we should be grateful. I have prayed for some really stupid things in my life. And I am so glad the Lord overruled and said, "Oh, Greg, forget it. I'm not going to do that to you. I love you too much."

So what we want to do is get into an alignment with the will of God. How do you learn about God's will, about His purpose, His character and mind, His heart, and His plan? Through the pages of Scripture and through spending time talking to Him.

There's really no point in praying for God to give you something if Scripture states that what you want is immoral or clearly outside of God's will. For instance, let's say that two people are in an immoral relationship. They don't need to bother praying that God will bless this union, because the Bible clearly says, "Thou shall not commit adultery."

But there are certain things God tells us we can *always* pray for—because they are always His will. For example, He tells us we can pray for wisdom. James says, "If any of you lacks wisdom, he should ask God, who gives generously to all without finding fault, and it will be given to him" (James 1:5, NIV).

We can always pray for His provision. Philippians 4:19 says, "My God will meet all your needs according to his glorious riches in Christ Jesus" (NIV). This verse doesn't say that God will provide for our "greeds." If He turns down a request, we don't need that thing the way we think we do.

We can always pray for protection. Psalm 91:5-7 says, "Do not be afraid of the terrors of the night, nor fear the dangers of the day, nor dread the plague that stalks in darkness, nor the disaster that strikes at midday. Though a thousand fall at your side, though ten thousand are dying around you, these evils will not touch you" (NLT).

Prayer is not our permission to order God around. He is not "our bellhop who art in heaven." Prayer is not moving God your way; it is moving yourself His way. And that is the amazing thing about prayer. When you spend time in prayer, God will help you turn your faulty thinking upside down, and you'll begin to discover the joys of praying according to His will.

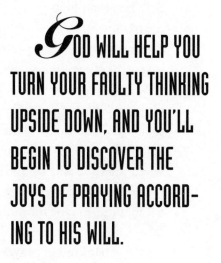

GOD WILL HELP YOU TURN YOUR FAULTY THINKING UPSIDE DOWN, AND YOU'LL BEGIN TO DISCOVER THE JOYS OF PRAYING ACCORDING TO HIS WILL.

3. Pray earnestly—even when you don't feel like it.
Remember what we read in Acts 12:5: "Constant prayer was offered to God for him by the church" (NKJV).

The word *constant* not only speaks of a regular, continuous prayer but in the original language can be translated "earnestly" or even "with agony." It is a word that implies a soul's stretching out or reaching forward to accomplish or touch something.

Our natural impulse is to be lazy. We might pray, "Lord, would you do this? Thank you. Amen." Or "Lord, save the world. Amen." But the right approach to prayer is specific, focused, and heartfelt. "Lord, I am bringing this person before you today. Lord, I pray you will save her soul. I pray that you will bring her to a realization of her own need for you. Lord, I pray you will send Christians who speak the truth to cross her path today. . . ."

4. Pray with persistence.

This point is related to the last one. How easy it is for us to ask with passion—but then give up quickly when we don't see change immediately. God answers prayer on His timetable, not on ours. And He has told us that it's OK to ask more than once. In fact, in the parable of the widow knocking on the judge's door, Jesus was commanding us to be persistent. And Jesus said, "Man ought always to pray and never give up" (Luke 18:1, paraphrased).

Notice that Peter was not released until the very night before his planned execution. The Lord delayed His answer. The Christians were praying, and nothing was happening. They kept praying, and Peter was still in prison. But they kept praying still. And when the time was right, God answered.

Perhaps you have been praying for a loved one's salvation for a long time, maybe for months or even years. Keep praying—if it takes thirty years. Don't do the ordinary thing and give up or give in. That kind of prayer will never change the world. But persistent, passionate prayer will avail much in God's time. And that's a promise.

5. Pray with others—not just by and for yourself.

Often our impulse is to mind our own business when it comes to prayer, but upside-down prayer seeks others who share our burden—and shares theirs as well.

"Constant prayer was offered to God for [Peter] by the church." There is power in united prayer. It's important that the church pray together—in regular worship services and outside regular services. Church people need to pray for each other and for the world.

When we hold our crusades, we encourage people to pray together for unbelievers. We pass out a card and ask each person to write down the names of five people they know who are not Christians. Then they will gather in groups of three or four and pray for these people.

Why is that important? Because Jesus said, "If two of you agree on earth concerning anything that they ask, it will be done for them by My Father in heaven" (Matt. 18:19, NKJV).

Jesus is not simply emphasizing the idea of two people in agreement *in general.* He is implying that these are two people with the same God-given burden who are sure of His will, in agreement with the Spirit of God and with one another.

With whom are you praying? Are you taking advantage of joint prayers? Sometimes we can have faith for something that someone else does not have faith for. And when we extend our prayers beyond our own private agenda, we put ourselves in a position to be used by God. Praying with someone is not a small thing. It is one of the greatest things you have to offer a brother or sister in the Lord.

6. Pray with faith in God—regardless of His answer.
So often we confuse the prayer of faith—the prayer that trusts in God—with the prayer of confidence in a specific outcome. And when God's answer does not match ours, we wonder if we didn't have enough faith. We wonder if God even heard our prayer. I prayed for a job at Microsoft, and I didn't get it. How much better to put our faith in God, not in what we think His answers should be.

ARE YOU TAKING ADVANTAGE OF JOINT PRAYERS? SOMETIMES WE CAN HAVE FAITH FOR SOMETHING THAT SOMEONE ELSE DOESN'T HAVE FAITH FOR.

In the story we read, Peter seemed to have this kind of faith. How do we know? Verse 6 says that Peter was sleeping. That's amazing in itself. Would you be able to sleep if you knew you were going to be put to death the next morning? Peter was probably the only Christian in Jerusalem asleep that night. Everyone else was praying for him. Then Peter thought he was having a vision when the angel led him out of prison. We might think that if Peter had had real faith, he would have known that it wasn't a vision, that he was really being rescued.

WHEN WE EXTEND OUR PRAYERS BEYOND OUR OWN AGENDA, WE PUT OURSELVES IN A POSITION TO BE USED BY GOD.

Peter's faith was in God, not in a specific answer to prayer. Keep in mind that the church must have also prayed for James as well as for Peter. Yet James was killed. And Peter knew this. His faith in God would not have been misplaced—even if he had been executed that night. Peter had faith that God heard his and the church's prayers. But he could sleep because his faith was big enough to trust God's will—*even if he wasn't rescued.*

True faith in prayer hinges on our trust in God, in His goodness and His rightness. It doesn't hinge on how much confidence we can muster that God is going to answer a specific prayer a certain way.

Miracles Knocking

Maybe you are in a situation right now and you're saying, "It is hopeless. I don't know what to do."

Pray.

"But I just—"

Pray. Let your prayer be unto God. Get your Christian friends to pray with you. Pray with fervor and with energy. Pray continually. Don't give up. You just don't know what the Lord is going to do.

At the beginning of this story we see a seemingly all-powerful Herod wreaking havoc on the church. Herod had on his side the power of the sword and the threat of prison. What did the church have? They had prayer. And they used it.

The story ends with Herod's giving a great speech that was met with the adulation of the people chanting, "The voice of a god and not of a man!" The Jewish historian Josephus adds the detail that when Herod gave this speech, he was dressed in a tunic that was made completely of silver and shone so brightly that the people hailed him as a god.

Picture this. Here was Herod in his silver frock. The sun was reflecting off him. The people were chanting in unison, "The voice of a god and not of a man!"

And then God's judgment came upon him, and he died. That is how the chapter ends.

Look at how things change. The chapter opened with James dead, Peter in prison, and Herod in triumph. It closed with Herod dead, Peter free, and the Word of God in triumph. In the end God will always have His way. It ain't over till it's over.

The kind of prayer that took place in the early church is the kind of prayer we need today. A miracle might be outside the very same door God seems to have shut. Prayer is how we open the door to receive it.

> *T*RUE FAITH IN PRAYER DOESN'T HINGE ON HOW MUCH CONFIDENCE WE CAN MUSTER THAT GOD IS GOING TO ANSWER A SPECIFIC PRAYER A CERTAIN WAY.

Maybe you're a pastor whose church is having conflict. Or maybe your attendance has dropped off. Have you prayed? Have you prayed with faith in God?

Today, God wants to do the same things in our world and in your life that He was doing in Peter's day. Be careful. Is there a miracle knocking?

THE LORD'S PRAYER

Question: How do you recommend that a church prioritize prayer?

Answer: In addition to our many prayer meetings through the week, we have done a special intercessory prayer meeting on Sunday morning.

We modeled it after the Lord's Prayer. The prayer Jesus taught us, which really is a model for all prayer, breaks into two sections. The first three statements ("Our Father who art in heaven, hallowed be Your name, Your kingdom come, Your will be done") deal with God's glory. The second ("Give us this day our daily bread, forgive us our debts, lead not into temptation") deal with our need.

So we would start with teaching segment number one. This would introduce the prayer, and the teacher (I would have three of our associate pastors teach this) would teach on coming before God with reverence and thanksgiving and ask for His will and kingdom in our life. Then there would be a musical break that would emphasize in song these themes, and individual people we had already picked from our congregation, who would be sitting on the platform, would come and pray relatively short prayers along those lines.

Then we would go to the next sections and include intercessory prayer for our leaders, nation, church, etc. There would be prayer for those in special need and so forth. It's a way to model prayer and at the same time drop it right in the lap of someone on Sunday morning who would not necessarily attend one of our other prayer meetings.

TWELVE

MORE THAN MUSIC
How to Worship in
Spirit and Truth

A FEW YEARS ago I was given an opportunity to go to a Paul McCartney concert at the Anaheim Stadium. I've liked many of his songs, especially ones he recorded with the Beatles. We have held our crusades at the same venue over the years, so I was intrigued by the idea of seeing a different event there. And the price was right; the seats were given to me free of charge.

As it turned out, a lot that went on felt very familiar. For example, Paul McCartney got on stage and went through his litany of Beatles songs, wildly shaking his hair as if he were still twenty.

But something happened toward the end of the concert that caught me a little off guard. As the strains of a well-known Beatle anthem began, suddenly the stage was lit up with a stained-glass motif, making it look quite a bit like a cathedral. And then thousands and thousands of Bic lighters lit the stadium, and everyone began to sway and sing along to the words of "Let It Be."

I didn't have a Bic lighter to hold up. But as I looked around at that scene, I thought, "This is about as close as this world gets to having a worship experience. The lights. The sense of unity. The voices lifted with affection and even a kind of reverence."

And then I was struck with how much more we Christians have in our worship experience. Think about it. We have a light much greater than a flimsy Bic. We have a Savior so much greater than any rock star. And when we gather together to sing, we really don't want to just "let it be." We want to change the world.

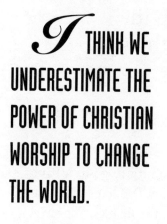

I THINK WE UNDERESTIMATE THE POWER OF CHRISTIAN WORSHIP TO CHANGE THE WORLD.

I think we underestimate the power of Christian worship to do just that—to change the world. For some reason, we stand in awe of the pop culture's power to influence kids through music. But the church is trying so hard to relate to a secular culture that too often we forget that this culture is an arena where our strengths lie as well. We forget that worship can be a powerful tool for evangelism.

Psalm 40:3 declares, "He has given me a new song to sing, a hymn of praise to our God. Many will see what he has done and be astounded. They will put their trust in the Lord" (NLT).

If we're going to turn the world upside down, we're not going to do it through human methods but through God's. And that means we should never underestimate the power of a simple song that is sung in His name.

Big Little Jesus Songs

The Bible tells us to give to God the sacrifice of praise that is the fruit of our lips (Heb. 13:15). But were you aware that this kind of worship experience is unique to the Christian faith? No other religion sings worship to their "leader" in the same way that Christians do. People of other faiths may chant. They may recite their prayers, but they don't clap, sing, and express adoration and praise the way Christians always have.

And why is this? We Christians actually have something wonderful to sing about. And we know that we have an actual Person to receive our praises.

I distinctly remember the first time I watched Christians worship. Before I became a Christian, I went to a high school Bible study. I didn't actually attend it, but I sat at a distance, where I could hear these teenagers singing what I thought were these silly little Jesus songs. I don't remember if anyone had a guitar. As they sang, I thought, *This is very strange. They are sitting on the front lawn of a high school campus singing songs about God. These guys are clearly mentally disturbed. I really feel sorry for them. Look at them!*

But over time, as I continued to watch and listen, it became clear to me that there was something very real and profound going on. It wasn't just that I could tell that these people really believed what they were singing. I could sense that Someone was really on the receiving end of their praise. They were clearly not just singing but communicating.

I COULD TELL THAT THESE PEOPLE BELIEVED WHAT THEY WERE SINGING. BUT, MORE THAN THAT, I SENSED THAT SOMEONE WAS ON THE RECEIVING END OF THEIR PRAISE.

And it was actually this—observing the true worship of Christians—that made me aware that there was a God and that I didn't know Him.

Remember when Paul and Silas began to praise God in jail? They had been arrested for preaching the gospel. Their backs had been ripped open with a Roman whip, their feet fastened in metal stocks and pulled as far apart as possible, causing excruciating pain. They were then thrown into a dark, cavelike hole filled with filth and stench. They could have become angry at God, but instead we read that they sang and rejoiced: "Around midnight, Paul and

Silas were praying and singing hymns to God, and the other prisoners were listening" (Acts 16:25, NLT). Instead of groans, songs issued from their mouths. Instead of cursing the men who had them arrested, they blessed God. Instead of complaining or calling on God to judge those who had inflicted their pain, Paul and Silas prayed. No wonder the other prisoners were listening to them.

When an earthquake shook the walls, the first thing the Philippian jailer said was, "What must I do to be saved?" It was obvious to him that Paul and Silas had been having a very real encounter with a very real God. Through worship the jailer had witnessed an intimate relationship between God and man in action, and it opened his heart to the truth of the gospel.

Compare what God accomplished through the apostle Paul's songs in a moldy cell to what Paul of the Beatles' songs accomplished!

Sometimes prior to a stadium crusade people have asked me, "Why do you have worship at these things? Many of the people coming aren't Christians anyway. They probably don't even know the songs. Why don't you just have performers or choirs sing?"

My answer is simple. When unbelievers find themselves surrounded by literally thousands of people truly worshiping God, immediately they say, "What is going on here?" They're aware that we're not just standing around singing songs, lighting Bics, or crooning the national anthem at a baseball game. We are singing to the Lord. And He is inhabiting the praises of His people.

Lessons from the Well

One of the key passages of Scripture on worship is found in a simple conversation Jesus had at a well with a woman who'd been married five times. We pick the conversation up in John chapter 4:

The woman said to Him, ". . . Our fathers worshiped on this mountain, and you Jews say that in Jerusalem is the place where one ought to worship." Jesus said to her, "Woman, believe Me, the hour is coming when you will neither on this mountain, nor in Jerusalem, worship the Father. You worship what you do not know; we know what we worship, for salvation is of the Jews. But the hour is coming, and now is, when the true worshipers will worship the Father in spirit and truth; for the Father is seeking such to worship Him. God is Spirit, and those who worship Him must worship in spirit and truth."
John 4:19-24, NKJV

What does it mean to worship in spirit and in truth? It simply means that we are to worship rightly with both our mind and our heart. You worship in truth when you worship the one true God and when you know who you're worshiping and why.

When we worship in truth, we are agreeing with God about who He is, what He can do and has done, and what He is asking of us. Then we respond by telling Him so. "Yes, Lord, You are very great. Yes, God, You are awesome, and I love You. I praise You and honor You for who You are and what You have done. I lift up Your name right now!"

WORSHIP IS GOING TO BE MORE EFFECTIVE WHEN IT IS BASED ON AN ACCURATE UNDERSTANDING OF WHO GOD IS.

This is why Bible study and worship go hand in hand and are both crucial to the church. Worship is going to be more effective when it is based on an accurate understanding of who God is. So as we learn more about His nature, His character, His plans, and His purposes, then our worship is in truth—a response to what we know is true about God.

Colossians 3:16 puts it all together and says, "Let the word of Christ dwell in you richly as you teach and admonish one another with all wisdom, and as you sing psalms, hymns and spiritual songs with gratitude in your hearts to God" (NIV). Notice the elements: teaching and worship. This is worshiping in truth, and it's why only a Christian is capable of truly worshiping God.

The second half of the equation, which the Word actually lists first, is worshiping in spirit. Our worship of God should engage the mind, but it should also engage the affections, the heart, and our emotions and spirit. That does not mean that worship has to necessarily be emotional or involve an outward emotional display to be "in spirit." But it does mean it can be.

If we see someone get excited at a football game and throw his hands in the air to cheer for his favorite player, we think nothing of it. But if someone comes to church and lifts his hands in reverence to the Creator of the universe, some will say, "Look at that fanatic!"

There is nothing wrong with expressing ourselves emotionally as we respond to our awesome God. In fact, the word *worship* comes from an old English word that could be translated "worth-ship." In other words, we praise and honor a God who is worth it, who deserves our praise. We are told in Revelation 5:12 that in heaven there is a loud voice saying, "Worthy is the Lamb, who was slain, to receive power and wealth and wisdom and strength and honor and glory and praise!" (NIV).

When God says, "worship in spirit and in truth," He's saying that we should above all worship sincerely. God doesn't want us to fake it with Him but to be honest in our worship. David had more problems than most people, and he poured them out even as he worshiped the Lord continually in his psalms. As a result of his worshiping with his spirit, again and again we see him come back to his senses about God's love for him.

The Pharisees thought they were experts on worship. They would even stand on the street corners and make sure that everyone knew they were worshiping. They would sound a trumpet and give their great gifts. They would recite their long prayers. But Jesus said, "Let me tell you something about these guys. You think they're true worshipers. But the truth is, they draw near to me with their mouth, but their hearts are far from me" (see Mark 7:6-7).

So we see that it is possible to appear to worship God but not be doing so in spirit and in truth.

Let's face it. The kind of praise that will change the world won't happen when people are dutifully singing out of a hymnal. We all have had times when we realize that we're just going through the motions. We're singing a song, not lifting our voice to our Savior. Or we're clapping and laughing without a thought for what we're actually celebrating.

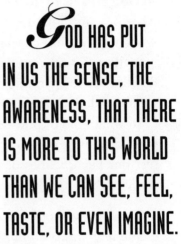

GOD HAS PUT IN US THE SENSE, THE AWARENESS, THAT THERE IS MORE TO THIS WORLD THAN WE CAN SEE, FEEL, TASTE, OR EVEN IMAGINE.

God wants us to engage in worship with intelligence as well as emotion as we learn to worship "in spirit and in truth."

Upside-Down Principles of Worship

The ability to worship is one of the distinguishing marks of humans as compared with animals. My dog doesn't sit in his backyard and lift his paws to the Lord and bark out his praises. Yes, he barks sometimes, but I guarantee he is not contemplating the wonders of eternity. He's probably thinking about food or strangers passing by.

In contrast, God has placed eternity in the human heart. That simply means that God has put in us the sense, the awareness, that there is more to this world than we can see, feel, taste, or even imagine.

A number of words are translated "worship" in the Bible. The one used most frequently, *shachah,* means to bow down and do homage. Unlike animals, human beings have a drive to bow down to something. To pay homage to something. To offer reverence and respect for God.

But we have something else animals don't have—pride. And so God asks us to do what we were uniquely created to do but what our sinful nature rebels against. In fact, many aspects of worship go against our natural tendencies. Worship is a spiritual act with spiritual consequences. And if we're not living upside down, if we're operating on the world's principles, then worship probably doesn't make much sense to us.

So what kind of praise is powerful, upside-down praise? And what kind of people offer it? When we look in the Scriptures, we see four key qualities of those people who changed the world through their upside-down praise of God.

*1. They lavishly and extravagantly praised
a God who needs nothing.*
Why does a God who has everything and needs nothing want us to worship Him?

A lot of people stumble over this. Our tendency is to praise people whom we think need it and who we believe look up to us and our opinion. We may praise a friend's golf swing as much for his sake as for any other reason. As a result, we can easily get stingy with God without even realizing it. *God doesn't need me to boost His ego!*

That's true. God may not need our worship, but He desires it. He wants a tender, intimate relationship with us, and praise is one way we express our affection. In fact, another word that is used for worship in the Bible is one that literally means to "kiss toward." So putting these two words together, we get a whole new idea of what intimate worship is and should be.

The Bible tells us in Psalm 63:3, "Because Your lovingkindness is better than life, my lips shall praise You" (NKJV).

That means that we need to verbally communicate our affection. A wife can feel that her husband doesn't love her because he never says it. Or we may know that our spouse loves us, but we still want to hear him or her say, "I love you. I appreciate you. I'm so glad you're in my life."

God knows that worship costs us something—time, concentration, and, sometimes, real effort. But that's also when our gift of affection or affirmation can mean the most to us—-and to Him.

Mary was an upside-down woman in the Bible. One time Jesus was in the home of Mary and her sister, Martha (see John 12). The Bible says that Mary got out a box of expensive ointment (some say it was worth an entire year's wages), broke it and anointed Jesus with it. The fragrance filled the room. She wiped His feet with her hair and tears.

Mary wanted to give Jesus something that was valuable and precious to her. So with complete abandon she poured a year's wages over his feet. But she didn't care about that. She was saying with these actions, "Lord, I want to show you in a tangible way my commitment to you."

In a similar way, when David bought a field from Ornan that he wanted to use for his worship of God, Ornan said, "You're the king. This is for the Lord. Take it." But David understood worship. He said, "I'm not going to give to the Lord that which costs me nothing. I will pay top dollar" (see 1 Chron. 21:24).

2. They worshiped the Lord even when they didn't feel like it.
An upside-down believer goes against his tendency to say, "Oh man. I have a cold. The car is not working properly. I'm not in the mood to worship today, so I won't."

Think about Job. In a matter of hours he lost his family, his possessions, and his health. Everything fell apart. And when it was all said and done, what did Job do? Curse God? No. The

Bible says he fell down and worshiped. He said, "Naked I came from my mother's womb, and naked shall I return there. The Lord gave, and the Lord has taken away; blessed be the name of the Lord" (Job 1:21, NKJV).

I worship God because He deserves my praise—not because I feel like it. That's important. You should worship Him because He is always worthy of your praise whether things are going badly or well. This doesn't mean that you worship and thank Him for the bad things. It means you give thanks in the midst of difficult circumstances. We're not required to give thanks for bad things like car wrecks and broken arms.

Ultimately we give thanks for the fact that God is still on the throne—no matter how bad things get. The Bible says, "Rejoice in the Lord always" (Phil. 4:4, NKJV). And when we praise God in spite of difficult circumstances, that's when non-Christians will listen to what we have to say.

Anybody can sing when things are going well. But when the bottom drops out, when hardship hits and you keep singing, that's something unique to the Christian—and it startles the world.

Back to the story of Paul and Silas in prison. After they've sung praises to God, there is a mighty earthquake. With the walls down, the other prisoners are free to escape. Realizing that the prisoners under his guard are escaping, the Philippian jailer prepares to commit suicide rather than face the penalty from his own superiors.

Suddenly, to his surprise, Paul shouts out, "Don't do yourself any harm—we are all still here!"

And do you know what the next words out of the jailer's mouth were? "Sirs, what must I do to be saved?" (He's certainly changed his tune—"Sirs"!)

The jailer is moved and deeply impressed by the faith of Paul and Silas—which has enabled them to worship God in such miserable circumstances and in such great pain. And they haven't escaped, even when they could have. All of this opens the jailer's heart to the message of the gospel (see Acts 16:25-33).

3. They wouldn't bow down to idols.
We were all created to worship. And everybody on the face of the earth *does* worship. We don't all worship the God of heaven. But we all worship someone or something. If you are not worshiping the true and living God, you will worship a god of your own making or some false god.

It may be a sports figure. It may be an actor or a musician. It may be your own body. But everybody bows at some kind of altar. Everyone, everywhere, worships. It's the fundamental drive of life. Even atheists, skeptics, Republicans, and Democrats worship. Insurance agents and lawyers worship. Because that is one of those unique distinctions of humanity.

The story is told of a Japanese warlord who was known as Hitioshi in the late 1500s. He decided that he wanted a colossal statue of Buddha created to put in a temple in Kyoto, Japan. So he got fifty thousand workers, who worked on it for five solid years—around the clock. They had just completed this colossal Buddhist statue and erected it in the temple, when the earthquake of 1596 struck. It brought the roof down on the shrine and ruined the statue. In a rage, Hitioshi fired an arrow at the fallen Buddha and yelled out, "I put you here at great expense, and you can't even look after your own temple."

Ultimately we give thanks for the fact that God is still on the throne—no matter how bad things get.

That's the problem with a false god. It can't hear you or see you. It's not even aware of you because it's not real.

But the true God, the living God, can not only take care of a temple; He can also take care of you.

4. They worshiped with their whole life.

Worship is not only what we do when we lift our hands or our voice. It's the way we live. We worship the Lord, or don't, through our life. We worship or not through the way we do our job. We worship or not through the way we give.

True worship is the living of our life in a way that is pleasing to God. Our singing and our prayer are only the outward manifestations of a life lived for the glory of God.

Hebrews 13:15-16 provides a good overview of what worship ought to be. "Through Jesus, therefore, let us continually offer to God a sacrifice of praise—the fruit of lips that confess his name. And do not forget to do good and to share with others, for with such sacrifices God is pleased" (NIV).

We can worship God just as much through the giving of our time and resources as we do through raising our hands and singing. Paul thanked the believers for the gift they had sent to him through a man named Epaphroditus. And in Philippians 4:18 Paul made this statement about this gift, showing that a gift can be an act of worship. He said, "I have received full payment and even more; I am amply supplied, now that I have received from Epaphroditus the gifts you sent. They are a fragrant offering, an acceptable sacrifice, pleasing to God" (NIV).

If you were to come to the church I pastor, Harvest Christian Fellowship, you would drive to Riverside, California, on a Sunday morning for one of our three services and pull into our parking lot. As you pulled in, someone standing out in the hot sun would direct you to a parking place. That man or woman is worshiping the Lord by giving time. If you take your children to their class, others will be waiting there to care for them. They are going to minister to your child until you return for them. They are worshiping the Lord with the gifts they have.

Then as you walked into the auditorium, an usher would welcome you, give you a bulletin, and help you find a seat. You would be led through the service by a worship team of skilled and God-honoring musicians. Then you would listen to me speak. And, we hope, all of it would be worship.

If you made a commitment to follow Christ, you would be met by a team of loving follow-up counselors, who would walk you through the basics of what it is to follow Jesus Christ.

First Corinthians 10:31 says, "Whatever you eat or drink or whatever you do, you must do all for the glory of God" (NLT).

Fullness of Joy

A final reason to worship is that it changes us. It changes our perspective on our problems, and it brings us into God's healing presence. David once wrote, "Better is one day in your courts than a thousand elsewhere" (Ps. 84:10, NIV).

But we don't worship God to *get* anything. The upside-down believer knows this. God doesn't want to be used as a means to an end. He *is* the end. He is the object of our aim. As A. W. Tozer said, "Whoever seeks God as a means toward desired ends will not find God. God will not be used."

God is looking for those who will worship in spirit and in truth. He is looking for those who are worshiping Him because He is more than worthy, who will sing their song in the night, who will worship with their whole life so that all the world will see and know that He inhabits His people's praise.

A FINAL REASON TO WORSHIP IS THAT IT CHANGES US. IT CHANGES OUR PERSPECTIVE ON OUR PROBLEMS, AND IT BRINGS US INTO GOD'S HEALING PRESENCE.

And for those who do, there's a sweet reward. When I bring pleasure to God, I find personal pleasure. "You will show me the path of life; in Your presence is fullness of joy; at Your right hand are pleasures forevermore" (Ps. 16:11, NKJV).

TO CLAP OR NOT TO CLAP

Question: Is it better to have a planned series of songs or "let the Spirit lead"? Or is this distracting? And how much singing or clapping is too much?

Answer: The Bible tells us, "Let all things be done decently and in order" (1 Cor. 14:40, NKJV).

In our church we have what we call a "worship team." This is made up of many talented musicians in our church who will spend hours together practicing and working on the songs that will be sung in our services. There is no excuse for sloppy playing or singing done in the name of "letting the Spirit lead." Scripture tells us to "Sing to Him a new song; play skillfully with a shout of joy" (Ps. 33:3, NKJV). Whatever we do should be done for the glory of God. We should work at what we do and improve in it, be it singing, playing a musical instrument, or preaching.

At the same time, we want to keep the door open for the leading of the Holy Spirit. Some of the most tender moments in worship often come after a message has been given. People want to respond to God as a result of what they have heard from His Word. There are times when I have preached, and a certain song will come to mind that really fits what has just been said. And there on the platform I whisper into the ear of our worship leader, "Let's sing this song now." Sometimes I even lead it myself.

We might only sing a single line of it that somehow expresses the prayer of our heart. One danger that must be avoided in well-crafted worship is that it turns into a performance. That group is there to facilitate and lead, not to perform. If the singers or musicians begin to play or sing in such a way that I find myself

watching them more than thinking about the one
I should be worshiping, then some adjustments need
to be made.

As in most things, balance is the key.

QUESTIONS PEOPLE ASK

What's it like to speak to fifty thousand people?
Is there a feeling of euphoria? Is it frightening? Is it the ultimate ego trip? For me it is really none of the above. When I walk up to speak at a crusade, I believe I have a simple objective: to proclaim a simple-yet-powerful message, the gospel. I need to stay within certain parameters to do so. In that setting I am, for all practical purposes, a delivery boy. This brings a great sense of responsibility there, for I know that people may have gotten a friend, family member, or coworker out to hear the gospel, possibly for the one time in that person's life. I don't want to bungle this. I want my message to be clear, understandable, loving, and biblical.

I don't think about the huge number of people I may be speaking to but rather about the individuals who may be present—the mother with two small children who is wondering what the purpose of life is; the businessman who may have reached many of his goals but is empty inside and can't understand why; the young teenager who has been so despondent that she has thought about or even attempted suicide; the elderly man or woman who knows eternity is getting closer. I try to speak personally to them because I know they are out there. I have received letters, E-mails, and phone calls and have had personal conversations with them. I've heard their stories of conversion.

Looking back over the years, I can now plainly see that God has been preparing me for both pastoring and evangelism. I feel

211

equally called to do both. Each brings its own joys and challenges. When I have been at home pastoring for a few months, I start getting that itch to go do some evangelism. Yet when I have been out crusading for a while, I look forward to returning home and teaching through a book of the Bible again.

Our congregation has been more than supportive of these crusades, and they pray constantly for us when we are out on the field. It is not unusual for us to take one hundred or more people from our congregation with us when we go to other cities for crusades. These people will have been trained and will go out on the streets and hand out invitations and gospel tracts, inviting people to the crusades at night. They will also help as counselors and ushers when needed. And they will pay their own way, just to have the opportunity to be used by God in this way.

We have recently done live Internet hookups so that people can join us in person during services as we have brought live updates of what God is doing. Considering the fact that we need to mobilize local churches when we come to town to do a crusade, it certainly helps, being a pastor myself, to speak to and encourage other pastors who have come on board to assist. Being a pastor of a local church also brings accountability and grounding. I plan on continuing to do both unless the Lord leads differently.

How do you balance quality and quantity?
Any pastor, teacher, and evangelist would rather speak to people than to empty seats. We all like to see growth in numbers, and we like the excitement that can generate. But my philosophy has always been to provide quality and leave the quantity up to God. I feel that if I do my best to provide the best spiritual meals I can, the people will naturally want to bring out their friends, and that has proved to be true.

We have never spent a dollar promoting our church in the community. We don't have ads in the religious section of our newspaper, nor do we try to get people to join up. Even when we were just a bunch of kids with no resources to speak of, we always tried our best to present the Lord's Word in the most contemporary and high-quality fashion possible. I don't understand it when people will let their facilities get run down—paint chipping, weeds growing, cobwebs building. Some might say, "We can't afford to keep it up!" Then get out there with a paintbrush, broom, or whatever, and do it yourself!

Having a background in graphics has always motivated me to put out printed materials that were totally contemporary. The same goes for music. So often in the church, we seem to always be a few years behind, and I think that's a shame. We certainly don't have to compromise our message in order to provide quality. I have found that many people who are not believers do not reject our message as much as the way we present it. It's not that they always are against what is in the box but rather against the paper we wrap it in.

What is your philosophy of preaching?

Preaching has been defined as truth through personality. Sometimes preachers will go too far one way or the other in this area. Technically it's impossible to provide too much truth, but it is possible to drone on and on about something that is true—until people have stopped listening. And when there's not personality in it, it's like the preacher who was asked to give a short talk before a luncheon. He had been given twenty minutes to speak, but he was going way over his allotted time. The moderator tried to get his attention, pointing to his watch, clearing his throat, but that preacher was in his own world, oblivious to the fact that people were falling asleep all around the room. The moderator tapped with his gavel, indicating that the preacher's time was up, but the preacher wouldn't stop talking. Finally, in complete frustration, the moderator threw his gavel at this long-winded preacher, missed him, and hit an elderly man who had fallen asleep in the front row. Waking from his sleep, the old man said, "Hit me again; I can still hear him!"

I cannot think of a torment worse for me personally than listening to bad preaching. And there certainly is a lot of it around today. To me, it is almost a crime to take the living, vibrant, powerful, life-changing Word of God and deliver it in a boring way. You should be arrested for impersonating a communicator. I do believe that as teachers we should work at what we do and seek to be the most effective communicators that we possibly can be. When you find yourself cutting corners on your preparation because you think you have mastered all the skills, then stop and repent. C. H. Spurgeon once said, "I dread getting to be a mere preaching machine without my heart and soul being exercised in this solemn duty—lest it should be a mere piece of clock work." You are not a machine. Some preachers have great truths but deliver them in a thoroughly boring way. These truths should grip and move you as you express them to the people. Again to quote Spurgeon, "The Holy Spirit will move them by first moving you. If you can rest without their being saved, they will rest, too. But if you are filled with an agony for them, if you cannot bear that they should be lost, you will soon find that they are uneasy, too. I hope you will get into such a state that you will dream about your child or your hearer perishing for lack of Christ, and start up at once and begin to cry, 'O God, give me converts, or I die.' Then you will have converts."

But there is also the problem of not enough truth and far too much personality. You could also call it pulpit personality. Of course we should use our voice and body language to express the message in a compelling way. But some speakers take on an entirely different personality in the pulpit. It's almost as if they are in some kind of trance. They talk faster than they can think, they get whipped up in some kind of frenzy, or they sound as if they've come from another planet. Yet the Scripture tells us,

"The spirits of the prophets are subject to the prophets (1 Cor. 14:32, NKJV). This simply means that you can control your volume, tone, voice inflection, and—brace yourself for this one— you can control how long you speak!

Do you have any "most embarrassing moments"?
In the early years, when we were establishing our church, I was goofing around in the sanctuary with a musician friend. It was a weekday, and the church was empty. I decided to imitate a screaming preacher, and I got a bit carried away. My friend was playing furiously on the piano, and I jumped up on one of our speakers and was yelling, preacher-style, at the top of my lungs when two very conservative older ladies suddenly appeared before me. There I was, with shoulder-length hair, a full beard, jeans (bell-bottoms, of course—it was the seventies), in full crazy-preacher stance on top of a speaker.

One of the ladies said, "Excuse me, could you tell me where the pastor of this church is?" I couldn't bear the thought of admitting I was the pastor. I said, "Uh, he's upstairs in the church office." So they went to the church office and talked with my associate pastor.

I have had more than my share of faux pas and bumbling of phrases over the years. The first time I spoke in front of Chuck Smith, I was very nervous and wanted to deliver a message he would really be impressed with. I was speaking from Ephesians 6 about spiritual warfare. I intended to say, "You need to watch out for the fiery darts of the wicked one!" But what came out was, "You need to watch out for the diery farts of the wicked one!" It's hard to recover after that. That is all people will remember about your message.

One Sunday morning I was dedicating a little baby to the Lord and intended to pray, "Father, bless this little baby today." Instead I prayed, "Little Father, bless this . . ." Little Father? People started cracking up during the prayer. But I had a worse experience one day after I had just delivered a passionate evangelistic message. I was going to pray and invite people to come and receive Jesus Christ into their life. But instead of saying, "Let's pray," I said, "Let's pee!" I'm glad no one took me up on that.

Where do you find good leadership?
We have never really had any problems finding good leadership over the years at Harvest Christian Fellowship. Most of our associate pastors came to Christ in our services. They began attending and getting involved. When people want to serve the Lord at Harvest, we require that they attend for a minimum of one year first. Ironically, those who want to serve the most are the ones who are sometimes only weeks old in the faith. But they need to get a good spiritual foundation first. We have a special series of classes they must go through as well. Some have faithfully served the Lord over the years and have risen through the ranks as they have proved themselves faithful.

People may be teaching home Bible studies or helping out with counseling during the week. They begin, for all practical purposes, to function like a pastor-in-training. We identify those who have come to this point and ask them to become a part of what we call a leadership network. Our future associate pastors come from this network. It has always seemed that when an opening for another associate came up, there would be two or three in our network who were ready and raring to go.

It is really not for us to make someone a minister of the gospel. That is the work of the Holy Spirit. Our job is to identify those whom God is raising up. Look at the pattern of identifying leadership given in Acts 13:2-4:

> *While they were worshiping the Lord and fasting, the*
> *Holy Spirit said, "Set apart for me Barnabas and Saul for*
> *the work to which I have called them." So after they had*
> *fasted and prayed, they placed their hands on them and*

sent them off. The two of them, sent on their way by the Holy Spirit, went down to Seleucia and sailed from there to Cyprus. NIV

Notice that it says, "The two of them, sent on their way by the Holy Spirit." God is the one who calls to ministry. We are simply to acknowledge or ratify what God has already done. The process of ordination really means very little apart from this calling from God. It is my conviction that there are many schooled, degreed, ordained men in the pulpit today who quite frankly have never been called by God. On the other hand, there are many so-called laypeople who *are* called.

One of the advantages of finding the leadership for our church in our own ranks is that we know exactly what we are getting. The cream just seems to rise to the top. The more traditional approach with many churches is to look over the resumés of prospective pastor candidates who have just graduated from seminary. Then, after deliberating over it with the board, a decision is made and a person is hired. The problem with this is that sometimes you don't really know what you are getting until much later. And it's a lot harder to let a person go than it is to hire him. Many of our associate pastors attended our church for upwards of twelve years before they came on staff. It's a biblical—and a very practical—way to go.

How do you handle growth?
A popular approach to ministry is to build a building first and hope people will fill it. It is even thought in some circles that the facilities themselves will attract certain people. I know of a pastor who once had a thriving congregation. The Lord was blessing them, and the church was growing. He decided they needed a large facility, much larger than the one they already had. In the excitement of the planning, they decided to build in an affluent area of town where many families lived. They thought that if the church had the finest day-care facilities and programs for the

whole family, they could attract those people who would in turn attend their Sunday services and handle the considerable debt they were about to commit to.

When it was all said and done, they built a huge six-thousand-seat sanctuary with escalators and marble slabs on the walls behind the pulpit. It was spacious, as nice as any upscale mall, but it had one small problem: The people did not fill it. This pastor arrived in his new oversized building with fewer people then he'd had in his other adequate building. His elders ended up asking him to leave.

I have always believed that building should take place to accommodate what God has done. When we have experienced new growth numerically, we have sought to build accordingly. I haven't always seen the growth coming. We always have new people coming in, but we also have others going out. Our growth over the years has always happened in spurts—and often at very unexpected times. It is all a mystery to me. My priority is to concentrate on the quality and leave the quantity up to God.

When a church begins to grow into what we now call a megachurch, one must adjust. There was a time when I knew most people in our congregation by name. Now it is not uncommon for someone to come up to me and say something like, "I've been going to Harvest for three years and have never met you!" Frankly, I feel a bit embarrassed when a person says this. I stand at the back door after the service and shake hands with people, just like countless other pastors on Sunday mornings. But I cannot possibly know every person in our congregation.

That is where good leadership comes in. The people are able to develop relationships with our lay leaders and associate pastors, and we're able to establish accountability. Each of our pastors at Harvest oversees a number of ministries. For instance, one associate may oversee the jail-and-prison ministry, the convalescent-home outreach, and the street-witnessing team. Another may oversee the new-convert counseling, ushers, etc. This way, when we have a staff meeting, I can talk to each one and get an overview of what is going on in the various ministries of our church. Under each of these pastors are key leaders who are over other leaders implementing their particular ministry. Then we have a team of three head pastors who oversee the others. It may sound confusing, but it all works quite well. I try not to micromanage but rather to enable and encourage the others in the calling God has put on their lives. I have been practicing this approach from the very beginning of our ministry, trying to identify the gifts of people and then turning those people loose where they can make the greatest difference.

When you take this approach, you need to know that people will fail at times. Yet if you can help them to fail forward, or learn from their mistakes, they can become a great asset to the work of the kingdom in the future. I was given a chance by a man named Chuck Smith in my early days of ministry. I want to do that for others as well. Now, as the years have passed, many of our associates have gone out and started their own churches that God is blessing. These are transferable principles because they are biblical ones.

My prayer and hope for you are that you will be actively involved in a Bible-teaching, gospel-preaching church. And that your church, operating by what this world may see as upside-down principles, will make an impact on your community. Let's do our part to turn this world upside down for Jesus Christ!

ABOUT THE AUTHOR

GREG LAURIE is senior pastor of Harvest Christian Fellowship in Riverside, California. He began his pastoral ministry at age nineteen by leading a Bible study of thirty people. Today that small group has grown into a church of some fifteen thousand.

Laurie also holds evangelistic events called Harvest Crusades around the country. Since 1990 more than 2 million people have attended, and more than 171,000 have indicated their decision to follow Jesus Christ.

From the early years of Laurie's ministry, his passion has been to preach the gospel to as many people as possible and to train and equip others to do the same. His style as a pastor and speaker is contemporary and straightforward, creating a nonthreatening environment that attracts people of all ages, particularly young people.

Laurie is also the featured speaker on an international daily radio program, *A New Beginning,* and serves as a board member of the Billy Graham Evangelistic Association. Laurie's other books include:

The God of the Second Chance: Experiencing Forgiveness
Life. Any Questions?
The Great Compromise
Every Day with Jesus
On Fire
Discipleship: Giving God Your Best

The New Believer's Growth Book
A Passion for God: The Practical Power of the Holy Spirit
  in Your Life
notes for the best-selling *New Believer's Bible*

Whether speaking or writing, Laurie is known for his ability to apply biblical principles to current events in a way that is relevant and easily understood by people of all ages and from all walks of life. Greg and his wife, Cathe, have two children and reside in southern California.